PassKey EA Review

Complete: Individuals, Businesses, and Representation

IRS Enrolled Agent Exam Study Guide
2014-2015 Edition

Authors:
Richard Gramkow, EA
Collette Szymborski, CPA
David V. Sherwood, CPA, EA
Christy Pinheiro, EA ABA®

PassKey Publications
Ladera Ranch, California

Table of Contents

Editor: Cynthia Willett Sherwood, EA, MSJ

This study guide is designed for test-takers who will take their enrolled agent exams in the 2014-2015 testing window (May 1, 2014-February 28, 2015).

PassKey EA Review Complete: Individuals, Businesses, and Representation: IRS Enrolled Agent Exam Study Guide 2014-2015 Edition

ISBN: 978-1-935664-29-1

First Printing. PassKey EA Review
PassKey EA Review® is a U.S. Registered Trademark

PassKey Publications, Ladera Ranch, CA
www.PassKeyPublications.com

Recent Praise for the PassKey EA Review Series

(All testimonials are unsolicited and from customers using their real names)

The best I've experienced!
Ramona L. Ashe (Santa Barbara, California)
I'm very impressed. Of the volumes of material available, I've found yours to be the absolute best. From an obviously strong knowledge base flows a strong demonstration of logic with superior attention to detail. Much more than a compilation of IRS publications, with thoughtful questions and detailed explanations to answers, your product puts others to shame.

The Workbook brings it all together in a great combo!
Amber Martin
I found the Workbook and the Complete set for all three parts so helpful I don't see how I can fail! The only way you could not become a better preparer for your clients is by not reading the material. It is so clear and helpful. I want to thank the authors for their great and clear explanations.

I passed!
D. Hudson (Philadelphia)
Using this and other resources, I was well prepared! The book was easy to read and the questions were similar to the test!

Passed SEE Part 1 first try.
Dean Manolis (Hammock, Florida)
I used this book (along with the Workbook) to pass the exam on the first try. The book is well organized and written. I have prepared taxes for five years, so while most of this information was not new, I found the PassKey EA review to be very useful and a good value. Highly recommended.

Thank you for a great product!
Kimberly Boyer (Brandon, Florida)
I used only your books, and I am proud to say that I passed all three of my exams in five weeks on the first try. I loved your books and have recommended them to others. They are very well written and easy to follow and understand. Thank you for a great product and helping me achieve my goals.

I passed on the first try!
Donald Taylor (New Bern, North Carolina)
With the help and assistance of your books, I passed on the first try on all exams and did them in three months. How's that for a 77-year-old?

PassKey Workbook has questions that help pass the EA exams!
Lyn Tontz (Corona, California)
Well organized and written with a lot of thought in helping the reader fathom the complexities of the U.S. Internal Revenue Code to pass the EA exam.

I love it.
Ke Huan-Ball (Oceanside, California)
I used this book to prepare for the EA Part 3 exam in less than four weeks, and I passed it. I love this book. I would like to recommend it to everyone who wants to take the EA exams.

Excellent material to pass EA exam.
Mohan Singh, MST, EA
PassKey EA Review Complete 2013-2014 Edition is very helpful. I passed all three exams. Detailed information in very simple language helps a lot. This is excellent material to become an EA. Thanks to all the team members who put their efforts into writing this book.

Excellent study material.
Elizabeth Combs (Smyrna, Tennessee)
This set of books was extremely clear, well formatted, and the authors seemed to have a good handle on what was important and likely to be on the test. I definitely recommend using the test workbook in conjunction with the main review book. I really appreciated that all of the questions in both books contained detailed explanations as to why answers were correct. Highly recommend this book!

I passed all my EA exams on my first attempt with only this book.
David Martinez
PassKey EA Review is all you need to study for the EA exam. The Workbook is important because it lets you practice before the exam and refresh all the knowledge you need for it. I am not affiliated with PassKey. I just took the time to put this review out there because PassKey EA Review deserves it. It is very affordable and got me through all my examinations, which I am very happy about.

Essential Figures for the 2014-2015 EA Exam Cycle
for Part One

Here is a quick summary of some of the important tax figures for the current enrolled agent exam cycle (May 1, 2014-February 28, 2015):

Income Tax Return Filing Deadline: April 15, 2014

Personal Exemption: $3,900

Personal Exemption Phaseout Thresholds:

- Married filing jointly or qualifying widow(er): $300,000-$422,500
- Head of household: $275,000-$397,500
- Single: $250,000-$372,500
- Married filing separately: $150,000-$211,250

Standard Deduction Amounts:

- Married filing jointly or qualifying widow(er): $12,200
- Head of household: $8,950
- Single: $6,100
- Married filing separately: $6,100
- Dependents: $1,000
- Blind taxpayers and senior citizens (over 65) qualify for an increased standard deduction. Additional amounts per taxpayer are:
    - $1,500: single or head of household
    - $1,200: married filing jointly, married filing separately, or qualifying widow(er)

Itemized Deduction Phaseout Thresholds:

- Married filing jointly or qualifying widow(er): $300,000
- Head of household: $275,000
- Single: $250,000
- Married filing separately: $150,000

Social Security Taxable Wage Base: $113,700

Medicare Taxable Wage Base: No limit

Earned Income Thresholds for Additional 0.9% Medicare Tax:

- Married filing jointly: $250,000
- Single, head of household, or qualifying widow(er): $200,000
- Married filing separately: $125,000

MAGI Thresholds for Net Investment Income Tax:

- Married filing jointly or qualifying widow(er): $250,000
- Single or head of household: $200,000
- Married filing separately: $125,000

Contribution Limits for Traditional or Roth IRA: $5,500 ($6,500 for taxpayers age 50 or over by the end of 2013)

AGI Ranges for Phase-out of Traditional IRA Deductions (if taxpayer and/or spouse is covered by an employer plan):

- Married filing jointly or qualifying widow(er): $95,000 to $115,000 (taxpayer covered)
- Married filing jointly or qualifying widow(er): $178,000 to $188,000 (spouse covered)
- Single or head of household: $59,000 to $69,000
- Married filing separately: $0 to $10,000

AGI Ranges for Phase-out of Roth IRA Contributions:

- Married filing jointly or qualifying widow(er): $178,000 to $188,000
- Single or head of household: $112,000 to $127,000
- Married filing separately: $0 to $10,000

Maximum Health Savings Account Contributions:

- Individual: $3,250
- Family: $6,450

Mileage Rates:

- Business miles: 56.5¢ per mile
- Medical or moving miles: 24¢ per mile
- Charitable purposes: 14¢ per mile

Earned Income Credit (EIC) Income Thresholds:

Earned income and adjusted gross income must each be less than:

- $46,277 ($51,567 MFJ) with three or more qualifying children
- $43,038 ($48,378 MFJ) with two qualifying children
- $37,870 ($43,210 MFJ) with one qualifying child
- $14,340 ($19,680 MFJ) with no qualifying children

Investment income must be $3,300 or less for the year in order to qualify for the EIC.

Alternative Minimum Tax (AMT) Exemption:

- $80,800 (MFJ or QW)
- $51,900 (Single or HOH)
- $40,400 (MFS)

"Kiddie Tax" Unearned Income Threshold: $2,000

Withholding Threshold for "Nanny Tax": $1,800

Foreign Earned Income Exclusion: $97,600

Maximum Education Credits and Deductions:

- Hope/American Opportunity Credit: $2,500 per student
- Lifetime Learning Credit: $2,000 per return
- Tuition and fees deduction: $4,000
- Student loan interest deduction: $2,500

Maximum Credit Amounts:

- Adoption Credit: $12,970 per child
- Child Tax Credit: $1,000 per child
- Credit for Child and Dependent Care Expenses: $3,000 (one child); $6,000 (two or more)
- Retirement Savings Contributions Credit: $1,000 ($2,000 MFJ)
- Nonbusiness Energy Property Credit: $500

Combined Estate and Gift Tax Exclusion: $5.25 million

GST Tax Exclusion: $5.25 million

Annual Gift Tax Exclusion: $14,000

Non-Citizen Marital Threshold for Gift Tax: $143,000

New Laws Affecting Individuals

Changes to federal tax law in 2013 include the following:

- **Same-sex couples:** The Supreme Court struck down the Defense of Marriage Act, which has major tax implications for same-sex couples who were married in any of the states where same-sex marriage is legal. For tax year 2013, these couples must file either jointly or as married filing separately. There are more than 200 federal tax laws that refer to a "husband and wife" which now apply to these same-sex spouses, including provisions related to estate/gift taxes, gain exclusion on home sales, and retirement plans. Same-sex couples who have not been legally married in a state that recognizes same-sex marriage will not be treated as married for federal tax purposes.

- **Limitation on itemized deductions and personal/dependency exemptions:** The American Taxpayer Relief Act of 2012 restored limitations on itemized deductions and personal and dependency exemptions for higher-income taxpayers.

- **Tax brackets:** The number of tax brackets increased to seven, with the highest income tax rate increased to 39.6%. For taxpayers subject to the 39.6% marginal rate, the top rate on long-term capital gains and qualified dividends rose from 15% to 20%.

- **Employee portion of Social Security tax increased:** The "payroll tax holiday" of 2011 and 2012 ended. The employee's share of Social Security tax reverted from 4.2% to 6.2% in 2013.

- **Affordable Care Act taxes:** Two new taxes mandated by the health care act were implemented: the additional Medicare Tax and the net investment income tax. Both affect higher-income taxpayers.

- **Medical expense deduction:** Taxpayers 64 and under may claim an itemized deduction for medical expenses only if they exceed 10% of adjusted gross income, rather than the prior threshold of 7.5%. Taxpayers 65 and over may continue to use the 7.5% threshold.

- **Simplified home office deduction:** The IRS introduced an optional safe harbor method for taxpayers to calculate the home office deduction.

- **FBAR filing:** Starting July 1, 2013, all *Foreign Bank and Financial Accounts* reports (FBAR) must be filed electronically.

Essential Tax Figures for Businesses
for Part Two

2013 Social Security Taxable Wage Base: $113,700. A combined tax rate of 12.4% applies up to this limit, consisting of employee and employer portions of 6.2% each. The Social Security tax rate for self-employed persons is 12.4%.

2013 Medicare Taxable Wage Base: No limit. A tax rate of 2.9% applies, consisting of employee and employer portions of 1.45% each. The Medicare rate for self-employed persons is 2.9%.

Section 179 Expense: $500,000 of qualified expenditures/phase-out at $2 million; up to $250,000 in expense for qualified leasehold improvement, restaurant, and retail improvement property.

Bonus Depreciation: Up to 50% for new assets placed in service in 2013.

Mileage Rates:

- Business miles: 56.5¢ per mile
- Medical or moving miles: 24¢ per mile
- Charitable purposes: 14¢ per mile

Maximum Exclusion for Employer-Provided Transportation Benefits:

- $245 per month for parking benefits
- $245 per month in combined highway vehicle transportation and transit passes

Limits on Employee Deferral Contributions to Defined Contribution and SIMPLE Plans: $17,500 (with additional $5,500 catch-up contributions for participants age 50 or over)

Limits on Contributions to Profit-sharing and SEP Plans: $51,000

Maximum Compensation for Employer Contributions to Profit-sharing Plans: $255,000

New Laws Affecting Businesses

Changes to federal tax law for tax year 2013 include the following:

- **Same-Sex Couples:** The Supreme Court struck down the Defense of Marriage Act, which has significant implications for same-sex couples who were married in any of the states where gay marriage is legal, as well as for employers. There are more than 200 federal tax laws that refer to a "husband and wife" which now apply to these same-sex spouses, including provisions related to estate/gift taxes and eligibility for health benefits and retirement plans.

- **Affordable Care Act Taxes:** Two new taxes were implemented: the additional Medicare Tax and the net investment income tax. An employer must withhold the additional Medicare Tax from salaries it pays in excess of $200,000 to an employee in a calendar year; the tax also applies to self-employed individuals. The net investment income tax affects certain estates and trusts as well as higher-income individual taxpayers.

- **Safe Harbor Rule for Real Estate Professionals:** If a real estate professional participated in rental real estate activity for more than 500 hours per year or more than 500 hours in any five of the last tax years prior to the current one, the rental income associated with that activity will be presumed to be derived from the ordinary course of trade or business. The income would not be considered net investment income for purposes of the net investment income tax.

- **New Regulations on Repairs vs. Improvements:** The IRS regulations will affect whether costs are expensed or capitalized, and they include certain safe harbor provisions. They are effective in 2014, but taxpayers have the option to apply them for tax years beginning January 1, 2012 or later.

- **Simplified Home Office Deduction:** The IRS introduced an optional safe harbor method for taxpayers to calculate the home office deduction.

- **Flexible Spending Arrangements (FSAs):** Employee salary reduction contributions to a health care FSA are capped at $2,500 ($5,000 for a married couple) and up to $500 of unused balance per account may be carried over to the following year. An employer must choose whether to allow a grace period or the new carryover option.

New Information for Part 3

Representation, Practices, and Procedures

Loving v. IRS (RTRP lawsuit): In February 2014, the D.C. Circuit Court of Appeals ruled against the IRS's attempt to regulate unenrolled tax return preparers. As of publication, the IRS had not announced whether it would appeal, but it is considered highly unlikely. The exam for registered tax return preparers was halted by the litigation in 2013. The judge's ruling permits the IRS to offer the RTRP exam on a voluntary basis; however, that is not expected to happen during 2014 as the program and testing would have to be restructured.

Filing season delayed: The IRS delayed the start of the 2014 filing return due to the federal government closure in October. The first date to file business returns was January 13. The first date to file individual income tax returns was January 31.

Fees: Application fees for installment agreements and offers in compromise both increased effective January 1, 2014. The fee for entering into an installment agreement was raised $15 to $120. The fee for processing an offer in compromise was raised $36 to $186.

Equitable relief: The IRS adopted final regulations for streamlined relief, including expanding the period for a former spouse to request equitable relief from two years to ten years.

Audits of small businesses: The Fast Track Settlement program was expanded nationwide to expedite case resolution of small businesses and self-employed taxpayers under examination.

EIC penalty: In December 2013, the IRS sent penalty letters to hundreds of preparers who failed to send Earned Income Credit checklist forms along with EIC claims on the 2012 tax returns they had prepared.

Online automation: The IRS announced a number of services would be shifted online, and some in-person or phone services reduced or eliminated. Most refund inquiries and all new EIN requests will be online only. Transcript requests can be made online in a new "Get Transcript" service, but may also be ordered via paper form. The IRS's walk-in offices will no longer prepare tax returns for qualified taxpayers, who will be directed to nearby VITA offices instead. The Practitioner Priority Service will be restricted to tax professionals only.

Direct Pay: In January 2014, the IRS launched its first free electronic payment option, Direct Pay. It allows individual taxpayers with a valid Social Security number to make IRS payments directly from their checking or savings accounts.

Ten Steps for the IRS EA Exam

STEP 1-Learn

Learn more about the enrolled agent designation and explore the career opportunities that await you after passing your EA exam.

STEP 2-Gather Information

Gather more information before you launch into your studies. The IRS publishes basic information about becoming an EA on its website at www.irs.gov/Tax-Professionals/Enrolled-Agents. You will also find information about the exam itself on the Prometric testing website at www.prometric.com/see. Be sure to download the *Candidate Information Bulletin*, which takes you step-by-step through the registration and testing process.

STEP 3-Obtain a PTIN

PTIN stands for *Preparer Tax Identification Number*. Before you can register for your EA exam, you must obtain a PTIN from the IRS. The PTIN sign-up system can be found at www.irs.gov/ptin.

STEP 4-Register with Prometric

Once you have your PTIN, you may register for your exam on the Prometric website by creating an account to set up your user ID and password. You must also complete Form 2587, *Application for Special Enrollment Examination*.

STEP 5-Schedule Your Test

After creating an account, you can complete the registration process by clicking on "Scheduling." Your exam appointment must be scheduled within one year from the date of registration. You can choose a test site, time, and date that are convenient for you. The testing fee is nonrefundable. During the 2013 to 2014 testing period, the fee for each exam part was $105.

STEP 6-Adopt a Study Plan

Focus on one exam part at a time, and adopt a study plan that covers each unit of your PassKey guides. A good rule of thumb is to study at least 60 hours for each of the three exam sections. Part 2: Businesses may require additional study preparation, as evidenced by the lower pass rates. For each of the tests, start studying well in advance of your scheduled exam date.

STEP 7-Get Plenty of Rest, Exercise, and Good Nutrition

Get plenty of rest, exercise, and good nutrition prior to the EA exam. You'll want to be at your best on exam day.

STEP 8-Test Day

Be sure to arrive early at the test site. Prometric advises to arrive at least 30 minutes before your scheduled exam time. If you miss your appointment and are not allowed to take the test, you'll forfeit your fee and have to pay for a new appointment. Remember to bring a government-issued ID with your name, photo, and signature. Your first and last name must exactly match the first and last name you used to register for the exam.

STEP 9-During the Exam

This is when your hard work finally pays off. Focus and don't worry if you don't know the answer to every question, but make sure you use your time well. Give your best answer to every question. All questions left blank will be marked as wrong.

Step 10-Congratulations. You Passed!

After celebrating your success, you need to apply for your EA designation. The quickest way is by filling out Form 23, *Application for Enrollment to Practice Before the Internal Revenue Service*, on the IRS website. You may also pay online. Once your application is approved, you'll be issued an enrollment card, and you'll be official—a brand new enrolled agent!

Introduction

Congratulations on taking the first step toward becoming an enrolled agent, a widely respected professional tax designation. The Internal Revenue Service licenses enrolled agents, known as EAs, after candidates pass a competency exam testing their knowledge of federal tax law.

The PassKey study guide is designed to help you study for the EA exam, which is formally called the *IRS Special Enrollment Examination* or *"SEE."* This guide is designed for the 2014 to 2015 testing season, which begins May 1, 2014 and closes February 28, 2015. Those who take the EA exam during this time period will be tested on tax law applicable to tax returns for the 2013 calendar year.

Exam Basics

The EA exam consists of three parts, which candidates may schedule separately and take in any order they wish. The computerized exam covers all aspects of federal tax law, with Part 1 testing the taxation of individuals; Part 2 testing the taxation of businesses; and Part 3 testing ethics as well as IRS regulations and procedures.

Each part of the EA exam features 100 multiple choice questions, with no written answers required. Eighty-five of the questions are scored; the other 15 are experimental questions that are not scored. You will not know which of the questions count toward your score and which do not.

Computerized EA Exam Format
Part 1: Individual Taxation-85 scored/15 experimental questions
Part 2: Business Taxation-85 scored/15 experimental questions
Part 3: Representation, Practice, & Procedures-85 scored/15 experimental questions

You will have 3.5 hours to complete each part of the exam. The actual seat time is four hours, which allows time for a pre-exam tutorial and a post-exam survey.

The testing company Prometric exclusively administers the EA exam at thousands of testing centers across the United States and in certain other countries. You can find valuable information and register online at ***http://www.prometric.com/IRS***.

Testing Center Procedures

The testing center is designed to be a secure environment. The following are procedures you will need to follow on test day:

1. Check in about a half-hour before your appointment time, and bring a current government-issued ID with a photo and signature. If you do not have a valid ID, you will be turned away and have to pay for a new exam appointment.
2. You will be given a locker for your wallet, phone, and other personal items. The EA exam is a closed-book test, so you are not allowed to bring any notes or reference materials into the testing room. You may bring your own soft earplugs, but the center also supplies noise-blocking headphones.

3. No food, water, or other beverages are allowed in the testing room.
4. You will be given scratch paper and a pencil to use, which will be collected after the exam.
5. You will be able to use an onscreen calculator during the exam, or Prometric will provide you with a handheld calculator. You cannot bring your own.
6. Before entering the testing room, you will be scanned with a metal detector wand.
7. You will need to sign in and out every time you leave the testing room. Bathroom breaks are permitted, but the test timer will continue to count down.
8. You are not allowed to talk or communicate with other test-takers in the exam room. Prometric continuously monitors the testing via video, physical walk-throughs, and an observation window.

Violation of any of these procedures may result in the disqualification of your exam. In cases of cheating, the IRS says candidates are subject to consequences that include civil and criminal penalties.

Exam-takers who require special accommodations under the Americans with Disabilities Act (ADA) must contact Prometric at 888-226-9406 to obtain an accommodation request form. A language barrier is not considered a disability.

Exam Content

Each May, using questions based on the prior calendar year's tax law, the IRS introduces multiple new versions of each part of the EA exam. If you fail a particular part of the exam and need to retake it, do not expect to see the identical questions the next time.

Prometric's website includes broad content outlines for each exam part. When you study, make sure you are familiar with the items listed, which are covered in detail in your PassKey guides. The IRS no longer releases test questions and answers from prior exams, although questions from 1999 to 2005 are still available on the IRS website for review. Be aware that tax law changes every year, so be familiar with recent updates and do not rely too heavily on these earlier questions and answers.

Your PassKey study guides present an overview of all the major areas of federal taxation that enrolled agents typically encounter in their practices and are likely to appear on the exam. Although our guides are designed to be comprehensive, we suggest you also review IRS publications and try to learn as much as you can about tax law in general so you are well-equipped to take the exam.

In addition to this study guide, we highly recommend that all exam candidates read:

- **Publication 17, *Your Federal Income Tax*** (for Part 1 of the exam), and
- **Circular 230, *Regulations Governing the Practice of Attorneys, Certified Public Accountants, Enrolled Agents, Enrolled Actuaries, and Appraisers before the Internal Revenue Service*** (for Part 3 of the exam).

You may download these publications for free from the IRS website.

Note: Some exam candidates take Part 3: Representation, Practice, and Procedures first, rather than taking the tests in order, since the material in Part 3 is considered less complex. However, test-takers should know that several questions pertaining to taxation of Individuals and Businesses are often included on the Part 3 exam.

Exam Strategy

Each multiple choice question has four answer choices. There are several different question formats, and examples of each format are featured in your PassKey study guides.

Format One-Direct Question

Which of the following entities are required to file Form 709, United States Gift Tax Return?

A. An individual

B. An estate or trust

C. A corporation

D. All of the above

Format Two-Incomplete Sentence

Supplemental wages **do not** include payments for_______________.

A. Accumulated sick leave

B. Nondeductible moving expenses

C. Vacation pay

D. Travel reimbursements paid at the federal government per diem rate

Format Three-All of the Following Except

There are five tests which must be met for you to claim an exemption for a dependent. Which of the following is **not** a requirement?

A. Citizen or Resident Test

B. Member of Household or Relationship Test

C. Disability Test

D. Joint Return Test

There may also be a limited number of questions that have four choices, with three incorrect statements or facts and only one a correct statement or fact, which you would select as the right answer.

During the exam, you should read each question thoroughly to understand exactly what is being asked. Be particularly careful when the question uses language such as "not" or "except."

If you are unsure of an answer, you may mark it for review and return to it later. Try to eliminate clearly wrong answers from the four possible choices to narrow your odds of selecting the right answer. But be sure to answer every question, even if you have to guess, because all answers left incomplete will be marked as incorrect. Each question is weighted equally.

With 3.5 hours allotted for each part of the exam, you have slightly more than two minutes per question. Try to answer the questions you are sure about quickly, so you can devote more time to those that include calculations or that you are not so sure about. Remember the clock does not stop for bathroom breaks, so allocate your time wisely.

To familiarize yourself with the computerized testing format, you may take a tutorial on the Prometric website. However, the tutorial only illustrates what the test screens look like; it does not allow you to revisit questions you have left open or marked for review, as you can do during the actual exam.

Scoring

The EA exam is not graded upon a curve, and the IRS does not reveal either a percentage of correct answers needed to pass or a predetermined pass rate. Each question on the exam is worth one point. The IRS determines scaled scores by calculating the number of questions answered correctly from the total number of questions in the exam and converting to a scale that ranges from 40 to 130. The IRS has set the scaled passing score at 105, which corresponds to the minimum level of knowledge deemed acceptable for EAs.

After you finish your exam and submit your answers, you will exit the testing room, and a Prometric staff member will print results showing whether you passed or failed. Test results are automatically shared with the IRS, so you do not need to submit them yourself.

If you pass, your printed results will show a passing designation but not your actual score. The printout also will not indicate which specific questions you answered correctly or missed.

If you fail, you will receive a scaled score between 40 and 104, so you will be able to see how close you are to the minimum score of 105. You will also receive the following diagnostic information from the IRS to help you know which subject areas to concentrate on when studying to retake the exam:

- *Level 1: Area of weakness where additional study is necessary. It is important for you to focus on this domain as you prepare to take the test again. You may want to consider taking a course or participating actively in a study group on this topic.*
- *Level 2: May need additional study.*
- *Level 3: Clearly demonstrated an understanding of subject area.*

These diagnostic indicators correspond to various sections of each part of the exam.

If necessary, you may take each part of the exam up to four times during the testing window between May 1 and February 28. You will need to re-register with Prometric and pay fees each new time you take an exam part.

You may carry over passing scores for individual parts of the exam up to two years from the date you took them.

Pass Rates

The yearly pass rates for the SEE vary by exam. In the 2012-2013 testing period, about 85% of test-takers passed Parts 1 and 3. The pass rate for Part 2 was much lower, averaging about 60%. Prometric notes that it can be misleading to compare pass rates for the various exams because the same individuals do not take each one. The number of candidates who take Part 1 is nearly double that of the candidates taking either Part 2 or Part 3.

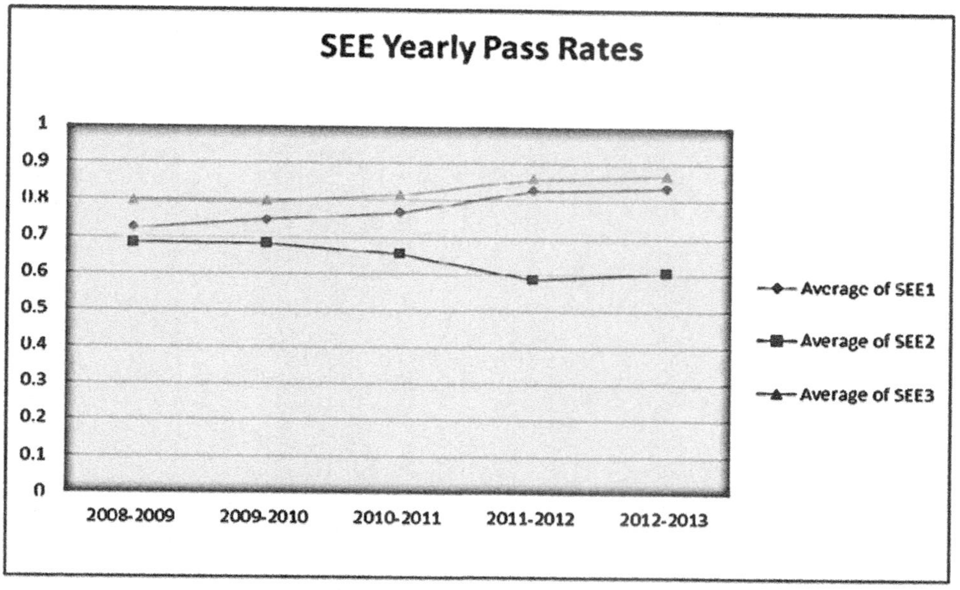

Applying for Enrollment

Once you have passed all three parts of the EA exam, you can apply to become an enrolled agent. The process includes an IRS review of your tax compliance history. Failure to timely file or pay personal income taxes can be grounds for denial of enrollment. The Return Preparer Office will review the circumstances of each case and make determinations on an individual basis. You may not practice as an EA until the IRS approves your application and issues you an enrollment card, a process that takes up to 60 days.

Successfully passing the EA exam can launch you into a fulfilling and lucrative new career. The exam requires intense preparation and diligence, but with the help of PassKey's comprehensive *EA Review*, you will have the tools you need to learn how to become an enrolled agent.

We wish you much success.

Part 1: Individuals

Unit 1: Tax Returns for Individuals

More Reading:
Publication 17, *Your Federal Income Tax*
Publication 501, *Exemptions, Standard Deduction, and Filing Information*
Publication 519, *U.S. Tax Guide for Aliens*
Publication 552, *Recordkeeping for Individuals*

Overview of EA Exam Part 1: Individuals

For Part 1 of the enrolled agent exam, you will be expected to know a broad range of information about preparing tax returns for individual taxpayers. This information includes the basics of filing status, requirements, and due dates; taxable and nontaxable income; deductions, credits, and adjustments to income; determining the basis of property; figuring capital gains and losses; rental income; retirement income; estate and gift taxes, and much more.

Specifically, Part 1 of the exam is broken down into the following sections and corresponding percentages of questions: *Preliminary Work and Taxpayer Data*, 15%; *Income and Assets*, 25%; *Deductions and Credits*, 25%; *Taxation and Advice*, 20%; and *Specialized Returns for Individuals, 15%.*[1] We begin with the preliminary work tax preparers are expected to do in order to prepare accurate tax returns.

Use of Prior Year Returns

When enrolled agents and other tax professionals prepare tax returns for clients, they are expected to perform due diligence in collecting, verifying, and gathering taxpayer data. Preparers are also expected to review prior year tax returns for compliance, accuracy, and completeness. A tax practitioner is required by law to notify a taxpayer of an error on a prior year tax return and the consequences of not correcting the error. However, a practitioner is not required to actually correct the error. The use of prior year returns can help prevent major mathematical errors and alert a tax preparer to issues specific to a particular client. In reviewing prior year tax returns, preparers need to determine whether there are items that affect the current year's return, including the following:

- Carryovers
- Net operating losses
- Credit for prior year minimum tax (Form 8801)
- Depreciation

Taxpayer Biographical Information

The following information is required to prepare an accurate tax return:

- Legal name
- Date of birth
- Marital status

[1]Specifications for tests administered during the May 1, 2013 to February 28, 2014 exam cycle.

- Residency status and/or citizenship
- Dependents
- Taxpayer identification number

The IRS requires each individual listed on a federal income tax return to have a valid taxpayer identification number (TIN). That includes the taxpayer, his or her spouse (if married), and any dependents.

The types of TINs are:

- Social Security number (SSN)
- Individual taxpayer identification number (ITIN)
- Adoption taxpayer identification number (ATIN)

Note: A taxpayer's personal information is considered highly sensitive and confidential. A preparer who wrongfully discloses taxpayer information could face criminal charges.

A taxpayer who cannot obtain an SSN must apply for an ITIN if he files a U.S. tax return or is listed on a tax return as a spouse or dependent. These taxpayers must file Form W-7, *Application for IRS Individual Taxpayer Identification Number*, and supply documentation that establishes foreign status and true identity.

Example: Laurie is a U.S. citizen with a Social Security number. She marries José, a citizen of Mexico, who has a daughter from a prior marriage. Laurie decides to file jointly with José and claim her stepdaughter as a dependent. In order to do so, they must request ITINs for José and his daughter.

An ITIN may also be required when a soldier marries a foreign spouse and brings him or her to the United States. In order to file a joint return, the couple would need to request an ITIN for the foreign spouse.

New ITIN Documentation Requirements: In 2013, the IRS instituted new procedures for taxpayers applying for ITINs. Form W-7 must include original documentation such as passports and birth certificates, or certified copies of these documents from the issuing agency. Notarized copies are no longer accepted. Military spouses and military dependents are exempt if they provide a copy of the spouse or parent's U.S. military ID, or if they apply from an overseas APO/FPO address. Nonresident aliens applying for ITINs for the purpose of claiming tax treaty benefits are also exempt from the new requirements, but the IRS says it will give heightened scrutiny to any documents submitted by these applicants.

Note: The issuance of an ITIN does not confirm an individual's immigration status as legal or give him the right to work in the United States. A taxpayer with an ITIN is not eligible to receive Social Security benefits or the Earned Income Credit.

ATINs: For an adopted child who does not yet have an SSN, a taxpayer may request an adoption taxpayer identification number (ATIN) if:

- The child is placed in the taxpayer's home for legal adoption.
- The adoption is a domestic adoption, or the adoption is a legal foreign adoption and the child has a permanent resident alien card or certificate of citizenship.

- The taxpayer cannot obtain the child's existing SSN even though he has made a reasonable attempt to obtain it from the birth parents, the placement agency, and other persons.
- The taxpayer cannot obtain an SSN for other reasons, such as the adoption not yet being final.

The taxpayer needs an ATIN to claim the adopted child as a dependent or to be eligible for the Child Care Credit, but an ATIN cannot be used to obtain the Earned Income Credit. However, if a child is born and dies within the same tax year and is not granted an SSN, the taxpayer may still claim that child as a dependent.

Example: Alice gave birth to a son on October 1, 2013. The baby had health problems and died three days later. He was issued a death certificate and a birth certificate, but not an SSN. Alice may claim her son as a qualifying child in 2013, even though he only lived a short time.

The tax return must be filed on paper with the birth and death certificate attached. The birth certificate must show that the child was born alive, as a stillborn infant does not qualify. The taxpayer would enter "DIED" in the space for the dependent's Social Security number on the tax return.

Recordkeeping for Individuals

Whether a paid tax return preparer is involved or not, a taxpayer is responsible for keeping copies of tax returns and maintaining other records for as long as they may be needed for the administration of any provision of the Internal Revenue Code. Generally, a taxpayer should keep copies of tax returns and supporting documentation for at least three years from the date the returns were filed or the date they were due, whichever is later.

The IRS does not require taxpayers to keep records in any particular way, but says individuals need good records to:

Identify sources of income: Taxpayers receive money or property from a variety of sources. Individuals need this information to separate business from nonbusiness income and taxable from nontaxable income.

Keep track of expenses: Tracking expenses as they occur helps taxpayers identify expenses that can be used to claim deductions.

Keep track of the basis of property: Taxpayers need to retain records showing the original cost or other basis of property they own and any improvements made to them.

Prepare tax returns: Good records help taxpayers and their preparers file accurate returns more quickly.

Support items reported on tax returns: If the IRS has questions about items on a return, a taxpayer should have records to substantiate those items.

Note: Even if a tax professional prepares and signs an individual's tax return, the taxpayer is ultimately responsible for the accuracy of its contents.

The IRS allows taxpayers to maintain records in any way that will help determine the correct tax. Electronic records are acceptable, so long as a taxpayer can reproduce the records in a legible and readable format. Basic records that all taxpayers should keep include items related to:

- **Income:** Forms W-2, Forms 1099, bank statements, brokerage statements, Schedules K-1.
- **Expenses:** Sales slips, invoices, receipts, canceled checks or other proof of payment, written communications from qualified charities, Forms 1098 to support mortgage interest and real estate taxes paid.
- **Home:** Closing statements, purchase and sales invoices, proof of payment, insurance records, receipts for improvement costs.
- **Investments:** Brokerage statements, mutual fund statements, Forms 1099, Forms 2439.

Basic Tax Forms for Individuals

Form 1040EZ: Form 1040EZ is the simplest tax return form. The one-page form is designed for single and joint filers with no dependents or large deductions. It shows the taxpayer's filing status, income, adjusted gross income, standard deduction, taxable income, tax, Earned Income Credit, amount owed or refund, and signature. A taxpayer may use Form 1040EZ if:

- Taxable income is below $100,000.
- The filing status is single or married filing jointly.
- The taxpayer is under age 65 and not blind.
- The taxpayer is not claiming any dependents.
- Interest income is $1,500 or less.
- The taxpayer claims no adjustments to income and no credits other than the Earned Income Credit.

Form 1040A: Form 1040A is a two-page form. Taxable income must be less than $100,000, and there can be no self-employment income. A taxpayer may not itemize deductions when using Form 1040A, and is limited to certain adjustments to income and credits.

Form 1040: Form 1040 is also called the "long form" and is designed to report all types of income, deductions, and credits. If a taxpayer cannot use Form 1040EZ or Form 1040A, he must use Form 1040.

The most common reasons a taxpayer must use Form 1040 are:

- Taxable income exceeds $100,000.
- He wants to itemize his deductions.[2]
- He is reporting self-employment income.
- He is reporting income from the sale of property (such as the sale of stock or rental property).

---

[2] When a married couple chooses to file separately, if one spouse itemizes deductions, the other must do so as well, meaning each spouse must use Form 1040.

Form 1040NR: Form 1040NR is used by nonresident aliens to report their U.S. source income. The IRS defines an alien as any individual who is not a U.S. citizen or U.S. national. A nonresident alien is an alien who has not passed the green card test or the substantial presence test, which are explained in detail in Unit 2. Form 1040NR is used by investors overseas, as well as nonresident taxpayers who earn money while in the U.S. The 1040NR is not used by U.S. citizens or U.S. residents.

A taxpayer must file Form 1040NR if any of the following apply:

- He was a nonresident alien engaged in a trade or business during 2013. This is true even if:
    - He has no income from a trade or business conducted in the United States.
    - He has no U.S. source income.
    - His income is exempt from U.S. tax under a tax treaty or any section of the IRC.

Example: Cisco Ramos is a boxing champion, and a legal citizen and resident of Panama. Cisco receives a non-immigrant visa to fight in a boxing match in the U.S., where he earns $500,000. After his appearance, he returns to Panama. Cisco is not eligible for an SSN and must request an ITIN to report his U.S. income. Without the ITIN, he would be subject to backup withholding on his U.S. earnings. Cisco's accountant reports his income and tax on Form 1040NR.

Tax Rates

An individual's federal taxable income is taxed at progressive rates in the United States. The more taxable income a taxpayer has, the higher the percentage of that income he pays in taxes. The IRS groups individuals by ranges of their taxable income level, or *brackets*, and applies increasing tax rates at each successive level. For tax year 2013, there are seven tax brackets for individuals: 10%, 15%, 25%, 28%, 33%, 35%, and 39.6%. Each year, the IRS adjusts the income ranges for inflation and issues tax tables that show how much tax is owed for specific amounts of taxable income, depending upon a taxpayer's filing status.

For example, in 2013 a single taxpayer with $8,000 of taxable income would be in the 10% tax bracket. If he had $40,000 of taxable income, he would be in the 25% tax bracket, while a taxpayer with more than $400,000 of taxable income would be in the highest tax bracket of 39.6%.

However, this does not mean that a taxpayer in the highest income range owes tax at 39.6% on all of his taxable income. The applicable tax rate for each successive bracket applies only to the additional amounts of taxable income that fall within that bracket.

Example: Jamie is single and had $37,000 of taxable income for 2013. For the first $8,925 she is taxed at a 10% rate. For the next segment of her taxable income, from $8,926 to $36,250, she is taxed at a 15% rate. Only for the remaining $750, from $36,251 to $37,000, is she taxed at 25%, which is referred to as her marginal rate.

In addition to the regular tax in the United States, there is a parallel tax called the alternative minimum tax (AMT). A taxpayer must pay either the regular tax or the AMT, depending on his individual situation. The AMT is covered in detail in Unit 15.

Due Dates and Extensions

The regular due date for individual tax returns is April 15; if April 15 falls on a Saturday, Sunday, or legal holiday, the due date is delayed until the next business day.

If a taxpayer cannot file his tax return by the due date, he may request an extension by filing Form 4868, *Application for Automatic Extension of Time to File*, which may be filed electronically. An extension grants a taxpayer an additional six months to file his individual tax return. For the 2013 tax year, extended individual tax returns are due by October 15, 2014.

Note: Although an extension gives a taxpayer extra time to *file* his return, it does not extend the time to *pay* any tax due. A taxpayer will owe interest on any amount that is not paid by the filing deadline, plus a late payment penalty, if he has not paid at least 90% of his total tax due by that date. Taxpayers are expected to estimate and pay the amount of tax due by the filing deadline.

The IRS will accept a postmark as proof of a timely-filed return. For example, if a tax return is postmarked on April 14 but does not arrive at the IRS Service Center until April 18, the IRS will accept the tax return as having been filed on time. E-filed tax returns are given an "electronic postmark" to indicate the day they are transmitted.

Filing Deadline Exceptions

Federal Disaster Areas: Taxpayers in presidentially declared disaster areas are often granted extensions to file and pay their income taxes and to make estimated tax payments. The IRS may also abate interest and any late filing or late payment penalties that apply to taxpayers in these disaster areas. This tax relief generally includes individuals and businesses located in a disaster area, those whose tax records are located in a disaster area, and relief workers.

For example, in 2013 Boston-area taxpayers affected by the April 15 bombing at the Boston Marathon were given until July 15, 2013 to file their 2012 taxes or make payments. Taxpayers in areas affected by the May 18, 2013 tornado in Oklahoma were given until Sept. 30, 2013 to make June and September estimated tax payments.

June 15 Deadlines: Three groups of taxpayers are granted an automatic two-month extension to file and pay any tax due:

- Nonresident aliens who have income that is not subject to U.S. withholding[3]
- U.S. citizens or legal U.S. residents who are living outside the United States or Puerto Rico and their main place of business is outside the United States or Puerto Rico
- Taxpayers on active military service duty outside the U.S.

A citizen or resident alien living abroad must attach a statement to his tax return explaining which situation qualifies him for the two-month extension. Even if he is allowed an extension, the taxpayer will have to pay interest on any tax not paid by the regular due date of his return.

---

[3] Nonresident employees (such as a nonresident alien who earns money while living or visiting the U.S.) who received income that is subject to U.S income tax withholding must file Form 1040NR by the regular due date of April 15.

Combat Zones: The deadline for filing a tax return or a claim for refund, and the deadline for payment of tax owed, are automatically extended for any service member, Red Cross personnel, accredited correspondent, or contracted civilian serving in a combat zone. These taxpayers have their tax deadlines suspended from the day they started serving in the combat zone until 180 days after they leave the combat zone.

Example: Philip is a Marine who has served in a combat zone since March 1, so he is entitled to extra time to file and pay his taxes. The 46 days between the date he entered the combat zone and the April 15 filing deadline are added to the normal extension period of 180 days, so he has a 226-day extension period after he leaves the combat zone. IRS deadlines for assessment and collection are also suspended during this period.

These deadline extensions also apply to spouses of armed services members serving in combat zones.

Penalties and Interest

The IRS can assess a penalty on individual taxpayers who fail to file, fail to pay, or both. The failure-to-file penalty is generally greater than the failure-to-pay penalty. If someone is unable to pay all the taxes he owes, he is better off filing on time and paying as much as he can, as the IRS will consider payment options with individual taxpayers.

Failure-to-File Penalty: The penalty for filing late is usually 5% of the unpaid taxes for each month or part of a month that a return is late. The penalty is based on the tax that is not paid by the due date, without regard to extensions. The penalty will not exceed 25% of a taxpayer's unpaid taxes.

If both the failure-to-file penalty and the failure-to-pay penalty apply in any month, the 5% failure-to-file penalty is reduced by the failure-to-pay penalty. However, if a taxpayer files his return more than 60 days after the due date or extended due date, the minimum penalty is the smaller of $135 or 100% of the unpaid tax.

If a taxpayer is owed a refund, he will not be assessed a failure-to-file penalty.

Failure-to-Pay Penalty: If a taxpayer does not pay his taxes by the due date, he could be subject to a failure-to-pay penalty of ½ of 1% (0.5%) of unpaid taxes for each month or part of a month after the due date that the taxes are not paid. This penalty can be as much as 25% of a taxpayer's unpaid taxes.

The failure-to-pay penalty rate increases to a full 1% per month for any tax that remains unpaid the day after a demand for immediate payment is issued, or ten days after notice of intent to levy certain assets is issued.

Relief from Joint Tax Liability

In certain cases, a spouse can be relieved of the tax, interest, and penalties on a joint return. When spouses file a joint return, they are both legally responsible for the entire tax liability. However, a spouse can file a claim for relief under three different grounds.

Innocent Spouse Relief: This is when a joint return has understated tax liability due to erroneous items attributable to a taxpayer's spouse or former spouse. Erroneous items include income received by a spouse that is omitted from the return. Deductions, credits, and property basis are also erroneous items if they are incorrectly reported on the joint return.

To be considered an innocent spouse, the taxpayer must establish that he did not know that there was an understated tax liability at the time of signing the joint return. The taxpayer must request relief within two years after the date on which the IRS first began collection activity.

Separation of Liability Relief: The above restrictions also apply to separation of liability relief, but in this case the taxpayer must no longer be married to; or must be legally separated from; or must be widowed; or must have lived apart for at least 12 months from the spouse with whom he filed the joint return.

The understated tax, plus interest and penalties, would be allocated to the taxpayer based on the amount for which he is responsible.

Equitable Relief: If a taxpayer does not qualify for the first two types of relief, he may be eligible for equitable relief. The IRS will review the facts and circumstances of the taxpayer's case and determine whether it would be unfair to hold him liable for the understated tax. Unlike the other two forms of relief, equitable relief may also be granted for an underpaid tax, meaning it was properly reported on a tax return but not paid. Further, in some cases the spouse requesting relief may have known about the understated or underpaid tax but did not challenge the treatment for fear of his spouse's retaliation.

Example: Diana is a victim of domestic violence who now lives apart from her husband. When she signed her joint return, she knew her husband was underreporting income from his business but was afraid of what would happen if she refused to sign. After the IRS discovered the understated tax, Diana filed for equitable relief and was able to document her history of spousal abuse. The IRS granted her request for relief of her portion of the understated tax, penalties, and interest.

Under new rules, the taxpayer has up to ten years to request equitable relief in certain circumstances. Form 8857, *Request for Innocent Spouse Relief*, is used to request all three types of relief.

Injured Spouse Claims

An injured spouse claim has a similar-sounding name, but is completely different than innocent spouse relief. To be considered an injured spouse, a taxpayer must meet the following criteria:

- Have filed a joint return
- Have paid federal income tax or claimed a refundable tax credit
- All or part of his refund was, or is expected to be, applied to his spouse's past financial obligations
- Not be responsible for the debt

A spouse who believes he is entitled to a portion of his refund may file Form 8379, *Injured Spouse Allocation*.

Example: Rolando filed a joint return with his wife, Valerie, who had unpaid student loans. Valerie incurred the student loan debt before she was married. Rolando files Form 8379 to request his portion of their tax refund as an injured spouse. The IRS will retain Valerie's portion of the couple's tax refund to offset her debt.

Note: *PassKey EA Review Book 3* has more detailed information about innocent spouse and injured spouse claims, since Part 3 of the exam typically tests these concepts more frequently than does the Part 1 exam.

Claims for Refunds

In order to claim a refund, a taxpayer must file an amended tax return within three years from the date the original return was filed or two years from the date the tax was paid, whichever is later. If a claim is not filed within the applicable period, a taxpayer generally will not be entitled to a refund.

Example: Don has not filed a tax return for a long time, and now he wants to file six years of delinquent tax returns: 2008 through 2013. Don files the returns and realizes that he was entitled to refunds for each year. If he files all the back tax returns by April 15, 2014, he will receive refunds for his 2010, 2011, 2012, and 2013 tax returns. His refunds for 2008 and 2009, however, have expired.

Example: Aisha's 2010 tax return was due April 15, 2011. She filed it on March 20, 2011. In 2013, Aisha discovered that she missed a deduction on her 2010 return, so she wants to amend it, expecting the correction to result in a large refund. If the return is postmarked on or before April 15, 2014, it will be within the three-year limit and she will be entitled to the refund. If she files the amended return after April 15, 2014, she will be too late to claim a refund.

If the taxpayer had an extension and filed his original return prior to the October 15 extension deadline, the three-year period begins October 15.

Example: Steve made estimated tax payments of $1,000 and requested an extension to file his 2010 income tax return. When he filed his return on September 7, 2011, he paid an additional $200 tax due. He later finds an error on the return. Three years after the extended due date, Steve files an amended return on October 15, 2014 and claims a refund of $700.

Extended Statute for Claiming Refunds

In some cases, a request for a tax refund will be honored past the normal deadline. These special cases involve:

- A bad debt from a worthless security (up to seven years prior)
- A payment or accrual of foreign tax
- A net operating loss carryback
- A carryback of certain tax credits
- Exceptions for military personnel
- Taxpayers in presidentially declared disaster areas
- Taxpayers who have been affected by a "terroristic or military action"

Time periods for claiming a refund are also extended when a taxpayer is "financially disabled." This usually requires that the taxpayer be mentally or physically disabled to the point that he is unable to manage his financial affairs.

Statute of Limitations for IRS Assessment and Collection

The IRS is required to assess tax or audit a taxpayer's return within three years after the return is filed. If a taxpayer files his tax return late, the IRS has three years from the later of:

- The due date of the return, or
- The date the return was actually filed.

If a taxpayer never files a return, there is no deadline for assessment of tax.

The IRS has six years to assess tax on a return if a substantial understatement is identified, meaning that income was understated by 25% or more. If the taxpayer files a fraudulent tax return, there is no deadline for IRS assessment or collection.

Example: Caroline filed her 2010 tax return on February 27, 2011. The three-year statute period for audit began April 15, 2011 and ends on April 15, 2014. After that date, the IRS must be able to prove fraud or a substantial understatement of income to audit the tax return.

The statute of limitations for IRS collection is ten years from the date tax is assessed. If a taxpayer never files a return, the IRS can attempt to collect indefinitely.

Estimated Taxes

The federal income tax is a "pay-as-you-go" tax, meaning a taxpayer must pay taxes as he earns or receives income throughout the year. If a taxpayer earns income that is not subject to withholding, such as self-employment income, rents, and alimony, or if his taxes withheld are insufficient to cover his tax liability, he may be required to make quarterly estimated tax payments. Estimated tax is used to pay income tax as well as self-employment tax and alternative minimum tax.

Safe Harbor Rule: Taxpayers can avoid making estimated tax payments by ensuring they have enough tax withheld from their income. A taxpayer with adjusted gross income of $150,000 or less ($75,000 or less if married filing separately) must generally make estimated tax payments if:

- He expects to owe at least $1,000 in tax (after subtracting withholding and tax credits)
- He expects the total amount of withholding and tax credits to be less than the smaller of:
    - 100% of the tax shown on his prior year return
    - 90% of the tax shown on his current year return

Example: Gerald earned $95,000 in 2013 and paid $8,200 in tax. Although he expects his income to increase in 2014, he will not be assessed a penalty for underpayment of estimated taxes provided he pays at least $8,200 in estimated tax during the year (100% of the tax shown on his prior year return).

A U.S. citizen or U.S. resident is not required to make estimated tax payments if he had zero tax liability in the prior year.

Example: Cassius, age 25 and single, earned $2,700 before he was laid off in 2012, and received $1,500 in unemployment compensation afterward. He did not have to pay income tax because his gross income of $4,200 was less than the filing requirement. In 2013, Cassius began working as a carpenter, but made no estimated tax payments during the year. Even though he owed $3,000 in tax at the end of the year, Cassius does not owe the underpayment penalty for 2013 because he had zero tax liability in the prior year.

A taxpayer will not face an underpayment penalty if the total tax shown on his return (minus the amount paid through withholding) is less than $1,000.

Example: Dominique has a full-time job as a secretary. She also earns money part-time as a self-employed manicurist. In 2013, she did not make estimated payments. However, Dominique made sure to increase her withholding at her job in order to cover any amounts that she would have to pay on her self-employment earnings. When she files her tax return, she discovers that she owes $750. She will not owe an underpayment penalty because the total tax shown on her return is less than $1,000.

If a taxpayer wishes to change his withholding amounts from his wages, he must use Form W-4, *Employee's Withholding Allowance Certificate*, and submit it to his employer, not to the IRS.

Safe Harbor Rule for Higher Income Taxpayers: An alternate safe harbor rule applies to higher income taxpayers with adjusted gross income of more than $150,000 ($75,000 or more if married filing separately). A taxpayer will not be assessed an estimated tax penalty if he pays the smaller of 90% of the tax shown on his current year return or 110%, rather than 100%, of the tax shown on his prior year return.

Example: Connie and Spencer are a married couple who work as self-employed business consultants. In 2013, their adjusted gross income was $175,000. In 2012, they paid $5,000 in federal income tax. They will not be subject to a penalty for underpayment of estimated tax if they pay at least $5,500 in tax on their 2013 return (110% of their 2012 tax liability.)

Estimated Payment Due Dates

The year is divided into four payment periods for estimated taxes, each with a specific payment due date. If the due date falls on a Saturday, Sunday, or legal holiday, the due date is the next business day. If a payment is mailed, the date of the U.S. postmark is considered the date of payment.

First Payment Due: April 15
Second Payment Due: June 15
Third Payment Due: September 15
Fourth Payment Due: January 15 (of the following year)

A taxpayer must complete Form 1040-ES, *Estimated Tax for Individuals,* to pay his estimated tax.

Estimated Taxes for Farmers and Fishermen

Special rules apply to the payment of estimated tax by qualified farmers and fishermen. If at least two-thirds of the taxpayer's gross income comes from farming or fishing activities, the following rules apply:

- The taxpayer does not have to pay estimated tax if he files his return and pays all tax owed by the first day of the third month after the end of his tax year (usually March 1, but the date is Monday, March 3 in 2014 because March 1 is a Saturday).
- The taxpayer does not have to pay estimated tax if his 2013 income tax withholding is at least two-thirds (.6667) of the total tax shown on his 2013 tax return or 100% of the total tax shown on his 2012 return.
- If the taxpayer must pay estimated tax, he is required to make only one estimated tax payment (called the "required annual payment") by the fifteenth day after the end of his tax year (usually January 15).

For this special tax treatment, qualified farming income includes gross farming income from Schedule F, gross farming rental income, gains from the sale of livestock, and crop shares for the use of a farmer's land.

Example: Jay is a self-employed owner of a commercial fishing vessel. All of his income is from commercial fishing, so he is not required to pay quarterly estimated taxes. Jay's records are incomplete, so he asks his tax accountant to file an extension on his behalf. Since Jay will be unable to file his tax return by March 3, 2014, his accountant notifies Jay that he is required to make a single payment of estimated taxes by January 15, 2014.

Example: Karla earns 100% of her income from growing organic strawberries. She is not required to pay quarterly estimated taxes. Karla filed her tax return on February 20, 2014 and enclosed a check for her entire balance due of $4,900. Since she filed before the March 3, 2014 deadline, she will not be subject to any penalty.

Backup Withholding

There are times an entity is required to withhold certain amounts from a payment and remit the amounts to the IRS. For example, the IRS requires backup withholding if a taxpayer's name and Social Security number on Form W-9, *Request for Taxpayer Identification Number and Certification*, does not match its records.

The IRS will sometimes require backup withholding if a taxpayer has a delinquent tax debt, or if he fails to report all his interest, dividends, and other income. Payments that may be subject to backup withholding include wages, interest, dividends, rents, royalties, and payments to independent contractors for services. The current backup withholding rate is 28% for all U.S. citizens and legal U.S. residents.

Unit 1: Study Questions

(Please test yourself and check the correct answers at the back of the study guide.)

1. Generally, how long should taxpayers keep the supporting documentation for their tax returns?

A. Four years from the date the return was filed or the return was due, whichever is later.
B. Three years from the date the return was filed or the return was due, whichever is later.
C. Two years from the date the return was filed or the return was due, whichever is later.
D. At least one year from the date the return was filed.

2. Which of the following taxpayers is required to have an individual taxpayer identification number (ITIN)?

A. A nonresident alien with an SSN who moves outside the U.S.
B. A nonresident alien who must file a return and is not eligible for a valid SSN.
C. Anyone who does not have a Social Security number.
D. All nonresident and resident aliens.

3. Clark and Christy are both age 34 and file jointly. They have no dependents. Their combined income is $31,000, which includes $35 in interest income. The remainder of their income is from wages. They want to take the standard deduction. What is the simplest tax form that Clark and Christy can use for their tax return?

A. Form 1040.
B. Form 1040A.
C. Form 1040EZ.
D. Form 1040NR.

4. The current backup withholding rate is _________.

A. 0%.
B. 13.5%.
C. 25%.
D. 28%.

5. Ricky files his 2013 tax return on February 15, 2014. He has a balance due of $800 on the return. How long can he wait to pay the amount owed and not incur a penalty?

A. He will owe a late payment penalty unless he pays his tax liability when he files his return.
B. He has until the due date of the return (not including extensions) to pay the amount owed and not pay a penalty.
C. He has until the due date of the return (including extensions) to pay the amount owed and not pay a penalty.
D. He does not have to pay the amount due by a certain date, because it is less than the safe harbor amount of $1,000.

6. All of the statements about estimated tax payments are correct except________:

A. An individual whose only income is from self-employment will generally have to pay estimated payments.
B. If insufficient tax is paid through withholding, estimated payments may still be necessary.
C. Estimated tax payments are required when the amount of taxes withheld is greater than the overall tax liability.
D. Estimated tax is used to pay not only income tax but self-employment tax and alternative minimum tax as well.

7. Which of the following is not an acceptable reason for extending the statute of limitations for claiming a refund past the normal deadline?

A. A bad debt from a worthless security.
B. Living in a presidentially declared federal disaster area.
C. Exceptions for military personnel.
D. Living outside the country for three years.

8. Cynthia is divorced, files as head of household, and has two dependents. She earned $43,000 in 2013 and plans to itemize her deductions. Which tax form should Cynthia use?

A. Form 1040.
B. Form 1040A.
C. Form 1040EZ.
D. Form 1040NR.

9. Isla files as single and has no refundable credits. Based on the figures below, is she required to pay estimated tax in 2014?

AGI for 2013	$73,700
Total tax on 2013 return	$9,224
Anticipated AGI for 2014	$82,800
Total 2014 estimated tax liability (using the 2014 estimated tax worksheet)	$11,270
Tax expected to be withheld in 2014	**$10,250**

A. Yes, she is required to make estimated tax payments.
B. No, she is not required to make estimated tax payments.
C. She qualifies for the safe harbor rule for higher income taxpayers and thus will not face an estimated tax penalty.
D. None of the above is correct.

10. If an individual requests an extension file his tax return, what is the extended due date?

A. April 15.
B. August 15.
C. October 15.
D. December 15.

11. Dottie is a U.S. resident who paid estimated tax in 2013 totaling $2,500. In 2014, she quit her business as a self-employed contractor and is now unemployed. Dottie expects to have zero tax liability in 2014. Which of the following statements is true?

A. She is still required to make estimated tax payments in 2014.
B. She is not required to make estimated tax payments in 2014.
C. She must pay at least $2,500 in estimated tax in 2014 or she will be subject to a failure-to-pay penalty.
D. She must make a minimum of $2,250 (90% × $2,500) in estimated tax payments in 2014 or she will be subject to an underpayment penalty.

12. Ernesto's 2010 tax return was due April 15, 2011. He filed it on March 20, 2011. Later, Ernesto discovered that he is eligible for a tax credit that will result in a refund. He neglected to take this credit on his 2010 return. What is the latest date that Ernesto can amend his 2010 tax return in order to receive a refund?

A. April 15, 2013.
B. April 15, 2014.
C. March 20, 2014.
D. October 15, 2014.

13. Which of the following statements is true regarding the filing of Form 4868, *Application for an Automatic Extension of Time to File U.S. Individual Income Tax Return?*

A. Form 4868 provides the taxpayer with an automatic six-month extension to file and pay.
B. Even though a taxpayer files Form 4868, he will owe interest and may be charged a late payment penalty on the amount owed if the tax is not paid by the due date.
C. Interest is not assessed on any income tax due if Form 4868 is filed.
D. A U.S. citizen, who is out of the country on vacation on the due date, will be allowed an additional twelve months to file so long as "Out of the Country" is written across the top of Form 1040.

14. What is the statute of limitations for IRS assessment on a tax return from which more than 25% of the taxpayer's income was omitted?

A. There is no statute of limitations on a return in which income was omitted.
B. Three years from the date the return was filed or the return was due, whichever is later.
C. Six years from the date the return was filed.
D. Ten years from the date the return was filed.

15. A taxpayer who claims a dependent can use any tax form except __________.

A. Form 1040.
B. Form 1040A.
C. Form 1040EZ.
D. None of the above. A taxpayer who is claiming a dependent can use any of these forms.

16. If a taxpayer files his tax return more than 60 days after the due date or extended due date, what is the minimum penalty he will face?

A. A minimum of 25% of his unpaid taxes.
B. A minimum of 5% of his unpaid taxes.
C. The smaller of $135 or 100% of the unpaid tax.
D. There is no penalty for filing a tax return late.

17. Leah is a self-employed architect and must make estimated tax payments. What is the due date for her third estimated tax payment for tax year 2013?

A. June 15, 2013.
B. August 15, 2013.
C. September 15, 2013.
D. October 15, 2013.

18. To prepare an accurate tax return, a preparer needs all of the following information about a client except __________:

A. Date of birth.
B. Citizenship or residency.
C. Social Security number or taxpayer identification number.
D. Mother's maiden name.

19. Ray and Maggie are married, but he and his wife are filing MFS. Their combined income was $100,000. Ray earned $60,000 in wage income and plans to itemize his deductions. Maggie has $40,000 in self-employment income and has nothing to itemize. Which is the simplest form that Maggie can use for her tax return?

A. Form 1040.
B. Form 1040A.
C. Form 1040EZ.
D. Either Form 1040 or Form 1040A.

20. All of the following statements regarding the ATIN are correct except________:

A. An ATIN may be used to claim the Earned Income Credit.
B. An ATIN may not be used to claim the Earned Income Credit.
C. An ATIN may be requested by a taxpayer who is unable to secure a Social Security Number for a child until his adoption is final.
D. An ATIN can be obtained even if an adoption has not been finalized.

21. Janice is a taxpayer who switched to a new tax preparer in 2014. In reviewing her prior year tax returns, he notices that she had not claimed a large deduction she was entitled to on her 2010 tax return. She had filed that return on extension on September 9, 2011. In order for Janice to receive a refund on the earlier return, the tax preparer must file Form 1040X no later than ________________:

A. October 15, 2013.
B. April 15, 2014.
C. September 9, 2014.
D. October 15, 2014.

22. Under new procedures implemented by the IRS, which of the following documents will be accepted as valid means of identification for a taxpayer applying for an ITIN?

A. Notarized copies of birth certificates and passports.
B. Original birth certificates and passports.
C. Certified copies of birth certificates and passports.
D. Both B and C.

23. Isaac is a calendar-year, self-employed farmer who files on the cash basis. All of the following statements are true except:

A. Isaac does not have to make any estimated payments if he files by April 15 and pays all his tax with his return.
B. Isaac is a qualified farmer if at least two-thirds of his previous year's gross income is from farming.
C. The required annual estimated tax payment for farmers is due on the fifteenth day after the close of their tax year.
D. The required annual payment is two-thirds of the current year's tax or 100% of the previous year's tax.

24. Rochelle is a United States citizen who lives in England. She owes $5,000 in tax for 2013. Which of the following is correct regarding her filing and payment requirements?

A. She must file and pay her taxes by April 15.
B. She is allowed an automatic two-month extension to file her tax return, but must pay her taxes by April 15.
C. She is allowed an automatic two-month extension to file and pay her taxes, but must attach a statement to her return explaining why she qualifies for the extension.
D. If she files by June 15, she will not owe any additional interest on her tax liability.

25. Benicio is single and earned $200,000 as a self-employed businessman in 2013. Under the estimated tax safe harbor rules for high income taxpayers, he can avoid an underpayment penalty if he pays __________ of his 2012 tax liability.

A. $1,000.
B. 90%.
C. 100%.
D. 110%.

26. Sally and Albert file a joint return. Their tax refund will be applied toward Albert's unpaid child support obligations from an earlier relationship. To request her portion of their refund, Sally should file ________________________:

A. As an innocent spouse.
B. As a damaged spouse.
C. As an injured spouse.
D. For equitable relief.

27. Catherine files an extension request (Form 4868), which allows her an additional six months to file her tax return. When she finally prepares her return, she realizes that she owes a substantial amount of tax. She pays the tax when she files the return, which she does before the extended due date. Which penalties, if any, is Catherine likely to owe?

A. She will owe interest on the amount owed and a late payment penalty.
B. She will owe interest on the amount owed and a late filing penalty.
C. She will owe interest on the amount owed, a late payment penalty, and a late filing penalty.
D. She will not owe any penalties because she filed before the extended due date and paid the taxes owed with the return.

Unit 2: Taxpayer Filing Status and Residency

For additional information read:
Publication 17, *Your Federal Income Tax*
Publication 501, *Exemptions, Standard Deduction, and Filing Information*
Publication 54, *Tax Guide for U.S. Citizens and Resident Aliens Abroad*
Publication 519, *U.S. Tax Guide for Aliens*

The IRS uses a taxpayer's filing status to determine filing requirements, standard deductions, eligibility for certain credits, and the amounts of tax owed. There are five filing statuses, with rules governing each, including special rules for annulled marriages and widows/widowers with dependent children.

In general, a taxpayer's filing status depends first on whether he or she is married or unmarried. For federal tax purposes, a marriage has traditionally been defined as a legal union between a man and a woman as husband and wife. However, for tax years 2013 and going forward, a marriage between same-sex spouses is also recognized as a legal union, so long as the marriage was performed in a domestic or foreign jurisdiction that recognizes the validity of same-sex marriage. This is true even if the same-sex couple lives in a state or country that does not recognize the legality of same-sex marriage.[4] Individuals who have entered into a registered domestic partnership, civil union, or other similar relationship that is not considered a marriage under state law are not considered married for federal tax purposes.

Single

A taxpayer is considered single for the entire tax year if, on the last day of the tax year, he or she is:

- Unmarried
- Legally separated or divorced, or
- Widowed (and not remarried during the year).

Example: Kenneth and Jennifer legally divorced on December 31, 2013. They do not have any dependents. They may not file jointly for 2013, but instead must each file as single.

Note: Annulled Marriages (Single): If a marriage is annulled, it is considered never to have existed. Annulment is a legal procedure for declaring a marriage null and void. If a taxpayer obtains a court decree of annulment that holds no valid marriage ever existed, the couple is considered unmarried even if they filed joint returns for earlier years.

[4] Revenue Ruling 2013-17 was issued in response to the Supreme Court ruling in June 2013 that struck down the Defense of Marriage Act (DOMA). In *Windsor vs. United States*, the court ruled that DOMA was unconstitutional because it violated equal protection. The ruling is intended to provide same-sex couples who are legally married equal treatment under federal law with in matters such as income tax, estate tax, and Social Security benefits.

Unlike divorce, an annulment is retroactive. Taxpayers who have annulled their marriage must file amended returns (Form 1040X) claiming single (or head of household status, if applicable) for all the tax years affected by the annulment that are not closed by the statute of limitations.

Example: Sara and Robert were granted an annulment on October 31, 2013. They were married for two years. They do not have any dependents. They must each file single for 2013, and the prior two years' tax returns must be amended to reflect single as their filing status.

Married Filing Jointly (MFJ)

The married filing jointly status typically provides more tax benefits than filing a separate return. Taxpayers may file jointly if they are married as of December 31 and:

- Live together as husband and wife or as a legally married same-sex couple
- Live together in a common law marriage recognized in the state where they now reside or in the state where the common law marriage began
- Live apart but are not legally separated or divorced
- Are separated under an interlocutory (not final) divorce decree

In addition, a widowed taxpayer may use the married filing jointly status if his spouse died during the year and he has not remarried as of the end of the year.

A U.S. resident or U.S. citizen who is married to a nonresident alien can elect to file a joint return as long as both spouses agree to be taxed on their worldwide income.

On a joint return, spouses report all of their combined income, allowable expenses, exemptions, and deductions. Spouses can file a joint return even if only one spouse had income. Both spouses must agree to sign the return and both are responsible for any tax owed, even if all the income was earned by only one spouse.

A subsequent divorce usually does not relieve either spouse of the liability associated with the original joint return (see exceptions related to innocent spouse relief covered later in the unit).

Married Filing Separately (MFS)

The MFS status is for taxpayers who are married and either:

- Choose to file separate returns, or
- Do not agree to file a joint return.

If one spouse chooses to file MFS, the other is forced to do the same, since a joint return must be signed by both spouses.

Example: Jerry and Danielle usually file jointly. However, Danielle has chosen to separate her finances from her husband. Jerry wishes to file jointly with Danielle, but she has refused. Danielle files using married filing separately as her filing status; therefore, Jerry is forced to file MFS as well.

The MFS filing status means the husband and wife report their own income, exemptions, credits, and deductions on separate returns, even if one spouse had no income. This filing status may benefit a taxpayer who wants to be responsible only for his own tax, or if it results in less tax than filing a joint return. Typically, however, a married couple will pay more tax on a combined basis when filing MFS than they would by filing MFJ.

Specific features of the MFS filing status include the following:

- The tax rates are generally higher than those applicable to MFJ.
- The exemption amount for the alternative minimum tax is half that allowed on a joint return.
- Various credits, including the Earned Income Credit and those for child care, education, adoption, and retirement savings, are either not allowed or are much more limited than on a joint return.
- The capital loss deduction is limited to $1,500, half that allowed on a joint return.
- The standard deduction is half the amount allowed on a joint return and cannot be claimed if the taxpayer's spouse itemizes deductions.

Example: Dinesh and Maya keep their finances separate and choose to file MFS. Dinesh plans to itemize his casualty losses, so Maya is forced to either itemize her deductions or claim a zero standard deduction.

One common reason a taxpayer may choose the MFS filing status is to avoid an offset of his refund against his current spouse's outstanding prior debt. This might include delinquent child support or student loans, or a tax liability a spouse incurred before the marriage.

Example: Tom and Judith were married in 2013. Tom owes delinquent taxes from a prior year. Judith chooses to file separately from Tom, so her refund will not be offset by his overdue tax debt. If they were to file jointly, their entire refund would be retained in order to pay the debt.

Same-Sex Spouses: Under new IRS guidelines, starting in tax year 2013, same-sex spouses who are legally married must file as either married filing jointly or married filing separately. They do not have the choice to file as single.

Example: Curtis and Antonio were legally married in New Hampshire in 2010. They live in South Dakota, which does not recognize same- sex marriage. Until now, each has filed as single. Curtis and Antonio must file jointly for tax year 2013.

For tax year 2012, same-sex spouses who filed their tax returns before September 16, 2013[5] may choose to amend their tax returns and file either as married filing separately or married filing jointly. They are not required to do so, however. The same holds true for returns for tax years 2011 and earlier, to the extent that the time period for filing an amended return has not yet expired. A taxpayer must generally file a claim for refund within three years from the date the original return was filed or within two years from the date the tax was paid, whichever is later.

Example: Curtis and Antonio consult Marilynne, an EA who prepares their tax returns. She does some research and finds that they would receive refunds if they amended their 2010 and 2012 tax returns to married filing jointly. However, they would not receive a refund on their 2011 return if they amended to MFJ status. Curtis and Antonio decide to amend their 2010 and 2012 tax returns, but not their 2011 returns.

Changing Filing Status: There are rules for when married taxpayers are allowed to change their filing status for a given year's return. Taxpayers generally cannot change from a joint return to

[5] The effective date of Revenue Ruling 2013-17.

a separate return after the due date of the return. For example, if a married couple filed their joint 2013 tax return on March 13, 2014 and subsequently decided they wanted instead to file MFS, they would have only until April 15, 2014 to file amended returns using the MFS filing status.

An exception allows a personal representative for a deceased taxpayer to change from a joint return elected by the surviving spouse to a separate return for the decedent, for up to a year after the filing deadline.

Example: Kurt and Susan have always filed jointly. Susan dies suddenly in 2013, and her will names Harriet, her daughter from a previous marriage, as the executor for her estate. Kurt files a joint return with Susan for 2013, but Harriet, as the executor, decides that it would be better for Susan's estate if her tax return were filed MFS. Harriet files an amended return claiming MFS status for Susan, and signs the return as the executor.

To change from separate returns to a joint return, taxpayers must file an amended return using Form 1040X, and may do so at any time within three years from the due date of the separate returns.

Head of Household (HOH)

The head of household status is available to taxpayers who meet all three of the following requirements:

- The taxpayer must be single, divorced, legally separated, or "considered unmarried" on the last day of the year.
- The taxpayer must have paid more than half the cost of keeping up a home for the year.
- The taxpayer must have had a qualifying person living in his home for more than half the year. There are exceptions for temporary absences, such as school, and for a qualifying parent, who does not have to live with the taxpayer.

A taxpayer who qualifies to file as head of household will usually have a lower tax rate than the rates for single or MFS, and will receive a higher standard deduction.

To be "considered unmarried" on the last day of the tax year, a taxpayer must meet all of the following conditions:

- File a separate return.
- Pay more than half the cost of keeping up the home for the tax year.
- Not live with his spouse in the home during the last six months of the tax year.
- Maintain the home as the main residence of a qualifying child, stepchild, or foster child for more than half the year.
- Be able to claim an exemption for the child (although there is an exception for divorced parents, explained later.)

Valid household expenses used to calculate whether a taxpayer is paying more than half the cost of maintaining a home include:

- Rent, mortgage interest, property taxes
- Home insurance, repairs, utilities
- Food eaten in the home

Valid expenses do not include clothing, education, medical treatment, vacations, life insurance, or transportation. Welfare payments are not considered amounts that the taxpayer provides to maintain a home.

For purposes of the HOH status, a "qualifying person" is defined as:

- A qualifying child,
- A married child who can be claimed as a dependent, or
- A dependent parent.

The qualifying person for HOH filing status must generally be related to the taxpayer either by blood, adoption, or marriage. However, a foster child also qualifies if the child was legally placed in the home by a government agency.

A taxpayer's qualifying person may include the taxpayer's child or stepchild; sibling or stepsibling; or a descendant of any of these. For example, a niece or nephew, stepbrother or stepsister, or grandchild may all be eligible as qualifying persons for the HOH filing status.

Example: Lewis's unmarried son, Aaron, lived with him all year. Aaron turned 18 at the end of the year. He does not have a job, did not provide any of his own support, and cannot be claimed as a dependent by anyone else. As a result, Aaron is Lewis's qualifying child. Lewis may use the HOH filing status.

An unrelated individual may still be considered a "qualifying relative" for a dependency exemption, but will not be a qualifying person for the HOH filing status.

Example: Jeffrey has lived with his girlfriend, Patricia, and her son, Nolan, for five years. Jeffrey pays all of the costs of keeping up their home. Patricia is unemployed and does not contribute to the household costs. Jeffrey is not related to Nolan and cannot claim him as a dependent. Jeffrey also cannot file as HOH because neither Patricia nor Nolan is a qualifying person for Jeffrey.

Example: Joan is a U.S. citizen who is single and lived with her friend, Wilson, all year. Joan had no income and received all of her financial support from Wilson. Joan falls under the definition of a qualifying relative, and Wilson can claim Joan as a dependent on his return. However, his support for Joan does not qualify Wilson to file as head of household.

Special Rules for HOH Status

Divorced or Noncustodial Parents: A taxpayer may file as HOH and not claim the qualifying child as his dependent. This happens most often with divorced parents.

Example: George and Elizabeth have been divorced for five years. They have a 12-year-old daughter named Rebecca who lives with her mother and only sees her father on weekends. Therefore, Elizabeth is the custodial parent. They agree, however, to allow George to claim the dependency exemption for Rebecca on his tax return. In 2013, George correctly files as single and claims Rebecca as his dependent. Elizabeth may still file as HOH if she otherwise qualifies.

The "considered unmarried" rules apply in determining who may claim a child for dependency and HOH purposes. A couple, even if not formally separated or divorced, must live apart for more than half the year in order for either spouse to claim HOH status.

Example: Luke and Pauline separated in February 2013 and lived apart for the rest of the year. They do not have a written separation agreement and are not yet divorced. Their six-year-old daughter, Kennedy, lived with Luke all year, and he paid more than half the cost of keeping up the home. Luke files a separate tax return and claims Kennedy as a dependent because he is the custodial parent. Luke can also claim HOH status for 2013. Although Luke is still legally married, he can file as HOH because he meets all the requirements to be "considered unmarried."

Example: Janine and Richard separated on July 10, but were not yet divorced at the end of the year. They have one minor child, Madeline, age eight. Even though Janine lived with Madeline and supported her for the remainder of the year, Janine does not qualify for HOH filing status because she and Richard did not live apart for the last six months of the year.

Death or Birth during the Year: A taxpayer may still file as HOH if the qualifying person is born or dies during the year. The taxpayer must have provided more than half of the cost of keeping up a home that was the individual's main home while he was alive.

Example: Velma has a son in September 2013 who dies within weeks of his birth. She may claim him on her tax return as a qualifying child even though he only lived a short while.

Dependent Parents: If a taxpayer's qualifying person is a dependent parent, the taxpayer may file HOH even if the parent does not live with the taxpayer. The taxpayer must pay more than half the cost of keeping up a home that was the parent's main home for the entire year. This rule also applies to a parent in a rest home. A qualifying "parent" may be a stepparent, in-law, or grandparent who is related to the taxpayer by blood, marriage, or adoption.

Example: Sharon is 54 years old and single. She pays the monthly bill for Shasta Pines Retirement Homes, where her 78-year-old mother lives. Sharon's mother has lived at Shasta Pines for two years and has no income. Since Sharon pays more than half of the cost of her mother's living expenses, Sharon qualifies for head of household filing status.

Example: Tina is single and financially supports her mother, Rue, who lives in her own apartment. Rue dies suddenly on September 15, 2013. Tina may claim her mother as a dependent and file as HOH in 2013.

Nonresident Alien Spouses: A taxpayer who is married to a nonresident alien spouse may elect to file as HOH even if both spouses lived together throughout the year.

Example: In 2012, Tim, a U.S. citizen, met and married Aom, a nonresident alien who is a citizen and resident of Thailand. The couple lived together in Thailand while Tim was on sabbatical from his university teaching position. They have a son who was born in 2013. Tim may file as HOH, even though he and Aom lived together all year, because Aom is a nonresident alien.

Qualifying Widow(er) With a Dependent Child

Qualifying widow(er) with a dependent child is the least common filing status. A qualifying surviving spouse receives the same standard deduction and tax rates as married taxpayers who file jointly. In the year of the spouse's death, a taxpayer can generally file a joint return. However, if a surviving spouse remarries before the end of the year, the married filing separately status must be used for the decedent's final return.

Example: Shelly and her husband, Rodney, have an infant son. Rodney dies of cancer in January 2013. Shelly remarries in December 2013. Since she remarried in the same year her former husband died, she no longer qualifies for the joint return filing status with her deceased husband. Shelly does qualify for MFJ with her new spouse. Therefore, Rodney's filing status for his final tax return in 2013 must be MFS.

For each of the two years following the year of the spouse's death, the surviving spouse can use the qualifying widow(er) filing status if he has a qualifying dependent and does not remarry. After two years, the taxpayer's filing status converts to single or HOH, depending upon which status applies. For example, if a taxpayer's spouse died in 2012 and he did not remarry, he could use the qualifying widow(er) filing status for 2013 and 2014 if he has a qualifying dependent.

Example: Barbara's husband dies on December 3, 2013. She has one dependent child, a 14-year-old daughter. Barbara does not remarry. Therefore, Barbara's filing status for 2013 is MFJ (the last year her husband was alive). In 2014 and 2015, she can file as a qualifying widow, which is a more favorable filing status than single or HOH.

To be eligible for the qualifying widow(er) filing status, the taxpayer must:

- Not have remarried before the end of the tax year.
- Have been eligible to file a joint return for the year the spouse died; it does not matter if a joint return was actually filed.
- Have a qualifying child for the year.
- Have furnished over half the cost of keeping up the child's home for the entire year.

Filing Requirements

Not every person is required to file a tax return. A taxpayer is required to file a tax return if his 2013 gross income exceeds the combined total of the standard deduction and personal exemption amounts. The IRS defines gross income as all income a taxpayer received in the form of money, goods, property, and services that is not exempt from tax. Sometimes, a taxpayer is required to file even though none of his income is taxable. The 2013 filing requirement thresholds, expressed as levels of gross income, are as follows:

- Single: $10,000
  - Single, 65 or over: $11,500
- Head of household (HOH): $12,850
  - Head of household, 65 or over: $14,350
- Married filing jointly (MFJ): $20,000
  - 65 or over, one spouse (MFJ): $21,200
  - 65 or over, both spouses (MFJ): $22,400
- Married filing separately (MFS): $3,900 (any age)
- Qualifying widow(er) with dependent child: $16,100
  - 65 or over: $17,300

Example: Laurel is 36, single, and had gross income of $17,500 last year. She does not have any children. She is required to file a tax return since her income was over $10,000. She will use the single filing status.

Example: Adrienne and Marvin are married and plan to file jointly. Adrienne is 64 and had gross income of $12,225 for the year. Marvin is 66 and had gross income of $6,500 for the year. Since their combined gross income was $18,725, they are not required to file a tax return. The filing requirement threshold for joint filers when one spouse is 65 or older is $21,200 in 2013.

Example: Wallace is 67 and single. His gross income was $11,900 during the tax year. Wallace is required to file a return because his gross income is over the filing threshold ($11,500 for 2013) for single taxpayers who are 65 and over.

Example: Rita is 66, married, and had $9,500 of wage income in 2013. Her husband, Roger, also 66, had $10,000 in wage income. They have no dependents. Normally, Roger and Rita would not have a filing requirement because their gross income is under the filing threshold for MFJ taxpayers 65 and over. However, Rita wants to file separately from her husband. She is therefore required to file a tax return because the filing threshold for MFS is $3,900. Roger must also file a tax return, because his filing status is MFS by default. Roger cannot choose to file jointly with his wife unless she agrees, since both spouses are required to sign a joint return.

Self-Employed Taxpayers: There are different requirements for taxpayers who are self-employed. Generally, a taxpayer is required to file a tax return if he has net self-employment earnings of $400 or more.

Dependents: A dependent is required to file an income tax return when he has any of the following:

- Unearned income of more than $1,000
- Earned income (such as wages) of more than $6,100
- Gross income of more than the larger of:
  - $1,000, or
  - Earned income (up to $6,100) plus $350

Definitions: Earned income includes employee compensation and self-employment earnings. Most other types of income are considered **unearned income**, including interest income, dividends, inheritances, and prizes.

Example: Cesar is a 16-year-old high school student who is claimed as a dependent on his parents' tax return. He works as a pizza delivery boy ten hours a week and earned $3,200 in wages in 2013. He also had $1,200 of interest income from a certificate of deposit that his grandmother gave him. Cesar is required to file a tax return because his unearned income exceeds $1,000.

Example: Taryn is 15 and is claimed as a dependent on her mother's tax return. Taryn babysat over the summer, worked at an ice cream parlor during the school year, and earned a total of $6,300. She had no other income. Taryn must file a tax return because her total earned income is more than $6,100.

Example: Marc is 20, single, and a full-time college student. Marc's parents claim him on their joint tax return. He received $200 in interest income and earned $2,750 in wages from a part-time job. Marc does not have to file a tax return because his total income of $2,950 is below the filing threshold for dependents.

Even if a taxpayer is not legally required to file a tax return, he should do so if he is eligible to receive a refund. A taxpayer should file a tax return if he:

- Had income tax withheld from his pay,
- Made estimated tax payments or had prior year overpayments,
- Qualifies for the Earned Income Credit, or
- Qualifies for any other refundable tax credits.

Example: Holly is single, has a young child and qualifies for head of household filing status. In 2013, she earns $12,000 in wages and $700 in self-employment income from cleaning houses. Although Holly makes less than the filing threshold for the HOH filing status, she must file a tax return because her net earnings from self-employment exceed $400. Even if Holly did not have self-employment earnings, she should still file a tax return, because she likely qualifies for the Earned Income Credit. The EIC is a refundable credit for low income wage earners, which could give Holly a refund.

Additional Filing Requirements

Sometimes a taxpayer is required to file a tax return even if the gross income threshold is not met, such as in the previous example of self-employment earnings of $400 or more. Other examples include the following:

- Church employees who are exempt from employers' Social Security and Medicare taxes and have wages above $108.28.
- If the taxpayer owes Social Security tax or Medicare tax on tips not reported to his employer.
- If the taxpayer must pay the alternative minimum tax.
- If the taxpayer owes additional tax in connection with a qualified plan, an IRA, a health savings account, or other tax-favored health plan.
- If the taxpayer received a Medicare Advantage MSA or health savings account distribution.
- If the taxpayer owes household employment taxes for a household worker such as a nanny.
- If the taxpayer must recapture an education credit, investment credit, or other credit.

Determining Residency

In addition to filing status, to file an accurate tax return, a taxpayer must determine whether he is considered a *resident* or a *nonresident*. For tax purposes, an alien is an individual who is not a U.S. citizen. Aliens are further classified as nonresident aliens and resident aliens. Residency status is important because these taxpayers are taxed in different ways:

- **Resident aliens** are generally taxed on their worldwide income, the same as U.S. citizens.
- **Nonresident aliens** are taxed only on their income from sources within the United States and on certain income connected with the conduct of a trade or business in the U.S.
- **Dual status aliens** are both nonresident and resident aliens during the same tax year, with different rules applying for the part of the year a taxpayer is a U.S. resident and the part of the year he is a nonresident.

Residency for IRS purposes is not the same as legal immigration status. An individual may be considered a U.S. resident for tax purposes based upon the time he spends in the United States, regardless of immigration status.

A nonresident alien could be someone who lives outside the U.S. and simply invests in U.S. property or stocks, and is therefore required to file a tax return to correctly report his earnings.

Residency Tests

If the taxpayer is an alien, he is considered a nonresident alien for tax purposes unless he meets at least one of two tests: the green card test or the substantial presence test.

Green Card Test: An alien taxpayer is considered a U.S. resident if he is a "lawful permanent resident" of the United States at any time during the tax year. A taxpayer generally has this status if he is a lawful immigrant and has been issued an alien registration card, also known as a green card. An alien who has been present in the United States at any time during a calendar year as a lawful permanent resident may choose to be treated as a resident alien for the entire calendar year.

Substantial Presence Test: An alien taxpayer without a green card is considered a U.S. resident for tax purposes only if he meets the substantial presence test for the calendar year. To meet this test, he must be physically present in the United States for at least:

- 31 days during the current year (2013), and
- 183 days during the three-year period that includes the current year (2013) and the two years immediately preceding the current year.

For purposes of the 183-day requirement, all the days present in the current year (2013) are counted, along with:

- 1/3 of the days present in the first year before the current year (2012), and
- 1/6 of the days present in the second year before the current year (2011).

Note: If an individual meets the requirements of the substantial presence test, he is considered for tax purposes a resident alien of the United States, even though he may be an undocumented immigrant. Filing a tax return as a resident does not affect or alter immigration status.

Numerous exceptions are considered when counting days for the substantial presence test. Days in the United States are not counted if the alien taxpayer:

- Regularly commutes to work in the U.S. from a residence in Canada or Mexico (deemed a "closer connection to home country").

- Is in the U.S. as a crew member of a foreign vessel.
- Is unable to leave because of a medical condition that arose while in the United States.
- Is a professional athlete in the U.S. to compete in a charitable sports event. These athletes exclude only the days in which they actually competed in the sports event, but do not exclude days used for practice, travel, or promotional events.
- Is an exempt individual. Exempt individuals include aliens who are:
  - Foreign government-related individuals in the U.S. temporarily, such as diplomats.
  - Teachers on temporary visas. Scholars are exempt for two years.
  - Students on temporary visas who do not intend to reside permanently in the U.S. Students are exempt from the substantial presence test for five years.

If the taxpayer does not meet either the green card test or the substantial presence test, he is considered a nonresident alien for tax purposes. Unlike U.S. citizens and U.S. residents, nonresident aliens are subject to U.S. income tax only on their U.S. source income.

Example: Juliana is a Brazilian citizen who was physically present in the United States for 15 days in each of the years 2011, 2012, and 2013. She is not a green card holder. Juliana earned $32,000 in 2013 as a Portuguese translator for the U.S. government. Since the total days she was present in the U.S. for the three-year period do not meet the substantial presence test, Juliana is not considered a resident for tax purposes for 2013 and her earnings are taxed as a nonresident. Juliana is required to file Form 1040NR, *U.S. Nonresident Alien Income Tax Return*.

Tax Residency through Marriage

A nonresident alien who does not meet the substantial presence test and does not have a green card may still elect to be treated as a resident for tax purposes if he is married to a U.S. citizen or resident. This election can be made only if:

- At the end of the year, one spouse is a nonresident alien and the other is a U.S. citizen or resident, and
- Both spouses agree to file a joint return and to treat the nonresident alien as a resident alien for the entire tax year.

Example: Lola and Bruno are married and both are nonresident aliens at the beginning of the year. In February, Bruno becomes a legal U.S. resident alien and obtains a green card and a Social Security number. Lola and Bruno may both choose to be treated as resident aliens for tax purposes by attaching a statement to their joint return. Lola is not eligible for a Social Security number, so she must apply for an ITIN. Lola and Bruno must file a joint return for the year they make the election, but they can file either joint or separate returns for later years.

Example: Mei, a citizen of South Korea, is temporarily in the U.S. as a graduate student on an F-1 visa status. She has resided continuously in the U.S. since arriving on August 15, 2008. She was in the U.S. all of 2013. Because international students are exempt from the substantial presence test for five years, Mei became a resident alien for federal income tax purposes in 2013. Mei is married to Quon, who lives in South Korea and is a nonresident alien. Mei and Quon can both elect to be treated as U.S. residents for tax purposes on a jointly filed return.

Students: Most international students and scholars fall under the status of nonresident aliens. An international student is anyone who is temporarily in the U.S. on an F, J, M, or Q visa. Immediate family members of a student, including spouses and unmarried children under age 21 who reside with the student, are also considered students for tax purposes. Any part of a calendar year in which the student is present in the U.S. counts as a full year.

Example: Nayan is a graduate student at the local university. She came to the U.S. in 2008 from India as an F-1 student. She studied in the U.S. until the end of 2009 and then returned home. She re-entered the U.S. as a J-1 student in 2013. For federal income tax purposes, Nayan is a nonresident alien because she has been in the U.S. for less than five years as a student.

Dual Status Aliens: A taxpayer is considered a dual status alien when he has been both a resident alien and a nonresident alien in the same tax year. The most common dual-status tax years are the years of arrival and departure. A taxpayer's status on the last day of the year determines whether he is a resident alien or a nonresident alien for the tax year.

For the part of each year the taxpayer is a nonresident alien, he is taxed only on his U.S.-source income. For the part of each year the taxpayer is a resident alien, he is taxed on his worldwide income. This applies even if the income was earned earlier in the year while the taxpayer was a nonresident alien but was received after he became a resident for tax purposes.

Example: Abbas became a U.S. resident for tax purposes on January 1, 2013. On January 15, 2013, he received $2,000 in income for contract work he did the previous year. Even though the income was earned while he was a nonresident alien, it was received after he became a resident. The income is reported and taxed on Form 1040, not on Form 1040NR.

Tax Treaties: The United States has income tax treaties with a number of foreign countries. Under these treaties, residents of foreign countries may be taxed at reduced rates, or be exempt from U.S. income taxes on certain items of income they receive from U.S-source income. These reduced rates and exemptions vary among countries and specific items of income.

Treaty provisions generally are reciprocal. Therefore, a U.S. citizen or resident who receives income from a treaty country and who is subject to taxes imposed by foreign countries may be entitled to certain credits, deductions, exemptions, and reductions in the rate of taxes of those foreign countries.

Income received by a nonresident alien that is effectively connected with a trade or business in the United States is, after allowable deductions, taxed at the rates that apply to U.S. citizens and residents. Withholding would be made at the highest applicable rate.

Note: Other income or gains from U.S. sources is generally subject to withholding at 30%, unless a lower treaty rate applies.

Unit 2: Study Questions

1. Helen, age 65, and Edward, age 72, were married in 2013. They have no dependents. Helen had gross income of $2,000 and Edward had gross income of $28,000 for the year. Edward wants to file jointly, but Helen wants to file separately. Which of the following statements is true?

A. Edward is required to file a tax return using the MFS status. Helen is not required to file a return.
B. Edward may still file jointly with Helen and sign on her behalf, so long as he notifies her in writing.
C. Edward and Helen are both required to file tax returns, and they must both file MFS.
D. Edward and Helen may both file as single.

2. Munir is a citizen of Pakistan who is granted a green card and comes to the U.S. to work as an engineer. Munir arrives in the U.S. on November 1, 2013. He earns $26,000 in U.S. wages in November and December. Which of the following is true?

A. He is not required to file a U.S. tax return.
B. He is required to file a U.S. tax return, and he must file using Form 1040NR.
C. He is required to file a U.S. tax return, and he must file using Form 1040 (or Form 1040A or Form 1040EZ.
D. He is not required to file a U.S. tax return in 2013, but he will be required to file a return in 2014.

3. A person who is not required to file a tax return should still file a return for all of the following reasons except to ________.

A. Report self-employment net earnings of $400 or more.
B. Claim a refund of withheld taxes.
C. Claim the Earned Income Credit.
D. Claim the Additional Child Tax Credit.

4. Annie's husband, Enzo, has neither a green card nor a visa. He was physically present in the United States for 150 days in each of the years 2011, 2012, and 2013. Is Enzo a resident alien under the substantial presence test?

A. Yes, he is a resident alien for tax purposes.
B. No, he is a nonresident alien for tax purposes.
C. Enzo is a nonresident alien for tax purposes, but he may elect to file as a resident with his spouse.
D. None of the above is correct.

5. Janet and Harry are married and file jointly. During 2013, Janet turned 67 and Harry turned 66. Janet's gross income was $19,000, and Harry's gross income from self-employment was $620. Harry had no other income. Based on this information, which of the following statements is true?

A. Janet and Harry are not required to file tax returns.
B. Janet and Harry are required to file tax returns.
C. Only Janet is required to file a tax return.
D. Only Harry is required to file a tax return.

6. Which of the following statements is true regarding the head of household filing status?

A. The taxpayer must be single on the first day of the year in order to qualify for head of household filing status.
B. The taxpayer's spouse must live in the home during the tax year.
C. The taxpayer's dependent parent does not have to live with the taxpayer in order to qualify for head of household filing status.
D. The taxpayer must have paid roughly half of the cost of keeping up the house for the entire year.

7. Dana's husband died on January 24, 2013. She has one dependent son who is eight years old. What is Dana's best filing status for tax year 2013?

A. Married filing jointly.
B. Single.
C. Qualifying widow.
D. Head of household.

8. Trinity, age 22, is single and a full-time college student who is claimed as a dependent on her father's tax return. In 2013, Trinity earned $6,150 in wages from her part-time job as an administrative assistant. She has no other income. Is she required to file a tax return?

A. Yes, she is required to file a tax return.
B. No, she is not required to file a tax return.
C. Trinity is only required to file a tax return if she is a full-time student.
D. Trinity should file a return because she will receive a refund, but she is not required to file.

9. Malik and his wife, Stacey, are married. In 2013, she earned $4,600 in wages before she quit her job. Malik worked as a bartender and earned $11,000 in wages for the year. He owes Social Security and Medicare tax on $2,500 in tip income he did not report to his employer. Do Malik and Stacey have to file a tax return?

A. No, because their gross income is below the threshold for MFJ.
B. Yes, because their gross income is above the threshold for MFJ.
C. Yes, because Malik owes Social Security tax on his unreported tip income.
D. Stacey is not required to file, if Malik files separately and chooses not to report the tip income.

10. Clarence takes care of his ten-year-old grandson. How long must his grandson live in Clarence's home in order for Clarence to qualify for head of household status?

A. At least three months.
B. More than half the year.
C. The entire year.
D. More than 12 months.

11. When may a taxpayer amend a joint tax return from "married filing jointly" to "married filing separately" after the filing deadline?

A. Never.
B. Only within the statute of limitations for filing amended returns.
C. Only with annulled marriages.
D. Only when an estate's personal representative changes a joint return elected by the surviving spouse to a separate return for the decedent.

12. In order to qualify a taxpayer as head of household, a person must be ________ .

A. A minor child.
B. A blood relative.
C. The taxpayer's dependent or the taxpayer's qualifying child.
D. A minor child or a full-time student.

13. Huang is a student temporarily in the U.S. on an F-1 Visa. You are his tax preparer and you are trying to determine residency for tax purposes. Huang was present in the U.S. all year. How long is he exempt from the substantial presence test?

A. One year.
B. Three years.
C. Five years.
D. There is no exemption to the substantial presence test.

14. Victor is 39 years old and has lived apart from his wife, Eleanor, since February 1, 2013. Their divorce was not yet final at the end of 2013 and they were not legally separated under a separate maintenance decree. They have two minor children. Since they split up, one child has lived with Victor and the other with Eleanor. Victor provides all of the support for the minor child living with him. Eleanor refuses to file jointly with Victor in 2013. The most beneficial filing status that Victor qualifies for is _______________:

A. Married filing separately.
B. Single.
C. Head of household.
D. Married filing jointly.

15. Mary and Troy are married and live together. Mary earned $7,000 in 2013, and Troy earned $42,000. Mary wants to file a joint return, but Troy refuses to file with Mary and instead files a separate return. Which of the following statements is true?

A. Mary may file a joint amended tax return and sign Troy's name.
B. Mary and Troy must both file separate returns.
C. Mary may file as single because Troy refuses to sign a joint return.
D. Mary does not have a filing requirement.

16. Kathy's marriage was annulled on February 25, 2014. She was married to her husband in 2011 and filed jointly with him in 2011 and 2012. She has not yet filed her 2013 tax return. Kathy has no dependents. Which of the following statements is true?

A. She must file amended returns, claiming single filing status for all open years affected by the annulment.
B. She is not required to file amended returns, and she may file jointly with her husband in 2013.
C. She is not required to file amended returns, and she must file married filing separately on her 2013 return.
D. She is not required to file amended returns, and she should file as single on her 2013 return.

17. Lisa married Stuart in 2010. Stuart died in 2012. Lisa has not remarried and she has one dependent child. Which filing status should Lisa use for her 2013 tax return?

A. Single.
B. Married filing jointly.
C. Head of household.
D. Qualifying widow with dependent child.

18. Which dependent relative may qualify a taxpayer for head of household filing status?

A. An adult stepdaughter who lives in her own apartment as she looks for work and is supported by the taxpayer.
B. A family friend who lives with the taxpayer all year.
C. A parent who lives in his own home and not with the taxpayer.
D. A child who lived with the taxpayer for three months of the tax year.

19. Dwight and Angela are married, but they choose to file separate returns for 2013, because the IRS is investigating Dwight for a previous tax issue. Dwight and Angela file their separate returns on time. A few months after the investigation is over and Dwight's previous tax issue has been resolved, he wishes to file amended returns and file jointly with his wife in order to claim the Earned Income Credit. Which of the following is true?

A. Dwight is prohibited from changing his filing status in order to claim this credit.
B. Dwight and Angela may amend their MFS tax returns to MFJ in order to claim the credit.
C. Dwight may amend his tax return to MFJ filing status, but he may not claim the credit.
D. Angela may not file jointly with Dwight after she has already filed a separate tax return.

20. The two filing statuses that generally result in the lowest taxes are married filing jointly and ___________.

A. Married filing separately.
B. Head of household.
C. Qualifying widow(er) with dependent child.
D. Single.

21. Madison and Todd are not married and do not live together, but they have a twc-year-old daughter named Amanda. Madison and her daughter lived together all year while Todd lived alone in his own apartment. Madison earned $13,000 working as a clothing store clerk. Todd earned $48,000 managing a hardware store. He paid over half the cost of Madison's apartment for rent and utilities. He also gave Madison extra money for groceries. Todd does not pay any expenses or support for any other family member. Which of the following is true?

A. Todd may file as head of household.
B. Madison may file as head of household.
C. Todd and Madison may file jointly.
D. Neither may claim head of household filing status.

22. A U.S. resident or citizen who is married to a nonresident alien can file a joint return so long as both spouses ____________.

A. Sign the return and agree to be taxed on their worldwide income.
B. Are living overseas.
C. Have valid Social Security numbers.
D. Are physically present in the United States.

23. Carol and Raul were married four years ago and have no children. They split up in 2012, but did not file for divorce. Although they lived apart during all of 2013, they are neither divorced nor legally separated. Which of the following filing statuses can they use?

A. Single or married filing separately.
B. Married filing jointly or married filing separately.
C. Married filing separately or head of household.
D. Single or qualifying widow(er).

24. Louisa legally separated from her husband during 2013. They have a 10-year-old son. Which of the following would prevent Louisa from filing as head of household?

A. Louisa has maintained a separate residence from her husband since November 2012.
B. Her son's principal home is with Louisa.
C. Louisa's parents assisted with 40% of the household costs.
D. Her son lived with Louisa from July 3, 2013 to December 31, 2013.

25. Taxpayers are considered to be married for the entire year if:

A. One spouse dies during the year and the surviving spouse does not remarry.
B. The spouses are legally separated under a separate maintenance decree.
C. The spouses are divorced on December 31 of the tax year.
D. The spouses had their marriage annulled December 31 of the tax year.

26. Alexandra's younger brother, Sebastian, is 17, and lived with friends in January and February of 2013. From March through July of 2013, he lived with Alexandra. On August 1, Sebastian moved back in with his friends and stayed with them the rest of the year. Since Sebastian did not have a job, Alexandra gave him money every month. She had no other dependents. Which of the following statements is true?

A. Alexandra may file as head of household for 2013.
B. Alexandra may file jointly with Sebastian in 2013.
C. Alexandra cannot file as head of household in 2013.
D. Sebastian may file as head of household in 2013.

27. The married filing separately (MFS) status is for taxpayers who:

A. Are legally divorced on the last day of the year.
B. Are married and choose to file separate returns.
C. Are unmarried, but engaged to be married.
D. Are unmarried, but have a dependent child.

28. Which of the following is not a valid expense used to calculate whether a taxpayer is paying more than half the cost of maintaining a home to qualify for the HOH filing status?

A. Food eaten in the home.
B. Home mortgage payment.
C. Property taxes.
D. Clothing.

29. All of the following individuals are required to file an income tax return except:

A. A taxpayer who owes household employment tax for a nanny.
B. A church employee who is exempt from payroll taxes and who earned $106 in wages in 2013.
C. A 74-year-old qualifying widower who earned $17,000 in 2013.
D. A single taxpayer who earned $6,500 in 2013 and who owes tax on a health savings account.

30. Kylie is an 18-year-old senior in high school. She works as a grocery store bagger on weekends and earned $1,400 in 2013. She also received $1,100 for a winning scratch-off lottery ticket. Her parents claim her as a dependent on their tax return. Does Kylie have to file her own return?

A. Yes, because of the amount of her unearned income.
B. Yes, because of the combined amount of her unearned and earned income.
C. No, because her earned income is below the threshold for a dependent.
D. No, because it is illegal for a high school student to play the lottery.

Unit 3: Personal and Dependency Exemptions

For additional information read:
Publication 501, *Exemptions, Standard Deduction, and Filing Information*
Publication 504, *Divorced or Separated Individuals*

Exemptions are like tax deductions, as they reduce taxable income. Exemption amounts are indexed for inflation and are generally updated every year. For tax year 2013, the exemption amount is $3,900 per person.

Taxpayers may qualify to claim two kinds of exemptions:

- **Personal exemptions,** which taxpayers claim for themselves.
- **Dependency exemptions,** which taxpayers claim for their dependents.

Only one exemption is allowed per person.

Married Couples: On a joint tax return, a married couple is allowed two personal exemptions, one for each spouse. One spouse is never considered the dependent of the other spouse.

Example: Jenny married Rick in April of 2013. Jenny and Rick may claim two personal exemptions on their jointly filed return. Because they are married, they cannot claim each other as a dependent.

If a married couple files separate returns, each spouse can claim a personal exemption for himself or herself. However, if a spouse files a separate return, he may claim an exemption for his spouse only if that spouse had no gross income, is not filing a return, and could not be claimed as the dependent of another taxpayer.

A taxpayer who is divorced or legally separated at the end of the tax year cannot claim an exemption for his (former) spouse. If a taxpayer's spouse dies during the year and the surviving spouse does not remarry before the end of the year, he can claim an exemption for the deceased spouse on a jointly filed return.

Example: Barrett's wife died in 2013. He did not remarry. Barrett may claim personal exemptions for himself and his deceased wife on their jointly filed return for 2013.

A taxpayer can claim one dependency exemption for each qualified dependent. Examples of dependents include a child, stepchild, brother, sister, or parent.

Example: Hao and Bình are married and have four dependent children. On their jointly filed return, they may claim six exemptions: four dependency exemptions for their children and two personal exemptions for themselves.

Phase-out of Exemptions: In 2013, the phase-out of personal and dependency exemptions has been reinstated for taxpayers with adjusted gross income above specified thresholds. For an individual subject to this limitation, the total exemption amount that can be claimed is reduced by 2% for each $2,500 increment by which his AGI exceeds the applicable threshold.

For married couples filing jointly, exemptions are fully phased out once their AGI reaches $422,500; for a single filer, exemptions are fully phased out when AGI reaches $372,500.

Exemption Phase-out Thresholds	
Filing Status	**AGI Phase-out**
MFJ, QW	$300,000-$422,500
HOH	$275,000-$397,500
Single	$250,000-$372,500
MFS	$150,000-$211,250

Example: Evan and Martina file jointly. They have no children. Each is allowed a $3,900 personal exemption, for a total of $7,800. Their AGI for 2013 is $340,000, or $40,000 above the threshold at which the phase-out begins for their filing status. For each $2,500 of that $40,000, their $7,800 exemption is reduced by 2%. The percentage reduction is 32% [($40,000 ÷ $2,500) × 2%], or $2,496. Evan and Martina's personal exemption amount is reduced to $5,304 ($7,800 - $2,496 = $5,304.)

Primary Tests for Dependency

In order to determine if a taxpayer may claim a dependency exemption for another person, there are three main tests:

- Dependent taxpayer
- Joint return
- Citizenship or residency

#1. Dependent Taxpayer Test: If a taxpayer can claim another person as a dependent, even if the taxpayer does not do so, the dependent cannot take a personal exemption on his own tax return or claim another person as a dependent, even if he has a qualifying child or qualifying relative. Thus, there is only one personal exemption that applies to a person who qualifies as a dependent, whether he files his own return or is listed as a dependent on someone else's return.

Example: Eva is a 17-year-old single mother who has an infant son. Eva is claimed as a dependent by her parents, so she cannot claim an exemption for herself, and she is prohibited from claiming her infant son as a dependent on her own tax return.

Sometimes an individual meets the rules to be a qualifying dependent of more than one person. Regardless, only one person can claim an individual as a dependent on his tax return.

Example: Dan and Linda live with their daughter, Savannah. They are not married, so each files as single. Savannah is a qualifying child for both Dan and Linda, but only one of them can claim her as a dependent on their tax return.

#2. Joint Return Test: A dependent cannot file a joint return with his spouse. In other words, if an individual files a joint return, he cannot be claimed as a dependent by another taxpayer.

Example: Ellen is 18 years old and had no income in 2013. She got married on November 1, 2013. Ellen's new husband had $26,700 of income and they file jointly, claiming two personal exemptions on their tax return. Ellen's father supported her throughout the year and even paid for their wedding. However, her father cannot claim Ellen as his dependent because she is filing jointly with her new husband.

This test does not apply if the joint return is filed by the dependent only to claim a refund and neither spouse would have a tax liability, even if they filed separate returns.

Example: Greg and Taylor are both 18 and married. They live with Taylor's mother, Michelle. In 2013, Greg earned $1,800 from a part-time job. Neither Greg nor Taylor is required to file a tax return, but they file a joint return to obtain a refund of the taxes that were withheld from Greg's wages. As the exception to the joint return test applies, Michelle may claim exemptions for both Greg and Taylor on her tax return, if all the other tests for dependency are met.

#3. Citizenship or Residency Test: The dependent must be a citizen or resident of the United States, or a citizen or resident of Canada or Mexico (with an exception for foreign-born adopted children.)

Example: Maurice is an American citizen. He provides all of the financial support for his two children, ages six and 12, who live in Canada with their mother. Maurice may claim his children as dependents.

Dependency Relationships

A taxpayer cannot claim a person as a dependent unless that person is either his **qualifying child** or his **qualifying relative**. There are very specific tests to identify the difference between the two.

Note: Both qualifying children and qualifying relatives must meet all of the general dependency requirements already specified: the dependent taxpayer, joint return, and citizenship or residency tests.

Qualifying Child

The tests for a qualifying child are more stringent than the tests for a qualifying relative. Having a qualifying child entitles a taxpayer to claim a dependency exemption as well as numerous tax credits, including the Earned Income Credit and the Child Tax Credit. Having a qualifying relative, on the other hand, does not qualify a taxpayer for these credits.

There are five tests for a qualifying child:

- Relationship
- Age
- Residency
- Support
- Tie-breaker (for a qualifying child of more than one person)

#1. Relationship Test: The qualifying child must be related to the taxpayer by blood, marriage, or legal adoption.

Qualifying children include:

- A child or stepchild
- An adopted child
- A sibling or stepsibling
- A descendant of one of the above (such as a grandchild, niece, or nephew)
- An eligible foster child

#2. Age Test: In order to be a qualifying child, the dependent must be:

- Under the age of 19 at the end of the tax year, or
- Under the age of 24 at the end of the tax year and a full-time student, or
- Permanently and totally disabled at any time during the year, regardless of age.

A child is considered a full-time student if he attends a qualified educational institution full-time for at least five months during the year.

Example: Andrew is 45 years old and totally disabled. Karen, his 37-year-old sister, provides all of Andrew's support and cares for him in her home, where he lives with her full-time. Despite Andrew's age, since he is completely disabled he is considered a qualifying child and a dependent for tax purposes. Karen may claim Andrew as her qualifying child and may file as head of household.

A child who is claimed as a dependent must be younger than the taxpayer who is claiming him, except in the case of dependents who are disabled. For taxpayers filing jointly, the child must be younger than one spouse listed on the return, but does not have to be younger than both spouses.

Example: Owen and Sydney are 22 years old, married, and file jointly. Sydney's 23-year-old brother, Parker, is a full-time student and lives with Owen and Sydney, who provide all of his support. Parker is not disabled. Owen and Sydney are both younger than Parker. Therefore, Parker is not their qualifying child, even though he is a full-time student.

Example: Lucius, age 34, and Paige, age 21, are married and file jointly. Paige's 23-year-old nephew, Jason, is a full-time student, single, and lives with Lucius and Paige. They provide all of Jason's support. In this case, Lucius and Paige may claim Jason as a qualifying child on their joint tax return because he is a full-time student and is younger than Lucius.

#3. Residency Test: A qualifying child must live with the taxpayer for more than half the tax year (over six months).

Example: Marty's nine-year-old granddaughter, Quinn, lives with him for five months of the year, with her mother for three months, and with her aunt for four months. Quinn is not Marty's qualifying child because the residency test is not met. However, she may be Marty's qualifying relative if other tests are met.

Exceptions apply for children of divorced parents, kidnapped children,[6] and temporary absences, and for children who were born or died during the year.[7]

---

[6] A child who has been kidnapped can be treated as meeting the residency test if he was kidnapped by someone other than a family member and if he lived with the taxpayer for more than half of the year in the year in which the kidnapping occurred.

A temporary absence includes illness, college, vacation, military service, and incarceration in a juvenile facility. It must be reasonable to assume that the child will return to the home after the temporary absence.

Example: Scott is unmarried and lives with his 10-year-old son, Elijah. Scott provides all of Elijah's support. In 2013, Elijah became very ill and was hospitalized for seven months. Elijah is still considered Scott's qualifying child, because the hospitalization counts as a temporary absence from home. Scott may claim Elijah as his qualifying child and also file for head of household status.

#4. Support Test: A qualifying child cannot provide more than one-half of his own support. A full-time student does not take scholarships (whether taxable or nontaxable) into account when calculating the support test.

Note: The definition of "support" includes only income that is actually used for living expenses. For example, if a child earns income that is saved in a bank account rather than spent on the child's living expenses, the amounts are not included in the support test.

Example: Douglas and Andrea file jointly. They have a daughter named Isabella, age 29. She earned $4,000 before she was laid off in March and moved back in with her parents. Douglas and Andrea therefore provided the majority of Isabella's support for the rest of the year. Isabella got a new job in December and moved out. She is not a qualifying child for federal tax purposes. Isabella meets the support test, as well as the residency test. However, she does not meet the age test.

Example: Samuel has an 18-year-old daughter named Tiffany. Samuel provided $4,000 toward his teenage daughter's support for the year. Tiffany also has a part-time job and provided $13,000 of her own support. Therefore, Tiffany provided over half of her own support for the year. Tiffany does not pass the support test, and consequently, she is not Samuel's qualifying child. Tiffany can file a tax return as single and claim her own exemption.

Example: Penelope, age 15, had a small role in a television series. She earned $40,000 as a child actor, but her parents put all the money in a trust fund for her. She lived at home all year. Penelope meets the support test since her earnings were not used for her own support. She meets the tests for a qualifying child, so she can be claimed as a dependent by her parents.

Payments received from a child placement agency for the support of a foster child are considered support provided by the agency, rather than support provided by the child.

Example: Gina is a foster parent who provided $3,000 toward her 10-year-old foster son's support for the year. The state of Nevada provided $4,000, which was considered support provided by the state, not by the child. Gina's foster child did not provide more than half of his own support for the year. Therefore, Gina may claim her son as a qualifying child if all the other tests are met.

This special tax treatment applies for all years until the child is returned; there is a determination the child is dead; or the year the child would have reached age 18.

[7] A taxpayer cannot claim an exemption for a stillborn child. The child must be born alive, even if he lived only for a short time.

#5. Tie-Breaker Test: Only one person can claim a qualifying child, even if the child qualifies for more than one person. If more than one taxpayer attempts to claim the same child, the tie-breaker rules apply, meaning the child is treated as a qualifying child in the following sequence:

- By the child's parents, if they file a joint return
- If only one of the taxpayers is the child's parent, by that parent
- By the parent with whom the child lived the longest during the year
- By the parent with the highest AGI, if the child lived with each parent for the same length of time during the tax year
- By the taxpayer with the highest AGI, if neither of the child's parents can claim the child as a qualifying child
- By a taxpayer with a higher AGI than either of the child's parents who can also claim the child as a qualifying child but does not

Example: Sophia is single and has a three-year-old son named Preston. They live with Sophia's father, Theodore (the child's grandfather). Sophia claims Preston as her qualifying child, which means the child may not be the qualifying child of Theodore, the grandfather.

Example: Penny and her sister, Rosa, live together. Their seven-year-old niece, Brianna, lived with her aunts all year because Brianna's mother is incarcerated. Penny's AGI is $12,600. Rosa's AGI is $19,000. Brianna is a qualifying child of both Penny and Rosa because she meets the relationship, age, residency, and joint return tests for both aunts. However, Rosa has the primary right to claim Brianna as her qualifying child because her AGI is higher than Penny's.

Qualifying Relative

A person who is not a qualifying child may still qualify as a dependent under the rules for qualifying relatives. Even an individual who is not a family member can be a qualifying relative. Unlike a qualifying child, a qualifying relative can be any age. To be claimed as a qualifying relative, the dependent must meet the four following tests:

- Not a qualifying child
- Member of household or relationship
- Gross income
- Support

#1. Not a Qualifying Child Test: If a child is already a qualifying child for any taxpayer, he cannot also be a qualifying relative.

#2. Member of Household or Relationship Test: A dependent who is not related to the taxpayer must have lived with the taxpayer the entire tax year in order to meet the member of household or relationship test.[8] A family member who is related to the taxpayer in any of the following ways does not have to live with the taxpayer to meet this test:

- A child, stepchild, foster child, or descendant of any of them (for example, a grandchild)
- A sibling, stepsibling, or half sibling

[8] If a relationship violates local laws, this test is not met. For example, if a taxpayer's state prohibits cohabitation, the person cannot be claimed as a dependent, even if all other criteria are met.

- A parent, grandparent, stepparent, or other direct ancestor (but not a foster parent)
- A niece or nephew, son-in-law, daughter-in-law, father-in-law, mother-in-law, brother-in-law, or sister-in-law

Example: Ernie's 12-year-old nephew, Josh, lived with him for three months in 2013. For the rest of the year, Josh lived with his mother, Natalie, in another state. Natalie is Ernie's 32-year-old sister. Even though Josh and Natalie lived in another state, Ernie still provided all of their financial support. Josh is not Ernie's qualifying child because he did not live with Ernie for more than half the year and therefore does not meet the residency test. However, Josh is Ernie's qualifying relative.

Note: For the relationship test, family members do not include cousins, who are treated as unrelated persons. A cousin must live with the taxpayer for the entire year and also meet the gross income test in order to qualify as a dependent.

Any relationship that is established by marriage does not end as a result of death or divorce. For example, if a taxpayer supports his mother-in-law, he can continue to claim her as a dependent even if he and his ex-spouse are divorced or if he becomes widowed.

Example: Mia and Caleb have always financially supported Mia's elderly mother, Gertrude, and claimed her as their dependent on their jointly filed returns. In 2011, Mia dies and Caleb becomes a widower. Caleb remarries in 2013, but continues to support his former mother-in-law. Caleb can still claim Gertrude on his tax returns, even though he has remarried.

Example: Tomás lived all year with his girlfriend, Ava, and her two children in his home. Their cohabitation does not violate local laws. Ava does not work and is not required to file a 2013 tax return. Ava and her two children are not related to Tomás as family members, but they may be qualifying relatives if they meet all the other tests.

#3. Gross Income Test: A qualifying relative cannot earn more than the personal exemption amount, which is $3,900 in 2013.

#4. Support Test: In order to claim an individual as a qualifying relative, the taxpayer must provide more than half of the dependent's total support during the year. Support includes amounts from Social Security and welfare payments, even if that support is nontaxable. Support does not include nontaxable scholarships. Support *can* include the fair market value (FMV) of lodging.

Example: Morgan provided $4,000 toward her father's support during the year. In 2013, Morgan's father received earned income of $600, nontaxable Social Security benefits of $4,800, and tax-exempt interest of $200. He used all these for his support. Morgan cannot claim an exemption for her father because the $4,000 she provided is not more than half of her father's total support of $9,600.

Multiple Support Agreements

There are special rules for claiming a dependency exemption for a qualifying relative when a taxpayer has a multiple support agreement. A multiple support agreement is when two or more people jointly provide for a person's support. This happens commonly when adult children are taking care of their parents.

In order for the dependency exemption to apply under a multiple support agreement, family members together must pay more than half of the person's total support, but no one member individually may pay more than half. In addition, the taxpayer who claims the dependent must provide more than 10% of the person's support.

Only one family member can claim the dependency exemption in a single year. Different qualifying family members can claim the dependency exemption in other years.

Example: Benjamin, Matthew, and Pamela are siblings who support their disabled mother, Abigail. Abigail is 83 and lives with Benjamin. In 2013, Abigail receives 20% of her financial support from Social Security, 40% from Matthew, 30% from Benjamin, and 10% from Pamela. Under the IRS rules for multiple support agreements, either Matthew or Benjamin can take the exemption for their mother if the other signs a statement agreeing not to do so. Pamela may not claim the dependency exemption because she does not provide more than 10% of the support for her mother.
Example: Graciela and Pilar are sisters who help support their 64-year-old father, Alonso. Each provides 20% of his care. The remaining 60% is provided equally by two persons not related to Alonso. He does not live with them. Because more than half of his support is provided by persons who cannot claim an exemption for him, no one can take the dependency exemption.

Divorced and Separated Parents

Generally, to claim a child as a dependent, the child must live with the taxpayer for more than half the year. However, special rules apply if the dependent is supported by parents who are divorced or separated, or who live apart.

In most cases, the child is the qualifying child of the custodial parent. However, the custodial parent may allow the noncustodial parent to claim the dependency exemption. The noncustodial parent must attach Form 8332, *Release/Revocation of Release of Claim to Exemption for Child by Custodial Parent*, to his tax return to claim the dependency exemption.

A child may be treated as the qualifying child of the noncustodial parent if all the following conditions apply:

- The parents are divorced or legally separated or they lived apart at all times during the last six months of the year.
- The child received over half of his support for the year from the parents (multiple support agreement rules do not apply in this case).
- The child is in the custody of one (or both) parents.
- The custodial parent signs a written declaration (Form 8332 or a similar statement) that he will not claim the child as a dependent for the year and the noncustodial parent attaches this declaration to his return.

This rule is an exception to the normal residency test for a qualifying child. It does not apply to determination of head of household filing status or to eligibility for the Earned Income Credit. These benefits may only be claimed by the custodial parent, even if the noncustodial parent claims the dependency exemption.

Example: Gary and Frieda are divorced and have one child. Frieda is the custodial parent, but she agrees to release the dependency exemption to Gary by signing Form 8332. Gary files as single and claims his son as his dependent. Frieda may still file as head of household, even though she does not claim the dependency exemption for her son because she maintained the home where he lived for most of the year.

If a divorce decree does not specify which parent is the custodial parent or which parent receives the dependency exemption, the exemption goes to the parent who has physical custody for the majority of the year.

Example: Alexis and Nathan are divorced. They have one child named Dylan. In 2013, Dylan lived with Alexis for 300 nights and with Nathan for 65 nights. Therefore, Alexis is the custodial parent and has the right to claim Dylan as her qualifying child. However, Alexis may choose to release the exemption to Nathan by signing Form 8332.

If the child lived with each parent for an equal number of nights during the year, the custodial parent is deemed to be the parent with the higher adjusted gross income.

Rules for Alien Exemptions

A resident alien may claim the same exemptions as U.S. citizens.

A nonresident alien, whether single or married, may claim only one personal exemption for himself, as long as he cannot be claimed as a dependent on any other U.S. tax return. He generally cannot claim any dependency exemptions.

Nonresident aliens who are married generally cannot file jointly and instead must file MFS.

Exceptions to these rules include the following:

- Residents of Canada and Mexico may claim additional exemptions for a spouse and dependents if:
    - The spouse had no gross income,
    - The spouse was not the dependent of another U.S. taxpayer, and
    - The dependents otherwise qualify as dependents.
- Residents of South Korea may claim additional exemptions for spouses and dependents if they meet the conditions outlined above, and if the spouse and children lived with the taxpayer at some time during the year.
- Students and business apprentices who are residents of India may claim an exemption for spouses and dependents if they meet certain conditions, including that the children claimed as dependents are U.S. citizens or resident aliens.

Unit 3: Study Questions

1. Alyssa is 18 years old and a full-time student who is claimed as a dependent on her parents' tax return. Over the summer, she worked in store and earned $7,000. Alyssa wants to file a tax return to report her wages and receive a refund. How many exemptions may she claim on her return?

A. Zero.

B. One.

C. Two.

D. Three.

2. Dani and Ted were divorced years ago. They have six-year-old twins who live with Dani. Her AGI is $41,000, and Ted's AGI is $48,000. Although Dani is the custodial parent, their divorce decree states that Ted may claim the children on his tax return. However, Dani refuses to sign Form 8332. Which of the following is true?

A. Ted can claim one child as a dependent.

B. Ted and Dani can each claim the children as dependents on their respective tax returns.

C. Dani is the custodial parent and refuses to sign Form 8332, so Ted may not claim a child on his return.

D. Neither Dani nor Ted can claim the children as dependents.

3. Haley is 23 and a full-time college student. During 2013, she lived at home with her parents for four months and lived in the dorm for the rest of the year. She also worked part-time and earned $6,000, but that income did not amount to half of her total support. Can Haley's parents still claim her as a dependent?

A. No, because Haley earned more than the personal exemption amount.

B. No, because Haley did not live with her parents for more than half the year, and she does not meet the age test.

C. Yes, Haley's parents can claim her as a qualifying child.

D. Yes, Haley's parents can claim her as a dependent, but only as a qualifying relative.

4. Ingrid and Bill file for divorce in 2012. Ingrid has one son from a prior marriage named Greg, age 15. After the divorce is final, Ingrid develops a drug problem and disappears. In 2013, Greg lives for nine months with his former stepfather, Bill, who provides all of Greg's support. Which statement is true?

A. Bill may claim Greg as his qualifying child.

B. Bill may claim Greg as his dependent but not as a qualifying child because the divorce dissolved any legal relationship between them.

C. Bill may not claim Greg as his dependent because they are not related persons.

D. Only Ingrid can claim Greg as her dependent.

5. Amber lives with Chad, her 16-year-old son. She provided $5,100 toward his support for the year. Chad also has a part-time job and provided $12,900 toward his own support. Can Amber claim her son as a dependent?

A. Yes, she can claim her son as a qualifying child, because he is a minor.

B. Yes, she can claim Chad as a qualifying relative.

C. No, Chad provided more than half of his own support for the year. Therefore, he is neither Amber's qualifying child nor her qualifying relative.

D. None of the above.

6. Joseph, 52, is a single father who lives with an adopted son named Wyatt who has Down syndrome. Wyatt is 32 years old and permanently disabled. Wyatt had $800 in interest income and $5,000 in wages from a part-time job in 2013. Which of the following statements is true?

A. Joseph can file as head of household, with Wyatt as his qualifying child.
B. Joseph does not qualify for head of household, but he could still claim Wyatt as his qualifying relative, because Wyatt does not meet the age test for a qualifying child.
C. Joseph can file as head of household, with Wyatt as his qualifying relative.
D. Joseph must file as single, and he cannot claim Wyatt because Wyatt earned more than the standard deduction amount.

7. The personal exemption phase-out begins when AGI is over ____ for MFJ taxpayers:

A. $250,000.
B. $275,000.
C. $300,000.
D. $422,500.

8. Ursula lives with her son, Dave, who is 34 years old, not disabled, and has a part-time job. Ursula provides more than half of Dave's support. She may claim Dave as a qualifying relative, as long as he does not earn ______ or more in 2013.

A. $0.
B. $3,500.
C. $3,900.
D. No limit.

9. Clifford and Lily divorced three years ago. They have one child who lived with Clifford for ten months during 2013. The child lived with Lily the other two months. The divorce decree states that Lily, not Clifford, is supposed to be the custodial parent. Who is considered the custodial parent for IRS purposes?

A. Lily.
B. Clifford.
C. Neither.
D. Both.

10. Cheryl is 46 and unmarried. Her nephew, Bradley, lived with her all year and was 18 years old at the end of the year. Bradley did not provide more than half of his own support. He had $4,200 of income from wages and $1,000 of investment income. Which of the following is true?

A. Bradley is Cheryl's qualifying child.
B. Bradley is not a qualifying child; however, Cheryl can claim him as a qualifying relative.
C. Bradley is not a qualifying child or qualifying relative, because he had income that exceeded the personal exemption amount.
D. Cheryl can claim Bradley only if he is a full-time student, since he is no longer a minor child.

11. Sean's wife, Jackie, died in 2013. Sean did not remarry during the year, and he has one dependent child who is 16 years old. Based on this information how many exemptions can Sean claim on his 2013 tax return?

A. Only the personal exemption for himself.
B. Only the personal exemption for himself and the dependency exemption for his son.
C. Exemptions for himself, his son, and his deceased wife.
D. A personal exemption for himself and a partial exemption for his deceased wife.

12. Stacy is unmarried and files as head of household. She has four dependent children that live with her, all of whom are under 17. Stacy's mother, Racine, also lives with them. Racine has no income, and Stacy provides all of her mother's financial support. Based on this information, how many dependency exemptions may Stacy claim on her return?

A. Two.
B. Three.
C. Five.
D. Six.

13. In a multiple support agreement, a taxpayer must provide more than _________% of support to claim a dependent.

A. 10%.
B. 15%.
C. 50%.
D. 75%.

14. John provides the sole support for his mother. To claim her as a dependent on his Form 1040, John's mother must be a resident or citizen of which of the following countries?

A. United States.
B. Mexico.
C. Canada.
D. Any of the above.

15. Jacob is filing as head of household. He has three children who qualify for him to claim dependency exemptions, and his AGI in 2013 was $315,000. The personal exemption amount in 2013 is $3,900 and the phase-out begins at AGI of $275,000 for his filing status. What personal exemption amount may Jacob claim?

A. $5,088.
B. $10,608.
C. $11,700.
D. $15,600.

16. Terrence is single and 18 years old. He works a part-time job at night and goes to school full-time. His total income for 2013 was $10,500. Terrence lives with his parents, who provided the majority of his support. His parents are claiming him as a dependent on their 2013 tax return. Which of the following statements is true?

A. He is not required to file his own return.
B. His parents may not claim him as a dependent because he earned more than the standard deduction amount for 2013.
C. He is required to file his own return, and he may also take an exemption for himself.
D. His parents may claim Terrence as their qualifying child. He is required to file a tax return, but he cannot claim a personal exemption for himself.

17. Dina Wiley has three children: Luther, Tim, and Mary. Each child contributes toward Mrs. Wiley's support. Luther and Tim each provide 45%, and Mary provides 10%. Which of Mrs. Wiley's children would be eligible to claim a dependency exemption for her in 2013 under a multiple support agreement?

A. Luther or Tim.
B. Both Luther and Tim.
C. Luther, Tim, or Mary.
D. None of the three are eligible to claim the dependency exemption because no one child provided more than half of his or her mother's support.

18 Roy is a client who tells you that his wife died in February 2013. Based on this information, Roy can claim ________________:

A. Only the personal exemption for himself.
B. Only the personal exemption for his wife.
C. Personal exemptions for both himself and his wife.
D. A person exemption for himself and a partial exemption for his wife, prorated based on the number of months she lived in 2013.

19. Tony and Isabelle are the sole support of all the following individuals. (All are U.S. citizens but none lives with them, files a tax return, or has any income.)

- Jennie, Tony's grandmother
- Julie, Isabelle's stepmother
- Jonathan, father of Tony's first wife
- Timothy, Isabelle's cousin

How many exemptions may Tony and Isabelle claim on their joint return?

A. 3.
B. 4.
C. 5.
D. 6.

20. Which of the following is not a correct statement about the rules for exemptions in 2013?

A. A single taxpayer would have his personal and dependency exemptions phased out entirely if his adjusted gross income was $375,000.
B. A couple filing jointly would have their exemptions partially phased out if their adjusted gross income was $375,000.
C. A taxpayer may take any personal exemption he is entitled to, regardless of adjusted gross income.
D. Filing status and AGI determine the threshold levels at which exemptions are phased out.

21. Giovanni and Lucia are married and classified as nonresident aliens for U.S. tax purposes. How many exemptions would they qualify for when they file their U.S. tax return(s)?

A. None.
B. One each on returns filed separately.
C. One each on a joint return.
D. It depends how many dependents they have.

Unit 4: Taxable and Nontaxable Income

For additional information read:
Publication 525, *Taxable and Nontaxable Income*
Publication 15-B, *Employer's Tax Guide to Fringe Benefits*
Publication 3, *Armed Forces' Tax Guide*

The Internal Revenue Code (IRC) describes types of income that are taxable and nontaxable. Over the course of the next few units, we will cover the most common types of both. In this unit, we focus on various forms of employee compensation, but we start with a look at broader concepts regarding the taxability of income.

The IRS's position is that all income is taxable unless it is specifically excluded. An exclusion is not the same as a deduction, and it is important to understand the distinction because many deductions are phased out as a taxpayer's gross income increases. Excluded income, on the other hand, retains its character without regard to the amount of the taxpayer's gross income.

Most types of excluded income do not have to be reported on a tax return.

Example: Brock is a popular recording artist who made more than $600,000 in taxable income last year. Because of his high income, Brock is phased out for many deductions. However, in 2013 Brock is involved in an auto accident and sustains major injuries. Brock sues the other driver and receives a settlement of $80,000 from the insurance company. The insurance settlement is excluded income because compensation for physical injuries is not taxable to the recipient.

Calculating Taxable Income

For a taxpayer to figure out how much tax he owes, he first needs to determine his **gross income**. Gross (or total) income is all income a taxpayer receives in the form of money, goods, property, and services that is not exempt from tax. In addition to wages, salaries, commissions, tips, and self-employment income, this includes other forms of compensation such as taxable fringe benefits and stock options.

Next, the taxpayer calculates his **adjusted gross income (AGI)** by subtracting from gross income certain specific deductions or adjustments. These deductions include IRA contributions, certain expenses for self-employed individuals, alimony payments, and moving expenses. The amount of a taxpayer's AGI is important because it helps determine eligibility for certain deductions and credits.

Finally, the taxpayer calculates his **taxable income** by subtracting additional deductions (standard or itemized) and exemptions from AGI. The amount of taxable income is used to determine the taxpayer's gross income tax liability before applicable credits.

How to Calculate Taxable Income and Tax Liability

Start with GROSS INCOME

MINUS - Adjustments to Income ("Above the Line" Deductions)

= ADJUSTED GROSS INCOME (AGI)

MINUS - Greater of Itemized Deductions or Standard Deduction

MINUS - Personal and Dependency Exemptions

= TAXABLE INCOME

× Tax Rate

= GROSS TAX Liability

MINUS - Credits

= Net Tax Liability or Refund Receivable

Earned Income vs. Unearned Income

Earned income such as wages, salaries, tips, professional fees, or self-employment income is received for services performed. *Unearned income* includes interest, dividends, retirement income, alimony, and disability benefits.

Earned income is generally subject to Social Security and Medicare taxes (also called FICA taxes). Investment income and other unearned income are generally not subject to FICA taxes.

Constructive Receipt of Income

The doctrine of constructive receipt requires that cash-basis taxpayers be taxed on income when it becomes available, regardless of whether it is actually in their physical possession. Income received by an agent for a taxpayer is constructively received in the year the agent receives it.

Example: On December 30, 2013, a customer gives Jerrald a $500 check for repairing a plumbing leak. Jerrald leaves town to celebrate New Year's Eve and does not deposit the check until January 2, 2014. He is considered to have constructive receipt in 2013 and must include the $500 in gross income on his 2013 tax return.

Note: Most individuals are cash-basis taxpayers who report income when it is actually or constructively received during the tax year. This concept of constructive receipt would not apply to accrual-basis taxpayers who recognize income when earned rather than when received.

Funds must be available without substantial limitations. If there are significant restrictions on the income or if the income is not accessible to the taxpayer, it is not considered to have been constructively received. Income is also not considered to have been constructively received if a taxpayer declines it, as in the case of a prize or an award.

Example: Opal won front-row concert tickets valued at $1,200 from a local radio station. Opal would be required to pay taxes based on the fair market value of the tickets. However, on the day of the concert, the radio station does not receive the tickets in time from the promoter and Opal is not able to attend the concert. Since she never actually received the proceeds, the prize is not taxable to her because she never had constructive receipt of it.

Claim of Right Doctrine

Under the claim of right doctrine, income received without restriction (over which the taxpayer has complete control) must be reported in the year received, even if there is a possibility it may have to be repaid in a later year.

If there is a dispute and income is later repaid, the repayment is deductible in the year repaid. As a result, the taxpayer is not required to amend his reported gross income for the earlier year.

Example: In 2013, Courtney sells a painting in her art gallery for $25,000. She properly includes $25,000 in her gross income and pays taxes on the income for the 2013 tax year. On March 1, 2014, the customer discovers the painting is a forgery and returns it for a full refund of $25,000. Since Courtney pays back the $25,000 in 2014, she is entitled to deduct the amount from her gross income in 2014.

Worker Classification

For federal tax purposes, the IRS classifies workers in two broad categories: employees or independent contractors. These workers are taxed in different ways, and it is critical for businesses to identify the correct classification for each individual to whom it makes payments for services. In general, a business must withhold and remit income taxes, Social Security and Medicare taxes, and pay unemployment tax on salaries and wages paid to an employee. A business generally does not have to withhold or pay taxes on payments to independent contractors.

Self-Employed Taxpayers

Self-employment income is earned by taxpayers who work for themselves. A taxpayer who has self-employment income of $400 or more in a year must file a tax return and report the earnings to the IRS.

Taxpayers who are independent contractors usually receive Forms 1099-MISC from their clients or customers showing the income they were paid. The amounts from the Forms 1099-MISC, along with any other business income payments, are reported by most self-employed individuals on Schedule C, *Profit or Loss from Business*, of Form 1040. Self-employed farmers or fishermen report their earnings on Schedule F, *Profit or Loss from Farming,* of Form 1040.

Self-employment income also includes:

- Income of ministers, priests, and rabbis for the performance of services such as baptisms and marriages.

- The distributive share income allocated by a partnership to its general partners or by a limited liability company to its members. The income is reported on IRS Schedule K-1.

A taxpayer does not have to conduct regular full-time business activities in order to be considered self-employed. A taxpayer may have a side business in addition to a regular job, and this is also considered self-employment.

Example: James earned $45,000 as a full-time employee for Regal Roofing. He also did handyman projects on the weekends for clients. James received payments of $9,000 from several different individuals for his handyman work. He did not receive Forms 1099-MISC for the $9,000, but must report these payments as self-employment income on Schedule C.

Self-Employment Tax

Self-employment tax (SE tax) is imposed on self-employed individuals in a manner similar to the Social Security and Medicare taxes that apply to wage earners. For an employee, half of these taxes are paid by the employer and the other half are withheld from the employee's wages. Self-employed individuals are responsible for paying the entire amount of Social Security and Medicare taxes applicable to their net earnings from self-employment.

The tax rate for 2013 is 15.3% up to $113,700 of a taxpayer's combined earned income, including wages, tips, and net earnings from self-employment. If the taxpayer's combined earned income exceeds $113,700, a rate of 2.9%, representing only the Medicare portion, applies to the excess earnings. There is no cap on the 2.9% Medicare tax. Starting in 2013, a 0.9% additional Medicare tax is applied to self-employment income above a certain threshold. This new tax is covered in more detail in Unit 15.

If a taxpayer has wages in addition to self-employment earnings, the Social Security tax on the wages is paid first.

Example: In 2013, Devon has a full-time job and also makes money as a self-employed musician. His wages from his job are $75,000. He has $45,000 in net earnings from his music business for total income of $120,000. Devon does not owe Social Security taxes on his earnings that exceed $113,700. His employer withholds 7.65% in Social Security and Medicare taxes on his $75,000 in wages. That means Devon must pay Social Security and Medicare taxes of 15.3% on his first $38,700 in self-employment earnings ($113,700 - $75,000 = $38,700) and Medicare tax of 2.9% on the remaining $6,300 in earnings ($120,000 - $113,700).

There are two adjustments related to the self-employment tax that reduce overall taxes for a taxpayer with self-employment income.

- First, the taxpayer's net earnings from self-employment are reduced by 7.65%. Just as the employer's share of Social Security tax is not considered wages to the employee, this reduction removes a corresponding amount from the net earnings before the SE tax is calculated.
- Second, the taxpayer can deduct the employer-equivalent portion of his self-employment tax in determining his adjusted gross income.

Self-employment tax is calculated on IRS Schedule SE.

More Than One Business: If a taxpayer owns more than one business, he must net the profit or loss from each to determine the total earnings subject to SE tax. However, married taxpayers cannot combine their income or loss from self-employment to determine their individual earnings subject to SE tax.

Example: Tanner is a sole proprietor who owns a barbershop. He has $19,000 in net income in 2013. His wife, Erin, has a candle-making business, which has a loss of $12,000 in 2013. Tanner must pay self-employment tax on $19,000, regardless of how he and Erin choose to file. That is because married couples cannot offset each other's income from self-employment. The income of each business is allocated to the individual.

Example: Darren is a single taxpayer who is a sole proprietor with two small businesses, a computer repair shop and a car wash business. The computer business has net income of $45,000 in 2013, while the car wash has a net loss of $23,000 in 2013. Darren only has to pay self-employment tax on $22,000 ($45,000 - $23,000) of income because he may net the income and losses from both his businesses.

Employee Compensation

Wages, salaries, bonuses, tips, and commissions are compensation received by employees for services performed. This compensation is taxable income to the employee and a deductible expense for the employer. Employers are required by January 31 to issue Forms W-2, which show the amounts of wages paid to employees for the previous year.

Social Security/Medicare Taxes: Employers are required by law to withhold Social Security and Medicare taxes from an employee's wages. If the employer fails to withhold these taxes, the employee is required to file Form 8919, *Uncollected Social Security and Medicare Tax on Wages.*

Note: If a taxpayer has more than one employer and his total compensation is over the Social Security base limit for the year ($113,700 in 2013), too much Social Security tax may have been withheld. In this case, a taxpayer may claim the excess as a credit against his income tax. If he files Form 1040, he would enter the excess amount on line 69. He could also file Form 843, *Claim for Refund and Request for Abatement*, and attach his Forms W-2 for the year.

Advance Wages: If an employee receives advance wages, commissions, or other earnings, he must recognize the income in the year it is constructively received, regardless of whether he has earned the income. If the employee is later required to pay back a portion of the earnings, the amount would be deducted from his taxable wages at that time.

Example: Maddox requests a salary advance of $1,000 on December 18, 2013, so he can take a two-week vacation. Maddox must recognize the income on his 2013 tax return, even though he will not actually earn the money until 2014 when he returns from his vacation.

Supplemental Wages

Supplemental wages are compensation that is paid to an employee in addition to his regular pay. These amounts are listed on the employee's Form W-2 and are taxable just like regular wages, even if the pay is not actually for work performed. Vacation pay and sick pay are examples of supplemental wages that are taxable just like any other wage income, even though the employee has not technically "worked" for the income. Supplemental wages may also include:

- Bonuses, commissions, prizes
- Severance pay, back pay, and holiday pay
- Payment for nondeductible moving expenses

Property in Lieu of Wages

An employee who receives property for services performed must generally recognize the fair market value of the property when it is received as taxable income. However, if an employee receives stock or other property that is restricted, the property is not included in income until it is available to the employee without restriction.

Example: Barry's company gives him $5,000 worth of stock, a total of 500 shares. He cannot sell or exercise the shares for five years. If Barry quits his job, he forfeits the shares. He does not have to recognize the stock as income in the year he receives it because the stock is subject to restrictions. Barry will report it as taxable income when the restrictions lapse and he gains complete control over the stock.

Garnished Wages

An employee may have his wages garnished for various reasons, such as when he owes child support, back taxes due, or other debts. Regardless of the amounts garnished from the employee's paycheck, the full amount of his gross wages must be included in the employee's taxable wages at year-end.

Example: Holden's employer garnishes part of his salary for back child support. Since the amount would have normally been included in Holden's paycheck, he must recognize the income as if he had received it himself.

Tip Income

Tips received by food servers, baggage handlers, hairdressers, and others for performing services are taxable income. An individual who receives $20 or more per month in tips must report the tip income to his employer.

Example: Lydia works two jobs, as an administrative assistant during the week and as a bartender on the weekends. She reports her tip income, $3,000, to her employer. Her Forms W-2 show wage income of $21,000 (assistant) and $8,250 (bartender). Lydia must report $29,250, the total amount earned at both jobs, on her Form 1040. Since she reported the tip income to her employer, her bartending tips are already included on her Form W-2 for that job.

An employee who does not report all of his tips to his employer generally must report the tips and related Social Security and Medicare taxes on his Form 1040. Form 4137, *Social Security and Medicare Tax on Unreported Tip Income,* is used to compute the additional tax. An employee who receives less than $20 per month in tips while working one job does not have to report the tip income to his employer. Tips of less than $20 per month are exempt from Social Security and Medicare taxes, but are still subject to federal income tax and must be reported on Form 1040.

Noncash tips (for example, concert tickets or other items) do not have to be reported to the employer, but they must be reported and included in the taxpayer's income at their fair market value.

Definition: The IRS defines **fair market value** (FMV) in this way: The price at which a property would change hands between a buyer and a seller when both have reasonable knowledge of all the necessary facts and neither is being forced to buy or sell. If parties with adverse interests place a value on property in an arm's-length transaction, that is strong evidence of FMV. If there is a stated price for services, this price is treated as the FMV unless there is evidence to the contrary.

Taxpayers who are self-employed and receive tips must include their tips in gross receipts on Schedule C.

Taxable Fringe Benefits for Employees

Employers often offer fringe benefits to employees; common fringe benefits include health insurance, retirement plans, and parking passes.

Although most employee fringe benefits are nontaxable, some benefits must be reported on the employee's Form W-2 and included in his taxable income.

Examples of taxable fringe benefits include:

- Off-site athletic facilities and health club memberships
- The value of employer-provided life insurance over $50,000
- Any cash benefit or benefits in the form of a credit card or gift card
- Season tickets to sporting events, although single tickets can be excluded in certain cases
- Transportation benefits, if the value of a benefit for any month is more than a specified nontaxable limit
- Employer-provided vehicles, if they are used for personal purposes

Example: Tanning Town Inc. owns a tropical resort that its employees may use free of charge. Sam visits the resort with his family for two weeks. The fair market value of the stay is $5,000 and must be included in his taxable wages.

Example: Great American Bank pays for country club memberships for all its top executives. Membership costs $8,000 a year per person. The bank executives use the club to entertain prospective clients and investors. Even though the club membership is used for business purposes, this type of fringe benefit is taxable compensation to the employees.

Nontaxable Fringe Benefits for Employees

Most fringe benefits are not taxable and may be excluded from an employee's income. For example, the value of accident or health plan coverage provided by an employer is not included in an employee's income.

The following are some common types of nontaxable employee fringe benefits.

Retirement Plans

Employer contributions on behalf of their employees' qualified retirement plans are not taxable to the employees when they are made. However, when an employee receives distributions from a retirement plan, the amounts received are taxable income.

Retirement plans may also allow employees to contribute part of their pretax compensation to the plan. This type of contribution is called an elective deferral and is excluded from taxable compensation for income tax purposes, but subject to Social Security and Medicare taxes.[9]

Cafeteria Plans

A cafeteria plan provides employees an opportunity to receive certain benefits on a pretax basis. Participants in a cafeteria plan must be permitted to choose from at least one taxable benefit (such as cash) and one qualified (nontaxable) benefit. Qualified benefits include:

- Accident, dental, vision, and medical benefits (but not Archer medical savings accounts or long-term care insurance)
- Health care flexible spending accounts (FSA, as opposed to a health savings account that a taxpayer may establish and fund on his own. An employee who is covered by an FSA generally cannot make contributions to an HSA.)
- Adoption assistance
- Dependent care assistance

Employee contributions are usually deducted based upon salary reduction agreements.

Salary reduction contributions are not considered actually or constructively received by the employee and therefore are not considered to be taxable wages. Thus, they are generally not subject to income tax withholding, or to FICA (Social Security and Medicare taxes) or FUTA (unemployment tax). An employer may choose to make benefits available to employees, their spouses, and dependents.

Flexible Spending Arrangement (FSA): An FSA is a form of cafeteria plan benefit that reimburses employees for expenses incurred for certain qualified benefits, such as health benefits. The benefits are subject to annual maximum limits and have traditionally also been subject to an annual "use-or-lose" rule, with a short grace period after year-end to use any remaining balance. Starting in 2013, employee salary reduction contributions to a health care FSA are capped at $2,500 ($5,000 for a married couple, even if they work at the same company.) Up to $500 of unused FSA money per account may be carried over to the following year. An employer must choose between either the grace period or the carryover option.

Adoption Assistance: An employee can exclude amounts paid or reimbursed by an employer under a qualified adoption assistance program ($12,970 in 2013).

Dependent Care Assistance: An employee can exclude up to $5,000 in 2013 ($2,500 if MFS) of benefits received under a dependent care assistance program each year. Amounts paid directly to the taxpayer or to a daycare provider qualify for exclusion.

---

[9] The tax provisions of retirement plans are covered in detail in Unit 16.

Highly Compensated Employees (HCEs)

There cannot be special rules that favor eligibility for highly compensated employees to participate, contribute, or benefit from a cafeteria plan. If a benefit plan favors HCEs, the value of their benefits become taxable. This is to discourage companies from offering spectacular tax-free benefits to their highly compensated executives, while ignoring the needs of lower-paid employees.

An HCE is any of the following:

- An officer,
- A shareholder who owns more than 5% of the voting power or value of all classes of the employer's stock,
- An employee who is highly compensated based on the facts and circumstances; or
- A spouse or dependent of a person described above.

Employer-provided benefits also cannot favor "key employees," defined as:

- An officer with annual pay of more than $165,000 in 2013, or
- An employee who is either a 5% owner of the business or a 1% owner of the business whose annual pay was more than $150,000 in 2013.

> **Example:** Fengrew Inc. is a C corporation with 300 employees, 45 of whom are considered highly compensated employees. Fengrew's cafeteria plan and its benefits are available to all full-time employees; therefore, the discrimination rules do not apply, and the employees' benefits are not taxable.

A plan is considered to have favored HCEs if over 25% of all the benefits are given to HCEs.

Other Types of Employee Fringe Benefits

Educational Assistance: An employer can offer employees educational assistance for the cost of tuition, fees, books, supplies, and equipment. The payments may be for either undergraduate or graduate-level courses, and do not have to be work-related.

In 2013, $5,250 may be excluded per year per employee. If an employer pays more than $5,250, the excess is taxed as wages to the employee. The cost of courses involving sports, games, or hobbies is not covered, unless they are related to the business or are required as part of a degree program. The cost of lodging, meals, and transportation is also not included.

Tuition Reduction: An educational organization can exclude the value of a qualified undergraduate tuition reduction to an employee, his or her spouse, or a dependent child. Graduate education only qualifies if it is for the education of a graduate student who performs teaching or research activities for the educational organization.

Meals and Lodging: An employer may exclude the value of meals and lodging provided to employees if they are provided:

- On the employer's business premises, and
- For the employer's convenience.

For lodging, there is an additional rule: it must be required as a condition of employment. Lodging can be provided for the taxpayer, the spouse, and the taxpayer's dependents and still not be taxable.

Example: Henry is a project supervisor for Franklin Construction. He is provided free hotel lodging at remote job sites, where he is required to stay for many months while timber is cleared and the grounds are prepared for construction projects. The value of the lodging is excluded from his income, because it is for his employer's convenience.

The exclusion from taxation does not apply if the employee can choose to receive additional pay instead of lodging.

Meals may be provided to employees for the convenience of the employer on the employer's business premises for a number of reasons, such as when:

- Police officers and firefighters need to be on call for emergencies during the meal period
- The nature of the business requires short meal periods
- Eating facilities are not available in areas near the workplace
- Meals are furnished immediately after working hours because the employee's duties prevented him from obtaining a meal during working hours

Example: Paramedic Transport regularly provides meals to employees during working hours so that paramedics are available for emergency calls during the meal. The meals are therefore excludable from the employees' wages.

Meals furnished to restaurant employees before, during, or after work hours are also considered furnished for the employer's convenience.

Transportation: Employers may provide transportation benefits to their employees up to certain amounts without having to include the benefits in the employees' taxable income. Qualified transportation benefits include transit passes, paid parking, and a ride in a commuter highway vehicle between the employee's home and workplace.

In 2013, employees may exclude from taxable income:

- \$245 per month in combined commuter highway vehicle transportation and transit passes, and
- \$245 per month in parking benefits.

An employer may also reimburse an employee up to \$20 per month for reasonable expenses incurred when using a bicycle to commute to work.

However, the use of a company car for commuting purposes or other personal use is a taxable benefit. Therefore, the value of the vehicle's use for either of these purposes is considered taxable wages to the employee.

Example: Joe is employed by a lumber company. He drives an employer-provided pickup truck, hauling equipment on job sites and delivering lumber to customers. In 2013, Joe drives the truck 20,000 miles, of which 4,000, or 20%, are personal miles (4,000/20,000 = 20%). The truck has an annual lease value of \$4,100. Personal use is therefore valued at \$820 and is included in Joe's wages.

Cell Phones: The value of the business use of an employer-provided cell phone may be excluded from an employee's income to the extent that, if the employee paid for its use, the payment would be deductible. There must be substantial "noncompensatory" reasons for use of a phone that relate to the employer's business.

Legitimate reasons include the employer's need to contact the employee in the event of work-related emergencies and the employee's need to be available to speak with clients when away from the office. If a cell phone is provided simply to promote goodwill, to boost an employee's morale, or to attract a prospective employee, it is not considered noncompensatory, and the value of a cell phone must be added to an employee's wages.

No-Additional-Cost Services: Nontaxable fringe benefits also include services provided to employees that do not impose any substantial additional cost because the employer already offers those services in the ordinary course of doing business. Employees do not need to include these no-additional-cost services in their income.

Typically, no-additional-cost services are excess capacity services, such as airline, bus, or train tickets; hotel rooms; or telephone services provided free or at a reduced rate to employees working in those lines of business.

Example: Bella is a flight attendant with Jet Way Airlines. She is allowed to fly for free on stand-by flights when there is an extra seat. This fringe benefit is allowed at no additional cost to the employer and is therefore nontaxable to the employee.

If an employee is provided with the free or low cost use of a health club on the employer's premises, the value is not included in the employee's compensation. The gym must be used primarily by employees, their spouses, and their dependent children. However, if the employer pays for a fitness program or use of a facility at an off-site location, the value of the program is included in the employee's compensation.

Group-term Life Insurance Coverage: Up to $50,000 of life insurance coverage may be provided as a nontaxable benefit to an employee. The value of insurance coverage that exceeds $50,000 is a taxable benefit.

Moving Expense Reimbursements: Reimbursements of moving expenses, if paid under an accountable plan for expenses that would otherwise have been deductible by the employee, generally are not taxable to the employee.

Definition: An **accountable plan** is an employee reimbursement allowance arrangement or a method for reimbursing employees for business travel expenses that complies with IRS regulations. The rules for accountable plans are covered below.

Employee Achievement Awards: Employers may generally exclude from an employee's taxable wages the value of awards given for length of service or safety achievement. The tax-free amount is limited to the following:

- $400 for awards that are not qualified plan awards.[10]
- $1,600 for all awards, whether or not they are qualified plan awards.

[10] A qualified plan award is one that does not discriminate in favor of highly compensated employees. In this context, an HCE is defined as a 5% owner at any time during the year or the preceding year or an employee who received more than $115,000 in pay for the preceding year, unless he was not also in the top 20% of employees when ranked by pay in the preceding year.

The exclusion for employee awards does not apply to awards of cash, gift cards, or items such as vacations or tickets to sporting events.

Employee Discounts: Employers may exclude the value of employee discounts from wages up to the following limits:

- For services, a 20% discount of the price charged to nonemployee customers.
- For merchandise, the company's gross profit percentage multiplied by the price nonemployee customers pay.

De Minimis (Minimal) Benefits: This is a property or service an employer provides that has so little value that accounting for it would be impractical. Examples of de minimis benefits include the following:

- Occasional personal use of a company copying machine
- Holiday gifts with a low fair market value
- Beverages such as coffee or soft drinks for employees

Cash and gift cards are not excludable as de minimis benefits, no matter how small the amounts, except for occasional meal money or transportation fare.

Reimbursement of Business Expenses

When a business reimburses its employees for certain business expenses, such as meals and travel, reimbursements are not taxable income if employees meet all of the following requirements of an accountable plan:

- Have incurred the expenses while performing services as employees
- Adequately account for travel, meal, entertainment, and lodging
- Provide evidence of their employee business expenses, such as receipts or other records
- Return any excess reimbursement within a reasonable period of time

Under an accountable plan, a business may advance money to employees; the cash advance must be reasonably calculated to equal the anticipated expenses and it must be advanced within a reasonable period of time. If any expenses reimbursed under this arrangement are not substantiated, they are considered taxable income for the employee.

Example: Vivianna runs a tax preparation business. She advances $250 to her employee, Mel, so that he can become a notary. Mel spends $90 on a notary course and then another $100 to take the notary exam. Mel returns the unused funds ($60) as well as copies of his receipts to Vivianna. The expenses are qualified expenses under an accountable plan, so the amounts paid are not taxable income for Mel.

Qualifying expenses for travel are excludable from an employee's income if they are incurred for temporary travel on business away from the area of the employee's tax home. Travel expenses paid in connection with an indefinite work assignment are not excludable. Any work assignment in excess of one year is considered "indefinite." Travel expense reimbursements include:

- Costs to travel to and from the business destination (such as flights and mileage reimbursements)
- Transportation costs while at the business destination (such as taxi fares and shuttles)

- Lodging, meals, and incidental expenses
- Cleaning, laundry, and other miscellaneous expenses

Example: Woody works for a travel agency in Detroit. He flies to Seattle to conduct business for an entire week. His employer pays the cost of transportation to and from Seattle, as well as lodging and meals while there. The reimbursements for substantiated travel expenses are excluded from Woody's income.

Taxation of Clergy Members

There are special rules regarding the taxation of clergy members, defined as individuals who are ordained, commissioned, or licensed by a religious body or church denomination. A clergy member's salary is reported on Form W-2 and is taxable. Offerings and fees received for performing marriages, baptisms, and funerals must also be reported as self-employment income on Schedule C.

Housing Allowance: A clergy member who receives a housing allowance may exclude the allowance from gross income to the extent it is used to pay the expenses of providing a home. The exclusion for housing is limited to the lesser of:

- Fair market rental value (including utilities), or
- The actual cost to provide the home.

The housing allowance cannot exceed reasonable pay and must be used for housing in the year it is received. Salary, other fees, and housing allowances must be included in income for purposes of determining self-employment tax.

Example: William is an ordained minister who receives $32,000 in salary in 2013. He receives an additional $4,000 for performing marriages and baptisms. His housing allowance is $500 per month, for a total of $6,000 per year, and is excluded from his gross income. William must report the $32,000 as wages and the $4,000 as self-employment income. The $6,000 housing allowance is subject to self-employment tax, but not income tax.

Example: Abby is a full-time ordained minister. Her church allows her to use a cottage that has a rental value of $5,000. She is paid a salary of $12,000. Her self-employment income is $17,000 ($5,000 + $12,000).

If a clergy member is a member of a religious order that has taken a vow of poverty, he is exempt from paying SE tax on his earnings for qualified services. The earnings are tax-free because they are considered the income of the religious order rather than of the individual clergy member.

Combat Pay and Veterans' Benefits

Wages earned by military personnel are generally taxable. However, there are a number of special rules for military personnel regarding taxable income.

Combat zone wages (combat pay) are not taxable income. Hazardous duty pay is also excludable for certain military personnel. Enlisted personnel who serve in a combat zone for any part of a month may exclude their pay from tax. For officers, pay is excluded up to a certain amount, depending on the branch of service.

Example: Lee is a Navy pilot who served in a combat zone from January 1, 2013 to November 3, 2013. He is only required to report his income for December 2013, because all of the other income is excluded from taxation as combat zone pay. Even though Lee only served three days in November in a combat zone, his income for the entire month of November is excluded.

Similarly, veterans' benefits paid by the Department of Veterans Affairs to a veteran or his family are not taxable if they are for education, training, disability compensation, work therapy, dependent care assistance, or other benefits or pension payments given to the veteran because of disability.

Disability Payments

Disability retirement benefits are taxable as wages if a taxpayer retired on disability before reaching the minimum retirement age. Once the taxpayer reaches retirement age, the payments are no longer taxable as wages. They are then taxable as pension income.

Disability payments from an insurance policy are excluded from income if the taxpayer pays the premiums for the policy. If an employer pays the premiums, the employee must report the payments as taxable income. If both an employee and his employer have paid premiums for a disability policy, only the employer's portion of the disability payments would be reported as taxable income.

Note: Sick pay is not the same as disability pay. Sick pay is always taxable as wages, just like vacation pay.

Worker's compensation paid to a taxpayer under a worker's compensation act or other statute is fully exempt from tax.

Life Insurance Payments

Life insurance payments generally are not taxable to the recipient. This is true even if the proceeds were paid under an accident or health insurance policy. However, income interest received as a result of life insurance proceeds may be taxable. Further, if a taxpayer surrenders a life insurance policy for cash, he must include in income any proceeds that are more than the cost of the policy.

Sometimes, a taxpayer will choose to receive life insurance proceeds in installments rather than as a lump sum. In this case, part of the installment generally includes interest income. If a taxpayer receives life insurance proceeds in installments, he can exclude part of each installment from his income. To determine the excluded part, the amount held by the insurance company (generally the total lump sum payable at the death of the insured person) is divided by the number of installments to be paid. The taxpayer would include any amount over this excluded portion as taxable interest income.

Example: Libby's brother died in 2013, and she is the beneficiary of his life insurance. The face amount of the policy is $75,000, and Libby chooses to receive 120 monthly installments of $1,000 each. The excluded part of each installment is $625 ($75,000 ÷ 120), or $7,500 for an entire year. The rest of each payment, $375 a month (or $4,500 for an entire year), is taxable income to Libby.

Unit 4: Study Questions

1. Income was constructively received in 2013 in each of the following situations except:

A. Wages were deposited in the taxpayer's bank account on December 26, 2013, but were not withdrawn by the taxpayer until January 3, 2014.
B. A taxpayer was informed his check for services rendered was available on December 15, 2013. The taxpayer did not pick up the check until January 30, 2014.
C. A taxpayer received a check by mail on December 31, 2013, but did not deposit the check until January 5, 2014.
D. A taxpayer's home was sold on December 28, 2013. The payment was not received by the taxpayer until January 2, 2014 when the escrow company released the funds.

2. Marisol received the following income and fringe benefits in 2013:

- $30,000 in wages
- $2,000 Christmas bonus
- Parking pass at $90 per month
- Employer contributions to her 401(k) plan in the amount of $900 for the year
- Free use of an indoor gym on the employer's premises, FMV valued at $500

How much income must Marisol report on her 2013 tax return?

A. $30,000.
B. $32,000.
C. $32,500.
D. $34,480.

3. Which of the following tip income is exempt from federal income tax?

A. Tips of less than $20 per month.
B. Noncash tips.
C. Tips not reported to the employer.
D. All tips are taxable.

4. Which of the following fringe benefits is taxable (or partially taxable) to the employee?

A. Health insurance covered 100% by the employer.
B. Employer-provided parking at $275 per month.
C. Group-term life insurance coverage of $50,000.
D. Employer contributions to an employee's 401(k) plan.

5. Chaz is a naval officer who was injured while serving in a combat zone. He was later awarded Veterans Affairs (VA) disability benefits. How are these payments reported on Chaz's tax return?

A. 100% of the disability benefits may be excluded from income.
B. Up to 50% of the disability benefits may be excluded from income.
C. 100% of the benefits may be excluded from income for enlisted personnel but not for officers.
D. The disability benefits are taxable.

6. Max owns a restaurant. He furnishes one of the waitresses, Caroline, two meals during each workday. Max encourages (but does not require) Caroline to have her breakfast on the business premises before starting work so she can help him answer phones. She is required to have her lunch on the premises. How should Max treat this fringe benefit to Caroline?

A. Caroline's meals are not taxable.
B. All of Caroline's meals at the restaurant are taxable.
C. Caroline's lunch is not taxable, but her breakfast is.
D. Caroline's meals are taxed at a flat rate of 15%.

7. Which of the following types of fringe benefits are deductible by an employer but not taxable to the employee?

A. De minimis fringe benefit.
B. Use of an employer's apartment, vacation home, or boat.
C. Membership in a country club or athletic facility.
D. A gift card.

8. What is adjusted gross income?

A. The sum of all sources of taxable income that the taxpayer receives during the year.
B. The amount of earned income a taxpayer receives during the year.
C. Another term for taxable income.
D. Gross income minus certain allowable deductions or adjustments, calculated before exemptions and the standard deduction or itemized deductions are taken.

9. Randall is an ordained minister in the Evangelical Church of Chicago. He owns his own home and his monthly house payment is $900. His monthly utilities total $150. Fair rental value in his neighborhood is $1,000. Randall receives a housing allowance from his church in the amount of $950 per month. What amount of his housing allowance would he include in his gross income?

A. $0.
B. $100 per month.
C. $150 per month.
D. $950 per month.

10. Salvador is an enlisted soldier in the U.S. Army who served in a combat zone from January 1 to September 2 of 2013. He returned to the United States and received his regular duty pay for the remainder of the year. How many months of his income are taxable in 2013?

A. Zero. All the income is tax-free.
B. Three months are subject to tax.
C. Four months are subject to tax.
D. Twelve months are subject to tax.

11. Self-employment income does not include:

A. Income of ministers, priests, and rabbis for the performance of services such as baptisms and marriages.
B. The share of partnership income allocated to general partners on Schedule K-1.
C. Wages earned by a temporary employee.
D. Payments to independent contractors.

12. Antonio is employed as an accountant by a large firm. When Antonio travels for his audit work, he submits his travel receipts for reimbursement by his firm, which has an accountable plan for its employees. Which of the following statements is true?

A. Under an accountable plan, the reimbursed amounts are not taxable to Antonio.
B. Under an accountable plan, Antonio may still deduct his travel expenses on his tax return.
C. Under an accountable plan, Antonio's employer may not deduct the travel expenses, even though Antonio was reimbursed in full.
D. Under an accountable plan, reimbursed expenses are taxable to the employee, and the employer may also deduct the expenses as they would any other current expense.

13. Which of the following fringe benefits provided by the employer will result in taxable income to the employee?

A. A cell phone used by a salesperson to talk to clients while on the road.
B. Reimbursements paid by the employers for qualified business travel expenses.
C. Use of a company van for commuting.
D. Occasional coffee, doughnuts, and soft drinks.

14. Debby broke her leg in a car accident in 2013 and was unable to work for three months. She received an accident settlement of $13,000 from her car insurance company. During this time she also received $7,500 in sick pay from her employer. In addition, she received $5,000 from the accident policy she had purchased herself. How much of this income is taxable income to Debby?

A. $5,000.
B. $7,500.
C. $12,500.
D. $18,000.

15. Any taxpayer who has self-employment income of ______ or more in a year must file a tax return and report the earnings to the IRS.

A. $0.
B. $400.
C. $600.
D. $3,900.

16. Brendan, a flight attendant, earned wages of $30,000 in 2013. The airline provided free transportation on standby from his home in Little Rock to the airline's hub in Charlotte. The fair market value of the commuting flights was $5,000. Brendan also received reimbursements under an accountable plan of $10,000 for overnight travel, but only spent $6,000. He returned the excess to his employer. Brendan was injured on the job and received workers' compensation of $4,000. What amount must he include in gross income?

A. $30,000.
B. $34,000.
C. $35,000.
D. $37,000.

17. Elaine is a cash-basis taxpayer and sells cosmetics on commission. Elaine receives $10,000 in income from commissions, plus an advance of $1,000 in December 2013 for future commissions in 2014. She also receives $200 in expense reimbursements from her employer after turning in her receipts as part of an accountable plan. How much income should Elaine report on her 2013 tax return?

A. $0.
B. $11,000.
C. $11,200.
D. $10,200.

18. Sheila and Ralph are married and both have life insurance. In December 2013, Ralph dies and Sheila, as the beneficiary, is awarded the life insurance. The face amount of the policy is $270,000. Instead of a lump sum, Sheila chooses to receive 180 monthly installments of $1,800, starting January 1, 2013. How should Sheila treat these installments on her 2013 tax return?

A. All of the payments are excluded from income.
B. $18,000 is excluded from income per year, and $3,600 must be recognized as interest income.
C. $21,600 is included in Sheila's income.
D. $18,000 are excluded from income, and the remainder is taxed as a capital gain.

19. Alfonso receives supplemental wages and a holiday bonus in 2013. Which items listed below are not considered taxable income to Alfonso?

A. Holiday bonus.
B. Overtime pay.
C. Vacation pay.
D. Travel reimbursements.

20. Rob owns a business that has a $10,000 profit in 2013. His wife, Cecilia, has a business loss of $12,000 for 2013. They both file Schedules C to report their self-employment income. Which statement is true?

A. On their joint return, they will not have to pay self-employment tax because the losses from Cecilia's business offsets Rob's income.
B. They can file MFS and offset each other's self-employment tax.
C. Rob must pay self-employment tax on $10,000, regardless of his wife's losses.
D. If they choose to file separate returns, they may split the profits and losses equally between their two businesses.

Unit 5: Interest and Dividend Income

For additional information read:
Publication 550, *Investment Income and Expenses*

Taxpayers who lend or deposit cash or invest in securities such as stocks, bonds, and mutual funds may earn income from interest, dividends, and capital appreciation. This unit covers interest and dividend income. Other types of income from investments, such as gains resulting from sales, are covered in Unit 7.

Interest Income

Interest is a form of income that may be earned from deposits, such as in bank and money market accounts, notes receivable, and investments in instruments such as bonds. Some interest income is taxable, and some is not.

Certain distributions commonly referred to as dividends are actually reported as taxable interest income. These include "dividends" on deposits or share accounts in cooperative banks, credit unions, domestic savings and loan associations, and mutual savings banks. A taxpayer may also have taxable interest from certificates of deposits (CDs) and other deferred interest accounts.

Interest income is generally reported to the taxpayer on Form 1099-INT by the financial institution or other payer. If a taxpayer does not receive Form 1099-INT from a payer, he still must report all taxable interest income.

If taxable interest income exceeds $1,500, the taxpayer cannot file Form 1040EZ and must report the interest on Schedule B, *Interest and Ordinary Dividends*, and file Form 1040 or Form 1040A.

Example: Leona has five savings accounts in different banks. The total amount of interest earned from the accounts is $1,950. Leona will receive five Forms 1099-INT. She will list each payer and amount on Schedule B and file it with her tax return.

Interest on U.S. Treasury Bills, Notes, and Bonds: Interest on U.S. obligations, such as U.S. Treasury bills, notes, and bonds issued by any agency of the United States, is taxable for federal income tax purposes.

The Series EE bond is the most common type of U.S. savings bond. These bonds are issued at a discount, and the difference between the purchase price and the amount received when the bonds are redeemed (or "cashed in") is interest income.

Series I bonds are issued at face value with a maturity period of 30 years. The face value and accrued interest are payable at maturity. Individual taxpayers can generally report interest income from a Series EE or Series I savings bond either:

- When the bond matures or is redeemed (whichever occurs first), or
- Each year as the bond's redemption value increases.

However, a taxpayer must use the same reporting method for all the Series EE and Series I bonds he owns. When a taxpayer redeems savings bonds, he should receive a Form 1099-INT from the bank or other payer.

Series HH U.S. savings bonds are issued at face value and pay interest twice a year. Taxpayers must report the interest in the year it is paid.

Interest earned on other U.S. obligations, such as U.S. Treasury bills, notes, and bonds, is taxable when it is received.

Interest on Education Savings Bonds

Taxpayers may purchase and eventually redeem certain Series EE or I bonds on a tax-free basis to pay qualified higher education expenses. The expenses must be for the taxpayer, his spouse, or dependents for whom an exemption is claimed.

For 2013, the amount of the interest exclusion is phased out for taxpayers filing jointly or qualifying widow(er) taxpayers whose modified AGI is between $112,050 and $142,050. If modified AGI is $142,050 or more, no exclusion is allowed. Married taxpayers who file separately (MFS) do not qualify for the education savings bond interest exclusion. For taxpayers using single or head of household status, the interest exclusion is phased out when modified AGI is between $74,700 and $89,700. If modified AGI is $89,700 or more, no exclusion is allowed.

The exclusion is calculated and reported on Form 8815, *Exclusion of Interest from Series EE and I U.S. Savings Bonds Issued After 1989*. There are certain rules that must be followed in order for the educational exclusion to qualify:

- The bonds must be purchased by the owner. They cannot be a gift.
- Qualified higher education expenses must be reduced by certain tax-free benefits received and by expenses used to claim the American Opportunity and Lifetime Learning credits.
- The total interest received may only be excluded if the combined amounts of the principal and the interest received do not exceed the taxpayer's qualified higher education expenses.

Example: In February 2013, Daniel and Blythe, a married couple, cash a Series EE savings bond they bought ten years ago. They receive proceeds of $8,124, representing principal of $5,000 and interest of $3,124. In 2013, they have modified adjusted gross income of $100,000 and they pay $4,000 of their daughter's college tuition. They are not claiming an education credit for that amount, and their daughter does not have any tax-free educational assistance in the form of scholarships or grants. Daniel and Blythe can exclude $1,538 ($3,124 × [$4,000 ÷ $8,124]) of interest in 2013. They must pay tax on the remaining $1,586 ($3,124 – $1,538).

Interest on a Certificate of Deposit: Interest earned on a certificate of deposit (CD) is generally taxable when the taxpayer receives it or is entitled to receive it without paying a substantial penalty.

The interest a taxpayer pays on funds borrowed from a financial institution to meet the minimum deposit required for a CD and the interest a taxpayer earns on the CD are two separate items. The taxpayer must include the total interest earned on the CD in income. If the taxpayer itemizes deductions, he can deduct the interest paid as investment interest, up to the amount of net investment income.

Example: Sienna wanted to invest in a $10,000 six-month CD. She deposited $5,000 in a CD with a credit union and borrowed $5,000 from another bank to make up the $10,000 minimum deposit required to buy the six-month CD. The certificate earned $575 at maturity in 2013, but Sienna actually received a net amount of $265 for the year. This represented the $575 Sienna earned on the CD, minus $310 interest charged on the $5,000 loan. The credit union gives Sienna a Form 1099-INT for 2013 showing the $575 interest she earned. The other bank gives Sienna a statement showing that she paid $310 interest for 2013. Sienna must include the total interest amount earned, $575, in her interest income for 2013. She can deduct the interest expense of $310 only if she itemizes deductions.

Gift for Opening a Bank Account: If a taxpayer receives noncash gifts or services for making deposits or for opening an account in a savings institution, the value of the gift may have to be reported as interest. For deposits of less than $5,000, gifts or services valued at more than $10 must be reported as interest. For deposits of $5,000 or more, gifts or services valued at more than $20 must be reported as interest. The value of the gift is determined by the financial institution.

A cash bonus for opening a new checking or credit card account is also taxable interest. Similarly, reward points or airline miles that a bank offers as a gift to customers who open new accounts are taxable. However, cash back and reward points earned on credit and debit card purchases are not taxable interest income.

Tax-Exempt Interest

Interest earned on debt obligations of state and local governments is generally exempt from federal income tax but may be subject to income taxes by state and local governments. However, interest on federally guaranteed state and local obligations issued after 1983 is generally taxable. In addition, even if interest on an obligation is nontaxable, the taxpayer may need to report a capital gain or loss when the investment is sold.

The taxpayer's Form(s) 1099-INT may include both taxable and tax-exempt interest. Tax-exempt interest must be reported on Form 1040, line 8b. It is used in calculating the taxability of certain income items, such as Social Security benefits.

Dividend Income

A dividend is a distribution of cash, stock, or other property from a corporation or a mutual fund. The payer will generally use Form 1099-DIV to report dividend income to taxpayers. If a taxpayer does not receive Form 1099-DIV from a payer, he still must report all taxable dividend income.

Generally, if a taxpayer's total dividend income is more than $1,500, it must be reported on Schedule B, *Interest and Ordinary Dividends*. Otherwise, it can be reported directly on Form 1040 or 1040A. Dividends are not subject to employment taxes.

Ordinary Dividends

Ordinary dividends are corporate distributions in cash (as opposed to property or stock shares) that are paid to shareholders out of earnings and profits. Unless they are qualified dividends, they are taxed as ordinary income rather than as capital gains, and are therefore subject to the taxpayer's normal tax rates. Ordinary dividends are reported on Box 1a of Form 1099-DIV.

Definition: Ordinary income is income that is subject to regular income tax rates, rather than the lower tax rates that apply to capital gains. Ordinary income includes all types of income other than capital gains, such as wages, self-employment income, and interest.

Nondividend Distributions: Distributions that are not paid out of earnings and profits are nondividend distributions. They are considered a recovery or return of capital and therefore are generally not taxable. However, these distributions reduce the taxpayer's basis. Once basis is reduced to zero, any additional distributions are capital gains and are taxed as such. Nondividend distributions are reported on Box 3 of Form 1099-DIV.

Qualified Dividends: Qualified dividends are reported to the taxpayer on box 1b of Form 1099-DIV. These are ordinary dividends that are given preferred tax treatment as capital gains if specific criteria are met. Qualified dividends are subject to a 15% tax rate if the taxpayer's regular tax rate is 25% or higher. If the taxpayer's regular tax rate is under 25%, the qualified dividends are subject to a zero percent rate, which means they are essentially nontaxable.

In order for the dividends to qualify for these preferred rates, the following are the most common requirements that must be met:

- The dividends must have been paid by a U.S. corporation or a qualified foreign corporation.
- The taxpayer must generally have held the stock for more than 60 days during the 121-day period that begins 60 days before the ex-dividend date.

The ex-dividend date is the date following the declaration of a dividend. When figuring the holding period for qualified dividends, the taxpayer may count the number of days he held the stock and include the day he disposed of the stock. The date the taxpayer *acquires* the stock is not included in the holding period. A longer holding period may apply for dividends paid on preferred stock.

Example: Israel bought 5,000 shares of Sundowner Corp. stock on July 9, 2013. Sundowner paid a cash dividend of 10 cents per share. The ex-dividend date was July 17, 2013. Israel's Form 1099-DIV from Sundowner shows $500 in dividends. However, Israel sold the 5,000 shares on August 12, 2013. Israel held his shares of Sundowner for only 34 days of the 121-day required holding period, which began on May 18, 2013 (60 days before the ex-dividend date) and ended on September 15, 2013. Israel has no qualified dividends from Sundowner because he held the stock for less than the required 61 days. He does not qualify for the preferred tax treatment that is given to qualified dividends.

Mutual Fund Distributions

A taxpayer who receives mutual fund distributions during the year should also receive Form 1099-DIV identifying the types of distributions received. Mutual fund distributions are reported based upon the character of the income source and may include ordinary dividends, qualified dividends, capital gain distributions, exempt-interest dividends, and nondividend distributions.

Capital gain distributions from a mutual fund are always treated as long-term, regardless of the actual period the mutual fund investment is held. Distributions from a mutual fund investing in tax-exempt securities are tax-exempt interest and retain their tax-exempt character for the payee. Even so, the taxpayer must report them on his tax return.

If a mutual fund or Real Estate Investment Trust (REIT) declares a dividend payable to shareholders in October, November, or December but actually pays the dividend during January of the following year, the shareholder is considered to have received the dividend on December 31 of the prior tax year and must report the dividend in the year it was declared.

Mutual fund distributions may be reported on Form 1040 or Form 1040A, but not on Form 1040EZ.

Stock Dividends: A stock dividend is a distribution of stock, rather than money, by a corporation to its own shareholders. A stock dividend is generally not a taxable event and does not affect the shareholder's income in the year of distribution because he is not actually receiving any money.

When a stock dividend is granted, the total basis of the shareholder's stock is not affected, but the basis of individual shares is adjusted by the inclusion of the newly issued shares.[11]

Example: Razor Ball Corporation declares a year-end stock dividend. Scarlett is a shareholder in Razor Ball and owns 100 shares. Her basis in the shares is $5,000, or $50 per share. Scarlett receives a stock dividend of 100 shares. After the dividend, Scarlett owns 200 shares. Her overall basis in the shares does not change (it is still $5,000), but her new basis in each individual share is $25 per share. Scarlett does not have any taxable income as a result of the stock dividend.

If a shareholder has the option to receive cash instead of stock, the stock dividend is taxable in the year it is distributed. The recipient of the stock must include the FMV of the newly issued stock in his gross income and that amount is the basis of the shares received.

Example: The Pacheco Corporation declares a year-end stock dividend and gives its shareholders the option of receiving cash instead of stock. Therefore, the stock dividend becomes a taxable event. Dale owns 1,000 shares in Pacheco, and his basis in the shares is $10,000, or $10 per share. Dale decides to take the stock instead of cash and receives an additional 100 shares. The FMV of the stock at the time of the distribution is $15 per share. Dale must recognize $1,500 in income ($15 FMV × 100 shares = $1,500), which is his basis in the new shares.

Constructive Distributions

Certain transactions between a corporation and its shareholders may be regarded as constructive distributions. They may be considered dividends or nondividend distributions, and may be taxable to the shareholders. Examples of constructive distributions include:

- **Payment of personal expenses:** If a corporation pays personal expenses on behalf of an employee-shareholder, the amounts should be classified as a distribution rather than expenses of the corporation.

[11] Basis and how it is calculated is discussed in detail in Unit 6, *Basis of Property*.

- **Unreasonable compensation:** If a corporation pays an employee-shareholder an unreasonably high salary considering the services actually performed, the excessive part of the salary may be treated as a distribution.
- **Unreasonable rents:** If a corporation rents property from a shareholder and the rent is unreasonably higher than the shareholder would charge an unrelated party for use of the property, the excessive part of the rent may be treated as a distribution.
- **Cancellation of a shareholder's debt:** If a corporation cancels a shareholder's debt without repayment by the shareholder, the amount canceled may be treated as a distribution.
- **Property transfers for less than FMV:** If a corporation transfers or sells property to a shareholder for less than its FMV, the excess may be treated as a distribution.
- **Below market or interest-free loans**: If a corporation gives a loan to a shareholder on an interest-free basis or at a rate below the applicable federal rate, the uncharged interest may be treated as a distribution.

Example: Maureen's father owns 95% of Fallon Orthotics Corporation, and she and her siblings own the remaining 5%. She performs data processing and other secretarial functions on a part-time basis for the corporation, and is paid a salary of $200,000 a year. The corporation also pays for various personal expenses Maureen incurs, such as monthly payments on the car she uses to commute to work. The IRS would likely consider Maureen's salary as unreasonably high based on her duties, meaning that a portion of the salary and the personal expenses would be reclassified as constructive distributions.

Unit 5: Study Questions

1. Which of the following dividends are reported as interest income on a taxpayer's return?

A. Stock dividends.
B. Dividends earned on deposits in credit unions.
C. Preferred dividends.
D. Qualified dividends.

2. Six years ago, Derrick bought a U.S. Series EE savings bond and decided to report the interest earned each year until maturity. This year, he bought another Series EE savings bond. How should Derrick report the interest on this new bond?

A. He should wait until the second bond matures to report all the interest earned at that time.
B. He should report the interest earned each year until maturity.
C. He can use either method to report interest earned, as long as he makes the election on a timely filed return.
D. This type of interest is now exempt from federal income tax.

3. Alec received a Form 1099-DIV from his brokerage firm showing that he earned $1,200 of ordinary dividends (Box 1a) in 2013. How should this income be handled on Alec's tax return?

A. He must report the dividend income on Schedule B, but it is not taxable.
B. He must report the dividend income on Schedule B. It is taxable as ordinary income.
C. He may report the dividend income on page one of his Form 1040. It is taxable as ordinary income.
D. He does not have to report the dividend income until he sells the stock from the corporations that distributed the dividends.

4. Araceli received $500 in interest from bonds issued by the state of New Jersey. How should she report this on her Form 1040?

A. It must be reported on her tax return, but it is not taxable income.
B. It must be reported as interest income, and it is 100% taxable.
C. She does not have to report the bond interest.
D. None of the above.

5. CJ opened a savings account at his local bank and deposited $800. He received a $15 calculator as a gift for opening the account, which earned $20 of interest in 2013. CJ also received $100 of municipal bond interest in his mutual funds account. How much taxable interest income must CJ report on his Form 1040?

A. $15.
B. $20.
C. $35.
D. $135.

6. All of the following statements about stock dividends are correct except:

A. When a stock dividend is granted, the basis of the stockholder's existing shares is adjusted to reflect issuance of the new shares.
B. A stock dividend occurs when a corporation distributes stock to its own shareholders.
C. A taxpayer generally recognizes income only when he sells the stock received in a stock dividend distribution.
D. A stock dividend is never taxable if a taxpayer has the choice to receive cash instead of stock.

7. Miguel deposited $4,000 of his own funds and also borrowed $12,000 from the bank to buy a six-month certificate of deposit for $16,000. The certificate earned $375 at maturity in 2013, and Miguel received $175, which represented the $375 he earned minus $200 in interest charged on the $12,000 loan. The bank gives Miguel a Form 1099-INT showing the $375 interest he earned. The bank also gives him a statement showing that he paid $200 in interest. How should Miguel report these amounts on his tax return?

A. He should report $175 of interest income.
B. He must report $375 of interest income. The $200 he paid to the bank is not deductible.
C. He must report $375 of interest income and may deduct $200 on his Schedule A, subject to the net investment income limit.
D. He does not have to report any income from this transaction.

8. Kent invested in a mutual fund in 2013. The fund declared a dividend, and Kent earned $19. He did not get a Form 1099-DIV for the amount, and he did not withdraw the money from his mutual fund. Kent sold his investment in the mutual fund on January 2, 2014. Which of the following statements is true?

A. The dividend is not reportable in 2013 because Kent did not receive the money yet.
B. The dividend is not reportable in 2013 because Kent did not receive a 1099-DIV.
C. The dividend is taxable and must be reported in 2013.
D. The dividend is taxable and must be reported in 2014.

9. Toni files as head of household and has modified AGI of $72,000 in 2013. She owns a Series EE savings bond, which she purchased as an investment to help pay for her daughter Tyler's education. She redeems the bond in 2013 and immediately uses all the funds to pay college tuition for Tyler. The bond's interest is reported on _____________.

A. Toni's tax return, and it is 100% taxable.
B. Tyler's tax return, and it is 100% taxable.
C. Toni's tax return, and it is exempt from taxes.
D. Nothing. It is not taxable and not required to be reported, so long as Toni uses all the funds to pay for qualified higher education costs.

10. A taxpayer must generally have held stock for ________________ in order for his dividend income to be considered qualified dividends.

A. More than 30 days during the 121-day period that begins 60 days before the ex-dividend date.
B. More than 60 days during the 121-day period that begins 60 days before the ex-dividend date.
C. More than 120 days.
D. More than one year.

11. In 2013, Remy had the following transactions from which she earned interest:

- Interest of $700 from a certificate of deposit that matured in September.
- Upon maturity of the first CD, she invested the proceeds in a second certificate with a maturity in March 2014. As of December 31, this certificate has accrued interest of $400.
- She loaned $2,000 to a family member who repaid the loan and related interest of $120 with a check dated December 31 that Remy received on January 4, 2014.

What is the amount of taxable interest income that Remy must report for the year?

A. $1,100.
B. $1,220.
C. $700.
D. $820.

12. Robert is a 5% employee-shareholder of a family-owned corporation. Which of the following would the IRS likely classify as a constructive distribution?

A. Use of a company vehicle for making sales calls.
B. Payment of his monthly homeowner's association dues.
C. Dental benefits paid through a cafeteria plan.
D. All of the above.

13. Marcelo opened a savings account at his local bank and deposited $800. The account earned $20 interest in 2013. Marcelo also received 10,000 frequent flier miles as a gift for opening the account. The bank values the miles at $75. On his credit card account, Marcelo received $100 worth of reward points for charging $10,000 in purchases, which he used to pay a portion of his credit card bill. How much interest income must Marcelo report on his Form 1040?

A. $20.
B. $75.
C. $95.
D. $195.

14. All of the following statements about dividends are correct except:

A. A taxpayer will pay a higher tax rate on an ordinary dividend than on a qualified dividend.
B. A taxpayer will pay a higher tax rate on a qualified dividend than on an ordinary dividend.
C. The ex-dividend date is the date following the declaration of a dividend.
D. When figuring the holding period for qualified dividends, the taxpayer may count the number of days he held the stock and include the day he disposed of the stock.

Unit 6: Basis of Property

For additional information read:
Publication 551, *Basis of Assets*
Publication 544, *Sales and Other Dispositions of Assets*

The tax treatment of an asset varies based on whether the asset is personal-use, business property, or investment property. When an asset is sold, the difference between the asset's basis and the selling price may be a taxable gain or loss.

In order to correctly calculate gains and losses, you must first understand the concept of basis.

Study Note: Understanding basis and how it is applied to various types of property is critical to your success in passing Parts 1 and 2 of the EA exam. You will be expected to calculate basis in multiple questions.

The initial basis of an asset is usually its cost. However, there are instances in which basis is determined based upon the fair market value of the asset when acquired by the taxpayer, rather than its cost, such as when property is acquired by gift or inheritance. The cost basis of an asset may include:

- Sales taxes charged during the purchase
- Freight-in charges
- Installation and testing fees
- Delinquent real estate taxes that are paid by the buyer of a property
- Legal and accounting fees

Example: Raoul purchases a new car for $15,000. The sales tax on the vehicle is $1,200. He also pays a delivery charge to have the car shipped from another dealership to his home. The freight charge is $210. Therefore, Raoul's basis in the vehicle is $16,410 ($15,000 + $1,200 + $210).

Example: Hilda is a self-employed writer. She purchases a new printer for her home office. The printer costs $540, with an additional $34 for sales tax. Therefore, Hilda's basis in the item is $574 ($540 + $34).

In order to correctly report a taxable gain or loss related to disposition of an asset, a taxpayer needs to identify:

- The asset's basis or adjusted basis:
  - As described above, the initial basis of an asset is usually its purchase cost, including certain ancillary charges.
  - Adjusted basis includes the original basis plus any increases or decreases resulting from events, transactions, or tax benefits that occur after the original purchase or acquisition by the taxpayer (such as subsequent improvements, depreciation deductions, casualty losses, rebates, and insurance reimbursements.)
- The asset's holding period:
  - Short-term property is held one year or less.
  - Long-term property is held more than one year.
- The proceeds from the sale.

Example: Brian buys a house for $120,000. The following year, he paves the driveway, which costs $6,000. Brian's adjusted basis in the home is now $126,000 ($120,000 original cost + $6,000 for major improvements).

Example: Whitney purchases a commercial washing machine for her pet grooming business. The washer costs $1,230, with an additional $62 of sales tax and freight and installation charges of $96, all of which increase the basis. Whitney receives a manufacturer's rebate check for $300 several weeks later, which decreases the basis. Her basis in the washer is figured as follows:

Cost:	$1,230
Sales tax:	$62
Installation:	$96
Rebate:	($300)
Adjusted Basis:	**$1,088**

Depreciation

Depreciation is an income tax deduction that allows a business to recover the cost or basis of property used in the business over time. It is an annual allowance for the wear and tear, deterioration, or obsolescence of assets. The amount allowed as an annual depreciation deduction is intended to roughly approximate the reduction in the value of assets as they age. Property ceases to be depreciable when the business has fully recovered the property's cost or when the taxpayer sells or retires it from service, whichever happens first.

Some types of property, such as land, cannot be depreciated. Most other types of tangible property, such as buildings, machinery, vehicles, furniture, and equipment, are depreciable.

Study Tip: Depreciation is a business concept, so it is tested most often on Part 2: Businesses of the EA exam. For Part 1 of the EA exam, test-takers must understand depreciation primarily in the context of rental income, which is covered in Unit 9.

Basis of Real Property (Real Estate)

The basis of real estate usually includes a number of costs in addition to the purchase price. If a taxpayer purchases real property (such as land or a building), certain fees and other expenses are included in the cost basis. They may include real estate taxes the seller owed at the time of the purchase, if the real estate taxes were paid by the buyer.

Example: Tara sells Lawrence a home for $100,000. She had fallen behind on her property tax payments, so Lawrence agrees to pay $3,500 of delinquent real estate taxes as a condition of the sale. Because the Internal Revenue Code does not allow a taxpayer to deduct property taxes that are not his legal responsibility, Lawrence must add the property taxes paid to his basis. His basis in the home is $103,500 ($100,000 + $3,500).

If a property is constructed rather than purchased, the basis of the property includes the expenses of construction. This includes the cost of payments to contractors, building materials, and inspection fees.

Demolition costs and other costs related to the preparation of land prior to construction must be added to the basis of the land, rather than to any buildings constructed on it later.

Example: Wanda pays $50,000 for an empty lot where she plans to build her home. She also pays $2,800 for the removal of tree stumps and $6,700 to demolish an existing concrete foundation on the lot. These costs must be added to the basis of the land, not to the basis of the house. Therefore, Wanda's basis in the land is $59,500 ($50,000 + $2,800 + $6,700).

Settlement Costs: Generally, a taxpayer must include settlement costs for the purchase of property in his basis. The following fees are some of the closing costs that can be included in a property's basis:

- Abstract fees
- Charges for installing utilities
- Legal fees (including title search and preparation of the deed)
- Recording fees
- Surveys
- Transfer taxes
- Owner's title insurance

Also included in a property's basis are any amounts the seller legally owes that the buyer agrees to pay, such as recording or mortgage fees, charges for improvements or repairs, and sales commissions. A taxpayer cannot include fees incidental to getting a loan in the basis of the property financed with proceeds from the loan.

Basis of Securities

A taxpayer's basis in securities (such as stocks or bonds) is usually the purchase price plus any additional costs (e.g., brokers' commissions).

When a taxpayer sells securities, his investment broker should provide Form 1099-B, *Proceeds from Broker and Barter Exchange Transactions,* by January 31 following the end of the tax year, showing the proceeds of the sale. The IRS also receives a copy of Form 1099-B. If Form 1099-B does not identify a taxpayer's basis, he must keep track of this information. If a taxpayer cannot provide evidence of his basis in an asset sold, the IRS may deem it to be zero.

Note: The IRS now requires stockbrokers and mutual fund companies to report the basis for most stock purchased in 2011 and all stock purchased in 2012 and later years. The reporting is made to investors and to the IRS.

A taxpayer may own more than one block of shares in a particular company's stock. Each block may differ from the others in its holding period (long-term or short-term), its basis (amount paid for the stock), or both.

When directing a broker to sell stock, a taxpayer may specify which block, or part of a block, to sell; this is called *specific identification*. The specific identification method requires good recordkeeping; however, it simplifies the determination of the holding period and the basis of stock sold, and gives the taxpayer better control over the recognition of taxable income and losses when selling part of an investment.

If the taxpayer cannot identify a specific block at the time of sale, shares sold are treated as coming from the earliest block purchased; this method is called First In, First Out (FIFO).

Example: Amber buys two blocks of 400 shares of stock (800 shares total), the first in May 2011 for $11,200 and the second in June 2012 for $11,600. In September 2013, she sells 400 shares for $11,500 without specifying which block of shares she is selling. The sold shares are therefore treated as coming from the earliest block purchased. Since the basis and holding period defaults to the original block of shares, Amber realizes a long-term gain of $300 ($11,500 - $11,200).

Example: Tia bought 50 shares of stock of Coffee Corp. in 2006 for $10 a share. In 2007, Tia bought another 200 shares of Coffee Corp. for $11 a share. In 2009, she bought 100 shares for $9 a share. In 2013, she sells 130 shares. She cannot identify the exact shares she sold, so she must use the stock FIFO method to determine the basis of the shares that she sold. Tia figures her stock basis as follows:

Shares purchased:

Year	# of shares	Cost per share	Total cost
2006	50	$10	$500
2007	200	$11	$2,200
2009	100	$9	$900
Total shares	**350**		

The basis of the stock sold is figured as follows:	
50 shares (50 × $10) of stock bought in 2006	$500
80 shares (80 × $11) of stock bought in 2007	$880
Total basis of stock sold in 2013	**$1,380**

Events that occur after the purchase of stock can require adjustments (increases or decreases) to the basis per individual share. For example, the original basis per share can be changed by events such as stock dividends and stock splits. Stock dividends and stock splits usually are not taxable events. However, a stock dividend may be taxable when shareholders have the option to receive cash or other property instead of stock.

- **Stock dividends** are additional shares a company grants to its shareholders in lieu of paying cash dividends. These additional shares increase the number of shares owned by an individual shareholder, so his original basis is spread over more shares, which decreases the basis per individual share.
- A **stock split** is similar to a stock dividend, and occurs when a company issues additional shares of stock for every existing share an investor holds. Stock splits are a way for a company to lower the market price of its stock. For example, in a 2-for-1 stock split, a corporation issues one share of stock for every share outstanding. This decreases a shareholder's basis per individual share by half. An original basis of $200 for 100 shares

becomes $200 for 200 shares in a 2-for-1 stock split. However, the total basis in the stock remains the same even though the basis per share decreases.

Example: Victoria pays $1,050 for 100 shares of stock, plus a broker's commission of $50. Her basis in the 100 shares is $1,100 ($1,050 cost + $50 broker's commission) or $11 ($1,100/100) per share. Victoria receives ten additional shares of stock as a stock dividend. Her $1,100 basis must be spread over 110 shares (100 original shares plus the 10-share stock dividend). Her basis per share decreases to $10 ($1,100/110).

Example: Sean buys 100 shares of MaxiWin Corp. for $50 per share. His cost basis is $50 × 100 shares or $5,000. In 2013, MaxiWin declares a 2-for-1 stock split, and Sean receives 100 additional shares of stock. Therefore, his new basis in each individual stock is $25 = ($5,000 ÷ [100+100]).

Stock Options

A taxpayer may purchase options to buy or sell property, such as stocks or commodities, through an exchange or in the open market. He may realize a gain or loss from the sale or trade of an option itself, or he may exercise the option to buy or sell the underlying property and realize a gain or loss from disposition of that property.

In addition, companies may grant options to their employees, as compensation for their service and as an incentive that allows them to purchase the company's stock at a later date. If an employee receives stock options, he may have income when the options are granted, when he exercises them (to buy the company's stock), or when he sells or otherwise disposes of the options or the stock. The nature, timing, and amount of income depend on whether the options are considered to be statutory or nonstatutory options. There are two types of statutory stock options:

- As discussed in Unit 5, **incentive stock options (ISOs),** which allow employees to purchase stock at a pre-established price (exercise price) that may be below the actual market price on the date of exercise.
- Options granted under **employee stock purchase plans (ESPPs)**.

For either of these types of options, the taxpayer must be an employee of the company granting the option, or a related company, at all times during the period beginning on the date the option is granted and ending three months before the option is exercised.

Otherwise, the option is a nonstatutory stock option.The tax advantage of a statutory stock option is that income is not reported when the option is granted or when it is exercised. Income is only reported once the stock is ultimately sold. However, the bargain element of an ISO, representing the difference between the exercise price and the market value of the stock on the exercise date, is considered a tax preference item for purposes of alternative minimum tax.

The employee's basis in the stock is the actual amount paid at exercise plus any amounts paid for the option itself or in connection with the exercise of it. Thus, the employee may have taxable income or a deductible loss when he sells the stock that he bought by exercising the option. The income or loss will generally be treated as capital gain or loss if the employee satisfies a holding period requirement and does not sell the stock until the end of the one-year period after the stock was transferred to him or the two-year period after the option was granted. Otherwise, all or a portion may be treated as ordinary income or loss.

Example: The Bodysculpt Cardio Company has an employee stock purchase plan (ESPP). The option price is the lower of the stock price at the time the option is granted or at the time the option is exercised. The value of the stock when the option was granted was $25. Bodysculpt Cardio deducts $5 from Morgan's pay every week for 48 weeks (total = $240 ($5 × 48)). The value of the stock when the option is exercised is $20. Morgan receives 12 shares of Bodysculpt stock ($240 ÷ $20). Her holding period for all 12 shares begins the day after the option is exercised, even though the money used to purchase the shares was deducted from her pay on 48 separate days. Morgan's basis in each share is $20.

Nonstatutory Stock Options (NSOs): A nonstatutory or nonqualified stock option also allows an employee to purchase stock at a pre-established exercise price. If the option is actively traded on an established market or its FMV is otherwise readily determinable, the employee must recognize compensation income, either at the date of grant if there are no restrictions that affect its value to the employee, or at a later date when any restrictions no longer apply.

If the option's FMV is not readily determinable at the date of grant, the difference between the exercise price and the market value of the stock on the exercise date must be recognized as ordinary income in the year the option is exercised. The employee's basis in the stock is the market value of the stock at grant or exercise (which was used to determine his tax liability) plus any amount paid for the option itself.

Basis Other Than Cost

The following are examples of situations in which an asset's basis is determined by something other than purchase cost.

Property in Exchange for Services: If a taxpayer receives property in payment for services, he must include the property's FMV in income, and this becomes his basis in the property. If two people agree on a cost for services beforehand, the agreed-upon cost may be used to establish the amount included as income and as the asset's basis.

Example: Cassidy is a CPA who prepares tax returns for a long-time client named Katie. Katie loses her job and cannot pay Cassidy's bill, which totals $400. Katie offers Cassidy an antique vase in lieu of paying her invoice. The fair market value of the vase is approximately $525. Cassidy agrees to accept the vase as full payment on Katie's delinquent invoice. Cassidy's basis in the vase is $400, the amount of the invoice that was agreed upon by both parties.

Basis After Casualty Loss: If a taxpayer has a casualty loss, he increases the basis in the property by the amount spent on repairs that restore the property to its pre-casualty condition. However, he must also decrease the basis of the property by any related insurance proceeds.

Example: Ira paid $5,000 for a car several years ago. It was damaged in a flood, so he spends $3,000 to repair it. He does not have flood insurance on the car. Therefore, his new basis in the car is $8,000 ($5,000 + $3,000).

Basis After Mortgage Assumption: If a taxpayer buys property and assumes an existing mortgage on it, the taxpayer's basis includes the amount paid for the property plus the amount owed on the mortgage. The basis also includes the settlement fees and closing costs paid to buy the property. However, fees and costs for obtaining a loan on the property (points) are not included in a property's basis.

Example: Sondra buys a building for $20,000 cash and assumes a mortgage of $80,000 on it. Therefore, her basis is $100,000.

Basis After Involuntary Conversion: An involuntary conversion occurs when a taxpayer involuntarily sells, exchanges, or otherwise loses property. This might happen as a result of a disaster, such as a fire, drought, or flood. Involuntary conversions may also occur as a result of theft or condemnation of property. The basis of replacement property is the same as the basis for the converted property, meaning any gain is deferred until a taxable sale or exchange occurs. A taxpayer may also have taxable gain if the amount of an insurance reimbursement exceeds his basis of the asset lost.

Example: An earthquake destroys Joy's greenhouse that had a basis of $6,000. She receives insurance proceeds of $8,000 and uses $6,000 of the amount to buy a new greenhouse. Joy must report a $2,000 gain from the conversion ($8,000 - $6,000) since she did not use all of the insurance proceeds to replace the greenhouse.

Basis of Property Transferred from a Spouse: The basis of property transferred by a spouse (or former spouse if the transfer is due to divorce) is the same as the spouse's adjusted basis. Generally, there is no gain or loss recognized on the transfer of property between spouses (or between former spouses if the transfer is because of divorce). This rule applies even if the transfer was in exchange for cash, the release of marital rights, the assumption of liabilities, or other considerations.

Example: Before they divorced, Margot and Zachary jointly owned a home that had a basis of $50,000 and an FMV of $250,000. When they divorced last year, Margot transferred her entire interest in the home to Zachary as part of their property settlement. Zachary's basis in the home is the same as their original joint basis of $50,000.

Basis of Inherited Property

The basis of inherited property is generally the FMV of the property on the date of the decedent's death, regardless of what the deceased person paid for the property. This means that if the property is sold by the beneficiary, gain will be calculated based on the change in value from the date of death.

This usually results in a beneficial tax situation for anyone who inherits property because the taxpayer generally gets an increased or "stepped up" basis. However, there are cases in which this rule can work against taxpayers.

Although the value of most property such as stocks, collectibles, and bonds increases over time, there are also instances in which a property's value drops. This creates a "stepped down" basis.

Example #1: Sasha's uncle bought 300 shares of stock many years ago for $500. Sasha inherited the stock when her uncle died. On the date of his death, the stock was valued at $9,000, so Sasha's basis is $9,000. She later sells the stock for $11,000. She has a gain of $2,000 ($11,000 - $9,000).

Example #2: With the same facts as above, if Sasha were to sell the stock for $8,000, she would have a loss of $1,000.

Example #3: Sasha's aunt also bought 100 shares of stock many years ago for $10,000. Sasha inherited the stock when her aunt died. On the date of her aunt's death, the value of the stock was $500, meaning Sasha's basis in the stock is stepped-down for tax purposes to $500. She later sells the stock for $500. She cannot report a loss on the stock.

Although the basis of an estate is usually determined on the date of death, a special rule allows the personal representative of the estate to elect a different valuation date of six months after the date of death. For assets disposed of within six months after death, the value at the date of disposition is used. To elect the alternate valuation date, the estate value and related estate tax must be less than they would have been on the date of the taxpayer's death.

If a federal estate tax return (Form 706) does not have to be filed for the deceased taxpayer, the basis in the beneficiary's inherited property is the FMV value at the date of death and the alternate valuation date does not apply.

Basis of Property Received as a Gift

The basis of property received as a gift is determined differently than property that is purchased. The taxpayer must know the donor's adjusted basis in the property when it was gifted, its fair market value on the date of the gift, and the amount of gift tax paid on it, if any, by the donor.

Generally, the basis of gifted property for the donee is equal to the donor's adjusted basis. This is called a "transferred basis." For example, if a taxpayer gives his son a car and the taxpayer's basis in the car is $2,000, the basis of the vehicle remains $2,000 for the son.

Example: Alicia's father gives her 50 shares of stock. Her father has an adjusted basis in the stock of $500. Alicia's basis in the stock, for purposes of determining gain on any future sale, is also $500 (transferred basis).

If the fair market value of the property on the date of the gift is less than the transferred basis, the donee's basis for gain is the transferred basis. However, if the donee reports a loss on the sale of gifted property, his basis is the lower of the transferred basis or the FMV of gifted property on the date of the gift.

The sale of gifted property can also result in no gain or loss. This happens when the sale proceeds are greater than the gift's FMV but less than the transferred basis.

Example: Benny's Aunt Roberta bought 100 shares of IBM stock when it was at $92 per share. Roberta's basis for the 100 shares is $9,200. Roberta gives the stock to Benny when it is selling at $70 and has an FMV of $7,000. In this case, Benny has a dual basis in the stock. He has one basis for purposes of determining a gain, and a different basis for determining a loss. Here are three separate scenarios that help illustrate how the gain or loss would be calculated when Benny sells the gifted stock:
Scenario #1: If Benny sells the stock for more than his aunt's basis, he will use her basis to determine his amount of gain. For example, if he sells the stock for $11,000, he will report a gain of $1,800 ($11,000 - $9,200).
Scenario #2: If Benny sells the stock for less than the FMV of the stock at the time of the gift ($7,000 in the example), he will use that basis to determine the amount of his loss. For example, if the stock continues to decline and Benny eventually sells it for $4,500, he can report a loss of $2,500 ($7,000 - $4,500).
Scenario #3: If Benny sells the stock for an amount between the FMV and the donor's basis, no gain or loss will be recognized. For example, if Benny sells the stock for $8,000, there will be no gain or loss on the transaction.

Unit 6: Study Questions

1. On February 11, 2013, Henry bought 1,000 shares of stock for $4 per share and paid an additional $70 for his broker's commission. What is Henry's basis in the stock?

A. $1,000.
B. $4,000.
C. $4,070.
D. None of the above.

2. Which of the following does not decrease the basis of an asset?

A. Depreciation.
B. Manufacturers' rebates.
C. Theft losses.
D. Assessments for local improvements.

3. On January 3, 2013, Brigit purchased 1,000 shares of stock at a cost of $5,100, including the commission. On August 14, 2013, she sold 500 shares for $3,300. What is the adjusted basis of the stock she sold?

A. $5,100.
B. $2,550.
C. $3,300.
D. $3,255.

4. Mackenzie purchases an empty lot for $50,000. She pays $15,000 in cash and finances the remaining $35,000 with a bank loan. The lot has a $4,000 lien against it for unpaid property taxes, which she also agrees to pay. Which statement below is correct?

A. Mackenzie's basis in the property is $50,000, and she may deduct the property taxes on her Schedule A as property taxes paid.
B. Mackenzie's basis in the property is $19,000.
C. Mackenzie's basis in the property is $54,000.
D. Mackenzie's basis in the property is $46,000.

5. On the one-year anniversary at her new job, Faith's employer gave her restricted stock in the company with the condition that it would be forfeited if she did not complete five years of service with the company. The stock's FMV is $30,000. How much should she include in her income for the current year, and what would be her basis in the stock?

A. Income of $30,000; no basis.
B. No income; basis of $30,000.
C. Income of $30,000; basis of $30,000.
D. Faith would not report any income or have any basis in the stock until she has completed five years of service.

6. Which statement is not correct about the basis of assets?

A. The basis of an asset is always equal to its cost.
B. The basis of stocks or bonds is the purchase price plus any additional costs such as brokers' commissions.
C. The adjusted basis of a property must be determined before figuring gain or loss on the sale or exchange of the property.
D. The cost basis of an asset includes sales tax and other expenses connected with the purchase.

7. If a taxpayer cannot determine his basis in a property and the property is sold, the IRS will deem the basis to be ________.

A. Zero.
B. Fair market value.
C. Actual cost.
D. Average cost.

8. Julian owned one share of common stock that he bought for $45. The corporation distributed two new shares of common stock for each share held. Julian then had three shares of common stock. What is Julian's basis for each share?

A. $5.
B. $45.
C. $15.
D. $135.

9. Deirdre bought 100 shares of Prestige Properties stock in 2006 for $10 a share. In January 2007, Deirdre bought another 200 shares of Prestige stock for $11 a share. In July 2007 she gave her son 50 shares. In December 2010 Deirdre bought another 100 shares of Prestige stock for $9 a share. In April 2013 she sold 130 shares. What is the basis of the 130 shares of stock Deirdre sold in 2013?

A. $880.
B. $1,380.
C. $1,300.
D. $1,000.

10. Stephen purchases a truck for $15,000 to use in his carpentry business. He pays $5,000 in cash and finances the remaining $10,000 with a five-year loan. He also pays taxes and delivery costs of $1,300 and $250 to install a protective bedliner. What is Stephen's basis for depreciation of the truck?

A. $6,550.
B. $10,000.
C. $16,550.
D. $16,300.

11. Which of the following is not added to the cost basis of a property?

A. Excise taxes.
B. Points on a loan.
C. Sales tax.
D. Freight charges.

12. David wishes to sell a home that he inherited from his mother. His mother had paid $45,000 for the home ten years ago. She put a new roof on the property two years ago at a cost of $10,500. The fair market value of the home on the date of his mother's death was $120,000. What is David's basis in the home?

A. $45,000.
B. $55,500.
C. $34,500.
D. $120,000.

13. Esteban installs artificial turf at a client's home at a cost of $1,500. After the installation, his client, Andie, receives a foreclosure notice and is unable to pay Esteban's bill. She has a golden-doodle show dog that just had puppies. The FMV of each puppy is $1,800. Esteban loves animals and decides to take one of the puppies as full payment on Andie's delinquent bill. What is Esteban's basis in his new dog?
A. $0.
B. $300.
C. $1,500.
D. $1,800.

14. Claire owned two shares of common stock. She bought one for $30 in 2008 and the other for $45 in 2009. In 2013, the corporation distributed two new shares of common stock for each share held. Claire had six shares after the distribution. How is the basis allocated between these six shares?

A. All six shares now have a basis of $12.50.
B. Three shares have a basis of $10 each and three have a basis of $15 each.
C. The shares are valued at $45 each.
D. None of the above.

15. On July 1, 2013 Miletech Corporation granted 1,000 non-qualified stock options to an executive with an exercise price of $23 per share. On December 31, 2013, the executive exercised all of his options when the market price per share was $43. What is the basis of his stock and what amount should be included on his Form W-2 as income in 2013?

A. Basis $23,000; income $0.
B. Basis $43,000; income $20,000.
C. Basis $0; income $0.
D. None of the above.

Unit 7: Capital Gains and Losses

For additional information read:
Publication 550, *Investment Income and Expenses*
Publication 523, *Selling Your Home*
Publication 544, *Sales and Other Dispositions of Assets*

Many of the items a taxpayer owns and uses for personal or investment purposes are capital assets; the net gains that result from their disposition may be subject to tax at favorable capital gains tax rates. Examples include:

- A main or vacation home
- Furniture
- Antiques
- A car or boat
- Stocks, bonds, and mutual funds (except when held for sale by a professional securities dealer)

Note: Losses from the sale of personal-use property, such as a home, furniture, or jewelry, are not deductible.

Example: Liam owns a Subaru that he uses to commute to work, run errands, and take on weekend ski trips. He purchased the car four years ago for $20,500. In 2013, he sells the car for $12,000. Liam cannot claim a loss from the sale of the car since it is his personal-use vehicle.

Example: Mason sold his personal computer to his friend for $750. Mason paid $5,000 for the computer five years ago. Mason used the computer to play games, surf the Internet, and pay bills on-line. He did not use the computer for business. Mason cannot deduct a loss on the sale of his personal computer.

A gain on the sale of personal-use property may be taxable, subject to certain exclusions.

Example: Priscilla collects antique coins as a hobby. She is not a professional dealer. Two years ago, Priscilla purchases an antique Roman coin for $50. In 2013, she is offered $1,000 for the coin, and she promptly sells it. Priscilla has a taxable capital gain that she must report on her tax return.

The applicable capital gains tax rate depends on the holding period and the taxpayer's ordinary income tax bracket.

Noncapital Assets

Assets held for business-use or created by a taxpayer for purposes of earning revenue (author's writings, copyrights, inventory, etc.) are considered noncapital assets. Gains and losses from the sale of business property are reported on Form 4797, *Sales of Business Property*, and in the case of individual taxpayers, the amounts flow through to Form 1040, Schedule D, *Capital Gains and Losses.*

Example: Tony is the sole proprietor of a health club. In 2013, he sells used fitness equipment to make room for new equipment. Since the equipment was business property, Tony reports the sale on Form 4797. Also during the year, Tony sells some stock at a substantial profit. He has a capital gain on the stock that he reports on Schedule D.

The following assets are noncapital assets:

- Inventory or any similar property held for sale to customers
- Depreciable property used in a business, even if it is fully depreciated
- Real property used in a trade or business, such as a commercial building or a residential rental
- Self-produced copyrights, transcripts, manuscripts, drawings, photographs, or artistic compositions
- Accounts receivable or notes receivable acquired by a business
- Stocks and bonds held by professional securities dealers
- Business supplies
- Commodities and derivative financial instruments

Unlike capital assets, the costs of many noncapital assets may be deducted as business expenses when they are sold.

Example: Michael is a self-employed fisherman who reports his income and expenses on Schedule F. In 2013, he sells some of his commercial fishing equipment. The fishing equipment is a noncapital asset, and the sale must be reported on Form 4797, *Sales of Business Property.* Also during the year, Michael sells his vacation home at a substantial loss. Unlike the fishing equipment, the vacation home is a capital asset, but since it is personal-use property, he cannot deduct the loss.

Holding Period (Short-Term or Long-Term)

When a taxpayer disposes of investment property, his holding period affects the tax treatment of his capital gain or loss. This is important because long-term capital gains are taxed at lower rates than short-term gains.

If a taxpayer holds investment property for more than one year, any capital gain or loss is long-term capital gain or loss. If a taxpayer holds investment property for one year or less, any capital gain or loss is short-term capital gain or loss.

Long-term = more than one year (at least a year and a day)
Short-term = one year or less

To determine how long a taxpayer has held an investment property, he must begin counting on the date after the day he acquires the property. The day the taxpayer disposes of the property is part of the holding period.

Example: Nicky bought 50 shares of stock on February 5, 2012 for $10,000. She sells all the shares on February 5, 2013 for $20,500. Nicky's holding period is not more than one year, and so she has a short-term capital gain of $10,500. The short-term gain is taxed at ordinary income tax rates. If Nicky had waited one more day, she would have received long-term capital gain treatment on her gain.

Example: Stuart bought 100 shares of stock on October 1, 2012 for $1,200. To determine his holding period, Stuart must start counting his holding period on October 2, 2012 (the day after the purchase). He sells all the stock on October 2, 2013 for $2,850. Stuart's holding period has been more than one year, and therefore, he will recognize a long-term capital gain of $1,650 ($2,850 - $1,200).

Stock shares acquired as a result of a stock dividend or stock split have the same holding period as the original shares owned.

Example: On September 10, 2010, Jamal bought 500 shares of Felton Software stock for $1,500, including his broker's commission. On June 6, 2013, Felton Software distributes a 2% nontaxable stock dividend (10 additional shares). Three days later, Jamal sells all his Felton Software stock for $2,030. Although Jamal owned the 10 shares he received as a nontaxable stock dividend for only three days, a long-term holding period applies to all of his shares in the stock. Because he bought the stock for $1,500 and then sold it for $2,030 more than a year later, Jamal has a long-term capital gain of $530 on the sale of the 510 shares.

The holding period for a gift is treated differently than the holding period for inherited and purchased property. If a taxpayer receives a gift of property, his holding period includes the donor's holding period. This concept is known as *tacking on* the holding period.

Example: Florence gives her niece, Marian, an acre of land. At the time of the gift, the land had an FMV of $23,000. Florence's adjusted basis in the land was $20,000. Florence held the property for six months. Marian holds the land for another seven months. Neither held the property for over a year. Regardless, Marian may "tack on" her holding period to her aunt's holding period. Therefore, if Marian were to sell the property, she would have a long-term capital gain or loss, because jointly they held the property for 13 months, or more than one year.

Determining Capital Gain or Loss

As described in the preceding unit, a taxpayer determines gain or loss on a sale or trade of stock or property by comparing the amount realized with the adjusted basis of the property.

Example: Corbin receives Form 1099-B showing a net sales price of $1,200 on the sale of 600 shares of Kominski Corporation. He bought the stock six years ago and sold it on September 25, 2013. His basis in Kominski, including commissions paid, is $1,455. He has a loss on the stock, which he will report on Schedule D.

Example: Nadine purchased 50 shares of Hammaker Corporation stock five years ago for $5,000. Two years ago, she purchased 750 shares of Shelby Ironworks stock for $8,200. In 2013, Nadine sells all her stock. Her Hammaker stock sells for $2,000 and her Shelby stock sells for $13,000. Nadine's gain and loss are both long-term, because she held both stocks for more than one year. Her long-term loss and long-term gain are netted against each other, resulting in a net long-term capital gain, as follows:

Stock	Basis	Sale Price	Gain (Loss)
Hammaker	$5,000	$2,000	($3,000)
Shelby	$8,200	$13,000	$4,800
Net Long-term Capital Gain			**$1,800**

A disposition of stock, and the related income or loss, must be reported in the year of sale, regardless of when the taxpayer receives the proceeds.

Capital losses are netted against capital gains. A taxpayer may deduct up to $3,000 ($1,500 for MFS) of net capital losses against ordinary income in a tax year. Unused losses in excess of this limit are carried over to later years. The carryover losses are combined with gains and losses that occur in the next year.

Amounts carried over retain their character as either long-term or short-term and are reported on Schedule D. Thus, a long-term capital loss carried over to the next tax year will reduce that year's long-term capital gains before it reduces that year's short-term capital gains. A capital loss can be carried over indefinitely during the taxpayer's life.

Example: Arthur purchased stock two years ago for $16,000. The stock declines in value, and he sells it in 2013 for $12,000. Arthur has a $4,000 long-term capital loss. He also has $60,000 in wages in 2013. He may claim $3,000 of his long-term capital loss against his ordinary income, thereby lowering his gross income to $57,000 ($60,000 - $3,000). The remainder of the long-term capital loss ($1,000) must be carried forward to a future year.

Worthless Securities

A taxpayer may choose to "abandon" a security that has lost its entire value in order to take advantage of the loss for tax purposes rather than retaining ownership. Stocks, stock rights, and bonds (other than those held for sale by a securities dealer) that became worthless during the tax year are treated as though they were sold for zero dollars on the last day of the tax year. To abandon a worthless security, a taxpayer must permanently surrender all rights to it and receive no consideration in exchange.

Example: Reginald owned 500 shares of WorldCom stock. The company files for bankruptcy and the bankruptcy court extinguishes all rights of the former shareholders. Reginald learns of the bankruptcy court's decision in December 2013. Rather than wait for a formal notice from the court, he chooses to abandon his WorldCom securities, knowing that his shares are worthless. He takes a capital loss on his 2013 tax return, reflecting the value of his worthless shares as "zero."

A loss from worthless securities gets special tax treatment. Unlike other losses, a taxpayer is allowed to amend a tax return for up to seven years in order to claim a loss from worthless securities. This is more than double the usual three-year statute of limitations for amending returns.

Capital Gains from Mutual Funds

A mutual fund is a regulated investment company generally created by pooling funds of investors to allow them to take advantage of a diversity of investments and professional management.

Two different types of transactions may result in taxable capital gains reporting by a taxpayer who invests in mutual funds.

First, profits resulting from investments made by the fund itself are reported to its own shareholders as capital gain distributions on Form 1099-DIV. The capital gain distributions are always taxed at long-term capital gains tax rates, without regard to how long a taxpayer has owned shares in the mutual fund.

In addition, if a taxpayer disposes of shares that represent all or a portion of his investment in the mutual fund itself, Form 1099-B will be issued. The taxable gain or loss that results from the sale or exchange of the taxpayer's shares in the mutual fund is reported on Form 1040, Schedule D.

Qualified Small Business Stock (Section 1244)

Investments in section 1244 small business stock (also called qualified small business stock or QSBS) are subject to tax rules that are favorable to the shareholder. Qualified small business stock must be issued by a domestic C corporation with gross assets of $50 million or less.

A loss on an investment in section 1244 small business stock is considered an ordinary loss rather than capital but any gain is a capital gain. This means that the losses are not subject to the capital loss limit ($3,000 per year), but gains are still given favorable capital gains rates. The amounts that can be deducted by taxpayers as an ordinary loss against ordinary gross income are $50,000 for a single filer and $100,000 for joint filers.

In order to qualify, the shareholder must be an individual or a partnership; other entities such as corporations do not qualify for this special treatment. Only the original purchaser of the stock can claim an ordinary loss, so the special treatment for losses does not apply to stock that is inherited or gifted to another person. Losses from the sale of section 1244 stock are reported on Form 4797, *Sales of Business Property*.

In addition to capital gain rates, gains on qualified small business stock are given the following preferential treatment:

- A taxpayer generally can exclude up to 50% of the gain from the sale or exchange of qualified small business stock held for more than five years.
- For stock acquired after September 27, 2010 and before January 1, 2014, the exclusion is 100%. The amount of gain eligible for the exclusion is limited to the greater of 10 times the taxpayer's basis in the stock or $10 million of gain from stock in that corporation.

Example: On December 15, 2013, Lenore purchases 100 shares of Button Makers USA, a domestic corporation with $20 million in annual revenue. The stock is qualified small business stock. Lenore must wait until December 16, 2018 to sell the stock in order to receive the 100% exclusion from gain.

Gains from qualified small business stock are reported on Schedule D, Form 1040.

Wash Sales

A wash sale occurs when an investor sells a security to claim a capital loss, only to repurchase it again very soon thereafter. A taxpayer cannot deduct a loss on the sale of an investment if an identical investment was purchased within 30 days before or after the sale.

A wash sale is considered to have occurred when a taxpayer sells a security and, within 30 days:

- Buys the identical security,
- Acquires a substantially identical security in a taxable trade, or
- Acquires a contract or option to buy the identical security.

If a taxpayer's loss is disallowed because of the wash sale rules, he must add the disallowed loss to the basis of the new stock or securities. The result is an increase in the taxpayer's basis in the new stock or securities. This adjustment postpones the loss deduction until the disposition of the new stock or securities.[12]

Example: Carlos sells 1,000 shares of Granger Corporation stock on December 4, 2013, resulting in a loss of $3,200. On January 2, 2014 he buys 1,000 shares of Granger stock. Because of the IRS wash sale rules, all of the $3,200 loss is disallowed, and he must add the disallowed loss to the basis of the newly-purchased shares. He cannot take the loss until he finally sells the repurchased shares at some later time.

For purposes of the wash sale rules, securities of one corporation are not considered identical to securities of another corporation. This means that a person can sell shares in one corporation and then purchase shares in a different corporation and this will not trigger a wash sale. Similarly, preferred stock of a corporation is not considered identical to the common stock of the same corporation.

It is considered a wash sale if a taxpayer sells stock and his spouse then repurchases identical stock within 30 days, even if the spouses file separate tax returns.

Home Sale Gain or Loss

The following are used to figure the gain or loss on the sale of a home:

- Selling price
- Amount realized
- Basis
- Adjusted basis

[12] Wash sale rules do not apply to trades of commodity futures contracts and foreign currencies. The rules also do not apply to dealers in stocks or securities.

Selling Price: The selling price is the total amount the taxpayer received for his main home. It includes money, all notes, mortgages, or other debts taken over by the buyer as part of the sale, and the fair market value of any other property or services that the seller received. Real estate sales proceeds are reported on Form 1099-S, *Proceeds From Real Estate Transactions*. If a taxpayer does not receive a Form 1099-S, he must rely upon sale documents and other records.

Amount Realized: The amount realized is the selling price minus selling expenses, which include commissions, advertising fees, legal fees, and loan charges paid by the seller, such as points.

Basis: The basis in a home is determined by how the taxpayer obtained the home. For example, if a taxpayer purchases a home, the basis is the cost of the home. If a taxpayer builds a home, the basis is the building cost plus the cost of land. If a taxpayer receives a home through an inheritance or gift, the basis is either its FMV or the decedent's or donor's adjusted basis.

Example: Eve is single. She sells her home for $350,000. She purchased the home 20 years ago for $50,000 and has lived in it continuously since then. She pays $4,000 in seller's fees to sell the home. Her amount realized in the sale is $346,000 ($350,000 - $4,000 = $346,000). Her basis is subtracted from her amount realized in order to figure her gain: ($346,000 - $50,000 basis) = $296,000.

The costs of obtaining a mortgage are not deductible and cannot be included in a home's basis. These costs include items such as termite inspections or title fees that would be required regardless of whether a taxpayer was financing the purchase. Points may be deducted as mortgage interest on Schedule A. The IRS defines points as prepaid interest paid by a home buyer at closing in order to obtain a mortgage or a lower interest rate.

If the taxpayer inherited the home, the basis is generally its FMV on the date of the decedent's death, or the later alternate valuation date chosen by the representative for the estate.

Adjusted Basis: The *adjusted basis* is the taxpayer's basis in the home increased or decreased by certain amounts. Increases include additions or improvements to the home. In order to be considered a basis increase, an addition or improvement must have a useful life of more than one year.

Repairs that simply maintain a home in good condition are not considered improvements and should not be added to the basis of the property. Decreases to basis include deductible casualty losses, credits, and product rebates. Depreciation reduces basis for business assets, such as rental property, but is never taken on personal-use property.

Formula for figuring adjusted basis:

Basis + Increases - Decreases = Adjusted Basis

Example: Immanuel purchased his home years ago for $125,000. In 2013, he added another bathroom to the property at a cost of $25,000. Immanuel's adjusted basis in the home is therefore $150,000 ($125,000 purchase price + $25,000 addition).

If the amount realized is less than the adjusted basis, the difference is a loss. A loss on the sale of a primary residence can never be deducted.

If the amount realized is more than the adjusted basis of the property, the difference is a gain. As described in detail in Unit 8, the taxpayer may be able to exclude all or part of the gain. If not excluded and the taxpayer owns a home for one year or less, the gain is reported as a short-term capital gain. If the taxpayer owns the home for more than one year, the gain is reported as a long-term capital gain.

Related Party Transactions

Special rules apply to related party transactions, which are between two parties who are joined by a special relationship. If a taxpayer sells an asset to a close family member or to a business entity that the taxpayer controls, he may not receive all the benefits of the capital gains tax rates, and he may not be able to deduct his losses. The rules were made to prevent related persons and entities from shuffling assets back and forth and taking improper losses.

50% Control Rule: If a taxpayer controls more than 50% of a corporation or partnership, any property transactions between the taxpayer and the business are subject to related party transaction rules.

In general, a loss on the sale of property between related parties is not deductible. When the property is later sold to an unrelated party, gain is recognized only to the extent it is more than the disallowed loss. If the property is later sold at a loss, the loss that was disallowed to the related party cannot be recognized.

If a taxpayer sells or trades property at a loss (other than in the complete liquidation of a corporation), the loss is not deductible if the transaction is between the taxpayer and the following related parties:

- Members of immediate family, including a spouse, siblings, ancestors, or descendants (children, grandchildren, etc.).

Note: For purposes of this rule, the following are not considered related parties: uncles, aunts, nephews, nieces, cousins, stepchildren, stepparents, in-laws, and ex-spouses.

- A partnership or corporation that the taxpayer controls. A taxpayer "controls" an entity when he has more than 50% ownership in it. This also includes partial ownership by other family members.
- A tax-exempt or charitable organization controlled by the taxpayer or a member of his family.
- Losses on sales between certain closely related trusts or business entities controlled by the same owners.

Example: Hillary buys stock from her brother, Clyde, for $7,600. Clyde's cost basis in the stock is $10,000. He cannot deduct the loss of $2,400 because of the related party transaction rules. Later, Hillary sells the same stock on the open market for $10,500, realizing a gain of $2,900. Hillary's reportable gain is $500 (the $2,900 gain minus the $2,400 loss not allowed to her brother).

Example: Vicky purchases stock from her father for $8,600. Her father's basis in the stock is $11,000. Vicky later sells the stock on the open market for $6,900. Her recognized loss is $1,700 (her $8,600 basis minus $6,900). Vicky cannot deduct the loss that was disallowed to her father.

In the case of a related party transaction, if a taxpayer sells multiple pieces of property and some are at a gain while others are at a loss, the gains will generally be taxable while the losses cannot be used to offset the gains.

Installment Sales

An installment sale is a sale of property in which at least one payment is expected to be received after the tax year in which the sale occurs. If a taxpayer sells property and receives payments over multiple years, he may use the installment method in order to defer tax by only reporting his gain as each installment is received.

A taxpayer's gain, or gross profit, is the amount by which the selling price exceeds the adjusted basis in the property sold. A gross profit percentage is calculated by dividing the gross profit from the sale by the selling price.

Study Note: Test-takers may be required to determine gross profit percentage for either Part 1 or Part 2 of the EA exam.

Each payment on an installment sale typically consists of the following three parts:

- Interest income
- Return of the adjusted basis in the property
- Gain on the sale (determined by applying the gross profit percentage to the amount of the payment received less the interest portion)

In each year the taxpayer receives a payment, he must report the interest income and the portion that relates to his gain on the sale. The taxpayer does not include in income the part that is the return of basis in the property.

Definition: When a taxpayer disposes of certain types of property that have been depreciated, the property may be subject to **depreciation recapture**, which requires that the taxpayer report all or a portion of the prior depreciation deductions as ordinary income in the year of the sale.

A taxpayer would calculate his installment sale income using the following formula:

Figuring Gross Profit Percentage

1. Enter the selling price for the property: ________________
2. Enter the adjusted basis for the property: ________________
3. Enter the selling expenses: ________________________________
4. Enter any depreciation recapture: ____________________
5. Add lines 2, 3, and 4. This is the adjusted basis for installment sale purposes. ________________
6. Subtract line 5 from line 1. This is the gross profit. ________________ (If zero or less, there is no gain, and a taxpayer would not use the installment method.)
7. Divide line 6 by line 1. This is the gross profit percentage.________________
8. Multiply line 7 by amount of the current year installment payment (exclusive of interest income). This is the installment gain recognizable for the year.____________

The selling price includes the cash and any other property to be received from the buyer, any existing mortgage or debt the buyer pays or assumes, and any selling expenses the buyer pays.

However, if the buyer assumes or pays off a mortgage or other debt on the property sold, the calculation of gross profit percentage is affected. The mortgage assumption is considered a recovery of basis in the year of sale and is subtracted before calculating the gross profit percentage, except to the extent that it exceeds the adjusted basis of the property for installment sale purposes.

In contrast, if the property is sold to a buyer who holds a mortgage on it and the mortgage is canceled rather than assumed, the cancellation is treated as a payment received in the year of the sale and is not subtracted in calculating the gross profit percentage.

If installment payments are made according to a schedule other than what was originally agreed, income is recognized according to the actual payments received. However, if the parties subsequently agree to adjust the selling price, the gross profit percentage must be recalculated, and income from future installments must be recognized based upon the adjusted gross profit.

Example: Ernesto sells property in an installment sale for $6,000. His gross profit is $1,500. The gross profit percentage on the sale is 25% ($1,500 ÷ $6,000). After subtracting interest, Ernesto reports 25% of each payment, including the down payment, as installment sale income in the year received. The remainder of each payment is the tax-free return of the property's basis.

Example: In 2012, Chloe sells an empty lot with a basis of $40,000 for $100,000. Her gross profit is $60,000. She receives a $20,000 down payment and the buyer's note for $80,000. The note provides for four annual payments of $20,000 each, plus 8% interest, beginning in 2013. Chloe's gross profit percentage is 60%. Exclusive of the interest income, she must report $12,000 of installment income on each $20,000 payment received.

If the taxpayer decides not to use the installment method, he must report all the gain in the year of the sale. Installment sale rules do not apply to property that is sold at a loss.

The installment method cannot be used for publicly traded securities, such as stocks and bonds. A taxpayer must report gain on the sale of securities in the year of the sale, regardless of whether the proceeds are received in the following year.

Example: Dillon owns 500 shares of stock, which he sells at a gain on December 29, 2013. Dillon does not receive the proceeds until January 15, 2014. Dillon is required to report the capital gain on the sale of the stock on his 2013 tax return. He cannot delay reporting the gain, and the sale is not considered an installment sale.

Installment sales to related persons are generally allowed. However, if a taxpayer sells property to a related person who then sells or disposes of the property within two years of the original sale, the taxpayer will lose the benefit of installment sale reporting.

Example: Lou sells a plot of land to his daughter, Melanie. The sale price is $25,000, and Lou realizes a profit on the sale of $10,000. Melanie agrees to pay in five installments of $5,000. A year later, she sells the property to another person. Lou must report the entire profit of $10,000 on the sale, even though he may not have received all the installment payments. The installment sale method is disallowed on the related party sale, because the property was disposed of before the two-year holding period.

Installment sales are reported on Form 6252, *Installment Sale Income*, which is attached to Form 1040. A taxpayer may also be required to complete Schedule D or Form 4797.

Reporting Asset Sales

Capital gains and losses are reported by using two forms:

- Schedule D, *Capital Gains and Losses*, and
- Form 8949, *Sales and Other Dispositions of Capital Assets.*

Schedule D is used to report gain or loss on the sale of investment property and other capital gain distributions. This schedule consolidates the individual transaction detail that is entered on Form 8949. Schedule D is divided into three parts:

- Part I, Short-Term Capital Gains and Losses (for assets held one year or less).
- Part II, Long-Term Capital Gains and Losses (for assets held more than one year).
- Part III, Summary. Part III also identifies the portion of capital gain that is subject to the 28% tax rate, which is applied to the sale of collectibles.

New for 2013, the totals from certain transactions can be reported directly on Schedule D without needing to report them on Form 8949. A taxpayer can do so if:

- He received a Form 1099-B that shows basis was reported to the IRS and does not show a nondeductible wash sale loss in box 5, and
- He does not need to make any adjustments to the basis or type of gain or loss (short-term or long-term) reported on Form 1099-B, or to his gain or loss.

Example: Carson receives a Form 1099-B reporting the sale of stock he had held for five years. It shows proceeds in box 21 of $8,000 and cost or other basis in box 3 of $3,000. Box 6b is checked, meaning that basis was reported to the IRS. Carson does not need to make any adjustments to the amounts reported on Form 1099-B, and this was his only 2013 transaction. He does not report the amounts on Form 8949. Instead, he enters the amounts directly onto his Schedule D.

Unit 7: Study Questions

1. What is the maximum number of years a taxpayer can carry over an unused capital loss?

A. One year.
B. Two years.
C. Five years.
D. As many years as required to utilize the entire deduction.

2. Five years ago, Marsha bought 100 shares of stock. Her sale date was March 10, 2013. Marsha's original cost for the stock was $10,110, plus an additional $35 in broker's fees. When she sold the stock, she received gross proceeds of $8,859. What is the net gain or loss from this transaction?

A. $1,286 of long-term capital loss.
B. $1,286 of short-term capital loss.
C. $1,251 of long-term capital loss.
D. $1,251 of long-term capital gain.

3. Mario purchased his home five years ago for $150,000. He sold it at a loss for $115,000 in 2013. Which of the following statements is true?

A. If he itemizes deductions, Mario may claim a loss of $35,000 on his 2013 tax return.
B. Mario may claim a loss of $3,000 in 2013, but must carry over the remainder to future years until the loss is completely deducted.
C. Mario can claim a loss of $35,000 because the home sale was an involuntary conversion.
D. Mario cannot claim a loss for the sale of his home.

4. Gianna purchased 200 shares of stock on January 2, 2013 for $1,000. She sold all the shares on December 31, 2013 for $2,500. On January 3, 2014, the shares were delivered and payment was submitted to Gianna's account. How should this sale be reported?

A. $1,500 long-term gain on her 2013 return.
B. $1,500 short-term gain on her 2013 return.
C. $1,500 long-term gain on her 2014 return.
D. $1,500 short-term gain on her 2014 return.

5. Ruben bought 100 shares of stock on October 1, 2012 when the share price was $26. He sold the stock for $20 a share on October 1, 2013. How should this trade be reported, and what is the nature of Ruben's gain or loss?

A. Short-term capital loss of $600.
B. Long-term capital loss of $600.
C. This is a wash sale, and there is no gain or loss.
D. Short-term capital loss of $500.

6. Tahir purchased 100 shares in Foresthill Mutual Fund in April 2013 for $750. He received a capital gain distribution of $120 in 2013. The $120 was reported to him on Form 1099-DIV. How should this be reported on his tax return?

A. He must reduce his stock's basis by $120.
B. He must report the $120 as interest income.
C. He must report the $120 as a long-term capital gain.
D. He must report the $120 as a short-term capital gain.

7. Fred is married and files jointly. He bought ten shares of Jixi Corporation stock on October 1, 2012. He sold them for a $7,000 loss on October 1, 2013. He has no other capital gains or losses. He also has $20,000 of wage income. How must Fred treat this transaction on his tax return?

A. He may deduct the $7,000 as a long-term capital loss on his 2013 return.
B. He may deduct the $7,000 as a short-term capital loss on his 2013 return.
C. He may deduct $3,000 as a short-term capital loss to offset his wage income on his 2013 return. The remaining amount, $4,000, must be carried over to future tax years.
D. He may not deduct any of the capital loss; it must be carried over to future tax years.

8. Erik sold his home for $275,000. His selling expenses were $10,000. What is the amount realized on this sale?

A. $265,000.
B. $275,000.
C. $285,000.
D. Some other amount.

9. Melissa purchased 1,000 shares of Devil Foods Company stock in 2011 at $10 per share. She sold 900 shares on January 15, 2013 at $9 per share, resulting in a $900 loss. Melissa's husband, Alex, purchased 900 shares of Devil Foods Company stock on February 10, 2013. Alex and Melissa keep their finances separate and will file MFS in 2013. Which of the following is true?

A. Melissa may deduct the $900 capital loss on her tax return.
B. Melissa has a wash sale and her loss is not deductible.
C. Alex may deduct the loss on his separate tax return.
D. None of the above.

10. Nikhil's adjusted basis in 500 shares of Edico Corporation was $2,550. He owned the shares for three months. If he sold 500 shares for $3,300, what is the resulting gain or loss?

A. $750 short-term gain.
B. $700 short-term gain.
C. $750 long-term gain.
D. $750 long-term loss.

11. Consuela purchased 1,000 shares of Hometown Mutual Fund on February 15, 2010 for $15 per share. On January 31, 2013, she sold all her shares for $3.75 per share. She also earned $45,000 in wages in 2013. She has no other transactions during the year. How should this transaction be reported on her tax return?

A. She has a capital loss of $11,250 that she can deduct against her wage income.
B. She must carry over the entire loss to a future tax year and offset future capital gains.
C. She may deduct a $3,000 capital loss on her 2013 tax return and the remainder of the loss will carry forward to subsequent years.
D. She may deduct a $5,000 capital loss on her 2013 tax return and the remainder of the losses will carry forward to subsequent years.

12. Which of the following losses is deductible?

A. A loss on the sale of a primary residence.
B. A loss on the sale of a vacation home.
C. A loss on the sale of a personal-use mobile home.
D. A loss on the sale of rental property.

13. Kayla's cost basis was $2,400 for 600 shares of stock she purchased in December 2010 and sold in September 2013. She sold the 600 shares for $4,400 and paid a $100 broker's commission. Her broker reported the gross proceeds of $4,400 on Form 1099-B. What was the amount and type of capital gain or loss?

A. $2,000 short-term gain.
B. $1,900 long-term gain.
C. $2,100 short-term gain.
D. $2,100 long-term gain.

14. For Mother's Day on May 12, 2013, Jonathan gives his mother, Caryna, a classic 1963 Corvette. Jonathan had purchased the car for $50,000 on January 4, 2013 and then worked for several months restoring it, spending $5,000 to do so. At the time of his gift, the car's FMV was $63,000. Caryna dislikes the Corvette's poor gas mileage and sells it on March 15, 2014 for $58,000. What is the nature and amount of Caryna's gain or loss?

A. $8,000 short-term loss.
B. $3,000 short-term gain.
C. $13,000 long-term gain.
D. $3,000 long-term gain.

15. Colin purchased 100 shares of Entertainment Digital Media stock for $1,000 on December 1, 2012. He sold these shares for $750 on December 22, 2013. Colin has seller's remorse, and on January 19, 2014 he repurchases 100 shares of Entertainment Digital for $800. Which of the following statements is true?

A. Colin may report a $250 capital loss in 2013.
B. Colin may report a loss in 2013 and a taxable gain in 2014.
C. Colin may not deduct his stock loss of $250 and must add the disallowed loss to his basis.
D. Colin may report a $250 capital loss in 2014.

16. When trying to determine the holding period for investment property, which of the following is important?

A. The cost of the property.
B. In the case of gifted property, the amount of the gift.
C. The date of acquisition.
D. The amount realized in the transaction.

17. Phil and Sharon owned a vacation home for 14 months before selling it for $254,000. Their adjusted basis in the home was $232,000, and they incurred $12,500 in selling expenses. Prior to the sale, they did not rent the home. What is the nature and amount of their gain?

A. $22,000 long-term capital gain.
B. $9,500 long-term capital gain.
C. $9,500 short-term capital gain.
D. $34,500 long-term capital gain.

18. Gerardo owns 100 shares of Wild Fishery stock, which he purchased five years ago for $1,500. In May 2013, Wild Fishery issues a stock dividend of 50 additional shares. Gerardo sells 60 shares on December 28, 2013. What is his adjusted basis in these 60 shares?

A. $500.
B. $600.
C. $900.
D. $2,250.

19. All of the statements are true about related party transactions except the following:

A. If a taxpayer controls more than 50% of a corporation or partnership, any property transactions between the taxpayer and business would be subject to the related party transaction rules.
B. Typically, a loss on the sale of property between related parties is not deductible.
C. The related party transaction rules apply to spouses, siblings and half-siblings, grandchildren, uncles, and aunts.
D. Related party transaction rules are designed to prevent improper deductions between two parties joined by a special relationship.

20. On Mar. 10, 2009, Hans bought 500 shares of Merring stock for $1,500. On June 6, 2012, Merring distributed to Hans a nontaxable stock dividend of ten additional shares. Three days later, he sold the stock for $2,030. What is the nature of his gain on the shares sold?

A. Long-term capital gain of $530.
B. Long-term capital gain of $500, short-term gain of $30.
C. Short-term capital gain of $530.
D. None of the above.

21. Conrad purchased Blue-Chip Corporation stock in 2009 and sold it in 2013. In 2013, he also traded in a copy machine that he had been using in his business since 2008 for a new model. On December 15, 2013, Conrad's mother gave him 35 shares of Energy Corp. stock that she had held for five years. Conrad sold the gifted stock two weeks after he received it from his mother. What is the holding period for all these assets?

A. All short-term.
B. Blue-Chip stock and copy machine are long-term and Energy Corp. stock is short-term.
C. All the stocks are long-term; the copy machine is short-term.
D. All are long-term.

22. Tariq bought two blocks (each of 400 shares) of Acme Co. stock. He purchased the first block in April 2008 for $1,200 and the second block in March 2013 for $1,600. In June of 2013, he sold 400 shares for $1,500, but is unable to specify which stocks he sold. Tariq's stock sale results in a _____.

A. Short-term loss of $100.
B. Short-term gain of $300.
C. Long-term loss of $100.
D. Long-term gain of $300.

23. Norma sells an empty lot with an adjusted basis of $20,000. Her buyer assumes an existing mortgage on the property of $15,000 and agrees to pay Norma $10,000, with a cash down payment of $2,000 and then $2,000 every year (plus 12% interest) in each of the next four years. What is Norma's gross profit and gross profit percentage on the installment sale?

A. The gross profit is $5,000, and the gross profit percentage is 20%.
B. The gross profit is $10,000, and the gross profit percentage is 100%.
C. The gross profit is $15,000, and the gross profit percentage is 20%.
D. The gross profit is $5,000, and the gross profit percentage is 50%.

24. Oliver operates a repair business as a sole proprietorship. In 2013, Oliver sold property that was acquired for use in the business for $15,000. The purchase price of the property was $12,000, and Oliver had claimed depreciation of $3,000 related to the property. He accepted a down payment of $5,000 from the buyer, along with a note requiring additional payments of $2,500 plus interest in each of the next four years. Based upon the information provided, what amount of taxable income will result from the installment sale of this property in 2013?

A. Capital gain of $1,000 and ordinary income of $3,000.
B. Capital gain of $5,000 and ordinary income of $1,000.
C. Capital gain of $2,000.
D. Capital gain of $1,000 and ordinary income of $1,000.

Unit 8: Nonrecognition Property Transactions

For additional information read:
Publication 544, *Sales and Other Dispositions of Assets*
Publication 523, *Selling Your Home*

For some transactions in which a taxpayer sells or exchanges property, gains may be nontaxable, partially taxable, or deferred. Three of the most common types of nonrecognition transactions involve:

- Sale of a main home (section 121, excluded gain)
- Like-kind exchanges (section 1031 exchange)
- Involuntary conversions (section 1033 exchange)

Sale of Main Home (Section 121)

In many cases, a taxpayer may exclude the gain from the sale of a main home. Up to $250,000 of gain may be excluded by single filers and up to $500,000 by joint filers. Generally, if the taxpayer can exclude all of the gain, it is not even necessary to report the sale. However, if part of the gain is taxable, the sale must be reported on Schedule D. Gain from the sale of a home that is not the taxpayer's main home must be reported as income.

The section 121 exclusion only applies to a "main home" and not to rental properties, vacation homes, or second homes. A taxpayer's main home is the residence where he lives most of the time. It does not have to be a traditional house. The main home can be a house, houseboat, mobile home, cooperative apartment, or condominium. To qualify as a home, it must have sleeping, kitchen, and bathroom facilities.

Example: Wayne owns and lives in a house in Detroit. He also owns a lake cottage, which he uses only during the summer. The house in Detroit is his main home; the lake cottage is not. Wayne sells the cottage and has $100,000 in gain. The gain cannot be excluded because the cottage is not his main home.

If the home was used for business purposes or as rental property, the gain is reported on Form 4797, *Sales of Business Property.* If a taxpayer took depreciation deductions because he used his home as a rental or for other business purposes, he cannot exclude the part of the gain equal to any deductible depreciation. Section 121 applies only to the nonbusiness portion of a home.

Example: Erica lives in one half of a duplex she owns and rents out the other half. She purchased the duplex in 2005 for $200,000. In 2013, Erica sells the duplex for $340,000, a gain of $140,000. Since half of the duplex counts as her main home, Erica may exclude only half of the gain ($70,000). She must report the other $70,000 as long-term capital gain.

Eligibility Requirements: To be eligible for the section 121 exclusion, a taxpayer must:

- Have sold his main home
- Meet ownership and use tests
- Not have excluded gain in the two years prior to the current sale of a home

Ownership and Use Tests

During the five-year period ending on the date of the sale, the taxpayer must have:

- Owned the home for at least two years (the ownership test), and
- Lived in the home as his main home for at least two years (the use test).

Example: For the past six years, Lindsay lived with her parents in the home her parents owned. On September 1, 2012, she bought the house from her parents. She continued to live there until December 14, 2013 when she sold it because she wanted a bigger house. Lindsay does not meet the requirements for exclusion. Although she *lived* in the property as her main home for more than two years, she did not *own* it for the required two years. Therefore, she does not meet both the ownership and use tests.

The required two years of ownership and use do not have to be continuous, as illustrated in examples on the next page.

A taxpayer meets the tests if he owned and lived in the property as his main home for either 24 full months or 730 days (365 × 2) during the five-year period.

Example: In 2005, Carter began living in an apartment he rented. The apartment was converted to a condominium, which he bought on December 1, 2010. In 2011, Carter became ill, and on April 14 of that year he moved into his daughter's home. On July 10, 2013, while still living in his daughter's home, Carter sold his condo. He can exclude all the gain on the sale because he meets the ownership and use tests. His five-year period is from July 11, 2008 to July 10, 2013 (the date he sold the condo). He owned the condo from December 1, 2010 until July 10, 2013 (more than two years). He lived there from 2005 until April 14, 2011 (more than two years).

Ownership and use tests can be met during different two-year periods, as illustrated in the preceding example.

Example: Irene bought a house in September 2009. After living there for ten months, she moved in with her boyfriend and kept her house vacant. They broke up and she moved back into her own house in 2012. She lived there for 16 months until she sold it in September 2013. Irene meets the ownership and use tests because during the five-year period ending on the date of sale, she owned the house for four years and lived in the house for a total of 26 months.

Short, temporary absences, even if the property is rented during those absences, are still counted as periods of use. Short absences include vacations and other seasonal absences. Longer breaks, such as a one-year sabbatical, are not included.

Example: Katarina bought her home on February 1, 2010. Each year, she left her home for a four-month vacation in Ecuador. Katarina sold the house on March 1, 2013. She may exclude up to $250,000 of gain. The vacations are considered short temporary absences and are counted toward her periods of use.

Married Homeowners: The ownership and use tests are applied differently to married homeowners. Married homeowners can exclude gain of up to $500,000 if they meet all of the following conditions:

- They file a joint return.
- Either spouse meets the ownership test (only one is required to own the home).
- Both spouses meet the use test.
- Neither spouse has excluded gain in the two years before the current sale of the home.

If they do not satisfy these requirements, the couple cannot claim the maximum $500,000 exclusion.

Example: After selling her main home in June 2013, Leigh has $350,000 of gain. She marries William in September 2013. Leigh meets the ownership and use tests, but William does not meet the use test. Leigh can exclude up to $250,000 of gain on her 2013 tax return, whether she files MFJ or MFS. The $500,000 exclusion for joint returns does not apply.

Example: Robert owns a home that he has lived in continuously for eight years. In June 2010, he marries Annabel. She moves in and they both live in the house until December 1, 2013 when the house is sold. Robert meets the ownership test and the use test. Annabel meets only the use test, because Robert is listed as the sole owner of the property. On a jointly filed return, they may claim the maximum $500,000 exclusion.

Legally married same-sex spouses are now eligible for the maximum $500,000 exclusion from gain.

Example: Brandon and Max were legally married in Vermont in 2012. In 2013, they sell the house they had co-owned and lived in for ten years. The house sold for $575,000 more than they paid for it. Brandon and Max may receive the maximum $500,000 exclusion for married couples when they file jointly in 2013. The remaining $75,000 of gain is taxable.

Unrelated Individuals: An unmarried couple or other taxpayers who own a home and live together may take the $250,000 exclusion individually on their separate returns if they meet the use and ownership tests.

Example: Greta and Carolyn are lifelong friends. They are both widowed and decide to purchase a home and live together. If they later sell the home, the ownership and use tests would apply to them individually. Each could claim an exclusion of up to $250,000 for her portion of the sale on her individual return.

Deceased Spouse: When a taxpayer's spouse dies, the taxpayer is considered to have owned and lived in a home during any period of time that the spouse owned and lived in it as a main home (provided that the taxpayer did not remarry before the date of sale). In effect, the holding period of the deceased spouse is tacked on for surviving spouses. As a result, the surviving spouse may exclude up to $500,000 of gain even if he sells the home within two years from when he first moved in.

Example: Alice owned and lived in her home for seven years. She married Stanley in April 2013, and he moved into the home with her. Alice died six months later, and Stanley inherited the property. He did not remarry. Stanley sells the home on December 1, 2013. Even though he did not own or live in the house for two years, he meets the test requirements because his period of ownership and use includes the period that Alice owned and used the property before her death. Stanley may exclude up to $500,000 of the gain.

This exclusion also applies to a home that is transferred by a spouse in a divorce. The receiving spouse is considered to have owned the home during any period of time that the transferor owned it.

Military Personnel Exception: Members of the armed forces are often required to move and might have a difficult time meeting the tests for ownership and use within the five-year period prior to sale of a home. The five-year period can be suspended for up to ten years for military and Foreign Service personnel, Peace Corps workers, and intelligence officers that are on official extended duty. This provides the taxpayer a better opportunity to meet the two-year use test even if he and/or his spouse did not actually live in the home during the normal five-year period required of other taxpayers.

Disability Exception: There is an exception to the use test if, during the five-year period before the sale of the home, a taxpayer becomes physically or mentally unable to care for himself, but he has owned and lived in the home for at least one year. The taxpayer is considered to have lived in the home during any time that he is forced to live in a licensed facility, including a nursing home. The taxpayer must still meet the two-year ownership test.

Reduced Exclusions: A taxpayer who owned and used a home for less than two years (and therefore does not meet the ownership and use tests) or who has used the home sale exclusion within the prior two-year period may be able to claim a reduced exclusion under certain conditions. This may apply if a home sale has occurred primarily because of "unforeseen circumstances" during the taxpayer's period of use and ownership. Unforeseen circumstances include the following:

- Death, divorce, or legal separation.
- Certain health reasons related to care for the taxpayer, a spouse, a child, or certain other related persons. The related person does not have to be a dependent in order for the reduced exclusion to apply.
- Unemployment or a job change. The job-related exclusion applies if a new job is at least 50 miles farther from the old home than was the former place of employment. If there was no former place of employment, the distance between the new place of employment and the old home must be at least 50 miles.
- Multiple births resulting from the same pregnancy.
- Damage to the residence resulting from a disaster, an act of war, or terrorism.
- Involuntary conversion of the property.

The circumstances may involve the taxpayer, his spouse, a co-owner, or a member of the taxpayer's household. The IRS also has the discretion to deem other circumstances as unforeseen.

For example, the IRS Commissioner declared the September 11, 2001 terrorist attack an unforeseen circumstance.

Example: Justin purchased his new home in Mississippi in June 2012, but he lost his job shortly after he moved. He found a new job in North Carolina and sold his house in April 2013. Because the distance between Justin's new place of employment and his former home is at least 50 miles, the sale satisfies the distance requirement. Justin's sale of his home is due to a change in place of employment, and he is entitled to claim a reduced exclusion on his gain from the sale.

The reduced exclusion amount equals the full $250,000 (or $500,000 for married couples filing jointly) multiplied by a fraction. The numerator is the shorter of:

- The period the taxpayer owned and used the home as a principal residence during the five-year period ending on the sale date, or
- The period between the last sale for which the taxpayer claimed the exclusion and the sale date for the home currently being sold.

The denominator is two years, or the equivalent in months or days. Thus, the amount of the reduced exclusion is figured by multiplying the full exclusion amount by the number of days or months the taxpayer owned and used the property, and dividing by either 730 days or 24 months.

Example: Carrie purchased her home on January 1, 2013 for $350,000. Her mother is diagnosed with cancer, and Carrie must move to care for her. Even though Carrie does not claim her mother as a dependent, the move still qualifies as an unforeseen circumstance. Carrie sells her home on May 1, 2013 for $430,000, realizing a gain of $80,000. She qualifies for the reduced exclusion, so part of her gain is nontaxable. She owned and occupied the home for 121 days (January 1 to May 1). She may exclude $41,438 ($250,000 × [121 ÷ 730]). Therefore, Carrie's taxable gain is $38,562 ($80,000 - $41,438). This amount is a short-term capital gain since she owned the house for less than one year.

Example: Sabrina, a single taxpayer, lived in her principal residence for one full year (365 days) before selling it at a $400,000 gain in 2013. She qualifies for the reduced exclusion because she is pregnant with triplets (multiple births exclusion). Sabrina can exclude $125,000 of gain ($250,000 × [365 ÷ 730]).

Land Sales: If a taxpayer sells the land on which his main home is located but not the house itself, he cannot exclude the gain. Similarly, the sale of a vacant plot of land with no house on it does not qualify for the section 121 exclusion.

Example: Theresa purchased an empty lot in 2009 for $90,000, planning to build her dream home. Construction was delayed and her house was never completed. In December 2013, Theresa sells the land for $150,000. She owned the property for more than a year, so she has $60,000 of long-term capital gain. None of the gain can be excluded from income, because there is no residence on the property.

If a taxpayer sells a vacant lot that is adjacent to his main home, he may be able to exclude the gain from the sale under certain circumstances. Gain from the sale of vacant land that was used in connection with a principal residence may be excluded if the land sale occurs within two years before or after the sale of the home. The sale of the land and the sale of the home are treated as one sale for purposes of the exclusion.

Like-Kind Exchanges (Section 1031 Exchange)

A Section 1031 "like-kind" exchange occurs when a taxpayer exchanges business or investment property for similar property. If the exchange qualifies under Section 1031 he does not pay tax on a resulting gain and may not deduct a loss until he disposes of the property received. To qualify for nonrecognition treatment, the exchange must meet all of the following conditions:

- The property must be held for investment or for productive use in a business. Property held for personal use, such as a personal residence, does not qualify.
- The property must not be "held primarily for sale" (such as inventory).
- There must be an actual exchange of two or more assets or properties (the exchange of cash for property is treated as a sale, not as an exchange).
- For instances in which a property is transferred in exchange for like-kind property to be received later (known as a deferred exchange), the property to be received must be identified in writing (or actually received) within 45 days after the date of transfer of the property given up.

Further, the replacement property in a deferred exchange must be received by the earlier of:

- The 180th day after the date on which the property given up was transferred, or
- The due date, including extensions, of the tax return for the year in which the transfer of that property occurs.

Taxpayers report like-kind exchanges on Form 8824, *Like-Kind Exchanges*.

Qualifying Exchanges: To qualify under section 1031, an exchange must involve like-kind property, such as the trade of real property for real property or personal property for personal property.

Note: The term "personal property" does not refer to items used for personal use but rather to assets used in a business that are not real property.

An exchange of real property generally qualifies more easily as like-kind, regardless of how each property is used or whether each property is improved or unimproved. For instance, the exchange of a building for farmland would qualify, as would the exchange of an apartment building for an office building. However, the exchange of factory machinery (personal property) for a factory building (real property) is not a qualifying exchange.

In contrast, an exchange of personal property must involve items that are at least similar enough to both be categorized within one of several asset classes established by the IRS. For example, the exchange of a panel truck for a pickup truck may qualify as a trade of like-kind property, but the exchange of a pickup truck for a semi-truck likely would not.

Example: Casey exchanges a private jet with an adjusted basis of $400,000 for an office building valued at $375,000. The exchange of personal property (an airplane) for real property (the building) does not qualify for section 1031 treatment.

Nonqualifying Exchanges: The exchange of equipment or business assets that are used within the United States for similar items used outside the United States would not be considered an exchange of qualifying like-kind property. Similarly, real estate within the United States and real estate outside the United States is not like property and an exchange would not qualify for section 1031 treatment.

Other exchanges that do not qualify for section 1031 treatment include the following types of property:

- Livestock of different sexes
- Securities, bonds, stocks, or notes
- Currency
- Partnership interests

Boot: Although the Internal Revenue Code itself does not use the term "boot," it is frequently used to describe cash or other property added to an exchange in order to compensate for a difference in the values of properties traded. An exchange may still be valid under section 1031, but the taxpayer who receives boot may have to recognize taxable gain to the extent of the cash and the FMV of unlike property received. The amount considered boot would be reduced by qualified costs paid in connection with the transaction.

Example: Sloan wishes to exchange his rental property in a 1031 exchange. The relinquished property has an FMV of $60,000 and an adjusted basis of $30,000. The replacement property Sloan receives has an FMV of $50,000, and he also receives $10,000 in cash as part of the exchange. Sloan, therefore, has a gain of $30,000 on the exchange (combined value of $60,000 received less his basis of $30,000 in the property exchanged), but he is required to pay tax on only $10,000, the cash (boot) received in the exchange. The rest of his gain is deferred until he disposes of the property at a later date.

When an exchange involves property that is subject to a liability, assumption of the liability is treated as if it were a transfer of cash and thus considered boot by the party who is relieved of the liability. If each property in an exchange is transferred subject to a liability, a taxpayer is treated as having received boot only if he is relieved of a greater liability than the liability he assumes.

Basis of Property Received in a Like-Kind Exchange: The basis of the property received is generally the adjusted basis of the property transferred.

Example: Judy has a rental house with an adjusted basis of $70,000. In 2013, she trades the rental house for an empty lot with an FMV of $150,000. Judy's basis in the lot is $70,000, equal to the adjusted basis of the property she exchanged.

If a taxpayer trades property and also pays money as part of the exchange, the basis of the property received is the basis of the property given up, increased by any additional money paid.

Example: Jorge trades a plot of land with an adjusted basis of $30,000 for a different plot of land in another town with an FMV of $70,500. He pays an additional $4,000 in cash. Jorge's basis in the new land is $34,000: his $30,000 basis in the old land plus the $4,000 cash.

Example: Peyton bought a new diesel truck for use in her catering business. She received credit of $13,600 for trading in her old truck and also paid $43,000 cash. The old truck cost $50,000 two years ago and Peyton had taken depreciation deductions of $39,500 on it. She has a $3,100 gain on the exchange ($13,600 trade-in allowance minus her $10,500 adjusted basis for the old truck) but recognition of the gain is postponed under the rules for like-kind exchanges.

If a taxpayer receives boot in connection with an exchange and recognizes gain, the basis of the property received is equal to the basis of the property given up plus the amount of gain recognized.

Related Party Transactions: Like-kind exchanges are allowed between related parties, including family members. However, if either party disposes of the property within two years after a 1031 exchange, the exchange is usually disqualified from nonrecognition treatment; any gain or loss that was deferred in the original transaction must be recognized in the year the disposition occurs.

For purposes of this rule, a related person includes a close family member (such as a spouse, sibling, parent, or child). It also includes a corporation or partnership in which a taxpayer holds ownership or interests of more than 50%.

The two-year holding period rule may not apply:

- If one of the parties involved in the exchange dies
- If the property is subsequently converted in an involuntary exchange (such as a fire or a flood)
- If it can be established to the satisfaction of the IRS that the exchange and subsequent disposition were not done mainly for tax avoidance purposes

The IRS gives close scrutiny to exchanges between related parties because they can be used by taxpayers to evade taxes on gains.

Involuntary Conversions (Section 1033)

An involuntary conversion occurs when a taxpayer's property is lost, damaged, or destroyed, and the taxpayer receives an award, insurance money, or some other type of payment, as a result of:

- Casualty or theft,
- Disaster,
- Condemnation, or
- Threat of condemnation.

Gain or loss from an involuntary conversion of property is usually recognized for tax purposes unless the property is a main home. A taxpayer reports the gain or deducts the loss in the year the gain or loss is realized. A taxpayer cannot deduct a loss from an involuntary conversion of personal-use property unless the loss resulted from a casualty or theft.

However, under section 1033, a taxpayer can defer reporting gain on an involuntary conversion if he receives proceeds from insurance or another source and invests in property that is similar to the converted property.

Example: A hurricane destroys Denise's residential rental property that has an adjusted basis of $50,000. The insurance company gives Denise a check for $100,000, which is the FMV of the home. Denise buys a replacement rental property six months later for $100,000. Her gain on the involuntary conversion is $50,000 ($100,000 insurance settlement minus her $50,000 basis). However, Denise does not have to recognize any taxable gain because she reinvested all the insurance proceeds in another, similar property. This is an example of a qualified 1033 exchange.

Example: Lane and Candace are married and file jointly. They paid $100,000 for their home ten years ago. They receive an insurance payment of $700,000 after their home is destroyed in a mudslide, for a $600,000 gain on the conversion. They may exclude $500,000 of the gain under section 121, leaving $100,000 as taxable long-term capital gain. If they reinvest the insurance proceeds under the rules for involuntary conversions, they may defer the remainder of the gain.

Replacement Period: The replacement period for an involuntary conversion generally ends two years after the end of the first tax year in which any part of the gain is realized.

Example: Barney owns a drywall repair business. On September 1, 2013, a flood destroys a storage shed filled with his supplies. Barney's insurance company reimburses him for the loss. He has until December 31, 2015 to replace the shed and supplies using the insurance proceeds. Barney is not required to report the insurance proceeds on his 2013 tax return. If he reinvests all the proceeds in a replacement property, he will not have any taxable gain.

Real property that is held for investment or used in a trade or business is allowed a three-year replacement period. The replacement period is four years for livestock that is involuntarily converted because of weather-related conditions. If a main home is damaged or destroyed and is in a federally-declared disaster area, the replacement period is extended to four years. A five-year replacement period has been applied to certain extreme disaster areas, including Hurricane Katrina, the May 2007 Kansas storms and tornadoes, and the Midwestern area disasters of 2008, but only if the replacement property is purchased in the same area.

Property Type	Replacement Period
Most property except those noted below	Two years
Real property that is held for investment or business use, such as residential rentals and office buildings	Three years
Sale of livestock due to weather-related conditions	Four years
Property in federally-declared disaster areas	Four to five years

If a taxpayer reinvests in replacement property similar to the converted property, the replacement property's basis is the same as the converted property's basis on the date of the conversion, subject to the following adjustments:

The basis is **decreased** by the following:

- Any loss a taxpayer recognizes on the involuntary conversion
- Any money a taxpayer receives that he does not spend on similar property

The basis is **increased** by the following:

- Any gain a taxpayer recognizes on the involuntary conversion
- Any additional costs of acquiring the replacement property

Example: Franco owns an apartment building in Texas with a basis of $250,000. He receives an insurance settlement of $400,000 after the building is destroyed by a tornado. A year later, Franco purchases another apartment building in Wisconsin for $380,000. Franco's realized gain on the involuntary conversion is $150,000 ($400,000 - $250,000 basis). He must recognize $20,000 of gain because he received an insurance payment of $400,000 but only spent $380,000 on the replacement property ($400,000 - $380,000). His basis in the new property is $250,000, which is calculated as the cost of the new property in Wisconsin minus the deferred gain ($380,000 - $130,000 = $250,000). If Franco had used all the insurance proceeds and invested it in the new property, he would not have to report any taxable gain.

Condemnations

A condemnation is a type of involuntary conversion. Condemnation is the process by which private property is taken from its owner for public use. The property may be taken by the government or by a private organization that has the legal power to seize it. The owner generally receives a condemnation award (money or property) in exchange for the property that is taken. A condemnation is like a forced sale, with the owner being the seller and the government or other third party being the buyer.

Example: The local government informs Trevor that his farmland is being condemned to create a public park. The government takes Trevor's property and pays him $400,000. Trevor's basis in the farmland was $80,000. He decides not to purchase replacement farmland. Therefore, he has a taxable event, and he must recognize $320,000 as income ($400,000 - $80,000 = $320,000). However, if Trevor were to purchase replacement property with the condemnation award, he would have a nontaxable section 1033 exchange.

Amounts taken out of a condemnation award to pay debts on the property are considered paid to the taxpayer and are included in the amount of the award.

Example: The state condemned Nan's property in order to build a light rail system. The court award was set at $200,000. The state paid her only $148,000 because it paid $50,000 to her mortgage company and $2,000 in accrued real estate taxes. Nan is considered to have received the entire $200,000 as a condemnation award.

The time period for replacing condemned property is the same as other qualified section 1033 exchanges, two years after the end of the first tax year in which any part of the gain on the condemnation is realized. For real property held for business use or investment, the replacement period is three years instead of two.

Example: Joel owns a pool hall. In February 2013, the building is condemned by the city because asbestos is discovered in the building. He receives his condemnation award in May 2013. He has until December 31, 2016 to replace the condemned pool hall with a similar building.

Condemnation of a Main Home: If a taxpayer has a gain because his main home is condemned, he can generally exclude the gain as if he had sold the home under the section 121 exclusion. Single filers can exclude up to $250,000 of the gain and joint filers up to $500,000.

Unit 8: Study Questions

1. Isaiah has lived in and owned his home for 15 months when he decides to move in with his girlfriend, so he sells his home for $285,000. His adjusted basis in the home is $160,000. What is the amount and nature of his taxable gain on the sale?

A. $0.
B. $35,000 long-term capital gain.
C. $125,000 long-term capital gain.
D. $125,000 short-term capital gain.

2. Lucille owns a home in the Vail ski area. She stays at the ski home most weekends and spends the entire months of December, January, and February there. When she is not at the ski home, she lives in a four-room apartment that she rents in Denver. What is Lucille's main home for purposes of the section 121 exclusion?

A. Her ski home in Vail.
B. Her apartment in Denver.
C. She is considered a transient for tax purposes.
D. None of the above.

3. Bailey exchanges his residential rental property (adjusted basis $50,000, FMV $80,000) for a different rental property (FMV $70,000). What is Bailey's basis in the new property?

A. $50,000.
B. $70,000.
C. $80,000.
D. $100,000.

4. All of the following would generally be acceptable as "unforeseen circumstances" for a taxpayer to take a reduced exclusion on the sale of his primary residence except:

A. The home is condemned by the city.
B. A legal separation.
C. The birth of twin girls.
D. Moving to another state to be closer to grown children.

5. Heather is single and bought her first home in 2003 for $350,000. She lived continuously in the house until she sold it in 2013 for $620,000. Which of the following is true?

A. Heather may exclude $250,000 of gain and report the remaining gain as a long-term capital gain.
B. Heather may exclude the entire gain. There is no amount that needs to be reported.
C. Heather may not exclude any of the gain.
D. Heather may exclude $250,000 of gain. The remaining amount must be reported as a short-term capital gain.

6. Aiden exchanges a residential rental property in Las Vegas with a basis of $100,000 for an investment property in Miami Beach valued at $220,000 plus $15,000 in cash. What is Aiden's taxable gain on the exchange, and what is the basis of the new property in Miami Beach?

A. Taxable gain: $15,000; basis: $115,000.
B. Taxable gain: $0; basis: $235,000.
C. Taxable gain: $15,000; basis: $135,000.
D. Taxable gain: $15,000; basis: $220,000.

7. Geoff sold his main home in 2013 at a $29,000 gain. He meets the ownership and use tests to exclude the gain from his income. However, he used one room of the home for business in 2011 and 2012. His records show he claimed $3,000 of depreciation for a home office. What is Geoff's taxable gain on the sale, if any?

A. $0.
B. $1,000.
C. $2,000.
D. $3,000.

8. A tornado destroyed Bryant's home on July 15, 2011. He wants to replace the home using a section 1033 exchange for involuntary conversions. What is the latest that Bryant can replace the property in order to defer any gain from his insurance reimbursement?

A. By December 31, 2013.
B. By July 15, 2014.
C. By July 15, 2013.
D. By December 31, 2015.

9. Bob and Grace were married in January 2009. They purchased their first home in March 2009 for $150,000. In February 2013, Bob and Grace legally separated, and the court granted Grace ownership of the home as part of the divorce settlement. The divorce became final in June 2013, and the fair market value of the home was $370,000 when ownership was transferred to Grace. She sells the house on December 23, 2013 for $480,000. What is Grace's taxable gain in the transaction?

A. $0.
B. $80,000.
C. $120,000.
D. $210,000.

10. Mitchell and Kay are married and file jointly. They owned and used a house as their main home for 15 months. Mitchell got a new job in another state and they sold their home. What is the maximum amount that can be excluded from income under the rules regarding a reduced exclusion?

A. $22,727.
B. $250,000.
C. $312,500.
E. $500,000.

11. Jonah exchanged a rental building for another rental building. The original cost of the old building was $16,000, and he had made $10,000 of improvements prior to the exchange. He exchanged it for a building worth $36,000. Jonah did not recognize any gain from the exchange. What is his basis in the new property?

A. $26,000.
B. $36,000.
C. $10,000.
D. $16,000.

12. Which of the following transactions does not qualify for a section 1031 like-kind exchange?

A. An exchange of a boutique in Manhattan for 20 acres of farmland.
B. An exchange of an apartment building in New Mexico for an office building in Alaska.
C. An exchange of a business desk for a business printer.
D. An exchange of inventory for different inventory.

13. Shane and Phyllis move after living in their home for 292 days, because Phyllis became pregnant with triplets and they needed a larger home. The gain on the sale of the home is $260,000. Since they have lived there for less than two years but meet one of the exceptions, what is the actual amount of their reduced exclusion? (Two years = 730 days)

A. $60,000.
B. $200,000.
C. $260,000.
D. $500,000.

14. Allen is a flight instructor. He trades in a small plane (adjusted basis $300,000) for another, larger plane (FMV $750,000) and pays $60,000 of cash in addition. He uses the plane 100% in his flight instruction business. What is his basis in the new plane?

A. $300,000.
B. $360,000.
C. $690,000.
D. $750,000.

15. Gino bought a house for $189,000 in July 2010. He lived there continuously for 13 months and then moved in with his girlfriend. They later separated, and Gino moved back into his own house and lived there for 12 months until he sold it in July 2013 for $220,000. What is the amount and nature of his gain?

A. Gino has no taxable gain, because the sale qualifies for a section 121 exclusion.
B. $31,000 long-term capital gain.
C. $31,000 short-term capital gain.
D. $30,000 long-term capital gain.

16. Katherine owns a yacht that she uses for personal use. Her purchase price was $150,000. A storm destroys the yacht in 2013. Katherine collects $175,000 from her insurance company and promptly reinvests all the proceeds in a larger, new yacht, which costs her $201,000. What is her basis in the new yacht?

A. $175,000.
B. $176,000.
C. $201,000.
D. $226,000.

17. Annalise sold her primary residence in Utah and moved to Iowa. She had purchased the house in 2000 for $200,000, and she sold it in 2013 for $550,000, net of selling expenses. During the time she lived in the house, she paid $25,000 for improvements and $15,000 for repairs. Assuming that Annalise utilizes the maximum available exclusion, what amount would she report as taxable gain?

A. $100,000.
B. $60,000.
C. $75,000.
D. $0.

18. Christian owned an office building with an adjusted basis of $400,000. The building was destroyed by a fire in 2013, and Christian receives an insurance reimbursement of $600,000. He purchases a new office building for $450,000 and invests the rest of the insurance proceeds in stocks. Which of the following statements is true?

A. He has $200,000 of taxable gain he must recognize on his tax return.
B. He has $150,000 of taxable gain he must recognize on his tax return.
C. He does not have a taxable gain, because he reinvested the insurance proceeds in qualifying investment property.
D. He has $50,000 of taxable gain he must recognize on his tax return.

Unit 9: Rental and Royalty Income

For additional information read:
Publication 527, ***Residential Rental Property***
Publication 946, ***How to Depreciate Property***
Publication 525, ***Taxable and Nontaxable Income***

Rental income is any payment received for the use or occupation of property. In most cases, taxpayers must include amounts received as rent in their gross income.

Property owners can deduct the expenses of managing, conserving, and maintaining their rental properties. Common rental expenses include:

- Mortgage interest and property taxes
- Maintenance, repairs, and cleaning fees
- Advertising
- Utilities
- Insurance
- Depreciation

Advance Rent: Taxpayers must report rental income when it is constructively received, i.e. available without restrictions. This includes advance rent, which is any amount received before the period that it covers. Thus, a taxpayer must include advance rent in income in the year he receives it, regardless of the period covered or the accounting method used.

Example: Gene rents out a duplex. On December 20, 2013, his tenant pays two months of rent in advance for January and February because she is leaving town on vacation. Gene must report the advance rent as income in 2013, not in 2014.

Lease Cancellation: If a tenant pays to cancel a lease, the amount received for the cancellation is rental income. The payment is included in the year received regardless of the taxpayer's accounting method.

Security Deposits: A security deposit is not considered income upon initial receipt, if the deposit is refundable to the tenant at the end of the lease. However, if the taxpayer keeps the security deposit because the tenant did not live up to the terms of the lease or because he damaged property, the deposit amount is recognized as income in the year it is forfeited by the tenant.

Property or Services in Lieu of Rent: If a taxpayer receives property or services as payment for rent instead of cash, the fair market value must be recognized as rental income. If the tenant and landlord agree in advance to a price, the agreed-upon price is deemed the fair market value unless there is evidence to the contrary.

Example: Beth's tenant, Chris, is a professional chimneysweep. Chris offers to clean all of Beth's chimneys in her apartment building instead of paying three months' rent in cash. Beth accepts Chris's offer. Beth must recognize income for the amount Chris would have paid for three months' rent. However, Beth may deduct that same amount as a business expense for maintenance of the property.

If a tenant pays expenses on behalf of the landlord, the landlord must recognize the payments as rental income. The landlord can deduct the expenses as rental expenses.

Example: Rosetta owns an apartment building. While she is out of town, the furnace in the apartment building breaks down. Kerry, Rosetta's tenant, pays for the emergency repairs out-of-pocket and deducts the furnace repair bill from his rent payment. Rosetta must recognize as rental income both the actual amount of rent received in cash from Kerry and the amount he paid for the repairs. Rosetta can deduct the cost of the furnace repair as a rental expense.

Insurance Premiums Paid in Advance: If a cash-basis taxpayer pays an insurance premium for more than one year in advance, he may only deduct the part of the premium payment that applies to that year. He cannot deduct the total premium in the year he pays it.

Local Benefit Taxes: In most cases, a taxpayer cannot deduct charges for local taxes that increase the value of a rental property, such as assessments for streets, sidewalks, or water and sewer systems. These charges are nondepreciable capital expenditures that must be added to the basis of the property. Only taxes to maintain or repair such infrastructure, or to pay interest charges related to financing its construction, may be deducted.

Vacant Property: A taxpayer cannot deduct any loss of rental income for the period a property is vacant. However, if the taxpayer is actively trying to rent the property, he can deduct ordinary and necessary expenses as soon as the property is made available for rent.

Example: Rodrigo purchased a rental property and made the property available for rent on March 1, 2013 by advertising it in the local newspaper. He found a tenant who moved in on June 1, 2013. Even though the rental was unoccupied from March through May, Rodrigo may still deduct the mortgage interest and other expenses related to the property during that period.

Depreciation of Rental Property

A taxpayer begins to claim deductions for depreciation of a rental property when he places it in service for the production of income. Rental property is considered "placed in service" when it is ready and available for rent. Depreciation ends when a taxpayer has either fully recovered his cost or other basis or when the property is retired from service, whichever happens first. Three basic factors determine how much depreciation a taxpayer can deduct:

- Basis
- Recovery period for the property
- Depreciation method used, including certain conventions

The cost of land is never depreciated because land does not wear out, become obsolete, or get used up.

Most residential rental buildings are depreciated over 27.5 years and nonresidential buildings are generally depreciated over 39 years.

Example: In 2008, Lance purchased a home for \$180,000. On the date of purchase, the assessed value of the land was \$30,000. After living in the home for five years, Lance converted it to a rental property on April 1, 2013. Since the cost of land is not depreciated, Lance includes only the cost of the house when calculating the basis for depreciation. The allocated cost of the house is \$150,000 (\$180,000 - \$30,000). In 2013, the county assessor's office assigned the home an FMV of \$185,000, of which \$40,000 was for land and \$145,000 for the house. The basis for depreciation of the house is the FMV on the date of conversion (\$145,000), because it is less than Lance's allocated cost (\$150,000). Lance uses \$145,000 to calculate depreciation, which is reported on Schedule E, *Supplemental Income and Loss (From rental real estate, royalties, partnerships, S corporations, estates, trusts, REMICs, etc.)*
Example: In 2013, Shannon buys a rental property for \$200,000. It has an assessed value of \$160,000, of which \$136,000 is for the house and \$24,000 is for the land. Shannon can allocate 85% (\$136,000 ÷ \$160,000) of the purchase price to the house and 15% (\$24,000 ÷ \$160,000) of the purchase price to the land. Therefore, her basis in the house is \$170,000 (85% of \$200,000) and her basis in the land is \$30,000 (15% of \$200,000). Shannon may use \$170,000 as her basis for depreciation on the property.
Example: A residential rental building with a cost basis of \$137,500 would generate depreciation of \$5,000 per year (\$137,500/27.5 years).

Repairs vs. Improvements

A taxpayer can deduct the cost of repairs to rental property, but cannot deduct the cost of improvements. Instead, the taxpayer recovers the cost of an improvement by taking depreciation deductions over its applicable recovery period.

A repair keeps an asset or property in operating condition. It does not add to the value of the asset or substantially prolong its life. Repainting, fixing leaks, and replacing broken windows are examples of repairs.

Example #1: Keith owns a rental home. A baseball broke a window, so he replaced it with an upgraded model: an insulated double-pane window that helps control heating and cooling costs. Even though this window is a substantial upgrade from the previous one, it is still considered a repair, because the old window was broken and needed to be replaced. If Keith were to replace all the windows in the house, the upgrade would be considered an improvement, and he would be required to depreciate the cost.
Example #2: Keith also replaces the entire roof at a cost of \$7,000. This is considered a substantial improvement, and the cost of the roof must be depreciated over time rather than deducted against current income.

An improvement results in "betterment" to a property, "restores" a property, or "adapts" a property to a new or different use. Examples include:

- Additions of a bedroom, bathroom, deck, or garage
- Installation of central air conditioning, new plumbing, wall-to-wall carpeting, or upgraded wiring
- Construction of a retaining wall, fence, or swimming pool

Example: Glenna owns a rental home. In 2013, she spent $7,000 to replace the carpet, $2,540 to pave the driveway, and $200 to repair a couple of broken gutters. Only the gutter repair ($200) can be expensed on her 2013 tax return. The costs of the new carpet and the new driveway must be capitalized and depreciated over time.

The capitalized cost of an improvement is depreciated separately from the asset or property that is being improved.

Note: In September 2013, the IRS released new rules governing repairs, which went into effect January 1, 2014. Among the highlights, materials and supplies costing $200 or less may be immediately deductible. For the 2013 tax year, taxpayers have the choice of using the previous repair rules or the new ones. For this year's EA exam, test-takers should have a general understanding of the difference between a repair and an improvement, but should not need more specific information about the new regulations.

Rental Rules

The tax treatment of rental income, expenses, and losses depends on several factors: whether a taxpayer is a real estate professional or actively manages a property; whether there is any personal use of the rental property, and if so, whether the dwelling is considered a "home"; and whether the rental activity is for profit. We will briefly review the rules related to each of these situations next.

Passive Activity Limits: The deductibility of losses from passive activities is limited, and a taxpayer usually cannot deduct losses from passive activities to offset his nonpassive income (such as wages). In general, a trade or business activity is considered a passive activity if the taxpayer does not materially participate in it. A taxpayer materially participates in an activity if he is involved in the operation of that activity on a regular, continuous, and substantial basis. Generally, losses from passive activities that exceed income from passive activities in the same year are disallowed. The disallowed losses are carried forward to the next taxable year and can be used to offset future income from passive activities.

The passive activity loss rules for taxpayers involved in rental activities are an exception, as most rental activities are considered passive activities, even if the taxpayer does materially participate in them. However, when a taxpayer *actively participates* in a rental real estate activity, he may be able to deduct up to $25,000 of losses against his nonpassive income. It should be noted that active participation is a different, and less stringent, standard than material participation.

In order to actively participate, a taxpayer must own at least 10% of the rental property and must make management decisions in a significant and bona fide way, such as approving new tenants and establishing the rental terms.

> **Note:** If the IRS determines that a taxpayer has not actively participated, rental losses are disallowed, and he is not eligible for the special $25,000 loss allowance.

The full $25,000 allowance is available for taxpayers, whether single or MFJ, whose modified adjusted gross income (MAGI) is $100,000 or less. If a taxpayer is married and files a separate return but lived apart from his spouse for the entire tax year, the taxpayer's special allowance for rental losses cannot exceed $12,500; this full allowance would be available if his MAGI is $50,000 or less. However, if the taxpayer lived with his spouse at any time during the year and is filing MFS, the taxpayer cannot use any of his passive rental losses to offset nonpassive income.

> **Definition: MAGI** is a taxpayer's adjusted gross income with certain deductions added back in. These may include IRA contributions, rental losses, student loan interest, and qualified tuition expenses, among others. A taxpayer's MAGI is used as a basis for determining whether he qualifies for certain tax deductions.

Rental losses that cannot be deducted due to the limitations described above can be carried forward indefinitely and used in subsequent years, subject to the same limitations.

> **Example:** Philip and Susanne own a residential rental property that they manage themselves. This year, they have wages of $98,000 and a rental loss of $26,800. Because they meet both the active participation and the MAGI tests, they are allowed to deduct $25,000 of the rental loss as an offset to their nonpassive income (wages). The remaining amount over the $25,000 limit ($1,800) that cannot be deducted in the current year is carried forward and may be used in the following year.

For every $2 by which a taxpayer's MAGI exceeds $100,000, the allowance is reduced by $1. If MAGI is $150,000 or more (or $75,000 or more if married filing separately), the $25,000 allowance is fully phased out.

> **Example:** Hal and Lorena file jointly and have MAGI of $140,000. They have $25,000 in losses from the residential rental property that they actively manage. Because they actively manage the property, they potentially qualify for deduction of up to $25,000 in losses against their nonpassive income. However, because their joint income is over $100,000, they are subject to the phase-out. Therefore, Hal and Lorena's deduction for rental losses is reduced by $20,000 (0.5 × ($140,000 - $100,000). They can deduct $5,000 ($25,000 - $20,000) against their nonpassive income. The additional $20,000 of losses is carried forward to the following year.

Real Estate Professionals: If a taxpayer qualifies as a real estate professional, the losses from rental real estate activities in which he materially participates are not considered passive activity losses and are fully deductible.

A taxpayer qualifies as a real estate professional if he satisfies both of the following tests:

- More than half of the taxpayer's personal services in all businesses for the year are performed in real estate and rental activities.
- The taxpayer spends more than 750 hours in real property businesses and rentals in which he materially participates.

Note: A new rule in 2013 provides a safe harbor for real estate professionals: Participation in rental real estate activity must be more than 500 hours during the tax year or more than 500 hours in any five tax years during the ten tax years immediately prior to the current one.

If the tests for material participation are not met, rental losses are considered passive and are deductible only up to $25,000 based upon the passive activity rules outlined above.

Self-employed real estate professionals, brokers, and dealers report their active rental income on Schedule C, *Profit or Loss from Business*. Their income is subject to self-employment tax. Real estate professionals include the owners of hotels and apartment buildings.

Example: Evelyn is a licensed real estate agent. She sells properties and also owns several apartment buildings. She works as a real estate agent full-time and manages all the rental properties herself. Evelyn reports her rental income on Schedule C. Her losses are not limited, and the income is subject to self-employment tax.

If a taxpayer is not a real estate professional and he provides only basic services to tenants, such as trash collection, he reports rental income and expenses on Schedule E, Form 1040. It is not subject to self-employment tax.

Example: Joseph owns two residential rental properties and provides basic services to his tenants. He manages them and collects rents. He also has a full-time job as a restaurant manager. He is not a real estate professional. Joseph must report his rental income and losses on Schedule E. His rental income is considered passive activity income, and it is not subject to self-employment tax.

Not Rented for Profit: A taxpayer who does not rent his property to make a profit can deduct rental expenses only up to the amount of his rental income. The IRS calls this a "not-for-profit rental." He cannot deduct a loss or carry forward to the next year any rental expenses that are more than his rental income for the year. The taxpayer reports the rental income on Form 1040; if he itemizes deductions, he can deduct expenses for mortgage interest and real estate taxes on Schedule A. He may also report his other rental expenses as miscellaneous itemized deductions on Schedule A, but the deductibility is subject to the 2% floor.

The IRS will presume a taxpayer is renting property to make a profit if his rental income is greater than his rental expenses for at least three out of five years.

If a taxpayer is just starting his rental activity and does not have three years showing a profit, he can elect to postpone the decision of whether the rental is for profit by filing Form 5213, *Election to Postpone Determination as to Whether the Presumption Applies that an Activity is Engaged in for Profit*. This gives the taxpayer five years to determine whether his rental is for profit or not for profit.

Renting Part of Property: A taxpayer who rents part of a property must divide certain expenses between the part of the property used for rental purposes and the part used for personal purposes, as though there were actually two separate pieces of property. Expenses related to the part of the property used for rental purposes can be deducted as rental expenses on Schedule E. This includes a portion of expenses that normally are nondeductible personal expenses, such as painting the outside of a house.

If an expense applies to both rental use and personal use, such as a heating bill for the entire house, the taxpayer must divide the expense between the two. The two most common methods for dividing such expenses are based on:

- The number of rooms in the house, and
- The square footage of the house.

Example: Pablo rents out a bedroom in his house. The room is 12 × 15 feet, or 180 square feet. Pablo's entire house, including this room, is 1,800 square feet. Pablo can deduct as a rental expense 10% of any expense that must be divided between rental use and personal use. Pablo's 2013 heating bills for the entire house totaled $600, and therefore $60 ($600 × .10) can be considered a rental expense. The balance, $540, is a personal expense that Pablo cannot deduct.

A common situation involves a duplex in which the landlord lives in one unit and rents out the other side. Certain expenses, such as mortgage interest and real estate taxes, apply to the entire property and must be split to determine rental and personal expenses.

Example: Gillian owns a duplex with two units of the same size. She lives in one side and rents out the other. In 2013, Gillian paid $12,000 of mortgage interest and $4,000 of real estate taxes for the entire property. Gillian can deduct $6,000 of mortgage interest and $2,000 of real estate taxes on Schedule E. She can claim the other $6,000 of mortgage interest and $2,000 of real estate taxes attributable to her personal use on Schedule A as itemized deductions.

If a taxpayer owns a partial interest in rental property, he can deduct expenses paid according to the percentage of ownership.

Personal Use of Dwelling Unit: When a taxpayer has a residence (whether a main home or a second home) that is used personally at certain times and rented out at other times, he must divide his expenses between rental use and personal use. Rental expenses generally will be no more than a taxpayer's total expenses multiplied by the following fraction: the denominator is the total number of days the dwelling is used and the numerator is the total number of days actually rented at a fair rental price. Any day the unit is rented at a fair rental price is a day of rental use. Any day the unit is available for rent but not actually rented is not a day of rental use.

Example: Carol owns a vacation home in Hawaii that she rented for 90 days in January, February, and March. She may deduct the rental expenses on Schedule E only for those 90 days. However, she may deduct expenses for mortgage interest and real estate taxes for the other 275 days of the year on her Schedule A.

If a taxpayer uses a property for both rental and personal purposes, the tax treatment of expenses depends on whether his personal use is considered to be usage as a "home." It is considered usage as a home if he uses the property for personal purposes during the year for more than the greater of:

- Fourteen days, or
- 10% of the total days it is rented at a fair rental price.

Days of personal use are counted when:

- The taxpayer or a member of his family uses the property without paying a fair rental price.

- Anyone uses the property at less than fair rental price.
- Use of the property is donated to a charitable organization.

However, any day the taxpayer spends working on repairs and maintaining the property is not counted as personal use, even if his family is also staying there.

Example: Mike owns a mountain cabin at Lake Tahoe that was used as follows in 2013: He rented it for 60 days during the ski season; spent a week at the cabin cleaning and making repairs before the rental period began; and donated a week of rental use to a local charity. In apportioning expenses:

- 7/67 days would be treated as personal use; expenses such as mortgage interest and property taxes would be deductible in this ratio on Schedule A.
- The remaining 60/67 days would be treated as rental use and this fraction of total expenses incurred would be deductible on Schedule E.
- The seven days cleaning and making repairs would not count as either personal or rental use for purposes of allocating expenses.

Mike's cabin is not considered a "home," because his personal use was less than 14 days and less than 10% of the total days it was rented.

Renting a dwelling unit that is considered a home is not considered a passive activity. If a taxpayer's rental expenses are more than his rental income, he cannot use the excess expenses to offset income from other sources. However, excess deductions may be carried forward to the next year and treated as rental expenses for the same property, subject to the same limits.

Example: Jack owns a condo on Hilton Head Island. He uses it as a personal residence four months out of the year and rents it out to tenants the rest of the year. Jack's rental income is $8,000 in 2013, and his rental expenses are $10,000. Jack cannot deduct the full $10,000 of rental expenses, but he can carry over the remaining $2,000 and deduct that amount from future rental income on the condo.

Minimal Rental Use: If a taxpayer rents a main home or vacation home for fewer than 15 days, he does not have to recognize any of the income as taxable. He also cannot deduct any rental expenses. This is called the "15 day rule."

Example: Brynn owns a condo on the Gulf Coast. While she was away on vacation, she rented her condo for 14 days, charging $100 per day for a total of $1,400. She also had $320 in expenses during that time. Brynn does not report any of the income or expenses based on the exception for minimal rental use.

Converting to Rental Use: If a taxpayer changes a main home or second home to rental use at any time other than the beginning of a tax year, he must divide his expenses between rental use and personal use. He can deduct as rental expenses only the portion that is for the part of the year the property was used or held for rental purposes.

For depreciation purposes, the property is treated as being placed in service on the conversion date. When a taxpayer converts property held for personal use to rental use, the basis for depreciation will be the lesser of fair market value or his adjusted basis on the date of conversion.

Royalty Income

Like rental income, royalty income is reported on line 17 of Form 1040. Royalties from copyrights, patents, and oil, gas, and mineral properties are taxable as ordinary income.

In many cases, a taxpayer reports details of royalties on Schedule E, *Supplemental Income and Loss*. However, self-employed writers, musicians, and inventors report income on Schedule C, *Profit or Loss from Business,* and are subject to self-employment tax.

Example: In 2013, Don's brother died. Don inherited a copyright from his brother who had written an instruction manual for woodworking. Don then leased the copyrighted material to schools and colleges for their use. Since he had not created the copyright himself, Don must report the royalty income on Schedule E.

Royalties from copyrights on literary, musical, or artistic works, or from patents on inventions, are paid to a taxpayer for the right to use his work over a specified period of time. Royalties generally are based on the number of units sold, such as the number of books, tickets to a performance, or machines sold.

Example: Marisa is the self-employed author of a popular series of books for young children. She receives royalties from her publisher based on the number of books she has sold over a certain period of time. Marisa must report these royalties as taxable income on her Schedule C.

A taxpayer is required to issue Form 1099-MISC, *Miscellaneous Income,* to each person to whom he has paid at least $10 in royalties for the year.

Unit 9: Study Questions

1. Reba converted her primary residence to rental use during the year. Her original cost was $189,000, of which $13,200 was allocated to the land and $175,800 was to the house. On the date of the conversion, the property had a fair market value of $158,000, of which $11,000 was allocable to the land and $147,000 to the house. What is Reba's basis for depreciation on Schedule E?

A. $147,000.
B. $189,000.
C. $175,800.
D. $158,000.

2. Matt and Diane are separated and have lived apart for three years. They file separate tax returns (MFS). They own a rental property jointly, actively participate in the rental activity, and share income and losses equally. The rental property had $30,000 in losses during the year. Matt has wage income of $48,000 in 2013. He has no other items of income or loss. What is the maximum amount of rental losses that Matt can claim on his separate return?

A. $15,000.
B. $25,000.
C. $12,500.
D. $0.

3. Amelia owns a 50% interest in a residential rental house. Last year she paid $968 to repair a broken window. She replaced it with a premium energy-saving window. What is the treatment of this expense?

A. She cannot deduct the cost since it was an improvement (an upgrade); she must add it to the basis of the property.
B. She can deduct $484 (50% × $968) as a rental expense on Schedule E.
C. She can deduct $968 as a rental expense on Schedule E.
D. She can deduct $968 on Schedule A as an itemized deduction.

4. What type of property is never depreciated?

A. Buildings.
B. Cars.
C. Computers.
D. Land.

5. In 2013, Jane is single and has $40,000 in wages, $2,000 of passive activity income from a limited partnership, and $3,500 of passive activity loss from a rental real estate activity in which she actively participated. Which of the following statements is true?

A. The first $2,000 of Jane's $3,500 passive loss offsets her passive income. Jane may deduct the remaining $1,500 loss from her $40,000 wages.
B. Jane may not deduct the passive loss from her $40,000 in wages.
C. Jane may not offset the rental loss with the passive income from the partnership, because it is not the same type of passive activity.
D. Jane must carry over her loss to the subsequent tax year.

6. Which of the following costs incurred on rental property should be classified as a capital improvement and must be capitalized and depreciated rather than expensed?

A. Replacing an entire deck.
B. Repairing a broken toilet.
C. Refinishing the wood floor in the family room.
D. Patching a hole in the wall.

7. Ian signs a three-year lease to rent a building he owns. In December 2013, he receives $12,000 for the first year's rent and $12,000 as rent for the last year of the lease. He also receives $1,500 in 2013 as a refundable security deposit. How much rental income must Ian include in his 2013 tax return?

A. $1,500.
B. $12,000.
C. $24,000.
D. $25,500

8. Pam purchased a heating, ventilating, and air conditioning (HVAC) unit for her rental property on December 15, 2013. It was delivered on December 28, 2013, and was installed and ready for use on January 2, 2014. When should the HVAC unit be considered placed in service for depreciation purposes?

A. December 15, 2013.
B. December 28, 2013.
C. January 1, 2014.
D. January 2, 2014.

9. Rosemary's home is used exclusively as her residence all year, except for 13 days. During this time, Rosemary rents her home to alumni while the local college has its homecoming celebration. She made $3,000 in rental income and had $500 in rental expenses. Which of the following statements is true?

A. All of the rental income may be excluded.
B. Rosemary may exclude only $2,500 of the rental income.
C. Rosemary may deduct her rental expenses when she reports her rental income on Schedule E.
D. Rosemary must recognize $3,000 in rental income.

10. Which IRS form is used to report passive rental income and losses?

A. Schedule E.
B. Schedule A.
C. Schedule C.
D. Schedule D.

11. Nick decides to convert his residence into a rental. He moves out of his home in May and starts renting it on June 1. He has $12,000 in mortgage interest for the year. How should Nick report his mortgage interest expense?

A. He should report the entire $12,000 on Schedule E.
B. He should report the entire $12,000 on Schedule A.
C. He can report $7,000 on Schedule E and $5,000 on Schedule A as mortgage interest.
D. He can report $8,000 on Schedule E and $4,000 on Schedule A as mortgage interest.

12. Thomas, who is single, owns a rental apartment building. He actively participates in the rental activity by collecting rent and performing repairs. In 2013, Thomas had a loss of $29,000 on this rental activity and had no other passive income. His income from wages was $60,000. How much of the rental loss may Thomas deduct on his 2013 return?

A. $0.
B. $6,000.
C. $25,000.
D. $29,000.

13. Which of the following describes depreciation?

A. A business expense that applies only to rental properties.
B. An improvement to an asset that must be capitalized.
C. A common type of accounting method used by most partnerships.
D. An annual tax deduction that accounts for the reduction in the value of an asset as it ages.

14. All of the following are true about not-for-profit rentals except:

A. Rental losses cannot be carried forward to the next year.
B. Profit is determined when rental income is greater than rental expenses for four out of five years.
C. A taxpayer with a not-for-profit rental can deduct expenses only up to his rental income.
D. A taxpayer with a new rental may elect to postpone the decision whether the activity is for profit or not for profit for five years.

15. In 2013 Travis and Brittany moved to Canada. They decided to rent their house in California instead of selling it. They had purchased the home in 2006 for $500,000 and had paid $80,000 for various improvements through 2012. The purchase price of $500,000 was attributable to fair market values of $100,000 for the land and $400,000 for the house. Their new tenant paid a refundable security deposit of $6,000 and moved in on July 1, 2013. The FMV of the property on July 1 was $525,000, comprised of $105,000 for the land and $420,000 for the house. The tenant then paid rent of $3,000 each month from July through December. Travis and Brittany incurred the following expenses in 2013 related to the house:

- Mortgage interest $10,000
- Property taxes $10,000
- Casualty insurance $1,000

In addition, they paid $500 for repairs during December. Exclusive of depreciation expense, what was Travis and Brittany's taxable rental income for 2013?

A. $13,000.
B. $7,000.
C. $1,500.
D. $7,250.

16. Based upon the information in question 15, what is the amount of basis on which depreciation should be calculated for the rental period?

A. $400,000.
B. $480,000.
C. $580,000.
D. $420,000.

Unit 10: Other Taxable Income

For additional information read:
Publication 525, *Taxable and Nontaxable Income*
Publication 4681, *Canceled Debts, Foreclosures, Repossessions, & Abandonments*
Publication 504, *Divorced or Separated Individuals*

In this unit, we will cover a number of other types of income that are reported on Form 1040.

Taxable Recoveries

A recovery is a return of an amount a taxpayer deducted or took a credit for in an earlier year. The most common recoveries are refunds, reimbursements, and rebates of deductions itemized on Schedule A. A taxpayer must include a recovery in income in the year he receives it, to the extent the deduction or credit reduced his tax in the earlier year.

Example: In 2012, Perla paid $1,700 for medical expenses. She subtracted $1,500, which was 7.5% of her adjusted gross income, to determine her medical expense deduction of $200. In 2013, Perla's medical insurance reimbursed $500 of her 2012 expenses. The only portion of the $500 reimbursement she must include in her income for 2013 is $200, the amount actually deducted.

State and local income tax refunds are reported as taxable income in the year received only if the taxpayer itemized deductions in the prior year in which those taxes were overpaid. The payer should send Form 1099-G, *Certain Government Payments*, to the taxpayer by January 31, and also send a copy to the IRS.

Example: Wally claimed the standard deduction on his 2012 federal tax return. In 2013, he received a refund of $600 for state income taxes he paid during 2012. The state tax refund is not taxable, as Wally received no federal tax benefit from his 2012 state tax payments because he did not itemize deductions for that year.

Refunds of federal income taxes are not included in a taxpayer's income because they are never allowed as a deduction. Taxable refunds, credits, or offsets of state and local income taxes are reported on line 10 of Form 1040.

Alimony

Alimony is taxable income to the recipient and deductible by the payer. In contrast, child support is not taxable income to the receiver and not deductible by the payer because it is viewed as a payment a parent makes simply to support his child.

Example: Mark and Sibba are divorced. Their divorce decree requires Mark to pay Sibba $200 per month as child support and $150 per month as alimony. Mark makes all of his child support and alimony payments on time. Therefore, in 2013, he may deduct $1,800 ($150 × 12 months) as alimony paid and Sibba must report $1,800 as alimony received. The amount paid as child support, $2,400 ($200 × 12), is not deductible by Mark and is not reported as income by Sibba.

Alimony received is reported on line 11 of Form 1040. Alimony paid is an adjustment to income for the payer, who does not have to itemize in order to deduct alimony payments made. The alimony paid is listed on the first page of Form 1040; Form 1040A or Form 1040EZ cannot be used.

If a divorce agreement specifies payments of both alimony and child support and only partial payments are made by the payer, the partial payments are considered child support until that obligation is fully paid. Any additional amounts paid are then treated as alimony.

Example: Elsa and Jessie are divorced. Their divorce decree requires Jessie pay Elsa $2,000 a month ($24,000 [$2,000 × 12] a year) as child support and $1,500 a month ($18,000 [$1,500 × 12] a year) as alimony. Jessie falls behind on his payments and pays only $36,000 during 2013. In this case, the first $24,000 paid is considered child support and only the remaining amount of $12,000 ($36,000 - $24,000) is considered alimony. Jessie can deduct $12,000 as alimony paid. Elsa must report $12,000 as alimony income received.

If an alimony payment is subject to reduction based on a contingency relating to a child (e.g., attaining a certain age, marrying), the amount subject to reduction is treated as child support.

If alimony payments continue after the receiving spouse dies, they will automatically be considered child support, not alimony.

In order for a payment to qualify as alimony:

- The divorce agreement may not include a clause indicating that the payment is something else (such as child support or repayment of a loan.)
- If the spouses are legally separated, they cannot live together when the payments are made.
- The payer must have no liability to make any payment (in cash or property) after the death of the former spouse.

Alimony does not include:

- Payments that are a former spouse's share of income from community property
- Payments to keep up the payer's property
- Free use of the payer's property
- Noncash property settlements

Property settlements are simply a division of property and are not treated as alimony. Property transferred to a former spouse incident to a divorce is treated as a gift.

Payments made to a third party can be considered alimony. For example, if under the terms of a divorce agreement a spouse pays the medical bills of his ex-wife, a cash payment to the hospital can count as alimony. For a jointly owned home, half of the mortgage payments and real estate taxes may be deducted as alimony, assuming the divorce decree or separation agreement requires a taxpayer to pay these expenses for his ex-spouse. The ex-spouse must include the payments as alimony received.

Government Benefits

Most government welfare benefits, including food stamps, heating assistance programs, and non-federal assistance benefits from states or local agencies, are exempt from federal taxation.

Worker's compensation, which provides wage replacement and medical benefits to injured workers, is not taxable income. In contrast, unemployment compensation is taxable and is reported on Line 19 of Form 1040.

> **Example:** Kiara was laid off from her job in 2013. She received $300 a week in unemployment compensation for 26 weeks. When she was unable to find another job, she began receiving benefits from her state's WIC program, which provided vouchers for food for her and her toddler. The unemployment compensation would be taxable income, but the welfare benefits would not.

Social Security Income: Social Security income is reported to the taxpayer on Form SSA-1099, and these benefits are taxable in certain cases, depending upon a taxpayer's income and the amount of benefits received for the year. To determine if any percentage of his Social Security benefits is taxable, a taxpayer must compare the base threshold amount for his filing status with the total of:

- One-half of his benefits, plus
- All of his other income, including tax-exempt interest.

If the sum is less than the base amount for his filing status, none of the Social Security is taxable. If the sum is more than the base amount for his filing status, a percentage of the Social Security is taxable.

Base Amounts for Calculating Taxability of Social Security
MFJ: $32,000
Single, HOH, QW, or MFS (and lived apart from his/her spouse all year): $25,000
MFS (if lived with spouse at any time during the year): $0

The taxpayer calculates the taxable portion on a worksheet in the *Instructions for Form 1040*, or Publication 915, *Social Security and Equivalent Railroad Retirement Benefits.* The taxable portion of Social Security benefits is never more than 85% and in most cases is less than 50%.

Spouses who file jointly must combine their incomes and Social Security benefits when figuring the taxable portion of their benefits, even if one spouse did not receive any benefits.

> **Example:** Bo and Yvonne are both over 65. They file jointly and both received Social Security benefits during 2013. At the end of the year, Bo received a Form SSA-1099 showing net benefits of $7,500. Yvonne received a Form SSA-1099 showing net benefits of $3,500. Bo also received wages of $20,000 and taxable interest income of $500. He did not have any tax-exempt interest.
>
> | | |
> |---|---|
> | 1. Total Social Security benefits: | $11,000 |
> | 2. Enter one-half of SS | $5,500 |
> | 3. Enter taxable interest and wages | $20,500 |
> | 4. Sum ($5,500 + $20,500) | $26,000 |
>
> Bo and Yvonne's benefits are not taxable for 2013 because the total above is not more than the base amount ($32,000) for married filing jointly.

A taxpayer reports Social Security benefits on line 20a and the taxable amount on line 20b, Form 1040.

Educational Assistance

Many types of educational assistance are tax-free if they meet certain requirements.

Scholarships and fellowships: A scholarship is an amount paid to an undergraduate or graduate student to pursue studies. A fellowship is an amount paid to an individual to pursue research.

A scholarship or fellowship is excluded from income only if:

- The taxpayer is a degree candidate at an eligible educational institution that has been nationally accredited.
- It does not exceed qualified educational expenses.
- It is not designated for other purposes, such as room and board.
- It does not represent payment for teaching, research, or other services.

Qualified educational expenses include tuition, required fees, and course-related expenses such as books.

Example: Aubrey is a graduate student who received a scholarship of $3,000. Under its terms, she must serve as a part-time teaching assistant. From the $3,000 scholarship, she receives $1,250 for teaching, which is listed as income on her Form W-2. She had expenses of more than $5,000 for tuition and course-related books. Aubrey may exclude $1,750 of the scholarship funds from income, but the $1,250 is taxable and must be included in her gross income.

An athletic scholarship is tax-free only if it meets the requirements described above.

Pell Grants: A Pell grant is a need-based grant that is treated as a scholarship for tax purposes. It is tax-free to the extent it is used for qualified educational expenses during the specified grant period.

Payment to Service Academy Cadets or Midshipmen: An appointment to a United States military academy is not a scholarship or fellowship. Cadets and midshipmen receive free tuition and room and board, which is not taxable. However, they also receive government pay while at the military academy, and these amounts are classified as taxable income.

Veterans' Educational Benefits: Veterans' benefits for education are tax-free if administered by the Department of Veterans Affairs.

Example: Moises served in Afghanistan and has since returned to college. He receives two education benefits under the GI bill: a $1,534 monthly basic housing allowance and $3,840 tuition paid directly to his college. Neither of these benefits is taxable to Moises, and he is not required to report them on his tax return.

Qualified Tuition Programs (QTPs): QTPs, also known as Section 529 plans, are established and maintained by states or educational institutions. They allow a taxpayer to either prepay a student's qualified educational expenses at an eligible educational institution or contribute to an account that will be used to pay future expenses. The amounts contributed to a QTP are not deductible for federal tax purposes.

Eligible institutions include virtually all accredited colleges, universities, vocational schools, and other postsecondary educational institutions. Qualified expenses include tuition, fees, books, computer equipment and software, and room and board for any time the beneficiary is enrolled in college. A beneficiary may be anyone the taxpayer designates: himself, a child, a grandchild, or an unrelated person.

Distributions from a 529 plan are reported on Form 1099-Q. The part of a distribution representing the amount paid or contributed to the plan is not included in income. The beneficiary also generally does not have to include in taxable income any earnings distributed from a 529 plan if the total distribution is less than or equal to a student's qualified education expenses (after reduction of the latter by other tax-free education assistance received during the year). If the total distribution is greater than a student's adjusted qualified expenses, an allocable portion of the earnings is taxable.

Other Income (Line 21)

"Other income" includes items that do not have separately identified lines on Form 1040. Generally, these amounts are reported on line 21. Examples, which we cover in detail next, include:

- Cancellation of debt income
- Gambling winnings
- Hobby income
- Certain types of court awards
- Prizes and awards
- Jury duty pay

The taxpayer is required to report this income, whether or not he receives a document from the payer reporting the amount paid.

Cancellation of Debt Income

Generally, if a taxpayer's debt is canceled or forgiven, the taxpayer must include the debt forgiveness or cancellation of debt (COD) in his gross income. The canceled debt should be reported to the taxpayer on Form 1099-C by the creditor. If the debt is a nonbusiness debt, the canceled debt amount is reported as "other income" on line 21 of a taxpayer's Form 1040. However, there is no taxable income from a canceled debt if it is intended as a gift (for example, if a taxpayer owes his parents money but they choose to forgive the debt.)

Cancellation of debt may include any indebtedness for which a taxpayer is personally liable or which attaches to the taxpayer's property such as an auto loan, credit card debt, mortgage, or home equity loan. Taxation related to canceled debt may depend on whether the debt is recourse or nonrecourse. Recourse debt holds the borrower personally liable for any amount not satisfied by the surrender of secured property. If a lender forecloses on property subject to a recourse debt and cancels the portion of the debt in excess of the FMV of the property, the canceled portion is treated as ordinary income. This amount must be included in gross income unless it qualifies for an exception or exclusion. The taxpayer must generally report two transactions:

1. The cancellation of debt income
2. Gain or loss on the sale or repossession, generally equal to the difference between the FMV of the property at the time of the foreclosure and the taxpayer's adjusted basis in the property

If a personal asset such as a vehicle is repossessed, the repossession is treated as a sale, and a gain or loss must be computed. A loss related to a personal asset would be nondeductible.

Example: Doreen bought a new car for $15,000. She made a $2,000 down payment and borrowed the remaining $13,000 from her bank. Doreen is personally liable for the car loan (recourse debt). The bank repossessed her car because she stopped making payments. The balance due on the loan at the time of the repossession was $10,000. The FMV of the car when repossessed was only $9,000. Since a repossession is treated as a sale, the gain or loss must be computed. Doreen compares the amount realized ($9,000) with her adjusted basis ($15,000) to determine that she has a $6,000 nondeductible loss. She also has ordinary income from cancellation of debt. That income is $1,000 ($10,000 canceled debt - $9,000 FMV). Doreen must report the canceled debt as income on line 21 of her Form 1040.

Example: Zach lost his sailboat because he could no longer make his payments. At the time of repossession, he owed a balance of $170,000 to the lender, and the FMV of the sailboat was $140,000. Zach is personally liable for the debt (recourse loan), so the abandonment is treated as a sale. The "selling price" from the repossession is $140,000, and Zach must recognize $30,000 in debt forgiveness income.

A nonrecourse debt is a type of loan that is secured by collateral in which the borrower does not have liability for the loan. Many mortgages are nonrecourse. This means that if the borrower defaults, the lender can seize the home, but cannot seek out the borrower for any further compensation, even if the FMV of the home does not cover the remaining loan balance.

If the taxpayer abandons property that secures debt for which the taxpayer is not personally liable (a nonrecourse loan), the abandonment is treated as a sale or exchange. If a loan is nonrecourse and the borrower does not retain the asset, the borrower does not have to recognize cancellation of debt income.

A taxpayer may question the taxability of canceled debt because it can apply in a tax year in which cash is not received. In a situation where property is surrendered or repossessed, such as a foreclosure, the taxpayer may feel that by giving up the property, he should be relieved from any further obligation. However, subject to the exceptions described below, canceled debt is taxable because the benefit to the taxpayer is the relief from personal liability to pay the debt.

Example: Phoebe borrows $10,000 to take a vacation and defaults on the loan after paying back only $2,000. She has the ability to pay back the loan but chooses not to. The lender writes off the remaining balance of the loan. Therefore, there is a cancellation of debt of $8,000, which is taxable income to Phoebe.

There are several circumstances in which canceled debt is not taxable:

Insolvency: If a taxpayer is insolvent when the debt is canceled, the canceled debt is not taxable. A taxpayer is insolvent when his total debts are more than the FMV of his total assets. For this purpose, the taxpayer's assets include the value of everything he owns, including pensions and retirement accounts.

> **Example:** In 2013, Darla had $5,000 of credit card debt, which she did not pay. She received a Form 1099-C from her credit card company showing canceled debt of $5,000. Immediately before the cancellation Darla's total liabilities were $15,000 and the FMV of her total assets was $7,000. Therefore, at the time the debt was canceled, Darla was insolvent to the extent of $8,000 ($15,000 total liabilities minus $7,000 FMV of her total assets). Darla can exclude the entire $5,000 canceled debt from income.

Bankruptcy: Debts discharged through bankruptcy court in a Title 11 bankruptcy case are not considered taxable income. The taxpayer must attach Form 982, *Reduction of Tax Attributes Due to Discharge of Indebtedness,* to his federal income tax return to report debt canceled in bankruptcy.

Cancellation of Student Loans: Certain student loans contain a provision that all or part of the debt incurred to attend a qualified educational institution will be canceled if the student later works for a specified period of time in certain professions. The canceled debt does not have to be recognized as income on a taxpayer's return

> **Example:** Tatum is a medical student completing her residency. In return for forgiveness of her student loans, she agrees to work for four years as a pediatrician in a state program in Minnesota that serves rural and poor communities. The canceled debt does not have to be recognized as income.

Qualified Farm Indebtedness: If a taxpayer incurred the canceled debt in a farming business, it is generally not considered taxable income.

Home Mortgage Debt: Normally, when a bank forecloses on a home and sells it for less than the borrower's outstanding mortgage, it forgives the unpaid mortgage debt and the canceled debt is taxable income to the homeowner. However, a taxpayer may exclude income realized as a result of loan modification or foreclosure of a taxpayer's principal residence. The principal residence is the home where the taxpayer ordinarily lives most of the time. This exclusion does not apply to second homes or vacation homes. Further, the exclusion does not apply unless it is directly related to a decline in the home's value or the taxpayer's financial condition.

Qualified principal residence indebtedness (QPRI) is a mortgage secured by a taxpayer's principal residence that was taken out to buy, build, or substantially improve that residence and may also include debt from refinancing. QPRI cannot be more than the cost of the home plus improvements. The maximum amount that can be treated as QPRI is $2 million ($1 million if MFS). If only part of a loan is qualified principal residence indebtedness, the exclusion from income for QPRI applies only to the extent the amount canceled exceeds the amount of the loan that is not QPRI. However, the remaining part of the loan may qualify for a different exclusion (such as the exclusion for insolvency).

Example: Ken incurred debt of $800,000 when he purchased his home for $880,000. He made a down payment of $80,000 and financed the rest with a mortgage. When the FMV of the property was $1 million, Ken refinanced the debt for $850,000. At the time of the refinancing, the balance of the original loan was $740,000. Ken used the $110,000 he obtained from the refinancing ($850,000 minus $740,000) to buy a luxury car and take a vacation to the Bahamas. Two years after the refinancing, Ken lost his job. Ken's home declined in value to $750,000. Based on Ken's circumstances, the lender agreed to a short sale of the property for $735,000 and to cancel the remaining $115,000 of the $850,000 debt. Ken can exclude only $5,000 of the canceled debt from his income using the exclusion for canceled QPRI ($115,000 canceled debt minus the $110,000 amount of the debt that was not QPRI). Ken must include the remaining $110,000 of canceled debt in income.

The taxpayer must report the amount of debt forgiven on his return by completing Form 982, *Reduction of Tax Attributes Due to Discharge of Indebtedness.*

Example: Adam's home is subject to a $320,000 mortgage. Adam's creditor forecloses in April 2013. The residence is later sold for $280,000 in December 2013. Adam has $40,000 of income from discharge of indebtedness and may claim the exclusion by filing Form 982 with his 2013 tax return.

The Home Affordable Modification Program (HAMP) attempts to help financially distressed homeowners lower their monthly mortgage payments. If a borrower continues to make timely payments on the loan for three years, he can have his mortgage reduced by a predetermined amount (known as the PRA Forbearance Amount). The loan holder is then reimbursed through incentive payments by the HAMP program administrator. To the extent the mortgage reduction exceeds the incentive payments, the borrower may be required to include the excess amount in gross income as a discharge of indebtedness. However, the borrower may be eligible to exclude the discharge of indebtedness income from gross income if:

- The mortgage loan is QPRI and the loan is modified before January 1, 2014, or
- The discharge of indebtedness occurs when the borrower is insolvent.

Any portion of the discharge of indebtedness that is excluded from income must also be reflected as a reduction in basis.

Canceled Debt that is Otherwise Deductible: If a taxpayer uses the cash method of accounting, he should not recognize canceled debt income if payment of the debt would have otherwise been a deductible expense.

Example: Jiao is a self-employed interior designer. She receives $2,200 in accounting services for her business on credit. Later, Jiao loses a major account and has trouble paying her debts, so her accountant forgives the amount she owes. Jiao does not include the canceled debt in her gross income because payment of the debt would have been deductible as a business expense.

Gambling Winnings

Gambling income may include winnings from lotteries, raffles, horse races, and casinos. Gambling winnings should be reported to a taxpayer on Form W-2G if he wins:

- $600 or more from gambling
- $1,200 or more from bingo or slot machines
- $1,500 or more from keno
- Any amounts subject to federal income tax withholding

A taxpayer must report and pay tax on all gambling winnings, regardless of whether he receives a Form W-2G.

Gambling losses are deductible on Schedule A as a miscellaneous deduction that is not subject to the 2% limit, but the deduction is limited to the amount of gambling winnings.

Example: Yolanda had $1,000 in gambling winnings and $3,000 in gambling losses in 2013. Her deduction for gambling losses cannot exceed $1,000, the amount of her gambling winnings. In order to claim the deduction, Yolanda must itemize and list her gambling losses on Schedule A, Form 1040.

The taxpayer must keep an accurate diary or similar record of gambling winnings and losses, along with tickets, receipts, canceled checks, and other documentation. He is not required to include these supporting records with his tax return, but they should be retained in case of an audit.

Hobby Income

A hobby is an activity typically undertaken primarily for pleasure. Even though it may produce income, a hobby is not considered a business because it is not carried on to make a profit. The IRS presumes that an activity is "carried on for a profit" if it makes a profit during at least three of the last five tax years, including the current year. Income from a hobby is taxable and reported on Form 1040, Line 21 as "other income." Hobby income is generally not subject to self-employment tax, and the use of losses from a hobby to offset income is limited. Expenses related to a hobby activity are deductible, but only up to the amount of hobby income.

Example: Chester breeds aquarium fish as a hobby. Twice a year, he goes to an Exotic Fish convention and sells some of his fish. Although he makes money on occasion, he mainly does this activity for pleasure. Chester plans to continue attending the conventions whether he makes money or not. Therefore, the income is hobby income. The convention costs are hobby expenses and only deductible up to the amount of his hobby income.

Court Awards and Damages

Court awards for compensation for lost wages or profits are generally taxable as ordinary income, as are punitive damages.

Compensatory damages for personal physical injury or physical sickness are not taxable income, whether they are from a settlement or from an actual court award.

Example: Felix was injured in a car accident in 2013. His legs were broken, and he suffered other serious physical injuries. He received an insurance settlement for his injuries totaling $950,000. This is nontaxable income because it is payment for a physical injury.

Compensatory damages for "emotional distress" are generally included in taxable income. Emotional distress itself is not a physical illness or ailment. However, when there is medical care due to that emotional distress, the damages received for medical care are not taxable.

Example: Kristina won a court award for emotional distress caused by unlawful discrimination. The emotional distress resulted in her hospitalization for a nervous breakdown. The court awarded Kristina damages of $100,000, including $20,000 to refund the cost of her medical care for the nervous breakdown. In this case, $80,000 ($100,000 - $20,000) would be considered a taxable court award. The $20,000 of damages for her medical care would not be taxable.

Prizes and Awards

Prizes and awards are usually taxable. If the prize or award is in the form of property rather than cash, the fair market value of the property is treated as the taxable amount. The winner may avoid taxation of the award by rejecting the prize. The taxpayer may also avoid taxation by having the payer directly transfer the prize to a charity or other nonprofit organization.

Example: A national education association chooses Jerry, a college instructor, as its teacher of the year. He is awarded $3,000, but he does not accept the prize. Instead, Jerry directs the association to transfer his winnings to a college scholarship fund. Jerry never receives a check or has control over the funds. Therefore, the award is not taxable to him.

Employee awards for safety, length-of-service, or achievement are generally not taxable to the employee unless they exceed specified limits.

Additional Line 21 Income Items

Other types of income that are taxable to the recipient and reported on line 21 include the following:

- Strike benefits
- Jury duty pay (when it is not turned over to the employee's employer and deducted as an adjustment to income)
- Fees paid by an estate to a personal representative/executor
- Taxable distributions from a Coverdell education savings account or a qualified tuition program if they are more than the 2013 qualified higher education expenses for a designated beneficiary
- Gifts or gratuities received by a host or hostess of a party or event where sales are made

Example: Kathleen hosts a party for 15 women, which includes a cooking demonstration by a Pampered Chef consultant. At the end of the evening, the women order $1,000 worth of cookware and other products from the consultant. Kathleen receives a gift of $215 of products for hosting the party, which she must report as income at its fair market value.

Bartering Income

Bartering is an exchange of property or services, usually without an exchange of cash. Barter may take place on an informal, one-on-one basis between individuals and businesses, or it may occur on a third-party basis through a barter exchange company.

Taxpayers may barter for a variety of goods and services: computer services for auto repairs, or dental work for carpet cleaning, for example. The FMV of the goods or services exchanged must be reported as income by each party in the year of the exchange. If the parties have agreed ahead of time as to the value of services exchanged, the agreed-upon value will be accepted as the fair market value.

Example: Brayden builds custom kitchen cabinets. Annemarie is a veterinarian. In 2013, Brayden builds new cabinets for Annemarie's kitchen, and Annemarie performs hip dysplasia surgery on Brayden's German shepherd. They agree in advance that the cost for the kitchen cabinets and the surgery is $2,500. They each must report $2,500 of income on their 2013 tax returns.

Bartering income for services exchanged is reported on Schedule C.

Summary: Taxable vs. Nontaxable Income

TAXABLE INCOME	NONTAXABLE INCOME
Wages, salaries, tips, bonuses, vacation pay, severance pay, commissions	Gifts and inheritances
Interest	Life insurance proceeds
Unemployment compensation	Child support
Dividends	Certain veterans' benefits
Strike benefits	Interest on bonds
Bank "gifts" for opening accounts	Most employer-provided fringe benefits
Cancellation of debt income (unless excludable)	Welfare payments, food stamps, other forms of public assistance
Alimony	Compensation or court awards for physical injury or illness
Gains from sales of property, stocks and bonds, stock options, etc.	Worker's compensation
Social Security benefits (above the base amount)	Combat pay
Court awards for emotional distress, punitive damages, and lost wages	Scholarships, Pell grants, employer-provided educational assistance
Barter and hobby income	Canceled debt from a primary residence, bankruptcy, or insolvency
Prizes, awards, gambling winnings	Foreign earned income

Unit 10: Study Questions

1. Under Cary's divorce decree, he must pay his ex-wife, Eugenia, $30,000 of alimony per year. The decree also requires that Cary pay child support of $12,000 per year. The payments will stop after 15 years; if Eugenia dies before the end of the 15-year period, Cary must still pay Eugenia's estate the difference between $450,000 ($30,000 annually × 15 years) and the total amount paid up to that time. Eugenia dies at the end of the tenth year, and Cary must pay her estate an additional $150,000 ($450,000 – $300,000). How are the payments that occurred after Eugenia's death characterized for tax purposes?

A. Child support.
B. Alimony.
C. Other income.
D. Taxable income.

2. Karly was released from her obligation to pay a large credit card debt. She owed $10,000 to her credit card company, which agreed to accept $2,500 as payment in full. Karly was not insolvent and not in bankruptcy when the debt was canceled. What amount should be reported as "other income" on Karly's Form 1040, line 21?

A. $0.
B. $10,000.
C. $2,500.
D. $7,500.

3. Alexander, age 64, is single and retired. He earned the following income in 2013. To determine if any of his Social Security is taxable, Alexander should compare how much of his income to the $25,000 base amount?

Part-time job	$8,000
Bank interest	$5,000
Social Security	$11,000
Taxable pension	$6,000
Total	**$30,000**

A. $30,000.
B. $11,000.
C. $24,500.
D. $25,000.

4. Ed received $32,000 in wages in 2013. He also won a prize from his homeowner's association for developing a new water conservation plan. The prize was free landscaping service for a year, valued at $600. Ed also received $7,000 in child support and $2,000 in alimony from his ex-wife. Ed has full custody of his children. What is Ed's taxable income (before deductions and adjustments) for 2013?

A. $32,000.
B. $32,600.
C. $34,600.
D. $39,600.

5. Expenses related to a hobby activity are deductible, but only up to the amount of ______:

A. Taxable income.
B. Ordinary income.
C. Passive income.
D. Hobby income.

6. Isabella had $9,000 of gambling winnings during the year. She also incurred $15,000 of gambling losses. How should these transactions be reported on her tax return?

A. The $9,000 of winnings are reported as income, and the $15,000 of losses are reported as an adjustment to income on Form 1040.
B. The $9,000 of winnings are reported as income, and the $15,000 of losses are reported on Schedule A as an itemized deduction subject to the 2% limit.
C. The $9,000 of winnings are reported as income, and $9,000 of the losses are reported on Schedule A as an itemized deduction not subject to the 2% limit.
D. The $9,000 of winnings are reported as income, but the gambling losses are not deductible.

7. In 2013, Mina was discharged from her liability to repay $10,000 of credit card debt. The lender reported the discharged debt on Form 1099-C. Immediately prior to the debt cancellation, Mina had liabilities of $15,000 and the fair market value of her assets was $2,000. What portion of the canceled debt must Mina include in income?

A. $10,000.
B. $3,000.
C. $5,000.
D. $0.

8. Beth and Clifton's divorce decree requires Clifton to pay Beth $250 per month of child support and $1,500 per month of alimony. Clifton makes all of his child support and alimony payments on time during 2013. How much of these payments is Beth required to report as taxable income on her 2013 return?

A. $0.
B. $18,000.
C. $1,500.
D. $21,000.

9. How is barter income determined for tax purposes?

A. The IRS publishes a table showing the value of various types of goods and services that must be used when taxpayers barter. The table is updated annually for inflation.
B. The taxpayer exchanging the higher cost good or service determines the value of the item being bartered.
C. The taxpayer exchanging the lower cost good or service determines the value of the item being bartered.
D. The fair market value of the goods and services exchanged is included in gross income.

10. Paulo, 72, experiences age discrimination on his job and sues his company. After he files the lawsuit, he is attacked by the company owner, who breaks Paulo's arm. The court awards Paulo the following amounts:

- $4,000 for emotional distress
- $10,000 for loss of wages
- $35,000 for physical injury related to the assault
- $16,000 reimbursement for medical expenses

How much of this award is taxable to Paulo?

A. $4,000.
B. $10,000.
C. $14,000.
D. $49,000.

11. Which of the following is not taxable income to the recipient?

A. Long-term disability payments, from a policy paid by the recipient's employer.
B. Strike benefits.
C. Gains from the sale of stock.
D. $25,000 in group-term life insurance coverage provided by an employer.

12. Sven and Samantha file jointly and received the following income in 2013. How much income should be reported on their joint return?

- W-2 income for Samantha for wages of $40,000.
- W-2 for Samantha for $2,000, the value of a trip she won to the Bahamas. She is planning to take the trip in 2014.
- Court settlement of $10,000 paid to Sven from a car accident for serious injuries he suffered.
- $4,000 child support for Samantha's son from a previous marriage.

A. $40,000.
B. $42,000.
C. $46,000.
D. $52,000.

13. Alimony does not include:

A. Noncash property settlements.
B. Payments to a third-party on behalf of an ex-spouse.
C. Medical expenses paid on behalf of an ex-spouse.
D. Cash payments.

14. Which of the following would be considered taxable income to the recipient?

A. Life insurance proceeds paid to a beneficiary.
B. Adoption expense reimbursements.
C. Unemployment compensation.
D. Worker's compensation benefits.

15. Jeff, a married taxpayer who files separately from his wife, bought his house in Florida in 2004 for $4.5 million, and financed the purchase with a mortgage loan of the same amount that required payments of interest only for the first five years. In 2006, the house appraised for $5.5 million, and he refinanced, this time with an interest-only mortgage loan of $5 million. In 2013, the mortgage lender agrees to a short sale of the house for $3.2 million, and cancels the remaining $1.8 million (the amount by which the balance of the mortgage exceeded the sale proceeds.) Based upon the information provided, what portion of the amount forgiven can Jeff exclude from income?

A. $1.8 million.
B. $1.3 million.
C. $1 million.
D. $0.

16. Jean received the following income: wages, interest, child support, alimony, inheritance, workers' compensation, and lottery winnings. What amount of her income is taxable?

Jean's Income

Source	Amounts
Wages	$13,000
Interest	$15
Child support	$6,000
Alimony	$2,000
Inheritance	$10,000
Workers' compensation	$1,000
Lottery winnings	$5,000

A. $13,015.
B. $16,015.
C. $20,015.
D. $30,015.

17. During 2013 Anaya received payments of $20,000 for alimony and $15,000 for child support. Based on her divorce settlement, her ex-spouse was also required to pay $14,000 in mortgage payments for the house they owned jointly. What portion of the amounts above must Anaya include in income?

A. $49,000.
B. $27,000.
C. $35,000.
D. $34,000.

18. Bart had a $15,000 loan from his credit union, but stopped making payments. The credit union determined that the legal fees to collect might be higher than the amount Bart owed, so it canceled the remaining amount of $5,000 due on the loan. Bart did not file bankruptcy nor is he insolvent. How much income must he include from the debt cancellation?

A. $0.
B. $5,000.
C. $10,000.
D. $15,000.

19. Hank received Social Security in 2013 totaling $11,724. Also in 2013, Hank sold all of his stock and moved into senior housing. He received $31,896 of taxable income from the stock sale. What is the maximum taxable amount of Hank's Social Security benefits?

A. $31,896.
B. $20,172.
C. $11,724.
D. $9,965.

20. Brent, a dermatologist, agreed to exchange services with a handyman, Tevin. Brent removed a mole for Tevin and Tevin fixed Brent's running toilet. Brent generally charges $200 for mole removal, and Tevin generally charges $150 to fix a toilet. They agreed in advance that the fee would be $150. They did not exchange cash. How much income must Brent recognize for this barter transaction?

A. $50.
B. $150.
C. $200.
D. $250.

21. Ginny had the following income in 2013:

Source	**Amounts**
Wages	$14,000
Interest	$125
Gambling winnings	$1,000
Gambling losses	$2,000
Settlement for a bodily injury	$10,000
Child support payments	$1,000
Food stamp benefits	$5,000

How much gross income must Ginny report on her tax return?

A. $14,000.
B. $14,125.
C. $15,125.
D. $30,000.

22. Archer is a former National Football League cornerback. In 2013, he is awarded a sizable settlement in a class action lawsuit for concussion injuries. The settlement will be paid in installments over a period of ten years. How should Archer report the damages he is awarded on his income tax return?

A. He must include the entire amount of his settlement in his gross income for 2013.
B. He must include only the portion of the settlement paid to him each year when it is received.
C. He must report the settlement on his tax return, but it is not taxable income.
D. He may exclude the payments from his gross income.

Unit 11: Adjustments to Gross Income

For additional information read:
Publication 535, *Business Expenses*
Publication 521, *Moving Expenses*
Publication 970, *Tax Benefits for Education*

An adjustment to income reduces taxable income and thus the amount of tax owed. It is similar to a tax deduction, except that deductions, either itemized or the standard deduction amount, are entered in a different section of Form 1040. Adjustments are subtracted from gross (total) income in order to derive adjusted gross income (AGI), and deductions are subtracted from AGI. Because adjustments are taken before AGI is calculated, they are designated as "above-the-line" deductions.

Adjustments are beneficial because they not only reduce taxable income, but a lower AGI may increase a taxpayer's eligibility for certain credits and deductions and the amounts that he can claim. Unlike "below-the-line" deductions, adjustments are not added back when calculating the alternative minimum tax.

Adjustments may be taken by all taxpayers regardless of whether they itemize deductions or take the standard deduction.

	d	Total number of exemptions claimed		lines above ▶
Income	7	Wages, salaries, tips, etc. Attach Form(s) W-2		7
	8a	**Taxable** interest. Attach Schedule B if required		8a
Attach Form(s) W-2 here. Also attach Forms W-2G and 1099-R if tax was withheld.	b	**Tax-exempt** interest. **Do not** include on line 8a	8b	
	9a	Ordinary dividends. Attach Schedule B if required		9a
	b	Qualified dividends	9b	
	10	Taxable refunds, credits, or offsets of state and local income taxes		10
	11	Alimony received		11
	12	Business income or (loss). Attach Schedule C or C-EZ		12
	13	Capital gain or (loss). Attach Schedule D if required. If not required, check here ▶ ☐		13
If you did not get a W-2, see instructions.	14	Other gains or (losses). Attach Form 4797		14
	15a	IRA distributions 15a	b Taxable amount	15b
	16a	Pensions and annuities 16a	b Taxable amount	16b
	17	Rental real estate, royalties, partnerships, S corporations, trusts, etc. Attach Schedule E		17
Enclose, but do not attach, any payment. Also, please use **Form 1040-V.**	18	Farm income or (loss). Attach Schedule F		18
	19	Unemployment compensation		19
	20a	Social security benefits 20a	b Taxable amount	20b
	21	Other income. List type and amount		21
	22	Combine the amounts in the far right column for lines 7 through 21. This is your **total income** ▶		22
Adjusted Gross Income	23	Educator expenses	23	
	24	Certain business expenses of reservists, performing artists, and fee-basis government officials. Attach Form 2106 or 2106-EZ	24	
	25	Health savings account deduction. Attach Form 8889	25	
	26	Moving expenses. Attach Form 3903	26	
	27	Deductible part of self-employment tax. Attach Schedule SE	27	
	28	Self-employed SEP, SIMPLE, and qualified plans	28	
	29	Self-employed health insurance deduction	29	
	30	Penalty on early withdrawal of savings	30	
	31a	Alimony paid b Recipient's SSN ▶	31a	
	32	IRA deduction	32	
	33	Student loan interest deduction	33	
	34	Tuition and fees. Attach Form 8917	34	
	35	Domestic production activities deduction. Attach Form 8903	35	
	36	Add lines 23 through 35		36
	37	Subtract line 36 from line 22. This is your **adjusted gross income** ▶		37

Common Adjustments to Gross Income

There are many types of adjustments to gross income, and we will cover the most common ones in this unit. These are the adjustments listed in the order they are reported on Form 1040:

- Educator expenses (Line 23)
- Certain business expenses of reservists, performing artists, and fee-basis government officials (Line 24)
- Health savings account deduction (Line 25)
- Moving expenses (Line 26)
- Deductible part of self-employment tax (Line 27)
- Self-employed SEP, SIMPLE, and qualified plans (Line 28)
- Self-employed health insurance deduction (Line 29)
- Penalty on early withdrawal of savings (Line 30)
- Alimony paid (Line 31a)
- IRA deduction (Line 32)
- Student loan interest deduction (Line 33)
- Tuition and fees (Line 34)
- Domestic production activities deduction (Line 35)
- Write-in adjustments (Line 36)
    - Archer MSA deduction
    - Jury duty pay remitted to an employer
    - Repayment of unemployment benefits
    - Other adjustments

Note: Form 1040 is needed for most adjustments; Form 1040-EZ cannot be used. Form 1040A can be used if a taxpayer is reporting the following adjustments: educator expenses, IRA deduction, student loan interest deduction, and tuition and fees.

Line 23: Educator Expenses

An eligible educator is allowed to deduct up to $250 of unreimbursed expenses for books, supplies, computer equipment (including related software and services), other equipment, and supplementary materials used in the classroom. Since this is an adjustment to income, teachers can deduct these expenses even if they do not itemize deductions.

For courses in health and physical education, expenses are deductible only if they are related to athletics. Nonathletic supplies for physical education and expenses related to health courses do not qualify. Materials used for home schooling cannot be deducted.

An eligible educator must work at least 900 hours a school year in a school that provides elementary or secondary education (K-12). College instructors do not qualify.

An educator includes a:

- Teacher or instructor
- Counselor
- Principal
- Teacher's aide

Example: Devina is a third grade teacher who worked 1,600 hours during the tax year. She spent $262 on supplies for her students. Of that amount, $212 was for educational software. The other $50 was for supplies for a unit she teaches on health. Only the $212 is a qualified expense that she can deduct.

On a joint tax return, if both taxpayers are eligible, they each may take the deduction, up to a maximum of $500. Any expenses that exceed the adjustment to income may be deducted as unreimbursed employee expenses on Schedule A, subject to the 2%-of-AGI limit.

Line 24: Certain Business Expenses of Reservists, Performing Artists, and Fee-Basis Government Officials

Certain employees are allowed to claim specified work-related expenses as an adjustment to income, rather than as a deduction on Schedule A. This adjustment applies only to reservists (members of the reserve component of the Armed Forces of the United States, National Guard, or the Reserve Corps of the Public Health Service); qualified performing artists; and state or local government officials who are compensated on a fee basis.

Line 25: Health Savings Account Deduction

A health savings account (HSA) allows a taxpayer to save funds intended to pay for health care expenses on a tax-preferred basis. The taxpayer can then take tax-free withdrawals from the HSA based on the amount of his qualifying medical expenses.

HSA contributions are deductible from gross income. An HSA must be established exclusively for paying medical expenses for the taxpayer, his spouse, and his dependents. HSA accounts are usually set up with a bank, an insurance company, or through an employer.

To qualify, the taxpayer:

- Must not be enrolled in Medicare.
- May not be claimed as a dependent on anyone else's 2013 tax return.
- Must be covered under a high deductible health plan and have no other health coverage, other than for a specific disease or illness; a fixed amount for a certain time period of hospitalization; or liabilities incurred under worker's compensation laws or tort liabilities.

An employee and his employer are both allowed to contribute to the employee's HSA in the same year. If an employer makes an HSA contribution on behalf of an employee, it is excluded from the employee's income and is not subject to income or payroll taxes.

For 2013, a taxpayer can contribute up to $3,250 (or $6,450 for joint filers). Taxpayers who are 55 and over may contribute an extra $1,000 to their HSAs. Excess contributions over these limits are subject to a 6% penalty.

2013 Health Savings Account (HSA) Contribution Limits

Taxpayer	Minimum Deductible	Maximum Out-of-Pocket	Contribution Limit	55 and Over
Single	$1,250	$6,250	$3,250	+$1,000
Family	$2,500	$12,500	$6,450	+$1,000

Allowable medical expenses are those that would generally qualify for purposes of the deduction for medical and dental expenses and which are not paid or reimbursed by his high deductible health plan. Withdrawals from an HSA for purposes other than payment of allowable medical expenses are subject to income tax. They may also be subject to a 20% penalty, except in the following instances:

- When a taxpayer turns age 65 or older
- When a taxpayer becomes disabled
- When a taxpayer dies

A taxpayer should receive Form 5498-SA from the HSA trustee showing the amount of contributions for the year. The deduction for an HSA is reported on Form 8889, *Health Savings Accounts*.

To claim the HSA deduction for a particular year, the HSA contributions must be made on or before that year's tax filing date (without extensions). For 2013, HSA contributions must be made on or before the filing deadline of April 15, 2014.

Line 26: Moving Expenses

If a taxpayer moves due to a change of job or business location, he may deduct qualifying moving expenses that his employer does not reimburse.

A taxpayer who starts a first job or returns to full-time work after a long absence can also qualify for the deduction. Moving expenses incurred within one year of the date the taxpayer first reported to work at the new location can generally be deducted. There is no requirement that the job be in the same field.

If a taxpayer does not move within one year of the date he begins the new job, the moving expenses are not deductible unless he can prove that circumstances prevented moving within that period. Failing to sell a former home, for example, would not be an adequate reason.

To qualify for the moving expense deduction, the taxpayer must satisfy these tests:

- The move must be related to work or business, and
- The taxpayer must meet the tests for time and distance.

Time Test: This test is different for employees than for those who are self-employed. For employees, moving costs are deductible only if the taxpayer works full-time at the new work location for at least 39 weeks in the first 12 months. For joint filers, only one spouse has to qualify for the time test in order to deduct moving expenses.

Self-employed taxpayers must work full-time for at least 39 weeks in the first 12 months at the new location, and at least 78 weeks within the first 24 months at the new location. For this test, any combination of full-time work as an employee or as a self-employed person qualifies.

Example: Randy quit his job and moved from Missouri to Georgia to begin a full-time job as a mechanic for Custom Motorcycles. He worked at the motorcycle shop 40 hours each week. Shortly after his move, Randy also opened a part-time motorcycle repair business from his home garage on weekends. Because Randy's principal place of business is Custom Motorcycles, he satisfies the time test by meeting the 39-week test as an employee. However, if Randy is unable to satisfy the requirements of the 39-week test during the 12-month period, he may instead be able to satisfy the 78-week test because he also works as a self-employed person.

If a taxpayer fails to meet the time test, he must report the moving expenses as "other income" in a later tax year, or amend the tax return on which the moving expenses were claimed.

Exceptions to the Time Test: A taxpayer does not have to meet the time test and may still deduct moving expenses, if any of the following applies:

- The taxpayer is in the armed forces and moved because of a permanent change of station.
- The taxpayer's main job location was outside the United States and he moved back to the United States because he retired from his position.
- A taxpayer is the surviving widow(er) of a person whose main job location at the time of death was outside the United States.
- The taxpayer's job at the new location ends because of death or disability.
- The taxpayer is transferred or laid off for a reason other than willful misconduct.

Example: Darrell's company transfers him from New York to Tennessee, and he deducts his moving expenses. Darrell expects to continue his full-time employment in Tennessee and does not expect it to be a temporary move. A few months later, his employer is forced into bankruptcy and closes the entire Tennessee division. Darrell is laid off. He does not have to satisfy the time test.

Example: Shelby moves from Michigan to Ohio for a new job as a building manager. Six months after she starts the job, she dies. On Shelby's final tax return, her executor may deduct her moving expenses since the job ended due to her death.

Exceptions for Seasonal Work and Temporary Absences: For purposes of the moving expense deduction, if a taxpayer's trade or business is seasonal, the off-season weeks when no work is available may still be counted as weeks during which he worked full-time. In order to qualify, the off-season must be less than six months and the taxpayer must work full-time before and after the off-season.

Example: Chelsea moves from North Dakota to Jackson Hole, Wyoming for a job at a ski resort. She works full-time during the ski season and is off for five months during the summer. Chelsea may still count this time as full-time work, since her regular employment is expected to be seasonal.

A taxpayer is still considered to be employed on a full-time basis during any week he is temporarily absent from work because of illness, labor strikes, natural disasters, or similar causes.

Distance Test: Under the distance test, the new job must be at least 50 miles farther from the taxpayer's old home than the old job location was from the taxpayer's old home. If the taxpayer had no previous workplace, the new job must be at least 50 miles from the old home (see the diagram for clarification).

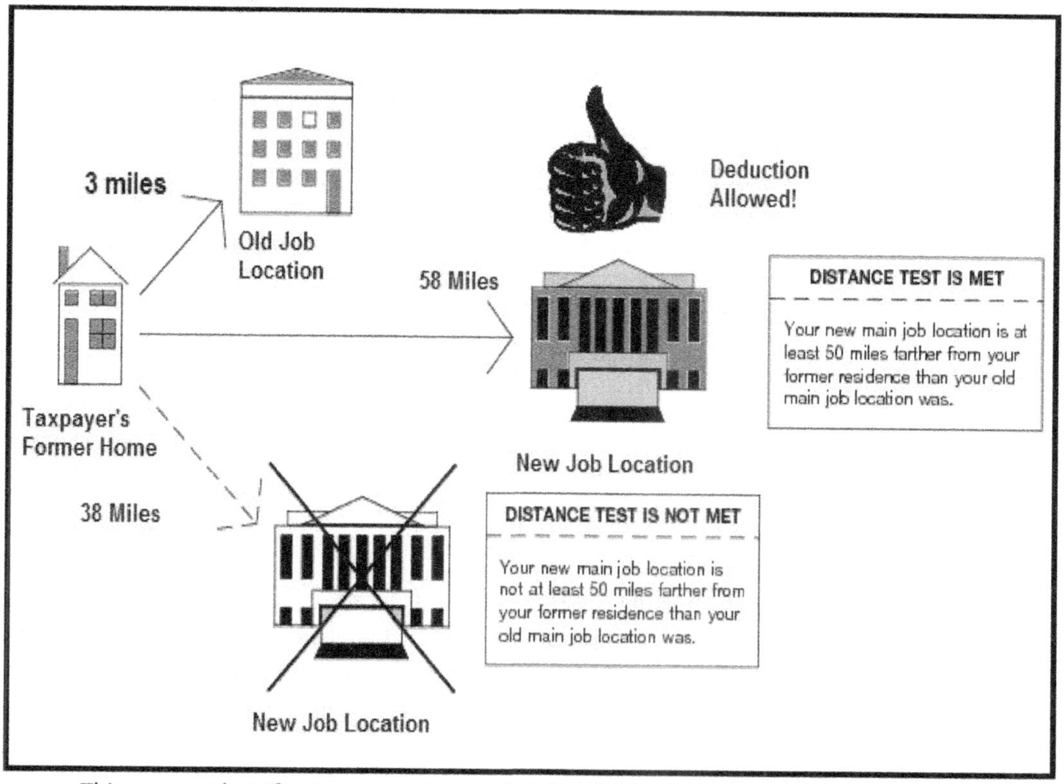

This means that if a taxpayer starts a job for the first time, the place of work must be at least 50 miles from his former home to meet the distance test.

Example: Abe moved to a new city and took a job as an attorney in a different law firm. His old job was six miles from his former home. Therefore, in order to deduct his moving expenses, his new job location must be at least 56 miles from that former home.

Members of the armed forces moving because of a permanent change of station or a military order are not required to meet the distance test or the time test.

Qualifying Moving Expenses: Only certain expenses qualify for the moving expense deduction. These include:

- The cost of packing and moving household effects and family members.
- Storage costs (only while in transit and for up to 30 days after the day of the move).
- The cost of connecting or disconnecting utilities required because a taxpayer is moving his household goods, appliances, or personal effects.
- The cost of shipping a car or a pet to a new home.

- Travel expenses (including lodging but not meals) for one trip per person. Family members are not required to travel together.

Actual car expenses such as gas and oil are tax deductible if accurate records are kept, or a taxpayer can use the standard mileage rate instead. Parking fees and tolls are also tax deductible, but general car repairs, maintenance, insurance, and depreciation of a taxpayer's car are not deductible moving expenses.

Example: In February 2013, Ethan and Jackie moved from Rhode Island to Alabama where Ethan was starting a new job. He drove the family car to Alabama, a trip of 1,100 miles. His actual expenses were $281.50 for gas, plus $40 for tolls and $150 for lodging, for a total of $471.50. One week later, Jackie flew from Rhode Island to Alabama. Her only expense was a $400 plane ticket. The couple's moving expense deduction is $871.50 (Ethan's $471.50 + Jackie's $400).

Nondeductible Moving Expenses: Moving expenses that cannot be deducted include:

- Pre-move house-hunting expenses
- Temporary living expenses
- Meals while traveling
- Expenses of buying or selling a home, home improvements to help sell a home, or a loss on a home sale
- Real estate taxes
- Car tags and driver's license renewal fees
- Storage charges except those incurred in transit or for a foreign move

Employer-Reimbursed Moving Expenses: When an employer reimburses a taxpayer for deductible moving expenses, the reimbursement is excluded from taxable income. However, if an employer reimburses an employee for nondeductible expenses (such as the expense incurred from breaking a lease), the reimbursement is taxable as wages and must be included on the employee's Form W-2.

Example: Gabriel has been offered a job at XelCorp Engineering. He agrees to accept the offer if XelCorp pays all his moving expenses. The cost of his professional movers was $9,600, which the company pays. This amount is deductible by XelCorp as a business expense and not taxable to Gabriel, since it is a deductible moving expense. XelCorp also reimburses Gabriel for a $7,500 loss on the sale of his home. Because this is reimbursement of a nondeductible expense, it is taxable and must be included on Gabriel's Form W-2. The $7,500 is deductible to XelCorp, but it is categorized as a wage expense and subject to payroll tax.

Moving expenses are reported on Form 3903, *Moving Expenses.*

Line 27: Deductible Part of Self-Employment Tax

A self-employed taxpayer can subtract from income 50% of self-employment tax, equal to the amount of Social Security and Medicare taxes that an employer normally pays for an employee, which is excluded from an employee's income. The deduction is figured on Schedule SE.

Line 28: Self-Employed Retirement Plans

Self-employed individuals can deduct contributions to the following types of retirement plans:

- Simplified Employee Pension (SEP) plans
- Savings Incentive Match Plan for Employees (SIMPLE) plans
- Qualified plans

A taxpayer must have self-employment income in order to contribute to his own plan.

Line 29: Self-Employed Health Insurance Deduction

A self-employed taxpayer may be able to deduct up to 100% of his health insurance premiums as an adjustment to income. Premiums paid by the taxpayer for his spouse and dependents under age 27 at the end of the year are also deductible. However, the deduction is limited to the net profit or other earned income from the business under which the health coverage is arranged, less the deductions on Lines 27 and 28 of Form 1040. The taxpayer must either:

- Be self-employed and have a net profit for the year;
- Be a partner with net earnings from self-employment; or
- Have received wages from an S corporation in which he was a more-than-2% shareholder.

Long-term care insurance is also considered health insurance for purposes of this deduction. The policy can be in the name of the business or in the name of the business owner.

A self-employed taxpayer may not take the deduction if either he or his spouse (if MFJ) is eligible to participate in an employer-sponsored and subsidized health insurance plan, even if they decline coverage.

Line 30: Penalty on Early Withdrawal of Savings

If a taxpayer withdraws money from a certificate of deposit (CD) or other time-deposit savings account prior to maturity, he usually incurs a penalty for early withdrawal. This penalty is charged by the bank or other financial institution and withheld from a taxpayer's proceeds.

Taxpayers can take an adjustment to income for early withdrawal penalties. The penalties are reported on a taxpayer's Form 1099-INT, *Interest Income*, or on Form 1099-OID, *Original Issue Discount*, which list interest income as well as the penalty amount.

> **Example:** Early in 2013, Gloria invested in a $15,000 one-year certificate of deposit. In November, she had an unexpected medical expense and had to liquidate the CD. She paid a penalty of three months' interest, which totaled $150. Gloria can claim the penalty ($150) as an adjustment to income.

The penalty for early withdrawal from an IRA or a retirement plan is not deductible.

Line 31: Alimony Paid

As described in the preceding unit, alimony received is taxable income. Alimony paid is generally treated as the mirror image and is a deductible expense that is claimed on Page 1 of Form 1040.

By definition, alimony is a payment to a former spouse under a divorce or separation instrument. The payments do not have to be made directly to the ex-spouse. For example, payments made on behalf of the ex-spouse for expenses such as medical bills, housing costs, and other expenses can also qualify as alimony.

Example: Yvette's divorce settlement requires that she pay her ex-husband $16,000 a year. Per the divorce agreement, she also must pay his ongoing medical expenses. In 2013, the medical expenses were $9,500. She can deduct the full amount ($25,500) as an adjustment to income because it is required by her divorce agreement.

Voluntary payments that are not required by a divorce decree or separation instrument do not qualify as alimony.

Example: Under the terms of Anthony's divorce decree, he must pay his ex-wife $12,600 in 2013. As a favor, he also makes $2,400 in payments to cover part of her vehicle lease so she can keep steady employment. Anthony may take the $12,600 as an adjustment to income. He cannot count the lease payments because they were not required by the divorce agreement.

Line 32: IRA Deduction

An individual retirement arrangement (IRA) offers tax advantages for setting aside money for retirement. Some taxpayers may claim a deduction for the amounts contributed to a traditional IRA as an adjustment to gross income.[13] Amounts that do not qualify for deduction include:

- Contributions to a Roth IRA
- Contributions to a traditional IRA that are nondeductible because the taxpayer and/or spouse is covered by an employer-sponsored retirement plan and modified adjusted gross income (MAGI) exceeds certain limits
- Contributions that apply to the previous tax year
- Rollover contributions

Deductions are allowed in full for contributions to a traditional IRA by a taxpayer (and spouse, if married) who is not covered by a retirement plan at work. If the taxpayer (and/or spouse) is covered by a retirement plan at work, deductions are phased out at certain income levels.

For 2013, the most a taxpayer can contribute to his traditional IRA generally is the smaller of the following amounts:

- $5,500 ($6,500 if age 50 or older), or
- The amount of taxable compensation.

Contributions can be made to a traditional IRA at any time during the year or by the due date for filing the return, not including extensions.

Example: Kenji wants to make a contribution to his traditional IRA for 2013 but is unsure how much to contribute. He sees his accountant in February, and Kenji decides he wants to contribute the maximum amount. He files his tax return on March 1 and takes the deduction for his contribution. Kenji has until April 15, 2014 to make a tax deductible contribution for the 2013 tax year.

---

[13] The rules regarding IRA contributions, withdrawals, and rollovers to IRAs are covered in detail in Unit 16.

Line 33: Student Loan Interest Deduction

Generally, personal interest (other than mortgage interest) is not deductible. However, interest on a qualified student loan is deductible. A "qualified student loan" is used solely to pay qualified higher education expenses for the taxpayer, his spouse, or his dependents. A taxpayer can claim the deduction for 2013 if:

- He paid interest on a qualified student loan on which he was legally obligated.
- His filing status is not married filing separately.
- Neither he (nor his spouse if filing jointly) can be claimed as a dependent on someone else's return.

The maximum deduction for student loan interest in 2013 is $2,500. This limit begins to phase out for joint filers with modified adjusted gross income of $125,000 and phases out completely at MAGI of $155,000. For single taxpayers, the MAGI phase-out range is from $60,000 to $75,000.

Example: Veronica and her husband file jointly. Their modified adjusted gross income is $162,000. She completed her doctorate and paid $3,400 in student loan interest in 2013. Due to their high MAGI, they may not deduct any of their student loan interest as an adjustment to income.

In order for student loan interest to qualify, the student must have been enrolled at least half-time in a higher education program leading to a degree, certificate, or other recognized educational credential. A student who used the loan to take classes for other purposes does not qualify.

Example: Peter graduated from a technical college where he had been enrolled full-time in a certificate program for automotive repair. Peter may take the student loan interest deduction.

Qualified higher education expenses are costs of attending an eligible educational institution, including graduate schools, such as:

- Tuition and fees
- Room and board
- Books, supplies, and equipment
- Other necessary school-related expenses, such as transportation

Qualified expenses must be reduced by the amounts of tax-free items used to pay them, such as the following:

- Employer-provided educational assistance benefits
- Tax-free withdrawals from a Coverdell Education Savings Account
- U.S. savings bond interest already excluded from income
- Tax-free scholarships and fellowships
- Veterans' educational assistance benefits
- Any other nontaxable payments (except gifts or inheritances) received for educational expenses

Example: In 2013, Katelyn's educational expenses are $7,200. She also receives a gift of $1,000 from her aunt and $1,000 in veterans' educational assistance. Therefore, Katelyn's qualified higher education expenses are $6,200 because veterans' assistance benefits must be subtracted. The gift from her aunt does not have to be subtracted.

A student loan is not eligible if it is from certain related persons (such as family members or certain corporations, partnerships, or trusts). Loans from an employer plan also do not qualify. The student loan interest deduction limit is per return, not per student. For example, if a taxpayer has three children and pays $2,000 in student loan interest for each of them, the maximum deduction is still only $2,500.

Summary: Student Loan Interest Deduction

Rules	Description
Max. benefit	$2,500 per tax return, per year
Loan qualifications	The student loan: • Must have been taken out solely to pay qualified education expenses, and • Cannot be from a related person or made under a qualified employer plan.
Student qualifications	The student must be the taxpayer, a spouse, or a dependent; and enrolled at least half-time in a degree program when the loan was incurred.
Time limit	The taxpayer can deduct interest paid during the remaining period of the student loan.
MAGI Phase-out ranges	Single: $60,000-$75,000; MFJ: $125,000-$155,000. MFS does not qualify.

Line 34: Tuition and Fees

Taxpayers may deduct qualified tuition and related higher education expenses paid for academic periods beginning in 2013 and the first three months of 2014. For 2013, the deduction is either $2,000 or $4,000, depending on MAGI, determined as follows:

- $4,000 if MAGI is $65,000 or less ($130,000 if MFJ)
- $2,000 if MAGI is $80,000 or less ($160,000 if MFJ)

The deduction is eliminated completely once a taxpayer's MAGI exceeds $80,000 for single filers and $160,000 for joint filers.

A qualified student is:

- The taxpayer
- The taxpayer's spouse (if filing jointly)
- The taxpayer's dependent

Qualifying Expenses: The expenses that qualify for the tuition and fees deduction are more limited than the expenses that qualify for the student loan interest deduction. Generally, for the tuition and fees deduction, qualified education expenses are only amounts paid for tuition expenses at an eligible college or vocational institution.

Qualified expenses do not include amounts paid for:

- Room and board, medical expenses (including student health fees), transportation, or other personal expenses
- Course-related books, supplies, equipment, and nonacademic activities and fees, unless they are required as a condition of enrollment
- Any course or other education involving sports, games, or hobbies, or any noncredit course

A taxpayer cannot claim the tuition and fees deduction based on expenses that have already been paid with a tax-free scholarship, fellowship, grant, or education savings account funds such as a Coverdell education savings account, tax-free savings bond interest, or employer-provided education assistance.

Restrictions: A taxpayer filing MFS cannot take the tuition and fees deduction. If a taxpayer is claimed as a dependent on someone else's return, he cannot take the deduction for himself. Nonresident aliens also do not qualify for this deduction.

A taxpayer cannot claim the tuition and fees deduction and an education credit for the same student. A taxpayer who is eligible to claim the American Opportunity Credit or Lifetime Learning Credit[14] is allowed to figure his return both ways and choose the deduction that results in the lowest tax.

Line 35: Domestic Production Activities Deduction

The domestic production activities deduction (DPAD) is a tax deduction available to manufacturing businesses that have employees in the United States. Its aim is to stimulate domestic production. A sole proprietor could qualify for this deduction, if his business has employees and pays wages.[15]

Line 36: Other Adjustments

Line 36 of Form 1040 is reserved for more obscure deductions. There is a dotted line on the form that allows the taxpayer to manually indicate what type of adjustment is being taken. It may also be completed using most tax preparation software programs. These are some of the miscellaneous adjustments that may be entered on line 36:

1. **Archer MSA:** An Archer MSA is a tax-exempt account, similar to a health savings account, that can be set up with a U.S. financial institution and in which a taxpayer can save money exclusively for future medical expenses.
2. **Jury Duty Pay Remitted to an Employer:** Jury duty pay is reported as taxable income on Form 1040. However, some employees continue to receive their regular wages when they serve on jury duty even though they are not at work, and their jury pay is turned over to their employers. In that case, the amount is reported as a write-in adjustment.
3. **Repayment of Unemployment Benefits:** A taxpayer who repaid unemployment benefits may report the amount as an adjustment to income in the year it is repaid.

---

[14] These education credits are discussed in Unit 14, *Tax Credits*.

[15] The DPAD is tested on Part 2: Businesses of the EA exam.

Unit 11: Study Questions

1. Caylie had an HSA account set up with her employer that had $3,000 in the account at the end of 2013. She then quit her job and withdrew all the funds from her HSA. She did not use the $3,000 for qualifying medical expenses. What is the consequence of this action?

A. Nothing; taxpayers are allowed to withdraw from their HSA accounts at any time.
B. Nonmedical withdrawals from an HSA are prohibited and will result in a forfeiture of the funds.
C. Withdrawals from an HSA for non-eligible expenses are subject to income tax and a 20% penalty.
D. Withdrawals from an HSA for non-eligible expenses are subject to income tax and a 6% penalty.

2. Jermaine and Anna have MAGI of $45,000. They are married and file a joint return. Two years ago, they took out a loan so their daughter, Miranda, could earn her degree. Miranda is their dependent. In 2013, they paid $3,000 in student loan interest. How much student loan interest can Jermaine and Anna deduct on their tax return?

A. $0.
B. $1,000.
C. $2,500.
D. $3,000.

3. Contributions to a traditional IRA can be deducted for a given tax year if they are made:

A. Any time during the year or by the due date of the return, not including extensions.
B. Any time during the year or by the due date of the return, including extensions.
C. By December 31.
D. Any time during the year, but only while the taxpayer is employed.

4. All of the following statements are correct except:

A. A school counselor may qualify for the educator expense deduction.
B. A part-time teacher may qualify for the educator expense deduction.
C. A school principal may qualify for the educator expense deduction.
D. A college instructor may qualify for the educator expense deduction.

5. Dave and Bea file jointly. In March 2013, they move from Arizona to Connecticut, where Dave is starting a new job. Dave drives the car to Hartford. His expenses are $400 for gas, $40 for tolls, $150 for lodging, and $70 for meals. A week later, Bea drives to Hartford. Her expenses are $500 for gas, $40 for tolls, $35 for parking, $100 for lodging, and $25 for meals. A week later, they pay $600 to ship their pet, a miniature horse, to Connecticut. How much can they deduct for moving expenses?

A. $590.
B. $1,265.
C. $1,865.
D. $1,960.

6. Sammy took out a student loan for $90,000 to help pay his tuition at a university. He graduated and began making payments on his student loan in 2013. Sammy made 12 payments in 2013, which included $1,600 of interest and $2,000 of principal. How much is Sammy's student loan interest deduction?

A. $1,600.
B. $2,000.
C. $2,500.
D. $2,600.

7. Under his divorce decree, Rick must pay the medical expenses of his former spouse, Linda. In January 2013, Rick sends a check totaling $4,000 directly to General Medical Hospital in order to pay for Linda's emergency surgery. Which of the following statements is true?

A. This payment qualifies as alimony, and Linda must include the $4,000 as income on her return.
B. This payment does not qualify as alimony, but Rick can claim a deduction for the medical expenses on his return.
C. Linda must include the $4,000 as income on her return, but Rick cannot deduct the expense as alimony because it was paid to a third party.
D. None of the above.

8. An adjustment to income is considered the most beneficial type of deduction because_____________:

A. It favors taxpayers who choose to itemize their deductions.
B. It is simpler to figure out qualifying expenses for adjustments to income than it is other deductions.
C. It lowers a taxpayer's adjusted gross income, and thus can affect the amounts of certain credits and deductions he may be able to claim.
D. There is no significant difference between an adjustment to income and a regular tax deduction.

9. Which of the following statements is true?

A. Credit card interest can be deductible as student loan interest if qualifying educational expenses are paid.
B. On a joint return, a taxpayer may deduct student loan interest paid on behalf of his spouse.
C. The maximum deduction for student loan interest is $5,000 per student.
D. Taxpayers may deduct student loan interest even if they are not liable for the loan.

10. Which item qualifies as a deductible education expense for the tuition and fees deduction?

A. College club dues.
B. Student health fees.
C. Room and board.
D. Student activity fees required as a condition for enrollment.

11. What is the maximum educator's expense deduction for two teachers who are married and file jointly?

A. $100.
B. $250.
C. $500.
D. $750.

12. Chuck and Mallory are married and file jointly. Chuck is self-employed and his net profit was $50,000 in 2013. They pay $500 per month for health insurance coverage. Mallory was a homemaker until she got a job working for a local construction company. Mallory and Chuck became eligible to participate in her employer's health plan on March 1, 2013, but they did not want to switch doctors, so she declined the coverage. Which of the following statements is true?

A. They may deduct $500 for both January and February, and $250 per month for each of the last ten months of the year, as self-employed health insurance premiums on Chuck's Schedule C.
B. They may deduct $1,000 in self-employed health insurance premiums, which is for January and February, the two months they were not eligible to participate in an employer plan.
C. They may deduct 100% of their health insurance premiums because they declined the employer coverage.
D. They may deduct 50% of their health insurance premiums on Chuck's Schedule C.

13. Drew borrowed $15,000 from his sister to pay for college. He signed a notarized loan statement and is making regular payments of $500 per month including 10% interest. In 2013, he paid $1,400 in student loan interest. Which of the following is true?

A. Drew can deduct all the interest as qualified student loan interest.
B. Drew can deduct $2,500 of the interest as qualified student loan interest.
C. Drew cannot deduct the interest.
D. Drew can deduct $6,000 ($500 × 12 months).

14. Lynn was offered a position in another city. Her new employer reimburses her for the $9,500 loss on the sale of her home because of the move. How should this reimbursement be treated?

A. The employer can reimburse Lynn and make the payment nontaxable through an accountable plan, if properly documented.
B. Because this is a reimbursement of a nondeductible expense, it is treated as wages and must be included on Lynn's Form W-2.
C. The reimbursement is tax-exempt because it is a qualified moving expense.
D. The expense is nontaxable so long as Lynn's employer makes the payment directly to her mortgage lender.

15. George paid $14,000 in alimony to his wife during the year. Which of the following is true?

A. George can only deduct alimony if he itemizes deductions on his tax return.
B. The deduction for alimony is entered on Schedule A as an itemized deduction.
C. George can deduct alimony paid, even if he does not itemize.
D. George can deduct alimony paid on Form 1040A.

16. Marshall lost his job last year and withdrew money from a number of accounts. He paid the following penalties:

- $100 penalty for early withdrawal from a certificate of deposit (CD)
- $200 penalty for early withdrawal from a traditional IRA
- $50 late penalty for not paying his rent on time

How much of these amounts can Marshall deduct as an adjustment to income on his Form 1040?

A. $0.
B. $100.
C. $200.
D. $250.

17. Kyle has an HSA, and he becomes permanently disabled in 2013. Which of the following statements is true?

A. Kyle may withdraw money from his HSA for nonmedical expenses, but the withdrawals will be subject to income tax and also an additional penalty of 20%.
B. Kyle may withdraw money from his HSA for nonmedical expenses. The withdrawals will be subject to income tax, but will not be subject to penalty.
C. Kyle may not take nonmedical distributions from his account.
D. Kyle must be at least 65 to take nonmedical distributions from an HSA.

18. Chase is moving for a new job. He has the following expenses:

Moving truck rental	$500
Moving family and pets	$300
Storage unit while moving	$200
Breaking his existing apartment lease	$400
Pre-move house-hunting	$500

Assuming that Chase passes all the required tests, what is his allowable moving expense deduction?

A. $500.
B. $800.
C. $1,000.
D. $1,900.

19. Jasmine is a part-time art teacher at an elementary school. She spends $185 on qualified expenses for her art students and $75 on materials for a health course that she also teaches. She worked 440 hours as an educator during the tax year. How much can she deduct in educator expenses as an adjustment to income?

A. $0.
B. $185.
C. $250.
D. $260.

20. Emilio is a sophomore at his state university's degree program in anthropology. In 2013, he paid $3,000 in tuition and $10,000 to live in optional on-campus housing. In addition to tuition, he is required to pay a fee of $300 to the university for the rental of the equipment he will use in this program. How much of these expenses qualify for the tuition and fees deduction?

A. $3,000.
B. $3,300.
C. $13,000.
D. $13,300.

21. Bruce makes an excess contribution to his HSA, by accidentally contributing over the maximum allowable amount. What is the penalty on excess contributions if Bruce does not correct the problem?

A. No penalty.
B. 6% penalty.
C. 10% penalty.
D. 20% penalty.

22. Deborah was self-employed in 2013 and had self-employment tax of $4,896. Which of the following statements is true?

A. She may deduct 100% of the self-employment tax she paid on Schedule C.
B. She may deduct 50% of the self-employment tax she paid on Schedule C.
C. She may deduct 50% of the self-employment tax she paid as an adjustment to income on Form 1040.
D. She may not deduct self-employment tax.

23. Marina is a software specialist who works and lives in Boston. A company offers her a new job in Raleigh, North Carolina, more than 700 miles away. As part of the offer, she negotiates a deal to work part-time for the first six months. Marina's husband is a stay-at-home father to the couple's two young children. The family makes the move from Boston to Raleigh, and Marina begins work at her new job. Does she meet both the time and distance tests in order to deduct her moving expenses as an adjustment to income?

A. No, she does not meet the distance test.
B. No, she does not meet the time test or distance test.
C. She meets the distance test, but not the time test.
D. Marina meets both tests and is able to deduct her moving expenses.

Unit 12: Standard Deduction & Itemized Deductions

For additional information read:
Publication 502, *Medical and Dental Expenses*
Publication 600, *State and Local General Sales Taxes*
Publication 936, *Home Mortgage Interest Deduction*
Publication 526, *Charitable Contributions*

A taxpayer generally may choose either to claim a standard deduction amount or to itemize deductions. The choice should be based on which option results in a lower tax liability.

The standard deduction is a specific dollar amount that reduces the amount of income on which a taxpayer is taxed. Using the standard deduction eliminates the need for a taxpayer to itemize his actual allowable deductions, such as medical expenses, charitable contributions, or state and local taxes. The standard deduction amounts are based on a taxpayer's filing status and are adjusted every year for inflation.

Depending on the option selected, either the applicable standard deduction amount or the taxpayer's total itemized deductions is subtracted from his adjusted gross income.

2013 Standard Deduction	
Filing Status	**Amount**
Single or MFS	$6,100
MFJ or QW	$12,200
HOH	$8,950

Additional standard deduction amounts are available to taxpayers who at the end of the year are:

- 65 or older, and/or
- Blind or partially blind

The additional standard deduction amount in these cases is $1,200 per taxpayer for married filers and $1,500 for single and head of household filers. A taxpayer who is both blind and 65 or older may take the basic standard deduction and additional standard deduction amounts for both age and blindness.

The additional amount for blindness is allowed if the taxpayer is blind on the last day of the tax year, even if he was not blind the rest of the year. A taxpayer must obtain a certified statement from an eye doctor indicating that:

- The taxpayer cannot see better than 20/200 in the better eye, even when corrected with eyeglasses, or
- The taxpayer's field of vision is not more than 20 degrees (the taxpayer has disabled peripheral vision).

Example: Wade, 46, and Christine, 33, file jointly. Neither is blind. They decide not to itemize their deductions. Their standard deduction in 2013 is $12,200.

Example: Gilbert and Lisa are married and do not itemize deductions. Because they file jointly, their base standard deduction is $12,200. Lisa, age 59, is blind, so she can claim an additional standard deduction amount of $1,200. Gilbert turns 65 on December 31, 2013. Since he is 65 at the end of the tax year, he, too, can claim an additional standard deduction amount of $1,200. Therefore, their total standard deduction in 2013 is $14,600 ($12,200 + $1,200 + $1,200).

The standard deduction for a deceased taxpayer is the same as if the taxpayer had lived the entire year, with one exception: If the taxpayer died before his sixty-fifth birthday, the higher standard deduction for being 65 does not apply.

Example: Richard is single and died on November 1, 2013. He would have been 65 if he had reached his birthday on December 12, 2013. He does not qualify for a higher standard deduction because he died before his sixty-fifth birthday. His standard deduction would be $6,100 on his final tax return filed by his executor.

Standard Deduction for Certain Dependents

The standard deduction for a dependent who can be claimed on another person's return is limited to the greater of:

- $1,000, or
- The dependent's earned income (such as wages) plus $350, but not more than the regular standard deduction amount. For a single person, this is generally $6,100.

Example: Georgia is single, 22, and a student with a part-time job. Her parents supported her, so they claim her as a dependent on their 2013 tax return. Georgia also files a return and takes the standard deduction. She has interest income of $120, wages of $780 from her part-time job, and taxes withheld from her wages totaling $35. Her standard deduction is $1,130 ($780 wages + $350).

The standard deduction is higher if the dependent is 65 or older and/or blind.

Example: Amy is 19, single, and legally blind. She is claimed on her parents' 2013 return. Amy has interest income of $1,300 and wages from a part-time job of $2,900. Her base amount for the standard deduction is $3,250 ($2,900 + $350). Because Amy is blind, she is allowed an additional standard deduction amount of $1,500. Her standard deduction is $4,750 ($2,900 + $350 + $1,500).

Itemized Deductions

Itemized deductions may be taken instead of the standard deduction, and allow taxpayers to reduce their taxable income based on specific personal expenses. If a taxpayer's total itemized deductions are greater than his applicable standard deduction amount, they will result in lower taxable income and a lower tax liability.

In most cases, a taxpayer may choose whether to claim itemized deductions or the standard deduction, depending on which is more beneficial. However, taxpayers are required to itemize in the following cases:

- If married and filing separately and one spouse itemizes, the other spouse also must itemize.
- If the taxpayer is a nonresident or dual-status alien (who is not married to a U.S. citizen or resident).
- If the taxpayer files a tax return for a period of less than 12 months due to a change in accounting methods.

If a taxpayer itemizes deductions, he must complete and file Schedule A along with his Form 1040. We will review the specific requirements for various itemized deductions in this and the next unit.

Pease Limitation on Itemized Deductions

In 2013, certain itemized deductions for higher income taxpayers are limited. The so-called Pease limitation[16] reduces the total amount of a higher income taxpayer's itemized deductions by the lesser of:

- 3% of the amount by which the taxpayer's AGI exceeds a specific threshold, or
- 80% of the total amount of the otherwise allowable itemized deductions.

Pease Limitation Threshold Amounts

Filing Status	2013 AGI Threshold
Single	$250,000
MFJ or QW	$300,000
HOH	$275,000
MFS	$150,000

The limitation does not apply to the following itemized deductions:

- Medical expenses
- Investment interest expense
- Casualty or theft losses
- Gambling losses

The limitation applies to all other itemized deductions, including charitable contributions; mortgage interest; state, local, and property taxes; and miscellaneous itemized deductions.

Example: Lynn and Adrian have $425,000 in adjusted gross income in 2013. They have $60,000 of itemized deductions from real estate taxes, mortgage interest, and charitable contributions. They are required to reduce their itemized deductions by whichever is the lesser of:

- 3% over the amount by which their AGI exceeds the applicable threshold of $300,000 ($125,000 × .03 = $3,750), or
- 80% of their total itemized deductions ($60,000 × .80 = $48,000).

They may deduct $56,250 ($60,000 - $3,750).

---

[16] Named for former congressman Donald Pease and first enacted in 1990. It was suspended from 2010 to 2012, but reinstated as part of the American Taxpayer Relief Act of 2012.

Medical and Dental Expenses

Medical and dental expenses (other than self-employed health insurance premiums) are deductible only if a taxpayer itemizes deductions. Further, most taxpayers can deduct only the amount of unreimbursed medical expenses that exceeds 10% of adjusted gross income. This is an increase in 2013 from the previous threshold of 7.5%.

Example: Tracy, age 53, had unreimbursed medical expenses totaling $2,500 in 2013. Her AGI was $40,000. Tracy cannot deduct any of her medical expenses on Schedule A because they are not more than 10% of her AGI ($40,000 × .10 = $4,000).

Example: Manuel, age 46, paid $12,000 in out-of-pocket expenses for knee surgery in 2013. His AGI was $100,000. The amount in excess of $10,000 (AGI of $100,000 × .10), or $2,000, is allowed as an itemized deduction.

For tax years 2013 through 2016, a taxpayer (and his spouse if married) age 65 or over is temporarily exempt from the increase in the threshold from 7.5% to 10%. The 7.5% floor continues to apply if either spouse reaches age 65 by the end of the tax year.

Example: Meredith, age 64, and Rudy, age 66, had unreimbursed medical expenses of $8,000 in 2013. Their AGI was $70,000. Because Rudy is 65 or older, they may use the 7.5%-of-AGI threshold and deduct $2,750 on their Schedule A, the amount in excess of the 7.5% floor ($70,000 × .75 = $5,250).

A change in the applicable AGI percentage can occur because of marriage to, or divorce from, a spouse age 65 or older.

Example: In 2013, Neil, age 60, marries Cora, age 67. Their unreimbursed medical expenses total 9% of their AGI. They may deduct the amount that exceeds the 7.5% floor because Cora is age 65 or over. In 2015, Neil and Cora divorce. Neil, who is now age 62, may deduct only the amount of his unreimbursed medical expenses that exceeds 10% of his AGI, while Cora may continue to use the 7.5% floor. In 2017, regardless of age, each is subject to the 10% floor.

Qualified Medical Expenses: The taxpayer may only include medical expenses paid during the year, regardless of when the services were provided. Qualified medical expenses include expenses paid for:

- The taxpayer, or the taxpayer's spouse
- Dependents (the individual must have been a dependent at the time the medical services were provided or at the time the expenses were paid)

If a child of divorced or separated parents is claimed as a dependent on either parent's return, each parent may deduct medical expenses he or she individually paid for the child. This is true even if the other parent claims the child's dependency exemption. There is also an exception for medical expenses paid on behalf of a former spouse pursuant to a divorce decree.

Example: Raymond and Carmen are divorced. Their son, Colby, lives with Carmen, who claims him as a dependent. Carmen deducts Colby's annual medical and dental bills, including orthodontia expenses for his braces. However, in April, Colby falls on the playground and fractures his arm. The out-of-pocket expenses are $5,500. Colby's father, Raymond, pays for the emergency room visit and the expenses related to the injury, and may deduct them even though he does not claim his son as a dependent.

A taxpayer can deduct medical expenses paid on behalf of an adopted child, even before the adoption is final.

A taxpayer can deduct medical expenses paid for a dependent parent. All the standard rules for a dependency exemption apply, so the dependent parent does not have to live with the taxpayer to qualify.

Example: Julie pays all the medical expenses for her father, age 62, who is her dependent but does not live with her. The medical expenses are deductible on Julie's tax return as an itemized deduction to the extent they exceed the 10% threshold.

Qualifying Medical Expenses: Qualifying medical expenses include the costs of diagnosis, cure, mitigation, treatment, or prevention of disease, and the costs of medical (but not cosmetic) treatments. They include the costs of:

- Medically necessary equipment, supplies, and diagnostic devices
- Dental and vision care
- Transportation to obtain medical care
- Qualified long-term care insurance

Deductible medical expenses may include:

- Fees paid to doctors, dentists, surgeons, chiropractors, psychiatrists, psychologists, and nontraditional medical practitioners
- In-patient hospital care or nursing home services, including the cost of meals and lodging charged by the hospital or nursing home
- Lactation supplies
- Treatment at alcohol or drug addiction centers, participation in smoking-cessation programs, and prescription drugs to alleviate nicotine withdrawal
- Weight-loss programs prescribed by a physician (but not payments for diet food items)
- Insulin and prescription drugs
- Admission and transportation to a medical conference relating to a chronic disease (but not the costs for meals and lodging while attending the conference)
- Veterinary care when it relates to the care of animals trained to assist persons who are visually-impaired, hearing-impaired, or disabled

Note: Medical expenses must be primarily to alleviate or prevent a physical or mental defect or illness. Medical expenses do not include expenses that are merely beneficial to general health, such as vitamins, spa treatments, gym memberships, or vacations. In addition, the cost of over-the-counter medications cannot be deducted.

Medical Insurance: If a taxpayer receives insurance reimbursement for medical care expenses, those amounts are not deductible.

Qualifying medical expenses include medical insurance and long-term care insurance premiums that the taxpayer paid with after-tax dollars. A taxpayer may not deduct insurance premiums paid by an employer-sponsored plan unless the premiums are included in Box 1 of his Form W-2.

Note: The value of a taxpayer's annual health care coverage is reported in Box 12 on Form W-2. The amount includes the portions paid by both the employer and the employee. It is a provision of the Affordable Care Act to try to show taxpayers the cost of their health care. Although this amount is reported on the Form W-2, it does not mean the amount is taxable; it is for informational purposes only.

Long-term Care Services: A taxpayer may include in medical expense deductions limited amounts paid for qualified long-term care services and insurance premiums. Long-term care services include necessary diagnostic, preventive, therapeutic, rehabilitative, maintenance, and personal care services that are required by a chronically ill individual and provided under a plan of care by a licensed health care practitioner. The deductibility of costs of qualified long-term care premiums is limited by the age of the taxpayer, from $360 (age 40 or under) to $4,550 (age 71 or over). The expenses generally cannot include costs that would be reimbursed under Medicare.

Other Medical Expenses: If a taxpayer or a dependent is in a nursing home and the primary reason for being there is medically related, the entire cost, including meals and lodging, is a medical expense.

A taxpayer can deduct legal fees that are necessary to authorize treatment for a mental illness. However, legal fees for the management of a guardianship estate or for conducting the affairs of a person being treated are not deductible as medical expenses.

Medical Expenses of Deceased Taxpayers: In addition to expenses paid before a taxpayer's death, his survivor or personal representative can elect to treat medical expenses paid by the estate within one year after his death as if the taxpayer had paid when the medical services were provided.

Example: Anne had heart surgery in November 2013 and incurred $20,000 in medical bills. When she died on January 2, 2014, her 2013 medical bills had not yet been paid. The executor of Anne's estate may elect to deduct her medical expenses on her 2013 tax return, even though the medical expenses were paid by the estate in 2014.

Cosmetic Surgery: Cosmetic surgery is only deductible if it is used to correct a defect or disease. A cosmetic procedure simply for the enhancement of someone's physical appearance is not a deductible medical expense.

Example: Bethany undergoes surgery to remove a breast as part of treatment for cancer. A surgeon reconstructs her breast to correct a deformity that is directly related to the disease. The cost of the surgery is deductible as a medical expense.

Medically-Related Transportation, Meals, and Lodging: Vehicle mileage may be deducted if transportation is for medical reasons, such as trips to and from doctors' appointments. If a taxpayer uses his own car for medical transportation, he can deduct actual out-of-pocket expenses for gas and other expenses, or he can deduct the standard mileage rate for medical expenses, which is 24 cents per mile in 2013. A taxpayer may also deduct the costs of taxis, buses, trains, planes, or ambulances, as well as tolls and parking fees.

A taxpayer can deduct the cost of meals and lodging at a hospital or similar institution if the principal reason for being there is to receive medical care. The care must be provided by a doctor, hospital, or medical care facility, and there must not be any significant element of personal pleasure or recreation.

The IRS imposes a $50 limit per person, per night, for lodging related to medical care. There is no deduction for meals that are unrelated to inpatient care.

Capital Improvements for Medical Reasons: Capital improvements such as home improvements are usually not deductible. However, a home improvement may qualify as a deductible expense if its main purpose is to provide medical care to the taxpayer or to dependent family members.

The deduction for capital improvements is limited to the excess of the actual cost of the improvements over the related increase in the fair market value of the home. Home improvements that qualify as deductible medical expenses may include:

- Wheelchair ramps
- Lowering of kitchen cabinets
- Railings and support bars
- Elevators
- Special lift equipment

Tenants may deduct the entire cost of disability-related improvements, since they are not the owners of the property.

Example: Lonnie, age 61, has a heart condition. He cannot easily climb stairs or get into a bathtub. On his doctor's advice, he pays for installation of a special sit-in bathtub and a stair lift in his rented house. The landlord did not pay any of the cost. Lonnie can deduct the entire amount as a medical expense, subject to the 10% threshold.

Deductible Taxes

Taxpayers can deduct certain taxes if they itemize deductions. To be deductible, a tax must have been imposed on the taxpayer and paid by the taxpayer during the tax year. Deductible taxes include:

- State, local, and foreign income taxes
- State and local sales taxes
- Real estate taxes
- Personal property taxes (such as DMV fees)

State and Local Taxes: Taxpayers are allowed to deduct either state and local sales taxes or state and local income taxes,[17] depending on which provides the larger deduction, but not both.

[17] The option to deduct state and local sales taxes instead of state income taxes has been extended through 2013 as part of the American Taxpayer Relief Act of 2012.

Income taxes paid include taxes withheld from salaries and wages, amounts paid for prior years, and estimated tax payments.

Real Estate Taxes: State, local, or foreign real estate taxes that are based on the assessed value of the taxpayer's real property (such as a house or land) are deductible. If the taxes are paid from a mortgage escrow account, the taxpayer can only deduct the amount actually paid out of the escrow account during the year to the taxing authority.

Some real estate taxes are not deductible, including taxes imposed to finance improvements to property, such as assessments for streets, sidewalks, and sewer lines. In addition, itemized charges for services and homeowners' association fees are not deductible.

Example: Genevieve makes the following payments: state income tax, $2,000; real estate taxes, $900; local benefit tax for improving the sewer system, $75; homeowners' association fee, $250. Her total deductible taxes are $2,900 ($2,000 + $900 = $2,900). The $75 local benefit tax and the $250 homeowners' association fee are not deductible.

If a property is sold, the real estate taxes are prorated between the buyer and the seller according to the number of days that each owned the property, and adjustments are charged or credited on the settlement statement depending upon which party is responsible for paying the taxing authority.

Personal Property Taxes: Personal property taxes are deductible if they are:

- Charged on personal property, including cars, boats, or items used in a business such as equipment and furniture;
- Based on the value of the property; and
- Charged on a yearly basis, even if collected more or less than once a year.

Foreign Income Taxes: Generally, a taxpayer can choose between claiming the Foreign Tax Credit or claiming an itemized deduction on Schedule A for income taxes paid to a foreign country, depending on which option results in the lowest tax. The rules regarding which foreign taxes qualify for either the credit or the deduction are covered in Unit 15.

Interest

Certain types of interest payments are deductible as itemized deductions on Form 1040, Schedule A:

- Home mortgage interest
- Points
- Mortgage insurance premiums
- Investment interest expense

Home Mortgage Interest

Home mortgage interest is paid on a loan secured by a taxpayer's home. The loan may be a mortgage, a second mortgage, a home equity loan, or a line of credit. A taxpayer is allowed to deduct the interest related to a primary residence and a second home.

A second home can include any other residence a taxpayer owns and treats as a home, but the taxpayer does not have to actually use the second home during the year in order to deduct the mortgage interest paid on the related loan.

A taxpayer may deduct real estate taxes on more than two properties, but may not deduct mortgage interest on more than two homes.

An empty lot does not qualify for the mortgage interest deduction. If a taxpayer builds a house that becomes a qualified home when ready for occupancy, he can deduct mortgage interest for a period of up to 24 months from when construction begins. A taxpayer may deduct late charges on the loan as mortgage interest.

Example: Reese owns his home and pays his mortgage on a monthly basis. In 2013, he falls behind on his mortgage payments and sends in his payment late on two occasions. The mortgage company charges Reese a $35 fee for each late payment. The late fees are deductible as mortgage interest.

Mortgage Deduction Limits: If all of the taxpayer's mortgages fit into one or more of the following three categories, he can deduct all of the interest:

- Mortgages obtained on or before October 13, 1987 (grandfathered debt).
- Mortgages obtained after October 13, 1987 to buy, build, or improve a home (called home acquisition debt), but only if these mortgages plus any grandfathered debt total $1 million ($500,000 if MFS) or less.
- Mortgages obtained after October 13, 1987 for purposes other than to buy, build, or improve the home (called home equity debt), but only if these mortgages are $100,000 ($50,000 if MFS) or less.

If one or more of the taxpayer's mortgages does not fit in at least one of these categories, his interest deductions will be limited.

Example: Shirley has a mortgage of $800,000 against her primary residence and another of $500,000 against a vacation home. Both loans were used solely to acquire the homes. The loan amounts add up to $1.3 million. Since the total loan amounts exceed the $1 million limit for home acquisition debt, Shirley's mortgage interest deduction is limited.

Interest on Home Equity Debt: The interest paid on home equity debt related to a main home and a second home is deductible, but only for debt equal to the smaller of:

- The $100,000 ($50,000 if MFS) limit described above, or
- The total of each home's fair market value reduced by its grandfathered debt and home acquisition debt.

Example: Carla bought her home ten years ago for cash. Its fair market value is now $80,000. She did not have a mortgage until last year when she took out a $45,000 loan, secured by her home, to pay for her daughter's college tuition. This loan is home equity debt. Since it is less than the $100,000 limit, the mortgage interest on the equity line is deductible.

Example: Kody bought his home five years ago. Its FMV is now $110,000, and the current balance on his original mortgage is $95,000. His bank offers him a home equity loan with borrowings up to 125% of the FMV of the home. To consolidate some of his other debts, Kody takes out a new $42,500 home equity loan [(125% × $110,000) – $95,000]. Kody's home equity loan exceeds the FMV of the home less the balance of his home acquisition debt ($110,000 - $95,000 = $15,000). Therefore, his deductible mortgage interest relating to the home equity loan is limited to the interest on $15,000.

A taxpayer may deduct the interest on home equity debt, subject to the limits described above, no matter how he uses the proceeds.

Example: Jeremy and Ashley obtained two home equity loans totaling $90,000. They used the loans to pay off gambling debts, credit card payments, and medical expenses. The couple can deduct the interest on their home equity loans because the total does not exceed $100,000.

Points: Points are charges a borrower pays to obtain a loan. They generally represent prepaid interest that a borrower pays at closing in order to obtain a lower interest rate. Points may also be called loan origination fees, including VA and FHA fees; maximum loan charges; premium charges; loan discount points; or prepaid interest.

Loan fees paid for specific services, such as home appraisal fees, document preparation fees, VA funding fees, or notary fees, are not interest and are not deductible. In order to deduct points, the following requirements must be met:

- The mortgage must be secured by the taxpayer's main home, and the mortgage must have been used to buy, build, or improve the home.
- The points must not be an excessive or unusual amount for the local area.
- The points paid must not be more than the amount of unborrowed funds.
- The points must be computed as a percentage of the loan principal, and they must be listed on the settlement statement.

If all these requirements are met, the taxpayer can either deduct points in connection with the acquisition or construction of the home either in the year paid or over the life of the loan.

Points paid to refinance a mortgage are generally not fully deductible in the year paid, unless the proceeds are used to improve a main home and the requirements outlined above are met. A second home would not qualify for this exception.

Mortgage Insurance Premiums: A taxpayer can deduct qualified mortgage insurance[18] premiums for coverage related to home acquisition debt that was arranged after 2006. The deduction is phased out for higher income taxpayers.

Form 1098: If a taxpayer paid more than $600 during the year for mortgage interest (including points and mortgage insurance premiums) in connection with any single mortgage, the amounts should be reported to the taxpayer on Form 1098, *Mortgage Interest Statement,* by the financial institution that received the payments.

---

[18] A lender may require mortgage insurance to protect itself in case a borrower defaults. It generally allows the homebuyer to make a smaller down payment than would otherwise be required.

Investment Interest Expense

When a taxpayer borrows money to buy property held for investment, interest he pays on that borrowed money is investment interest expense and may be deductible. The amount of investment interest expense a taxpayer can deduct each year is limited to the amount of net investment income earned. However, he can carry forward any disallowed investment interest expense to the next year.

Example: Mariko borrows money from a bank to buy $3,000 worth of short-term bonds. The bonds mature during the year and Mariko makes $400 of investment interest income. She also has $210 in investment interest expense, which she paid on the loan originally taken out to buy the bonds. Mariko must report the full amount of $400 as investment interest income. She may deduct the $210 in investment interest expense on Schedule A.

Example: Jackson borrows money from a bank in order to buy $10,000 worth of U.S. gold coins. During the year, the coins lose value and he has no investment income. Jackson paid $326 of investment interest expense on the loan he used to buy the coins. He may not take a deduction for the investment interest expense because he has no investment income, but he may carry over to the next tax year the investment interest expense that he could not deduct.

The deductible amount of investment interest expense and any disallowed amount that may be carried over to the following year are calculated on Form 4952, *Investment Interest Expense Deduction.*

A taxpayer cannot deduct interest related to passive activities or incurred to produce tax-exempt income as investment interest expense.

Nondeductible Interest and Investment Expenses: The following expenses cannot be deducted:

- Interest on personal loans, such as car loans
- Fees for credit cards and finance charges for nonbusiness credit card purchases
- Loan fees for services needed to get a loan
- Interest on a debt the taxpayer is not legally obligated to pay
- Service charges
- Interest to purchase or carry tax-exempt securities
- Late payment charges paid to a public utility
- Expenses relating to stockholders' meetings or investment-related seminars
- Interest expenses from single-premium life insurance, endowment, and annuity contracts
- Interest incurred from borrowing against an insurance policy
- Short-sale expenses
- Fines and penalties paid to any government entity for violations of the law

Example: José and Blanca file a joint return. During the year, they paid:

1. $3,180 of home mortgage interest reported to them on Form 1098
2. $400 of credit card interest
3. $1,500 to the home mortgage lender for an appraisal fee
4. $2,000 of interest on a car loan

Only their home mortgage interest ($3,180) is deductible.

Charitable Contributions

Taxpayers who itemize deductions can deduct certain charitable contributions to qualified organizations. Taxpayers may contribute cash, property (such as clothing and furniture), securities, or other assets. A taxpayer can only deduct a contribution in the year it is actually made.

In order to claim deductions for noncash donations, the donated items must be in good condition. In most cases, the taxpayer will be able to claim a deduction for the fair market value of the contribution (generally what someone would be willing to pay at a garage sale or thrift store). No deduction is allowed for items that are in poor or unusable condition.

Deductible contributions may include:

- Unreimbursed expenses that relate directly to the services the taxpayer provided for the organization.
- The amount of a contribution in excess of the fair market value of items received, such as merchandise and tickets to a charity ball or a sporting event.
- Transportation expenses, including bus fare, parking fees, tolls, and either the actual cost of gas and oil or a standard mileage deduction of 14 cents per mile in 2013.

Volunteer Expenses: A taxpayer may not deduct a monetary value for the hours he spends volunteering.

Example: Emily is an attorney who donates time to her local church for its legal needs. In 2013, she spent ten hours drafting documents for the church, which is a qualified organization. She also had $200 of out-of-pocket expenses because she purchased a new printer for the church. The printer was delivered directly to the church rectory for its use. Emily can take a charitable deduction for $200, the amount she spent on behalf of her church. She cannot deduct the value of her time.

A taxpayer may deduct expenses incurred while traveling to perform services for a charitable organization only if there is no significant element of personal pleasure in the travel. However, a deduction will not be denied simply because the taxpayer enjoys providing the services. The taxpayer can take a charitable contribution deduction for the expenses if he is on-duty in a genuine and substantial sense throughout the trip.

Example: Francine regularly volunteers at her local animal shelter. She uses her own car to travel to and from the shelter. She is not reimbursed for mileage. Francine also fosters kittens on behalf of the shelter. She pays for cat food and other supplies out-of-pocket. Francine may deduct her mileage and her unreimbursed expenses as a charitable contribution, but may not deduct the value of her time.

Exchange Students: A taxpayer may deduct some expenses paid for a foreign or American student who is living with him. The student must be sponsored by a qualifying organization, not be related to the taxpayer, and be part of a program to provide educational opportunities.

> **Example:** The Jensen family hosts a high school student from Portugal in their home for nine months during 2013. The student is sponsored by AFS, a qualifying organization. They may deduct up to $50 a month in expenses while the student lives with them.

Nonqualifying Organizations

Not all nonprofit organizations qualify as charitable organizations for purposes of donors being able to claim tax deductions. An organization may qualify for nonprofit status so that its own activities are not subject to income tax, but this designation does not automatically provide qualification for purposes of deductible contributions.

The following are examples of items that do not qualify as deductible charitable contributions:

- Gifts to civic leagues, social and sports clubs, and Chambers of Commerce
- Gifts to groups run for personal profit
- Gifts to political groups, candidates, or political organizations
- Gifts to homeowners' associations
- Donations made directly to individuals
- The cost of raffle, bingo, or lottery tickets, even if the raffle is part of a qualified organization's fundraiser
- Dues paid to country clubs or similar groups
- Gifts and dues to labor unions (although union dues may be deductible on Schedule A as a miscellaneous itemized deduction)
- Blood donated to a blood bank or to the Red Cross
- Any part of a contribution that benefits the taxpayer, such as the FMV of a meal eaten at a charity dinner

> **Example:** Renee paid the Chamber of Commerce a $30 entry fee to run in a 10K race it was sponsoring on behalf of a cancer-related charity. The Chamber is not a qualifying charitable organization, so none of Renee's entry fee is tax deductible as a charitable contribution. If the race had been organized by the charity itself, part of her entry fee may have been deductible.

> **Example:** Bill goes to a church fundraiser that includes a bingo game. Bill spends $200 on bingo cards, but does not win anything. Even though the $200 went to the church, the cost of the bingo game is not considered a charitable gift and is therefore not deductible.

Substantiation Requirements for Charitable Gifts

There are strict recordkeeping requirements for taxpayers who claim deductions for charitable contributions, depending upon the nature and amounts.

Cash Donations of Less than $250: Cash contributions include those paid by cash, check, debit card, credit card, or payroll deduction. If the value of an individual donation is less than $250, the taxpayer must keep a reliable written record such as the following:

- A bank, credit union, or credit card statement that shows the name of the qualified organization, the date of the contribution, and the amount of the contribution.
- A receipt (or a letter or other written communication) from the qualified organization showing its name, the date of the contribution, and the amount of the contribution.
- For payroll deductions, a pay stub or Form W-2, plus a pledge card or other document showing the name of the qualified organization.
- For text donations, a telephone bill, so long as it shows the name of the qualified organization, the date of the contribution, and the amount given.

Example: Gary donates $10 per week to the Humane Society. He always pays by check, and he keeps the canceled check as a record of his contribution. This is a valid method of recordkeeping for donations under $250.

Cash Donations of $250 or More: For cash donations of $250 dollars or more, the taxpayer must have a receipt or written acknowledgement from the organization that includes:

- The amount of cash the taxpayer contributed.
- The date of the contribution.
- Whether the qualified organization gave any goods or services as a result of the contribution (other than certain token items and membership benefits.) The absence of this simple statement by a charity has led to court cases in which major cash contributions have been challenged, and in some cases, disallowed.
- If applicable, a description and a good faith estimate of the value of goods or services provided by the organization as a result of the contribution.

The taxpayer must obtain the receipt on or before:

- The date the taxpayer files his tax return for the year he makes the contribution, or
- The due date, including extensions, for filing the return.

If the donation is via payroll deduction, any amount of $250 or more must be substantiated with a pay stub or W-2, and a statement about whether goods or services were given by the qualified organization.

Noncash Contributions of Less than $250: For each contribution of less than $250, the taxpayer must obtain a receipt from the receiving organization and keep a list of the items donated.

Noncash Donations of $250 to $500: For each contribution of at least $250 but not exceeding $500, the taxpayer must have the same documentation as described above for noncash contributions less than $250. In addition, the organization's written acknowledgement must state whether the taxpayer received any goods or services in return and include a description and a good faith estimate of the fair market value of any such items.

Noncash Donations Over $500: If a taxpayer's total deduction for all noncash contributions for the year is more than $500, he must also file Form 8283**,** *Noncash Charitable Contributions.*

Noncash Donations Over $5,000: If any single donation or a group of similar items is valued at over $5,000, a qualified appraiser is required to make a written appraisal of the donated property. The taxpayer must also complete Form 8283, Section B, and attach it to his tax return. He generally does not have to attach the appraisal itself, but must retain a copy for his records. For donations of artwork valued at over $20,000 or property valued at over $500,000, the appraisal itself must be included with the tax return.

Donated Motor Vehicles, Boats, and Airplanes: Special rules apply to any donation of vehicles, including boats and airplanes. If the taxpayer claims a deduction of more than $500, he can only deduct the smaller of:

- The gross proceeds from the sale of the item by the charity, or
- The fair market value on the date of the contribution.

The charitable organization should provide Form 1098-C, *Contributions of Motor Vehicles, Boats, and Airplanes,* which shows the gross proceeds from the sale of the vehicle donated. If the taxpayer does not attach Form 1098-C, the maximum deduction that can be taken for the donation is $500. Vehicles that are not in working condition may have zero donation value.

Example: Kevin donates his used motorcycle to his church fundraiser. The FMV of the motorcycle is $2,500. The church sells the motorcycle 60 days later for $1,700 and sends Kevin a Form 1098-C. He may deduct only $1,700 on his Schedule A (the smaller of the FMV or the gross proceeds from the sale), and must attach a copy of the Form 1098-C to his tax return.

Two exceptions apply to the rules regarding vehicle donations:

- If the charity keeps the vehicle for its own use, the taxpayer can generally deduct the vehicle's FMV.
- If the charity gives or sells the vehicle directly to a needy person, the taxpayer can generally deduct the vehicle's FMV.

Limits on Deductible Contributions: A taxpayer may not deduct aggregate charitable contributions that exceed 50% of his adjusted gross income. For example, if a taxpayer had $100,000 of adjusted gross income in 2013, the maximum charitable contributions he could deduct would be $50,000 (50% of AGI). Any amounts disallowed as a result of this limit could be carried forward to future years.

The **50% contribution limit** applies to contributions made to churches; hospitals; most schools; state or federal government units; and corporations, trusts, or foundations organized solely for charitable, religious, educational, scientific, or literary purposes or for the prevention of cruelty to children or animals. Certain organizations that foster national or international amateur sports competition also qualify.

A taxpayer's deductible contributions to certain other types of nonprofit organizations are limited to either 30% or 20% of his AGI.

The **30% limit** applies to organizations that include the following:

- Veterans organizations
- Fraternal societies (such as the Knights of Columbus or Elks)
- Nonprofit cemeteries

In addition, a **separate 30% limit** applies in the following cases:

- Gifts for use by the charitable organization (such as the donation of a refrigerator that the organization uses for itself)
- Gifts of appreciated property (also called capital gain property)

The **20% limit** applies to contributions of capital gain property to organizations subject to the 30% limit.

Example: Howard's adjusted gross income is $50,000. During the year, he gave appreciated stocks with an FMV of $15,000 to his church, which is a 50% limit organization. Howard also gave $10,000 cash to a veteran's organization. The $10,000 gift is subject to the 30% limit based on the nature of the organization. The $15,000 gift of appreciated property is subject to the separate 30% limit. However, both gifts are fully deductible by Howard because neither is more than the 30% limit that applies ($15,000 in each case), and together they are not more than the 50% limit of Howard's AGI ($50,000 × 50% = $25,000).

Charitable Contribution Carryovers: To the extent a taxpayer's deductions for contributions are limited, they may be carried over to subsequent years. However, the carryover period is generally limited to five years. Any carryover amounts that cannot be deducted within five years due to the AGI limits are lost.

Any contributions made by the taxpayer and carried over to future years retain their original character. For example, contributions made to a 30% organization continue to be subject to the 30% -of-AGI limit.

Unit 12: Study Questions

1. Which of the following taxes can taxpayers deduct on Schedule A?

A. Federal income tax.
B. Real estate tax.
C. Taxes on alcohol and tobacco.
D. Foreign sales taxes.

2. Angie and Sheldon, both age 41, file a joint return and claim their two children as dependents. They have adjusted gross income of $68,400. Last year the family accumulated $6,620 of unreimbursed medical and dental expenses that included the following:

- Prescription eyeglasses for Angie: $320
- Prescription contacts for Sheldon: $1,000
- Sheldon's smoking-cessation program: $5,300

The total of Sheldon and Angie's deductible medical expenses is _____.

A. $6,620.
B. $6,300.
C. $5,620.
D. $0.

3. Max and Wendy are both 30 years old and file jointly for 2013. They decide not to itemize their deductions. Max is legally blind. What is their standard deduction amount in 2013?

A. $8,950.
B. $12,200.
C. $13,400.
D. $13,700.

4. All of the following home improvements may be itemized and deducted as medical expenses except __________:

A. The cost of installing porch lifts and other forms of lifts.
B. The cost of lowering cabinets to accommodate a disability.
C. The cost of making doorways wider to accommodate a wheelchair.
D. An elevator that costs $4,000 and adds $5,000 to the FMV of the home.

5. Which of the following taxpayers must either itemize deductions or claim zero as their deduction?

A. Mindy, who files a joint return with her husband.
B. Leslie, who claims two dependents and files Form 1040.
C. Pearl, whose itemized deductions are more than the standard deduction.
D. Gabe, whose wife files a separate return and itemizes her deductions.

6. All of the following are deductible medical expenses except _____.

A. Transportation for medical care.
B. Nursing home care.
C. Smoking-cessation programs.
D. Nonprescription nicotine gum and patches.

7. All of the following factors determine the amount of a taxpayer's standard deduction except _____.

A. The taxpayer's filing status.
B. The taxpayer's adjusted gross income.
C. Whether the taxpayer is 65 or older, or blind.
D. Whether the taxpayer can be claimed as a dependent.

8. Which of the following are not included in the Pease limitation that reduces the amount of total itemized deductions for certain higher income taxpayers?

A. Gambling losses, investment interest expense, and medical expenses.
B. Charitable contributions, employee business expenses, and medical expenses.
C. Charitable contributions, theft losses, and the mortgage interest deduction.
D. Miscellaneous itemized deductions, casualty losses, and real estate taxes.

9. Which of the following taxes can taxpayers deduct on Schedule A?

A. Local sales taxes.
B. Fines for speeding.
C. Social Security taxes.
D. Homeowners' association fees.

10. Which of the following taxpayers is required to itemize deductions?

A. Sophie, who has one dependent child.
B. Andrea, who wants to deduct the alimony she paid to her ex-husband.
C. Gabrielle, whose itemized deductions are more than the standard deduction.
D. Samir, who is a nonresident alien.

11. Justin, age 37, had the following medical expenses in 2013:

- $450 for contact lenses
- $800 for eyeglasses
- $9,000 for treatment of a broken leg, of which $8,000 was paid for by his insurance
- $200 for prescription drugs
- $1,900 for a doctor-prescribed back brace
- $200 for child care while in the hospital

What is his medical expense deduction before limitation based on the 10%-of-AGI threshold?

A. $1,900.
B. $4,350.
C. $4,550.
D. $12,350.

12. Dora, age 72, paid medical expenses of $3,500. Her AGI is $40,000. Taking into account the AGI limit, how much can Dora deduct on her Schedule A?

A. $0.
B. $500.
C. $2,313.
D. $2,500.

13. For a tax to be deductible, all of the following must be true except ________.

A. The tax must be imposed during the tax year.
B. The taxpayer must be legally liable for the tax.
C. The tax must be paid during the tax year.
D. The tax must be paid by the taxpayer.

14. Which of the following is a correct statement about the medical expense deduction in 2013?

A. James, age 64, married Sara, age 65, in 2013. His deductible medical expenses are reduced by 10% of his AGI.
B. Edita is age 65, single, and blind. Her deductible medical expenses are reduced by 7.5% of her AGI. She will also receive an additional standard deduction of $1,500 for blindness, even if she itemizes deductions.
C. Alvin is age 28 and disabled. His deductible medical expenses are reduced by 7.5% of his AGI.
D. Kiara is age 64 and disabled. Her deductible medical expenses are reduced by 10% of her AGI.

15. Iris is single and has the following income and expenses:

- Wages: $70,000
- Net investment interest income: $3,000
- Mortgage interest: $24,000
- Investment interest expense: $5,000
- Personal credit card interest: $3,400
- Car loan interest: $1,200
- Late fees on her mortgage: $50

What is Iris's total allowable deduction for interest expense on her Schedule A?

A. $24,000.
B. $27,000.
C. $27,050.
D. $32,400.

16. Christopher and Ariel file a joint return. During the year, they paid:

- $5,000 in home mortgage interest
- $600 in credit card interest
- $4,000 in auto loan interest
- $3,000 in loan interest on an empty lot that was purchased to build a second home

How much can they report as deductible mortgage interest?

A. $0.
B. $5,000.
C. $8,000.
D. $8,600.

17. Which of the following taxes is not deductible on Schedule A?

A. Property taxes paid on a vacation home.
B. Special assessments to improve the sidewalks.
C. Property taxes based on a vehicle's value.
D. Property taxes paid on a home in Mexico.

18. Amelia donates $430 in cash to her church. Which of the following is required on the receipt to substantiate the donation correctly for IRS recordkeeping requirements?

A. The reason for the contribution.
B. Amelia's home address.
C. The amount of the donation.
D. Amelia's method of payment.

19. Nirali is single. Her AGI is $315,000 in 2013 and she has $85,000 of allowable deductions for charitable contributions, state income tax, real estate taxes, and mortgage interest. The threshold for the Pease limitation is $250,000 for single taxpayers. What is the total amount she may deduct on her Schedule A?

A. $52,000.
B. $75,500.
C. $83,050.
D. $85,000.

20. Martin contributes to many organizations. In 2013, he donates $5,000 in cash to his church and $4,000 to his local Chamber of Commerce. He also contributes land with a fair market value of $16,000 to his church. Martin has a basis of $5,000 in the land. His AGI for the year is $45,000. What is the maximum amount he can deduct for charitable contributions?

A. $9,000.
B. $18,500.
C. $22,500.
D. $25,000.

21. Harvey refinanced his home and paid closing costs in 2013. He used the proceeds from the refinance to put on a new roof on his vacation cottage and to pay off his credit cards. He paid the following fees:

- $400 Loan origination fee (points)
- $500 Home appraisal fee
- $45 Document prep fee
- $60 Loan closing fee
- $70 Title insurance

How much of the fees Harvey paid to the bank for the loan is deductible in 2013?

A. $0.
B. $400.
C. $900.
D. $945.

22. Lindy donates her used car to a qualified charity. She bought it three years ago for $15,000. A used car guide shows the FMV for this type of car is $5,000. Lindy's friend, Buck, offered her $4,500 for the car a week ago. Lindy receives a Form 1098-C from the organization showing the car was sold for $1,900. How much is Lindy's charitable deduction?

A. $15,000.
B. $5,000.
C. $4,500.
D. $1,900.

23. Nathaniel owns a home and also owns a cabin in the mountains. The cabin sat empty all year. Which of the following statements is true?

A. Only the mortgage interest and property tax on his main home is deductible.
B. The interest and property tax on both his main home and the cabin are deductible.
C. The mortgage interest on both homes is deductible, but the property tax on the cabin is not.
D. The mortgage interest and property tax on his main home is deductible, and the property tax on the cabin is deductible. Mortgage interest on the cabin is not deductible.

24. Sam donated to all of the following nonprofit organizations in 2013. What is his total qualified deduction?

Amount	**Organization**
$100	Methodist church
$120	County animal shelter
$75	Salvation Army
$25	American Red Cross
$50	Political party
$300	Chamber of Commerce
$670	**Total Contributions**

A. $320.
B. $370.
C. $220.
D. $670.

25. All of the following statements regarding home equity debt are correct except:

A. There is a $150,000 limit on the amount of debt that can be treated as home equity debt for purposes of the mortgage interest deduction.
B. The taxpayer does not have to use the home equity loan on improvements to the home for it to be eligible as deductible interest.
C. The debt must not exceed the property's fair market value.
D. Both B and C.

26. When is an appraisal required for a charitable donation?

A. For any noncash contribution valued at more than $1,000.
B. For any noncash contribution valued at more than $5,000.
C. For any noncash contribution valued at more than $10,000.
D. For any vehicle donation.

27. In 2013 Henry, age 65, experienced numerous health problems. As a result, Henry and his wife Marie, age 59, incurred the following medical expenses:

Physician and hospital fees	$10,000
Dental and orthodontic fees	$5,000
Medical and dental insurance premiums	$12,000
Eyeglasses and contact lenses	$1,000
Health club dues	$1,000
Prescription medications	$3,000
Nonprescription drugs and medicines	$1,000

They also drove 3,000 miles in connection with medical visits, and incurred parking and toll charges of $100. The insurance premiums were paid through Henry's employer-sponsored health insurance plan and were not reported as income in box 1 of his Form W-2. Henry and Marie had adjusted gross income of $100,000 in 2013. What is the amount of their medical expense deduction for the year on Schedule A?

A. $9,820.
B. $19,820.
C. $12,320.
D. $33,820.

28. Oscar donated a leather coat to a thrift store operated by his church. He paid $450 for the coat three years ago. Similar coats in the thrift store sell for $50. What is Oscar's charitable deduction?

A. $0.
B. $50.
C. $400.
D. $450.

29. Carroll, age 64, and his wife, Ellen, age 66, file jointly. Which of the following is true regarding their qualified medical expenses, if they itemize deductions?

A. They may deduct 7.5% of their qualified medical expenses, if they itemize their deductions.
B. They may deduct 10% of their qualified medical expenses, if they itemize deductions.
C. They may deduct only the amount by which their total medical expenses for the year exceed 7.5% of adjusted gross income.
D. They may deduct only the amount by which their total medical expenses for the year exceed 10% of adjusted gross income.

30. Julio spent the entire day attending his human rights organization's regional meeting as a delegate. He spent $50 on travel to the meeting and $25 on materials for the meeting. In the evening, Julio went to the theater with two other meeting attendees. He spent $50 on movie tickets. The charity did not reimburse Julio for any of his costs. How much can Julio deduct as a charitable expense?

A. $25.
B. $50.
C. $75.
D. $125.

31. All of the following statements about itemized deductions are true except:

A. A married couple who file jointly will always owe less tax by itemizing deductions rather than by taking the standard deduction.
B. The Pease limitation on itemized deductions affects single taxpayers with adjusted gross income of $250,000 or more.
C. Taxpayers are allowed to deduct either state and local sales taxes or state and local income taxes, but not both.
D. A taxpayer may not deduct mortgage interest on more than two homes.

32. Vera and Jack are married and file jointly. They contributed $15,000 in cash to their synagogue during 2013. They also donated $3,000 to a private foundation that is a nonprofit cemetery organization to which a 30% contribution limit applies. Their adjusted gross income for 2013 was $30,000. Vera and Jack's deductible contributions for 2013 and carryover to the next year are:

A. $18,000 with zero carryover to next year.
B. $15,000 with $2,100 carryover to next year.
C. $7,500 with $2,100 carryover to next year.
D. $15,000 with $3,000 carryover to next year.

Unit 13: Other Itemized Deductions

For additional information read:
Publication 587, *Business Use of Your Home*
Publication 547, *Casualties, Disasters, and Thefts*
Publication 529, *Miscellaneous Deductions*

In addition to the deductions described in Unit 12, taxpayers may be able to claim the following:

- Casualty or theft losses
- Miscellaneous expenses subject to a 2%-of-AGI limit
- Miscellaneous expenses not subject to the 2%-of-AGI limit

Casualty and Theft Losses

A casualty is the damage, destruction, or loss of property resulting from an identifiable event that is sudden, unexpected, or unusual. Examples include a car accident, fire, earthquake, flood, theft, act of vandalism, or act of terrorism.

Losses that do not meet this definition and are thus not deductible include:

- Damage done by pets
- Progressive deterioration, such as the following:
    - Termite or moth damage
    - Damage or destruction of trees and plants by a fungus, disease, or pests
    - Loss of property caused by drought
    - Damage to a water heater that bursts
    - Steady weakening of a building due to wind and weather conditions
- A car accident if the taxpayer's willful act or negligence caused it
- Arson if committed by or on behalf of the taxpayer
- Accidental breakage of china, dishes, or other items during regular use
- Losses in real estate value from market fluctuations
- Lost property, unless it is the result of a sudden, unexpected, and unusual event

Example: A car door accidentally slams on Julia's hand, breaking the setting of her diamond ring. The diamond falls from the ring and is never found. The loss is deductible as a casualty because it is the result of an identifiable event that is sudden, unexpected, or unusual.

In order to deduct a casualty or theft loss, the taxpayer must be able to prove:

- The type of casualty loss (car accident, fire, storm, etc.) and the date of occurrence
- That the taxpayer was the legal owner of the property, or at least legally liable for the damage (such as leased property when the lessee is responsible for damage)
- Whether the loss was subject to any insurance reimbursement

Example: Gregory rents a car from Reliable Rentals. He declines insurance coverage and signs a contract stating he will be responsible for any damage. The rental car is stolen, and Gregory must reimburse Reliable Rentals. His car insurance does not have rental car coverage, so he is liable for the full amount. Gregory may deduct the loss as a casualty loss, subject to the applicable rules.

Casualty losses are deductible only for actual damage to a property. Payments for the cost of cleaning up or making repairs are not part of a casualty loss itself, but generally may be used as a measure in determining a decrease in the FMV of a property.

When calculating a decrease in the FMV of a property, a taxpayer may not consider the following:

- The actual replacement cost of stolen or destroyed property
- An item's sentimental value
- Related expenses such as the cost of temporary housing or a rental car
- A decline in market value of property near a casualty area

Example: Don purchased an antique vase at a garage sale for $600. Later, he discovered the vase was a rare collectible and its FMV was $20,000. The vase was stolen two months later. His casualty loss is limited to the $600 he paid for it, which is his basis in the property. Don cannot claim a casualty loss deduction for $20,000, the value of the item.

Example: Nicole purchased a condo for $200,000. Two months later, a hurricane destroyed five properties on her block. An appraisal showed that properties within a five-mile radius had declined 15% in fair market value because people were afraid to purchase homes in "hurricane territory." The reduction in the home's FMV is not a deductible casualty loss.

Casualty losses are subject to the "single event rule." This means that events closely related in origin are considered a single event. For example, it is a single casualty when the damage comes from two or more closely related causes, such as wind and flood damage from the same storm. A single casualty may also damage two or more pieces of property, such as a hailstorm that damages both a taxpayer's home and his car parked in the driveway.

Reporting a Casualty Loss or Gain: A taxpayer must complete Form 4684, *Casualties and Thefts*, to report a gain or loss resulting from a casualty or theft. The net deductible amount can be claimed by an individual taxpayer only if he itemizes deductions. A loss on personal use (nonbusiness) property is subject to certain limits described below. It is calculated on Part A of Form 4684 and reported on line 20 of Schedule A.

A loss on property used in a trade or business or for income producing purposes is calculated on Part B of Form 4684 and reported as a miscellaneous deduction either on line 23 of Schedule A (subject to the 2%-of-AGI threshold) if the property was used performing services as an employee or on line 28 of Schedule A (and not subject to the 2% threshold).

If an insurance reimbursement for a casualty loss exceeds the taxpayer's basis in the property, he will have a gain that may need to be reported. However, reporting the gain on damaged, destroyed, or stolen property can be postponed if the insurance reimbursement is spent to restore the property or to purchase similar property within a specified period of time.

Example: Forty years ago, Al bought a vacation cottage for $18,000. A storm destroyed the cottage, now valued at $250,000. Al received $146,000 from his insurance company. He had a gain of $128,000 ($146,000 – $18,000 basis). Al spent the full $146,000 to rebuild his cottage. Since he used the insurance proceeds to rebuild his cottage, he can postpone reporting or recognizing the gain until the cottage is sold.

The replacement period begins on the date the property was damaged, destroyed, or stolen, and ends two years after the close of the first tax year in which any part of the gain is realized.

For a main home or its contents located in a federally declared disaster area, the replacement period is generally four years rather than two. For disaster area losses, taxpayers may choose to deduct the loss on the previous year's tax return, rather than in the year the disaster loss occurred. This may result in a lower tax for that year, often producing or increasing a cash refund.

Nonbusiness Casualty Loss Limits

A taxpayer can deduct casualty and theft losses related to personal-use property only to the extent they exceed two separate limits:

$100 Rule: First, each separate casualty or theft loss is deductible only to the extent that it exceeds $100. It does not matter how many pieces of property are damaged, destroyed, or stolen in a single event; the taxpayer has to reduce his total loss for each event by $100.

Example: A fire damaged Dick's house in January, causing $3,000 in damage. In September, a storm damaged his house again, causing $5,000 in damage. Dick must reduce each loss by $100.

10% Rule: Second, a taxpayer may deduct the total of all casualty or theft losses during the year (after the reduction of each one by $100) only to the extent the total is more than 10% of his AGI. This rule does not apply to a net disaster loss within a federally declared disaster area.

However, married couples filing jointly who have a loss from the same event are treated as if they were one person; the $100 limit is applied only once to each shared loss event and the 10% limit is applied to their joint AGI to determine deductibility of their aggregate losses.

For losses on personal-use property, this is how the taxpayer determines his deduction:

1. Calculate the *lesser* of the FMV or adjusted basis of the item prior to the loss.
2. Subtract any payments/reimbursements from insurance.
3. Subtract $100 for each event.
4. Subtract 10% of the taxpayer's AGI.

Example: Raquel bought a new leather sofa four years ago for $3,000. In April, a fire destroyed the sofa. Raquel estimates that it would now cost $5,000 to replace it. However, if she had sold the sofa before the fire, she probably would have received only $1,900 because the sofa was already four years old. Raquel's casualty loss is $1,900 (the FMV of the sofa before the fire), subject to the $100 and 10% rules. Her loss is not $3,000 (her basis) and it is not $5,000 (the replacement cost). Raquel's AGI for 2013 was $15,000, so her deductible loss is $300. This is the amount by which $1,800 (the loss of $1,900 less $100) exceeds 10% of her AGI.

Insurance Reimbursements: Taxpayers can deduct qualified casualty and theft losses to their homes, household items, and vehicles. However, if the property is covered by insurance, a taxpayer may not deduct a loss unless he files a claim for reimbursement. If the taxpayer decides not to file an insurance claim but has a deductible, he may claim the amount of the insurance deductible as his loss, since that amount would not have been covered by the policy anyway.

Example: A small fire causes $8,000 in damage to Maria's home. She does not want her homeowner's insurance premium to go up, so she declines to file a claim and pays to repair the damage out-of-pocket. Maria cannot deduct the full amount of the loss because she did not file an insurance claim. However, she may deduct the amount of her insurance deductible, subject to the $100 and 10%-of-AGI limitations.

A taxpayer does not have to reduce his casualty loss by insurance payments received to cover living expenses in the following situations:

- When a taxpayer loses use of his main home because of a casualty.
- When government authorities do not allow a taxpayer access to his main home because of a casualty or a threat of one.

If the insurance payments are more than the temporary increase in his living expenses, a taxpayer must generally include the excess in his income. However, if the casualty occurs in a federally declared disaster area, the excess insurance payments are not taxable. The taxable part of the insurance payment should be included in income for the year the taxpayer gains use of his main home, or in a later year when the taxable part of the insurance payment is received.

Example: A tornado damages Olivia's main home in August 2011. After repairs were made, she moved back into her home in November 2012. She received insurance payments in 2011 and 2012 that were $1,500 more than the temporary increase in her living expenses. Olivia includes this amount in income on her 2012 Form 1040. In 2013, she receives another $500 to cover her living expenses in 2011 and 2012. She must include that payment on her 2013 tax return.

Theft Losses: A theft loss may be deducted in the year the theft is discovered, regardless of when it actually occurred. The taking of property must be illegal under the law of the state where it occurred, and it must have been done with criminal intent. Qualifying theft losses include those resulting from blackmail, burglary, embezzlement, extortion, kidnapping for ransom, larceny, robbery, and mail fraud. A taxpayer is not required to show that someone was convicted for theft.

If a taxpayer takes a deduction for stolen property and authorities later recover the property, he must report the recovery as income in the year the property is recovered, but only to the extent of the amount that actually reduced his tax in an earlier year.

Insurance Cost: The cost of insurance or other protection is not deductible as a casualty loss, but it is deductible as a business expense by business taxpayers.

Example: Jordan pays for renter's insurance to cover the furniture and appliances in his home from theft or other disaster losses. Jordan may not deduct the cost of the renter's insurance as a casualty loss.

Miscellaneous Expenses Subject to the 2% Limit

Certain miscellaneous expenses, including unreimbursed employee expenses, are deductible on Schedule A to the extent they exceed 2% of a taxpayer's AGI.

Example: Andy's AGI is $45,000, and he has $1,100 in miscellaneous deductible work-related expenses. He must first determine the 2%-of-AGI limit (2% × $45,000 = $900). He can therefore deduct only $200 of those expenses ($1,100 - $900 = $200).

Unreimbursed Employee Business Expenses

An employee may deduct certain work-related expenses as itemized deductions. These expenses are first reported on Form 2106, *Employee Business Expenses*, and the amount is transferred to Line 21 on Schedule A. The taxpayer can deduct only unreimbursed employee expenses that are:

- Paid or incurred during the tax year,
- For carrying on the business of being an employee, and
- Ordinary and necessary.

An expense does not have to be required to be deductible. However, it must be a common expense that would be accepted in the taxpayer's trade or profession.

The following are examples of unreimbursed employee expenses that may be deductible:

- Business bad debts of an employee
- Business liability insurance premiums
- Malpractice insurance
- Depreciation on an asset the employer requires for work
- Dues to professional societies or to a chamber of commerce
- Subscriptions to professional journals
- Expenses of looking for a new job in the taxpayer's present occupation
- Licenses and regulatory fees
- Union dues
- Work clothes and uniforms (if required and not suitable for everyday use)
- Tools and supplies used for work
- Passport for a business trip
- Work-related education
- Travel, transportation, meals, and lodging related to the taxpayer's work

Meals and Entertainment Expenses: An employee may deduct unreimbursed business-related meals and entertainment expenses he incurred for entertaining a client, customer, or another employee. The deduction for business meals and entertainment is generally limited to 50% of the unreimbursed cost. The taxpayer must apply the 50% limit before including the expenses on Schedule A (and applying the 2%-of-AGI limit).

The taxpayer can deduct meals and entertainment expenses only if they meet the following tests:

- The main purpose of the meal or entertainment was the active conduct of business,
- The taxpayer conducted business during the entertainment period, and
- The taxpayer had more than a general expectation of some other specific business benefit at a future time.

Employee Travel Expenses: A taxpayer may not deduct commuting expenses, which are expenses incurred when an employee travels from his home to his main workplace. However, there are numerous instances where an employee may deduct mileage or other travel expenses relating to his employment. Deductible employee travel expenses may include those related to:

- Going from one work location to another in the course of business
- Visiting clients or customers
- Going to a business meeting away from the regular workplace
- Traveling from a first job to a second job in the same day
- Going from the taxpayer's home to a temporary workplace

Any amounts reimbursed by an employer are not deductible by the employee.

Tax Home and Work Location: A taxpayer's tax home is his principal place of work, regardless of where he actually lives. A taxpayer's tax home is used to determine if travel expenses are deductible.

Travel and meal expenses are considered deductible if the taxpayer is traveling away from his tax home, which is determined based on the following two factors:

- The travel is away from the general area or vicinity of the taxpayer's tax home.
- The trip is long enough or far enough away that a taxpayer cannot reasonably be expected to complete the roundtrip without sleep or rest.

Example: Seville is a truck driver who lives in Tucson, Arizona with his family. He is employed by a trucking firm that has its main terminal in Phoenix. At the end of his long trucking runs, Seville returns to the terminal in Phoenix and spends one night there before returning home. Seville cannot deduct any expenses he has for meals and lodging in Phoenix or the cost of traveling from Phoenix to Tucson. This is because Phoenix is Seville's tax home.

When a taxpayer is traveling away from his tax home, he can deduct ordinary and necessary expenses incurred while traveling on business, such as:

- The cost of getting to a business destination (air, rail, bus, car, ferry, etc.)
- Meals and lodging while away from home (the deduction for business meals is generally limited to 50% of the unreimbursed cost)
- Taxi fares
- Dry cleaning and laundry
- Use of a car while at the business location
- Computer rental fees
- Baggage charges, including shipping samples and display materials to the destination
- Tips on eligible expenses

Special Department of Transportation Rules: Certain taxpayers subject to the Department of Transportation's "hours of service" limits may deduct 80% of meal expenses while traveling away from their tax home. These workers include the following:

- Certain air transportation workers such as pilots, crew, and mechanics regulated by the Federal Aviation Administration
- Interstate truck operators and bus drivers regulated by the Department of Transportation
- Certain railroad employees such as engineers and conductors regulated by the Federal Railroad Administration
- Certain merchant mariners regulated by the Coast Guard

Temporary Work Assignments: There are special rules for temporary work assignments that are expected to last for one year or less. When a taxpayer is working away from his main place of business and the job assignment is temporary, his tax home does not change. The taxpayer can deduct his travel expenses because the job assignment is of a temporary nature, and therefore, the travel is considered business-related.

However, travel expenses paid in connection with an indefinite work assignment are not deductible. Any work assignment longer than one year is considered indefinite. A taxpayer cannot deduct travel expenses at a work location if it is realistically expected that he will work there for more than one year.

Example: Terry is a construction worker who lives and works primarily in Los Angeles. Because of a shortage of jobs, he agrees to work at a construction site in Fresno for ten months. Since the job lasts less than one year, the Fresno job is considered temporary and Terry's tax home is still in Los Angeles. Therefore, his travel expenses, including meals and lodging, are deductible while traveling between his temporary place of work and his tax home in Los Angeles.

Special Rule for Military Members: Members of the armed forces on a permanent duty assignment overseas are not considered to be traveling away from home. Therefore, they cannot deduct their travel expenses for meals and lodging while on permanent duty assignment.

Convention Travel

A taxpayer may deduct the cost of travel and attendance to conventions in the U.S. or the "North American area," including Canada and Mexico.[19] For cruises, there is a $2,000 annual cap on deductions or $4,000 if both spouses went on qualifying cruise ship conventions and they are filing jointly. The IRS imposes strict substantiation requirements on taxpayers who claim this deduction. A deduction is not allowed for conventions focused exclusively on investments or financial planning.

Home Office

If a taxpayer uses a portion of his home regularly and exclusively for business purposes, he may be able to deduct a portion of the operating expenses and depreciation of the home. In order to qualify as a home office, the space must be used exclusively and regularly:

---

[19] The IRS maintains a list of these countries, many of which are tourist destinations and not normally associated with the "North American area." Examples include Aruba, Jamaica, Costa Rica, Barbados, Bermuda, Panama, the Marshall Islands, and the Netherlands Antilles (Revenue Ruling 2011-26).

- As the taxpayer's principal place of business, or
- As a place to meet with patients or clients in the normal course of business, or
- In the case of a separate structure not attached to the home, in connection with the trade or business.

The regular and exclusive use must be for the convenience of the employer, and not just helpful to the employee's job.

The home office deduction is calculated based on the percentage of the home that is used for business. A taxpayer can use any reasonable method to compute business percentage, but the most common methods are to:

- Divide the square footage of the home used for business by the total square footage of the home, or
- Divide the number of rooms used for business by the total number of rooms in the home (if all rooms in the home are about the same size.)

Taxpayers may not deduct expenses for any portion of the year during which there was no business use of the home.

Example: Lillian is a part-time medical transcriptionist with a qualified home office. The entire square footage of her home is 1,200 square feet. Her home office is 240 square feet, so her home office percentage is 20% (240 ÷ 1,200) of the total area of her home. Her business percentage is 20%.

Simplified Option: Starting in 2013, the IRS has developed a new simplified option for taxpayers who claim the home office deduction. The criteria for who qualifies remain the same, but the calculation and recordkeeping requirements have been simplified.

Highlights include:

- A deduction of $5 per square foot for the space in the home that is used for business, with a maximum allowable square footage of 300 square feet (for a maximum deduction of $1,500)
- No depreciation deduction or recapture of depreciation upon sale of the home
- Home-related itemized deductions, such as for mortgage interest and real estate taxes, may be claimed in full on Schedule A, without allocation of portions to the home office space

Each year, a taxpayer must choose whether to elect the simplified method or the regular method for calculating the home office deduction. If he chooses the regular method after having used the simplified method, depreciation is calculated using an optional depreciation table for the property.

Job Search Expenses

A taxpayer may deduct job search expenses if the expenses relate to the same occupation. Expenses can be deducted even if the taxpayer does not find a new job.

If the job search qualifies, the taxpayer can deduct the costs of using an employment agency or career counselor, of traveling to interviews, and of printing and mailing resumes.

The following expenses are not deductible:

- Job search expenses for a new occupation
- Living expenses incurred during a period of unemployment between the end of a job and the next period of employment
- Job search expenses incurred by a taxpayer looking for a job for the first time

Job-Related Education

The cost of courses designed to maintain or improve the skills needed for a taxpayer's present job (or required by his employer or the law) is deductible as an employee business expense. The education must meet at least one of the following tests:

- The education must maintain or improve skills required for the taxpayer's current line of work.
- The education must be required by law or by the taxpayer's employer as a condition of his employment.

If a taxpayer has a regular job and enrolls in work-related education courses on a temporary basis, he can also deduct the round-trip costs of transportation between his home and school. This is true regardless of the location of the school, the distance traveled, or whether the taxpayer attends school on non-work days.

In some cases, a taxpayer may be able to take an education credit for his education expenses, and may choose between the credit and the miscellaneous itemized deduction, depending upon which produces a lower tax.

Note: A taxpayer cannot deduct the cost of travel that in itself constitutes a form of education. For example, an individual who works as a Chinese-English interpreter cannot deduct the costs of a personal vacation to China, simply because it might benefit his language skills.

Uniforms

The cost of uniforms and other special work clothes required by an employer can be deducted as a work-related expense. The uniforms must not be suitable for everyday use. The taxpayer may also deduct the cost of upkeep, including laundry and dry cleaning bills.

Examples of employees who may deduct the cost of their uniforms include delivery workers, firefighters, health care workers, law enforcement officers, letter carriers, professional athletes, and transportation workers. Musicians and entertainers can deduct the cost of theatrical clothing and accessories that are not suitable for everyday wear. An employee can also deduct the cost of protective clothing, such as safety shoes or boots, safety glasses, hard hats, and work gloves.

Full-time active-duty military personnel cannot deduct the cost of their uniforms. However, they may be able to deduct the cost of insignia, shoulder boards, and related items.

Gifts to Clients

A taxpayer may deduct no more than $25 for business gifts he gives to a single client or customer during the tax year. A gift to a member of the customer's family is generally considered a gift to the customer himself. If both a taxpayer and his spouse give gifts, they are treated as one taxpayer, even if they have separate businesses. Incidental costs such as packaging and shipping expenses are generally not included in determining the cost of a gift for purposes of the $25 limit.

Example: Noelle tutors students to prepare them for their SAT exams. She gives eight students dictionaries in December to thank them for their business. Each gift is worth $29. Noelle may deduct $200 on her tax return ($25 × 8 = $200.)

Investment Expenses

Investment expenses directly connected with the production of investment income are allowed as a deduction. Examples include investment counseling fees and the rental of a safe deposit box to keep investment documents.

Hobby Expenses

As described in Unit 10, an activity is considered a hobby rather than a business when it is not carried on to make a profit. Expenses related to a hobby are deductible, but only up to the amount of hobby income.

Example: In 2013, Kathryn earned $2,000 from selling her quilts at craft shows and had $5,000 in expenses. She would be able to claim $2,000 of these expenses, the amount equal to her hobby income. However, her deduction is further limited to the amount by which this item and any other applicable miscellaneous deductions exceed 2% of her AGI. Kathryn's AGI was $40,000 in 2013, and she had no other miscellaneous itemized deductions to report. Therefore, her deductible hobby expenses are limited to $1,200 ($2,000 - $800 (2% × $40,000 AGI)).

Legal Fees

Most legal expenses are not deductible by individual taxpayers because they are considered personal expenses. But some legal expenses are deductible if they are incurred when a taxpayer is attempting to produce or collect taxable income, such as legal advice related to collecting alimony or earning investments.

To be deductible, tax advice fees must be separately stated on an attorney's bill. A taxpayer can deduct fees for legal advice on federal, state, and local taxes of all types, including income, estate, gift, and property taxes, even if the advice is related to a divorce.

Example: The lawyer handling Ben's divorce consults another law firm, which handles only tax matters, to obtain information on how the divorce will affect his taxes. Since Ben consulted with the second law firm specifically to discuss tax issues, he can deduct the part of the fee paid to the second firm and separately stated on his bill as an itemized deduction, subject to the 2% limit.

Example: Jenna pays an attorney $4,500 for handling her divorce. This fee is not deductible. She pays an additional $1,500 fee for services in collecting alimony that her former husband refuses to pay. Jenna can deduct the fee for collecting alimony ($1,500), subject to the 2% limit, if it is separately stated on the attorney's bill.

Tax Preparation Fees

A taxpayer may generally deduct tax preparation fees in the year he pays them. For example, on his 2013 tax return, a taxpayer may deduct fees paid in 2013 for preparing his 2012 return. The fees include the cost of tax preparation software and tax publications and any fee the taxpayer paid for electronic filing of his return. A taxpayer may also deduct fees paid to appraisers, actuaries, and accountants for services in determining the correct tax.

Miscellaneous Deductions Not Subject to the 2% Limit

There are some miscellaneous expenses that a taxpayer can deduct on Line 28 of Schedule A, without regard to the 2% limit. These expenses include:

Gambling losses to the extent of gambling winnings: The full amount of a taxpayer's gambling winnings is reported on line 21 of his Form 1040. Gambling losses are deducted on Schedule A, up to the total amount of gambling winnings. Taxpayers must have kept a written record of their losses. Gambling losses in excess of winnings are not deductible.

Work-related expenses for individuals with a disability: These are expenses that enable a disabled person to work, such as special equipment or attendant care services at their workplace.

Example: Erin has a visual disability. She requires a large screen magnifier in order to see well enough to perform her work. Erin purchased her screen magnifier for $550. She may deduct its cost as an itemized deduction not subject to the 2% floor.

Amortizable premium on taxable bonds: If the amount a taxpayer pays for a bond is greater than its stated principal amount, the excess is called a bond premium. Annual amortization of the premium is treated as a miscellaneous itemized deduction not subject to the 2% limit.

Casualty or theft losses from income-producing property: A taxpayer can deduct a casualty or theft loss as a miscellaneous itemized deduction not subject to the 2% limit if the damaged or stolen property was income-producing property (meaning property held for investment, such as stocks, bonds, gold, silver, vacant lots, and works of art).

Estate tax on income in respect of a decedent: Income in respect of a decedent (IRD) is income owed to a decedent at the time he died. If a decedent's estate has paid federal estate taxes on IRD assets, a beneficiary may be able to claim an IRD tax deduction, not subject to the 2% floor.

Deductions for Nonresident Aliens

Specific limitations on deductions apply to nonresident aliens who are required to file Form 1040NR. They may not claim the standard deduction. Further, except for personal exemptions and certain itemized deductions, they may claim deductions only to the extent they are connected with income related to their U.S. trade or business. The following itemized deductions are allowed:

- State and local income taxes
- Qualifying charitable contributions to U.S. nonprofit organizations
- Casualty and theft losses
- Miscellaneous itemized deductions

Itemized deductions related to mortgage interest are not allowed.

Bad Debt Deductions

There are two kinds of bad debts: business and nonbusiness. If a taxpayer cannot collect money owed to him, he may have a bad debt. To deduct a bad debt, the taxpayer must have a basis in it: the taxpayer must have already included the amount in income or must have already loaned out the cash.

Note: Unlike the other deductions discussed in this and the prior unit, bad debt deductions usually are not itemized on Schedule A. Deductible business bad debts are generally reported on an individual taxpayer's Schedule C (or other corresponding schedule such as Schedule E or F, depending on the type of business). As discussed earlier in this unit, business bad debts incurred by an employee are an exception, and may be deductible as miscellaneous itemized deductions, subject to the 2% limit. Deductible nonbusiness bad debts are reported on Schedule D.

Business Bad Debts: A business bad debt is a loss from the worthlessness of a debt that either was created or acquired in operating a trade or business or was closely related to the business when it became partly or totally worthless. Business bad debts are typically the result of credit sales to customers, but they can also be the result of loans to suppliers, clients, employees, or distributors. Goods and services customers have not paid for are shown in the business's books as either accounts receivable or notes receivable.

If the business is unable to collect any part of these accounts or notes receivable, the uncollectible part is a business bad debt. However, the business can take a bad debt deduction for these accounts and notes receivable only if the amount owed was included in gross income either for the year the deduction is claimed or for a prior year. Thus, a business that uses the cash method of accounting would normally report income when payment is received and would not usually have a bad debt deduction for amounts owed that are not received because those amounts would not previously have been included in income.

Nonbusiness Bad Debts: All other bad debts are nonbusiness bad debts. In order to be deductible, a nonbusiness bad debt must:

- **Be totally worthless:** A partly worthless nonbusiness debt cannot be deducted.
- **Be genuine:** A debt is genuine if it arises from a debtor-creditor relationship based on a valid and enforceable obligation to repay a fixed or determinable sum of money. There must be a profit motive in order for the loan to qualify as a true debtor-creditor relationship. If a taxpayer lends money to a relative or friend with the understanding that it will not be repaid, it is considered a gift and not a loan. Unless a taxpayer has documentation that proves otherwise, the IRS generally considers loans to relatives or friends to be gifts. For example, when minor children borrow from their parents, there is no genuine debt, and bad debt cannot be deducted.
- **Have basis to the taxpayer:** The taxpayer must have already included the amount in income or loaned out cash. Thus, a cash method taxpayer generally cannot take a bad debt deduction for unpaid salaries, wages, rents, fees, interest, dividends, and similar items.
- **Be claimed only in the year the debt becomes worthless:** The taxpayer does not have to wait until a debt is due to determine it is worthless, if there is proof that the debt is already worthless (for example, if the debtor dies or declares bankruptcy). A debt becomes worthless when there is no longer any chance that the amount owed will be paid.

It is not necessary to go to court if it can otherwise be demonstrated that a debt would be uncollectible. However, the taxpayer must document that he has taken reasonable steps to collect the debt. Bankruptcy of a debtor is generally good evidence of the worthlessness of at least a part of an unsecured debt.

Example: In January 2013, Stephanie loans her friend, Jed, $14,000 to buy a car. Jed signs a note and promises to pay the entire debt back with interest by December 31, 2013. Jed has a stroke in June 2013 and cannot pay his debts so he files for bankruptcy. Stephanie does not have to wait until the debt comes due. The bankruptcy means the loan has become worthless, since there is no longer any chance the amount owed will be paid. Stephanie can deduct the nonbusiness bad debt.

A loan guarantee is generally not a true debtor-creditor relationship. If a taxpayer simply guarantees a debt (by cosigning on the loan) and the debt becomes worthless, the taxpayer cannot take a bad debt deduction.

Example: Lucas and Jason are co-workers. As a favor to Jason, Lucas co-signs on an auto loan. Jason does not pay the loan and declares bankruptcy. Lucas is forced to pay off the note to maintain his credit. Since he did not enter into a formal guarantee agreement to protect an investment or to make a profit, Lucas cannot take a bad debt deduction.

A legitimate nonbusiness bad debt is reported as a short-term capital loss on Form 8949, *Sales and Other Dispositions of Capital Assets,* and Schedule D. It is subject to the capital loss limit of $3,000 per year, or $1,500 if the taxpayer files MFS. The taxpayer must include a detailed bad debt statement with a description of the debt, the amount, and the date it became due; the name of the debtor; the efforts made to collect the debt; and the reason the debt is worthless.

Nondeductible Expenses

The IRS has a lengthy list of expenses that cannot be deducted. These are just a sample of expenses that are not allowed:

- Lunch with coworkers or meals while working late
- Club dues
- Residential telephone lines and home security systems
- Home repairs, insurance, and rent
- Losses from the sale of a home, furniture, or personal car
- Brokers' commissions
- Burial or funeral expenses, including the cost of cemetery lots
- Fees and licenses, such as car licenses, marriage licenses, and dog tags
- Fines and penalties, such as parking tickets
- Investment-related seminars
- Life insurance premiums and personal disability insurance premiums

Unit 13: Study Questions

1. Alfred lives in Baltimore where he has a seasonal job for eight months each year and earns $25,000. He works the other four months in Miami, also at a seasonal job, and earns $9,000. Where is Alfred's tax home?

A. Miami.
B. Baltimore.
C. Alfred is a transient for tax purposes.
D. Alfred has no tax home.

2. Joshua's adjusted gross income is $20,000, and he has the following expenses in 2013:

- Income tax preparation fee: $100
- Safe deposit box rental to store bonds: $75
- Life insurance premiums: $600
- Home security system: $175
- Loss on sale of personal vehicle: $1,800
- Investment journals and newsletters: $250
- Investment advisory fees: $200
- Attorney fees for preparation of a will: $1,000

What is the total of Joshua's qualified miscellaneous itemized expenses (before the application of the AGI limitation)?

A. $2,400.
B. $1,225.
C. $800.
D. $625.

3. All of the following may be claimed as miscellaneous itemized deductions except ____________.

A. Unreimbursed commuting expenses to and from work.
B. Subscription fees for professional journals.
C. Expenses of looking for a new job in the same career field.
D. Work-related expenses for individuals with a disability.

4. Patrice's antique Persian rug was damaged by a new puppy. Patrice estimates the loss at $4,500. Her AGI for the year is $30,000. How much of the casualty loss may she deduct?

A. $0.
B. $4,500.
C. $4,400.
D. $1,400.

5. Using the simplified option to calculate a home office deduction, the maximum area that can be taken is ________________:

A. 100 square feet.
B. 250 square feet.
C. 300 square feet.
D. 500 square feet.

6. Eli purchased a used car for $11,000 in 2013. He did not purchase auto insurance, and three months later he totaled his car in an auto accident. The car's FMV on the date of the accident was $10,000. He was able to sell the car to a salvage yard for $300. Eli's AGI for 2013 was $50,000. What is Eli's deductible loss?

A. $0.
B. $4,200.
C. $4,600.
D. $9,700.

7. Isaac's home was damaged by a tornado. He had $90,000 worth of damage, but $80,000 was reimbursed by his insurance company. Isaac's employer had a disaster relief fund for its employees. Isaac received $4,000 from the fund and spent the entire amount on repairs to his home. What is Isaac's deductible casualty loss before applying the deduction limits?

A. $0.
B. $4,000.
C. $6,000.
D. $10,000.

8. Harriet is an attorney who reports the income from her practice on the accrual basis. In 2013, she receives $2,000 from the settlement of a bankruptcy case of a former client who owed her $15,000. What amount of bad debt deduction can Harriet claim?

A. $15,000.
B. $13,000.
C. $2,000.
D. None, because she uses the accrual basis.

9. All of the following may be claimed as miscellaneous itemized deductions except ______________.

A. Funeral expenses.
B. Union dues.
C. Laundry costs for uniforms.
D. Investment expenses.

10. Kim uses her home office while she works as a translator for an online company. She meets the requirements for deducting expenses for the business use of her home. Her home office is 480 square feet and her home is 2,400 square feet. She chooses not to use the simplified option for calculation. What is Kim's business use percentage in order to figure her allowable deduction?

A. 5%.
B. 10%.
C. 15%.
D. 20%.

11. Connor is deaf. He purchased a special device to use at work so he can identify when his phone rings. He paid for the device out-of-pocket, and his employer did not reimburse him. How should Connor report this on his tax return?

A. Connor may deduct the purchase as an itemized deduction, not subject to the 2% floor.
B. Connor may deduct the purchase as an itemized deduction, subject to the 2% floor.
C. Connor may not deduct the purchase because he is not totally disabled.
D. Connor may not deduct the purchase because he is not self-employed.

12. Which of the following will qualify for a deduction on Schedule A as an employee business expense?

A. Employer-reimbursed expenses under a tuition reimbursement (nontaxable) program.
B. Taking classes that maintain or improve skills needed in the taxpayer's present work.
C. Taking classes that are required by a taxpayer's employer or the law to keep his present salary, status, or job.
D. Both B and C.

13. Simon's AGI is $75,000. Therefore, the first__________ of miscellaneous employee work-related expenses is not deductible.

A. $1,000.
B. $1,500.
C. $5,625.
D. $7,500.

14. Harini is working on a temporary work assignment in another city. She is not sure how long the assignment will last. She travels overnight every week. So far, the work assignment has lasted 11 months in 2013, and Harini has incurred $800 in travel expenses and $300 in meal expenses. What is her deductible expense for this activity in 2013?

A. $0.
B. $800.
C. $950.
D. $1,100.

15. Brady's toolshed caught fire in 2013. The shed is not attached to his primary residence. Brady estimates the property damage at $6,000. He fixes the damage himself, so he does not file an insurance claim. Brady pays $3,000 for the cost of the materials and estimates the value of his labor to be $2,800. His insurance company has a $1,000 deductible for any casualty loss claim filed. What is Brady's deductible casualty loss before any deductions or income limitations?

A. $0.
B. $1,000.
C. $5,800.
D. $6,000.

16. All of the following miscellaneous itemized deductions are subject to the 2% of AGI limit except ______________________________.

A. Tax preparation fees.
B. Malpractice insurance.
C. Baggage fees during a business trip.
D. Gambling losses to the extent of gambling winnings.

17. Which of the following expenses does not qualify as a deductible transportation expense?

A. Getting from one client to another in the course of a taxpayer's business or profession.
B. Commuting expenses.
C. Traveling overseas to sign a business contract with a foreign supplier.
D. Going to a business meeting out-of-state.

18. Marissa works as a tax preparer. In 2013, her employer requires preparers to take several courses in order to keep their current positions. Marissa incurred the following expenses when she took these courses:

$100 Required supplies
$550 Tuition
$120 Required books
$50 Credit card interest from paying tuition
<u>$65 Bus passes to and from school</u>
$885 Total educational expenses

What is Marissa's deductible work-related educational expense on her Schedule A before the 2% limitation?

A. $550.
B. $670.
C. $835.
D. $885.

19. If a taxpayer's home is destroyed in a flood and the area is later declared a federally declared disaster area, how long would the taxpayer typically have to purchase replacement property?

A. One year.
B. Two years.
C. Four years.
D. Ten years.

20. During the year, Leon paid $350 to have his tax return prepared. He also paid union dues of $450 and paid an attorney $3,000 to draft his will. What are Leon's total miscellaneous itemized deductions on his Schedule A before the 2% limitation?

A. $350.
B. $450.
C. $800.
D. $3,800.

21. Sandy has the following income and losses in 2013:

- $45,000 in wages
- $10,000 in gambling winnings
- $13,000 in gambling losses
- $1,500 in attorney fees for a divorce

How should these transactions be treated on her tax return?

A. She should report $55,000 of income and $10,000 of miscellaneous itemized deductions on Schedule A, not subject to the 2% floor.
B. She should report $53,000 of income and $13,000 of miscellaneous itemized deductions on Schedule A, subject to the 2% floor.
C. She should report $55,000 of income and $13,000 of miscellaneous itemized deductions on Schedule A, subject to the 2% floor.
D. She should report $45,000 of income and $14,500 of miscellaneous itemized deductions on Schedule A, not subject to the 2% floor.

22. Enrique and Crystal had adjusted gross income of $75,000 in 2013 and incurred the following miscellaneous expenses:

Homeowners' association dues	$1,000
Fine from homeowners' association for violation of bylaws	$100
Loss from burglary of their home	$9,000
Tax preparation fees	$250

Based upon the information provided, what is the amount of expenses they can deduct for 2013?

A. $1,750.
B. $10,250.
C. $1,350.
D. $1,400.

23. Brooke had adjusted gross income of $20,000 in 2013. Her home sustained damage from a storm, and she incurred a loss of $3,000. Her home insurance policy had a deductible of $2,500 for this type of loss, so she elected not to file a claim. Based upon the information provided, what is the amount of casualty loss Brooke can deduct for the year?

A. $900.
B. $3,000.
C. $2,000.
D. $400.

24. All of the following statements are true except:

A. A taxpayer may deduct job-related expenses, subject to the 2%-of-AGI limit.
B. Job search costs, such as the use of an employment agency, are deductible expenses.
C. The job search does not have to result in a new job for the taxpayer in order for his expenses to be deductible.
D. A taxpayer may deduct expenses related to the search for a job in a new occupation.

25. Wes had a fire in his garage that destroyed his car and two antique desks. He had recently bought the car for $30,000. The FMV of the car just before the fire was $27,500. Its FMV after the fire was $500 (scrap value.) He had purchased the desks for $2,500, and their FMV just before the fire was $5,000. Wes's insurance company reimbursed him a total of $24,000. Wes's AGI in 2013 was $70,000. What is his casualty loss deduction?

A. $0.
B. $3,500.
C. $1,000.
D. $900.

26. Ali is a single taxpayer who has AGI of $100,000 in 2013. He loaned $8,000 to his friend Karyn in 2011 and Karyn has not repaid him. What amount of bad debt deduction can Ali claim?

A. $1,500.
B. $3,000.
C. $8,000.
D. $0.

27. Bon-Hwa is a nonresident alien who files Form 1040NR. Which of the following is he not allowed to claim as an itemized deduction on his income tax return?

A. A loss on a stolen laptop and audiovisual equipment used in his business in the U.S.
B. A charitable deduction to the American Cancer Society.
C. Mortgage interest on his main home.
D. Amounts paid for his state income tax.

28. Addison is a real estate agent who sold seven homes to buyers in 2013. She may deduct a total of __________ for giving each buyer a housewarming present worth $80.

A. $0.
B. $25.
C. $175.
D. $560.

29. Marilyn won the lottery and then made personal loans to several friends. Each loan was a true debtor-creditor relationship but not business related. She could not collect on many of these loans. How does Marilyn report these transactions?

A. The losses from the uncollectible loans are not deductible, since they were personal loans.
B. The losses are deductible as nonbusiness bad debts on Schedule D.
C. The losses are deductible as a business expense on Schedule C.
D. The losses are deductible on Schedule A as casualty losses.

30. Blair teaches high school Spanish classes. In order to improve her Spanish language skills, she spends two months during the summer of 2013 in Madrid. She incurs the following costs:

- Airfare: $5,000
- Apartment rental: $4,000
- Meals: $3,000
- Other miscellaneous costs: $1,500

Before application of the 2% threshold, what amount can Blair claim as a miscellaneous deduction for work-related education expenses?

A. $13,500.
B. $12,000.
C. $9,000.
D. $0.

31. Hector works as part of the crew on an Amtrak train. He regularly travels away from his tax home on long train trips. In 2013, he incurs $3,760 of unreimbursed meal expenses during his business travels. Before application of the 2% threshold, how much may Hector deduct on his Schedule A?

A. $1,880.
B. $2,820.
C. $3,008.
D. $3,760.

32. Which of the following expenses are itemized deductions subject to the 2%-of-AGI limitation?

A. Home office expense, hobby expenses, educator expenses.
B. Donation to a qualified charity, gambling losses, business-related entertainment expenses.
C. Cost of safety goggles required for work, tax preparation fee, dues to a professional society.
D. Impairment-related work expenses of a disabled employee, legal fee to collect alimony, union dues.

33. Stanton is a salesman in Oregon who attends a four-day convention for his industry in Las Vegas. He has the following expenses that are not reimbursed by his employer:

- $400 roundtrip airfare
- $25 baggage fee
- $125 car rental
- $650 hotel
- $300 business meals
- $120 entertainment expenses with prospective clients

What amount may Stanton deduct on his Schedule A, before applying the 2%-of-AGI floor?

A. $1,200.
B. $1,410.
C. $1,500.
D. $1,620.

Unit 14: Tax Credits

For additional information read:
Publication 972, *Child Tax Credit*
Publication 503, *Child and Dependent Care Expenses*
Publication 596, *Earned Income Credit*
Publication 970, *Tax Benefits for Education*

A tax credit directly reduces a taxpayer's liability on a dollar-for-dollar basis, which means it is usually more valuable than a tax deduction of the same dollar amount that only reduces the amount of taxable income. Various types of tax credits are either refundable or nonrefundable.

Nonrefundable Tax Credits

A nonrefundable tax credit reduces a taxpayer's liability for the year to zero but not beyond that, so any remaining credit is not refunded to the taxpayer. Among the most common nonrefundable tax credits are:

- Foreign Tax Credit (covered in Unit 15)
- Credit for Child and Dependent Care Expenses
- Child Tax Credit
- Adoption Credit
- American Opportunity Credit (partially refundable)
- Lifetime Learning Credit
- Retirement Savings Contributions Credit
- Residential energy credits

Credits cannot be claimed if the taxpayer is filing Form 1040EZ.

Refundable Tax Credits: A refundable tax credit can reduce a taxpayer's liability to zero and also generate a payment to the taxpayer for the amount by which the credit exceeds the amount of tax he would otherwise owe. Refundable tax credits include the following:

- Additional Child Tax Credit
- Earned Income Credit

Credit for Child and Dependent Care Expenses

The Child and Dependent Care Credit allows a taxpayer a credit for a percentage of child care expenses for children under age 13 and for disabled dependents of any age. This is a nonrefundable credit for child care expenses that allow taxpayers to work or to seek work. The credit offsets regular tax and the alternative minimum tax.

The credit ranges from 20% to 35% of qualifying expenses, depending on a taxpayer's income. For taxpayers with AGI of $43,000 or more, the credit is 20% of qualifying expenses but it is not phased out at higher income levels. For 2013, the limit on qualifying expenses is $3,000 for one child and $6,000 for two or more children.

If a taxpayer receives a reimbursement under a flexible spending account, the amount is treated as being pre-tax and the taxpayer must deduct the reimbursed amount from his qualified expenses to determine the credit.

A taxpayer must pass five eligibility tests to qualify for the Credit for Child and Dependent Care Expenses:

- Qualifying person test
- Earned income test
- Work-related expense test
- Joint return test
- Provider identification test

Qualifying Person Test: For purposes of this credit, a qualifying person is:

- A dependent child under the age of 13
- A spouse who is physically or mentally unable to care for himself
- Any other disabled person who is unable to care for himself and that the taxpayer either claims as a dependent or could claim if not for certain specified circumstances

Example: Samuel paid someone to care for his wife, Janet, so he could work. Janet is permanently disabled and requires an in-home care aide. Samuel also paid to have someone prepare meals for his 12-year-old daughter, Jill. Both Janet and Jill are qualifying persons for the credit.

Earned Income Test: Both the taxpayer and his spouse if married must have earned income during the year to qualify for this credit. This generally means both spouses must work. The credit is not available to MFS filers. The taxpayer's spouse is treated as having earned income for any month he is:

- A full-time student, or
- Disabled.

Example: Jessica and Quincy are married. Quincy worked as a custodian in 2013. Jessica attended school full-time from January 1 to June 30. She was unemployed during the summer and did not attend school the rest of the year. Jessica can be treated as having earned income for the six months she attended school full-time.

Work-Related Expense Test: Child and dependent care expenses must be work-related to qualify for this credit, meaning a taxpayer must be working or searching for work. Expenses incurred so that a spouse may do volunteer work or take care of personal business, or so that a married couple can go on a "date night" do not qualify.

Example: Patsy is a stay-at-home mom who volunteers several hours a week for a local autism information hotline. Her husband works full-time as a maintenance worker. They pay a babysitter to stay with their young daughter during the hours Patsy volunteers. The couple does not qualify for the credit because the babysitting expense is not work-related. Since Patsy does not have a job, is not disabled, and is not a full-time student, the child care expenses are ineligible.

Example: Darcy's four-year-old son attends a daycare center while she works three days a week. The daycare charges $150 for three days a week and $250 for five days a week. Sometimes Darcy pays the extra money so she can run errands on her days off. This extra charge is not a qualifying expense. Darcy's deductible expenses are limited to $150 a week, the amount of her work-related daycare expense.

The following kinds of expenses qualify for the credit:

- Education: Preschool or other programs below the level of kindergarten; before or after-school care for a child in kindergarten or above
- Care outside the home for a child under 13 or in a care center for a disabled dependent
- Transportation for a care provider to take a qualifying person to or from a place where care is provided
- Fees and deposits paid to an agency or preschool to acquire child care
- Household services, if they are at least partly for the well-being and protection of a qualifying person

Example: Roger's 10-year-old child attends a private school. In addition to paying for tuition, Roger pays an extra fee for before and after-school care so he can be at work during his scheduled hours. Roger can count the cost of the before and after-school program when figuring the credit but cannot count the cost of tuition.

Example: Edna is single and her elderly mother, Lorraine, is her dependent. Lorraine is completely disabled and must be in an adult daycare. Edna pays $8,000 per year for Lorraine to be in the adult daycare. Edna may take the credit, because Lorraine is disabled and incapable of self-care.

Examples of child care expenses that do not qualify include:

- Tuition costs for children in kindergarten and above
- Summer school or tutoring programs
- The cost of sending a child to an overnight camp (but day camps generally do qualify)
- The cost of transportation not provided by a care provider
- A forfeited deposit to a daycare center (since it is not for care and therefore not a work-related expense)

Example: Ellie is divorced and has custody of her 12-year-old daughter, Destiny, who takes care of herself after school. In August, Ellie spends $2,000 to send Destiny to an overnight camp for two weeks. She also sends Destiny to a Girl Scout day camp for a week in July while Ellie is working. The cost of the Girl Scout camp is $75. Ellie may only count the $75 toward the credit because the cost of sending a child to an overnight camp is not considered a work-related expense. Next summer, when Destiny turns 13, she will no longer be a qualifying child under the rules for this credit.

Care expenses do not include amounts paid for food, clothing, education, or entertainment. Small amounts paid for these items, however, can be included if they are incidental and cannot be separated from the cost of care.

Example: Krista takes her three-year-old child to a nursery school that provides lunch and educational activities as part of its program. The meals are included in the overall cost of care, and they are not itemized on her bill. Krista can count the total cost when she figures the credit.

Payments for child care will not qualify for the credit if made to a family member who is either:

- The taxpayer's own child under age 19
- Any other dependent listed on the taxpayer's tax return

Taxpayers may combine costs for multiple dependents. For example, if a taxpayer pays daycare expenses for three qualifying children, the $6,000 limit on qualifying expenses does not need to be divided equally among them.

Example: Alec has three children. His qualifying daycare expenses are $2,300 for his first child; $2,800 for his second child; and $900 for his third child. Alec can use the total amount, $6,000, when figuring his credit.

Example: Diego and Valeria both work and have three children. They have $2,000 in daycare expenses for their first child; $3,000 for their second child; and $4,000 for their third child. Although their total child care expenses are $9,000, they may only use the first $6,000 as their basis for the credit.

Example: Lori is a single mother with a five-year-old son. She takes him to daycare five days per week so she can work. Lori makes $46,000 in wages and spends $5,200 per year on daycare. The maximum amount of qualifying expenses she can claim for the credit is $3,000 since she only has one qualifying child, even though her actual expenses exceed that amount.

Joint Return Test: The joint return test specifies that married couples who wish to take the credit must file jointly. However, a married taxpayer can be "considered unmarried" for tax purposes if he qualifies for head of household filing status.

With divorced or separated taxpayers, only the custodial parent is allowed to take the credit.

Provider Identification Test: This test requires that taxpayers provide the name, address, and taxpayer identification number of the person or organization who provided the care for the child or dependent.

If a daycare provider refuses to supply its taxpayer identification information, the taxpayer may still claim the credit. He must report whatever information he has (such as the provider's name and address) and attach a statement to Form 2441, *Child and Dependent Care Expenses,* explaining the provider's refusal to supply the information.

Child Tax Credit

Taxpayers with income below certain threshold amounts may claim the Child Tax Credit for each qualifying child under the age of 17. This is a nonrefundable credit for up to $1,000 per qualifying child. A taxpayer whose tax liability is zero cannot take the Child Tax Credit because there is no tax to reduce. However, he may be able to take the Additional Child Tax Credit, which is refundable. The Child Tax Credit is reduced if the taxpayer's modified adjusted gross income is above the threshold amounts shown below:

- Married filing jointly: $110,000
- Single, head of household, or qualifying widow(er): $75,000
- Married filing separately: $55,000

The credit is phased out by $50 for each $1,000 of MAGI that exceeds the threshold amounts listed above. In addition, the Child Tax Credit is limited to the amounts of regular income tax and any alternative minimum tax owed.

Example: Cordell and Roxana file jointly and have two children who qualify for the Child Tax Credit. Their MAGI is $86,000 and their tax liability is $954. Even though their AGI is less than the threshold limit of $110,000, they can only claim $954, reducing their tax to zero. Cordell and Roxana cannot claim the maximum Child Tax Credit of $1,000 per child, but they may be eligible for the Additional Child Tax Credit.

Example: Clint files as head of household and has three children who qualify for the Child Tax Credit. His MAGI is $54,000 and his tax liability is $4,680. Clint is eligible to take the full credit of $1,000 per child ($3,000) because his MAGI is less than $75,000 and his tax liability is greater than $3,000.

Definition of a Qualifying Child: To be eligible to claim the Child Tax Credit, the taxpayer must have at least one qualifying child. To qualify, the child must:

- Be claimed as the taxpayer's dependent.
- Meet the relationship test: be the son, daughter, adopted child, stepchild, foster child, brother, sister, stepbrother, stepsister, or descendant of any of them (for example, a grandchild, niece, or nephew).
- Meet the age criterion: be under age 17 at the end of the year.
- Not have provided over half of his own support.
- Have lived with the taxpayer for more than six months of the tax year.[20]
- Be a U.S. citizen, a U.S. national, or a resident of the U.S. Foreign-born adopted children qualify if they lived with the taxpayer all year, even if the adoption is not yet final.

Example: Ed's son, Jeff, turned 17 on December 31, 2013. He is a U.S. citizen and has a valid SSN. According to the Child Tax Credit rules, he is not a qualifying child because he was not under age 17 at the end of 2013.

Example: Laura's adopted son, Nash, is 14. He is a U.S. citizen and lived with Laura for the entire tax year. Laura provided all of her son's support. Nash is a qualifying child for the Child Tax Credit because he was under age 17 at the end of the tax year; he meets the relationship requirement; he lived with Laura for more than six months of the year; and Laura provided his complete support.

Additional Child Tax Credit: The Additional Child Tax Credit is available for certain individuals who do not qualify for the full amount of the nonrefundable Child Tax Credit. In order to claim the Additional Child Tax Credit, a taxpayer must be able to claim the Child Tax Credit, even if he does not qualify for the full amount. Since the Additional Child Tax Credit is refundable, it can produce a refund even if the taxpayer does not owe any tax.

The Additional Child Tax Credit allows eligible taxpayers to claim up to $1,000 for each qualifying child after subtracting the allowable amount of Child Tax Credit. For taxpayers with earned income over $3,000, the credit is based on the lesser of:

[20] There are special rules for children of divorced or separated parents, as well as children of parents who never married. In some cases the noncustodial parent may be entitled to claim the dependency exemption for a child and thus the Child Tax Credit and Additional Child Tax Credit. In addition, there is an exception for an infant who is born during the tax year and has not lived long enough to meet the six-month requirement.

- 15% of the taxpayer's taxable earned income that is more than $3,000, or
- The amount of unused Child Tax Credit (caused when tax liability is less than the allowed credit).

Example: May and Dimitri have two children, MAGI of $66,000, and owe tax of $850. Because their tax liability is less than the full amount of the Child Tax Credit, they may be able to take the Additional Child Tax Credit of up to $1,150 ($2,000 - $850).

Schedule 8812, *Child Tax Credit,* is used to report both the Child Tax Credit and the Additional Child Tax Credit.

Note: In September 2013, the IRS released Form 8967, *Paid Preparer's Child Tax Credit Checklist.* It is a three-page form that a preparer should use as due diligence in determining whether a taxpayer is eligible for the Child Tax Credit. The form includes questions about each of the eligibility tests. The preparer is required to document the client's answers as well as the answers to any additional questions he asks. The preparer should keep the form for his own records, but must make it available upon IRS request. Form 8967 will be mandatory in tax year 2014, but it is optional for preparers in tax year 2013.

Adoption Credit

In 2013, a nonrefundable credit of up to $12,970 per child can be taken for qualified expenses paid to adopt a child. For a special needs child, the maximum credit amount is allowed even if the taxpayer incurs a lesser amount of adoption expenses.

If a taxpayer receives employer-provided adoption benefits that are excluded from income, he may still be able to take the Adoption Credit. However, the exclusion and the credit cannot be claimed for the same expenses, and any allowable exclusion must be claimed before any allowable credit. The exclusion is limited to the same dollar amount as the credit. Further, both the exclusion and the credit are phased out ratably when modified adjusted gross income is between $194,580 and $234,580. The phase-out ranges are the same for all taxpayers, regardless of filing status. Married taxpayers generally must file jointly to claim either the credit or the exclusion.

Although the Adoption Credit is nonrefundable, any unused credit may be carried forward for up to five years. Qualified adoption expenses are directly related to the adoption of a child. These include:

- Adoption fees
- Court costs
- Attorney fees
- Travel expenses related to the adoption, including meals and lodging
- Re-adoption expenses to adopt a foreign child

Qualified adoption expenses do not include:

- Illegal adoption expenses
- A surrogate parenting arrangement
- Adoption of a spouse's child

An eligible child is:

- Under 18 years old, or
- Physically or mentally disabled, regardless of age.

Special Needs Child: A taxpayer may claim the full credit for a special needs child regardless of actual expenses paid or incurred. A special needs child must be a United States citizen or resident when the adoption effort begins. Further, one of the following must apply:

- A state has determined the child cannot or should not be returned to his parents' home, or
- A state has determined the child will not be adopted unless assistance is provided to the adoptive parents.

In making the determination about special needs, a state may take into account the following factors: a child's ethnic background and age; whether he is a member of a minority or sibling group; and whether he has a physical, mental, or emotional handicap.

Example: Noel and Cassie adopt a special needs child, and the adoption is finalized in 2013. Their actual adoption expenses are $7,500. They are allowed to take the full $12,970 credit in 2013.

Unsuccessful Adoptions: A taxpayer who has attempted to adopt a child in the U.S. and been unsuccessful is still eligible for the credit or exclusion. Eligible expenses may include those related to unsuccessful attempts to adopt as well as an adoption attempt that is ultimately successful.

However, if the eligible child is from a foreign country, the taxpayer cannot take the credit or exclusion unless the adoption becomes final. A foreign child is defined as a child who was not a citizen or resident of the United States at the time the adoption effort began.

Timing of Payment: For a domestic adoption, qualified expenses paid before the year in which the adoption becomes final may be claimed in the year after the expenses were paid. Once the adoption becomes final (or if it is unsuccessful), the taxpayer can claim the expenses in the year paid. For a foreign adoption, expenses paid before or during the year of finality are allowable in that year.

Education Credits

Two education credits are available based on qualified expenses a taxpayer pays for postsecondary education:

- **American Opportunity Credit**
- **Lifetime Learning Credit**

If a taxpayer does not qualify for either of these education credits, he may still qualify for the tuition and fees deduction (as an adjustment to income, covered in Unit 11), which can reduce the amount of taxable income by up to $4,000. However, a taxpayer cannot claim the tuition and fees deduction in the same year that he claims either of the education credits. A taxpayer must choose to take either the tax credit(s) or the deduction, and should consider which provides the greatest tax benefit.

Certain general rules apply to both of these credits, in addition to specific rules for each. A taxpayer may take education credits for himself, his spouse, and his dependents who attended an eligible educational institution during the tax year. Eligible educational institutions include colleges, universities, vocational schools, and community colleges. Taxpayers can claim payments that are prepaid for an academic period that begins in the first three months of the next calendar year.

Example: Tom paid $1,500 in December 2013 for college tuition for the spring semester that begins in January 2014. Tom can claim $1,500 of education credits on his 2013 return, even though he will not start college until 2014.

A taxpayer cannot claim education credits if he:

- Can be claimed as a dependent on someone else's tax return
- Files as married filing separately
- Has MAGI above the specified limit for his filing status
- Has a spouse who was a nonresident alien for any part of the tax year

To claim the credit for a dependent's education expenses, the taxpayer must claim the dependent on his return, but he does not necessarily have to pay for all of the dependent's qualified education expenses.

If a taxpayer does not claim an exemption for a dependent who is an eligible student, the student may be able to claim an education credit on his own return.

Example: Cathy has a 19-year-old son named Trent who is a full-time college student. Trent's grandmother paid his tuition directly to the college. For purposes of claiming an education credit, either Cathy or Trent is treated as receiving the money as a gift and paying for the qualified tuition and related expenses. If Cathy claims Trent as a dependent, she may claim an education credit. Alternatively, if Trent claims an exemption for himself on his own return and his mother does not, he can claim the credit.

If a taxpayer has education expenses for more than one student, he may be eligible to take the American Opportunity Credit for one student and the Lifetime Learning Credit for another student on the same tax return.

Example: Reed pays college expenses for himself and his dependent daughter, Ivy, age 18. Reed goes to graduate school and qualifies for the Lifetime Learning Credit. Ivy is an undergraduate and qualifies for the American Opportunity Credit. Reed can take both credits on his tax return for each eligible student, Ivy and himself.

Form 8863 is used to figure and claim both education credits. Qualified education expenses are tuition and related expenses, such as books and other course materials required as a condition of enrollment.

Example: Elias is a college senior studying to be a dentist. This year, in addition to tuition, he pays a fee to the university for the rental of the dental equipment he is required to use in the program. Elias's equipment rental fee is a qualified education expense.

Expenses that do not qualify include:

- Room and board
- Medical expenses, including student health fees
- Insurance
- Transportation

- Personal, living, or family expenses

Any course of instruction or other education involving sports, games, or hobbies is not a qualifying expense unless the course is part of the student's degree program (or if taken to improve job skills in the case of the Lifetime Learning Credit.) Qualified education expenses must be reduced by the amount of any tax-free educational assistance received, such as Pell grants, tax-free portions of scholarships, and employer-provided educational assistance.

Tuition expenses are reported to the student on Form 1098-T, *Tuition Statement*, issued by the school.

Example: Faith received Form 1098-T from the college she attends. It shows that her tuition was $9,500 and that she received a $1,500 tax-free scholarship. Her maximum qualifying expenses for the education credit are $8,000 ($9,500 - $1,500).

Example: In 2013, Jacqueline paid $3,000 for tuition and $5,000 for room and board at her university. She was also awarded a $2,000 tax-free scholarship and a $4,000 student loan. To qualify for an education credit, she must first subtract the tax-free scholarship from her tuition, her only qualified expense. A student loan is not considered tax-free educational assistance because it must be paid back. To calculate her education credit, Jacqueline has $1,000 in qualified expenses ($3,000 tuition - $2,000 scholarship).

American Opportunity Credit (AOC)

The American Opportunity Credit (AOC) allows taxpayers to claim a credit of up to $2,500 based on qualified tuition and related expenses paid for each eligible student. The credit covers 100% of the first $2,000 and 25% of the second $2,000 of eligible expenses per student, up to the amount of tax.

In 2013, under certain conditions, 40% of the AOC is refundable, which means the taxpayer can receive up to $1,000 even if no taxes are owed.

Requirements for the AOC are as follows:

- **Degree requirement:** The student must be enrolled in a program that leads to a degree, certificate, or other recognized educational credential.
- **Workload:** The student must take at least one-half of the normal full-time workload for at least one academic period beginning during the tax year.
- **No felony drug conviction:** The student must be free of any felony conviction for possessing or distributing a controlled substance.
- **First four years of education:** The credit can only be claimed for expenses related to a student's four years of undergraduate education. A student in graduate school does not qualify for this credit.

The credit phases out for joint filers with modified adjusted gross income between $160,000 and $180,000 and for single filers with MAGI between $80,000 and $90,000. Couples with MAGI above $180,000 and single filers with MAGI above $90,000 do not qualify.

If a student does not meet all of the conditions for the American Opportunity Credit, he may still be able to take the Lifetime Learning Credit.

Lifetime Learning Credit

The Lifetime Learning Credit is a nonrefundable tax credit of 20% of qualified tuition and fees, up to $10,000, paid during the tax year. The maximum credit is $2,000 per tax return, not per student. A family's maximum credit is the same regardless of the number of qualified students. The requirements for the Lifetime Learning Credit differ from those for the AOC as follows:

- **No workload requirement:** A student is eligible no matter how many or how few courses he takes.
- **Non-degree courses eligible:** A student qualifies if he is simply taking a course to acquire or improve job skills.
- **All levels of postsecondary education:** A student may be an undergraduate, graduate, or professional degree candidate.
- **Unlimited number of years:** There is no limit on the number of years for which the credit can be claimed for each student.

Example: Lai works full-time and takes one course a month at night school. Some of the courses are not for credit, but she is taking them to advance her career. The education expenses qualify for the Lifetime Learning Credit, but not for the American Opportunity Credit.

Example: Roland attends Creek Community College after spending six months in prison for a felony cocaine conviction. He paid $4,400 for the course of study, which included tuition, equipment, and books required for the course. The school requires that students pay for books and equipment when registering for courses. The entire $4,400 is an eligible educational expense under the Lifetime Learning Credit. Roland does not qualify for the American Opportunity Credit because he has a drug conviction.

For 2013, the Lifetime Learning Credit is phased out for single filers with modified adjusted gross income between $53,000 and $63,000. For joint filers, the phase-out is between $107,000 and $127,000 of MAGI.

Earned Income Credit

The Earned Income Credit (EIC), also known as the Earned Income Tax Credit (EITC),[21] is a fully refundable federal income tax credit for lower income people who work and have earned income and adjusted gross income under certain thresholds. There are very strict rules and income guidelines for the EIC. To claim the EIC, a taxpayer must meet all of the following tests:

- Have a Social Security number. Any qualifying child must also have a valid SSN.
- Have earned income from wages, combat pay, or self-employment.
- Not have investment income that exceeds $3,300.
- Not file as MFS.
- Not be claimed as a dependent by another taxpayer.
- Be a U.S. citizen or legal resident all year (or a nonresident alien married to a U.S. citizen or resident alien filing MFJ).

[21] The IRS uses both terms. For consistency's sake, we refer to this credit as the Earned Income Credit (EIC).

Qualifying Income for the EIC: Only earned income, such as wages, tips, union strike benefits, and net earnings from self-employment, qualifies for the EIC.

Earned income does not include the following:

- Social Security benefits
- Workfare payments
- Alimony or child support
- Pensions or annuities
- Unemployment benefits
- Inmate wages, including amounts paid while in work release programs or halfway houses

Income from investments does not qualify as earned income for the EIC. A taxpayer with investment income above $3,300 is disqualified from claiming the EIC.

Income that is excluded from tax is generally not considered earned income for the EIC. Nontaxable combat pay is an exception, if the taxpayer elects to treat it as earned income.

Qualifying Children: Low-income taxpayers without children may qualify for the EIC in certain cases, but the rules are stricter and the amount of the credit is lower.

A taxpayer with a qualifying child may claim the EIC without any age limitations, but a taxpayer without a child can only claim the EIC if all of the following tests are met:

- Must be at least age 25 but under 65 at the end of the year (if married, either spouse can meet the age test)
- Must live in the United States for more than half the year
- Must not qualify as a dependent of another person
- Cannot file Form 2555 (related to foreign earned income exclusion[22])

The definition of a qualifying child for purposes of the EIC is stricter than it is for the dependency exemption. The taxpayer's qualifying child must meet the following four tests:

- Relationship test
- Age test
- Joint return test
- Residency test

Relationship Test: The child must be related to the taxpayer in one of the following ways:

- Son, daughter, stepchild, eligible foster child, adopted child, or descendant of any of them (for example, a grandchild), or
- Brother, sister, half-brother, half-sister, stepbrother, stepsister, or descendant of any of them (for example, a niece or nephew).

Example: Rusty is 27 and supports his younger sister, Colleen, who is 16. He has taken care of her since their parents died five years ago. Colleen is Rusty's qualifying child for purposes of the EIC.

An adopted child is generally treated as the taxpayer's own child. However, special rules apply for foreign adoptions. Any qualifying child listed on Schedule EIC also must have a valid SSN. Since

[22] A taxpayer who elects not to exclude foreign income from his gross income may still be eligible for the EIC.

an ATIN is not sufficient, the taxpayer can elect to amend the tax return and claim the EIC once a foreign adoption is final and an SSN is granted.

A foster child must be placed in the taxpayer's home by an authorized placement agency or by court order in order to be eligible.

Age Test: To qualify for the EIC, the child must be:

- Age 18 or younger, or
- A full-time student age 23 or younger, or
- Any age, if permanently disabled.

In addition, the qualifying child must be younger than the taxpayer claiming him, unless the child (dependent) is permanently disabled.

Example: Garth, age 45, supports his older brother, Jeremiah, age 56. Jeremiah, who is mentally challenged and permanently disabled, lives with Garth. In this case, Jeremiah meets the criteria to be Garth's qualifying child for purposes of the EIC.

Joint Return Test: The qualifying child (dependent) may not file a joint return with a spouse, except to claim a refund.

Example: Margaret's 18-year-old son and his 18-year-old wife had $800 of interest income and no other income. Neither is required to file a tax return. Taxes were taken out of their interest income due to backup withholding, so they file a joint return to get a refund of the taxes withheld. The exception to the joint return test applies, so Margaret's son may still be her qualifying child if all the other tests are met.

Residency Test: The child must have lived with the taxpayer in the United States for more than half of 2013. For purposes of the EIC, U.S. military personnel stationed outside the United States on extended active duty are considered to live in the U.S. during that duty period, so their children meet the residency test.

A child who was born or died in 2013 meets the residency test for the entire year if the child lived with the taxpayer the entire time he was alive in 2013.

Example: Tawanda gave birth to a baby girl in March 2013. The infant died one month later. The child is still a qualifying child for purposes of the EIC because she meets the other tests for age and relationship.

EIC Income Limits: Both the taxpayer's earned income and his adjusted gross income must be less than the following limits:

- $46,227 ($51,567 MFJ) with three or more qualifying children
- $43,038 ($48,378 MFJ) with two qualifying children
- $37,870 ($43,210 MFJ) with one qualifying child
- $14,340 ($19,680 MFJ) with no qualifying children

Example: Graham is single and his AGI is $39,000. He has one qualifying child. Graham cannot claim the EIC because his AGI exceeds the income threshold for single filers.

The maximum amount of the Earned Income Credit ranges from $487 for a taxpayer with no qualifying children to $6,044 for a married couple with three or more children.

EIC Fraud and Penalties: Taxpayers who improperly claim the EIC with a reckless or intentional disregard of the rules cannot take the credit for the next two years. Those who fraudulently claim the EIC may be banned from taking the credit for ten years.

Note: Tax preparers face significant due diligence requirements in preparing EIC cla ms for their clients. Preparers must use Form 8867, *Paid Preparer's Earned Income Credit Checklist,* to determine eligibility. The four-page, five-part form is required for each client who is claiming the EIC each year. The preparer must attach the checklist to the tax return of any client who is claiming the EIC. A preparer who fails to meet his EIC due diligence requirements is subject to a $500 penalty per failure

Retirement Savings Contributions Credit

Qualified individuals are allowed a nonrefundable credit of up to $1,000 ($2,000 MFJ) for eligible contributions to an IRA or an employer-sponsored retirement plan. The amount of the credit is the eligible contribution multiplied by the applicable credit rate, which is based on filing status and AGI.

Note: The IRS also refers to this credit as the "Saver's Credit." Either term may be used on the EA exam.

To be eligible for the Retirement Savings Contributions Credit, a taxpayer must be at least 18 years old and must not be a full-time student or claimed as a dependent on another person's return. AGI cannot be more than:

- $59,000 for married filing jointly
- $44,250 for head of household
- $29,500 for single, married filing separately, or qualifying widow(er)

Example: Truman is 24 and earns $35,000 during the year. He is single and contributes $3,000 to his 401(k) plan at work. Truman is not eligible for the credit because his income exceeds the threshold limit of $29,500.

Eligible contributions include those to both traditional IRAs and Roth IRAs; elective deferrals to 401(k) or other qualified employer-sponsored retirement plans; and voluntary employee contributions to other qualified retirement plans. Most workers who contribute to traditional IRAs already deduct all or part of their contributions.

The Saver's Credit is in addition to these deductions. When figuring the credit, a taxpayer generally must subtract the amount of distributions received from his retirement plans received in the two years before the year the credit is claimed; the year the credit is claimed; and the period after the end of the credit year but before the due date, including extensions, for filing the return for the credit year.

Example: Rashid and Angela filed joint returns in 2011 and 2012, and plan to do so in 2013 and 2014. Rashid received a taxable distribution from a qualified plan in 2011 and a taxable distribution from an eligible deferred compensation plan in 2012. Angela received taxable distributions from a traditional IRA in 2013 and tax-free distributions from a Roth IRA in 2013. Rashid contributes to an IRA in 2013, and he and Angela qualify for the credit. Their adjusted gross income in 2013 is $53,000, below the Saver's Credit income limit. Rashid and Angela must reduce the amount of their contributions in 2013 by the total of the distributions they received in 2011, 2012, 2013, and 2014.

The Saver's Credit amount can be as low as 10% or as high as 50% of a maximum annual contribution of $2,000 per person, depending on filing status and AGI.

Residential Energy Credits

A taxpayer who purchases certain qualified energy-efficient improvements for his main home may qualify for a nonrefundable tax credit. There are two types of residential energy credits:

- Residential Energy Efficient Property Credit
- Nonbusiness Energy Property Credit

Both credits are calculated and claimed on IRS Form 5695, *Residential Energy Credits.*

Residential Energy Efficient Property Credit: Taxpayers may claim this credit for certain alternative energy equipment property placed in service in 2013. The credit is equal to 30% of the cost of the following qualifying property:

- Solar energy systems (water heating and electricity)
- Fuel cells
- Small wind energy systems
- Geothermal heat pumps

There is no limit on the amount of credit for most types of property. If the credit is more than the tax owed, the unused portion may be carried forward to subsequent years. The credit is allowed for new construction as well as improvements to existing homes located in the United States.

Nonbusiness Energy Property Credit: This credit is equal to 10% of the cost of qualified energy efficient improvements to existing homes only. Taxpayers may be able to claim the actual cost of certain types of property. Each type of property has a different dollar limit, with various credit amounts allowed for items like water heaters and heating and air conditioning systems. The total combined amount that can be claimed is $500 for all tax years after 2005. Only $200 of this limit may be used for windows.

Other Energy Credits: The IRS also allows credits for other energy-related expenses:

- **Plug-in Electric Motorcycles and 3-Wheeled Vehicles:** This is a 10% tax credit; golf carts and other low-speed vehicles do not qualify.
- **Alternative Fuel Vehicle Property:** This is a 30% credit for the cost of installing qualified clean-fuel vehicle refueling property at a taxpayer's principal residence. The credit is limited to $1,000 per taxable year for nonbusiness taxpayers.

Unit 14: Study Questions

1. Gail's earned income from wages is $7,000 in 2013. She has interest income of $3,350. She is single and has a valid Social Security number. She does not have any dependents. Which of the following statements is true?

A. Gail qualifies to claim the Earned Income Credit.
B. Gail does not qualify for the Earned Income Credit.
C. Gail qualifies for the Earned Income Credit and the Child Tax Credit.
D. None of the above.

2. Orlando is a university senior studying to be an optometrist. Which of the following expenses is a qualifying expense for the American Opportunity Credit?

A. The rental of the vision equipment he is required to use to enroll in this program.
B. Student health fees.
C. Room and board.
D. A physical education course not related to his degree program.

3. Which of the following individuals could be a qualifying child for the Child Tax Credit?

A. An 18-year-old dependent who is a full-time student.
B. A six-year-old nephew who lived with the taxpayer for seven months.
C. A child actor who is 15 years old and provides over half of his own support.
D. A foster child who has lived with the taxpayer for four months.

4. For purposes of the EIC, which of the following types of income are considered earned income?

A. Alimony.
B. Interest and dividends.
C. Workfare payments.
D. Household employee income reported on Form W-2.

5. Beatrice has three dependent children, ages 10, 12, and 18, who live with her. Assuming she meets the other criteria, what is the maximum Child Tax Credit she can claim on her 2013 tax return?

A. $0.
B. $1,000.
C. $2,000.
D. $3,000.

6. Which of the following individuals is eligible for the American Opportunity Credit?

A. Garrett, who is enrolled full-time as a postgraduate student pursuing a master's degree in biology.
B. Lucy, who is taking a ceramics class at a community college.
C. Doug, who is a full-time undergraduate student and was convicted of a felony for distributing a controlled substance.
D. Beth, who is taking three-quarters of the normal full-time course load required for a computer science degree program and who attended classes the entire school year.

7. In 2013, Dylan and Hannah adopt a special needs child who is completely disabled. Their adoption expenses are $7,000, and their travel expenses related to the adoption are $1,200. Their modified AGI for 2013 is $175,000. What is their maximum Adoption Credit in 2013?

A. $7,000.
B. $8,200.
C. $12,970.
D. None of the above.

8. Based on the Child and Dependent Care Credit rules, which of the following individuals meets the eligibility test for a qualifying person?

A. Jeremy, 5, who is taken care of by his mother at home all day.
B. Virgil, 21, a full-time student supported by his parents.
C. Leroy, 80, who lives at home with his son but is not disabled.
D. Leanne, 52, who is disabled and is married to Jake, an employed carpenter.

9. In 2013, Tyrone paid $5,000 of his own funds to cover the cost of his college tuition. Tyrone also received a Pell grant for $3,000 and a student loan for $4,000, which he used for housing costs. What are Tyrone's total qualified tuition and related expenses for an education credit?

A. $12,000.
B. $9,000.
C. $5,000.
D. $2,000.

10. All of the following items are deductible as education-related expenses for the Lifetime Learning Credit except:

A. Required books.
B. On-campus child care in order to attend class.
C. Tuition.
D. Required fees.

11. Brett and Amy arranged daycare for their three-year-old son so they could work. Their child care expenses were $3,000 in 2013. Amy also paid a deposit of $100 to the daycare and an enrollment fee of $35. Brett was reimbursed for $1,200 by his flexible spending account at work. How much of the child care expenses can they use to determine their Child and Dependent Care Credit?

A. $1,800.
B. $1,900.
C. $1,935.
D. $3,135.

12. Samira and Rishi are married and file jointly. Their daughter, Chetana, was enrolled full-time in college for all of 2013. Samira and Rishi obtained a loan in 2013 and used the proceeds to pay for Chetana's tuition and related fees. They repaid the loan in 2014. When will they be entitled to claim an education credit?

A. They cannot claim an education credit.
B. 2014.
C. 2013.
D. Both 2013 and 2014.

13. Edwin is a bookkeeper. He takes an accounting course at the local community college to improve his work-related skills. Edwin is not a degree candidate. Which educational credit does he qualify for?

A. The American Opportunity Credit.
B. The College Saver's Credit.
C. The Lifetime Learning Credit.
D. The Mortgage Interest Credit.

14. To qualify for the Earned Income Credit, which of the following is true?

A. The taxpayer must have a dependent child.
B. The taxpayer must be a U.S. citizen or legal U.S. resident all year.
C. The taxpayer's filing status can be MFS or MFJ.
D. The taxpayer's only income may be from Social Security benefits.

15. Nina pays for daycare costs for the following individuals so she can work. Each is a qualifying individual for purposes of the Child and Dependent Care Credit except:

A. Nina's husband, who is totally disabled.
B. Nina's son, age 13, who is Nina's dependent.
C. Nina's nephew, age 12, who is also Nina's dependent.
D. Nina's niece, who is 35, lived with her all year, and is completely disabled.

16. Zoe attends Valley Oaks College full-time, pursuing an undergraduate degree in business. Because she changed majors in her junior year, she is now in her fifth year of college. She has a $4,000 Pell grant for the 2013 school year. Her parents have taken the American Opportunity Credit for Zoe the past four years. Calculate the amount her parents can claim for the AOC in 2013 based upon the following expenses for Zoe's education:

- Tuition: $15,000
- Room and board: $12,000
- Medical insurance: $1,000

A. $0.
B. $2,000.
C. $2,500.
D. $4,800.

17. Which of the following expenses is not a qualified expense for purposes of the Adoption Credit?

A. Court costs.
B. Re-adoption expenses to adopt a foreign child.
C. Attorney fees for a surrogate arrangement.
D. Travel expenses.

18. Which of the following filing conditions would not prevent an individual from qualifying for the Earned Income Credit for 2013?

A. MFS filing status.
B. A taxpayer with a qualifying child who is 23 and a full-time student.
C. Investment income of $3,800.
D. A taxpayer who is 68 years old without a qualifying child.

19. Generally, which is most beneficial to taxpayers when it comes to reducing income tax liability: a nonrefundable credit, a refundable credit, or a deduction?

A. A nonrefundable credit.
B. A refundable credit.
C. A deduction.
D. All are equally beneficial in reducing income tax liability.

20. Couples who file jointly may be eligible to claim up to ___________ per year for contributions to an IRA under the Retirement Savings Contributions Credit?

A. $500.
B. $1,000.
C. $2,000.
D. $5,000.

21. In 2013, what is the maximum amount of the American Opportunity Credit?

A. $2,500 per tax return.
B. $2,500 per student.
C. $2,000 per tax return.
D. $1,000 per student.

22. Arlene is single. She has a 16-year-old grandson who lived with her from May through December of 2013. She provided 90% of his support and he provided the other 10%. Arlene's MAGI was $85,000 in 2013. Calculate the amount of her Child Tax Credit.

A. $250.
B. $500.
C. $1,000.
D. She is not entitled to the credit because a grandson is not a qualifying child for the Child Tax Credit.

23. All of the following are qualified expenses for purposes of the Child and Dependent Care Credit except__________:

A. A $500 payment to a grandparent for child care while the taxpayer is employed.
B. A $300 payment to a daycare center while the taxpayer is looking for employment.
C. A $500 child care expense while the taxpayer obtains medical care.
D. A $600 adult daycare expense for a disabled spouse while the taxpayer works.

24. What is the maximum amount of Nonbusiness Energy Property Credit a taxpayer can claim for qualified improvements to his main home?

A. No maximum limit.
B. $5,000.
C. $1,000.
D. $500.

25. Orrin was audited in 2013, and the IRS determined that he claimed the Earned Income Credit erroneously due to reckless disregard of the EIC rules. For how many years is Orrin prohibited from claiming the EIC?

A. None.
B. Two years.
C. Five years.
D. Ten years.

26 The following taxpayers contributed to their employers' 401(k) plan. Which qualifies for the Retirement Savings Contributions Credit based on his or her adjusted gross income?

A. Ed, who is single and has AGI of $35,200.
B. Sybil, who is married, files jointly, and has AGI of $55,000.
C. Bert, who is married, files separately, and has AGI of $30,600.
D. Carl, who is a qualifying widower and has AGI of $32,000.

27. What is the maximum amount of the Lifetime Learning Credit in 2013?

A. $2,000 per student.
B. $2,500 per student.
C. $1,000 per student.
D. $2,000 per tax return.

28. Which is the following is true regarding a paid preparer's EIC due diligence requirements?

A. He is subject to a $50 penalty for each failure to meet his due diligence requirements.
B. He is required to complete the EIC checklist for every client who is claiming the Earned Income Credit. The preparer must retain a copy for his records and make it available to the IRS upon request.
C. He is required to complete and attach Form 8867, the EIC checklist, to the tax return of every client who is claiming the Earned Income Credit.
D. He is required to complete and attach Form 8867, the EIC checklist, to the tax return of every client, regardless of whether the taxpayer is claiming the Earned Income Credit.

29. What is the maximum amount of the Adoption Tax Credit for 2013?

A. $12,650 per child.
B. $12,970 per child.
C. $13,190 per child.
D. $13,360 per child.

30. Scott is 43 and unmarried. Scott's half-brother, Hayden, turned 16 on December 30, 2013. Hayden lived with Scott all year, and he is a U.S. citizen. Scott claimed Hayden as a dependent on his return. Which of the following is true?

A. Hayden is a qualifying child for the Child Tax Credit.
B. Hayden is not a qualifying child for the Child Tax Credit because he is too old to be eligible.
C. Hayden is not a qualifying child for the Child Tax Credit because siblings do not qualify.
D. Hayden only qualifies for the Child Tax Credit if he is a full-time student.

Unit 15: Additional Taxes and Credits

More Reading:
Publication 54, *Tax Guide for U.S. Citizens and Resident Aliens Abroad*
Publication 519, *U.S. Tax Guide for Aliens*
Publication 514, *Foreign Tax Credit for Individuals*
Tax Topic 556, *Alternative Minimum Tax*
www.irs.gov/uac/Affordable-Care-Act-Tax-Provisions-Home

In this unit, we cover a variety of other taxes and credits, including the new net investment income tax and the additional Medicare tax; the taxation and reporting of foreign income; and the "nanny" tax and "kiddie" tax. We start with a look at the alternative minimum tax (AMT).

Alternative Minimum Tax

As described in the preceding units, federal tax law provides special treatment for certain types of income and allows deductions and credits for certain types of expenses. These tax benefits can significantly reduce the regular income tax liabilities for some taxpayers. The AMT limits the extent to which these tax benefits can be used to reduce the total amount of income tax paid by higher-income taxpayers. Congress adopted the AMT in 1969 in an attempt to ensure that individuals and corporations pay at least a minimum amount of tax.[23]

When calculating the AMT, many common items considered in the computation of the regular income tax liability are either adjusted downward or eliminated entirely. These include personal exemptions; the standard deduction or certain itemized deductions, such as state, local, and foreign taxes; miscellaneous itemized deductions subject to the 2% floor; investment interest expense; and mortgage interest on home equity debt if the loan was not used to buy or improve the home. In addition, the benefits of the following tax preference items must be eliminated when calculating the AMT:

- Depletion
- Excess intangible drilling costs
- Interest on private activity bonds
- Accelerated depreciation on property placed in service before 1987
- Exclusion of gain on qualified small business stock

The AMT is a parallel tax system, with every taxpayer responsible for paying the higher of the regular tax or a calculated tentative minimum tax. The AMT is the excess of the tentative minimum tax over the regular income tax. Thus, the AMT is owed only if the tentative minimum tax is greater than the regular tax.

In general, the tentative minimum tax is computed by:

1. Starting with AGI less itemized deductions for regular tax purposes (or with AGI for taxpayers who are not claiming itemized deductions)

[23] The American Taxpayer Relief Act included provisions for the AMT to be indexed for inflation, meaning the income threshold for an individual to be subject to the AMT will rise automatically each year.

2. Eliminating or reducing certain adjustments and preferences (the exclusions, deductions, and credits that are allowed in computing the regular tax, such as those mentioned above), to derive alternative minimum taxable income (AMTI),
3. Subtracting the AMT exemption amount,
4. Multiplying the amount computed in (3) by the applicable AMT rate, and
5. Subtracting the AMT Foreign Tax Credit.

The AMT exemption in step 3 is an amount that is deducted from alternative minimum taxable income before calculating the tentative minimum tax. The exemption phases out after a taxpayer's AMTI reaches a certain level, which is based on his filing status. For 2013, the following AMT exemption amounts apply and are phased out at a rate of 25% when AMTI is within the indicated ranges:

Filing Status	AMT Exemption	Exemption Phase-out Range
MFJ or QW	$80,800	$153,000 to $477,100
MFS	$40,400	$76,950 to $238,550
Single or HOH	$51,900	$115,400 to $323,000

Tax preparation software will automatically compute whether a taxpayer owes the AMT. A taxpayer who prepares his own return without using software may need to complete Form 6251, *Alternative Minimum Tax-Individuals*, to determine whether he owes the AMT.

If a taxpayer received or claimed any of the following items in the tax year, he is required to complete Form 6251:

- Accelerated depreciation
- Stock received through incentive stock options that were not disposed of in the same year
- Tax-exempt interest from private activity bonds
- Intangible drilling, circulation, research, experimental, or mining costs
- Amortization of pollution-control facilities or depletion
- Income (or loss) from tax-shelter farm activities or passive activities
- Interest from long-term contracts not figured using the percentage of completion-method
- Interest paid on a home mortgage not used to buy, build, or substantially improve the taxpayer's home
- Investment interest expense reported on Form 4952
- Net operating loss deduction
- Alternative minimum tax adjustments from an estate, trust, electing large partnership, or cooperative
- Section 1202 exclusion
- Any general business credit in Part 1 on Form 3800
- Empowerment zone and renewal community employment credit
- Qualified electric vehicle credit
- Alternative fuel vehicle refueling property credit
- Credit for prior year minimum tax

Credit for Prior Year Minimum Tax

A nonrefundable credit may be available to individuals, estates, and trusts for alternative minimum tax paid in prior years to the extent that a taxpayer's regular tax in the current year is greater than his tentative minimum tax. If applicable, the credit is calculated on Form 8801, *Credit for Prior Year Minimum Tax – Individuals, Estates, and Trusts*.

The AMT is caused by two types of adjustments and preferences: exclusion items and deferral items. Exclusion items are those that affect only a single tax year and therefore cause a permanent difference between regular taxable income and AMTI. For individual taxpayers, an example is the deduction for state and local income taxes. These taxes are never deductible for AMT purposes, and they are added back to AGI in the calculation of AMTI in the year they are paid.

Deferral items are adjustment and preference items, such as depreciation, that affect more than one tax year. Because they affect the difference between regular taxable income and AMTI in multiple tax years, they generally do not cause a permanent difference in taxable income over time. The minimum tax credit is allowed only for the portion of AMT caused by deferral items, which generate credit for future years.

Example: Leland and Erika are married and file jointly. They had an AMT liability in 2012 after they exercised incentive stock options. They use Form 8801 to calculate how much of their AMT was related to that and other deferral items and discover they have a credit they can carry forward to 2013.

AMT adjustments/preferences that are exclusion items and are not used to determine the minimum tax credit are as follows:

- Personal exemption
- Standard deduction
- Itemized deductions
- Percentage depletion
- Certain tax-exempt interest
- Exclusion of gain from qualified small business stock

All other items are deferral items and are used to calculate the credit.

Affordable Care Act Taxes

The Affordable Care Act (ACA)[24] contains 20 new taxes or tax increases that are, or will be, administered by the IRS. The law mandates that all U.S. citizens and residents have health insurance, or pay a fine for not doing so. The ACA is being implemented in stages, with several key provisions having gone into effect in 2013.[25] In earlier units we described the increased threshold

[24] Although commonly known as Obamacare, the actual name of the 2010 health care law is the Patient Protection and Affordable Care Act, often shortened to the Affordable Care Act or ACA.

[25] Additional provisions of the law take effect in 2014. These include the tax on individuals who do not maintain health care coverage, which is called the "shared responsibility payment"; and the premium tax credit for certain taxpayers who acquire health insurance through the federal marketplace. However, full implementation will be delayed until 2016 for an employer mandate that requires all businesses with 50 full-time equivalent employees to provide health insurance for their full-time employees or pay a monthly "employer shared responsibility payment."

for deduction of medical expenses and the new $2,500 limit for contributions to flexible spending accounts. Two additional ACA taxes are imposed on higher-income taxpayers: the net investment income tax and the additional Medicare tax.

Net Investment Income Tax (NIIT)

Starting January 1, 2013, the net investment income tax applies to individuals, estates, and trusts. For individuals, a 3.8% tax is imposed on the lesser of:

- The individual's net investment income for the year, or
- Any excess of the individual's modified adjusted gross income for the tax year over the following thresholds:

Filing Status	Threshold Amount
MFJ or QW	$250,000
MFS	$125,000
Single or HOH	$200,000

These threshold amounts are not indexed for inflation. The NIIT is only imposed on U.S. citizens and resident aliens; nonresident aliens are not subject to the NIIT.

Net investment income that is subject to the tax includes:

- Interest, unless it is otherwise tax-exempt
- Dividends
- Capital gains
- Rental and royalty income
- Non-qualified annuities
- Income from businesses involved in trading of financial instruments or commodities
- Income from businesses that are passive activities for the taxpayer

Net investment income does not include wages, self-employment income, Social Security benefits, veterans' benefits, unemployment compensation, alimony payments, or distributions from IRAs or certain qualified retirement plans.

Example: Trey is single and earned a salary of $175,000 in 2013. He also had $15,000 of income from dividends and capital gains, for MAGI of $190,000.This amount is less than the $200,000 threshold for single filers, so Trey is not subject to the net investment income tax.

Example: Leanna is single and earned a salary of $175,000 in 2013. She also received $80,000 of rental income, for MAGI of $255,000, which exceeds the threshold for single filers by $55,000. The net investment income tax is based on the lesser of $55,000 (the amount by which her MAGI exceeds the threshold for single filers) or $80,000 (her NII). Leanne owes NIIT of $2,090 ($55,000 × 3.8% = $2,090).

To the extent that gains are not otherwise offset by capital losses, the following are common examples of items included in computing net investment income:

- Gains from the sale of stocks, bonds, and mutual funds

- Capital gain distributions from mutual funds
- Gains from the sale of investment real estate
- Gains from the sale of interests in partnerships and S corporations, to the extent the partner or shareholder was a passive owner

The NIIT does not apply to any amount of gain that is excluded from gross income for regular income tax purposes. Thus, the gain on the sale of a principal residence is not considered in the calculation of the NIIT, except to the extent that it exceeds the amount excluded from taxation (typically the first $250,000, or $500,000 if MFJ.)

Example: Reza and Zari are married and file jointly. They sell their main home that they have lived in for five years for $1.8 million and realize a gain of $850,000 on the sale. They may exclude $500,000 under section 121, so their gain subject to regular income tax is $350,000. They also have $75,000 of net investment income from other sources, for a total of $425,000. Their MAGI is $525,000, which exceeds the MFJ threshold amount of $250,000 by $275,000. They are subject to the NIIT on the lesser of $425,000 (NII) or $275,000 (the amount of excess MAGI). Reza and Zari owe NIIT of $10,450 ($275,000 × 3.8% = $10,450.)

A gain from the sale of a second home that is not a primary residence would not be eligible for section 121 exclusion and therefore would also be subject to the NIIT.

Federal income tax credits generally may be used to offset net investment income.

Investment interest expense, investment advisory and brokerage fees, expenses related to rental and royalty income, and tax preparation fees may also be deducted to determine gross investment income, which is used to arrive at net investment income.

The NIIT is subject to estimated tax provisions, so taxpayers may need to adjust their withholding or estimated payments to avoid underpayment penalties. Employers are not required to withhold the tax from an employee's wages. The tax is computed on Form 8960, *Net Investment Tax: Individuals, Estates, and Trusts.*

Additional Medicare Tax

Starting in 2013, an additional Medicare tax of 0.9% applies to a taxpayer's earned income that exceeds the following thresholds:

Filing Status	Threshold Amount
MFJ	$250,000
MFS	$125,000
Single, HOH, or QW	$200,000

The thresholds are not adjusted for inflation. A taxpayer's earned income (including wages, taxable fringe benefits, bonuses, tips, commissions, and self-employment income) that is subject to Medicare tax is also subject to the additional Medicare tax to the extent it exceeds the applicable threshold amount for his filing status. Box 5 on an employee's Form W-2 shows the amount of income from an employer that is subject to Medicare taxes.

An employer is required to withhold the additional Medicare tax if an employee is paid more than $200,000, regardless of an employee's filing status or whether the employee has wages paid by another employer. There is no employer share of the additional Medicare tax. Self-employed taxpayers cannot deduct one-half of the 0.9% additional Medicare tax.

A taxpayer may be subject to the additional Medicare tax even if amounts are not withheld from his wages.

Example: Steven is single and earned $145,000 of salary in 2013. Because his earnings are below the $200,000 threshold for single filers, his company did not withhold any amount for the additional Medicare tax. He also had $85,000 in self-employment income. Steven's total earned income is $230,000. He would be required to pay additional Medicare tax on the $30,000 of earned income that exceeds the $200,000 threshold. Steven would owe $270 in additional Medicare tax on his 2013 income tax return ($30,000 × .9% = $270).

Example: Steven gets married on December 31, 2013 to Elaine, who earned wages of $7,000 during the year. Because they are married as of the last day of the year and file jointly, their threshold for the additional Medicare tax is $250,000. Their combined earned income is $237,000, below the $250,000 threshold for MFJ. Steven and Elaine do not owe the additional Medicare Tax.

Example: Quan and Kim-Ly are married and file jointly. Quan earned $120,000 of salary in 2013, and Kim-Ly earned $190,000. Their employers do not withhold amounts for the additional Medicare tax, because neither has earnings above $200,000. However, their combined earned income is $310,000, which is above the $250,000 threshold for joint filers by $60,000. Quan and Kim-Ly will owe $540 of additional Medicare tax on their 2013 income tax return ($60,000 × .9% = $540.)

If an employer withholds amounts for an employee who earns more than $200,000 but the employee and his spouse's combined earnings are less than the $250,000 MFJ threshold, they can apply the overpayment against any other type of tax that may be owed on their income tax return.

The additional Medicare tax is computed on Form 8959, *Additional Medicare Tax.*

Kiddie Tax

Years ago, wealthy families could transfer investments to their minor children and save tax dollars because the investment income would be taxed at the children's lower rates. Congress closed this tax loophole, and now investment income earned by dependent children may be taxed at the parent's rate. This law became known as the kiddie tax. The kiddie tax does not apply to earned income; it applies only to investment income, such as interest, dividends, and capital gains distributions. Part of a child's investment income may be taxed at the parent's marginal tax rate if:

- The child's investment income is more than $2,000.
- The child is under age 18 or a full-time college student under age 24.
- The child is required to file a tax return for the tax year.
- At least one of the child's parents was alive at the end of the year.
- The child does not file a joint return for the tax year.

Parents can avoid paying the kiddie tax only if the child is age 18 or older and has enough earned income to provide greater than half of his own support. In that case, the tax would be based on the child's tax rate and not the parent's.

The first $1,000 of investment income a child or college student earns is offset by the $1,000 standard deduction for dependents (assuming the child has no earned income), and the next $1,000 is taxed at the child's rate. All of the child's investment income in excess of $2,000 is taxed at the parent's tax rate.

Example: Bill and Donna have a 15-year-old son named Jack. In 2013, Jack has $2,500 of interest income from a CD his grandfather gave him. He does not have any other income. The first $1,000 of investment income is not taxable, because the standard deduction for dependents is $1,000. The next $1,000 is taxed at the 10% income tax rate. The remainder, $500, is taxed at his parents' marginal rate.

A child's investment income is subject to the net investment income tax, which is calculated using only the child's income and not the parent's. The NIIT applies only if the child's net investment income exceeds the $200,000 threshold for single filers.

In certain cases, parents may elect to include their child's investment income on their own tax return, and the child will not have to file a return. The same age restrictions as listed above apply, and the following conditions must also be met:

- The child's only income was from interest and dividends, including capital gain distributions and Alaska Permanent Fund dividends.
- The child's gross income for 2013 was less than $10,000.
- The child would otherwise be required to file a 2013 return and does not file a joint return.
- There were no estimated tax payments for the child for 2013.
- There was no federal income tax withheld from the child's income.

To make this election, the parents must attach Form 8814, *Parents' Election to Report Child's Interest and Dividends,* to their Form 1040.

If the kiddie tax is applicable, Form 8615, *Tax for Certain Children Who Have Unearned Income,* must be completed.

Nanny Tax (Household Employees)

A taxpayer who has household employees may need to pay employment taxes. This obligation is commonly referred to as the "nanny tax." If a taxpayer pays a household employee cash wages (including amounts paid by check, money order, etc.) of $1,800 or more, he must withhold the employee's share of Social Security and Medicare taxes, and remit them along with the employer's matching share, for a total of 15.3%, unless he chooses to pay both the employer's and employee's shares. If the amount of wages paid to an employee during the year is less than this threshold, no Social Security or Medicare taxes are owed.

Note: Even if the employer is not required to pay FICA taxes, the wages may be taxable to the employee.

An employer is not required to withhold income tax from a household employee's wages. However, income tax may be withheld at the employee's request.

If a taxpayer pays wages of $1,000 or more to a household employee in a quarter, he must also pay federal unemployment tax. The tax applies to the first $7,000 of wages per employee, at a rate that ranges from .06% to 6% depending upon whether the wages are subject to state unemployment taxes.

A worker is the taxpayer's employee if the taxpayer can control not only what work is done but how it is done, regardless of whether the work is full-time or part-time; the employee is paid on an hourly, daily, weekly, or per job basis; or the employee is hired through an agency. Examples of household employees include babysitters, housekeepers, private nurses, yard workers, and drivers.

Example: Lena hires Candy to babysit her three children and do light housework in her home. Lena sets Candy's schedule and gives specific direction about household and child care duties. Lena also provides all the equipment and supplies Candy needs to do her work. Candy is Lena's household employee.

A self-employed worker, such as a daycare provider who cares for several children from different families in her own home, is not a taxpayer's household employee.

Example: Lena also hires Robby to care for her lawn. Robby runs a lawn care business and provides services to many other clients. He hires his own workers, instructs them how to do their jobs, and provides his own tools and supplies. Neither Robby nor his workers are Lena's household employees.

Wages paid to a taxpayer's spouse, parent, or child under the age of 21 are exempt from the nanny tax rules. A taxpayer may not claim a dependency exemption for a household employee such as a nanny, even if the employee lives with the taxpayer.

A taxpayer who is required to pay Social Security and Medicare taxes or federal unemployment taxes for household employees, or who withholds income tax for them, must file Schedule H, *Household Employment Taxes,* with his Form 1040. The taxpayer will need an employer identification number (EIN) to file Schedule H. He also must file Form W-2, *Wage and Tax Statement,* and furnish a copy of the form to the employee.

First-Time Homebuyer Credit Repayment

First-time homebuyers who claimed a special tax credit in 2008 are required to repay a portion of the funds received over a 15-year period. The First-Time Homebuyer Credit took the form of a loan in 2008. For example, a homebuyer who claimed the maximum credit of $7,500 must repay $500 per year as an additional tax. The amount is entered on line 59b on Form 1040.

A taxpayer who claimed the credit and sells a home purchased in 2008 must complete Form 5405, *First-Time Homebuyer Credit and Repayment of the Credit*. The repayment is limited to the amount of gain on the sale, if the sale is to an unrelated taxpayer. The credit was also available in 2009 and 2010, but has since expired. A taxpayer who purchased his home and received the credit in either 2009 or 2010 does not have to repay the credit unless he sold the home within a three-year period following the purchase.

Example: Alexa purchased her home in 2008 and claimed the full amount of the First-Time Homebuyer Credit. She still lives in the home and uses it as her primary residence. She is required to pay back her credit in equal yearly installments of $500 over a period of 15 years. When she files her 2013 tax return, the repayment is listed on her Form 1040 as an additional tax.

Foreign Income and Taxes

Generally, all income of U.S. citizens (and U.S. resident aliens) is subject to tax by the United States, regardless of where the individual lives and even if the income is earned outside the United States. "Foreign earned income" is income received for services performed in a foreign country while the taxpayer's tax home is also in a foreign country. It does not matter whether the income is paid by a U.S. employer or a foreign employer.

Foreign Earned Income Exclusion: If a taxpayer is eligible for the foreign earned income exclusion, his income up to a certain threshold is not taxed. For 2013, the maximum foreign earned income exclusion is $97,600. If married taxpayers file jointly and both individuals live and work abroad, each can claim the foreign earned income exclusion.

Example: Brenda and Sonny are married and file jointly. In 2013, they were both employed in Peru, with Brenda earning $80,000 and Sonny earning $26,000. Each qualifies for the foreign earned income exclusion. Brenda also has $6,000 in work-related expenses. She cannot deduct any of her expenses, because she is already excluding all of her income from taxation by taking the foreign earned income exclusion.

Nonresident aliens do not qualify for the foreign earned income exclusion. A taxpayer must be either a U.S. citizen or a legal resident alien of the United States who lives and works abroad and must pass one of two tests in order to claim the exclusion:

- **Bona Fide Residence Test:** A U.S. citizen or U.S. resident alien who is a bona fide resident of a foreign country for an uninterrupted period that includes an entire tax year.
- **The Physical Presence Test:** A U.S. citizen or U.S. resident alien who is physically present in a foreign country or countries for at least 330 full days during 12 consecutive months. A taxpayer may qualify under the physical presence test, and the income may span a period of multiple tax years. If so, the taxpayer must prorate the foreign earned income exclusion based on the number of days spent in the foreign country.

Note: The exclusion does not apply to the wages and salaries of members of the Armed Forces and civilian employees of the U.S. government.

The foreign earned income exclusion is calculated using Form 2555, *Foreign Earned Income,* which must be attached to Form 1040. If a choice is made to exclude foreign earned income, the choice remains in effect for subsequent years, unless revoked.

Foreign Housing Exclusion or Deduction: In addition to the foreign earned income exclusion, taxpayers can claim an exclusion or a deduction for foreign housing costs. The housing exclusion only applies to amounts paid by an employer. The housing deduction applies only to amounts paid with self-employment earnings. Qualified housing expenses include reasonable expenses paid for housing in a foreign country. Only housing expenses for the part of the year that the taxpayer actually qualified for the foreign earned income exclusion are considered.

Example: Sergio is a U.S. citizen who lived in Vietnam all of 2013 and was employed by a Vietnamese company. He lived rent-free in an apartment provided by his employer. Sergio received salary of $85,000, and the fair rental value of his housing was $20,000, for a total of $105,000 of earned income. He qualifies for the foreign earned income exclusion and the foreign housing exclusion.

Foreign Income Taxes: Generally, income taxes paid to a foreign country can be deducted as an itemized deduction on Schedule A or as a credit against U.S. income tax. A taxpayer can choose between these options and use whichever one results in the lowest tax.

Foreign Tax Credit: U.S. citizens and resident aliens are eligible for the Foreign Tax Credit, which is designed to relieve taxpayers of the double taxation burden that occurs when their foreign source income is taxed by both the U.S. and a foreign country. Nonresident aliens are not eligible.

Four tests must be met to qualify for the credit:

- The tax must be imposed on the taxpayer.
- The taxpayer must have paid, or accrued (if an accrual basis taxpayer), the tax.
- The tax must be a legal and actual foreign tax liability.
- The tax must be an income tax.

Although taxpayers can choose between taking the deduction or the credit for all foreign taxes paid, in most cases it is to their advantage to take the Foreign Tax Credit since a credit directly reduces tax liability. A taxpayer cannot claim both the deduction and the tax credit on the same return, but may alternate years, taking a credit in one year and a deduction in the next year.

Taxpayers also may not claim the Foreign Tax Credit for taxes paid on any income that has already been excluded using the foreign earned income exclusion or the foreign housing exclusion. Unlike the foreign earned income exclusion, which only applies to income that is earned while a taxpayer is living and working overseas, the Foreign Tax Credit applies to any type of foreign income, including investment income. Foreign tax paid may be reported to the taxpayer by a financial institution on Form 1099-INT or Form 1099-DIV.

Taxpayers may claim the credit on line 47 of Form 1040 if, among other conditions, all foreign income is specified passive category income and total taxes paid do not exceed $300 ($600 MFJ). If the tax paid exceeds $300 ($600 MFJ), the taxpayer must file Form 1116, *Foreign Tax Credit*, to claim the credit.

Example: Yusuf and Fatima are married and file jointly. They own a number of foreign stocks, and their Form 1099-DIV shows foreign tax paid of $590. The couple is not required to complete Form 1116, because their foreign taxes are less than $600.

Example: Colette is a shareholder of a French corporation. She receives $300 in earnings from the corporation. The French government imposes a 10% tax ($30) on Colette's earnings. She must include the gross earnings ($300) in her income. The $30 of tax withheld is a qualified foreign tax for purposes of the Foreign Tax Credit.

Certain taxes do not qualify for the Foreign Tax Credit, including interest or penalties paid to a foreign country, taxes imposed by countries involved with international terrorism, and taxes on foreign oil or gas extraction income. The Foreign Tax Credit is nonrefundable, but the taxpayer is allowed a one-year carryback and a ten-year carryforward of any unused credit amount.

Reporting Foreign Accounts and Assets

U.S. citizens and residents are required to report information concerning their foreign accounts to the IRS on their federal income tax returns. Taxpayers filing Form 1040 or Form 1040A do so by completing boxes 7a and 7b of Schedule B, *Interest and Ordinary Dividends.*

Statement of Specified Foreign Financial Assets: Taxpayers who hold foreign financial assets with an aggregate value that exceeds $50,000 ($100,000 MFJ) on the last day of the tax year, or that exceeds $75,000 ($150,000 MFJ) at any time during the tax year also must file Form 8938, *Statement of Specified Foreign Financial Assets,* with their returns. A taxpayer who is not required to file a return for the year does not need to file Form 8938, even if the value of his specified foreign assets is greater than one of the reporting thresholds.

FBAR: In addition to the Form 8938 requirement, there is a reporting mandate for taxpayers with foreign accounts of more than $10,000. Under the Bank Secrecy Act, these taxpayers must file FinCEN Form 114, *Report of Foreign Bank and Financial Accounts* (FBAR), on-line with the Treasury Department's Financial Crimes Enforcement Network (FinCEN). This requirement applies to bank accounts, brokerage accounts, mutual funds, trusts, and other types of foreign financial accounts. Taxpayers may be required to file the report even if their accounts produce no taxable income. U.S. citizens, residents, entities, and estates are required to file an FBAR if they:

- Had a financial interest in or signature authority over at least one financial account located outside of the United States; and
- The aggregate value of all foreign financial accounts exceeded $10,000 at any time during the calendar year.

Because foreign financial institutions may not be subject to the same reporting requirements as financial institutions located within the United States, the FBAR is designed to help the U.S. government identify persons or entities that use offshore accounts to hide income or illicit funds.

The FBAR is due by June 30 of the year following the year in which the account holder meets the $10,000 threshold. Unlike income tax returns, the FBAR is not considered to have been filed timely based upon its postmarked date. The Treasury Department office in Detroit must actually receive the report by June 30. Further, the taxpayer cannot request an extension of the FBAR due date, even if he has a six-month extension to file his tax return. As of July 1, 2013, all FBAR forms are required to be filed electronically.

Failure to file a required FBAR can subject a taxpayer to severe civil and criminal penalties. Criminal penalties may include a fine of up to $250,000 and five years in prison.

Unit 15: Study Questions

1. Which of the following statements regarding the Foreign Tax Credit is correct?

A. The Foreign Tax Credit is a refundable credit.
B. The Foreign Tax Credit is available to U.S. citizens and nonresident aliens.
C. Taxpayers may choose to take a deduction for foreign taxes paid rather than the Foreign Tax Credit.
D. Taxpayers may claim both a deduction and a tax credit for foreign taxes paid, provided the taxes were paid to different countries.

2. Colton is 22, a full-time student, and is claimed as a dependent on his parents' tax return. He also has a part-time job at a local mall. Colton has $210 of dividend income in 2013. What is the maximum amount of wages that Colton can earn in 2013 without triggering the kiddie tax?

A. $350.
B. $2,000.
C. $6,100.
D. No maximum.

3. Ella hired a part-time nanny to work in her home. She paid the nanny $1,500 of wages in 2013. Which of the following statements is true?

A. Ella is not required to issue a Form W-2 to the nanny, and does not have to report or pay Social Security and Medicare taxes on the nanny's wages.
B. The income is not taxable to the nanny.
C. No reporting is required by either party if the wages are paid in cash.
D. Ella can deduct the nanny's wages as a business expense on Schedule C.

4. The additional Medicare tax is:

A. 0.9% on a taxpayer's earned income above a certain threshold.
B. 3.8% on a taxpayer's earned income above a certain threshold.
C. 0.9% on a taxpayer's investment income above a certain threshold.
D. 3.8% on a taxpayer's investment income above a certain threshold.

5. All of the following statements are correct about the alternative minimum tax except:

A. Congress passed the alternative minimum tax to ensure that individuals and corporations that benefit from certain exclusions, deductions, or credits pay at least a minimum amount of tax.
B. The tentative minimum tax is figured in addition to a taxpayer's regular tax.
C. The AMT is the excess of the tentative minimum tax over the regular tax.
D. The AMT is permanently indexed for inflation.

6. Allen and Dorrie are married and file jointly. Dorrie's MAGI was $137,000 in 2013. Allen's MAGI was $165,000. They had $12,500 in net investment income. How much net investment income tax do they owe, if any, in 2013?

A. $2,451.
B. $1,976.
C. $475.
D. They do not owe the net investment income tax.

7. In 2013, when does an employer have to withhold and pay Social Security and Medicare taxes for a household employee?

A. When the taxpayer pays any employee for household services.
B. When the taxpayer pays a household employee $1,000 or more in wages a year.
C. When the taxpayer pays a household employee $1,800 or more in wages a year.
D. When the taxpayer pays his 20-year-old daughter to care for her younger siblings.

8. Natalie is a U.S. citizen who lives and works in Australia, which is her tax home. She does not maintain a residence in the U.S. In 2013, she received the following income:

- $12,500 of annuity income
- $2,000 of taxable interest
- $90,000 of wages

Natalie wants to take the foreign earned income exclusion on her individual tax return. What is the total amount of qualifying foreign earned income that she may report on her Form 2555 (Form 1040)?

A. $104,500.
B. $92,000.
C. $90,000.
D. $97,600.

9. Malia and Johnny are married and file jointly. Malia has $133,000 of self-employment income. Box 5 of Johnny's W-2 shows compensation of $184,000. Compute the amount of their additional Medicare tax, if any.
A. $2,853.
B. $1,053.
C. $603.
D. They do not owe the additional Medicare tax.

10. Which of the following taxpayers would not be eligible for the Credit for the Prior Year Minimum Tax by filing Form 8804?

A. An S corporation.
B. A trust.
C. An estate.
D. An individual.

11. Niki is 26, single, and purchased her first home in 2008. She applied for the $7,500 First Time Homebuyer Credit in 2008. Regarding this now-expired tax credit, how could it affect her individual tax return in 2013?

A. Expired credits have no effect on current-year returns.
B. In 2008, this credit took the form of a loan that was required to be repaid. Niki must pay a portion of this loan back on her 2013 tax return.
C. This credit is a refundable credit and does not need to be repaid until Niki sells or disposes of the property.
D. This expired credit will only affect Niki's current year return if she purchases a second home. In that case, the credit would be prorated.

12. What is the Foreign Tax Credit (FTC)?

A. The FTC applies to taxpayers who have paid foreign taxes to a foreign country on foreign-sourced income and are subject to U.S. tax on the same income.
B. The FTC applies to taxpayers who have paid U.S. taxes while living and working overseas.
C. The FTC applies to taxpayers who have paid U.S. taxes while living and working overseas and who are subject to U.S. tax on their worldwide income.
D. The FTC applies to nonresident aliens who have paid foreign taxes to a foreign country on foreign-sourced income and are subject to U.S. tax on the same income.

13. Faheema is single. She has the following income in 2013:

- $73,000 interest income
- $200,000 gain from selling her main home that she had lived in and owned for seven years
- $245,000 MAGI

Calculate Faheema's net investment income tax, if any, for 2013:

A. $0.
B. $1,710.
C. $2,774.
D. $10,374.

14. Which of the following is not an item that might trigger an AMT liability for individual taxpayers?

A. Investment interest expense on Schedule A.
B. Miscellaneous expenses on Schedule A.
C. Personal exemptions.
D. Casualty losses on Schedule C.

15. Jim, a U.S. citizen who lives in Iowa, has a bank account located in Austria. On December 31, 2013, the account has a balance of $23,000. What are Jim's reporting requirements for this account?

A. He is not required to report the funds in this account.
B. He must file Form 8938, *Statement of Specified Foreign Financial Assets*, with the IRS when he files his tax return.
C. He must file an FBAR, *Report of Foreign Bank and Financial Accounts*, with the Treasury Department by June 30, 2014.
D. He must file an FBAR, *Report of Foreign Bank and Financial Accounts*, with the Treasury Department by June 30, 2014, and file Form 8938, *Statement of Specified Foreign Financial Assets*, with the IRS when he files his tax return.

16. Which of the following taxpayers would be subject to the additional Medicare tax?

A. Randy, who files as head of household and earned $180,000 in wages and $50,000 in investment income.
B. Kerrie, who is single and earned $196,000 in compensation, fringe benefits, and bonuses.
C. Liz, who files separately from her husband and earned $140,000 in wages.
D. None of the above.

17. Roman is single. In 2013, he sold a house he had lived in for 15 years at a gain of $486,000. He also had the following income:

- $85,000 salary
- $4,000 bonus
- $1,500 gain from sale of stock
- $9,600 rental income
- $300 interest income from a CD

Roman's MAGI was $336,400. What is Roman's net investment income tax, if any, for 2013?

A. $114.
B. $5,183.20.
C. $18,468.
D. He does not owe the net investment income tax.

18. The AMT was adopted by Congress in an attempt to ensure that individuals ______________.

A. Pay a minimum amount of tax.
B. Pay zero tax.
C. Do not cheat on their taxes.
D. Pay tax at a lower rate than taxpayers in other countries.

19. Which of the following is a correct statement about the net investment income tax?

A. The tax is 3.8% of the excess of MAGI over a threshold amount.
B. The tax is 3.8% of net investment income.
C. The tax is 3.8% of the greater of net investment income or the excess of MAGI over a threshold amount.
D. The tax is 3.8% of the lesser of net investment income or the excess of MAGI over a threshold amount.

20. In determining a taxpayer's credit for prior year minimum tax, which of the following would not be considered?

A. Depreciation.
B. Mortgage interest.
C. Incentive stock options.
D. All of the above.

21. Which of the following types of a child's investment income would preclude his parents from electing to report that investment income on their tax return?

A. Royalties.
B. Capital gain distributions.
C. Interest.
D. Alaska Permanent Funds dividends.

22. Which of the following taxpayers would not be subject to the net investment income tax?

A. An estate.
B. A nonresident alien.
C. A C corporation.
D. Both B and C.

Unit 16: Retirement Accounts

> **More Reading:**
> **Publication 590, *Individual Retirement Arrangements (IRAs)***
> **Publication 575, *Pension and Annuity Income***
> **Publication 560, *Retirement Plans for Small Business***

There are a variety of retirement accounts that individuals can establish for themselves and retirement plans that can be established by employers and self-employed individuals. In this unit, we primarily cover traditional individual retirement arrangements (IRAs) and Roth IRAs, as they are tested heavily on Part 1 of the EA exam. We will also briefly address other types of retirement plans.

Form 1099-R, *Distributions From Pensions, Annuities, Retirement or Profit-Sharing Plans, IRAs, Insurance Contracts, etc.*, is used to report distributions of $10 or more from a retirement plan or an IRA.

> **Note:** Beginning September 16, 2013, the rules regarding IRAs and retirement plans apply to same-sex spouses who were legally married in any state that recognizes same-sex marriage. A same-sex spouse is entitled to all spousal benefits and protections provided to opposite-sex spouses from traditional IRAs, Roth IRAs, and qualified retirement plans.

Traditional IRA: Amounts in a traditional IRA, including contributions and earnings, are generally not taxed until they are distributed. In most cases, a taxpayer can deduct his traditional IRA contributions as an adjustment to gross income. However, the adjustment is phased out at higher income levels.

Roth IRA: Contributions to a Roth IRA are paid with after-tax income and are not deductible. In contrast to a traditional IRA, withdrawals from a Roth IRA are generally not taxed. Income limits apply in determining who is eligible to participate in a Roth IRA.

> **Example:** In 2013, Leo contributes $2,200 to a traditional IRA and $1,000 to a Roth IRA. Subject to further limitation based upon his income level, the most Leo will be able to deduct as an adjustment to income is the $2,200 contribution to his traditional IRA. Roth IRA contributions are never deductible.

A taxpayer cannot claim the adjustment for an IRA contribution on Form 1040EZ; he must use Form 1040, Form 1040A, or Form 1040NR.

2013 IRA Contribution Limits

The limits for contributions to an IRA in 2013 are the lesser of qualifying taxable compensation (as described below) and the following amounts:

Under 50 years of age:

- $5,500 per taxpayer
- Filing jointly (Both 50 or under): $11,000

50 years and over:

- $6,500 per taxpayer
- Filing jointly (Both 50 or older): $13,000

Traditional IRA Rules

To make contributions to a traditional IRA:

- The taxpayer must be under age 70½ at the end of the year.
- The taxpayer must have qualifying taxable compensation, such as wages, salaries, commissions, tips, bonuses, or self-employment income.

If either the taxpayer or his spouse is covered by an employer plan and his income is too high, his deductible IRA contribution will be phased out.

For purposes of making an IRA contribution, taxable alimony (but not child support payments) counts as qualifying compensation. This allows taxpayers to build retirement savings in IRAs even if they rely on alimony income for support. Nontaxable combat pay also qualifies as compensation for this purpose.

Example: Stan is an Army medic serving in a combat zone for all of 2013. Although none of his pay is taxable, it is still considered qualifying compensation for purposes of an IRA contribution.

Compensation for purposes of contributing to an IRA does not include:

- Rental income
- Dividend and interest income
- Pension or annuity income
- Deferred compensation
- Prize winnings or gambling income
- Items (except for nontaxable combat pay) that are excluded from income, such as foreign earned income and housing costs

Example: Larry is 54 and wants to contribute to his traditional IRA. He received $10,000 in rental income; $8,000 in interest income; and $3,000 in wages from a part-time job. The rental and interest income are not considered for purposes of determining his IRA contribution. Therefore, the maximum he can contribute to his traditional IRA is $3,000, the amount of his wages.

IRAs cannot be owned jointly; each spouse must have a separate IRA account. However, a married couple who files jointly may contribute to each of their IRA accounts, even if only one taxpayer has qualifying compensation.

Example: Joaquin, 49, and Meg, 51, are married and file jointly. Joaquin works as a paramedic and makes $46,000 per year. Meg is a homemaker and has no income. Even though Meg has no taxable compensation, they may contribute to her IRA account. Their combined maximum contribution for 2013 is $12,000. Joaquin may contribute $5,500, and Meg may contribute $6,500 because she is over 50 years old.

Contributions can be made to a traditional IRA at any time on or before the due date of the return (not including extensions). For the 2013 tax year, a taxpayer may make an IRA contribution up until April 15, 2014. This makes an IRA contribution a rare opportunity for late-stage tax planning because it can occur after the tax year has already ended.

A taxpayer can even file his return claiming a traditional IRA contribution before the contribution is actually made. However, if a contribution is reported on the taxpayer's return but it is not made by the deadline, the taxpayer must file an amended return.

Example: Paul files his 2013 tax return on March 5, 2014 and claims a $4,000 deduction for an IRA contribution. Paul may wait as late as April 15, 2014 (the due date of the return) to make the IRA contribution.

If a person's only qualifying compensation for the year is from self-employment and the self-employment activity generates a loss for that year, he would not be able to contribute to an IRA. However, if the taxpayer has wages in addition to self-employment income, a loss from self-employment would not be subtracted from the wages when figuring total compensation income for purposes of determining any limitation on his IRA contribution.

Example: Marcy is 45 and earns $10,000 in wages working part-time for a library. She also works as a self-employed photographer, but her photography business has a loss of $5,400. Even though Marcy's net income for 2013 is only $4,600 ($10,000 wages – $5,400 loss from self-employment), her qualifying compensation for purposes of an IRA contribution is still $10,000, the amount of her wages. This means that Marcy can make a full IRA contribution of $5,500 in 2013.

For married taxpayers filing a joint return, the combined IRA contributions cannot exceed their combined qualifying compensation.

Example: Elliott and June are both age 49 and married. Elliott has $23,000 in pension income for the year. June has $13,000 in pension income and $7,000 in wages. Only June's wages count as qualifying compensation. If they file jointly, they can contribute a maximum of $7,000 to their IRAs. One of them can contribute up to the maximum annual amount ($5,500), and the other can contribute up to $1,500 (equal to the remaining amount of June's qualifying compensation), or they could split the $7,000 in another manner.

If married taxpayers choose to file separately, they must consider only their own qualifying compensation for IRA contribution purposes.

Example: Greg is 35, works full-time, and earned $55,000 in 2013. His wife, Laverne, is 34 and earned $3,600 in 2013. They choose to file separately. Therefore, Laverne is limited to a $3,600 IRA contribution, the amount of her qualifying compensation. Greg may contribute the full $5,500 to his own IRA account.

Splitting Contributions Between IRA Accounts: A person may have IRA accounts with multiple financial institutions and may split his annual contributions between accounts; his aggregate contributions for the year are subject to the limits described above. Further, a taxpayer may choose to split his contributions between a traditional IRA and a Roth IRA; again, his combined contributions are subject to the maximum annual contribution limits outlined above.

Example: Alan is 32. He has a traditional IRA through his bank and a Roth IRA through his stockbroker. Alan can contribute to both of his retirement accounts, but the combined contributions for 2013 cannot exceed $5,500. Alan decides to contribute $3,000 to his Roth IRA and $2,500 to his traditional IRA.

Example: Naomi, 25, has $3,000 of interest income and no other income in 2013. Naomi marries Carl during the year. Carl has taxable wages of $34,000 and he plans to contribute $5,500 to his traditional IRA. If he and Naomi file a joint return, each can contribute $5,500 to a traditional IRA. Naomi, who has no qualifying compensation, can use Carl's compensation, reduced by the amount of his IRA contribution ($34,000 – $5,500 = $28,500), to determine her maximum contribution to a traditional IRA.

Deductibility of Traditional IRA Contributions

A taxpayer may not be able to deduct all of his traditional IRA contributions. Deductibility is based on income, filing status, and whether the taxpayer or his spouse is covered by an employer retirement plan. A taxpayer is permitted to contribute to a traditional IRA regardless of whether he or his spouse is covered by an employer retirement plan; however, the deductible portion of the contribution may be limited.

If a taxpayer exceeds the income limits for making a fully deductible contribution to a traditional IRA, the excess portion can still be made as a nondeductible or after-tax contribution. Regardless of whether a portion of the contribution is nondeductible, the related earnings will grow on a tax-deferred basis.

Taxpayer (and Spouse) Not Covered by an Employer Plan: If neither the taxpayer nor his spouse is covered by an employer plan, there is no limitation on the deductibility of his or their traditional IRA contributions, other than as stated above. Thus, he or they can deduct the smaller of:

- $5,500 ($6,500 if age 50 or older) or $11,000 ($13,000 if age 50 or older) if filing jointly, or
- 100% of qualifying compensation.

Taxpayer (or Spouse) Covered by an Employer Plan: If either a taxpayer or his spouse, or both, is covered by (participates in) an employer retirement plan, the tax-deductible contribution to a traditional IRA is phased out at the following levels of modified adjusted gross income (MAGI):

2013 Phase-outs for Taxpayers Covered by an Employer Plan	
Filing Status	**MAGI Range**
MFJ or QW	$95,000 - $115,000
MFS (living with spouse)	$0 - $10,000
Single, HOH, or MFS (living apart)	$59,000 - $69,000

2013 Phase-outs for Taxpayers Not Covered By an Employer Plan	
Filing Status	**MAGI Range**
MFJ (spouse covered by employer plan)	$178,000 - $188,000
MFS (spouse covered by employer plan)	$0 - $10,000
Single, QW, HOH, MFJ or MFS (spouse not covered)	No limit

If a taxpayer makes nondeductible contributions to a traditional IRA, he must attach Form 8606, *Nondeductible IRAs.* Form 8606 reflects a taxpayer's cumulative nondeductible contributions, which is his tax basis in the IRA. If a taxpayer does not report nondeductible contributions properly, all future withdrawals from the IRA will be taxable unless the taxpayer can prove, with satisfactory evidence, that nondeductible contributions were made.

Example: Tamara is single and earned $95,000 in 2013. She is covered by a retirement plan at work, but she still wants to contribute to a traditional IRA. She is phased out for the deduction because her income exceeds the threshold for single filers covered by an employer plan. If she contributes to a traditional IRA in 2013, she must file Form 8606 to report her nondeductible contribution.

Married taxpayers who file MFS generally have a much lower phase-out range than those with any other filing status. However, if a taxpayer files a separate return and did not live with his spouse at any time during the year, the taxpayer is not treated as married for IRA purposes, and the phase-out range is the same as would apply for a single taxpayer.

Example: Don, age 43, and his wife are not divorced but they have lived in separate residences for the past three years. In 2013, Don earns $40,000 and files MFS. He is covered by an employer retirement plan, but is nevertheless allowed to deduct his full IRA contribution of $5,500. This is because he did not live with his spouse at any time during the year, and therefore is not subject to the lower IRA phase-out limits that normally apply to MFS filers.

Study Tip: Test-takers should memorize the various IRA phaseout ranges, as they are often tested on the EA exam.

Required Minimum Distributions

A person cannot keep funds in a traditional IRA account indefinitely. When the account owner reaches 70½ years of age, the funds must be distributed in annual required minimum distributions (RMDs). The first RMD payment can be delayed until April 1 of the year following the year the taxpayer turns 70½. The distribution for each subsequent year must be made by December 31. The amount of each RMD is based on IRS tables.[26]

Failure to take an RMD can result in a penalty tax equal to 50% of the amount the taxpayer should have withdrawn but did not. He must file IRS Form 5329, *Additional Taxes on Qualified Plans*, to report the excise tax that applies as a result of the failure to take the RMD.

Example: Dinah was born on October 1, 1942. She reaches age 70½ in 2013. Her first RMD must be distributed to her by April 1, 2014 in order to avoid the 50% excise tax. As of January 1, 2013, her IRA account balance was $79,500. The applicable distribution period per the IRS tables for someone her age (71) on that date is 26.5 years. Her required minimum distribution for 2013 is $3,000 ($79,500 ÷ 26.5).

[26] An RMD is calculated by dividing the balance of the IRA account by a life expectancy factor that the IRS publishes in tables within Publication 590, *Individual Retirement Arrangements (IRAs).*

Taxability of Distributions

Distributions from a traditional IRA are generally taxable in the year they are received, subject to the following exceptions:

- Rollovers to another retirement plan or account (other than conversions to a Roth IRA, as discussed below)
- Qualified charitable distributions
- Tax-free withdrawal of contributions
- Distributions of nondeductible contributions

Qualified Charitable Distributions (QCD): A taxpayer who is 70½ or older may choose to make a qualified charitable distribution (QCD) of up to $100,000 ($200,000 for MFJ taxpayers) from his IRA to qualified charitable organizations. The IRA trustee must make the distribution directly to the qualified charity (the taxpayer cannot request a distribution and then donate the money later). Likewise, any tax withholdings on behalf of the owner from an IRA distribution cannot qualify as QCDs.

Penalty on Early Distributions

A taxpayer may withdraw funds at any time from a traditional IRA account. However, distributions before age 59½ will generally be subject to an extra 10% tax, in addition to normal income tax on the amount distributed. There are some exceptions to the general rule for early distributions. An individual may not have to pay the additional 10% tax in the following situations:

- The taxpayer has unreimbursed medical expenses that exceed 10% of adjusted gross income.
- The distributions do not exceed the cost of the taxpayer's medical insurance.
- The taxpayer is disabled.
- The distributions are not more than qualified higher education expenses.
- The distributions are used to buy, build, or rebuild a first home.
- The distributions are used to pay the IRS due to a levy.
- The distributions are made to a qualified reservist (an individual called up to active duty).

Even though distributions in these situations will not be subject to the additional 10% tax, they will be subject to income tax at the taxpayer's normal rates.

Distributions that are properly rolled over into another retirement plan or account (other than conversions to a Roth IRA) are generally not subject to either income tax or the 10% additional penalty.

Example: Lauren, age 39, takes a $5,000 distribution from her traditional IRA account. She does not meet any of the exceptions to the 10% additional tax, so the $5,000 is an early distribution. Lauren must include the $5,000 in her gross income and pay income tax on it. In addition, she must pay a 10% penalty tax of $500 (10% × $5,000).

Roth IRA Rules

Unlike a traditional IRA, none of the contributions to a Roth IRA are deductible, but the entire balance is generally tax-free at the time of withdrawal. However, distributions generally cannot be made until after a five-year holding period and after the taxpayer has reached age 59½.

Further, income limits apply, which means high income earners may be prohibited from contributing to Roth IRAs. In 2013, the following income limits apply to Roth IRAs:

Filing Status	Full Contribution	Phase-out Range	No Roth IRA Allowed
Single, HOH filers[27]	Less than $112,000	$112,000 - $127,000	$127,000 or more
MFJ and QW filers	Less than $178,000	$178,000 - $188,000	$188,000 or more
MFS (lived with spouse)	N/A	$0 - $10,000	$10,000 or more

The major differences between a Roth IRA and a traditional IRA are as follows:

- Contributions to a Roth IRA are not deductible by the taxpayer, and participation in an employer plan has no effect on the contribution limits.
- There are no required minimum distributions from a Roth IRA. No distributions are required until a Roth IRA owner dies.
- Contributions to a Roth IRA can be made by individuals who are over the age of 70½.

IRA Rollovers

A rollover is a transfer from one retirement plan or account to another retirement plan or account. If executed properly, most rollovers are nontaxable events. However, taxpayers may also choose to convert a traditional IRA into a Roth IRA. In this case, the conversion will result in taxation of any previously untaxed amounts in the traditional IRA.

If a taxpayer receives an IRA distribution and wishes to make a nontaxable rollover, he must complete the transaction by the 60th day following the day he receives the distribution.

Example: On September 4, 2013, Adam begins a new job. He decides to transfer the balance of his traditional IRA account to his new employer's plan. Adam receives a distribution from his IRA of $50,000 in cash and $50,000 in stock. On October 9, he rolls over the entire amount of $100,000 into his new employer's plan. Because the transaction is completed within 60 days, it is nontaxable.

If a taxpayer sells the distributed property (such as stocks distributed from an IRA) and rolls over all the proceeds into another traditional IRA or qualified retirement plan within the required time frame, no gain or loss is recognized. The sale proceeds (including any increase in value) are treated as part of the distribution and are not included in the taxpayer's gross income.

The IRS allows only one rollover per IRA account in a 12-month period. However, a direct "trustee-to-trustee" transfer can be done more than once a year. This is when an IRA's current custodian (such as a bank) directly transfers the funds to a new custodian.

A taxable distribution paid from an employer-sponsored retirement plan is subject to mandatory tax withholding of 20%, even if the taxpayer intends to roll it over. If the taxpayer does roll it over and wants to defer tax on the entire taxable portion, he will be forced to add funds from other sources equal to the amount of tax withheld. In order to avoid this mandatory withholding, a taxpayer may request a "direct rollover." The distribution is then made directly from the custodian

[27] This phase-out range also applies to MFS taxpayers who did not live with their spouses at any time during the year.

for the employer-sponsored plan to the custodian for the employee's IRA or his new employer's retirement plan. Under this option, the 20% mandatory withholding does not apply.

Rollover after the Death of an IRA Owner

After the death of a traditional IRA's owner, a surviving spouse has two options: he can elect to treat the IRA as being his own by changing the ownership designation, or he can roll over the IRA balance to his own IRA account or certain other types of retirement plans.

Example: Allison, 42, and Lorenzo, 53, are married. Allison dies in 2013, and at the time of her death she has $50,000 in her traditional IRA account. Lorenzo chooses to roll over the entire $50,000 into his own IRA account, thereby avoiding taxation on the income until he retires and starts taking distributions.

For a beneficiary other than a surviving spouse, there are a number of factors that determine the period over which amounts remaining in an IRA upon the owner's death would be payable. These include whether the owner died on or before the date he was required to begin taking distributions, whether the beneficiary is an individual (or the owner's estate), and the life expectancies of the owner and the beneficiary in the year of death.

If a Roth IRA owner dies and the sole beneficiary is the spouse, he can delay distributions until the owner would have reached 70½ or treat the IRA as his own. For other beneficiaries, the account balance must generally be distributed by the end of the fifth calendar year after the owner's death, or be paid as an annuity over the beneficiary's life expectancy beginning the year following the year of death.

Conversion of a Traditional IRA to a Roth IRA

If a taxpayer wishes to convert all or a portion of his traditional IRA to a Roth IRA, he is required to pay income taxes on the amount of pretax (deductible) contributions converted, as well as the growth in value resulting from earnings on those contributions. After the funds are converted to a Roth IRA, additional earnings are tax-free, and distributions are generally not subject to tax. However, penalties apply if the taxpayer withdraws from the Roth IRA within five years of the conversion.

Example: Nancy converts her traditional IRA to a Roth IRA in 2013. The traditional IRA has a balance of $100,000. The entire balance represents deductible contributions and earnings that have not previously been taxed. She reports the amount of the balance that was converted as taxable income in 2013.

A Roth conversion is reported on Form 8606, *Nondeductible IRAs*.

An inherited traditional IRA is generally not eligible to be converted to a Roth IRA unless it is inherited from a spouse. Non-spousal beneficiaries (for example, a child who inherits a traditional IRA from a deceased parent) are not allowed to convert to a Roth IRA.

Traditional IRA vs. Roth IRA		
Issue	**Traditional IRA**	**Roth IRA**
Age limit	A person over 70½ cannot contribute.	No age limit.
2013 contribution limits	The lesser of $5,500 (or $6,500 if age 50 or older by the end of 2013) and qualifying taxable compensation.	Same.
Are contributions deductible?	Yes, depending on AGI, filing status, and whether the taxpayer and/or spouse is covered by an employer retirement plan.	No. Contributions to a Roth IRA are never deductible.
Filing requirements	No filing requirement unless nondeductible contributions are made. Nondeductible contributions must be reported on Form 8606.	Filing requirement related to conversion of a traditional IRA to a Roth IRA. None related to contributions made directly to a Roth IRA.
Mandatory distributions	A person must begin receiving required minimum distributions by April 1 of the year following the year he reaches age 70½.	There are no required distributions unless the IRA owner dies.
How distributions are taxed	Distributions from a traditional IRA are taxed as ordinary income.	Distributions from a Roth IRA are generally not taxed.
Income limits	Phase-out of deductibility is based upon AGI if taxpayer and/or spouse is covered by an employer plan.	There are income limits for contributions, but none affect conversion of a traditional IRA to a Roth IRA.

Excise Tax on Excess Contributions

If a taxpayer accidentally contributes more to his IRA than is allowed, the excess contribution is subject to a 6% excise tax. Contributions made in the year a taxpayer reaches age 70½ or thereafter are also considered excess contributions. However, the IRS will allow a taxpayer to correct an excess contribution if certain rules are followed.

If he makes a contribution that exceeds the annual maximum or his qualifying compensation, the excess contribution and all related earnings must be withdrawn from the IRA before the due date (including extensions) of the tax return for that year. If a taxpayer corrects the excess contribution within this period, the 6% penalty will apply only to the amounts earned on the excess contribution. The taxpayer must also report the earnings on the excess contribution as taxable income for the year in which the withdrawal is made.

For each year that the excess amounts remain in the IRA, the taxpayer must pay the 6% tax. However, this tax can never exceed 6% of the value of the taxpayer's IRA at the end of the tax year.

Example: Betsy, age 66, is self-employed and owns several rental properties. She contributes $6,500 to her traditional IRA in December 2013. She files for an extension to prepare her tax return. When she gives her records to her accountant, he discovers that her taxable income from self-employment is only $3,000 and her rental income is $38,000. Only the self-employment income counts as compensation for purposes of contributing to her IRA, so she has inadvertently made an excess contribution of $3,500. Betsy must withdraw the excess contribution and any earnings on it by the extended due date of her return or face an excise tax of 6% on both.

Prohibited Transactions

Generally, a prohibited transaction is the improper use of an IRA by the owner, a beneficiary, or a disqualified person (typically a fiduciary or family member). Prohibited transactions related to an IRA include:

- Borrowing money from it
- Selling property to it
- Using it as security for a loan
- Buying property for personal use with IRA funds

Example: Jada uses her traditional IRA as collateral for an auto loan. This is a prohibited transaction.

If a prohibited transaction occurs at any time during the year, the account ceases to be treated as an IRA and its assets are treated as if having been distributed on the first day of the year. If the total fair market value as of that date is more than the taxpayer's basis in the IRA, the excess amount is reportable as taxable income. It may also be subject to the additional 10% tax on early distributions.

Retirement Plans for Businesses

Retirement plans for businesses include Simplified Employee Pension (SEP) plans, Savings Incentive Match Plan for Employees (SIMPLE) plans, and qualified plans. The term "qualified" refers to certain IRS requirements that the plan and the employer must adhere to in order to obtain tax-favored status. SEP and SIMPLE plans must also meet certain requirements, but they are much less complex than those that apply to qualified plans.

Study Note: Business retirement plans are covered in greater detail, and from the employer's perspective, in *PassKey EA Review Book 2: Businesses*, as much of the related information is tested on Part 2 of the EA exam.

If retirement plans are structured and administered properly, businesses can deduct contributions they make on behalf of their employees or, if self-employed, themselves. Both the contributions and the earnings are generally tax-free until distribution. Further, some plans also allow employees to make contributions, most commonly in pre-tax dollars (so that a portion of their salaries are not taxed until the amounts are later distributed to them by the plan).

SEP Plans: SEPs provide a simplified method for employers to make contributions to a retirement plan for themselves and their employees. Instead of setting up a profit-sharing plan with a trust, an employer can adopt a SEP agreement and make contributions directly to individual SEP-IRA accounts (similar to a traditional IRA as described previously) for himself and each eligible employee. A SEP plan is funded exclusively by employer contributions; employee contributions are not permitted.

SIMPLE Plans: An employer can generally set up a SIMPLE plan if the business has 100 or fewer employees who received at least $5,000 in compensation during the preceding year. Under a SIMPLE plan, employees can choose to make salary reduction contributions rather than receiving these amounts as part of their regular pay. An employer can contribute matching or nonelective contributions. A SIMPLE plan can be structured in one of two ways: using SIMPLE IRAs (again, similar to traditional IRAs as described previously) or as a SIMPLE 401(k) plan (similar to the qualified 401(k) plans described below).

Qualified Retirement Plans

There are two basic kinds of qualified retirement plans: defined contribution plans and defined benefit plans, and different rules apply to each. An employer is allowed to have more than one type of qualified plan, but contributions cannot exceed annual limits. Contributions for self-employed taxpayers are limited to 100% of compensation. If the business does not have any income for the year, no contribution can be made.

All qualified plans are subject to federal regulation under the Employee Retirement Income Security Act (ERISA). The federal government does not require an employer to establish a retirement plan, but it provides minimum federal standards for qualified plans.

Defined Benefit Plans

A defined benefit plan (often called a traditional pension plan) promises a specified benefit amount or annuity for each participant after retirement. Benefits are typically based on formulas that consider the participant's years of service with the employer and his earnings history. The federal government and most state and local governments provide defined benefit plans for their employees. However, fewer businesses now offer defined benefit plans because they are costly to administer and inflexible. The benefits promised by many defined benefit plans are protected by federal insurance. Contributions to a defined benefit plan are not optional. Contributions are typically based on actuarial calculations that estimate the amounts necessary to pay benefits in the future.

Defined Contribution Plans

A defined contribution plan provides an individual account for each participant in the plan depending upon how the plan is structured. It provides benefits to each participant based on the amounts contributed to the participant's account, along with subsequent investment income or losses, and, in some instances, allocations of forfeitures among participant accounts.

The participants, the employer, or both may contribute to the individual participant accounts. Examples of defined contribution plans include profit-sharing plans, 401(k) plans, 403(b) plans, and 457 plans.

Contributions: Depending upon how the plan is structured, salary reduction/elective deferral contributions are employee contributions based on a percentage of the employee's compensation, and are generally made on a pre-tax basis. In 2013, an employee can contribute a maximum of $17,500 ($23,000 for employees age 50 and over) to his defined contribution plan account. This limitation applies to the aggregate amounts of contributions to any qualified plans, SEPs, and SIMPLE plans in which the individual participates during the year. However, the contribution cannot exceed the amount of the employee's compensation. Depending on the individual plan, the employer may provide matching contributions for employees who make elective deferrals.

Example: Jon earns $80,000 per year as an insurance executive. He participates in his company's profit-sharing 401(k) plan. He contributes 3% of his pre-tax wages to the plan in 2013, or $2,400 ($80,000 × .03). Jon's company contributes a matching 3% to his individual 401(k) account.

Distributions: Distributions to participants may be made either on a periodic basis, such as annuity payments, or as a lump sum. As is the case with distributions from traditional IRA accounts (as well as SEP and SIMPLE plans), distributions generally are not permitted prior to when the participant retires or otherwise terminates employment; dies; becomes disabled; or reaches age 59½. Earlier distributions are generally subject to an additional 10% penalty tax.

Required minimum distributions from defined contribution plans must generally begin by April 1 of the year following the later of the calendar year when the taxpayer retires or the year in which the taxpayer reaches age 70½.

Example: In 2013, Jon retires at age 63 after working 35 years at the insurance company. He would have been required to take distributions by April 1 of the year following the calendar year in which he reaches age 70½. However, he chooses to begin taking distributions from his 401(k) account in the same year he retires.

Note: For purposes of the net investment income tax, net investment income does not include distributions from a qualified retirement plan, such as a 401(k), or from traditional or Roth IRAs. However, these distributions are taken into account when determining the modified adjusted gross income threshold.

Loans from Qualified Plans

A qualified plan may allow its participants to borrow specified portions of their individual account balances, subject to certain restrictions. A loan can generally be no more than the lesser of $50,000, or the greater of $10,000 or 50% of the vested portion of the participant's account balance. If a loan is not repaid according to the specified payment terms, it may be considered a taxable distribution. This may apply if a participant terminates employment with the employer that sponsors the plan.

Hardship Distributions: A 401(k) plan may allow participants to receive hardship distributions because of an immediate and heavy financial need, such as sudden medical or funeral expenses.

Hardship distributions are limited to the amount of the employee's elective deferrals and generally do not include any income earned on the deferred amounts. The amount of the distribution may include amounts necessary to pay taxes or penalties anticipated to result from the distribution, including the 10% penalty levied on early distributions.

Example: Kendra's home is in foreclosure, and she is in immediate danger of being evicted. She requests a hardship distribution from her 401(k), which is granted. Since she is under age 59½, Kendra will likely have to pay the 10% early distribution penalty.

Unit 16: Study Questions

1. Lucas, an unmarried college student working part-time, earns $3,500 in 2013. He also receives $500 of interest income and $4,000 from his parents to help pay tuition. What is his maximum IRA contribution in 2013?

A. $0.
B. $3,500.
C. $5,500.
D. $6,500.

2. Vic, age 36 and single, is in the Marines. He has the following income in 2013:

- $30,500 of nontaxable combat pay
- $2,100 of regular wages
- $4,600 of interest income

What is the maximum amount that Vic can contribute to a traditional IRA?

A. $2,100.
B. $4,600.
C. $5,500.
D. $6,500.

3. Rafael, 40, earns $26,000 in 2013. Although he is allowed to contribute up to $5,500 to his IRA, he only has enough cash to contribute $2,500. On May 15, 2014, Rafael expects to get a big bonus, and he wishes to make a catch-up contribution for 2013. Rafael filed a timely extension for his tax return. Which of the following is true?

A. Rafael can contribute an additional $3,000 in May 2014 for his 2013 tax year so long as he files his tax return by the extended due date.
B. Rafael cannot contribute an additional $3,000 for his 2013 tax year after April 15, 2014.
C. Rafael can contribute an additional $3,000 in May 2014 for his 2013 tax year only if he files his return by April 15, 2014.
D. Rafael cannot make a 2013 contribution to his IRA after December 31, 2013.

4. Celeste, age 50 and single, worked for a telephone company in Spain and earned $48,500 for which she claimed the foreign earned income exclusion. In addition she earned $3,200 as an employee of an answering service while she was in the U.S. She also received alimony of $400 for the year. What is the maximum amount she may contribute to a traditional IRA for 2013?

A. $3,200.
B. $3,600.
C. $5,500.
D. $6,500.

5. Kristin, 42, is a full-time graduate student with $1,200 in wages. She marries Omar, 50, during the year. Omar has taxable compensation of $46,000 in 2013. What is the maximum they can contribute to their traditional IRA accounts in 2013 if they file jointly?

A. $1,200.
B. $6,700.
C. $11,000.
D. $12,000.

6. An excess contribution to an IRA is subject to tax. Which of the following is true?

A. The taxpayer will not have to pay the 6% tax on the excess contribution if he withdraws the excess contribution and any earnings on the excess contribution before the due date of the tax return for the applicable year, including extensions.
B. The 6% tax is due on both the excess contribution and any earnings on the excess contribution, even if the taxpayer withdraws the excess contribution from the account.
C. A taxpayer will not have to pay the 6% tax on the excess contribution if he withdraws the excess contribution and any earnings on the excess contribution before the due date of the tax return for the year, not including extensions.
D. A taxpayer will not have to pay the 6% on earnings on the excess contribution if he is disabled.

7. Jody is single, age 51, and has the following compensation in 2013:

- $1,600 annuity income
- $3,000 wages
- $2,300 alimony
- $3,000 interest income
- $6,000 rental income

What is the maximum amount that Jody can contribute to her traditional IRA in 2013?

A. $3,000.
B. $5,500.
C. $5,300.
D. $6,500.

8. Elizabeth and Landon are age 62, married, and lived together all year. They both work and each has a traditional IRA. In 2013, Landon earned $4,000 in wages and received $11,000 in annuity income. Elizabeth earned $52,000. They prefer to file separately. If they file separate returns, what is the maximum that Landon can contribute to his IRA?

A. $1,000.
B. $4,000.
C. $5,500.
D. $6,500.

9. Frank, 72, and Sue, 61, are married and file jointly. In 2013, Frank earned wages of $30,000 and Sue earned $5,000. If Frank and Sue file jointly, how much can they contribute to their traditional IRAs?

A. $5,500.
B. $6,500.
C. $11,500.
D. $13,000.

10. Miguel is 47. In 2013, he contributed $1,500 to a Roth IRA. He also wants to contribute to a traditional IRA account. What is the maximum he can contribute to a traditional IRA in 2013, assuming he had sufficient qualifying compensation?

A. $0.
B. $3,000.
C. $4,000.
D. $5,000.

11. Which of the following distributions from a traditional IRA is subject to an additional 10% penalty?

A. Distributions made prior to age 59½.
B. Distributions made after age 70½.
C. Distributions made to an unrelated beneficiary after the IRA owner's death.
D. Distributions made due to an IRS levy.

12. Annette, age 40, and Gil, age 48, are married and file jointly. Annette is covered by a retirement plan at work, but Gil is not. In 2013, Annette contributed $2,000 to her traditional IRA and $3,500 to a traditional IRA for Gil. Annette has modified AGI of $90,000; Gil has modified AGI of $98,000. What is their allowable IRA deduction?

A. $5,500.
B. $3,500.
C. $2,000.
D. $0.

13. Shari received a distribution in 2013 from her IRA and wants to roll it over to an IRA account with another bank. How long does she have to complete the rollover in order to avoid income tax on the distribution?

A. 30 days.
B. 60 days.
C. Until the end of the year.
D. Until the due date of her return.

14. Janelle borrowed $100,000 and pledged the balance in her traditional IRA as security on the loan. At the beginning of 2013, the IRA had a balance of $70,000; at the time of the loan transaction, its balance was $80,000; and at the end of 2013, its balance was $75,000. Which of the following would result from this transaction?

A. She would have taxable income of $75,000.
B. She would have taxable income of $70,000.
C. She would have taxable income of $80,000.
D. She would have to pay an additional 10% penalty on her 2013 contribution to the IRA.

15. AJ was born on June 6, 1943. By what date must he take the first required minimum distribution from his traditional IRA?

A. April 1, 2013.
B. December 31, 2013.
C. December 31, 2014.
D. April 1, 2014.

16. Doris is 58 and took a distribution of $8,000 from her traditional IRA in 2013. She had qualified higher education expenses of $6,000 during the year. What tax treatment would apply to the IRA distribution?

A. The entire distribution would be subject to regular tax plus an additional 10% penalty.
B. The distribution would not be taxable.
C. A portion of the distribution ($2,000) would be subject to regular tax and the additional 10% applicable to early distributions would apply to the entire amount.
D. The entire distribution would be subject to regular tax and the additional 10% tax would apply to $2,000.

17. Which of the following is considered an excess contribution to an IRA?

A. A contribution to a traditional IRA by a taxpayer in the year he has reached age 70½.
B. A rollover to a Roth IRA.
C. A contribution to a Roth IRA by a taxpayer who is age 75.
D. A contribution made by a taxpayer who only has alimony income.

18. Megan, age 36, is married and files jointly. She contributes $5,500 to a traditional IRA, and she also is a participant in her employer's retirement plan. She and her husband had modified adjusted gross income of $104,000 in 2013. Which of the following is correct regarding her IRA contribution?

A. It is fully deductible.
B. It is partially deductible.
C. It is not deductible.
D. She would be subject to a 6% penalty if she contributed to her IRA in 2013.

19. Tiana, age 44, earned $39,000 in wages as an administrative assistant in 2013. What is the maximum amount she can contribute to her 401(k) account?

A. $1,170.
B. $17,500.
C. $23,000.
D. $39,000.

20. Which of the following statements is correct regarding loans from a qualified plan?

A. Loans from a qualified plan are never permitted.
B. Loans are permitted up to the full amount of the employee's contributions to the qualified plan.
C. Loans are permitted but may generally not exceed $50,000 or 50% of the vested portion of the employee's account balance.
D. Loans are permitted but only under specific and defined circumstances of hardship.

Unit 17: Estate and Gift Taxes

> **More Reading:**
> **Publication 559, *Survivors, Executors, and Administrators***
> **Publication 950, *Introduction to Estate and Gift Taxes***

Estates in General

An estate is a separate legal entity that is created when a taxpayer dies. The estate tax is a tax on the transfer of assets or property from an individual's estate to his beneficiaries after his death.

> **Study Note:** For Part 1 of the EA exam, you will be required to understand how estate and gift taxes affect individual taxpayers. For Part 2 of the exam, you will be tested on the treatment of estates and trusts as legal entities.

After a person dies, a personal representative, such as an executor named in his will or an administrator appointed by a court, will typically manage the estate and settle the decedent's financial affairs. If there is no executor or administrator, another person with possession of the decedent's property may act as the personal representative.

The following tax returns may need to be filed:

- **Form 1040:** Final income tax return for the decedent (for income received before death).
- **Form 1041**, *U.S. Income Tax Return for Estates and Trusts*: Fiduciary income tax returns for the estate for the period of its administration.
- **Form 706**, *United States Estate (and Generation-Skipping Transfer) Tax Return*: If the gross estate (based on the fair market value of its assets) exceeds the applicable threshold, this return is used to report tax on the taxable estate (the gross estate less certain deductions).

Either the personal representative or a paid preparer must sign each required return. The personal representative is also responsible for determining any estate tax liability before the estate's assets are distributed to beneficiaries. The tax liability for an estate attaches to the assets of the estate itself. If the assets are distributed to the beneficiaries before the taxes are paid, the beneficiaries may be held liable for the tax debt, up to the value of the assets distributed.

> **Example:** James was unmarried when he died on April 20, 2013. His only daughter, Lillian, was named as the executor of his estate. James earned wages in 2013 before his death, so a final tax return is required for 2013. Lillian asks her accountant to help prepare her father's final Form 1040, which will include all the taxable income that James received in 2013 before his death. The accountant also helps Lillian with the valuation of her father's estate. After determining the fair market value of all her father's assets, they conclude that James's gross estate is valued at approximately $7 million. As this exceeds the threshold of $5.25 million for 2013, an estate tax return (Form 706) is also required to be filed, and Lillian is responsible for filing both returns.

Final Income Tax Return (Form 1040)

The taxpayer's final income tax return is filed on the same form that would have been used if the taxpayer were still alive, but "deceased" is written after the taxpayer's name. The filing deadline is April 15 of the year following the taxpayer's death, the same deadline that applies for individual income tax returns.

The personal representative must file the final individual income tax return of the decedent for the year of death and any returns not filed for preceding years. If an individual died after the close of a tax year but before the return for that year was filed, the return for that year will not be the final return. The return for that year will be a regular return and the personal representative must file it.

Example: Stephanie dies on March 2, 2013. At the time of her death, she had not yet filed her 2012 tax return. She earned $51,000 of wages in 2012. She also earned $18,000 in wages between January 1, 2013 and her death. Therefore, Stephanie's 2012 and 2013 tax returns must be filed by her representative. The 2013 return would be her final individual tax return.

On a decedent's final tax return, the rules for personal exemptions and deductions are the same as those that apply for any individual taxpayer. The full amount of the applicable personal exemption may be claimed on the final tax return, regardless of how long the taxpayer was alive during the year.

Income in Respect of a Decedent

Income in respect of a decedent (IRD) is any taxable income that was earned but not received by the decedent by the time of death. IRD is not taxed on the final return of the deceased taxpayer. IRD is reported on the tax return of the person (or entity) that receives the income. This could be the estate, the surviving spouse, or another beneficiary, such as a child. Regardless of the decedent's accounting method, IRD is subject to income tax when the income is received.

IRD retains the same tax nature that would have applied if the deceased taxpayer were still alive. For example, if the income would have been short-term capital gain, it is taxed the same way to the beneficiary. IRD can come from various sources, including:

- Unpaid salary, wages, or bonuses
- Distributions from traditional IRAs and employer-provided retirement plans
- Deferred compensation benefits
- Accrued but unpaid interest, dividends, and rent
- Accounts receivable of a sole proprietor

Example: Carlos was owed $15,000 in wages when he died. The check for these wages was not remitted by his employer until three weeks later and was received by his daughter and sole beneficiary, Rosalie. The wages are considered IRD, and Rosalie must recognize the $15,000 as ordinary income, the same tax treatment that would have applied for Carlos.

Example: Beverly died on April 30. At the time of her death, she was owed (but had not yet received) $1,500 of interest on bonds and $2,000 of rental income. Beverly's beneficiary will include $3,500 f IRD in gross income when the interest and rent are received. The income retains its character as interest income and passive activity rental income.

IRD is included in the decedent's estate and may be subject to estate tax. If it is received by a beneficiary and subject to income tax on the beneficiary's return, the beneficiary may take a deduction for estate tax paid on the IRD. This deduction is taken as a miscellaneous itemized deduction on Schedule A and is not subject to the 2% floor.

Distributions of retirement plan benefits or distributions from taxable IRA accounts to the decedent's beneficiaries are generally taxable when received. The decedent's surviving spouse may be able to defer taxation by rolling over the assets of a taxable IRA to another IRA or to a qualified plan. Qualified distributions from a Roth IRA or of previously nondeductible contributions to a traditional IRA are generally not taxable.

Form 1041, Tax Return for Estates and Trusts

An estate is a taxable legal entity that exists from the time of an individual's death until all assets have been distributed to the decedent's beneficiaries. As investment assets will usually continue to earn income after a taxpayer has died, this income, such as rents, dividends and interest, must be reported. Form 1041 is a fiduciary return used to report the following items for a domestic decedent's estate, trust, or bankruptcy estate:

- Current income and deductions, including gains and losses from disposition of the entity's property and excluding certain items such as tax-exempt interest (collectively, *distributable net income* or DNI);
- A deduction for income either held for future distribution or distributed currently to the beneficiaries (income distribution deduction) that is limited to DNI; and
- Any income tax liability.

Current income would include IRD, if it was received by the estate rather than specific beneficiaries. Expenses of administering the estate can be deducted either from the estate's income on Form 1041 in determining its income tax, or from the gross estate on Form 706 in determining the estate tax liability, but cannot be claimed for both purposes. Schedule K-1 is used to report any income that is distributed or distributable to each beneficiary and is filed with Form 1041, with a copy also given to the beneficiary.

Note: Estates and certain trusts are subject to the additional tax of 3.8% on net investment income that became effective in 2013 as a result of the Affordable Care Act. The provisions for this tax are generally similar to those for individuals, as discussed in Unit 15, and it must be reported on Form 8960, *Net Investment Tax: Individuals, Estates, and Trusts.* The additional tax applies to estates that have undistributed net investment income and also have adjusted gross income over the threshold amount ($11,950 for 2013) at which the highest tax bracket begins.

Estates are allowed some of the same tax credits that are allowed to individuals. The credits are generally allocated between the estate and the beneficiaries. However, estates are not allowed the credit for the elderly or the disabled, the Child Tax Credit, or the Earned Income Credit.

The due date for Form 1041 is the fifteenth day of the fourth month following the end of the entity's tax year, but is subject to an automatic extension of five months if Form 7004 is filed. The tax year may be either a calendar or a fiscal year, subject to the election made at the time the first return is filed. An election will also be made on the first return as to method (cash, accrual, or other) to report the estate's income.

Form 1041 must be filed for any domestic estate that has gross income for the tax year of $600 or more or a beneficiary who is a nonresident alien (with any amount of income).

Estate Tax

Estate tax may apply to the decedent's taxable estate, which is the gross estate less allowable deductions.

Gross Estate: The gross estate is based upon the fair market value of the decedent's property, which is not necessarily equal to his cost, and includes:

- The FMV of all tangible and intangible property owned partially or outright by the decedent at the time of death
- Life insurance proceeds payable to the estate or, for policies owned by the decedent, payable to the heirs
- The value of certain annuities or survivor benefits payable to the heirs
- The value of certain property that was transferred within three years before the decedent's death

The gross estate does not include property owned solely by the decedent's spouse or other individuals. Lifetime gifts that are complete (so that no control over the gifts was retained) are not included in the gross estate.

Deductions from the Gross Estate: Once the gross estate has been calculated, certain deductions (and in special circumstances, reductions to value) are allowed to determine the taxable estate. Deductions may include:

- Funeral expenses paid out of the estate
- Estate administrative expenses (if not deducted on Form 1041)
- Debts owed at the time of death
- The marital deduction (generally, the value of property that passes from the estate to a surviving spouse)
- The charitable deduction (generally, the value of property that passes from the estate to qualifying charities)
- The state death tax deduction (generally, any inheritance or estate taxes paid to any state)

The following items are not deductible from the gross estate:

- Federal estate taxes paid

- Alimony paid after the taxpayer's death (these payments are treated as distributions to a beneficiary)

Property taxes are deductible only if they accrue under state law prior to the decedent's death.

Decedent's Medical Expenses: Debts not paid before death, including medical expenses subsequently paid on behalf of the decedent, are liabilities that can be deducted from the gross estate on the estate tax return. However, if medical expenses for the decedent are paid out of the estate during the one-year period beginning with the day after death, the personal representative can alternatively elect to treat all or part of the expenses as paid by the decedent at the time they were incurred, and deduct them on the decedent's final tax return (1040).

Marital Deduction: Transfers from one spouse to the other are typically tax-free. The marital deduction allows spouses to transfer an unlimited amount of property to one another during their lifetimes or at death without being subject to estate or gift taxes.

To receive an unlimited deduction, the spouse receiving the assets must be a U.S. citizen and a legal spouse, and must have outright ownership of the assets. The unlimited marital deduction is generally not allowed if the transferee spouse is not a U.S. citizen (even if the spouse is a legal resident of the United States).

Note: If the receiving spouse is not a U.S. citizen, assets transferred tax-free are limited to an annual exclusion, which is $143,000 in 2013.

Form 706: Estate Tax Return

An estate tax return is filed using Form 706, *United States Estate (and Generation-Skipping Transfer) Tax Return.* After the taxable estate is computed, it is added to the value of lifetime taxable gifts. The applicable estate tax rate is applied to derive a tentative tax, from which any gift taxes paid or payable are subtracted to determine the gross estate tax. The maximum estate tax rate is 40% in 2013.

However, all or a portion of the gross estate tax may be eliminated after consideration of the estate's available:

- **Basic exclusion amount**: This amount is adjusted for inflation each year and may be used to reduce or eliminate gift and/or estate taxes. For 2013, the basic estate tax exclusion amount is $5.25 million.
- **Deceased spousal unused exclusion (DSUE):** This is the unused portion of the decedent's predeceased spouse's basic exclusion (the amount that was not used to offset gift or estate tax liabilities). The predeceased spouse must have died on or after January 1, 2011 and a portability election generally must have been made on Form 706 filed to claim the DSUE on behalf of the surviving spouse's estate.

Only estates valued in excess of the sum of these amounts need to file a return and pay estate tax. Essentially, this means that a surviving spouse's estate valued up to $10.5 million could be excluded from taxation if both spouses died during 2013, neither spouse had used any of his basic exclusion amount to offset gift tax liabilities, and a portability election for the DSUE was properly made on Form 706 for the first spouse's estate.

Example: Marlene dies in 2013 and leaves an estate valued at $3 million. She had not previously used any of her basic exclusion amount to avoid paying gift taxes, so the entire exclusion amount of $5.25 million is available to her estate. As this amount exceeds the estate's value, no estate tax is owed and an estate tax return does not need to be filed.

Example: Matt dies in early 2013 and leaves a gross estate valued at $9 million. His assets transfer to his wife, Leslie, and none are taxed because of the unlimited marital deduction. Thus, none of the $5.25 million basic exclusion amount available to Matt's estate is used (and none had been used to offset gift tax liabilities during his lifetime). Leslie dies later in the year. Assuming the appropriate portability election was made when Form 706 was filed for Matt's estate and Leslie had not used any of her basic exclusion amount, Matt's unused basic exclusion is added to Leslie's basic exclusion, for a total exclusion amount of $10.5 million. If Leslie's estate is valued at less than $10.5 million, the full amount can be excluded and no estate tax will be owed.

Applicable Credit: The gross estate tax described above is reduced by the *applicable credit*, also referred to as the *unified credit*, which is a tax credit amount that corresponds with the basic exclusion amount and, if applicable, the DSUE available to a surviving spouse. An applicable credit amount of $2,045,800 in 2013 corresponds with the basic exclusion amount of $5.25 million.

Just as with the basic exclusion amount, any portion of the applicable credit amount used to avoid payment of gift taxes reduces the amount of credit available in later years that can be used to offset gift or estate taxes. For example, if someone had used the full $2,045,800 applicable credit to avoid payment of gift taxes during his lifetime, he would have exhausted his entire $5.25 million basic exclusion. If he then died in 2013, his estate would be liable for tax on the taxable estate without further offset.

Example: June, who is single, dies in 2013 and leaves an estate valued at $20 million. During her lifetime, she had used $1 million of her basic exclusion to offset payments of gift tax. That reduces the amount her estate may exclude to $4.25 million, which is then subtracted from her $20 million taxable estate. That leaves a total of $15.75 million to be taxed at a 40% rate, resulting in an estate tax liability of $6.3 million.

If required to be filed, the due date for Form 706 is nine months after the decedent's date of death. An automatic six-month extension may be requested by filing Form 4768. However, the tax is due by the due date and interest is accrued on any amounts owed that are not paid at that time. The assessment period for estate tax is three years after the due date for a timely filed estate tax return. The assessment period is four years for transfers from an estate.

Basis of Estate Property

The basis of property inherited from a decedent is generally one of the following:

- The FMV of the property on the date of death
- The FMV on an alternate valuation date, if elected by the personal representative

- The value under a special-use valuation method for real property used in farming or another closely-held business, if elected by the personal representative
- The decedent's adjusted basis in land to the extent of the value excluded from the taxable estate as a qualified conservation easement

Alternate Valuation Date: If elected, the alternate valuation date is six months after the date of death. The estate value and related estate tax must be less than they would have been on the date of the taxpayer's death.

Jointly Owned Property: Property that is jointly owned by a decedent and another person will be included in full in the decedent's gross estate unless it can be shown that the other person originally owned or otherwise contributed to the purchase price. The surviving owner's new basis of property that was jointly owned must be calculated. To do so, the surviving owner's original basis in the property is added to the value of the part of the property included in the decedent's estate. Any deductions for depreciation allowed to the surviving owner on that property are subtracted from the sum.

Example: Chen and Xia, brother and sister, owned as joint tenants with right of survivorship rental property they purchased for $60,000. Chen paid $45,000 (for 75% ownership of the property) of the purchase price and Xia paid $15,000 (for 25% ownership of the property). Under local law, each had a half interest in the income from the property and shared expenses equally. When Chen died, the FMV of the property was $100,000. Depreciation deductions allowed before his death were $20,000. Xia's original basis was $15,000. Upon Chen's death, she acquired his three-quarters' share of the property (.75 × $100,000 = $75,000), resulting in a basis of $90,000 ($75,000 + $15,000 = $90,000). After subtracting half of the depreciation deductions taken ($90,000 - $10,000), Xia's adjusted basis in the property after Chen's death is $80,000.

If property is jointly held between a husband and wife as tenants by the entirety or as joint tenants with the right of survivorship (if they were the only joint tenants), one-half of the property's value is included in the gross estate and there is a step-up in basis for that one-half. The other half is stated at the surviving spouse's cost basis, net of any deductions for depreciation allowed to the surviving spouse on that half. If the decedent holds property in a community property state, half of the value of the community property will be included in the gross estate of the decedent, but the entire value of the community property will receive a step-up in basis.

Generation-Skipping Transfer Tax (GST)

The generation skipping transfer tax (GST) may apply to gifts during a taxpayer's lifetime or transfers occurring after his death, called bequests, made to skip persons. A skip person is a person who belongs to a generation that is two or more generations below the generation of the donor. The most common scenario is when a taxpayer makes a gift or bequest to a grandchild.

The GST is assessed when a property transfer is made, including instances in which property is transferred from a trust. The GST is based on the amounts transferred to skip persons, after subtracting the allocated portions of the donor's available GST exemption. In 2013, the GST exemption is the same as the estate tax basic exclusion amount ($5.25 million) and the GST tax rate is set at the maximum estate tax rate of 40%.

The GST is imposed separately and in addition to the estate and gift taxes.

Example: Patrick sets up a trust that names his adult daughter, Helene, as the sole beneficiary of the trust. In January 2013, Patrick dies, and the trust passes to Helene. However, later in the year, Helene also dies, and now the trust passes to her children (Patrick's grandchildren). Patrick's grandchildren are skip persons for purposes of the GST, and the trust fund property may be subject to the GST.

Any payments for tuition or medical expenses on behalf of a skip person that are made directly to an educational or medical institution are exempt from gift tax and GST.

Example: Gordon wants to help support his grandchildren, but he tries to make sure that his gifts are not subject to gift tax, GST, or estate tax. In 2013, he pays his grandchild's college tuition in full and writes a check directly to the college for $25,000. There is no tax consequence for this gift, and no reporting is required.

Gift Tax

The gift tax is imposed on the transfer of property by one individual to another and applies whether the donor intends the transfer to be a gift or not. Gift tax is imposed on the donor, not the receiver, of the property. However, under special arrangements the donee may agree to pay the tax instead of the donor.

As discussed above, the estate tax and gift tax are subject to a combined basic exclusion amount ($5.25 million in 2013) and use of any portion of this exclusion amount to reduce payment of gift taxes during a taxpayer's lifetime will reduce the amount available upon death to reduce applicable estate taxes. For 2013, the maximum gift tax rate is 40%.

The following gifts are not taxable:

- Gifts that do not exceed the annual exclusion. In 2013, the exclusion is $14,000 per person.
- Tuition or medical expenses paid directly to the institution for someone else.
- Unlimited gifts to a spouse, as long as the spouse is a U.S. citizen (or gifts up to $143,000 to a spouse who is not a U.S. citizen)
- Gifts to a political organization for its use.
- Gifts to a qualifying charity.
- A parent's support for a minor child. This may include support required as part of a legal obligation, such as by a divorce decree.

Gift taxes are reported on Form 709, *United States Gift (and Generation-Skipping Transfer) Tax Return*. Form 709 must be filed if:

- A taxpayer gives more than the annual exclusion to at least one individual (except to a U. S. citizen spouse)
- A taxpayer "splits gifts" with a spouse

- A taxpayer gives a future interest[28] to anyone other than a U.S. citizen spouse

If required, Form 709 is due by April 15 of the following year. However, if the donor died during 2013, the filing deadline is the due date for his estate tax return (if earlier than April 15, 2014). Taxpayers who extend the filing of Form 1040 for six months using Form 4868 are deemed to have extended their gift tax returns, if no gift tax is due with the extension. If the taxpayer does not extend Form 1040, the gift tax return can be extended separately.

Example: Earlene gives her son, Dion, a gift of $14,000 in cash during the year. She also pays his college tuition, totaling $21,000. She writes the check directly to the college. Earlene also pays for Dion's medical bills by issuing the check directly to his doctor's office. None of these gifts are taxable, and no gift tax return is required.
Example: Dave is single. In 2013, Dave gives his adult son $18,000 to help start his first business. The money is not a loan, so Dave is required to file a gift tax return, since the amount exceeds the $14,000 annual exclusion amount.

Gifts by Married Couples: Both the basic exclusion amount and the annual exclusion for gifts to individuals apply separately to each spouse, and each spouse must separately file a gift tax return if he or she made reportable gifts during the year.

However, if a married couple or either spouse makes a gift to another person, the gift can be considered as being one-half from one spouse and one-half from the other spouse. This is known as gift splitting. Gift splitting allows married couples to give up to $28,000 to a person without making a taxable gift. Both spouses must consent to split the gift. If a married couple splits a gift, each spouse must file a gift tax return, even if one-half of the split gift is less than the annual exclusion.

Example: Harold and his wife, Margie, agree to split gifts of cash. Harold gives his nephew $21,000, and Margie gives her niece $18,000. Although each gift is more than the annual exclusion ($14,000), by gift splitting they can make these gifts without making a taxable gift. In each case, because one-half of the split gift is not more than the annual exclusion, it is not a taxable gift. However, each spouse is still required to file a gift tax return.
Example: Felicia gives her cousin, Jessie, $24,000 to purchase a new car. Felicia elects to split the gift with her husband, Ralph, and Ralph is treated as if he gave Jessie half the amount, or $12,000. Assuming they make no other gifts to Jessie during the year, the entire $24,000 gift is tax free. Since they have decided to split the gift, Jessie and Ralph are required to file gift tax returns.

Basis of Property Received as a Gift

For purposes of determining gain or loss on a subsequent disposition of property received as a gift, a taxpayer must consider:

- The gift's adjusted basis to the donor just before it was given to the taxpayer,
- The gift's FMV at the time it was given to the taxpayer, and

[28] A future interest is a gift that cannot be immediately used, possessed, or enjoyed.

- Any gift tax actually paid on appreciation of the property's value while held by the donor (as opposed to gift tax offset by the donor's applicable credit amount).

When a taxpayer sells property received as a gift, he calculates gain based upon the donor's adjusted basis plus any gift tax paid on the donor's appreciation. However, if the same property were sold at a loss, the taxpayer's basis would be the lower of the donor's adjusted basis or the FMV at the time of the gift.

Example: Edward's father gives him 20 shares of stock that are currently worth $900. Edward's father has an adjusted basis in the stock of $500. Edward's basis in the stock, for purposes of determining gain on any future sale of the stock, is $500.

Generally, the value of a gift is its fair market value on the date of the gift. However, the value of the gift may be less than its fair market value to the extent that the donee gives the donor something in return.

Example: Daniel sells his son, Jared, a house for $10,000. At the time, the fair market value of the house is $90,000. Daniel has made a gift to his son of $80,000 ($90,000 - $10,000 = $80,000).

Unit 17: Study Questions

1. Shawn, a single taxpayer, has never been required to file a gift tax return. In 2013, Shawn gave the following gifts:

- $18,000 of tuition paid directly to a state university for an unrelated person
- $14,500 paid to General Hospital for his brother's medical bills
- $50,000 of cash donations paid to his city's homeless shelter, a 501(c)(3) organization
- $15,000 as a political gift paid to the Libertarian Party (not a qualified charity).

Is Shawn required to file a gift tax return for 2013?

A. No.
B. Yes, because the donation to the political party is not an excludable gift.
C. Yes, because each of the gifts exceeded $14,000.
D. Yes, because the political gift is a reportable transaction.

2. Phil died in 2013. At the time of his death, he had assets of $4 million and liabilities of $500,000. He also had life insurance policies in place that paid $1 million to his children. He has not used any of his basic exclusion. Based upon the information provided, what is the taxable amount of Phil's estate that must be reported on Form 706?

A. $5 million.
B. $0.
C. $4 million.
D. $4.5 million.

3. During 2013, prior to his death in December, Herman gave $30,000 to each of his two granddaughters. He also paid $80,000 directly to Birchland College for their college tuition costs. When Herman died, how much of his basic exclusion amount would he have used up as a result of these gifts?

A. $60,000.
B. $140,000.
C. $32,000.
D. $112,000.

4. Which of the following is not income in respect of a decedent?

A. Wages earned before death but still unpaid at the time of death.
B. Vacation time paid after death.
C. Taxable IRAs and retirement plans.
D. A royalty check that was received before death but not cashed.

5. In general, who is responsible for paying gift tax?

A. The estate.
B. The donor.
C. The receiver of the gift.
D. The executor.

6. Delia's estate has funeral expenses for the cost of her burial. How should the executor deduct these costs?

A. Funeral expenses are an itemized deduction on Form 1040.
B. Funeral expenses are deducted on Form 1041.
C. Funeral expenses are deducted on Form 706.
D. Funeral expenses cannot be deducted as an expense.

7. Which of the following statements concerning the deceased spousal unused exclusion (DSUE) is not correct?

A. The DSUE allows an unlimited estate tax deduction for the spouse who dies last.
B. The predeceased spouse must have died on or after January 1, 2011.
C. The maximum DSUE available for a spouse who dies in 2013 is $5.25 million.
D. A portability election must be made, generally when filing Form 706.

8. When is an estate tax return due?

A. Four months after the close of the taxable year.
B. Six months after the close of the calendar year.
C. Nine months after the date of death.
D. Twelve months after the date of death

9. Duncan died in 2013. Following his death, the executor of his estate paid the following bills. Which of these is not an allowable deduction in determining Duncan's taxable estate?

A. Administration expenses.
B. State inheritance taxes.
C. Charitable contributions.
D. Alimony paid after the taxpayer's death.

10. In 2013, Jeffrey gives $25,000 to his girlfriend, Rachel. Which of the following statements is true?

A. The first $14,000 of the gift is not subject to the gift tax, but the remainder is subject to gift tax, and Rachel is responsible for paying it.
B. Rachel is required to file a gift tax return and pay tax on the entire gift.
C. Jeffrey is required to file a gift tax return, Form 709.
D. Jeffrey may choose to report the gift tax on Form 1040, Schedule A.

11. Dwayne died in April 2013. None of his basic exclusion amount was used to reduce or eliminate payment of gift or estate taxes. Form 706 was filed in November 2013 and the full amount of deceased spousal unused exclusion (DSUE) was reported thereon. His wife, Monica, died in December 2013. As was the case with Dwayne, none of her basic exclusion amount had been previously used to offset gift taxes that would otherwise have been payable. What amount must Monica's taxable estate exceed in order to be subject to estate tax?

A. $5.25 million.
B. $2,045,800.
C. $5 million.
D. $10.5 million.

12. Alana had gifts totaling $28,000 in 2013 that were subject to gift tax. When is her gift tax return due?

A. March 15, 2014.
B. April 15, 2014.
C. June 15, 2014.
D. September 15, 2014.

13. Dustin pays $15,000 in college tuition for his nephew, Rich, directly to Rich's college. Which of the following statements is correct?

A. The gift is taxable, and Rich must report the gift tax on his individual tax return (Form 1040).
B. The gift is not taxable, but Dustin must file a gift tax return.
C. The gift is taxable, and Dustin must file a gift tax return.
D. The gift is not taxable, and no gift tax return is required.

14. Which of the following items is not an allowable deduction from the gross estate?

A. Debts owed at the time of death.
B. Medical expenses.
C. Funeral expenses.
D. Federal estate tax.

15. The executor of Ophelia's estate is her sister, Elise. Elise decides to make a distribution of 100% of the estate's assets before paying the estate's income tax liability. Which of the following is true?

A. The beneficiaries of the estate can be held liable for the payment of the liability, even if the liability exceeds the value of the estate assets.
B. No one can be held liable for the tax if the assets have been distributed.
C. The beneficiaries can be held liable for the tax debt, up to the value of the assets distributed.
D. None of the above.

16. In which case must a gift tax return or returns be filed?

A. A married couple gives a gift of $14,000.
B. A married couple gives a gift of $15,000.
C. A single individual gives a gift of $4,000 to an unrelated person.
D. A wife gives a gift of $20,000 to her husband.

17. All of the following gifts are excluded from the determination of the gift tax except:

A. A gift made to a political organization for its own use.
B. A cash gift given to a nonresident alien spouse of a U.S. citizen.
C. A medical bill paid directly to a hospital on behalf of a relative.
D. A gift made to a qualifying charity.

18. Donald's will provides that each of his ten grandchildren is to receive $1 million. Assuming that none of his GST exemption amount has previously been used in connection with gifts to the grandchildren or other skip persons, what portion of the total amount distributed to the grandchildren after his death in 2013 would be subject to GST?

A. $7,954,200.
B. $5.25 million.
C. $10.5 million.
D. $4.75 million.

19. Janna is the executor for her father's estate. He died on November 5, 2013. Which of the following dates may she elect to use as an alternate valuation date for his estate?

A. January 1, 2014.
B. April 15, 2015.
C. May 5, 2014.
D. August 5, 2014.

20. Which of the following statements is incorrect regarding a married couple that uses gift splitting?

A. They must file a joint gift tax return.
B. They can give a gift of up to $28,000 to a single donee in 2013 without using any of their basic exclusion amounts to avoid paying gift tax.
C. They must file gift tax returns even if no gift tax is owed.
D. All of the statements are correct.

21. A taxpayer dies on May 4, 2013. Assuming that Form 706 needs to be filed for his estate, when is his estate tax due?

A. November 4, 2013.
B. January 1, 2014.
C. February 4, 2014.
D. April 15, 2014.

22. Ida died in 2013. Which of the following assets would not be included in the calculation of her gross estate?

A. Life insurance proceeds payable to Ida's children.
B. The value of property transferred to Ida's son five years before her death.
C. The value of property owned jointly by Ida and her spouse.
D. The value of Ida's traditional IRA.

Answers to Practice Questions: Individuals

Unit 1: Individuals Quiz Answers

1. The answer is B. Taxpayers should keep the supporting documentation for their tax returns for at least three years from the date the return was filed or three years from the date the return was due, whichever is later. This includes applicable worksheets, receipts, and other forms.

2. The answer is B. If a taxpayer must file a U.S. tax return or is listed on a tax return as a spouse or dependent and is not eligible for an SSN, he must apply for an ITIN.

3. The answer is C. Clark and Christy have no dependents, their combined income is less than $100,000, and they do not plan to itemize. In addition, their interest income is less than $1,500, so they may use Form 1040EZ to file their tax return.

4. The answer is D. The current backup withholding rate is 28%. The IRS may require backup withholding if a taxpayer has a delinquent tax debt; if he fails to report all his interest, dividends, and other income; or if his Social Security number does not match records provided to the IRS.

5. The answer is B. Ricky has until the original due date of the return (not including extensions) to pay the amount owed and not incur a penalty. Taxpayers should submit their payment of taxes due on or before April 15 (or the next business day if April 15 falls on a Saturday, a Sunday, or a legal holiday).

6. The answer is C. If a taxpayer's withholding exceeds his tax liability, no estimated payments would be required. The taxpayer would receive a refund of the overpaid tax when he files his tax return.

7. The answer is D. Living outside the country is not a valid reason to extend the statute of limitations for claiming a refund. In some cases, a request for a tax refund will be honored past the normal three-year deadline. Exceptions include those for military personnel, individuals who are financially disabled, taxpayers who live in presidentially declared disaster areas, and taxpayers who have bad debts from worthless securities.

8. The answer is A. Since Cynthia plans to itemize her deductions, she must file Form 1040.

9. The answer is B. Isla does not need to pay estimated tax because she expects her income tax withholding in 2014 ($10,250) to be greater than both 90% of the tax to be shown on her 2014 return ($11,270 × 90% = $10,143) and 100% of her 2013 tax liability ($9,224). Therefore, Isla qualifies for the safe harbor rule and is not required to make estimated tax payments. A taxpayer is not required to pay estimated tax for 2014 if:

- The taxpayer had no tax liability in the prior year,
- The taxpayer was a U.S. citizen or resident alien, and
- The 2013 tax year covered a 12-month period.

The taxpayer also does not have to pay estimated tax if she pays enough through withholding so that the tax due on the return is less than $1,000. In most cases, a taxpayer must pay estimated tax if she expects withholding (plus any refundable credits) to be less than the *smaller* of:

- 90% of the tax to be shown on the current year tax return, or
- 100% of the tax shown on the prior year tax return.

10. The answer is C. If a taxpayer cannot file his return by the due date, he may apply for an automatic six-month extension of time to file. With the extension, the taxpayer will have until October 15 to file. This is an extension of time for the taxpayer to file, not an extension of time to pay taxes that are due.

11. The answer is B. A taxpayer is not required to pay estimated tax if she expects to have zero tax liability.

12. The answer is B. If Ernesto has his amended return postmarked on or before April 15, 2014, it will be within the three-year limit and the return will be accepted. If the amended 2010 return is postmarked after that date, it will fall outside the three-year statute of limitations, and he will not receive the refund.

13. The answer is B. Even though a taxpayer files Form 4868, he will owe interest and a late payment penalty on the amount owed if he does not pay the tax owed by the regular due date.

14. The answer is C. If a taxpayer omitted 25% of his income or more, the IRS has up to six years to assess a deficiency.

15. The answer is C. A taxpayer who is claiming a dependent cannot use Form 1040EZ.

16. The answer is C. The minimum penalty is $135 or 100% of the unpaid tax for a taxpayer who files his return more than 60 days late.

17. The answer is C. The third quarter payment for estimated tax is due September 15, 2013. For estimated tax payments, a year is divided into four quarterly payment periods. Each period has a due date. The payments are due as follows:

Periods	Due Date
Jan. 1-March 31	April 15
April 1-May 31	June 15
June 1-Aug. 31	September 15
Sept. 1-Dec. 31	January 15 (following year)

18. The answer is D. To prepare an accurate return, a tax preparer must gather biographical information including a client's legal name, date of birth, marital status, citizenship or residency, dependents, and SSN or other TIN. A preparer does not need to know the maiden name of a client's mother.

19. The answer is A. Maggie will be forced to file Form 1040 for two reasons: she had self-employment income and Ray plans to itemize deductions. When a married couple files separate returns and one spouse chooses to itemize deductions, the other spouse cannot claim the standard deduction and therefore must itemize. If Maggie has no itemized deductions, then her deduction would be zero.

20. The answer is A. An ATIN may not be used to claim the Earned Income Credit. If the taxpayer is unable to secure a Social Security number for a child until the adoption is final, he may request an ATIN.

21. The answer is D. Form 1040X must be filed within three years of the date the original tax return was filed or the tax was paid, whichever is later. If a taxpayer filed his return before April 15, the three-year statute of limitation period starts from April 15. If a taxpayer requested an extension, as Janice had, the three-year period starts from October 15.

22. The answer is D. Under the IRS's new rules, only original documents of birth certificates and passports are accepted, or documents that have been certified by the original issuing agency. Notarized documents are no longer accepted.

23. The answer is A. If a farmer waits until April 15 to file his return, he must pay estimated taxes quarterly just like any other business. However, a farmer can either:

- Pay all his estimated tax by the fifteenth day after the end of his tax year (this date is usually January 15)
- File his return and pay all the tax owed by the first day of the third month after the end of his tax year (usually March 1).

24. The answer is C. A U.S. citizen or resident alien living outside the United States has an automatic two-month extension to file and pay her taxes. The same is true for members of the military who are serving outside the U.S. Rochelle must attach a statement to her tax return explaining why she qualifies for the extension. She will still owe interest on the tax that was due on April 15 but not paid until later.

25. The answer is D. To avoid an underpayment penalty, Benicio must pay the smaller of 110% of his 2012 tax liability or 90% of his expected tax for 2013. This estimated tax safe harbor rule applies to higher income taxpayers with adjusted gross income of more than $150,000 ($75,000 if filing a married filing separately return.)

26. The answer is C. Sally should file a claim as an injured spouse to request her portion of their tax refund. She would do so by filing Form 8379, *Injured Spouse Allocation.* Innocent spouse relief is when tax has been incorrectly reported on a joint return and one spouse is relieved of the obligation to pay the other spouse's tax liability.

27. The answer is A. Even though she files Form 4868, Catherine may owe interest and a late payment penalty on the amount owed if she does not pay the tax due by the regular due date of April 15. However, she will not be assessed a late filing penalty (failure-to-file) because she filed her tax return before the extended due date.

Unit 2: Individuals Quiz Answers

1. The answer is A. Since Edward and Helen are married, they may file either jointly or separately. If Helen does not agree to file jointly with Edward, Edward must file MFS. The filing requirement threshold for married filing separately is $3,900. Edward is required to file a return because his gross income exceeded this threshold. Helen is not required to file a tax return because her gross income in 2013 was $2,000.

2. The answer is C. Munir is required to file a U.S. tax return in 2013, and he must file using Form 1040, Form 1040A, or Form 1040EZ. Munir is a green card holder, and therefore he may choose to be treated as a U.S. resident for tax purposes, regardless of how much time he has been present in the United States. An alien who has been present in the United States at any time during a calendar year as a "lawful permanent resident" may choose to be treated as a resident alien for the entire calendar year. As a resident alien, Munir will be taxed on income from worldwide sources, including any income he earned while he was in Pakistan.

3. The answer is A. Even if a return does not have to be filed, individuals who want to claim tax refunds, the Earned Income Credit, or the Additional Child Tax Credit should still file a return. A taxpayer with self-employment earnings of $400 or more is *required* to file a tax return.

4. The answer is A. Enzo meets the substantial presence test and is considered a resident alien for tax purposes. He is considered to have been present in the United States for a total of 225 days. The full 150 days are counted for 2013; 50 days for 2012 (1/3 of 150); and 25 days for 2011 (1/6 of 150).

5. The answer is B. Janet and Harry must both file tax returns. Normally, Janet and Harry would not be required to file because their combined gross income was less than $22,400 in 2013, and they are both over 65. (This threshold applies if both spouses are 65 or over and they are filing jointly). However, because Harry's self-employment income exceeds $400, he is required to file. Further, if Janet did not wish to file a joint return with Harry, she would nevertheless be required to file separately because her income exceeds the applicable threshold of $3,900. Thus, they are both required to file tax returns.

6. The answer is C. A dependent parent does not have to live with a taxpayer in order for the taxpayer to elect the head of household filing status. This special rule applies to parents or grandparents who are related to the taxpayer by blood, marriage, or adoption if the taxpayer pays more than half of the qualifying parent's household costs.

7. The answer is A. If a taxpayer's spouse died during the year, the taxpayer is considered married for the whole year and may file as MFJ. So Dana may file a joint return for 2013.

8. The answer is A. A single dependent whose earned income was more than $6,100 in 2013 must file a return.

9. The answer is C. Even though their gross income is below the MFJ filing threshold of $20,000 for 2013, the couple must file a tax return because Malik owes Social Security and Medicare tax on his unreported tip income. (A taxpayer who fails to disclose tip income to his employer as required is also subject to IRS penalties.)

10. The answer is B. A relative must have lived with the taxpayer more than half the year (over six months) and be the taxpayer's dependent. A taxpayer's dependent parent is an exception and does not have to live with the taxpayer.

11. The answer is D. This is the only exception to a rule that generally prevents a taxpayer from amending his MFJ return to a MFS return.

12. The answer is C. The taxpayer may claim the person as a dependent unless the noncustodial parent claims the child as a dependent. Answer A is incorrect because a qualifying dependent does not have to be a minor in all cases. Answer B is incorrect because qualifying dependent may be related by blood, marriage, or adoption. Answer D is incorrect because a dependent parent may qualify a taxpayer for HOH status.

13. The answer is C. In determining residency status for tax purposes, students temporarily in the U.S. on an F, J, M, or Q visa are exempt from the substantial presence test for five years. In addition, an individual in either of the following categories is temporarily exempt from counting days toward the substantial presence test:

- Teacher or trainee
- Closer connection to home country

14. The answer is C. Victor qualifies for head of household filing status because he can be "considered unmarried" for tax purposes. His child lived with him for more than six months; he did not live with his spouse the last half of the year; and he paid more than half the cost of keeping up a home for the year for a qualifying child. Couples who are living apart but not yet divorced or legally separated are allowed to file jointly, but both spouses must agree to do so. Therefore, since Eleanor refuses to file jointly with Victor, the most beneficial filing status is head of household.

15. The answer is B. Married couples must agree to file jointly. If one spouse does not agree to file jointly, they are individually subject to the MFS filing threshold. In this case, both spouses are required to file tax returns because both are above the applicable earnings threshold for MFS.

16. The answer is A. Kathy must file amended tax returns for 2011 and 2012. She cannot file jointly with her husband in 2013. If a couple obtains a court decree of annulment, the taxpayer must file amended returns (Form 1040X) claiming single or head of household status for all tax years affected by the annulment that are not closed by the statute of limitations for filing an amended tax return.

17. The answer is D. In 2013, Lisa is eligible for qualifying widow with dependent child filing status. Lisa and Stuart qualified to file MFJ in 2012, the year he died, with Lisa signing the tax return as a surviving spouse. The year of death is the last year for which a taxpayer can file MFJ.

18. The answer is C. A parent is the only dependent relative who does not have to live with the taxpayer in order for the taxpayer to claim head of household status.

19. The answer is B. Dwight and Angela are allowed to amend their separate returns to a joint return in order to claim the credit. If a taxpayer files a separate return, he may elect to amend the filing status to married filing jointly at any time within three years from the due date of the original return (not including any extensions). However, the same does not hold true in reverse. Once a taxpayer files a joint return, he cannot choose to file a separate return for that year after the due date of the return (with a rare exception for deceased taxpayers.)

20. The answer is C. The married filing jointly and qualifying widow(er) with dependent child filing statuses generally result in the lowest tax.

21. The answer is D. Todd provided over half the cost of maintaining a home for Madison and Amanda, but he cannot file as head of household since Amanda did not live with him for more than half the year. Madison cannot file as HOH either, because she did not provide more than one-half the cost of keeping up the home for her daughter. However, either Todd or Madison may still claim Amanda as a dependent.

22. The answer is A. A U.S. resident or citizen who is married to a nonresident alien can elect to file a joint return so long as both spouses sign the return and agree to be taxed on their worldwide income. A Social Security number is not required, because a nonresident spouse that is ineligible for an SSN may request an ITIN.

23. The answer is B. As long as they are married and are neither divorced nor legally separated, Carol and Raul can file a joint return or file separately. They cannot file as single.

24. The answer is D. For Louisa to file as head of household, her home must have been the main home of her qualifying child for more than half the tax year. Since her son started living with her in July, he would not have been in the household sufficient time to qualify her for this filing status.

25. The answer is A. Taxpayers are considered married for the entire year if:

- They were married on the last day of the tax year, or
- One spouse died during the year and the surviving spouse has not remarried as of the end of the year.

26. The answer is C. Alexandra cannot claim head of household status because Sebastian lived with her for only five months, which is less than half the year.

27. The answer is B. The married filing separately (MFS) status is for taxpayers who are married and either:

- Choose to file separate returns, or
- Do not agree to file a joint return.

28. The answer is D. To qualify for head of household filing status, a taxpayer must have paid more than half the cost of maintaining a home. In making the calculation, valid expenses include rent, mortgage payments, property taxes, utilities, home insurance, home repairs, and food eaten in the home. Valid expenses do not include clothing, education, medical treatment, vacations, life insurance, or transportation.

29. The answer is B. Church employees who are exempt from Social Security and Medicare taxes and have wages of $108.28 or more for the year are required to file a tax return. In answer B, the church employee's wages were below that threshold. In all of the other answers, the taxpayer would be required to file a return.

30. The answer is A. Kylie has to file a tax return because of the amount of her unearned income: the $1,100 lottery prize. A dependent with unearned income of more than $1,000 is required to file a tax return. Her earned income—$1,400—was not high enough to trigger a filing requirement. In 2013, dependents with earned income of more than $6,100 are required to file.

Unit 3: Individuals Quiz Answers

1. The answer is A. Since Alyssa is claimed as a dependent on her parents' tax return, she cannot claim an exemption for herself. Therefore, her total number of exemptions is zero. She can still file a tax return in order to claim a refund of taxes withheld.

2. The answer is C. Without Form 8332, *Release/Revocation of Release of Claim to Exemption for Child by Custodial Parent,* signed and attached to the return, the IRS will not recognize the dependency exemption claimed by a noncustodial parent, regardless of what the divorce degree states. If a divorce decree does not specify which parent is the custodial parent or which parent receives the dependency exemption, the exemption automatically goes to the parent who has physical custody for the majority of the year.

3. The answer is C. Haley meets all the qualifying child tests: the relationship test; the age test (because she is under 24 and a full-time student); the residency test (because the time spent at college is a legitimate temporary absence); and the support test (because she did not provide over half of her own support).

4. The answer is A. Bill may claim his stepson as a qualifying child. A step relationship formed by a legal marriage is not dissolved by divorce or death. Since Greg did not live with Ingrid, Bill is the custodial parent, and he may claim his stepson as a qualifying child.

5. The answer is C. Chad provided more than half of his own support for the year, so he is not Amber's qualifying child or her qualifying relative. To meet the support test, the child cannot have provided more than half of his own support for the year.

6. The answer is A. Even though Wyatt is over the normal age threshold for a qualifying child, he is considered a qualifying child for purposes of the head of household filing status. This is because Wyatt is permanently disabled and Joseph provides his financial support and care.

7. The answer is C. In 2013, personal exemptions are subject to phase-out for taxpayers who have adjusted gross income above certain threshold amounts. For taxpayers who file jointly, the phase-out begins when AGI is above $300,000 and the personal exemptions are phased out completely when MAGI is $422,500. For single taxpayers, the phase-out range is from $250,000 to $372,500 of AGI.

8. The answer is C. There are two types of dependents: a qualifying child and a qualifying relative. Dave cannot be a qualifying child because he does not meet the age test, so he is a qualifying relative. The 2013 limit for gross income for qualifying relatives is $3,900. Therefore, if Dave earns $3,900 or more in 2013, his mother cannot claim him as a dependent on her tax return.

9. The answer is B. For IRS purposes, the custodial parent is the parent with whom the child lived for the greater part of the year. The other parent is the noncustodial parent. If the parents divorced or separated during the year and the child lived with both parents before the separation, the custodial parent is the one with whom the child lived for the greater part of the rest of the year.

10. The answer is A. Bradley is Cheryl's qualifying child because he meets the age test, support test, and relationship test. Also, because Bradley is single, he is a qualifying person for Cheryl to claim head of household filing status. Bradley is not required to be a full-time student, because the IRS says that any child under the age of 19 at the end of the tax year will be treated as a qualifying child if all the other tests are met. Bradley is only 18 years old, and therefore he passes the age test.

11. The answer is C. Sean may claim three exemptions on his tax return. Because they were married at the time of Jackie's death, Sean may file a joint return in the year of her death and claim a personal exemption for his deceased wife, along with a personal exemption for himself. He may also claim a dependency exemption for his son.

12. The answer is C. Stacy is entitled to claim five *dependency* exemptions. She may claim a dependency exemption for each of her children and one for Racine, her dependent parent. The total exemptions claimed on her return are six: one personal exemption for Stacy and five dependency exemptions.

13. The answer is A. In a situation involving a multiple support agreement, a taxpayer must have paid more than 10% of the support for a family member in order to claim the qualifying relative as a dependent. The taxpayer would not be entitled to the exemption if someone else provided more than 50% of the support for this family member.

14. The answer is D. A dependent must be a citizen or resident alien of the United States, Canada, or Mexico.

15. The answer is B. The amount Jacob can claim for personal exemptions is reduced but not eliminated based upon his AGI. Before any reduction, the total amount of exemptions for himself and his three children is $15,600 ($3,900 × 4). For head of household filers, the exemption deduction is reduced by 2% for each $2,500 over the threshold of $275,000 ($315,000 - $275,000 = $40,000)/$2,500 × 2% = 32%. $15,600 × 32% = $4,992. $15,900 - $4,992 = $10,608.) Jacob's allowable exemption amount is $10,608.

16. The answer is D. His parents may claim him as their qualifying child because he is under the age of 19 and does not provide more than half of his own support. He is required to file a tax return but cannot claim an exemption for himself. The gross income test only applies to a qualifying relative, not to a qualifying child.

17. The answer is A. Only Luther or Tim is eligible to claim the exemption under a multiple support agreement in 2013. Answer B is incorrect because only a single taxpayer may claim the exemption in a tax year. Mary is not eligible because she does not provide more than 10% of her mother's support.

18. The answer is C. In 2013, Roy can claim a personal exemption for his deceased wife and a personal exemption for himself. A taxpayer whose spouse dies during the year may file jointly in the year of death.

19. The answer is C. They may take three dependency exemptions on their tax return, and two personal exemptions for themselves. Tony and Isabelle may take dependency exemptions for all the dependents listed, except for Timothy, since he is Isabelle's cousin. Timothy would have to live with Tony and Isabelle all year for them to claim him as their dependent. Parents (or grandparents, in-laws, stepparents, etc.) do not have to live with a taxpayer to qualify as dependents. Tony can claim Jonathan, because Jonathan was once his father-in-law.

20. The answer is C. The phase-out of exemptions was reinstituted for 2013. The thresholds for phase-outs are determined by a taxpayer's filing status and AGI. At certain higher income levels, exemptions are phased out completely.

21. The answer is B. As nonresident aliens, each would qualify for one personal exemption only and would be required to file on separate tax returns. They would not be able to claim exemptions for their dependents.

Unit 4: Individuals Quiz Answers

1. The answer is D. A taxpayer need not have physical possession of income in order to have constructive receipt. However, income is not considered constructively received if the taxpayer cannot access the funds because of restrictions. Since the taxpayer's control of the receipt of the funds in the escrow account was substantially limited until the transaction had closed, the taxpayer did not constructively receive the income until the following year.

2. The answer is B. Only the wages and the bonus are taxable. The parking pass is a nontaxable transportation benefit, and the employer contributions are not taxable until Marisol withdraws the money from her retirement account. Marisol does not have to report the use of the gym, because it is on the employer's premises and therefore not taxable.

3. The answer is D. All tip income is subject to federal income tax, whether cash or noncash. An individual who receives less than $20 per month in tips while working one job does not have to report the tip income to his employer, but the income is still subject to federal income tax and must be reported on the taxpayer's Form 1040.

4. The answer is B. Employer-provided parking is an excludable benefit up to $245 per month. Therefore, the amount above $245 ($275 - $245 = $30) is taxable to the employee.

5. The answer is A. VA disability compensation is exempt from taxation if the veteran was terminated through separation or discharged under honorable conditions. The VA does not issue Form W-2, Form 1099-R, or any other tax-related document for veterans' disability benefits.

6. The answer is A. Meals furnished to Caroline are not taxable because they are for the convenience of the employer. Meals that employers furnish to a restaurant employee during, immediately before, or after the employee's working hours are considered furnished for the employer's convenience. Since Caroline is a waitress who works during the normal breakfast and lunch periods, Max can exclude from her wages the value of those meals. If Max allowed Caroline to have meals without charge on her days off, the value of those meals would be included in her wages.

7. The answer is A. A de minimis fringe benefit is deductible by the employer but not taxable to the employee. The IRS defines a de minimis benefit in this way: a benefit that, considering its value and the frequency with which it is provided, is so small as to make accounting for it unreasonable or impractical. For example, de minimis fringe benefits include occasional snacks, coffee, or doughnuts provided in a company's break room.

8. The answer is D. Adjusted gross income (AGI) is gross income (the sum of all income subject to taxation that the taxpayer receives during the year) minus certain allowable deductions or adjustments.

9. The answer is A. Clergy members may exclude from gross income for income tax purposes but not for self-employment tax purposes the rental value of a home or a rental allowance to the extent the allowance is used to provide a home, even if deductions are taken for home expenses paid with the allowance.

10. The answer is B. If a taxpayer serves in a combat zone as an enlisted person for any part of a month, all of his pay received for military service that month is excluded from gross income. Since Salvador served for a few days in September, all the income in September is excluded as combat pay and only October through December would be taxable.

11. The answer is C. Wage income is never considered self-employment income. The other examples listed are all types of self-employment income and subject to self-employment tax on Form 1040.

12. The answer is A. Under an accountable plan, employee reimbursements are not included in the employee's income. The employer can deduct the expenses as current expenses on its tax return. The employee is not required to be taxed on any amounts received in accordance with the terms of a qualified accountable plan.

13. The answer is C. Use of a company vehicle for commuting is not a qualified fringe benefit. Commuting expenses are not deductible. Use of a company van after normal working hours is personal use and not business use, so it would result in taxable income to the employee. The cell phone, reimbursements for business travel, and the occasional coffee and doughnuts are noncash fringe benefits that are not taxable.

14. The answer is B. Only Debby's sick pay is taxable as wages. Sick pay from an employer is taxable like wages and is therefore included in Debby's gross income. If a taxpayer pays the full cost of an accident insurance plan, the benefits for personal injury or illness are not included in income. If the employer pays the cost of an accident insurance plan, the amounts are taxable to an employee.

15. The answer is B. Any taxpayer who has self-employment income of $400 or more in a year must file a tax return and report the earnings to the IRS.

16. The answer is A. Brendan only has to include his wages in his 2013 return. The free flights offered on standby to airline personnel are considered no-additional-cost services and are not taxable to the employee. Reimbursements under an accountable plan and amounts paid for workers' compensation are nontaxable. Since Brendan returned the unspent amounts to his employer, the travel reimbursements qualify under an accountable plan, and the amounts spent are not taxable to him.

17. The answer is B. Elaine's commissions must be included in gross income, as well as advance payments in anticipation of future services, even by a cash-basis taxpayer. The expense reimbursements from her employer would not be included in gross income.

18. The answer is B. Life insurance proceeds are not taxable. However, interest or investment gains earned on a life insurance installment contract are taxable. The face amount of the policy is $270,000. Therefore, the excluded part of each installment is $1,500 ($270,000 ÷ 180 months), or $18,000 for an entire year. The rest of each payment, $300 a month (or $3,600 for an entire year), is interest income to Sheila.

19. The answer is D. Travel reimbursements, if paid through an accountable plan, are not included in an employee's wages.

20. The answer is C. Rob must pay self-employment tax on $10,000, regardless of how he and Cecilia choose to file. Taxpayers cannot combine both spouses' income or loss to determine their earnings subject to SE tax. However, if a taxpayer has more than one business, he must combine the net profit or loss from each to determine the total earnings subject to SE tax.

Unit 5: Individuals Quiz Answers

1. The answer is B. The dividends earned on deposits in credit unions are reported and taxed as interest income.

2. The answer is B. Savings bond owners must use the same interest-reporting method for all the Series EE and Series I bonds they own.

3. The answer is C. Ordinary dividends are taxable as ordinary income in the year they are earned. Only amounts over $1,500 must be reported on Schedule B, so Alec may report the $1,200 in dividend income directly on page one of his Form 1040.

4. The answer is A. Interest earned on state and local bonds is generally tax-exempt at the federal level. Although it is not taxable, it must be reported on the taxpayer's return.

5. The answer is C. A gift for opening a bank account is taxed as interest income. If no other interest is credited to CJ during the year, the Form 1099-INT he receives will include the fair market value of the calculator and show $35 of interest for the year. The $100 of municipal bond interest is not taxable for federal tax purposes, but it must be reported on the return.

6. The answer is D. If a taxpayer is given a choice between receiving cash or stock, a stock dividend is taxable in the year it is distributed. All of the other statements about stock dividends are correct.

7. The answer is C. Miguel must include the total amount of interest earned, $375, in his income. If he itemizes deductions on Schedule A, he can deduct $200 of interest expense, subject to the net investment income limit. He may not report the investment income and expenses on a net basis.

8. The answer is C. Kent earned the dividends in 2013, and whether or not he received a 1099-DIV is irrelevant. Mutual fund dividends are taxable in the year declared regardless of whether the taxpayer withdraws the dividends or reinvests them, so Kent must report the earnings in 2013.

9. The answer is C. As the buyer and owner of the bond, Toni reports the interest on her tax return, but excludes the interest from her taxable income because she paid for qualified higher education expenses the same year.

10. The answer is B. The taxpayer must generally have held the stock for more than 60 days during the 121-day period that begins 60 days before the ex-dividend date. The ex-dividend date is the date following the declaration of a dividend. When figuring the holding period for qualified dividends, the taxpayer may count the number of days he held the stock and include the day he disposed of the stock. The date the taxpayer acquires the stock is not included in the holding period. A longer holding period may apply for dividends paid on preferred stock.

11. The answer is C. The interest earned on the first certificate was received upon maturity, and was therefore taxable in 2013. The accrued interest on the second certificate would have been subject to penalty if the certificate had been redeemed prior to maturity, and was therefore not taxable. Remy did not have constructive receipt of the interest paid on the loan until 2014, and so it was not taxable in 2013.

12. The answer is B. The payment of personal expenses on behalf of an employee-shareholder is treated as a constructive distribution. In this case, it may be a taxable dividend to Robert or a nondividend distribution, depending upon whether the corporation has earnings and profits.

13. The answer is C. If no other interest is credited to Marcelo during the year, the Form 1099-INT he receives will show $95 of interest for the year. Marcelo must report the fair market value of the air miles on his tax return because a gift for opening a bank account is taxed as interest income. The IRS does not count reward points or cash back from a credit card as taxable interest income, so Marcelo does not have to report the $100 or pay tax on it.

14. The answer is B. Ordinary dividends are taxed at higher ordinary income rates than qualified dividends. If certain conditions are met, qualified dividends are given preferred tax treatment. They are either taxed at a capital gains tax rate of 15% or are nontaxable, depending on the taxpayer's regular tax rate.

Unit 6: Individuals Quiz Answers

1. The answer is C. Henry's basis in the stock is $4,070 ([1,000 × $4] = $4,000 + $70).

2. The answer is D. The basis of property must be increased for tax assessments the taxpayer is required to pay in order to finance local improvements, such as paving roads and building ditches. Basis is decreased for depreciation deductions, manufacturers' rebates received, and when the taxpayer incurs theft or other casualty losses.

3. The answer is B. Brigit's original basis in the total stock was $5,100, which is $5.10 per share, so her basis in the 500 shares she sold is 500 × $5.10, or $2,550.

4. The answer is C. Mackenzie's basis is determined as follows: ($50,000 + $4,000 = $54,000). She may not deduct the delinquent property taxes on her Schedule A. Any obligations of the seller that are assumed by the buyer increase the basis of the asset, and are not currently deductible. Since Mackenzie did not owe the property taxes but she still agreed to pay them, she must add the property tax to the basis of the property.

5. The answer is D. The stock is restricted, so Faith does not have constructive receipt of it. She should not report any income until she receives the stock without restrictions. Constructive receipt does not require physical possession of the item of income. However, there are substantial restrictions on the stock's disposition because Faith must complete another four years of service before she can sell or otherwise dispose of the stock.

6. The answer is A. In most situations, the basis of an asset is its cost, including any sales tax or brokers' commissions paid. However, the basis of some assets, including gifts and inherited property, may be determined based on the fair market value at the date of gift or inheritance, rather than the donor's or decedent's cost.

7. The answer is A. In order to compute gain or loss on a sale, a taxpayer must determine his basis in the property sold. If he cannot determine his basis in the property, the IRS will deem the basis to be zero.

8. The answer is C. Julian's basis in each share is $15 ($45 ÷ 3). If a taxpayer receives a nontaxable stock dividend, he divides the adjusted basis of the stock by the total number of shares of stock (old and new). The result is the taxpayer's basis for each share of stock.

9. The answer is B. If a taxpayer acquires and disposes of shares in the same stock at various times and in varying quantities and cannot specifically identify the shares disposed, the basis of the securities disposed is assumed to be the basis of the securities acquired first. This is referred to as the First In, First Out (FIFO) method. Deirdre cannot identify the shares she disposed of, so she must use the stock she acquired first to calculate the basis. The shares Deirdre gave her son had a basis of $500 (50 × $10). Deirdre calculates the basis of the 130 shares of stock she sold as follows:

Basis of first shares acquired (100 × $10)	$1,000
50 shares given to son (50 × $10)	$500
Balance of stock from 2006 (50 shares)	$500
Additional shares (80 × $11) sold (From 2007 purchase)	$880
Total basis of stock sold (130 shares)	**$1,380**

10. The answer is C. Stephen's basis in the truck includes the cost of acquiring the property and preparing it for use. Therefore, his basis is as follows: ($15,000 + $1,300 + $250) = $16,550. Any funds that are borrowed to pay for an asset are included in the basis.

11. The answer is B. Points related to a loan used to acquire property may be deductible in the year they are paid or amortizable over the term of the loan. They are not added to the basis of the property.

12. The answer is D. David's basis in the home is $120,000, the FMV on the date of his mother's death. Heirs can generally use a stepped up basis for inherited property, regardless of what the deceased person actually paid for the asset. The basis of inherited property is generally the FMV of the property on the date of the decedent's death. When the property is ultimately sold, the beneficiary's gain or loss will be calculated based on the change in value from the date of death.

13. The answer is C. If a taxpayer receives property as payment for services, he must include the property's FMV in income, and this becomes his basis. However, if the two parties agree on a cost beforehand, the IRS will usually accept the agreed-upon cost as the asset's basis.

14. The answer is B. The shares now are valued as follows: three with a basis of $10 each ($30 ÷ 3), and three with a basis of $15 each ($45 ÷ 3). If a taxpayer receives a nontaxable stock dividend, he must divide the adjusted basis of the old stock by the number of shares of old and new stock. The result is the taxpayer's basis for each share of stock.

15. The answer is B. The options were issued at an exercise price of $23, which means that $20,000 ($43 - $23 = $20 × 1,000), representing the difference between his exercise price and the stock's value at exercise, must be included in his W-2 for 2013. The basis of the stock would be the value on December 31, 2013 ($43,000), which includes the amount paid for the stock ($23,000) and the amount of taxable income recognized ($20,000). When the stock is later sold, the taxpayer would recognize gain or loss equal to the difference between his sales proceeds and his $43,000 basis in the stock.

Unit 7: Individuals Quiz Answers

1. The answer is D. Unused capital losses may be carried over indefinitely until they are utilized.

2. The answer is A. The answer is figured as follows: The original basis is increased by the broker's commission. Therefore, Marsha's adjusted basis is $10,145 ($10,110 + $35). The gross proceeds from the sale are $8,859, which is subtracted from the basis, resulting in a long-term capital loss of $1,286 ($10,145 - $8,859) because she held the stock for more than one year.

3. The answer is D. Losses on the sale of personal-use property, including residences, are never deductible.

4. The answer is B. The sale and income must be reported in the year the security is sold, regardless of when the proceeds were received. She held the shares for less than one year, so Gianna has a short-term gain that must be reported on her 2013 tax return.

5. The answer is A. Ruben has a short-term capital loss of $600 = (100 shares × $26) - (100 shares × $20). Ruben's holding period was not more than one year, which means that the loss must be treated as short-term. To determine holding period, begin counting on the day after the date the taxpayer acquires the property.

6. The answer is C. Mutual funds frequently distribute capital gains to shareholders. Capital gain distributions for mutual funds are always taxed as long-term capital gains, no matter how long a taxpayer has actually held the mutual fund shares.

7. The answer is C. Fred has a short-term capital loss because he did not hold the stock for over one year. He may deduct $3,000 of the loss in 2013, netting against his wage income. The remaining amount, $4,000, must be carried over to future tax years. A capital loss carryover retains its character as either long-term or short-term.

8. The answer is A. The amount realized on Erik's sale is $265,000, the selling price minus selling expenses.

9. The answer is B. The loss is disallowed. Melissa has a wash sale, because her spouse repurchased identical securities within 30 days. It does not matter if they file MFS. If a taxpayer sells stock and her spouse then repurchases identical stock within 30 days, the taxpayer has a wash sale.

10. The answer is A. The sales price is $750 more than the adjusted basis of the shares. The gain is short-term since Nikhil did not own the shares for more than one year.

11. The answer is C. Consuela cannot deduct all her stock losses in the current year. She may take a $3,000 capital loss on her 2013 tax return and the remainder of the losses will carry forward to subsequent years.

12. The answer is D. Losses on the sale of personal-use property, including a loss on the sale of a primary residence or a vacation home, are not deductible. Only losses associated with business property and investment property (such as stocks and bonds or rental property) are deductible.

13. The answer is B. The net sales price was $4,300 (gross proceeds of $4,400 less $100 commission), which was $1,900 more than her basis of $2,400 in the shares. She owned the shares for more than one year, so her gain was long-term.

14. The answer is D. Caryna recognizes a gain of $3,000 because her basis is the lower of Jonathan's adjusted basis of $55,000 and the FMV of $63,000 at the time of the gift. Even though Caryna owned the Corvette for less than a year, the gain is long-term because the time Jonathan owned the car, three months, is tacked on to the period of ten months that Caryna owned it. If a taxpayer receives a gift of property, his holding period includes the donor's holding period.

15. The answer is C. Because Colin bought substantially identical stock, this is considered a wash sale and he cannot deduct his loss of $250 on the sale. However, he must add the disallowed loss to the cost of the new stock to obtain his adjusted basis in the new stock.

16. The answer is C. To determine the holding period, a taxpayer must begin counting on the day after the acquisition date. If a taxpayer's holding period is not more than one year, the taxpayer will have a short-term gain or loss. The amount realized in the transaction has no bearing on the holding period.

17. The answer is B. The sale of a second home is a taxable event. Since Phil and Sharon owned the property for longer than one year, their gain is long-term. The gain is calculated as follows:

Sale price	$254,000
Less selling expenses	($12,500)
Net proceeds	($241,500)
Less adjusted basis in the property	$232,000
Taxable gain on the sale	**$9,500**

18. The answer is B. Gerardo's basis in the original stock was $1,500 for 100 shares, so his original basis per share was $15 ($1,500/100). The addition of 50 shares means Gerardo's adjusted basis per share decreased to $10 per share ($1,500/150). Therefore, his basis in the 60 shares he sold in December is $600 ($10 adjusted basis per share × 60).

19. The answer is C. Related party transaction rules do not apply to uncles, aunts, nieces, nephews, cousins, stepchildren, stepparents, and in-laws.

20. The answer is A. Although Hans owned the ten shares he received as a nontaxable stock dividend for only three days, all the stock is considered to have a long-term holding period. Because he bought the original shares for $1,500 and then sold them for $2,030 more than a year later, Hans has a long-term capital gain of $530 on the sale of the 510 shares.

21. The answer is D. All the property is long-term property. Generally, if a taxpayer holds investment property for more than one year, any gain or loss is a long-term gain or loss. If the taxpayer holds a property for one year or less, any gain or loss is a short-term gain or loss. However, if a taxpayer receives a gift of property, his holding period includes the donor's holding period. Since Conrad's mother had held the stock for a few years, Conrad's disposition would receive long-term treatment.

22. The answer is D. Tariq realized a long-term gain of $300 because the basis and holding period would automatically default to the original block of shares. A FIFO method is used if the taxpayer cannot specifically identify the shares sold.

23. The answer is D. Norma's gross profit is $5,000, and the gross profit percentage is 50%. Her selling price is $25,000 ($2,000 down payment + $8,000 to be paid over four years + $15,000 for buyer's assumption of mortgage). Therefore, Norma's gross profit is $5,000 ($25,000 – $20,000 adjusted basis). If the entire selling price were payable in cash, her gross profit percentage would have been 20% ($5,000/$25,000). However, if a buyer assumes or pays off a mortgage or other debt on a property, the calculation of the installment sale gross profit percentage is affected. The mortgage assumption is subtracted before calculating the gross profit percentage, except to the extent that it exceeds the adjusted basis of the property for installment sale purposes, to derive what the IRS calls "contract price," rather than selling price. The mortgage assumption is considered a recovery of the seller's basis in the year of sale. Although the mortgage assumption is considered a payment, none of the gross profit is recognized in connection with the assumption. Instead, in this case, the contract price is considered to be $10,000 ($25,000 selling price - $15,000 mortgage assumption). Therefore, Norma's gross profit percentage is 50% ($5,000 ÷ $10,000). Norma must report half of each payment received as gain from the sale. She must also report all interest received as ordinary income.

24. The answer is A. The amount of depreciation deducted for the property ($3,000) is recaptured and reported in 2013 as ordinary income. This amount is added back to the adjusted basis of $9,000 to determine the adjusted basis for the installment sale ($12,000). This amount is subtracted from the total proceeds of the sale ($15,000) to determine the gross profit of $3,000, which derives a gross profit percentage of 20%. This percentage is applied to the portion of proceeds received in 2013 ($5,000) to determine the amount of capital gain recognizable this year.

Supporting calculations:	
Original purchase price	$12,000
Less depreciation deductions	($3,000)
Adjusted basis at date of sale	$9,000
Depreciation recapture	$3,000
Adjusted basis for installment sale	$12,000
Proceeds of sale	$15,000
Gross profit	$3,000
Gross profit percentage	20%
Proceeds in 2013	$5,000
Capital gain to be recognized	**$1,000**

Unit 8: Individuals Quiz Answers

1. The answer is C. His gain is $125,000, the result of subtracting the adjusted basis in the home from the amount realized ($285,000 - $160,000 = $125,000). Since he does not meet the ownership or use tests or qualify for a reduced exclusion, he cannot exclude any of his gain under section 121. He owned the property for more than a year, so the gain is taxed as a long-term capital gain.

2. The answer is B. Lucille's main home is her rental apartment in Denver because she lives there most of the time. If she were to sell the ski home, she would not qualify for the section 121 exclusion on the sale because it is a vacation home and not her primary residence.

3. The answer is A. His basis in the new property is the same as the basis of the property given up ($50,000).

4. The answer is D. The move to be closer to grown children would not qualify. All of the following events would be qualifying events in order to claim a reduced exclusion from a premature sale:

- A divorce or legal separation.
- A pregnancy resulting in multiple births.
- Serious health reasons. (The person who is sick does not need to be the taxpayer's dependent.)

- The home is sold after being seized or condemned.
- A move due to a new job or new employment.

If any of these exceptions apply, the taxpayer may figure a reduced exclusion based on the number of days he owned and lived in the residence.

5. The answer is A. As a single taxpayer, Heather may exclude a maximum gain amount of $250,000 from the sale of her home. Her gain is $270,000 ($620,000 - $350,000). Her taxable gain is $20,000 ($270,000 gain - $250,000 exclusion). The $20,000 taxable gain must be reported as a long-term capital gain.

6. The answer is A. Aiden's total gain on the exchange is $135,000 ($220,000 value of new property + $15,000 cash - $100,000 basis in the old property). However, only the cash boot received is taxable. Aiden's basis in the new building is $115,000 (the original basis in the property he gave up plus the gain recognized as a result of the boot received.)

7. The answer is D. Geoff can exclude $26,000 ($29,000 - $3,000) of his gain. He has a taxable gain of $3,000. He must report the depreciation recapture as ordinary income. If a taxpayer took depreciation deductions because he used his home for business purposes or as a rental property, he cannot exclude the part of the gain equal to any depreciation allowed as a deduction.

8. The answer is A. Bryant must acquire qualifying replacement property by December 31, 2013 (two years from the end of the gain year) in order for the involuntary conversion to be a qualified section 1033 exchange. If Bryant's main home were in a federally declared disaster area, he could have four years to replace the property.

9. The answer is B. Grace meets the ownership and use tests, and the basis in the property remains the same. Transfers related to a divorce are nontaxable, and the FMV of the property at the time of the divorce has no bearing on the taxable outcome. The gain is figured as follows:

Original cost	$150,000
Sale price	$480,000
Total realized gain	$330,000
Sec. 121 exclusion	($250,000)
Taxable gain	$80,000

Since she owned the property for longer than one year, the taxable portion of Grace's gain would be reported as a long-term capital gain.

10. The answer is C. In this case, a reduced exclusion is available, even though the taxpayers did not live in the home for two full years. They qualify for a reduced exclusion because they are moving for a change in Mitchell's employment. Their maximum reduced exclusion is $312,500 [$500,000 × (15 months/24 months)]. The reduced exclusion applies when the premature sale is primarily due to a move for employment in a new location.

11. The answer is A. The basis in the new building is the same as his basis in the old building. The $10,000 of improvements is added to the $16,000 cost, so the adjusted basis of the old building was $26,000.

12. The answer is D. Inventory never qualifies for like-kind exchange treatment. The property must not be held "primarily for sale," such as merchandise, retail stock, or inventory. Generally, real property exchanges will qualify for like-kind treatment, even though the properties themselves might be dissimilar.

13. The answer is B. The couple has a reduced exclusion of $200,000 (292/730 multiplied by the $500,000 maximum exclusion available for married taxpayers). The remaining $60,000 would be considered taxable capital gain income and would be reported on Schedule D. This move qualifies for the reduced exclusion, because multiple births from the same pregnancy are considered an unforeseen circumstance.

14. The answer is B. Allen's basis is $360,000: the $300,000 basis of the old plane plus the $60,000 cash paid. The fair market value of the property has no bearing on Allen's basis in the new property.

15. The answer is A. This sale qualifies for section 121 treatment. Gino meets the ownership and use tests because, during the five-year period ending on the date of sale, he owned the house for three years and lived in it for a total of 25 months. The gain is not taxable and does not need to be reported.

16. The answer is B. Since Katherine purchased replacement property, the basis of the replacement property is the cost of the new yacht ($201,000) minus her deferred gain ($25,000), or $176,000. The deferred gain of $25,000 is calculated as follows: Insurance proceeds of $175,000 – cost of the old yacht of $150,000. Alternatively, the basis of the replacement property could be determined as follows: Basis of the old yacht ($150,000) plus cash paid in excess of insurance proceeds ($201,000 - $175,000 = $26,000).

17. The answer is C. Annalise's adjusted basis in the house would be the total of her original purchase price of $200,000 and the $25,000 cost of improvements. The cost of repairs would not be considered in determining her adjusted basis. Therefore, her gain on the sale would be $325,000, or the excess of her net proceeds over her adjusted basis. Since she met the requirements for ownership and use of the house as her primary residence, she qualifies for the maximum exclusion of $250,000 available to a single taxpayer, and the taxable portion of her gain would be $75,000.

Supporting calculations:	
Purchase price of house	$200,000
Cost of improvements	$25,000
Adjusted basis	$225,000
Net proceeds of sale	**$550,000**
Gain on sale	$325,000
Exclusion for single taxpayer	($250,000)
Taxable gain	**$75,000**

18. The answer is B. Christian's realized gain is $200,000 ($600,000 - $400,000) and his taxable gain is $150,000. He purchased another building for $450,000, so he may defer $50,000 of the gain under section 1033 for involuntary conversions. The remainder of the gain, $150,000 ($600,000 - $450,000), must be recognized because he did not reinvest the remaining proceeds in like-kind property. If Christian had reinvested all the proceeds in the new building, his entire gain would have been deferred.

Unit 9: Individuals Quiz Answers

1. The answer is A. When a taxpayer converts property held for personal use to rental use (for example, the rental of a former home), the basis for depreciation will be the lesser of fair market value or adjusted basis on the date of conversion. The basis for depreciation on the house is its fair market value on the date of the conversion ($147,000) because the FMV on the date of conversion is less than the amount of her original cost that was allocable to the house ($175,800).

2. The answer is C. Matt is allowed to claim a maximum of $12,500 in losses on his separately filed return. If a taxpayer actively participated in a passive rental real estate activity that produced a loss, he can deduct the loss to offset his nonpassive income, up to $25,000. Married persons filing separate returns who lived apart during the year are each allowed a maximum of $12,500 for losses from passive real estate activities. Married persons who file separate returns but lived together during the year are not allowed to take losses on rental real estate activity. Instead, the losses are suspended.

3. The answer is B. Generally, the expenses of renting a property, such as maintenance, insurance, taxes, and interest, can be deducted from rental income. If a taxpayer owns a partial interest in rental property, she can deduct expenses paid according to her percentage of ownership. This cost is a repair, not an improvement, because the window was broken. If all the windows had been replaced with energy-efficient windows, the cost would have been considered an improvement and added to the property's basis.

4. The answer is D. The cost of land is never depreciated.

5. The answer is A. Jane can use $2,000 of her rental loss to offset the passive activity income from the limited partnership. The remaining $1,500 loss can be offset against her $40,000 of wages. A taxpayer may deduct up to $25,000 per year of losses for rental real estate activities in which she actively participates. This special allowance is an exception to the general rule disallowing losses in excess of income from passive activities.

6. The answer is A. The replacement of the deck would be considered a depreciable improvement. The other choices are repairs and may be deducted as current expenses.

7. The answer is C. Ian must include $24,000 in his income in the first year. He must recognize all the advance rent as income in the year of receipt. The security deposit does not have to be recognized as income because it is refundable to the tenant.

8. The answer is D. Depreciation begins on the placed-in-service date when an asset becomes available for use. In most cases, the placed-in-service date and the purchase date are the same, but that is not necessarily the case. Since Pam did not have the HVAC unit ready for use until January 2, 2014, she must wait until 2014 to begin depreciating the unit.

9. The answer is A. All the rental income may be excluded under the "15 day rule." The home is primarily for personal use, and a rental period of less than 15 days is disregarded, which means the IRS does not consider it a rental. The rental income is not taxable, and the rental expenses (such as utilities or maintenance costs) are considered nondeductible personal expenses.

10. The answer is A. Rental income and expenses are reported on Schedule E, which is then attached to the taxpayer's Form 1040. Rental income is any payment received for the use or occupation of property, and is generally passive activity income. There is an exception for real estate professionals, who report rental income on Schedule C.

11. The answer is C. Nicklaus must allocate his expenses between personal use and rental use. He can deduct as rental expenses seven-twelfths (7/12) of annual expenses, such as taxes and insurance. Starting with June, he can deduct as rental expenses the amounts he paid for items generally billed monthly, such as utilities. When figuring depreciation, he should treat the property as placed in service on June 1.

12. The answer is C. Thomas may deduct $25,000 in rental losses. The remaining amount, $4,000 ($29,000 - $25,000), may be carried over to the following year.

13. The answer is D. Depreciation is an income tax deduction that allows a business to recover the cost of property over time.

14. The answer is B. The determination of whether a rental is for profit or not for profit is made when income exceeds rental expenses for three out of five years, not for four out of five years.

15. The answer is B. Travis and Brittany must report six months of rental income at $3,000 per month, or $18,000, but the security deposit of $6,000 is refundable and therefore not recognized as income in 2013. They can deduct 6/12 of the amounts incurred for mortgage interest, property taxes, and casualty insurance, or $10,500, plus the $500 cost of repairs while the house was rented. Thus, their reportable net rental income before considering depreciation would be $7,000.

Supporting calculations:	
Taxable rental income:	
Six months of rent (at $3,000)	$18,000
Less deductible expenses:	
Mortgage interest (for six months)	$5,000
Property taxes (for six months)	$5,000
Casualty insurance (for six months)	$500
Repair cost	$500
Expenses before depreciation	$11,000
Rental income before depreciation	**$7,000**

16. The answer is D. The basis for depreciation is the lesser of fair market value or the taxpayer's adjusted basis on the date the property was converted to rental use. The adjusted basis of the house on July 1, 2013 was $480,000 (original cost of $400,000 plus improvements of $80,000), but the FMV of $420,000 on the same date was lower. The basis of the land is not subject to depreciation.

Supporting calculations:	
Adjusted basis of house:	
Cost	$400,000
Improvements	$80,000
Total adjusted basis	$480,000
FMV on July 1, 2013	**$420,000**

Unit 10: Individuals Quiz Answers

1. The answer is A. For tax purposes, alimony cannot continue after the death of the receiving spouse. Since the payments are required even after Eugenia's death, none of the annual payments are considered alimony for tax purposes. The payments are considered "disguised child support" and cannot be deducted by Cary as alimony.

2. The answer is D. Karly would report $7,500 ($10,000 - $2,500) on line 21 of her Form 1040 as cancellation of debt income.

3. The answer is C. In order to figure out the taxable portion of Social Security, the taxpayer's total income, including tax-exempt interest, must be compared to the base amount for his filing status, which is $25,000. The amount of income that should be compared to the $25,000 base amount is calculated as follows:

Part-time job	$8,000
Interest	$5,000
½ of Social Security	$5,500
Taxable pension	$6,000
Total	**$24,500**

Alexander does not have to pay tax on his Social Security. His income plus one-half of Social Security is less than the base amount ($25,000). However, he is still required to file a tax return, because his overall income exceeds the minimum filing requirement.

4. The answer is C. The wages and the prize are both taxable income. Child support is not taxable to the receiver, nor deductible by the payer. The alimony is taxable to Ed and deductible by his ex-wife. The answer is figured as follows: ($32,000 + $600 + $2,000) = $34,600.

5. The answer is D. Expenses related to a hobby activity are deductible, but only up to the amount of hobby income. Hobby expenses are only deductible on Schedule A as an itemized deduction. If a taxpayer does not itemize, he cannot deduct hobby expenses.

6. The answer is C. The $9,000 of winnings are reported as income, and $9,000 of the losses are reported on Schedule A as an itemized deduction not subject to the 2% floor. The amount of losses deducted may not exceed gambling winnings.

7. The answer is D. The amount of Mina's insolvency immediately prior to the debt cancellation exceeded the amount of debt that was discharged. Therefore, the entire amount of the debt cancellation can be excluded from income.

Supporting calculations:	
Liabilities	$15,000
Fair market value of assets	($2,000)
Amount of insolvency	$13,000
Amount of debt cancellation	**$10,000**

8. The answer is B. Alimony is taxable income to the recipient and deductible by the payer. Therefore, Clifton may deduct $18,000 ($1,500 × 12 months) as alimony paid and Beth must report $18,000 as alimony received. The amount paid as child support, $3,000 ($250 × 12), is not deductible by Clifton and is not reported as income by Beth.

9. The answer is D. A taxpayer must include in gross income in the year of receipt the fair market value of goods and services provided under a bartering arrangement. Bartering involves the exchange of goods or services without exchanging money, such as a plumber fixing a leaky toilet in exchange for a dentist filling a cavity.

10. The answer is C. The amounts for loss of wages and emotional distress are taxable as ordinary income ($4,000 + $10,000 = $14,000). Damages for emotional distress are usually taxable, except for any amounts that were paid for medical care related to the emotional distress (such as a person who is treated for depression after an incident). The damages awarded for physical injury are not taxable.

11. The answer is D. An employer may provide up to $50,000 of life insurance coverage as a nontaxable benefit to an employee. The value of any insurance coverage that exceeds $50,000 is a taxable benefit. All of the other items are taxable.

12. The answer is B. The answer is $42,000 ($40,000 wages + $2,000 prize). Samantha must recognize the prize even though she has not taken the trip, because she had constructive receipt of the winnings. The accident settlement and the child support payments are not taxable.

13. The answer is A. Noncash property settlements do not qualify as alimony. Alimony does not include child support, noncash property settlements, payments to keep up the payer's property, or use of the payer's property. Payments made to a third party or medical expenses paid on behalf of a former spouse may qualify as alimony.

14. The answer is C. Unemployment compensation is taxable income.

15. The answer is C. Absent an additional exclusion based upon insolvency, the excludable amount is $1 million. The additional amount of $500,000 that was borrowed when the property was refinanced in 2006 exceeds the purchase cost and therefore was not qualified personal residence indebtedness eligible for exclusion. The remaining portion of the debt forgiveness ($1.3 million) exceeds the limitation of $1 million for a MFS taxpayer.

Supporting calculations:	
Balance of mortgage	$5,000,000
Proceeds of short sale	(3,200,000)
Amount of debt canceled	$1,800,000

Balance of mortgage	$5,000,000
Amount of QPRI	($4,500,000)
Portion that is not QPRI	$500,000

Amount of debt canceled	$1,800,000
Less portion not QPRI	($500,000)
Subtotal	$1,300,000
Less limit for MFS	($1,000,000)
Portion of QPRI not eligible for exclusion	**$300,000**

16. The answer is C. The wages, interest, alimony, and lottery winnings are taxable income ($13,000 + $15 + $2,000 + $5,000 = $20,015). Child support, inheritances, and workers' compensation are nontaxable income.

17. The answer is B. Anaya must report the cash alimony payments and one-half of the mortgage payments as taxable alimony. The child support payments are not taxable.

18. The answer is B. Bart's inability to pay his debt is not a result of bankruptcy or insolvency, so he must include the full amount of the canceled debt ($5,000) in his gross income.

19. The answer is D. The maximum amount that is ever taxable on net Social Security benefits is 85%, which in Hank's case is $9,965.

20. The answer is B. Brent must include $150 in income. He may also deduct the cost of the repair ($150) if it qualifies as a business expense. If a taxpayer exchanges services with another person and both have agreed ahead of time on the value of those services, that value will be accepted as fair market value unless the value can be shown to be otherwise.

21. The answer is C. The wages, gambling income, and interest income must all be reported. The accident settlement and the child support are not taxable. Food stamps and welfare payments also are not taxable income. The gambling losses do not affect the reporting of the gambling income. Gambling losses are a deduction on Schedule A, should Ginny choose to itemize. If Ginny does not itemize, the gambling losses are not deductible.

22. The answer is D. Gross income does not include the amount of damages received due to physical injuries or to sickness, regardless of whether they are paid as lump sums or as periodic payments.

Unit 11: Individuals Quiz Answers

1. The answer is C. Withdrawals from an HSA for non-eligible expenses are allowed, but the withdrawal is subject to a 20% penalty, in addition to regular income tax.

2. The answer is C. The maximum deduction for student loan interest is $2,500. The deduction is limited to the lesser of $2,500 or the amount of interest actually paid.

3. The answer is A. A taxpayer cannot deduct a contribution to an IRA after the due date of his tax return, even if he files for an extension. IRA contributions for tax year 2013 must be made by April 15, 2014.

4. The answer is D. College instructors do not qualify. An eligible educator must work 900 hours a year in a school that provides elementary or secondary education (K-12). Part-time teachers qualify, so long as they meet the yearly requirement for hours worked. The term educator includes teachers, instructors, counselors, principals, and aides.

5. The answer is C. The cost of meals is not deductible. The costs of travel, transportation, and lodging are all deductible. The costs of moving personal items and pets are deductible. The answer is figured as follows:

- Dave's deductible expenses $400 + $40 + $150 = $590
- Bea's deductible expenses $500 + $40 + $35 + $100 = $675

- Cost of shipping horse = $600
- Total deductible expenses: $590 + $675 + $600 = $1,865

If a married couple files jointly, either spouse can qualify for the full-time work test. Family members are not required to travel together.

6. The answer is A. Only the interest is deductible. A payment toward the principal on the loan is not a deductible expense. Student loan interest is interest a taxpayer paid during the year on a qualified student loan. It includes both required and voluntary interest payments.

7. The answer is A. The payment may be treated as alimony for tax purposes, because the medical payments are a condition of the divorce agreement. Payments to a third party on behalf of an ex-spouse under the terms of a divorce instrument can be alimony, if they qualify. These include payments for a spouse's medical expenses, housing costs (rent and utilities), taxes, and tuition. The payments are treated by the ex-spouse as if they were received directly, and included as income.

8. The answer is C. Adjustments are deducted from gross income to derive adjusted gross income (AGI), and itemized deductions are subtracted from AGI. The amount of a taxpayer's AGI is important, as it can affect his eligibility for certain deductions and the amounts that he can claim. For example, certain of these items are phased out at specified levels of AGI, and some itemized deductions must exceed specified percentages of AGI in order to be deductible. In addition, itemized deductions may be subject to the alternative minimum tax, or may total less than the taxpayer's applicable standard deduction.

9. The answer is B. On a joint return, a taxpayer may deduct student loan interest paid on behalf of his spouse or dependents. This deduction is a maximum of $2,500 in 2013. Credit card interest does not qualify, and taxpayers must be liable for the loan in order to deduct the interest expense.

10. The answer is D. Only the student activity fees qualify for the tuition and fees deduction. Deductions are not allowed for room and board and other basic expenses of going to college, other than required tuition and fees. Student activity fees, course-related books, supplies, and equipment may be deductible only if they are required by the institution as a condition of enrollment.

11. The answer is C. On a jointly filed tax return, if both taxpayers are teachers, they both may take the deduction, up to a maximum of $500 ($250 each).

12. The answer is B. Chuck and Mallory may only deduct $1,000 of self-employed health insurance for the two months that they were ineligible to participate in an employer plan. No deduction is allowed for self-employed health insurance for any month that the taxpayer has the option to participate in an employer-sponsored and subsidized plan. This is true even if the taxpayer declines the coverage. A self-employed taxpayer may deduct 100% of health insurance premiums as an adjustment to income but only if neither he nor his spouse was eligible to participate in an employer health plan.

13. The answer is C. Interest paid to a family member is not qualified interest for purposes of the student loan interest deduction. Related persons include a spouse, brothers and sisters, half-brothers and half-sisters, ancestors (parents, grandparents, etc.), and lineal descendants (children, grandchildren, etc.)

14. The answer is B. Expenses of buying or selling a home (including closing costs, mortgage fees, and points) are never deductible as moving expenses. If an employer pays or reimburses expenses, the amounts are treated as taxable compensation and must be reported as wages on Lynn's Form W-2.

15. The answer is C. George can deduct alimony paid, even if he does not itemize. He must file Form 1040 and enter the amount of alimony paid as an adjustment to income.

16. The answer is B. Early withdrawal penalties are deductible if made from a time deposit account, such as a certificate of deposit. The other types of penalties are not deductible.

17. The answer is B. Withdrawals for nonmedical expenses from an HSA are allowed but subject to income tax. Nonmedical distributions are also subject to an additional penalty tax of 20%, except when the taxpayer has turned 65, become disabled, or died. Kyle is disabled, so his withdrawals are not subject to penalty.

18. The answer is C. The cost of breaking a lease is not a deductible moving expense. House-hunting before a move is also not deductible. The other costs are deductible. Therefore, Chase may deduct the following: ($500 + $300 + $200 = $1,000).

19. The answer is A. Because Jasmine only worked 440 hours as an educator during the tax year, she cannot deduct her educator expenses as an adjustment to income. An educator must have at least 900 hours of qualified employment during the school year to take this deduction as an adjustment to income.

20. The answer is B. The rental fee and the tuition costs qualify for the tuition and fees deduction, and Emilio may deduct the cost on his tax return. Because the equipment rental fee must be paid to the university and is a requirement for enrollment and attendance, it is a qualified expense. Student activity fees and expenses for course-related books, supplies, and equipment can be included in qualified educational expenses if the fees and expenses paid to the institution are required. The housing is not a qualified educational expense.

21. The answer is B. A 6% penalty applies to excess contributions to a health savings account. Excess contributions made by an employer must be included in an employee's gross income. Excess contributions to an HSA are not deductible.

22. The answer is C. Deborah may deduct 50% of the self-employment tax she paid as an adjustment to income on page 1 of her Form 1040.

23. The answer is C. Marina is not able to deduct her moving expenses. She meets the distance test because her old home in Boston is more than 50 miles from her new office in Raleigh. However, to meet the time test, she must work full-time for a period of at least 39 weeks in the first 12 months. Since she is only working part-time for six months, this does not fulfill the requirements of the time test. A spouse does not need to be employed for a MFJ couple to deduct moving expenses.

Unit 12: Individuals Quiz Answers

1. The answer is B. Only the real estate taxes are deductible. Taxpayers can deduct real estate tax on Schedule A as an itemized deduction.

2. The answer is D. Angie and Sheldon cannot deduct any of their medical expenses. Only the portion of total medical expenses that exceeds 10% of the taxpayer's AGI is deductible. The total of Angie and Sheldon's medical expenses, $6,620, is less than $6,840 ($68,400 × 10%).

3. The answer is C. Based upon their MFJ status, Max and Wendy are entitled to a standard deduction of $12,200. Max is blind, so he is allowed an additional $1,200. Thus, their combined standard deduction is $13,400.

4. The answer is D. The deduction for capital improvements is limited to the excess of the actual cost of the improvements over the increase in the fair market value of the home. Since the increase in fair market value of the home exceeds the cost of the improvements, none of the cost can be deducted as a medical expense.

5. The answer is D. A married taxpayer who files separately and whose spouse itemizes deductions must either itemize his deductions or claim zero as his deduction. He is not permitted to utilize the standard deduction.

6. The answer is D. Taxpayers may deduct transportation related to medical care. The costs of nursing home care, smoking-cessation programs, and prescription drugs are also deductible. However, over-the-counter medicines are not deductible as medical expenses.

7. The answer is B. The standard deduction amount depends on the taxpayer's filing and dependent status, and whether the taxpayer is blind or at least 65 years old. It is not based on the taxpayer's income.

8. The answer is A. The Pease limitation does not apply to deductions for medical expenses, investment interest expense, casualty or theft losses, and allowable gambling losses. The Pease limitation places a limit on the following itemized deductions for higher income taxpayers: charitable contributions; mortgage interest; state, local, and property taxes; and miscellaneous itemized deductions. It reduces the total amount of otherwise allowable itemized deductions by 3% of the amount by which the taxpayer's AGI exceeds specific thresholds. The limitation cannot be more than 80% of the otherwise allowable itemized deductions.

9. The answer is A. Taxpayers have the option of claiming state and local sales taxes as an itemized deduction on Schedule A instead of claiming state and local income taxes. A taxpayer cannot claim both. The other expenses listed are not deductible on Schedule A.

10. The answer is D. A nonresident or dual-status alien (who is not married to a U.S. citizen or resident) must itemize deductions. He cannot use the standard deduction. The other taxpayers listed are not required to itemize their deductions but may elect to do so.

11. The answer is B. His medical expense deduction before limitation is $4,350 ($450 + $800 + $200 + $1,900 + $1,000). The child care cost is not deductible, even though it was incurred while Justin was obtaining medical care. The amount reimbursed by insurance is not deductible.

12. The answer is B. Dora can deduct only $500 of her medical expenses because that is the amount that exceeds 7.5% of her AGI ($40,000 AGI × 7.5 =$3,000), the applicable threshold since she is 65 or older.

13. The answer is A. Taxpayers can deduct tax imposed during a prior year, so long as the taxes were paid during the current tax year.

14. The answer is D. If a taxpayer or his spouse is age 65 or over, the floor for deducting medical expenses is 7.5% in 2013. Unless a taxpayer or his spouse is age 65 or older, the floor in 2013 is 10%, rather than 7.5%, of AGI. Being disabled is not an exception. A taxpayer cannot claim both itemized deductions and the standard deduction, regardless of whether or not she is blind.

15. The answer is C. The answer is $24,000 + $3,000 + $50 = $27,050. The deduction for investment interest expense is limited to net investment income. The excess amount of interest expense must be carried over to the next tax year and may be used to offset net investment income in future tax years. Late fees paid on a qualifying mortgage are deductible as interest. The credit card interest and car loan interest are not deductible.

16. The answer is B. Only their home mortgage interest ($5,000) is deductible as interest or Schedule A. The other types of interest are all personal interest, which is not deductible. Interest paid on a plot of land is not deductible as mortgage interest, even if the taxpayer later decides to build a home on the property. Only the interest that is secured by an actual home (not land) is deductible as mortgage interest.

17. The answer is B. The assessment to improve sidewalks is not deductible. Many local governments impose taxes that finance improvements to property, such as assessments for streets, sidewalks, and sewer lines. These taxes cannot be deducted, but should be added to the basis of the property.

18. The answer is C. A taxpayer can claim a deduction for a contribution of $250 or more only if she has a receipt or acknowledgment from a qualified organization. The receipt must include:

- The amount of cash contributed
- Whether the qualified organization gave the taxpayer any goods or services in return
- If applicable, a description and good faith estimate of the value of any goods or services provided in return by the organization

A receipt must also show the date of the donation and the name of the organization that was paid.

19. The answer is C. The Pease limitation reduces the value of itemized deductions by 3% of the AGI above $250,000 for single taxpayers ($300,000 for joint filers). The maximum reduction is 80% of the value of the total deductions. Nirali's AGI is $65,000 over the $250,000 threshold, so the reduction of itemized deductions is 3% of this amount ($315,000 - $250,000 = $65,000 × .03 = $1,950). That limits the total amount she may deduct to $83,050 ($85,000 - $1,950 = $83,050).

20. The answer is B. The contribution to the Chamber of Commerce is not deductible. The $5,000 contribution to his church is fully deductible. However, charitable gifts of appreciated property are subject to a maximum deduction of 30% of the taxpayer's adjusted gross income. Martin figures his charitable contribution as follows:

(AGI of $45,000 × 30%) =	$13,500
Cash contribution	$5,000
Total	$18,500
Carryover = $2,500 ($16,000 - $13,500)	

There is a five-year carryover period for any excess charitable contribution deductions.

21. The answer is A. Deductible fees are limited to home mortgage interest and certain real estate taxes. Points that represent interest on a refinancing are generally amortized over the life of the loan. Fees that are not associated with the acquisition of a loan (other than fees representing interest for tax purposes) generally only affect the basis of the home. Harvey may not deduct any of the expenses listed because the home loan is a refinance, not a purchase. If he had used part of the refinanced mortgage to improve his main home, he could have fully deducted the applicable portion of the points in the year he paid them. A new roof on a second home, however, does not qualify.

22. The answer is D. Lindy can only deduct $1,900 for her donation. She is allowed to take the lesser of the car's FMV or the amount for which the charity was able to sell the car. Since the car only sold for $1,900, that is the amount of the donation, regardless of other estimates of its value.

23. The answer is B. The mortgage interest and property tax on both his main home and the cabin are deductible. The mortgage interest on a second home is deductible, even if the taxpayer did not use the home during the year.

24. The answer is A. The contributions to the political organization and the Chamber of Commerce are not deductible on Schedule A. The deduction is figured: ($100 + $120 + $75 + $25 = $320).

25. The answer is A. The limit on the amount of debt that can be treated as home equity debt for purposes of the mortgage interest deduction is $100,000, not $150,000.

26. The answer is B. The IRS requires a taxpayer to obtain a written appraisal by a qualified appraiser for any noncash contribution of more than $5,000. The taxpayer must complete Form 8283, Section B, and attach it to his tax return. He must retain a copy of the appraisal for his own records, but in most cases does not have to include the appraisal with his tax return.

27. The answer is C. The insurance premiums are not deductible because they were paid through an employer health insurance plan and were not reported in box 1 of Form W-2. Neither club dues nor nonprescription medicines (except insulin) are deductible. The deductible costs listed total $19,100, and the 3,000 miles driven in connection with medical visits can be deducted at a standard mileage rate of $.24, or $720. Deductibility of the resulting total of $19,820 is limited to the amount in excess of 7.5% of adjusted gross income (because Henry is 65 or over), or $7,500, so the amount of their medical expense deduction calculated on Schedule A would be $12,320.

Supporting calculations:

Physician and hospital fees			$10,000
Dental and orthodontic fees			$5,000
Eyeglasses and contact lenses			$1,000
Prescription medications			$3,000
Parking and tolls			$100
Mileage at standard mileage rate of $.24			$720
Total deductible expenses			**$19,820**
Adjusted gross income	$100,000		
7.5% limit	($7,500)		
Limitation ($19,820 - $7,500)			
Medical expense deduction on Schedule A		$12,320	

28. The answer is B. Oscar's donation is limited to $50. Generally, the FMV of used clothing and household goods is far less than original cost. For used clothing, a taxpayer should claim as the value the price that a buyer typically would pay in a thrift shop or at a garage sale.

29. The answer is C. A taxpayer who is 65 and older (and his or her spouse, even if the spouse is younger than 65) may deduct only the amount by which total medical expenses for the year exceed 7.5% of adjusted gross income.

30. The answer is C. Julio's charitable contribution is $75 ($50 + $25 = $75). He can claim his travel and meeting expenses as charitable contributions, because they are directly related to his charitable activities. However, he cannot claim the cost of the evening at the theater, as that is a personal entertainment expense.

31. The answer is A. Each taxpayer's situation is different, meaning that it is difficult to predict, without actually making a comparison of the numbers, whether the standard deduction or itemized deductions will yield a lower tax liability. For example, if a married couple has no large deductions, such as for taxes, mortgage interest, or charitable contributions, their standard deduction may yield a greater tax benefit than their itemized deductions.

32. The answer is D. Vera and Jack cannot deduct more than $15,000, which is 50% of their income of $30,000. The remaining amount must be carried forward to a future tax year. The carryforward period is five years for most charitable deductions.

Unit 13: Individuals Quiz Answers

1. The answer is B. Baltimore is Alfred's main place of work because he spends most of his time and earns most of his income there. Therefore, Baltimore is Alfred's tax home for IRS purposes.

2. The answer is D. The expenses deductible as miscellaneous itemized expenses are the income tax preparation fee ($100); the safe deposit box rental ($75); the investment journals and newsletters ($250); and the investment advisory fees ($200). His total deduction before application of the 2% floor is $625.

3. The answer is A. The expense of commuting to and from work is not deductible.

4. The answer is A. A casualty loss is not deductible if the damage is neither unexpected nor unusual, such as when it is caused by a family pet.

5. The answer is C. If a taxpayer chooses the simplified option for calculating the home office deduction, the maximum allowable area is 300 square feet at $5 per foot, for a maximum deduction of $1,500.

6. The answer is C. Eli's deductible casualty loss on Schedule A is $4,600. This is a nonbusiness casualty loss, so Eli must first reduce his loss by $100 and then by 10% of his AGI. Although his basis is $11,000, he uses the FMV to determine his loss because it is lower.

Supporting calculations:

FMV	$10,000
Insurance	$0
Salvage value	($300)
Statutory reduction	($100)
10% of AGI	($5,000)
Deductible loss	$4,600

7. The answer is C. Isaac's casualty loss before applying the deduction limits is $6,000. Isaac must reduce his loss ($90,000) by the $80,000 insurance proceeds and the $4,000 he received from his employer.

8. The answer is B. Harriet can claim the difference between the $15,000 owed to her (and previously reported as accrual-basis income when earned) and the $2,000 received in the bankruptcy settlement as a business bad debt deduction. The former client's bankruptcy provides evidence to support the worthlessness of the remaining amount owed to Harriet.

9. The answer is A. Funeral expenses are not deductible as a miscellaneous itemized deduction. All of the other expenses listed are deductible as itemized deductions on Schedule A.

10. The answer is D. Kim uses 20% of her home for business, as her office is 20% (480 ÷ 2,400) of the total area of her home.

11. The answer is A. Connor may deduct the expenses for the special device as an impairment-related work expense. If a taxpayer has a physical or mental disability that limits employment, he can deduct the expense as a miscellaneous itemized deduction, not subject to the 2%-of-AGI floor.

12. The answer is D. A taxpayer can deduct the costs of qualifying work-related education as employee business expenses. Amounts that are reimbursed by an employer cannot be deducted by the taxpayer.

13. The answer is B. Simon's employee work-related expenses are subject to limit based upon 2% of adjusted gross income. Therefore, Simon must calculate his deduction on Schedule A by first subtracting 2% of his AGI (75,000 × 2% = $1,500) from the total amount of these expenses.

14. The answer is A. Harini cannot deduct any of the expenses, because travel expenses paid in connection with an indefinite work assignment are not deductible.

15. The answer is B. If a taxpayer's property is covered by insurance and the taxpayer declines to file an insurance claim, the eligible casualty losses are limited to the amount that is not normally covered by insurance, such as the amount of an insurance deductible.

16. The answer is D. Gambling losses, to the extent of gambling winnings, are not subject to the 2%-of-AGI limit.

17. The answer is B. A taxpayer can include in business expenses amounts paid for transportation primarily for and essential to a business or trade. A taxpayer cannot deduct personal commuting expenses, no matter how far his home is from his regular place of work.

18. The answer is C. Marissa may deduct all the costs as work-related educational expenses except the credit card interest, which is a personal expense and not deductible.

19. The answer is C. For most casualty losses, taxpayers have two years to purchase a replacement for damaged or destroyed property. However, in the case of most federally declared disaster areas, the period is four years. In certain extreme cases, including the taxpayers affected by Hurricane Katrina, the replacement period has been extended to five years.

20. The answer is C. The attorney's fee for drafting the will is not deductible. The tax preparation fees and union dues are deductible, but are subject to the 2%-of-AGI floor.

21. The answer is A. The full amount of income ($45,000 + $10,000 = $55,000) must be reported on Form 1040. The gambling losses are deductible on Schedule A, but only up to the amount of gambling winnings. Gambling losses are not subject to the 2% of income limitation. Attorney fees for a divorce are not deductible, but separate legal advice related to collecting alimony is deductible.

22. The answer is D. Neither the homeowners' association dues nor the fine are deductible. The tax preparation fees did not exceed 2% of adjusted gross income, and therefore are not deductible. The amount of the burglary loss, less $100, that exceeds 10% of adjusted gross income is deductible as a casualty loss.

Supporting calculations:

Loss from theft	$9,000
Less $100 threshold	($100)
Loss after $100 limit	$8,900
Adjusted gross income	$75,000
Multiply by 10% limit	$7,500
Casualty loss deduction ($8,900 - $7,500)	$1,400

23. The answer is D. Because the property was covered by insurance and Brooke did not file a claim, the casualty loss deduction is limited to the amount of the insurance deductible, as this amount would have been her out-of-pocket cost if a claim had been filed. This amount is further subject to a reduction of $100 and limited to the net amount that exceeds 10% of adjusted gross income.

Supporting calculations:

Loss from storm	$3,000
Limited to amount of deductible	$2,500
Less $100	($100)
Net loss	$2,400
Adjusted gross income	$20,000
Multiply by 10% limit	$2,000
Casualty loss deduction ($2,400 - $2,000)	$400

24. The answer is D. For job search expenses to be deductible, they must relate to the taxpayer's current occupation. A taxpayer may not deduct expenses if they are connected with the search for a job in a new field.

25. The answer is A. Wes does not have a deductible casualty loss. Since the fair market value of the car was lower than its cost, it is used as the starting point to determine his loss. Net of the salvage value, he had a loss of $27,000 on the car. His loss on the desks is limited to his original cost since it was lower than FMV. Thus he had total losses of $29,500 before the insurance reimbursement, and a net loss of $5,500. After subtracting the $100 deduction, he had potentially deductible losses of $5,400. However, his deduction is limited to the amount of the losses that exceeds 10% of his AGI, or $7,000.

Calculations	Car	Desks
Basis for the casualty loss	$27,000	$2,500
Insurance reimbursement	$24,000	
Net loss after insurance reimbursement ($29,500 - $24,000)	$5,500	
Subtract $100	$5,400	
AGI × 10% ($70,000 × 10%)	$7,000	
Allowable casualty loss	$0	

26. The answer is D. Based on the information presented, it appears unlikely that Ali would be able to claim a nonbusiness bad debt deduction. In order to do so, he would need to be able to demonstrate that: 1) he had a debtor-creditor relationship with Karyn that included a valid and enforceable obligation for her to repay the loan; 2) he had taken reasonable steps to collect the debt; and 3) the debt was totally worthless.

27. The answer is C. Nonresident aliens are limited as to the types of itemized deductions they may claim. Among other restrictions, they are not allowed to claim the deduction for mortgage interest.

28. The answer is C. Addison may deduct $175 for the presents because there is an annual limit of $25 per gift per customer (7 × $25 = $175.)

29. The answer is B. Nonbusiness bad debts are reported as short-term capital losses on Schedule D. They are subject to the capital loss limit of $3,000 per year.

30. The answer is D. Blair cannot claim a miscellaneous deduction for these costs. Although her travel to Spain may be somewhat educational, the related costs do not qualify as work-related education expenses.

31. The answer is C. Hector is an employee who falls under the special Department of Transportation hours of service rules, meaning he may deduct 80% of his unreimbursed meal expenses ($3,760 × .80 = $3,008), rather than the normal 50%.

32. The answer is C. This is the only answer where all three items are subject to the 2%-of-AGI floor. In answer A, educator expenses are an adjustment to income. In answer B, charitable donations are not a miscellaneous deduction and gambling losses are a miscellaneous deduction not subject to the 2% floor. In answer D, impairment-related work expenses of a disabled employee are a miscellaneous deduction not subject to the 2% floor.

33. The answer is B. Stanton may deduct 100% of the air fare, baggage fee, car rental fee, and hotel costs as unreimbursed employee expenses, before applying the 2%-of-AGI floor. However, he may deduct only 50% of the business meals and entertainment expenses, for a total of $1,410 ($400 + $25 + $125 + $650 + $150 meals + $60 entertainment).

Unit 14: Individuals Quiz Answers

1. The answer is B. Gail does not qualify for the Earned Income Credit in 2013 because her investment income exceeds $3,300.

2. The answer is A. Because Orlando's equipment rental fee must be paid to the university as a condition for enrollment, it is considered a qualified related expense. Qualified expenses do not include insurance or medical expenses (student health fees), room and board, transportation, or similar personal, living, or family expenses, or any course of instruction or other education involving sports, games, or hobbies, unless the course is part of the student's degree program.

3. The answer is B. A nephew who lived with the taxpayer for seven months may qualify. In order to qualify for the Child Tax Credit, the taxpayer must have a qualifying child who lived with him for more than six months and who is under the age of 17. The child cannot have provided more than half of his own support.

4. The answer is D. Household employee income is considered earned income, because it is a type of wages. Alimony, workfare payments, and interest and dividends are not considered earned income for purposes of the EIC.

5. The answer is C. Beatrice can claim $2,000 as a maximum credit, or $1,000 for each qualifying child. For purposes of this credit, she only has two qualifying children, because one of her dependents is already over 17 and therefore no longer eligible for the credit.

6. The answer is D. Beth is eligible for the American Opportunity Credit because she is taking at least one-half of the normal full-time workload for her course of study for at least one academic period beginning in 2013. Graduate courses do not qualify, and courses that do not lead to a degree, certificate, or other recognized credential also do not qualify for the AOC. Persons with felony drug convictions are ineligible for this credit.

7. The answer is C. Dylan and Hannah can take the full Adoption Credit because they adopted a special needs child. Under a special rule for taxpayers who adopt special needs children, the maximum Adoption Credit is allowed, even if the taxpayer has a lesser amount of adoption expenses.

8. The answer is D. Leanne meets the qualifying person test because she is the spouse of someone who works, and she is unable to care for herself.

9. The answer is D. The total qualified tuition payments are the net of the $5,000 tuition minus the grant of $3,000, which equals $2,000. The $3,000 Pell grant is tax-free, so it must be deducted from his overall qualifying costs. A student loan must be paid back, so it does not figure into the determination of educational expenses.

10. The answer is B. Daycare is not a qualifying education expense. For purposes of the Lifetime Learning Credit, qualified education expenses are tuition and certain related expenses required for enrollment or attendance at an eligible educational institution.

11. The answer is C. Their child care expenses are as follows: ($3,000 + $100 + $35) minus reimbursement of $1,200 = $1,935. If a taxpayer receives a reimbursement under a flexible spending account, the amount is treated as being pre-tax and the taxpayer must deduct the reimbursed amount from his qualified expenses to determine the credit. Fees and deposits paid to an agency or a daycare provider are qualifying expenses if the taxpayer must pay them in order to receive care.

12. The answer is C. Samira and Rishi are eligible to claim an education credit for 2013. The credit should be claimed for the year in which the taxpayer paid the expenses, not the year in which the loan is repaid.

13. The answer is C. Edwin qualifies for the Lifetime Learning Credit. He does not qualify for the American Opportunity Credit because he is not a degree candidate and because his course work-load does not meet the requirements. The "College Saver's Credit" does not exist. The Mortgage Interest Credit is not an education credit.

14. The answer is B. The taxpayer must be a U.S. citizen or legal resident all year. A taxpayer cannot claim the EIC if his filing status is MFS. Taxpayers do not need to have a dependent child in order to qualify for the Earned Income Credit; however, the EIC is greatly increased if the taxpayer has a qualifying child. A taxpayer must have earned income to qualify for the EIC; Social Security benefits do not qualify.

15. The answer is B. Nina's son does not qualify, because he is over the age limit for the credit. To qualify for the Child and Dependent Care Credit, the dependent must be under the age of 13 or completely disabled.

16. The answer is A. Zoe does not qualify for the AOC because she is in her fifth year of college and her parents have already claimed the credit the prior four years. If she had been eligible for the credit, she would have had $11,000 of eligible expenses. Room and board and medical insurance are not qualified expenses for the AOC, and the qualifying tuition cost must be reduced by any tax-free scholarships, such as the Pell grant. The AOC is a maximum credit of $2,500 per student (100% of the first $2,000 of eligible expenses and 20% of the next $2,000). Zoe qualifies for the Lifetime Learning Credit.

17. The answer is C. The cost of a surrogate is not a qualified adoption expense. Qualified adoption expenses are expenses directly related to the legal adoption of an eligible child. These expenses include adoption fees, court costs, attorney fees, travel expenses (including amounts spent for meals and lodging) while away from home, and re-adoption expenses to adopt a foreign child.

18. The answer is B. All the other choices are disqualifying for purposes of the EIC. At the end of the tax year, a qualifying child must be under age 19; under age 24 and a full-time student; or any age and disabled. A taxpayer claiming the EIC may have up to $3,300 of unearned income. He must be between the ages of 25 and 64 at the end of the year to qualify.

19. The answer is B. A refundable credit, such as the Earned Income Credit, is not limited by an individual's tax liability. The taxpayer can receive a refund even if he has zero tax liability.

20. The answer is C. MFJ taxpayers are allowed a nonrefundable credit of up to $2,000 for eligible contributions to an IRA or an employer-sponsored retirement plan. The credit is $1,000 per year for single filers.

21. The answer is B. In 2013, the maximum amount for the AOC is $2,500 per student. The taxpayer's family may have more than one eligible student per tax return.

22. The answer is B. Arlene is entitled to claim the Child Tax Credit because her grandson is a qualifying child for purposes of the credit: she provided more than half of his support, he is under 17, and he lived with her for more than half the year. However, Arlene cannot take the full $1,000 credit for her grandson because her income is above $75,000, the threshold for single, head of household, and qualifying widow(er) filers. The credit is reduced by $50 for each $1,000 of MAGI that exceeds the threshold amount. Thus, Arlene's credit is reduced by $500 (10 × $50).

23. The answer is C. Child care costs to obtain medical care are not a deductible expense. Deductible costs must be work related and for a child under 13, a disabled dependent, or a disabled spouse of any age. Child care costs incurred so that the taxpayer can volunteer, obtain medical care, run errands, or do other personal business do not qualify.

24. The answer is D. The total combined credit is $500 for all tax years after 2005.

25. The answer is B. Orrin cannot claim the EIC for two tax years. There are restrictions on EIC claims by taxpayers for whom a previous claim was denied or reduced due to any reason other than a math or clerical error. If a taxpayer was determined to have claimed the EIC due to reckless or intentional disregard of the EIC rules, he cannot claim the EIC for two tax years. If the error was due to fraud, the taxpayer cannot claim the EIC for ten tax years.

26. The answer is B. Sybil qualifies for the credit because her modified AGI is under $59,000, which is the threshold limit for married filing jointly. Ed, Carl, and Bert do not qualify because each has AGI that exceeds the applicable limit for his filing status.

27. The answer is D. The maximum credit is $2,000 per tax return. The credit is allowed for 20% of the first $10,000 of qualified tuition and fees paid during the year. The credit is per tax return, not per student, so only a maximum of $2,000 can be claimed each year, no matter how many qualifying students a taxpayer may have.

28. The answer is C. As part of his due diligence requirements, a paid preparer must complete and attach Form 8867, the Earned Income Credit checklist, to the tax return of every client who is claiming the EIC (not to all clients' returns, regardless of whether they are claiming the EIC). The checklist is a four-page form with questions the preparer must ask to determine client eligibility for the credit. A preparer faces a $500 fine for each failure to meet the EIC due diligence standards.

29. The answer is B. The maximum credit for 2013 is $12,970 per child. The other amounts listed were from other tax years. If a taxpayer adopts two children, he will be eligible for the full credit on each child. The credit phases out for taxpayers with MAGI starting at $194,580. Married taxpayers filing separately are not eligible for the Adoption Credit.

30. The answer is A. Hayden is a qualifying child for the Child Tax Credit because he was under age 17 at the end of 2013. Siblings can be qualifying children for purposes of this credit.

Unit 15: Individuals Quiz Answers

1. The answer is C. Taxpayers have the option to claim an itemized deduction for foreign taxes paid on Schedule A. They may choose either the deduction or the credit, whichever gives them the lowest tax. Taxpayers cannot claim both the deduction and a tax credit on the same return.

2. The answer is D. The kiddie tax only applies to investment income, not to wages. Therefore, Colton's income will not be subject to the kiddie tax. Under the provisions of the kiddie tax, unearned income that is in excess of $2,000 will be taxed at the parent's marginal rate.

3. The answer is A. Ella is not required to issue a Form W-2 to the nanny, and does not have to report or pay Social Security and Medicare taxes on the nanny's wages. If an employer pays a household employee wages of less than $1,800 in 2013, the employer is not required to report or pay Social Security and Medicare taxes on that employee's wages. However, employers who withhold federal income taxes from their employee's wages must issue a Form W-2. Regardless of whether Form W-2 is issued, the nanny must report the income on Form 1040.

4. The answer is A. The additional Medicare tax applies to 0.9% of a taxpayer's earned income above a threshold based on his filing status. For single, head of household, and qualifying widower filers, the threshold is $200,000. For married couples filing jointly, the amount is $250,000. For married couples filing separately, the amount is $125,000.

5. The answer is B. The tentative minimum tax is figured separately from the regular tax. The AMT is owed only if the tentative minimum tax is greater than the regular tax.

6. The answer is C. Allen and Dorrie owe tax on the lesser of their net investment income ($12,500) or the amount by which their combined MAGI of $302,000 exceeds the applicable threshold for joint filers of $250,000 ($52,000). Thus, they owe $475 of NIIT ($12,500 × 3.8% = $475.)

7. The answer is C. In 2013, the nanny tax applies when a taxpayer pays a household employee $1,800 or more in wages a year.

8. The answer is C. U.S. citizens and resident aliens who live abroad are taxed on their worldwide income. However, they may qualify to exclude a portion of their foreign earnings (up to $97,600 for 2013). A qualifying individual with qualifying income may elect to exclude foreign earned income, and this exclusion applies only if a tax return is filed and the income is reported. Natalie has $104,500 in gross income, but only her wages ($90,000) qualify for the foreign earned income exclusion.

9. The answer is C. Their combined compensation is $317,000, which is $67,000 above the applicable threshold of $250,000 for joint filers. Their additional Medicare tax is $603 ($67,000 × 0.9%).

10. The answer is A. Only individuals, estates, and trusts are eligible to claim the Credit for the Prior Year Minimum Tax by filing Form 8804. The credit is calculated differently for corporations, which use a different form and set of instructions to determine whether they are eligible for the credit.

11. The answer is B. If a taxpayer claimed the First-Time Homebuyer Credit in 2008, she must repay the credit as an additional tax on her tax returns for subsequent years. Niki is required to repay the credit in equal payments over 15 years

12. The answer is A. The Foreign Tax Credit applies to taxpayers who have paid foreign taxes to a foreign country on foreign-sourced income and are subject to U.S. tax on the same income.

13. The answer is B. The NIIT applies to the lesser of Faheema's investment income ($73,000) or her MAGI above the threshold for her filing status, which is $200,000 for a single filer ($245,000 MAGI - $200,000 threshold = $45,000.) Thus, her NIIT is calculated as follows ($45,000 × 3.8% = $1,710.) The $200,000 gain from selling her home is excluded from taxation under section 121 and is therefore not part of the calculation for the NIIT.

14. The answer is D. Unlike the other choices, business casualty losses are not an item that may trigger an AMT liability. Business-related casualty losses are not subject to phase-outs and are deductible in full. Certain other deductions or items of income are calculated differently under the AMT, which provides an alternative set of rules for calculating income tax.

15. The answer is C. There are two separate reporting requirements for taxpayers who hold certain types of foreign assets or who have certain amounts of funds in foreign bank accounts. An FBAR generally must be filed with the Treasury Department if a taxpayer has more than $10,000 in offshore bank accounts. Taxpayers also must file a statement with the IRS if they hold foreign financial assets with an aggregate value that exceeds $50,000 ($100,000 MFJ) on the last day of the tax year, or that exceeds $75,000 ($150,000 MFJ) at any time during the tax year. In Jim's case, since the funds in his foreign account total $23,000, he is only required to file an FBAR.

16. The answer is C. The additional Medicare tax is applied to MFS taxpayers whose earned income exceeds $125,000 in 2013. Liz will owe an additional .9% tax on the $15,000 of earned income that exceeds the $125,000 threshold ($15,000 × .9% = $135 additional Medicare tax.)

17. The answer is B. Roman may exclude $250,000 of the gain from the sale of his house, so his gain that is subject to regular income tax is $236,000. He has additional net investment income of $11,400 from the stock sale, rental income, and CD interest, for total NII of $247,400. His MAGI is $336,400, which exceeds the $200,000 threshold amount for single filers by $136,400. Roman is subject to the NIIT on the lesser of $247,400 (NII) or $136,400 (the amount of excess MAGI). Roman owes NIIT of $5,183.20 ($136,400 × 3.8% = $5,183.20).

18. The answer is A. The AMT was adopted by Congress in 1969 to ensure that individuals pay at least a minimum amount of tax. This means that individuals who reduce their taxable income using various methods (such as increasing their itemized deductions) may still be forced to pay tax.

19. The answer is D. For individuals, the net investment income tax is 3.8% of the lesser of net investment income, or the excess of modified adjusted gross income over a threshold amount. For example, the threshold for spouses filing joint returns is $250,000; the threshold is $200,000 for single filers.

20. The answer is B. Itemized deductions, such as mortgage interest, are exclusion items that are not used to determine the minimum tax credit. Other exclusion items include personal exemptions and the standard deduction. Items such as depreciation are deferral items and are used to calculate the credit.

21. The answer is A. The only types of a child's income that can be reported on a parent's tax return are interest, capital gain distributions, and Alaska Permanent Funds dividends. In order for parents to make this election, among other conditions, the child's gross income for the year must be less than $10,000.

22. The answer is D. The net investment income tax applies only to individuals, estates, and trusts. Only U.S. citizens and residents are subject to the tax.

Unit 16: Individuals Quiz Answers

1. The answer is B. His IRA contribution for 2013 is limited to $3,500, the total amount of his wages. The interest income and the gifted money from his parents are not qualifying compensation for IRA purposes.

2. The answer is C. Vic may contribute $5,500, the maximum contribution allowed for his age, because a taxpayer may elect to treat nontaxable combat pay as qualifying compensation for IRA purposes. The interest income is not considered compensation.

3. The answer is B. Rafael cannot contribute an additional $3,000 after April 15, 2014, regardless of whether he files an extension. If contributions to a traditional IRA for the year were less than the limit, a taxpayer cannot contribute more after the original due date of the tax return to make up the difference.

4. The answer is B. Foreign earned income and any other income that is excluded from tax (with the exception of nontaxable combat pay) is excluded for IRA contribution purposes. Alimony of $400 and wages of $3,200 earned in the U.S. are considered compensation for purposes of an IRA contribution.

5. The answer is D. They can contribute $12,000 if they file jointly. Kristin can contribute $5,500, and Omar can contribute $6,500 because he is 50. Even though Kristin only has $1,200 in compensation, she can use Omar's compensation to determine her maximum contribution.

6. The answer is A. The taxpayer will not have to pay the 6% tax on the excess contribution if the excess contribution and any earnings are withdrawn by the due date of his return, including extensions. If a taxpayer corrects the excess contribution in time, the 6% penalty will apply only to the earnings on the excess contribution.

7. The answer is C. Only Jody's wage income of $3,000 and the $2,300 of alimony qualify as compensation for purposes of an IRA contribution. The annuity income, rental income, and interest income do not qualify.

8. The answer is B. Since Landon is married and lived with his wife during the year but is filing separately, he can contribute no more than $4,000, the amount of his only qualifying compensation for IRA purposes.

9. The answer is B. Only Sue can contribute to a traditional IRA. Frank cannot contribute because he is over 70½ years old. However, Sue is over 50 and can utilize Frank's qualifying compensation in order to contribute the maximum of $6,500 to her IRA.

10. The answer is C. Assuming Miguel has sufficient qualifying compensation, he could contribute $4,000. The 2013 maximum for contributions to all types of IRAs is $5,500 for taxpayers under 50. Taxpayers are allowed to have different types of IRA accounts, but the maximum contribution limits apply to their total contributions for the year.

11. The answer is A. Distributions made prior to age 59½ are subject to a 10% early withdrawal penalty, if no exception applies. Exceptions that allow early distributions from an IRA, as well as from qualified retirement plans, include the following:

- Distributions made to a beneficiary or estate after death
- Distributions made because of permanent disability
- Distributions to the extent of deductible medical expenses (medical expenses that exceed 10% of adjusted gross income), whether or not the taxpayer itemizes deductions for the year
- Distributions made due to an IRS levy

The distributions listed above are not subject to the early distribution penalty, but they are subject to income tax at the taxpayer's normal tax rates.

12. The answer is D. Annette and Gil's allowable IRA deduction is zero because their modified AGI is over the phase-out limit of $188,000 for 2013. This limit applies when an MFJ taxpayer is not covered by an employer plan but his spouse is covered. Annette and Gil are still allowed to make nondeductible IRA contributions that would be reported on Form 8606.

13. The answer is B. Shari has 60 days to complete the rollover. If she does not complete the rollover within 60 days, the distribution is subject to income tax in 2013.

14. The answer is B. Pledging the IRA as security for a loan is considered a prohibited transaction that results in termination of the account's treatment as an IRA, and the FMV as of the beginning of the year is considered to be a taxable distribution. Assuming the entire balance of the account represented deductible contributions and earnings on them, Janelle would have had no basis in the account, and the entire $70,000 would be reportable as taxable income.

15. The answer is D. The first required minimum distribution from a traditional IRA must be taken by April 1 of the year following the year in which the taxpayer turns 70½. AJ turned 70½ on December 6, 2013.

16. The answer is D. As Doris is not yet age 59½, early distributions from her traditional IRA would typically be subject to the additional 10% tax in addition to regular tax at her marginal rate. However, the additional tax would apply only to the extent that her distributions exceeded her qualified higher education expenses for the year.

17. The answer is A. A taxpayer's contributions to a traditional IRA in the year he reaches age 70½ (and any later years) are considered excess contributions. An excess contribution and any earnings on it are subject to an additional 6% tax if the taxpayer does not withdraw the contribution and the earnings by the due date of the tax return, including extensions.

18. The answer is B. Contributions to a traditional IRA by an MFJ taxpayer who participates in an employer-sponsored retirement plan are allowed, but their deductibility is phased out, beginning at a MAGI threshold of $95,000 in 2013. When MAGI reaches $115,000, the IRA contribution is fully nondeductible. If a taxpayer makes nondeductible contributions to a traditional IRA, he must attach Form 8606, *Nondeductible IRAs*, to his tax return.

19. The answer is B. Tiana can defer up to $17,500 of her salary as a contribution to her 401(k) account in 2013. The limit increases to $23,000 for employees who are 50 and older. However, the amount deferred cannot exceed the amount of the employee's compensation.

20. The answer is C. Depending on its terms, a qualified plan may allow a participant to borrow funds from his account balance. A loan can be no more than the lesser of:

- $50,000, or
- The greater of $10,000 or 50% of the vested portion of the participant's account balance.

Unit 17: Individuals Quiz Answers

1. The answer is A. None of the gifts are taxable, and no reporting is required. Tuition or medical expenses paid for someone directly to an educational or medical institution are not counted as taxable gifts. Nor are gifts to a political organization for its own use or gifts to a qualified charity.

2. The answer is B. The amount of Phil's taxable estate is $4.5 million. However, because this amount is less than the basic exclusion amount of $5.25 million for 2013, an estate tax return is not required to be filed.

Supporting calculations:	
Assets	$4,000,000
Less liabilities	($500,000)
Life insurance proceeds	$1,000,000
Taxable estate	$4,500,000

3. The answer is C. Each granddaughter's cash gift of $30,000 would have been reduced by the annual exclusion amount of $14,000, and a portion of Herman's basic exclusion amount would have been used to avoid payment of gift tax on the excess amount of $16,000. Thus, he used a total of $16,000 for each granddaughter, or $32,000. Since the $80,000 was paid directly to Birchland College on behalf of the granddaughters, it was not subject to gift tax, and none of his basic exclusion amount would have been used as a result of these additional gifts. It should be noted that his cash gifts to the granddaughters would also be subject to generation-skipping tax.

4. The answer is D. Since the royalty check was received before the taxpayer died, it is not considered IRD income. Income in respect of a decedent is taxable income earned but not received by the decedent by the time of death. The fact that the royalty check was not cashed has no bearing on the nature of the income, and it should be reported as taxable income on the decedent's final income tax return (Form 1040).

5. The answer is B. The donor is generally responsible for paying gift tax.

6. The answer is C. No deduction for funeral expenses can be taken on Form 1041 or Form 1040. Funeral expenses may only be claimed as a deduction from the gross estate on Form 706.

7. The answer is A. The portability election allows a surviving spouse's estate the right to use a deceased spousal unused exclusion (DSUE), which is the remaining unused portion of the previously deceased spouse's basic exclusion amount. For example, assume that a spouse who dies in 2013 had used $2.25 million of his $5.25 million basic exclusion, either through gifts during his lifetime or in connection with his estate. Any portion of his estate that is transferred to his surviving spouse would be subject to the unlimited marital deduction, assuming the surviving spouse is a citizen of the United States. In addition, his estate can elect to transfer his DSUE of $3 million to the surviving spouse. This amount would be available to the estate of the surviving spouse, along with the surviving spouse's basic exclusion amount, when he or she dies. If a spouse dies in 2013 and a portability election is made, and the surviving spouse also dies in 2013, the estate of each could have a maximum of $5.25 million basic exclusion amount available, or a total of $10.5 million potentially available to the second spouse's estate, assuming that neither spouse had used any of his basic exclusion amounts to offset gift tax liabilities.

8. The answer is C. Estate tax returns are due nine months from the date of death, although the executor may request an extension of time to file.

9. The answer is D. Alimony paid after the taxpayer's death is not deductible from the gross estate. It is considered a distribution to a beneficiary. Deductions from the gross estate are allowed for:

- Funeral expenses paid out of the estate
- Administration expenses for the estate, including attorney's fees
- Debts owed at the time of death
- The marital deduction, charitable deduction, and state death tax deduction

10. The answer is C. Jeffrey is required to file a gift tax return. Gift tax is paid by the donor, not the recipient, of the gift. The first $14,000 of the gift is not subject to gift tax because of the annual exclusion. The remaining $11,000 is a taxable gift.

11. The answer is D. When Dwayne died in 2013, his estate qualified for the full basic exclusion amount of $5.25 million. As a result of having reported the DSUE when Form 706 was filed for his estate, the DSUE is available in addition to Monica's basic exclusion amount of $5.25 million. Therefore, the amount of her taxable estate would have to exceed $10.5 million in order to be subject to estate tax.

12. The answer is B. Gift tax returns are typically due on April 15 of the following calendar year, and payment of the tax is also due then, although the filing may be subject to a six-month extension. If the donor died during 2013, the filing deadline is the due date for his estate tax return (if earlier than April 15, 2014).

13. The answer is D. Tuition or medical expenses paid directly to a medical or educational institution for someone else are not included in the calculation of taxable gifts, and there is no reporting requirement.

14. The answer is D. Federal estate tax is not deductible from the gross estate. The other items listed are allowable deductions from the gross estate. The decedent's unpaid medical expenses represent liabilities that can be deducted from the gross estate. Alternatively, if the expenses are paid by the estate during the one-year period beginning with the day after death, the personal representative can elect to treat all or part of the expenses as paid by the decedent at the time they were incurred, and deduct them on the decedent's final tax return (1040).

15. The answer is C. The tax liability for an estate attaches to the assets of the estate itself. If the assets are distributed to the beneficiaries before the taxes are paid, the beneficiaries can be held liable for the tax debt, up to the value of the assets distributed.

16. The answer is B. In order to make a gift to one individual in excess of the annual exclusion of $14,000 and avoid using any of their basic exclusion amounts, a married couple can use gift splitting. Gift splitting allows married couples to give up to $28,000 to a person without making a taxable gift ($14,000 from each spouse), but they are each required to file a gift tax return. Alternatively, the gift of $15,000 could be considered to have been from only one spouse (without using gift splitting); that spouse would need to file a gift tax return because the gift exceeds the annual exclusion of $14,000. Gifts to a spouse generally do not require a return to be filed.

17. The answer is B. Although a full marital deduction is allowed for a spouse who is a U.S. citizen, a transfer of property to a noncitizen spouse is limited to $143,000 in 2013, and the excess amount would be subject to gift tax.

18. The answer is D. The aggregate portion of Donald's estate distributed to his grandchildren ($10 million) would be reduced by his exclusion amount for GST ($5.25 million in 2013) and the remainder of $4.75 million would be subject to GST.

19. The answer is C. An estate is normally valued on the date of the decedent's death. However, an executor may elect an alternate valuation date for an estate, which would be six months after the date of death. The estate value and related estate tax must be less than they would have been on the date of the taxpayer's death.

20. The answer is A. If a married couple uses gift splitting to reduce or eliminate gift tax applicable to a gift that exceeds the annual exclusion, each spouse must file a separate Form 709. Spouses may not file a joint gift tax return.

21. The answer is C. If required to be filed, Form 706, *United States Estate (and Generation-Skipping Transfer) Tax Return,* must be filed nine months after the date of a decedent's death. The estate tax would be owed at this time. An executor may request a six-month extension to file Form 706, but the tax would still be owed on the earlier date.

22. The answer is B. A taxpayer's gross estate includes the following:

- The FMV of all tangible and intangible property owned partially or outright by the decedent at the time of death
- Life insurance proceeds payable to the estate or, for policies owned by the decedent, payable to the heirs or beneficiaries
- The value of certain annuities or survivor benefits payable to the heirs or beneficiaries
- The value of certain property transferred within three years before the taxpayer's death (not five years as stated in answer B)

Part 2: Businesses

Unit 1: Business Entities and Requirements

> **More Reading:**
> **Publication 583, *Starting a Business and Keeping Records***
> **Publication 1635, *Understanding Your EIN***
> **Publication 334, *Tax Guide for Small Business***
> **Publication 1779, *Independent Contractor or Employee***
> **Publication 505, *Tax Withholding and Estimated Tax***

Overview of EA Exam Part 2: Businesses

For Part 2 of the enrolled agent exam, you will be expected to know a broad range of information about tax provisions that affect various types of businesses. You will need to understand the different types of businesses, including sole proprietorships, partnerships, corporations, and farming businesses, as well as trusts and estates, retirement plans, and tax-exempt organizations, and the special tax laws that apply to each.

Specifically, Part 2 of the exam is broken down into the following sections and corresponding percentages of questions: *Businesses* (Business entities; partnerships; corporations in general; forming a corporation; S corporations), 45%; *Business Financial Information* (business income; business expenses, deductions, and credits; business assets; analysis of financial records; advising the business taxpayer), 40%; *Specialized Returns and Taxpayers* (trust and estate income tax; exempt organizations; retirement plans; farmers), *15%.*[29]

We start with an overview of the different types of business entities. Each has its own drawbacks, risks, and benefits. We briefly review each type below and will examine the more complex entities in greater depth in later units.

Sole Proprietorship

A sole proprietorship is not a separate legal entity; it is an unincorporated business that is generally owned and controlled by one person. It may be a single-person business or it may have many employees, but there is only one owner who accepts all the risk and liability of the business. It is the simplest business type and also the easiest to start. An estimated 70% of businesses in the United States are sole proprietorships.

A sole proprietorship cannot be passed on to a new owner as the same business entity because, by definition, a sole proprietorship is owned and operated by a single, specific individual. If a business operated as a sole proprietorship is sold, it must be operated by the new owner as either a different sole proprietorship or as a different type of business entity.

A taxpayer does not have to conduct full-time business activities to be considered self-employed. Operating a part-time business in addition to having a regular job or business may also be self-employment, and may therefore constitute a sole proprietorship. An activity qualifies as a business if its primary purpose is for profit and if the taxpayer is involved in the activity with continuity and regularity. A hobby, which is not conducted for profit, does not qualify as a business.

[29]Prometric specifications for tests administered during the May 1, 2013 to February 28, 2014 exam cycle.

Sole proprietors often receive Forms 1099-MISC from their customers showing income they were paid. The amounts reported on Forms 1099-MISC, along with any other business income, are reported and taxed on the taxpayer's personal income tax return. Income and expenses from the sole proprietorship are reported on Schedule C, *Profit or Loss from Business,* of Form 1040.

A taxpayer may use the simplified Schedule C-EZ if he:

- Had business expenses of $5,000 or less
- Did not claim any depreciation expense
- Used the cash method of accounting
- Did not have inventory at any time during the year
- Did not have a net loss from the business and had no prior year passive activity losses
- Was the sole proprietor for only one business
- Had no employees during the year
- Did not deduct expenses for business use of his home and had no depreciation or amortization to report for the year

A self-employed individual with net earnings of $400 or more from self-employment is required to pay self-employment tax by filing Schedule SE, *Self-Employment Tax* with his Form 1040.

Example: Darlene works as an independent contractor for Conway Lighting Company. Conway sends Darlene a Form 1099-MISC that shows she received $25,000 for contract work in 2013. She also received payments of $7,000 from several individuals for contract work she completed on their homes. Although she did not receive Forms 1099-MISC for the $7,000, Darlene must include the payments as self-employment income, along with the $25,000 from Conway, on her Schedule C.

Married Couple Businesses

Often, a small business is operated by a husband and wife without incorporating or creating a formal partnership agreement. The business may be considered a partnership, whether or not there is a formal partnership agreement.

If both spouses materially participate as the only members of a jointly owned and operated business, the business may be treated as a *qualified joint venture*. This allows them to avoid the complexity of filing a partnership return, but still allows each spouse to take credit for self-employment earnings from the business for Social Security purposes. Items of business income, gain, loss, deduction, and credit are split between the spouses in accordance with their respective interests in the business. The spouses then file separate Schedules C and separate Schedules SE. This option is available only to married taxpayers who file joint tax returns.

Note: Federal tax law makes many references to laws specific to a "husband and wife." These laws now apply to same-sex spouses who were legally married in a state that recognizes same-sex marriage.

Partnerships

A partnership is a relationship that exists between two or more persons who join together to carry on a trade or business. Each person contributes money, property, labor, or skill and expects to share in the profits and losses of the business.

A partnership must file an annual information return to report the income, deductions, gains, and losses from its operations, but the partnership itself generally does not pay income tax. Instead, any profits or losses "pass through" to its partners, who are then responsible for reporting their respective shares of the partnership's income or loss on their individual returns.

Example: James and Madeline are father and daughter who operate Hunnicutt Business Consulting. Each is active in the business, and each has an equal share in partnership interests and profits. The partnership must file Form 1065 to report its income and loss for the year. The partnership must also issue a Schedule K-1 to each partner. In 2013, Hunnicutt had $80,000 in income. Since they share profits and losses equally, James and Madeline will each report $40,000 of self-employment partnership income on their individual tax returns. Partnership income is reported on page 2 of Schedule E, *Supplemental Income and Loss (From rental real estate, royalties, partnerships, S corporations, estates, trusts, REMICs, etc.)*

A partnership must always have at least one *general partner* whose actions legally bind the business and who is legally responsible for a partnership's debts and liabilities.

A limited partnership is a partnership that has at least one limited partner in addition to its general partner(s). A limited partnership allows an investor to own an interest in a business without assuming personal liability or risk beyond the amount of his investment. A *limited partner* has no obligation to contribute additional capital to the partnership, and therefore does not have an economic risk of loss for partnership liabilities.

A partnership can look very different depending on how it is structured; it can be anything from a small business run by a married couple to a complex business organization with hundreds of general partners and limited partners as investors. A partnership may have an unlimited number of partners.

An unincorporated organization with two or more owners is generally classified as a partnership for federal tax purposes if its members carry on a business and divide its profits. However, a joint undertaking merely to share expenses is not a partnership. For example, co-ownership of rental property is not considered a formal partnership unless the co-owners provide substantial services to the tenants.

Example: Anderson and Sally are good friends who own a rental property together. Each owns a 50% interest. Anderson takes care of the repairs, and Sally collects and divides the rent. They do not have any other business with each other. The co-ownership of the rental property is not considered a partnership for tax purposes. Instead, they would divide the income and expenses based on their ownership percentages, and each would report his respective share on Schedule E on his individual return.

A partnership's annual tax return is filed on Form 1065, *U.S. Return of Partnership Income.* Partners are not employees of the business, and they should not be issued Forms W-2. Instead, the partnership must furnish a copy of Schedule K-1 to each of its partners, showing the income and losses allocated to him. A partnership return must show the name and address of each partner and the partner's share of taxable income. The return must be signed by a general partner. A limited partner may not sign the return or represent a partnership before the IRS.

A **Limited Liability Partnership (LLP)** is an entity that is formed under state law by filing articles of organization as an LLP and is typically used for specific professional services, such as those offered by a law firm. Typically, an LLP allows each partner to actively participate in management affairs but still provides limited liability protection to each partner. A partner in an LLP generally would not be liable for the debt or malpractice of other partners and would only be at risk for his interest in the partnership's assets.

C Corporations

When forming a corporation, prospective shareholders provide money, property, or both in exchange for the issuance of the corporation's capital stock. A corporation is considered an entity separate from its shareholders and must elect a board of directors who are responsible for oversight of the company. A corporation conducts business, realizes net income or loss, and distributes profits to shareholders.

Most major companies are organized as C corporations. A C corporation may have an unlimited number of shareholders and may be either foreign or domestic. A C corporation must file annual income tax returns on Form 1120, *U.S. Corporation Income Tax Return,* to report its net income and losses, and pay tax on its income. Its after-tax profits may also be taxable income to its shareholders when distributed as dividends, resulting in double taxation.

The corporation does not receive a tax deduction when it distributes dividends to shareholders, and shareholders cannot deduct any losses of the corporation. A corporation generally takes the same deductions as a sole proprietorship to figure its taxable income, but is also allowed certain special deductions.

S Corporations

An S corporation is a distinct form of entity organized under applicable state law. For federal income tax purposes, an S corporation is generally not subject to tax; instead its income, losses, deductions, and credits are passed through to its shareholders in a manner similar to a partnership. However, the S corporation itself may be responsible for tax on certain built-in gains and passive investment income.

An S corporation is required to file an annual income tax return to report its income or loss using Form 1120S, *U.S. Tax Return for an S Corporation.* It also reports each shareholder's applicable share of income or losses on Schedules K-1. The shareholders report the pass-through income or loss on their individual tax returns. As a result, the shareholders of S corporations are generally able to avoid double federal taxation on their corporate income.

S corporations must meet the following requirements:

- Be a domestic corporation
- Have only allowable shareholders (partnerships, corporations, and nonresident aliens are not eligible)
- Have no more than 100 shareholders

- Have only one class of stock (voting and nonvoting stock are not considered to be separate classes of stock, as long as they have identical rights to distribution and liquidation proceeds)
- Not be an ineligible type of corporation (certain financial institutions, insurance companies, and domestic international sales corporations are not eligible for S corporation status)

Limited Liability Companies (LLC)

A limited liability company (LLC) is another type of corporation that may be formed under state law. Depending upon whether it has a single member (owner) or multiple members, it will be treated for federal tax purposes either as a part of the owner's individual tax return (a "disregarded entity," as described further below) or as a partnership, unless it elects to be treated as a corporation. Most LLCs are taxed as partnerships. Thus, like the owners of S corporations and partnerships, the members of an LLC can avoid double taxation. An LLC can provide the liability protection of a corporation with the tax benefits of a partnership. Unlike a partnership, none of the members of an LLC are personally liable for its debts.

If a limited liability company (LLC) is treated as a partnership for tax purposes, it must file Form 1065 annually and one of its owners must sign the return.

Personal Service Corporations (PSC)

The IRS classifies a business as a personal service corporation (PSC) if its principal activity during the prior tax year is performing personal services. Personal services include any activity performed in the fields of accounting, actuarial science, architecture, consulting, engineering, health (including veterinary services), law, and the performing arts. The majority of a PSC's stock is typically owned by employees, retired employees, or their estates.

Note: Unlike other corporations, personal service corporations are always taxed at a flat rate of 35%.

Farmers and Fishermen

Farming businesses are primarily engaged in crop production, animal production, or forestry and logging. They may include stock, dairy, poultry, fish, fruit, and tree farms, as well as plantations, ranches, timber farms, and orchards.

Congress has enacted many tax laws specific to farming that provide special tax treatment and reflect the highly unpredictable nature of the business. For example, farmers have a different schedule for paying estimated taxes; they may postpone gain or income in certain cases that other businesses cannot; they may deduct a higher percentage of mileage expenses than other businesses; and they are given special tax considerations when disaster strikes.

Farming and fishing businesses operating as sole proprietorships report income and loss on Schedule F, *Profit or Loss from Farming*, of Form 1040. A farmer is typically self-employed if he operates his own farm or rents farmland from others to engage in the business of farming. Self-employed farmers and fishermen must also complete Schedule SE to determine self-employment taxes due.

A farming business may also be organized as a partnership or a corporation.

Tax-Exempt Organizations (Nonprofit Entities)

The Internal Revenue Code (IRC)[30] outlines the requirements for tax-exempt organizations. They must be organized and operated exclusively for charitable, educational, or religious purposes, and none of their earnings may be used to benefit any private shareholder or individual.

Nonprofit organizations may be created as corporations, trusts, or unincorporated associations, but never as partnerships or sole proprietorships. Most organizations must request tax-exempt status by filing Form 1023, *Application for Recognition of Exemption.* However, churches, including synagogues, temples, and mosques, are treated as tax-exempt by default and do not have to apply for exemption.

An exempt organization must annually file Form 990, *Return of Organization Exempt from Income Tax,* to report its income and losses. Form 990 is usually an informational return only, but a nonprofit organization may be taxed on activities outside the scope of its tax-exempt status.

Entity Classification Election Rules

Certain business entities may choose how they will be classified for tax purposes by filing Form 8832, *Entity Classification Election*.

An LLC with a single owner is classified as an entity "disregarded" as being separate from its owner for income tax purposes, unless the owner files Form 8832 and chooses to be taxed as a corporation. Thus, a single-owner LLC owned by an individual is treated in a manner similar to a sole proprietorship and the owner is subject to the tax on net earnings from self-employment. Similarly, a single-owner LLC owned by a corporation or a partnership is included in the owner's tax return as if it were a division of the corporation or partnership.

A domestic LLC with at least two members is considered a partnership by default, unless it files Form 8832 and elects to be treated as a corporation.

An election to change an LLC's classification cannot take effect more than 75 days prior to the date the election is filed, nor can it take effect later than 12 months after the date the election is filed. Once a business entity chooses its classification, it cannot change the election again within five years (60 months).

Example: Kelly and Ned are married and own their own business. They form an LLC for liability protection. Kelly files Form 8832, and she elects to classify their business as a partnership for tax purposes. A few months later, Kelly changes her mind and wants to change the classification and be taxed as a corporation. Kelly must wait at least 60 months in order to change the election.

Employer Identification Number (EIN)

An employer identification number is used for reporting purposes. Unlike Social Security numbers that are assigned to individuals, EINs are assigned to business entities.

A business must apply for an EIN if any of the following apply:

- The business pays employees

[30] The Internal Revenue Code is the basis of federal tax law. It is enacted by Congress in Title 26 of the United States Code.

- The business operates as a corporation, exempt organization, trust, estate, or partnership
- The business files any of these tax returns:
    - Employment
    - Excise
    - Alcohol, Tobacco, and Firearms
- The business withholds taxes paid to a nonresident alien
- The business establishes a pension, profit sharing, or retirement plan

If a sole proprietor has no employees, he is not required to obtain an employer identification number (EIN). However, an EIN can be requested by a sole proprietor who simply wishes to protect his Social Security number for privacy reasons. This way, a sole proprietor can provide his EIN rather than his SSN to companies that need to issue him a Form 1099-MISC for independent contractor payments.

If a sole proprietor decides to form a business entity such as a partnership or corporation, he will be required to request an EIN for each separate entity. A new EIN is required for any of the following changes:

- When a sole proprietor or partnership decides to incorporate
- When a sole proprietor takes on a partner and becomes a partnership
- When a partnership becomes a sole proprietorship (for example, when one partner dies)
- When a sole proprietor files for bankruptcy under Chapter 7 or Chapter 11
- When a taxpayer terminates one partnership and begins another partnership
- When a business establishes a pension, profit sharing, or retirement plan

A business does not need to apply for a new EIN in any of the following instances:

- To change the name of a business
- To change the location or add locations (stores, plants, enterprises, or branches of the same entity)
- If a sole proprietor operates multiple businesses (including stores, plants, enterprises, or branches of the same entity)

Further, a single-member limited liability company (LLC) classified as a disregarded entity may use the owner's SSN or EIN and does not need a separate EIN, unless the business is required to file employment or excise tax returns.

Taxpayers can apply for an EIN online or manually file Form SS-4, *Application for Employer Identification Number.*

Business Recordkeeping

Adequate records help a taxpayer to monitor business operations, verify his income and expenses, and support expenses on his tax return. Except in a few cases, the law does not require a business to keep any specific kind of records or to use a particular recordkeeping system, so long as the system clearly shows a business's income and expenses.

The taxpayer's recordkeeping system should include a summary of business transactions, which is usually made in the taxpayer's books, such as accounting journals and ledgers. The books must show the business's gross income, as well as its deductions and credits. Additional documents must be kept to support these entries. These include sales slips, paid bills, invoices, receipts, deposit slips, canceled checks, credit card charge slips, cash register tapes, Forms 1099-MISC, invoices, mileage logs, and cell phone records.

Electronic records are acceptable so long as they provide a complete and accurate record of data that is accessible to the IRS in a legible format. They are subject to the same controls and retention guidelines as those used for the taxpayer's original hard copy books and records.

Taxpayers must keep records as long as they are needed for the administration of any provision of the Internal Revenue Code. Usually this means the business must keep records long enough to support income and deductions until the statute of limitations for a related tax return has expired.

Definition: A statute of limitation is a time period to review, analyze, and review tax-related issues. The Internal Revenue Code requires that the IRS assess, refund, credit, and collect taxes within specific time limits known as the statute of limitations. When they expire, the IRS can no longer assess additional tax, allow a claim for refund by the taxpayer, or take collection action.

Generally, a taxpayer must keep records for at least three years from when a tax return was due or was filed, whichever is later. If a business has employees, it must keep all employment tax records for at least four years.

Taxpayers must keep records relating to property until the statute of limitations expires for the year in which the property is sold or otherwise disposed of. These records are needed to figure any depreciation, amortization, or depletion deduction, and to figure basis for computing gain or loss. A taxpayer may need to keep records relating to the basis of property even longer since they may be important in determining the basis of replacement property.

Business funds should be kept separate from personal funds. The IRS is more likely to audit a business and deny deductions and losses if there is no clear separation between business and personal expenses. A separate bank account for business-related transactions is advisable, with business-related bills paid from it rather than from a personal account.

Financial Statements

Financial statements are the formal records of a business's financial activities. There are many types of financial statements, but the two most common ones used for tax reporting purposes are the income statement and the balance sheet.

Income Statement: The income statement is also called the profit and loss statement. It indicates the business's revenue, expenses, and net income or loss during a period, such as a month, quarter, or fiscal or calendar year.

Balance Sheet: The balance sheet is a summary of a business's assets, liabilities, and equity on a specific date, such as at the end of its fiscal year. A balance sheet provides a snapshot of the business's financial condition. Balance sheet accounts are carried forward from year to year, unlike income statement accounts, which are closed out at year-end and only reflect business operations within a specified period.

Business Reporting Requirements

Businesses are subject to a number of reporting requirements, including the following:

Forms 8300: When a business receives a cash payment of more than $10,000 from one transaction or from two or more related transactions, it must file Form 8300, *Report of Cash Payments Over $10,000 Received in a Trade or Business,* by the fifteenth day after the date of the cash transaction. By January 31 of the year following the reportable transaction, it must also provide to each person whose name is required to be included in Form 8300 a written statement that shows the aggregate amount of reportable cash transactions the business reported to the IRS for that person. These requirements are intended to assist in efforts to combat money laundering.

Forms W-4: When a business hires an employee, it must have the employee complete a Form W-4, *Employee's Withholding Allowance Certificate.*

Form W-4 tells the employer the employee's marital status, the number of withholding allowances the employee is claiming, and any additional amount to use when deducting federal income tax from the employee's pay.

If an employee fails to complete a Form W-4, the employer must withhold federal income taxes from his wages as if he were single and claiming no withholding allowances.

Forms W-2: A business must complete and file with the Social Security Administration Forms W-2, *Wage and Tax Statement,* showing the wages paid and taxes withheld for the year for each employee. A copy of the W-2 must be given to each current and former employee who received taxable wages or salaries during the year by no later than January 31 of the following year. Employers filing 250 or more Forms W-2 must file electronically unless granted a waiver by the IRS.

The Affordable Care Act requires employers with 250 or more workers to report on Form W-2 the cost of health care coverage under an employer-sponsored group health plan. The amount reported includes both the portion of cost paid by the employer and the portion paid by the employee.

Forms 1099: A business must report nonemployee compensation paid during the year to certain independent contractors by providing a Form 1099-MISC by January 31 of the following year. Copies of the 1099s must be sent to the IRS by February 28, or by March 31 if the business files them electronically. Specifically, the amounts that businesses are required to report on Forms 1099 include:

- Commissions, fees, and other compensation paid to a single individual when the total amount is $600 or more during the year
- Interest, rents, annuities, and income items paid to a single individual when the total amount is $600 or more

Payments to corporations are generally exempt from Form 1099 reporting requirements. Further, there is no requirement for payments issued in exchange for property, such as purchases of merchandise or equipment.

Forms 1099-MISC should only be used for payments that are made in the course of a trade or business. Personal payments are not reportable.

Example: Brett hires a painter to paint his home. The job costs $2,500. Brett is not required to report the payment to the painter, because it is for his personal residence. Since it was a personal payment, Brett cannot deduct the cost on his tax return. However, the painter is still required to report the income on his personal return. The following year, Brett calls the same painter to paint the interior of his business office, which he owns. The job costs $1,000. Since the cost is a business expense, Brett is required to issue a Form 1099-MISC to the contractor.

Employment Taxes and Self-Employment Tax

As discussed above, an employer uses information from the employee's Form W-4, as well as the IRS withholding tables, to calculate how much to withhold from each wage payment. The employer must also withhold the employees' share of Social Security and Medicare taxes from wages, and pay the corresponding employer's share of each tax.

Employers must report federal income taxes withheld and employment taxes on Form 941, *Employer's Quarterly Federal Tax Return*, or Form 944, *Employer's Annual Federal Tax Return.* Businesses must also make federal tax deposits of income and employment taxes electronically, generally by using the Electronic Federal Tax Payment System (EFTPS).

In 2013, only the first $113,700 of an individual's employee compensation and/or net earnings from self-employment are subject to the Social Security tax. There is no cap on the Medicare tax. Self-employed taxpayers can deduct half of their SE tax in figuring their adjusted gross income.

An individual general partner in a partnership is considered to be self-employed, and his income is subject to self-employment tax, just like a sole proprietor's. Income reported by the partnership to limited partners is considered passive activity income (and is generally not subject to self-employment tax).

Social Security and Medicare Taxes	
Social Security tax rate	**2013**
Employer's portion	6.2%
Employee's portion	6.2%
Total for self-employed taxpayer	12.4%
Maximum earnings subject to Social Security taxes	$113,700

Medicare Tax Rate	**2013**
Employer's portion	1.45%
Employee's portion	1.45%
Total for self-employed individual	2.9%
Maximum earnings subject to Medicare taxes	No limit

Starting in 2013, an additional Medicare tax of 0.9% applies to an individual taxpayer's earned income that exceeds the following thresholds:

Filing Status	Threshold Amount
MFJ	$250,000
MFS	$125,000
Single, HOH, or QW	$200,000

The thresholds are not adjusted for inflation. A taxpayer's earned income (including wages, taxable fringe benefits, bonuses, tips, commissions, and self-employment income) that is subject to Medicare tax is also subject to the additional Medicare tax to the extent it exceeds the applicable threshold amount for his filing status. Box 5 on an employee's Form W-2 shows the amount of income from an employer that is subject to Medicare taxes.

An employer is required to withhold the additional Medicare tax if an employee is paid more than $200,000, regardless of an employee's filing status or whether the employee has wages paid by another employer. There is no employer share of the additional Medicare tax. Self-employed taxpayers cannot deduct one-half of the 0.9% additional Medicare tax. A taxpayer may be subject to the additional Medicare tax even if amounts are not withheld from his wages.

If an employer withholds amounts for an employee who earns more than $200,000 but the employee and his spouse's combined earnings are less than the $250,000 MFJ threshold, they can apply the overpayment against any other type of tax that may be owed on their income tax return.

Backup Withholding: If a business does not have a Social Security number or taxpayer identification number for a payee such as an independent contractor, it must withhold federal income taxes at a 28% rate.

Trust Fund Recovery Penalty (TFRP)

Trust fund taxes refer to amounts withheld from employees' wages (Social Security, Medicare, and income tax) by employers and held in trust until they are remitted to the Treasury. If a business does not deposit its trust fund taxes in a timely manner, the IRS may assess a trust fund recovery penalty (TFRP). The amount of the penalty is equal to the unpaid balance of the trust fund taxes. The TFRP may be assessed against any person who:

- is **responsible** for collecting or paying withheld income and employment taxes, or for paying collected excise taxes, and
- **willfully fails** to collect or pay them.

Once the IRS asserts the penalty, it can take collection action against the personal assets of anyone who is deemed a "responsible person." It is not only the executives of businesses or the top finance and accounting personnel who may be held responsible for the TFRP. A "responsible person" may also include a person who signs checks for the company or who otherwise has authority to spend business funds, such as a bookkeeper.

For the IRS to determine that an individual willfully failed to pay the required taxes, the responsible person:

- Must have, or should have, been aware of the outstanding taxes, and
- Intentionally disregarded the law or been plainly indifferent to its requirements (no evil intent or bad motive is required).

Using available funds to pay other creditors when the business fails to pay employment taxes is an indication of willfulness.

Example: Greta ran her own accounting business and also processed the payroll for her local church. The church had four employees, including a choir director. Greta prepared and signed the payroll tax returns and all the checks and then gave them to the pastor to mail. The pastor did not mail the payroll tax reports or remit the payments to the IRS; instead, he used the money to purchase a new church organ. Greta knew the pastor was misusing the funds, but did not report the information to authorities. The IRS assessed the TFRP against the pastor, the church, and Greta. Even though Greta was just the bookkeeper, she knew that the pastor was improperly handling the payroll tax funds and she did nothing about it, so the IRS can assess the TFRP against Greta.

Federal Unemployment (FUTA) Tax

A business reports and pays FUTA tax separately from federal income tax, and Social Security and Medicare taxes. FUTA tax is paid only by the employer. The standard FUTA tax rate is 6% on the first $7,000 of each employee's wages. However, the employer may receive a credit of 5.4% when it files Form 940, *Employer's Annual Federal Unemployment (FUTA) Tax Return*, resulting in a net FUTA tax rate of 0.6%.

Employee and Worker Classification

Because businesses are responsible for withholding and/or paying income, employment, and FUTA taxes and reporting payments to independent contractors, they must accurately determine whether a person they pay is an independent contractor or an employee. A business is generally not required to withhold or pay taxes in connection with payments to independent contractors. However, it must understand the relationship that exists with each person it pays to perform services. A person performing services for a business may be:

- An independent contractor
- An employee
- A statutory employee
- A statutory nonemployee

The IRS evaluates three primary characteristics to determine the relationship between a business and workers it pays for services:

- **Behavioral Control:** Covers whether the business has a right to direct or control how the work is done.
- **Financial Control:** Covers whether the business has a right to direct or control the financial and business aspects of the worker's job.

- **Type of Relationship:** Relates to how the worker and the business owner perceive their relationship.

Whether a person is classified as an employee or an independent contractor depends on the facts and circumstances of each individual case.

Example: Rich, an electrician, submits a job estimate to a housing complex for electrical work at $16 per hour for 400 hours. He is to receive $1,280 every two weeks for the next ten weeks. Rich will receive $6,400, regardless of whether he works more or less than 400 hours to complete the work. He also performs electrical installations under contracts with other companies that he obtains through ads placed on Craigslist. Rich would likely be classified as an independent contractor.
Example: Donna is a salesperson employed full-time by an auto dealership. She is on duty in the showroom on certain assigned days and times. She uses lists of prospective customers that belong to the dealership. She develops leads and reports results to the sales manager. Because of her experience, she requires minimal assistance in closing and financing sales. She is paid a commission and is eligible for bonuses offered by the dealership. The business also pays the cost of her health and group-term life insurance. Donna is classified as an employee of the dealership.

Employers who misclassify workers as independent contractors rather than employees may face substantial tax penalties for failing to pay employment taxes and failing to file payroll tax forms.

Statutory Employees

Some workers are classified as statutory employees. They are issued Forms W-2 by their employers, but statutory employees report their wages, income, and allowable expenses on Schedule C, just like self-employed taxpayers. The difference is that statutory employees are not required to pay self-employment tax, because their employers must treat them as employees for Social Security tax purposes. Examples of statutory employees include:

- Full-time life insurance salespeople
- Traveling salespeople
- Certain commissioned truck drivers
- Directors (members of boards) of corporations
- Officers of nonprofit organizations
- Certain home workers who perform work on materials or goods furnished by the employer

If a person is a statutory employee, "statutory employee" in box 13 of Form W-2 should be checked.

Statutory Nonemployees

There are two main categories of statutory nonemployees: direct sellers and licensed real estate agents. They are treated as self-employed for federal tax purposes, including income and employment taxes, if:

- Payments for their services are directly related to sales, rather than to the number of hours worked, and

- Services are performed under a written contract providing that they will not be treated as employees for federal tax purposes.

Compensation for a statutory nonemployee is reported on Form 1099-MISC. The taxpayer then reports the income on Schedule C.

> **Example:** Adele works as a full-time real estate agent for Golden Gate Realtors. She visits Golden Gate's offices at least once a day to check her mail and her messages. She manages dozens of listings and splits her real estate commissions with Golden Gate. She does not work for any other real estate company. Adele is classified as a statutory nonemployee. Golden Gate issues Adele a Form 1099-MISC for commissions, and she files Schedule C to report her income and expenses.

Employing Family Members

The tax requirements for a business that employs family members may differ from those applicable to other employees. The rules vary depending on the family relationship and the type of business entity.

Child working for a parent: If the parent's business is one of three types (a corporation, an estate, or a partnership in which only one of the child's parents is a partner), payments for the child's services are subject to all federal taxes, including income, unemployment, Social Security, and Medicare.

If the parent's business is a sole proprietorship or a partnership in which each partner is the child's parent, payments for the child's services are subject to income tax withholding regardless of age. If the child is under 18, payments are not subject to Social Security and Medicare taxes. If the child is under 21, payments are not subject to FUTA tax.

> **Example:** Bradford and Cherie are married partners in a barbecue restaurant that they own and operate. Their daughter, Maisy, age 15, works as a hostess at the restaurant on the weekends. Her parents pay her $10 an hour. Bradford and Cherie must withhold income tax on Maisy's earnings. However, because of her age, her income is not subject to Social Security, Medicare, and unemployment taxes.

Parent working for a child: Payments are subject to income, Social Security, and Medicare taxes, but not FUTA tax, regardless of the business entity type.

Spouse employed by a spouse: Payments are generally subject to income, Social Security, and Medicare taxes, but not FUTA tax. However, FUTA tax is applicable if the spouse works for a corporation or a partnership in which the employing spouse is a partner.

Business Entities Snapshot				
Character	**Sole Proprietorship**	**C Corporation**	**S Corporation**	**Partnership**
Formation	No state filing required.	State filing required.	State filing required.	No state filing required.
Existence	Automatically dissolved upon death.	Perpetual life.	Perpetual life.	Varies from state to state.
Liability	Sole proprietor has unlimited liability because the sole proprietorship is not a separate legal entity.	Shareholders are not responsible for the debts of the corporation.	Shareholders are typically not responsible for the debts of the corporation.	General partners are liable for the debts of the partnership.
Operational Requirements	None.	Board of directors, annual meetings, and annual reporting required.	Board of directors, annual meetings, and annual reporting required.	No formal requirements.
Management	Sole proprietor has full control of management and operations.	Management reports to the directors, who are elected by the shareholders.	Management reports to the directors, who are elected by the shareholders.	Partners may have an oral or written operating agreement.
Taxation	Not a separate taxable entity. Sole proprietor pays all taxes on his/her individual return.	Taxed at the entity level. Dividends paid to owners are also taxable income for them.	Generally no tax at the entity level. Income/loss is passed through to shareholders.	Generally, no tax at the entity level. Income/loss is passed through to partners.
Pass Through?	Yes.	No.	Yes.	Yes.
Double Taxation	No.	Yes.	No.	No.
Transferability of Interest	No.	Yes.	Yes.	Varies.

Unit 1: Study Questions

(Please test yourself and check the correct answers at the back of the study guide.)

1. A domestic LLC with at least two members that does not file Form 8832 is automatically classified as __________ for federal income tax purposes.

A. An S corporation.
B. A partnership.
C. A qualified joint venture.
D. A personal service corporation.

2. Don and Selma are married and run a small pet grooming business together. They want to treat their business as a qualified joint venture. Which of the following is true?

A. They may choose to report their qualified joint venture as a sole proprietorship on two separate Schedules C, so long as they file jointly.
B. They may choose to report their qualified joint venture as a sole proprietorship on two separate Schedules C, so long as they file separate tax returns (MFS).
C. They must file a partnership tax return for their business activity.
D. They may file a single Schedule C, listing Don as the sole proprietor one year and Selma as the sole proprietor the next year.

3. In which of the following instances will a partnership not be required to obtain a new EIN?

A. The partners decide to incorporate.
B. The partnership is taken over by one of the partners and is subsequently operated as a sole proprietorship.
C. The general partner ends the old partnership and begins a new one.
D. The partnership adds other business locations.

4. Which of the following is considered a drawback of the C corporation entity?

A. It may have many different shareholders.
B. It may have investors who are nonresident aliens.
C. Profits are subject to double taxation, once at the corporate level and again at the shareholder level when distributed as dividends.
D. It is run by a board of directors.

5. A sole proprietor may not be required to file Schedule SE if his net earnings for 2013 were:

A. Less than $400.
B. $400 or more.
C. Less than $5,000 but more than $400.
D. More than $5,000.

6. Mandy and her friend, Tammy, work together, making beaded necklaces and selling them at craft shows. They run their business jointly and attempt to make a profit, but they do not have any type of formal business agreement. They share with each other the profits or losses of the business. They received $24,900 in 2013 from selling necklaces, and they had $1,900 of expenses. Where and how is the correct way for Mandy and Tammy to report their income?

A. Split the income and report the profits as other income on each taxpayer's individual Form 1040.
B. Each must report her own income and expenses on separate Schedule Cs.
C. Mandy and Tammy should calculate income and subtract expenses, and each should report the net amount as "other income" on her individual Form 1040.
D. Mandy and Tammy are working as a partnership and should report their income on Form 1065.

7. Julian is self-employed and has a small business selling used DVDs. The gross income from his business is $20,000 and his business expenses total $9,500. Which schedule must Julian complete to report his business income and expenses?

A. Schedule F.
B. Schedule C.
C. Schedule D.
D. Schedule A.

8. All of the statements are true about the following business entities except:

A. S and C corporations may have an unlimited number of shareholders.
B. An LLC typically provides the liability protection of a corporation but the tax benefits of a partnership.
C. "Pass through" entities include LLCs, LLPs, S corporations, and partnerships.
D. A sole proprietorship bears all the liabilities and risks of a business.

9. A sole proprietor would be required to obtain a new EIN in which of the following instances?

A. If he is required to file excise tax returns.
B. If he changes the name of his business.
C. If he changes location.
D. If he operates multiple locations.

10. A personal service corporation is always taxed at a_____________ rate.

A. 15%.
B. 28%.
C. 35%.
D. 39.6%.

11. Federal law requires businesses to provide a Form 1099-MISC for each independent contractor paid at least ________ for services during a year.

A. $400.
B. $500.
C. $600.
D. $1,000.

12. Dan is a full-time life insurance salesman and a statutory employee. He receives a Form W-2 for his earnings. How should he report his income?

A. On Form 1040 as regular wage income.
B. On Schedule C, not subject to self-employment tax.
C. On Schedule C, subject to self-employment tax.
D. On Schedule K.

13. The IRS evaluates all of the following characteristics to assess the relationship between a business and its workers except ________________:

A. Type of relationship.
B. Financial control.
C. Income level.
D. Behavioral control.

14. Caden, age 16, works behind the counter of a juice bar owned by his mother, a sole proprietor. Which of the following taxes, if any, should be withheld from his paycheck?

A. Income tax.
B. Income tax, Social Security and Medicare taxes.
C. Income tax, Social Security and Medicare taxes, and FUTA tax.
D. None of the above.

15. When a business receives a cash payment of more than $10,000 from a single transaction, it is required to file _________________.

A. Form 1099-MISC.
B. Form W-2.
C. Form 8300.
D. Form 941.

16. Which of the following organizations does not require an EIN?
A. An estate.
B. A C corporation.
C. Nonprofit organizations.
D. A sole proprietorship with no employees.

Unit 2: Accounting Periods and Methods

More Reading:
Publication 334, *Tax Guide for Small Business*
Publication 538, *Accounting Periods and Methods*

Tax Year

The tax year is an annual accounting period for reporting income and expenses. Individuals generally file their tax returns on a calendar-year basis. Certain businesses have the option to file their tax returns on either a calendar-year or a fiscal-year basis.

Calendar Tax Year: Twelve consecutive months beginning January 1 and ending December 31.

Fiscal Tax Year: Generally twelve consecutive months ending on the last day of any month except December. However, one variation of a fiscal year-end does not fall on the same date each year. A 52/53-week tax year is a fiscal tax year that varies from 52 to 53 weeks but does not necessarily end on the last day of the month. For example, some businesses choose to end their fiscal year on a particular day of the week, such as the last Friday in June or the Saturday that falls closest to January 31.

Example: Paula works for the state of California. The state's budget follows a fiscal year that runs from July 1, 2013 through June 30, 2014. This is a 12-month period not ending in December. Most federal and state government organizations operate on a fiscal-year basis, as do some corporations.

Short Tax Year: A tax year of less than 12 months. A short tax year may result in the first or last year of an entity's existence, or when an entity changes its accounting period (for example, from a fiscal year to a calendar year, or vice versa). Even if a business is not in existence for a full year, the requirements for filing the return and paying any tax liability are generally the same as if a full 12-month tax year had ended on the last day of the short tax year.

Example: Eduardo and Jared started a business partnership in 2011. Eduardo died on November 1, 2013; therefore, the partnership is no longer in existence. Jared decides to continue the business as a sole proprietor. He must request a new employer identification number since his business structure has changed. The partnership is dissolved, and a final partnership tax return must be filed for the short tax year from January 1, 2013 to November 1, 2013.

Example: Jillian formed Sorrento Rare Books on February 1, 2013. She immediately started having financial troubles and dissolved her corporation on October 31, 2013. Jillian must file a corporate return for a short tax year covering the nine-month period that Sorrento Rare Books was in existence.

A business adopts a tax year when it files its first income tax return. Any business may adopt the calendar year as its tax year. A new C corporation may generally elect to use a fiscal year instead. However, the IRS may require use of the calendar year in the following instances:

- The business keeps no books.
- There is no annual accounting period.

- The present tax year does not qualify as a fiscal year.
- The Internal Revenue Code or income tax regulations require use of a calendar year.

Form 1128, *Application to Adopt, Change, or Retain a Tax Year*, is used to request a change in the tax year.

If a business files its first tax return using the calendar tax year and later changes its business structure (such as moving from a sole proprietorship to a partnership), the business must continue to use the calendar year unless it receives IRS approval or is otherwise forced to change in order to comply with the IRC.

A taxpayer's death marks the end of his final tax year as an individual taxpayer and the following day is the beginning of the first tax year for his estate. The executor or personal representative of the estate is responsible for filing the individual's final income tax return (Form 1040), income tax returns for the estate (Form 1041), and possibly an estate tax return (Form 706).

Example: Desmond is an unmarried physician. He dies on July 1, 2013 and his son, Raleigh, is named the executor of his estate. Raleigh is responsible for filing Desmond's final individual tax return (Form 1040). The final Form 1040 covers the period from January 1 through July 1. In addition, he must file income tax returns for the estate for the period that begins on July 2 and ends when the estate's assets have been distributed. Raleigh must request an EIN for his father's estate, which is considered a separate entity for tax purposes. Desmond's assets are valued at approximately $15 million on the date of his death. Therefore, in addition to the income tax returns, an estate tax return must be filed.

The executor chooses the estate's tax period when he files its first income tax return. Generally, the estate's first tax year is any period of 12 months or less that ends on the last day of a month. If the executor selects the last day of any month other than December, the estate has adopted a fiscal tax year. The due date for Form 1041 is the fifteenth day of the fourth month following the end of the entity's tax year.

Required Tax Year

Partnerships, S corporations, and PSCs generally must use a required tax year. An entity does not have to use a required tax year if it receives permission from the IRS to use another permitted tax year or if it files an election under section 444 (as described further below). Unless it can establish a business purpose for using a fiscal year, an S corporation or PSC must generally use a calendar year.

A partnership, an S corporation, or a PSC can file Form 1128, *Application to Adopt, Change, or Retain a Tax Year* to support its business purpose for using a fiscal year. For example, a seasonal business (such as a ski resort) may elect a fiscal year based on a genuine business purpose. It is not considered a legitimate business purpose to elect a particular fiscal tax year so that partners or shareholders may defer income recognition.

Unless it can establish a business purpose for a different tax year, a partnership's required tax year must generally conform to its partners' tax years. If one or more partners with the same tax year owns a majority (more than 50%) interest in the partnership's capital and profits, the tax year of those partners is the required tax year for the partnership.

Example: Busy Bee Partnership has two partners, both of which are C corporations. Corporation A owns a 30% partnership interest in Busy Bee and operates on a calendar year. Corporation B owns the remaining 70% of the partnership interest and operates on a fiscal year ending February 28.

Partners	Partnership Interest	Tax Year
Corporation A	30%	Calendar year (Dec 31st)
Corporation B	70%	Feb 28 (fiscal year-end)

Since Corporation B owns a majority interest in Busy Bee Partnership, the partnership must file on the same tax year as Corporation B.

If there is no majority interest tax year, the partnership must use the tax year of all of the principal partners (those who have an interest of 5% or more in the partnership's capital and profits). If there is no majority interest tax year and the principal partners do not have the same tax year, the partnership must use the tax year that would result in the least aggregate deferral of income to its partners.

Example: Andrew and Bella each have a 50% interest in the Chef Supplies Partnership. Andrew uses the calendar year and Bella uses a fiscal year ending November 30. Chef Supplies must adopt a fiscal year ending November 30 because this results in the least aggregate deferral of income to the partners, as shown in the following table.

With Year End 12/31:

	Year End	Interest	Months of Deferral	Interest × Deferral
Andrew	31-Dec	50%	0	0
Bella	30-Nov	50%	11	5.5
Total Deferral				**5.5**

With Year End 11/30:

	Year End	Interest	Months of Deferral	Interest × Deferral
Andrew	31-Dec	50%	1	0.5
Bella	30-Nov	50%	0	0
Total Deferral				**0.5**

Section 444 Election

A partnership, an S corporation, or a PSC can request to use a tax year other than its required tax year by filing Form 8716, *Election to Have a Tax Year Other Than a Required Tax Year*. This is known as a section 444 election and it does not apply to any business that establishes a genuine business purpose for using a different tax year.

A partnership or an S corporation that makes this election must make certain required payments based upon the value of the tax deferral the owners receive by using a tax year different from the required tax year. A PSC that makes the election must make certain distributions to its owner-employees by December 31 of each applicable year. A business can request a section 444 election if it meets all of the following requirements:

- It is not a member of a tiered structure.
- It has not previously had a section 444 election in effect.
- It elects a year that meets the deferral period requirement.

The deferral period depends on whether the entity is using the election to retain its tax year or to adopt or change its tax year. If it intends to retain its tax year, it may only do so if the deferral period is three months or less. The deferral period is the number of months between the beginning of the retained year and the end of the first required tax year.

If the entity is requesting adoption or a change to a tax year other than the required tax year, the deferral period is the number of months from the end of the new tax year to the end of the required tax year. Generally, the IRS will allow a section 444 election only if the deferral period is less than the shorter of:

- Three months, or
- The deferral period of the tax year being changed.

Example: Davidson Partnership, a newly formed partnership owned by two calendar-year partners, begins operations on December 1, 2013. Davidson wants to make a section 444 election to adopt a September 30 tax year. Davidson's deferral period for the tax year beginning December 1, 2013 is three months, the number of months between September 30 and December 31.

The section 444 election remains in effect until it is terminated. If the election is terminated, another section 444 election cannot be made for any tax year. The election also ends automatically when any of the following occurs:

- The entity changes to its required tax year.
- The entity liquidates.
- The entity becomes a member of a tiered structure.
- The IRS determines that the entity willfully failed to comply with the required payments or distributions.
- The entity is an S corporation and the S election is terminated. However, if the S corporation immediately becomes a PSC, it can continue the prior section 444 election.
- A PSC ceases to be a PSC. Again, however, if a PSC becomes an S corporation, it can continue the prior election.

Filing Due Dates for Entities

Most individuals and partnerships use the calendar year, and the normal due date for filing their income tax returns is April 15 of the following year. For those on a fiscal year, returns are due on the fifteenth day of the fourth month following the end of the year. For these and other entities' returns, if the due date falls on a Saturday, Sunday, or legal holiday, it is delayed until the next business day.

If a corporation uses the calendar year, its tax returns are due on March 15 of the following year. If the corporation is on a fiscal year, the tax return is due on the fifteenth day of the third month following the end of the tax year.

Example: A calendar-year C corporation dissolved on July 22, 2013 and ceased all operations. Its final return is due by October 15, 2013 (the fifteenth day of the third month following the close of its short tax year). The return will cover the period from January 1, 2013 through July 22, 2013.

Nonprofit entities using the calendar year must file their information returns by May 15. For nonprofit entities using a fiscal year, returns are due on the fifteenth day of the fifth month following the end of the year.

Entities and individuals may request extensions of time to file their federal income tax returns. An extension does not grant the entity additional time to pay the tax due. The tax due must be paid by the filing deadline, or the entity will be subject to interest and penalties on the amount of unpaid tax.

Study Note: For Part 2 of the EA exam, you should memorize filing deadlines for partnerships, C corporations, and the other entities covered in this study guide.

Accounting Methods

An accounting method is a set of rules used to determine when and how income and expenses are reported. No single accounting method is required of all taxpayers. However, the taxpayer must use a system that reflects income and expenses, and it must be used consistently from year to year.

Businesses generally report taxable income under one of the following accounting methods:

- Cash method
- Accrual method
- Special methods of accounting for certain items of income and expenses
- Hybrid method using elements of the methods above

The special methods include, for example, those related to accounting for long-term contracts, farming operations, and installment sales. Different rules apply to each accounting method.

Note: The most common accounting method is the **cash method**, which is used by most individuals and many small businesses. The **accrual method** is used by most large corporations and is a more accurate method of recognizing income and expenses, because it reflects when taxable income is actually earned.

A business owner may use different accounting methods if he has two separate and distinct businesses. Two businesses will not be considered separate and distinct unless a separate set of books and records is maintained for each business.

Example: Blake is a self-employed enrolled agent. He prepares tax returns from January through April every year. He is also a motivational speaker who is booked for many paid engagements. He reports his tax preparation business using the accrual method and his speaking business using the cash method. He keeps separate books and records for each business. Blake may use different accounting methods because he has two separate and distinct businesses with separate sets of records.

Cash Method

The cash method of accounting is the simplest method to use, but the IRS restricts its use to businesses of certain types and sizes. The following businesses are required to use the accrual method rather than the cash method:

- A corporation (other than an S corporation) with average annual gross receipts exceeding $5 million
- A partnership with a corporate partner (other than an S corporation) with average annual gross receipts exceeding $5 million
- Any business that carries, produces, or sells inventory, unless the business has average annual gross receipts of $1 million or less
- Any tax shelter, regardless of its size
- Any corporation with long-term contracts

An entity (other than a tax shelter) with gross receipts that do not exceed the applicable threshold described above can use the cash method. Average annual gross receipts are determined by adding the gross receipts for the current tax year and the two preceding tax years and dividing the total by three.

Gross receipts for a short tax year are annualized. An entity that fails to meet the applicable gross receipts test for any tax year is prohibited from using the cash method and must change to the accrual method, effective for the tax year in which the entity fails to meet the test.

Example: Cameron and William Davis form the Davis and Davis Architectural Corporation, a C corporation, in 2013 and its annualized gross receipts for the year are $4.2 million. The corporation may use the cash method because it has gross receipts under $5 million and does not have any inventory.

Example: Green Bay Corporation produces inventory and its gross receipts are $200,000 for 2011, $800,000 for 2012, and $1,100,000 for 2013. The company's average annual gross receipts are therefore $700,000 ([$200,000 + $800,000 + $1,100,000] ÷ 3 = $700,000). Green Bay Corporation may continue to use the cash method.

Example: Crape Company makes golf car parts. The company carries inventory throughout the year. Crape's gross receipts have never exceeded $900,000. Therefore, even though it carries inventory, Crape may continue to use the cash method because its average annual gross receipts are less than $1 million.

A business that produces, purchases, or sells inventory and has average annual gross receipts in excess of $1 million is generally required to use the accrual method. However, certain types of businesses (called qualifying small business taxpayers) with average annual gross receipts between $1 million and $10 million may be exempt from this requirement and be allowed to use the cash method. To be eligible, a qualifying small business taxpayer's principal activity may not be in certain industries, including manufacturing, wholesale trade, or retail trade. Its principal activity should involve the provision of services, which may include providing property (inventory) related to those services, or the fabrication or modification of personal property.

Example: Corinne and her husband, Doug, run Bicycles-R-Us as a husband-and-wife business. Their primary business involves bicycle repair at several locations, but they also make retail sales of repair parts and bicycle accessories. Therefore, they do maintain an inventory. For the years 2011 through 2013, Bicycles-R-Us had average annual gross receipts of $1.3 million. Bicycles-R-Us can use the cash method, even though it sells inventory because its principal business is that of providing repair services and its related retail sales are relatively minor.

Exceptions to the Rules Outlined Above: The following entities may use the cash method of accounting:

- A qualified family farming corporation with gross receipts of $25 million or less
- A qualified personal service corporation
- Artists, authors, and photographers who sell works that they have created by their own effort

Under the cash method, taxpayers generally deduct expenses when they are paid, based upon the presumption that the expenses relate to the current tax year and that they would not be deductible if paid in advance. This means that businesses generally may not attempt to lower their taxable income by paying expenses applicable to future years. The taxpayer would instead capitalize costs paid in advance and deduct them in the years to which they apply. However, there is an exception called the 12-month rule, under which the cash-basis taxpayer is not required to capitalize amounts paid for periods that do not extend beyond the earlier of the following:

- 12 months after the benefit begins, or
- The end of the tax year after the tax year in which payment is made.

Example: Sherry is a calendar-year sole proprietor and pays $3,000 in 2013 for an insurance policy that is effective for three years (36 months), beginning on July 1, 2013. This payment does not qualify for the 12-month rule. Therefore, only $500 (6/36 × $3,000) is deductible in 2013, $1,000 (12/36 × $3,000) is deductible in 2014, $1,000 (12/36 × $3,000) is deductible in 2015, and the remaining $500 is deductible in 2016 when the policy expires.

Example: Garrison Partnership is a calendar-year business. It pays $15,000 on July 1, 2013 for a business liability policy that is effective for one year beginning on that date. The 12-month rule applies, and the full $15,000 is deductible in 2013.

Example: Mikayla is a sole proprietor who rents retail space for her eyebrow threading business. She pays two years of rent in advance in order to receive a substantial discount from her landlord. She cannot use the 12-month rule because the benefit from her advance payment exceeds the 12-month time period. She must recognize the rent expense over the two-year period.

Constructive Receipt of Income: Under the cash method, taxpayers report income when it is actually or "constructively" received during the tax year. Income is constructively received when the amount is credited to the taxpayer's account or made available without restriction so that the taxpayer or his agent has access to the funds. The taxpayer does not need to have physical possession of the payment.

Example: Patel Brothers Partnership operates on the cash method. Interest income is credited to Patel's bank account in December 2013, but the partners do not withdraw it until January 2014. The partnership must include the interest income in its gross income for 2013, not 2014. The partnership had ownership and control of the income in 2013, so it is taxable in the year received.

Income is not considered to be constructively received if control or use of it is restricted.

Example: Better Jail Bonds LLP is a cash-basis partnership that bills a customer on December 10, 2013. The customer sends the company a check postdated to January 2, 2014. The check is received on December 31, 2013 but cannot be deposited until 2014 because it was postdated. Better Jail Bonds would include this income in gross income for 2014, since constructive receipt did not occur until then.

Accrual Method

Under the accrual method of accounting, a business generally records income when a sale occurs or income is earned, regardless of when the business gets paid. Income is generally reported when one or more of the following occurs:

- Payment is received (subject to certain exceptions for advance payments as described in Unit 3)
- The taxpayer earns the income
- The income is due to the taxpayer
- Title has passed

A business that uses the accrual method must also report costs when they are incurred, either as expenses or as capitalized assets. It does not matter when the business actually pays for the expenses.

The accrual method gives a more accurate assessment of a business's financial situation than the cash method. Income earned in each period is more accurately matched against the expenses for that period, so a business gets a better picture of net profit or loss.

Example: Ali's Computer Inc. is a calendar-year, accrual-basis corporation. The business sold a computer on December 28, 2013 for $2,500. Ali billed the customer in the first week of January 2014, but did not receive payment until February 2014. Ali must include the $2,500 in his 2013 income, the year the company actually earned the income, even though the related billing and payment did not occur until the next year.

Hybrid Accounting Method

Businesses may also use a hybrid accounting method that is a combination of the cash, accrual, and perhaps other special methods, so long as the hybrid method clearly reflects income and is used consistently. However, the following restrictions apply:

- If inventory is necessary to account for income, the business must use the accrual method for purchases and sales. The cash method can be used for other income and expense items.
- If an entity uses the cash method for reporting income, it must use the cash method for reporting expenses.
- If an entity uses the accrual method for reporting expenses, it must use the accrual method for reporting income.

Changing Accounting Methods

When a business files its first tax return, it may choose any permitted accounting method. Subsequent changes, either in the overall accounting method or the treatment of a material item, generally require that the taxpayer obtain IRS approval. Prior approval is needed for:

- Changes from cash to accrual or vice versa, unless the change is required by tax law
- Changes in the method used to value inventory, such as switching from LIFO to FIFO (see discussion of these methods below)
- Changes in the method of depreciation or amortization

The taxpayer must file Form 3115, *Application for Change in Accounting Method*, to request a change in either an overall accounting method or the accounting treatment for an individual item. However, IRS consent is not required for the following:

- Making an adjustment in the useful life of a depreciable or amortizable asset (but a taxpayer cannot change the recovery period for MACRS or ACRS property)
- Correcting a math error or an error in figuring tax liability
- A change in accounting method when the change is required by tax law, such as when a business's average gross receipts exceed $5 million

Example: Gary is a general partner in Ultimate Consumer Goods and discovers an error in the useful life of a depreciable asset. The asset should have been depreciated over 15 years rather than five. Ultimate Consumer Goods does not have to ask the IRS for permission to correct the depreciation error.

Inventory Accounting

A business that produces or sells products must track its inventory in order to correctly calculate income. Businesses often make a full physical inventory count at the end of each tax year, as well as at other reasonable intervals. The recorded inventory balances are then adjusted to agree with the actual counts.

Physical inventory counts may identify irregularities such as theft, as well as damaged goods and obsolete products.

Example: Wrightwood Grocery Store takes a physical inventory once a month. During the physical inventory, store employees are required to record any damaged goods such as dented cans and ripped packaging. When the physical inventory is completed, the manager does a reconciliation to her records. She adjusts the books to reflect adjustments for shrinkage and damaged merchandise.

A taxpayer's inventory should include all of the following, if applicable:

- Merchandise or stock in trade
- Raw materials
- Work in process
- Finished products
- Supplies that physically become a part of items for sale (labels, packaging, etc.)

A taxpayer's inventory may include:

- Purchased merchandise if title has passed to the taxpayer, even if the merchandise is still in transit or the business does not have physical possession of it for another reason
- Goods under contract for sale that have not yet been segregated and applied to the contract
- Goods out on consignment
- Goods held for sale in display rooms or booths located away from the taxpayer's place of business

The following merchandise is not included in inventory:

- Goods the business has sold, if legal title (ownership) has passed to the buyer
- Goods consigned to the taxpayer
- Goods ordered for future delivery if the business does not yet have title

Land, buildings, and equipment used in a business are not included in inventory.

Shipping Terms and Transfer of Ownership

Certain shipping terms dictate when a taxpayer must take an item out of its inventory and recognize income from a sale. The terms indicate the point at which title (ownership) of goods transfers from seller to buyer. The three most common terms are:

1. **FOB Destination:** Title passes to the buyer at the point of destination (when the goods arrive at the buyer's location).
2. **FOB Shipping Point:** Title passes to the buyer at the point of shipment (when the goods leave the seller's premises). FOB shipping point is also called "FOB origin."

3. **C.O.D.** ("cash on delivery" or "collect on delivery"): Payment is made upon delivery and title passes at that time. For a business that sells by mail on a C.O.D basis, the merchandise is generally included in the seller's closing inventory until the buyer pays for it.

Example: Weitzman Furniture Company is a calendar-year, accrual-basis corporation that manufactures custom household furniture. It does not accrue income until the furniture has been delivered and accepted by the buyer. In 2013, the company receives an order for furniture to be custom manufactured for a total price of $20,000. Weitzman ships the furniture FOB destination to the customer on December 26, 2013, but it is not delivered and accepted by the customer until January 3, 2014. Weitzman will bill its customer for the $20,000 contract price and include this amount in its gross income for 2014, because the furniture had not been accepted and the title had not passed as of December 31, 2013.

Inventory Methods

The value of a business's inventory is a major factor in figuring taxable income. Several common methods are used to assign costs to the items in inventory. They include the specific identification method, the average cost method, FIFO, and LIFO.

Specific Identification Method: This method is used when it is possible to identify and match the actual cost to specific items in inventory. It is most useful with an inventory that includes a limited number of highly specific and high-dollar items, such as custom goods or rare items like artwork or gemstones. The business simply accounts for each individual item as it is sold.

Example: The Classic Custom Autos dealership sells rare collectible cars. Each car is tracked individually by its vehicle identification number and its actual cost. When a car is sold, the cost is taken out of inventory. This is an example of specific identification inventory valuation.

Average Cost Method: This method is commonly used when a business has quantities of items that are largely interchangeable rather than individually unique. It allows the business to calculate an average cost per unit without tracking the individual units as they are purchased, manufactured, or sold. The formula for figuring average cost is:

Average Unit Cost = (Total Cost of Units Purchased or Manufactured)/ (Total Quantity of Units)
Aggregate Inventory Cost = (Average Unit Cost) × (Units in Current Inventory)

Example: Anna owns a pet store. She purchases five dog leashes at $10 apiece. The following week, the price of the leashes goes up, and she purchases five more leashes at $20 apiece. Anna then sells five leashes the following week. The weighted average cost of Anna's inventory is calculated as follows:

Total cost of leashes:
(Five leashes at $10 each) = $50;
(Five leashes at $20 each) = $100
Total number of units = 10 leashes
Weighted average = $150 / 10 = $15

The average cost per leash for the 10 leashes Anna has purchased is $15. If she applies this average cost to the five leashes unsold at the end of the week, the calculated cost of the leashes on hand would be $75 ($15 × 5 leashes).

FIFO (First-in, First-out)

The first-in, first-out (FIFO) method is a variation of the average cost method in which it is assumed that inventory items are sold in the order they are acquired or produced, with the oldest goods sold first and the newest goods sold last. This assumption would mirror the actual flow of inventory items in certain businesses, such as rotating stock in a grocery store.

The actual quantities in inventory at the end of the tax year are assigned costs based upon the cost of items of the same type that the business most recently purchased or produced. The formula for figuring inventory based on the FIFO method is as follows:

Unit Cost Per Item = (Cost/Quantity) for the most recent lot of the item that was purchased or produced

Aggregate Inventory Cost = (Unit Cost Per Item × Quantity) for each item

In an economy with rising prices (inflation), the use of FIFO will typically assign a higher value to ending inventory than other methods and thus result in reporting lower cost of sales and higher taxable income.

FIFO Example: Rabbata Electronics, a cash-basis, calendar-year taxpayer, sells car audio equipment. Beginning inventory on January 1 included 300 car stereos with cost per unit of $20. On January 10 the business purchased 600 stereos at $20.10; on January 16 it purchased 400 stereos at $20.20; and on January 25 it purchased 500 stereos at $20.30. In January the business sold 1,200 car stereos. Under FIFO it is assumed that the oldest merchandise is sold first. Rabbata Electronics had a beginning inventory of 300 stereos. Those units are assumed to have been sold first, followed by the units purchased on January 10 and January 16. Thus, the cost assigned to the units on hand at the end of January is determined as follows:

Beginning inventory	**300**
January 10 purchases	600
January 16 purchases	400
January 25 purchases	500
Total units available	1,800
Units sold	(1,200)
Units in inventory at end of January	**600**

Composition based upon FIFO assumption:

January 25 purchases	500 @ $20.30 =	10,150
Unsold portion of January 16 purchases	100 @ $20.20 =	2,020
Total inventory at end of January	600	$12,170

LIFO (Last-in, First-out)

The last-in, first-out (LIFO) method assumes that the newest inventory purchased or produced is sold first, and the oldest inventory is sold last. Since the prices of goods, labor, and materials generally rise over time, this method will typically result in assigning a lower aggregate value to inventory on hand, higher amounts being recorded as the cost of sales, and lower taxable income. As a result, use of the LIFO method is subject to highly complex rules governing its calculation and close scrutiny by the IRS. The formula for figuring inventory using the LIFO method is as follows:

Unit Cost Per Item = (Cost/Quantity) for the oldest lot of the item that was purchased or produced
Aggregate Inventory Cost = (Unit Cost Per Item × Quantity) for each item

LIFO Example: Using the same background information for Rabbata Electronics outlined above but using a LIFO assumption rather than FIFO, the 300 units on hand at January 1 are assumed to have a LIFO cost per unit of only $10 because Rabbata has been in business for 20 years and the unit costs of its purchases have approximately doubled during that period due to inflation. Therefore, the cost assigned to the units on hand at the end of January is determined as follows:

Beginning inventory	**300**
January 10 purchases	600
January 16 purchases	400
January 25 purchases	500
Total units available	1,800
Units sold	(1,200)
Units in inventory at end of January	**600**

Composition based upon LIFO assumption:

Beginning inventory	300 @ 10.00 =	3,000
Unsold portion of January 10 purchases	300 @ 20.10 =	6,030
Total inventory at end of January	600	$9,030

In comparison to the earlier FIFO example, the aggregate cost assigned to ending inventory using LIFO would be lower. Since the income generated by Rabbata in January from selling 1,200 units would be the same using either inventory method, its taxable income would be higher using FIFO instead of LIFO.

Unless a business has used the LIFO method from its inception, it must obtain permission from the IRS to change to LIFO from another method of inventory valuation. Permission is requested by filing Form 970, *Application to Use LIFO Inventory Method.*

Differences between FIFO and LIFO

Economic Climate	FIFO	LIFO
Periods of rising prices (Inflation)	(+) Higher value of inventory	(-) Lower value of inventory
	(-) Lower cost of goods sold	(+) Higher cost of goods sold
Periods of falling prices (Deflation)	(-) Lower value of inventory	(-) Higher value of inventory
	(+) Higher cost of goods sold	(+) Lower cost of goods sold

Other Inventory Valuation Methods

In addition to the inventory accounting methods already described, the following methods, or conventions, are commonly used to assign value to inventory: cost, lower of cost or market, and retail.

Cost Method

All direct and indirect costs are included.

- For merchandise on hand at the beginning of the tax year, cost means the ending inventory price of the goods.
- For merchandise purchased during the year, cost means the invoice price minus appropriate discounts, plus transportation or other charges incurred in acquiring the goods. It may also include other costs that must be capitalized under the uniform capitalization rules (discussed later in the unit).
- For merchandise produced during the year, cost means all direct and indirect costs, including those that have to be capitalized under the uniform capitalization rules.

A trade discount is sometimes given for volume or quantity purchases. The cost of the actual value of inventory must be reduced by trade discounts.

Lower of Cost or Market Method

This method may be used for inventory, such as fashion clothing, that tends to lose value quickly. The market value of each item on hand is compared with its cost and the lower of the two is used as its inventory value. Market value is typically based upon the normal selling price at the date the inventory is being valued.

If inventory is offered for sale below market in the normal course of business, inventory can be valued at the lower price, less the direct cost of disposition. This method may also be used for items that cannot be sold at normal prices or are unusable because of damage, imperfections, changes of style, odd or broken lots, or other similar causes. In these cases, items should be valued at their actual selling price minus the direct cost of disposition, even if another method is used to value the rest of the entity's inventory. However, the lower of cost or market method cannot be used in conjunction with the LIFO method.

This method applies to the following:

- Goods purchased and on hand

- The basic elements of cost (direct materials, direct labor, and certain indirect costs) of goods being manufactured and finished goods on hand

Example: Graham makes motorcycle accessories at his factory. Under the lower of cost or market method, the following items would be valued at $600 in closing inventory.

Inventory Item	Cost	Market	Lower
Leather jacket	$300	$500	$300
Motorcycle helmets	$200	$100	$100
Leather motorcycle chaps	$450	$200	$200
Total	**$950**	**$800**	**$600**

Graham must value each item in the inventory separately. He cannot value the entire inventory at cost ($950) and at market ($800) and then use the lower of the two figures.

Retail Method

Under the retail method, the total retail selling price of goods on hand at the end of the tax year in each department or for each class of goods is reduced to approximate cost by using an average markup expressed as a percentage of the total retail selling price. For example, if a store marks up its merchandise by 35%, that percentage would be used as a basis for estimating the cost of its current inventory.

Cost of Goods Sold (COGS)

The methods described above to determine the value of a business's ending inventory allow calculation of cost of goods sold (COGS), which is deducted from a business's gross receipts to determine its gross profit. The following expenses related to inventory sold are included in COGS:

- The cost of products or raw materials, including freight
- Storage
- Direct labor costs for workers who produce the products
- Factory overhead

Example: In calculating COGS, American Custom Shoes includes the cost of leather and thread in the shoes it manufactures, as well as wages for the workers that produce the shoes. COGS is recorded as an expense as the company sells its goods.

The equation for cost of goods sold is as follows:

Beginning Inventory +
Inventory Purchases and Production Costs -
Ending Inventory =
Cost of Goods Sold

Example: Doggie Delights Inc. is an accrual-basis corporation that manufactures custom dog sweaters. The value of sweater inventory was $2,500 at December 31, and is $3,500 at January 31. In January, Doggie Delights has $20,000 of sales. In the same month, the corporation also has a number of expenses, including wages for the sweater designers ($5,000) and the cost of raw materials such as yarn, appliqué, and rhinestones ($3,000). The wages and the cost of the raw materials are directly related to the production of the inventory (the sweaters) and are included in the cost of goods sold calculation. Other costs not directly related to the manufacture of the sweaters, which might include items like a receptionist's salary ($1,500), telephone charges ($130), and advertising ($1,200) are also expensed, but are not part of COGS. The income statement for January would look like this:

Gross income from sales:	$20,000
COGS: ($2,500 + $5,000 + $3,000 - $3,500)	($7,000)
Gross profit	$13,000
Other expenses: ($1,500 + $130 + $1,200)	($2,830)
Income for January	**$10,170**

When a business incurs a casualty or theft loss of inventory, it increases the cost of goods sold by properly reporting beginning and ending inventories. Alternatively, the business may record the loss separately as a casualty or theft loss. If the entity chooses to report a casualty loss, it must adjust opening inventory to eliminate the loss items and avoid counting the loss twice.

Uniform Capitalization Rules (UNICAP)

The uniform capitalization rules (commonly referred to as UNICAP) provide detailed guidance regarding the direct costs and certain indirect costs related to the production of goods or the purchase of merchandise for resale that businesses must capitalize as part of the cost of inventory. These costs cannot be deducted when incurred. They must be capitalized and deducted later when the inventory is used or sold.

Example: MTG Studios produces movies for Hollywood. Film production is subject to the uniform capitalization rules, so MTG must capitalize all of its costs, including set design, costumes, special effects, film editing, and salaries for actors and production workers. When a film is finally completed and distributed, MTG Studios is allowed to deduct the production costs as COGS.

Example: Creative Costumes manufactures Halloween and stage costumes. During August, Creative Costumes purchases raw materials to produce costumes for the upcoming holiday. All the materials and shipping costs associated with the inventory must be capitalized rather than expensed. As the Halloween costumes are sold, Creative Costumes expenses the costs associated with the inventory as cost of goods sold. At the end of each month, Creative Costumes does a physical inventory count and adjusts COGS for any damaged or stolen inventory.

Businesses subject to the uniform capitalization rules include the following:

- Retailers or wholesalers that purchase merchandise for resale,
- Manufacturers that produce real or tangible property for sale; and

- Taxpayers who construct assets for their own trade or business.

However, the uniform capitalization rules do not apply to the following:

- Resellers of personal property with average annual gross receipts of $10 million or less for the three prior tax years.
- Personal or nonbusiness property (such as a hobby that produces occasional income).
- Research and experimental expenditures.
- Intangible drilling and development costs of oil and gas or geothermal wells.
- Property produced under a long-term contract.
- Timber raised, harvested, or grown, and the underlying land.
- Qualified creative expenses incurred as self-employed writers, photographers, or artists that are otherwise deductible on their tax returns.
- Loan originations.
- Property provided to customers in connection with providing services. It must be de minimis and not be included in inventory in the hands of the service provider.
- The costs of certain producers who use a simplified production method and whose total indirect costs are $200,000 or less.

Unit 2: Study Questions

1. Which of the following date ranges would be considered a fiscal tax year?

A. January 1, 2013 to December 31, 2013.
B. February 15, 2013 to February 15, 2014.
C. July 1, 2013 to June 30, 2014.
D. May 1, 2013 to May 31, 2014.

2. All of the following costs must be included in inventory except ________________:

A. Cost of shipping raw materials to the business's factory.
B. Cost of shipping finished product orders to customers.
C. Raw materials.
D. Direct labor costs.

3. Which of the following changes in accounting method does not require prior approval from the IRS?

A. A change from FIFO to LIFO inventory valuation.
B. A change from the cash method to the accrual method.
C. A change in the overall method of figuring depreciation.
D. A correction of a math error in depreciating an asset.

4. Which of the following entities may use the cash method of accounting?

A. A family farming corporation with average gross receipts of $22 million.
B. A C corporation with average gross receipts of $50 million.
C. A tax shelter with $50,000 in average gross receipts.
D. A corporation with long-term contracts and average gross receipts of $900,000.

5. Which would generally not be considered the end of an acceptable tax year?

A. January 31.
B. April 15.
C. December 31.
D. The last Friday in February.

6. Which of the following entities may not use the cash method of accounting?

A. A partnership that produces inventory for sale to customers and has $1.2 million in average annual gross receipts.
B. A C corporation without inventory that has $4.5 million in average annual gross receipts.
C. A qualified family farming corporation with $24 million in average annual gross receipts.
D. A sole proprietor with inventory and $500,000 in average annual gross receipts.

7. Under the lower of cost or market method of valuing inventory, what is the value of the inventory as a whole, based on the table below?

Item	Cost	Market
Shirts	$200	$500
Shoes	$300	$200
Shorts	$225	$150
Total	**$725**	**$850**

A. $725.
B. $850.
C. $750.
D. $550.

8. Helen is the owner of Banner Custom Sofas, a calendar-year, accrual-basis S corporation. She sells five sofas to Sonny's Interior Design on December 21, 2013 and bills Sonny's for $2,500 on that date. Sonny's pays the invoice on January 15, 2014. Banner would include this income in ___________:

A. 2013.
B. 2014.
C. 2015.
D. None of the above.

9. Vargas Cellular Corporation was organized on April 1, 2013. It elected the calendar year as its tax year. When is the first tax return due for Vargas Cellular for this short tax year?

A. April 15, 2013.
B. April 15, 2014.
C. March 15, 2014.
D. May 15, 2014.

10. Which of the following activities would make a taxpayer subject to the uniform capitalization rules?

A. An individual taxpayer produces items as a hobby and occasionally sells them at a profit.
B. A taxpayer produces property for sale to wholesale retailers.
C. A taxpayer acquires land and holds it for investment.
D. An individual taxpayer refurbishes multiple automobiles for his own use.

11. Ray operates a retail store using the accrual method and reports income on Schedule C, *Net Profit or Loss from Business*. He also runs a lawn care service that operates only in the summer months. Which of the following statements is true?

A. The lawn care business is required to use the accrual method of accounting because Ray has already elected this method for his other business, and all businesses operated by one individual must use the same method of accounting.
B. The lawn care business may use either the cash or accrual method, so long as both businesses have separate and distinct records.
C. Ray may keep one set of records for both businesses and use different methods of accounting.
D. Ray must combine the income for both businesses and keep one set of record books for both.

12. Ben owns a jewelry store. All of the following transactions are examples of constructive receipt of income in 2013 except ________________:

A. Ben receives a check payment on December 31, 2013, but does not deposit the check in the bank until January 2, 2014.
B. Ben receives a direct deposit of funds to his bank account on December 15, 2013, but does not withdraw any of the funds until March 2014.
C. Ben receives a signed IOU from a delinquent account in November 2013. He receives payment on this account on January 10, 2014.
D. An escrow agent receives a payment on Ben's behalf that is restricted for his use. It is an advance payment for a custom ring, but he cannot access any of the funds until the ring is delivered and inspected. On December 28, 2013, the ring is delivered and the restriction is lifted. Ben picks up the cash on January 9, 2014.

13. Chris is the owner-shareholder of Dress Down Fridays, a calendar-year S corporation. He manufactures clothing items for resale to the general public and also sells them to wholesale distributors. Chris is trying to figure out his inventory calculations in order to file his 2013 tax return. Which of the following items should be included in his year-end inventory?

A. 2,000 t-shirts out on consignment to a retailer.
B. The machinery used to manufacture the clothing.
C. An order of fabric that was in transit from a supplier, FOB destination (the title had not yet passed to Chris).
D. 1,000 shirts that were shipped COD to a retailer and had arrived there December 31.

14. Which of the following types of property are not exempt from the uniform capitalization rules?

A. Qualified expenses of a writer, photographer, or performing artist.
B. Timber and the underlying land.
C. Services provided to customers.
D. Audio recordings produced by a corporation.

15. Thomas is a cash-basis sole proprietor who reports income on Schedule C. He purchases a bulk order of watches for his mail order business. The watches cost $5,000, and the related shipping cost is $350. What is the correct treatment of the shipping cost he paid for delivery of the watches?

A. Thomas may elect to deduct the $350 shipping cost on his tax return as an expense.
B. Shipping cost paid on the watches must be added to the basis of the inventory.
C. Thomas cannot deduct the shipping cost and cannot capitalize it.
D. Thomas may elect to deduct the shipping cost as an itemized deduction on Schedule A.

16. A business must adopt its first tax year by ____________________:

A. The due date (including extensions) for filing a return.
B. The due date (not including extensions) for filing a return.
C. The date the EIN is established.
D. The first time the business pays estimated payments.

17. All of the following practices are acceptable methods of accounting for inventory except:

A. The taxpayer includes in inventory only the direct costs associated with manufacturing the goods.
B. The taxpayer has a theft loss of inventory when a disgruntled employee steals substantial amounts of merchandise. The taxpayer chooses to increase his cost of goods sold to account for the stolen items and properly reports his beginning and ending inventory.
C. The taxpayer values his inventory using the lower-of-cost or market method, applying the method to each item in his inventory.
D. The taxpayer has two businesses, and he keeps a separate set of books for each business. He chooses to use LIFO for the first business and FIFO for the second one.

18. All of the following activities are exempt from the uniform capitalization rules except:

A. Resellers of personal property with average annual gross receipts of $25 million.
B. Intangible drilling and development costs of oil and gas or geothermal wells.
C. Research and experimental expenditures.
D. Property produced under a long-term contract.

19. Tuxedo House, a clothing retailer, had the following expenses in 2013. Based on the information below, what is Tuxedo House's cost of goods sold for the year?

- Tuxedos purchased for resale $20,000
- Freight in $3,000
- Beginning inventory $15,600
- Ending inventory $12,000

A. $23,000.
B. $26,600.
C. $19,400.
D. $38,600.

Unit 3: Business Income

More Reading:
Publication 525, *Taxable and Nontaxable Income*
Publication 538, *Accounting Periods and Methods*
Publication 334, *Tax Guide for Small Business*
Publication 925, *Passive Activity and At-Risk Rules*

Gross income reportable by a business for tax purposes includes all types of income received, unless specifically exempt from taxation, in the form of money, property, or services. Sources of income for a business include the following:

- Income received for services
- Income received for manufacturing or selling merchandise
- Gains from the sale of business or investment property
- Income from the discharge of indebtedness (debt cancellation income)
- Income from an interest in an estate or trust
- Portfolio income from investments
- Fair market value of property or services received through bartering
- Rental activities and royalties

In addition to earning income that is exempt from tax, businesses may engage in transactions for which taxation of income is deferred to a later date. An example is a section 1031 exchange, which allows for deferral of income on the exchange of business or investment property.

In this unit, we will review the details of various types and treatments of business income.

Advance Payment for Services

An advance payment for services to be performed in a later tax year is generally taxable in the year it is received, even by an accrual-based taxpayer. However, if there is an agreement that the service will be completed by the end of the next tax year, recognition of the income can be delayed until the next year. The taxpayer cannot postpone the recognition of income beyond the next year.

Service Agreement: If a taxpayer receives an advance payment for a service agreement on property he sells, leases, builds, installs, or constructs, he can postpone reporting income, but only if he offers the property without a service agreement in the normal course of business. Postponement is not allowed if:

- The taxpayer will perform any part of the service after the end of the tax year immediately following the year he receives the advance payment.
- The taxpayer will perform any part of the service at any unspecified future date that may be after the end of the tax year immediately following the year he receives the advance payment.

Example: Ross is an accrual-based, calendar-year taxpayer who owns a television repair business. In 2013, he receives payments for one-year contracts that specify he will repair or replace certain TV components that break. Ross includes each payment evenly in gross income over a one-year period as it is earned.

Example: The Best Service Tennis Club is a calendar-year, accrual-based taxpayer that holds tennis clinics for new players. On November 1, the club receives payment for a one-year contract for 24 one-hour clinics beginning on that date. The club gives six clinics in 2013. The club must include one-fourth (6/24) of the payment in income for 2013 and three-fourths (18/24) of the payment in 2014, even if the club does not give all of the clinics by the end of 2014.

Guarantee or Warranty: Generally, an accrual-basis taxpayer cannot postpone reporting income received under a guarantee or warranty contract.

Advance Payment for Sales

Special rules apply to including income from advance payments on agreements for the future sale of goods to customers, such as gift certificates or cards that can be redeemed later for goods. The advance payment is generally included in income in the year it is received, even by a taxpayer reporting under the accrual method.

However, there is an alternative method in which the advance payment can be included in gross receipts under the method of accounting the taxpayer uses for tax purposes or the method of accounting used for financial reporting, whichever is earlier.

Example: Tangerine Specialty Foods uses the accrual method of accounting for tax and financial reporting purposes and accounts for the sale of goods when it ships the goods. A customer purchases a $100 gift card from Tangerine's website on December 28, 2013 using a credit card. Tangerine ships the gift card to the customer on January 3, 2014. Under the alternative method of reporting income for advance payment of sales, Tangerine may recognize the $100 in gross receipts in either 2013 (the tax year in which it received the payment) or 2014 (the tax year in which it shipped the gift card.)

Passive Activity Limits

Certain types of business activities are considered passive activities and are subject to passive activity limits on the deductibility of losses. The rules apply to individuals, estates, trusts (other than grantor trusts), personal service corporations, and closely held corporations. They also apply to owners of grantor trusts, partnerships, and S corporations. Before applying the passive activity limits, a taxpayer must determine the effects of at-risk limits,[31] which apply to individuals

[31] At-risk limits are explained in detail in later units pertaining to the specific types of entities that may be affected.

(including partners and S corporation shareholders), estates, trusts, and certain closely held corporations.

There are two kinds of passive activities:

- Trade or business activities in which the taxpayer does not materially participate during the year. The taxpayer materially participates in an activity if he is involved in the operations of the activity on a regular, continuous, and substantial basis.
- Rental activities, even if the taxpayer does materially participate, except for real estate professionals.

Study Note: There are additional exceptions related to limits on deductibility of passive losses from rental activities. These exceptions are more relevant to individual taxpayers and are generally tested on Part 1 of the EA exam.

The determination of whether a taxpayer materially participated is based upon satisfaction of at least one of several tests, including whether the taxpayer's participation in the activity:

1. Was for more than 500 hours.
2. Was substantially all the participation in the activity of all individuals for the tax year, including the participation of individuals who did not own any interest in the activity.
3. Was for more than 100 hours during the tax year, which was at least as much as any other individual for the year.
4. Included any five of the ten immediately preceding tax years.
5. Included a personal service activity in which he materially participated for any three preceding tax years.

If a taxpayer owned an activity as a limited partner, he is generally not treated as materially participating in the activity. However, he may be treated as materially participating if he met test (1), (4), or (5) above. Further, he would not be treated as a limited partner if he were also a general partner in the partnership at all times during the partnership's tax year.

A taxpayer's participation in an activity includes his spouse's participation.

A closely held corporation or a personal service corporation is treated as materially participating in an activity only if one or more shareholders who own more than 50% of the corporation materially participate in the activity.

Passive Activity Loss Limitations: Losses from passive activities that exceed the income from passive activities in a given year are generally disallowed. The taxpayer uses Form 8582, *Passive Activity Loss Limitations*, to summarize income and losses from passive activities and compute deductible losses, and Form 8582-CR, *Passive Activity Credit Limitations*, to summarize the credits from passive activities and compute the amount of passive activity credit allowed.

Disallowed passive losses are carried forward to the next taxable year. A similar rule applies to credits from passive activities. Generally, the taxpayer may deduct in full any previously disallowed passive activity losses in the year he disposes of his entire interest in the activity. Form 8582-CR may also be used to make an election to increase the basis of credit property upon disposal.

Example: Marjorie owns a 25% interest in a partnership that runs a hair salon and a 10% interest in an S corporation that runs a yoga studio. She has no involvement in the day-to-day operation of either business; therefore, her interest in each business is considered a passive activity. In 2013, the hair salon partnership has an ordinary loss of $40,000, of which $10,000 is allocated to Marjorie because of her 25% ownership. The dance studio business has ordinary income of $75,000, of which $7,500 is allocated to Marjorie because of her 10% ownership. As Marjorie's losses from passive activities for the year exceed her income from passive activities by $2,500 ($10,000 of loss minus $7,500 of income), deduction of the excess loss is disallowed. Marjorie may carry forward the $2,500 excess loss to the next year.

Definition: Ordinary income is income that is subject to regular tax rates, as opposed to capital gain income that is generally subject to more favorable tax rates.

A former passive activity is an activity that was a passive activity in an earlier tax year, but is not a passive activity in the current tax year. A prior year's disallowed loss from the activity can be deducted up to the amount of current year income from the activity.

Passive activity income does not include:

- Portfolio income, such as interest, dividends, annuities, and royalties not derived in the ordinary course of a trade or business, or gain or loss from the disposition of property that produces these types of income or that is held for investment.
- Personal service income. This includes salaries, wages, commissions, self-employment income from trade or business activities in which the taxpayer materially participated, deferred compensation, taxable Social Security and other retirement benefits, and payments from partnerships to partners for personal services.
- Any income from intangible property, such as a patent, copyright, or literary, musical, or artistic composition, if the taxpayer's personal efforts significantly contributed to the creation of the property.
- State, local, and foreign income tax refunds.
- Income from a covenant not to compete.
- Alaska Permanent Fund dividends.
- Cancellation of debt income, if at the time the debt is discharged, the debt is not allocated to passive activities.

Note: Although many of the items listed above seem passive in nature, they are by definition excluded from treatment as passive activities.

Grouping Business Activities

A taxpayer can treat one or more trade or business or rental activities as a single activity if the activities form an appropriate economic unit for measuring gain or loss under the passive activity rules. If two activities are grouped into one larger activity, he needs only to show material participation in the activity as a whole. If the two activities are separate, he must show material participation in each one.

Generally, when activities are grouped into appropriate economic units, they may not be regrouped in a later tax year. However, if any of the activities resulting from a grouping is not an appropriate economic unit and one of the primary purposes of the grouping is to avoid the passive activity rules, the IRS may regroup the activities.

Example: Malcolm owns a bagel shop and a movie theater at a shopping mall in Cincinnati and a bagel shop and a movie theater in Milwaukee. There may be more than one reasonable method for grouping Malcolm's activities, including the following: 1) the movie theaters and the bagel shops into one activity; 2) a separate movie theater activity and a separate bagel shop activity; 3) a Cincinnati activity and a Milwaukee activity; or 4) four separate activities.

Example: Roberta is a partner in Forever Young LLC, which sells skin care products to drug stores. She is also a partner in Verona Trucking. Forever Young LLC and Verona Trucking are under common control. Verona's main business is transporting goods for Forever Young, and it is the only trucking business Roberta is involved in. Roberta groups Forever Young's wholesale activity and Verona's trucking activity as a single activity.

In general, a rental activity cannot be grouped with a trade or business activity. However, they can be grouped together if the activities form an appropriate economic unit and:

- The rental activity is insubstantial in relation to the trade or business activity,
- The trade or business activity is insubstantial in relation to the rental activity, or
- Each owner of the trade or business activity has the same ownership interest in the rental activity, in which case the part of the rental activity that involves the rental of items of property for use in the trade or business activity may be grouped with the trade or business activity.

Example: Miles and Shira are married and file jointly. Miles is the only shareholder of Eco-Clean dry cleaners, an S corporation. Shira is the only shareholder of Fontana Properties, an S corporation that owns a commercial office building, part of which is rented to Eco-Clean. Fontana Properties' rental business and Eco-Clean's dry cleaning business are not insubstantial in relation to each other. Since Miles and Shira file a joint return, they are treated as one taxpayer for purposes of the passive activity rules. The same owner (Miles and Shira) owns both businesses, with the same ownership interest (100% in each). Miles and Shira may conclude that Fontana Properties' rental activity and Eco-Drycleaner's dry cleaning store form an appropriate economic unit and group them as a single business activity.

Rental Income

A business may have income from rental activity, for any amounts received or accrued as payment for the use of property. Rental income may also include advance payments and deposits from renters.

Rental income earned by a sole proprietor, and related expenses, are generally reported on the following forms:

- Schedule C, *Profit or Loss from Business*: Used for professional real estate dealers and by owners of hotels, boarding houses, or apartment buildings who provide services for tenants or guests. The services must be substantial and not simply those normally provided with the rental of rooms for occupancy only, such as maid service.
- Schedule E, *Supplemental Income and Loss (from rental real estate, royalties, partnerships, S corporations, estates, trusts, REMICs,* etc.): Used by taxpayers who are not professional real estate dealers or do not provide substantial services.

Generally, rental income earned by an individual taxpayer is not subject to employment taxes, unless the taxpayer is a professional real estate dealer. A taxpayer qualifies as a real estate dealer if he is primarily engaged in the business of selling real estate to customers.

Rental income reported on Schedule C, including rent received by a real estate dealer from real estate held primarily for sale to customers is subject to self-employment tax. Income reported on Schedule E typically is not subject to SE tax.

Example: Joe owns two residential rental properties. He manages them and collects rents. He also has a full-time job as a restaurant manager. He is not a real estate dealer. Joe must report his rental income and losses on Schedule E. His rental income is not subject to self-employment tax.

Lease cancellation payments received from a tenant are reported as income in the year received. Advance rental payments received under a lease must be recognized in the year received, regardless of which accounting method is used.

However, a security deposit is not considered income upon initial receipt, if the deposit is refundable to the tenant at the end of the lease. If the taxpayer keeps the security deposit because the tenant did not live up to the terms of the lease or because he damaged property, the deposit amount is recognized as income in the year it is forfeited by the tenant.

A taxpayer in the business of renting personal property, such as equipment, vehicles, or formal wear, includes the rental income on Schedule C. Advance payments for renting personal property must be reported in the year received.

Definition: Personal property is not the same as "personal-use" property that a taxpayer uses for personal purposes. In its most general definition, personal property includes any tangible asset other than real estate. The distinguishing factor between personal property and real property is that personal property is movable, while real property, such as land or buildings, generally remains in one location.

Investment Income

A business may earn interest or dividend income from investments or from lending money to others. A common example is when a C corporation owns stock in another corporation.

For most sole proprietors, dividend income is considered nonbusiness income and is reported directly on Form 1040. However, dividends are treated as business income by professional stockbrokers and securities dealers.

Bartering Income

Bartering occurs when a taxpayer exchanges goods or services without exchanging money. An example of bartering is a plumber doing repair work for a dentist in exchange for dental services. The fair market value of goods and services received in a barter exchange must be included in income by each party in the year received. If the parties agree in advance on the fair market value of goods and services exchanged, it may be used, absent conflicting evidence.

Example: Ethan is a self-employed social media marketer. He and Bryce, a house painter, are members of a barter club where members contact each another directly and bargain. In return for Ethan's marketing services, Bryce paints Ethan's office. Ethan must report the exchange as income on Schedule C. Bryce must also include in his income the fair market value of the services Ethan provided.

Definition: The IRS defines **fair market value** (FMV) as the price at which a property would change hands between a buyer and a seller when both have reasonable knowledge of all the necessary facts and neither is being forced to buy or sell.

Income from Canceled Debt

If a business-related debt is canceled or forgiven, other than as a gift or bequest, the business generally includes in income the amount of the cancellation of debt (COD). However, a cash-basis business is not required to realize income from a canceled debt to the extent that the payment of the debt would have led to a business deduction.

Example: Barbells Partnership is a cash-basis business. The company arranges computer repair services on credit but later has trouble paying its debts. The computer repair company forgives the repair bill. The partnership is not required to recognize the canceled debt as income because payment of the repair bill would have been deductible as a business expense anyway.

In the example above, the canceled debt of an accrual-basis business would be considered income, because a deduction for the repair expense already would have been recorded.

If a taxpayer owes a debt to a seller for property he bought and the seller reduces the amount owed, the taxpayer generally does not have income from the reduction. If the taxpayer is bankrupt or insolvent, the amount of the COD may be excluded from taxable income. If the taxpayer is not bankrupt or insolvent, the amount of the reduction is treated as a purchase price adjustment, and the buyer's basis in the property is reduced.[32]

Additional exclusions may apply to the discharge of qualified farm indebtedness and qualified real property business indebtedness. Taxpayers who use these exclusions are required to reduce specified tax attributes, including loss and credit carryforwards and the bases of assets, by corresponding amounts.

[32]An explanation of basis and how it is calculated can be found in Unit 7.

Business-Related Court Awards and Damages

Court awards and settlements that grant compensation for physical injuries or illness are generally excluded from taxation. Most other types of court awards and settlements are taxable income, such as:

- Damages for:
    - Patent or copyright infringement,
    - Breach of contract, or
    - Interference with business operations.
- Compensation for lost profits
- Interest earned on any type of court award
- Punitive damages related to business income or business activity[33]

Items Not Considered Business Income

Just as with individual taxpayers, certain types of business-related income and property transfers are not taxable or reportable. Others may be partially taxable, and in some instances the recognition of income is delayed until a later date. Examples include:

- Issuances of stock, including the sale of Treasury stock
- Most business loans (which create debt, not income)
- State and local taxes that are collected in connection with sales or the provision of services and remitted to state or local governments
- Like-kind exchanges of property
- Gain from an involuntary conversion, if the gain is reinvested properly

[33]Punitive damages may be awarded in addition to compensatory damages for actual monetary losses. Punitive damages are subject to income tax but are not subject to self-employment tax.

Unit 3: Study Questions

1. Which of the following is not passive activity income?

A. Income from a trade or business in which a taxpayer does not materially participate.
B. Interest income.
C. Rental income, if the taxpayer is a real estate professional.
D. Both B and C.

2. When is a business not required to realize income from a canceled debt?

A. Canceled debt is always taxable to a business.
B. A business does not have to recognize canceled debt income to the extent that the payment of the debt would have led to a business deduction.
C. Canceled debt is never taxable income to a business.
D. Canceled debt is taxable income for a sole proprietorship or partnership, but not for a C corporation or an S corporation.

3. The Mickelson Tool Corporation rents large tools and machinery for use in construction projects. The company always charges a refundable security deposit and a nonrefundable cleaning deposit when someone rents a machine. Mickelson Tool received the following amounts in 2013:

- Rental income: $50,000
- Security deposits: $4,050
- Cleaning deposits: $1,500

What amount should be included in the corporation's gross income?

A. $50,000.
B. $51,500.
C. $54,050.
D. $55,550.

4. Which of the following would not be considered income for tax purposes?

A. Interest earned on a court award.
B. Damages received in a lawsuit or as settlement for personal physical injuries.
C. Barter income from consulting services.
D. Legal damages awarded for copyright infringement.

5. Camille, a calendar-year, accrual-based taxpayer, owns a studio that teaches ballroom dancing. On October 1, 2013, she receives payment for a one-year contract for 96 one-hour lessons beginning on that date. She gives eight lessons in 2013 and the rest in 2014. How and when must she recognize this payment as income?

A. All income must be recognized in 2013.
B. All income may be deferred until 2014 since that is when most of the lessons are given.
C. 8/96 of the income must be recognized in 2013 and the rest, 88/96, in 2014.
D. All of the income can be split equally between 2013 and 2014.

6. Assume the same facts as in the previous question, except the payment is for a two-year contract for 96 lessons. Camille gives eight lessons in 2013; 48 lessons in 2014; and 40 lessons in 2015. How and when must she recognize this payment as income?

A. All of the income must be recognized in 2013.
B. 8/96 of the income must be recognized in 2013; 48/96 in 2014; and 40/96 in 2015.
C. 8/96 of the income must be recognized in 2013 and 88/96 in 2014.
D. All of the income can be deferred and split equally between 2014 and 2015.

7. Which of the following statements is not correct about grouping passive activities?

A. If two activities are grouped into one larger activity, the taxpayer will need only to show material participation in the activity as a whole.
B. A taxpayer may group two or more trade or business activities if they comprise an appropriate economic unit.
C. The IRS may challenge the grouping of passive activities.
D. A rental activity cannot be grouped with a trade or business activity.

8. Harley is a real estate professional who owns two duplexes and an office building, all of which he rents to tenants. He works on his rental activity full-time. How should Harley report his rental income?

A. On Schedule E.
B. On Schedule C.
C. On Schedule D.
D. Harley's rental income is not taxable because he is a real estate professional.

9. Losses from passive activities are generally deductible only up to the amount of __________ from passive activities in a given year.

A. Other losses.
B. Debt basis.
C. Capital gains.
D. Income.

10. When are advance rental payments taxable?

A. In the year they are received.
B. In the period in which they are accrued.
C. They are not taxable.
D. They are taxable when the checks are cashed.

11. Sa'id has an ownership stake in several businesses. He does not materially participate in any of them. In 2013, he had the following results from these activities:

- Appliance repair store: $20,000 loss
- Ice cream parlor: $31,000 income
- Cupcake store: $17,500 loss

What is the tax treatment of Sa'id's ownership of these businesses?

A. Taxable income of $31,000 and deductible losses of $37,500 in 2013.
B. Deductible loss of $6,500 in 2013.
C. No taxable income in 2013; carryover of passive activity loss of $6,500 to 2014.
D. Taxable income of $31,000 in 2013; carryover of passive activity loss of $37,500 to 2014.

12. Allen's Exotic Pets, a cash-basis taxpayer, purchases $1,000 worth of legal services on credit in 2013. His business is struggling, and he is unable to pay the bill. The law firm forgives the bill in 2014. What is the correct statement about how Allen's Exotic Pets should handle the canceled debt?

A. The company must recognize the canceled debt income in 2013.
B. The company must recognize the canceled debt income in 2014.
C. The company must recognize half the canceled debt income in 2013 and half in 2014.
D. The company does not have to recognize the canceled debt income because payment of the legal services bill would have been deductible as a business expense.

13. What is personal property?

A. Personal assets of a taxpayer.
B. Real property owned by a business taxpayer.
C. Assets that are moveable and tangible.
D. Real property owned by a nonbusiness taxpayer.

14. Which of the following is business income?

A. Like-kind exchanges of property.
B. Business loans.
C. The sale of Treasury stock.
D. A barter exchange of services between two sole proprietors.

Unit 4: Business Expenses

More Reading:
Publication 535, *Business Expenses*
Publication 538, *Accounting Periods and Methods*
Publication 587, *Business Use of Your Home*
Publication 463, *Travel, Entertainment, Gift, and Car Expenses*

Business expenses are the costs of carrying on a trade or business, and are usually deductible if the business operates to make a profit. However, some costs must be capitalized and depreciated or amortized. Expenses related to employee compensation and fringe benefits are discussed in Unit 5. This unit addresses general concepts and other types of business expenses.

As described in Unit 2, a cash-basis business generally claims deductible business expenses in the period they are paid.

Expenses Under the Accrual Method

Under the accrual method of accounting, a taxpayer generally deducts or capitalizes business expenses when both of the following apply:

- All events have occurred that fix the fact of liability, and the liability can be determined with reasonable accuracy.
- Economic performance has occurred: the property or services are provided or the property is used.

Example: Tessa is an accrual-based, calendar-year taxpayer. She orders office supplies in December 2013 and receives them later in the month. She does not pay the bill for the supplies until January 2014. She can deduct the expense in 2013 because all events have occurred to fix the liability, the amount of the liability can be determined, and economic performance occurred in 2013.

Exception for Recurring Items: Expenses for certain recurring items may be treated as incurred during the tax year even though economic performance has not occurred. In the above example, office supplies may qualify as a recurring item. If so, the taxpayer can deduct them in 2013, even if the supplies are not delivered until 2014 when economic performance occurs. The exception for recurring items applies if all of the following requirements are met:

- The all-events test described above has been met.
- Economic performance occurs by the earlier of the following dates:
  - 8½ months after the close of the year, or
  - The date the taxpayer files a timely return, including extensions, for the year.
- The item is recurring in nature and the taxpayer consistently treats similar items as incurred in the tax year in which the all-events test is met.
- And either:
  - The item is not material, or

- Accruing the item in the year in which the all-events test is met results in a better match against income than accruing the item in the year of economic performance.

A new expense or an expense that is not incurred every year can be treated as recurring if the taxpayer reasonably expects to incur it regularly in the future.

The exception does not apply to workers' compensation or tort liabilities.

Deductible Business Expenses: To be deductible, a business expense must be both *ordinary* and *necessary*. An ordinary expense is one that is common and accepted in the taxpayer's industry. A necessary expense is one that is helpful and appropriate for the particular trade or business. However, an expense does not have to be indispensable to be considered necessary.

Example #1: Louisa is an enrolled agent who sends newsletters to clients with year-end tax-saving tips. The newsletters are a marketing tool for her business and would be considered ordinary and necessary. She can deduct the printing and mailing costs as a business expense.
Example #2: Louisa renovates her home office and spends $8,000 on silk designer curtains for the windows. As she does not meet with clients in her home office, an expenditure of this size would likely not be considered reasonable, and therefore would not be deductible as a business expense.

In addition to being ordinary and necessary, the following rules apply to business expenses:

- Some costs must be capitalized rather than deducted. As described in Unit 2, certain costs that would otherwise be currently deductible are allocated to the cost of producing inventory or holding it for resale. If a cost is included in inventory, it may later be deductible as a component of cost of goods sold. Other costs must be capitalized and either amortized ratably to expense or added to the basis of an asset and recovered when the asset is disposed.
- Personal, family, and living expenses generally cannot be deducted as business expenses.

Business Organizational and Start-up Costs

The costs associated with starting a business generally must be treated as capital expenditures. However, businesses are allowed to deduct limited amounts of start-up and organizational costs.

Organizational Costs: The costs of organizing a corporation or partnership are deductible up to $5,000 in 2013. However, if the expenses incurred exceed $50,000, there is a dollar-for-dollar reduction until the current deduction is eliminated. Organizational costs that are not currently deductible may be amortized ratably over 180 months (15 years) on Form 4562, *Depreciation and Amortization*. The amortization period starts with the month the taxpayer begins operating the business.

To qualify as an organizational cost, an expense must be:

- For the creation of the business
- Chargeable to a capital account
- For a partnership, incurred by the due date of the tax return (excluding extensions) for the year business begins

- For a corporation, incurred before the end of the first tax year in which the corporation is in business

Examples of qualifying organizational costs include:

- The cost of temporary directors
- The cost of organizational meetings
- Filing fees for partnerships
- State incorporation fees for corporations
- Legal and accounting fees for setting up the business

Start-up Costs: Business start-up costs are the expenses incurred before a business actually begins operations, and include any amounts paid or incurred for:

- Creating an active trade or business; or
- Investigating the creation or acquisition of an active trade or business.

Start-up costs may include:

- An analysis or survey of potential markets
- Advertisements for the opening of the business
- Salaries and wages for employees who are being trained and their instructors
- Travel and other necessary costs for securing prospective distributors, suppliers, or customers
- Salaries and fees for executives and consultants, or for similar professional services

Example: Moonlight Corporation received its corporate charter on September 12, 2013. The company paid $15,500 for Internet and television advertising; $2,000 for training of employees; and $4,000 in consultant fees, all incurred before opening for business. Moonlight opens for business on January 8, 2014. The company can elect to deduct $5,000 as a start-up cost in the 2013 tax year. It can then amortize the remaining $16,500 beginning in January 2014.

Costs incurred in an attempt to purchase a specific business are capital costs that cannot be amortized.

Example: On May 3, 2013 Jackson hires an accounting firm and a law firm to help with the potential purchase of Hi-Oktane Inc., a company that makes energy drinks. The firms investigate the beverage industry and analyze the company's financial projections. In August, the law firm submits a letter of intent to purchase Hi-Oktane. The law and accounting firms continue to provide Jackson services, including a review of Hi-Oktane's books and records and the preparation of a purchase agreement. On November 2, 2013, Jackson signs a purchase agreement with Hi-Oktane. He may amortize all amounts paid or incurred to investigate the business before November 2. Amounts paid on or after that date relate to the attempt to purchase the business and therefore must be capitalized.

Start-up costs do not include deductible interest, taxes, or research and experimental costs.

As with organizational expenses, a business may deduct up to $5,000 of start-up expenses in the year they are incurred. If expenses exceed $50,000, there is a dollar-for-dollar reduction until the deduction is eliminated. Any remaining start-up expenses must be amortized ratably over 180 months (15 years) on Form 4562.

Example: Bronco Corporation has start-up expenses of $51,000 in 2013. Bronco is $1,000 over the $50,000 threshold so it must reduce its deduction for start-up expenses by the amount that it is over the threshold. Bronco can deduct $4,000 of its start-up expenses ($5,000 allowable deduction minus the excess $1,000). The remaining amount of start-up expenses, $47,000 ($51,000 - $4,000 allowable deduction) must be amortized over 180 months.

Example: Clean Water Inc. opened for business on November 1, 2013. Prior to opening, the company incurred $21,200 in start-up expenses for advertising and manager training. Since Clean Water had less than $50,000 of start-up costs, the company is allowed to deduct the full $5,000 on its 2013 tax return, and may also claim $180 of amortization [($21,200 - $5,000)/180 = $90 per month × 2 (two months, November and December)].

If a taxpayer completely disposes of a business before the end of the amortization period, he can deduct the remaining unamortized start-up costs. However, the business can deduct these deferred start-up costs only to the extent they qualify as a loss.

If a business never materializes after claiming start-up or organizational costs, the costs are treated differently depending on the entity type. In the case of a corporation, all investigatory costs are deductible as a business loss. In the case of an individual, the costs incurred before making a decision to acquire a business are considered personal costs and are generally not deductible.

Taxes

Businesses generally may deduct taxes in the year paid, regardless of which method of accounting the business uses. Under the accrual method, a business can deduct a tax before it pays it, if it meets the exception for recurring items discussed earlier in this unit. Further, an accrual-basis taxpayer may ratably accrue real estate taxes.

Real Estate Taxes: In order for real estate taxes to be deductible, the taxing authority must calculate the tax based on the assessed value of the real estate. If a property is sold, the deductible portion of the real estate taxes must be allocated between the buyer and the seller according to the number of days in the property tax year that each owned the property. The seller is treated as paying the taxes up to but not including the date of sale. The buyer is treated as paying the taxes beginning with the date of sale.

Businesses cannot deduct taxes charged for local benefits and improvements that tend to increase the value of property. These include assessments for streets, sidewalks, water mains, sewer lines, and public parking facilities. A business must instead increase the basis of its property by the amount of the assessment.

However, a business may deduct taxes for local benefits such as maintenance, repairs, or interest charges related to capital improvements.

Example: Lawrence owns a business office on Grand Street. In 2013, the city charges an assessment of $4,000 to each business on Grand Street to improve the sidewalks. Lawrence cannot deduct this assessment as a current business expense. Instead, he must increase the basis of his property by the amount of the assessment.

Example: Waterfront City converts a downtown area into an enclosed pedestrian mall. The city assesses the full cost of construction, financed with 10-year bonds, against the affected properties. The city pays the principal and interest with the annual payments made by the property owners. The assessments for construction costs are not deductible as taxes or as business expenses but are depreciable capital expenses. The part of each payment used to pay the interest on the bonds is deductible as taxes.

Personal Property Taxes: Taxes imposed by a state or local government on personal property used in a taxpayer's trade or business are deductible.

Income Taxes: Federal income taxes are never deductible. However, corporations and partnerships can deduct state and local income and franchise taxes. A self-employed individual who reports income on Schedule C can deduct state and local income taxes as an itemized deduction on Schedule A.

Example: Reiner Company is a calendar-year C corporation incorporated in Utah. Utah imposes a 5% state tax on Reiner's corporate earnings. In 2013, Reiner pays $12,000 in state income tax to Utah. This state tax would be deductible as a business expense on the corporation's federal tax return.

Sales Taxes: Sales taxes collected by a business in connection with the sale of goods or services to its customers are remitted to the taxing authorities, and are excluded from the business's gross receipts and its deductible expenses. When a business pays sales tax in connection with the purchase of goods or services, the tax is considered a component of the cost of the item purchased. Thus, if the item is depreciable property, the sales tax is added to its depreciable basis. If the item is merchandise for resale or to be used in the production of inventory, the tax is capitalized as a component of inventory. If the tax is related to a currently deductible business expense, it is likewise considered part of that expense.

Excise Taxes: Excise taxes that are ordinary and necessary expenses of carrying on a trade or business are deductible. Excise taxes are taxes paid when purchases are made on a specific item, such as gasoline, or activity, such as highway usage by trucks. When paid in connection with the purchase of a specific item an excise tax is considered part of the cost of that item. Therefore, it may be deductible currently or as the item is used, or be subject to capitalization, such as when the item is used in manufacturing inventory. Under the Affordable Care Act, indoor tanning salons are subject to a 10% excise tax, which is a deductible business expense.

Business Bad Debts

Most business bad debts are a result of credit sales of goods or services to customers for which payment has not been received. These are recorded in a business's books as either accounts receivable or notes receivable. If, after a reasonable period of time, a business has tried to collect the amount due but is unable to do so, the uncollectible part becomes a business bad debt.

A debt becomes uncollectible or worthless when there is no longer any chance the amount owed will be paid. A business does not have to wait for the debt to be due or to obtain a court judgment to show the debt is uncollectible.

A business bad debt is a loss from the worthlessness of a debt that was either:

- Created or acquired in a taxpayer's trade or business, or
- Closely related to the trade or business when it became partly or totally worthless.

To be considered closely related to a taxpayer's trade or business, the primary motive for incurring the debt must be business related.

A taxpayer may claim a business bad debt deduction only if the amount owed was previously included in his gross income. Thus, unlike an accrual-basis taxpayer, a cash-basis business typically would not record accounts receivable for credit sales, and would be less likely to have deductible business bad debts.

If a business loans money to a client, supplier, employee, or distributor for a business reason and the balance due later becomes worthless, the business may deduct the balance as a bad debt. However, the loan must have a genuine business purpose in order for this treatment to qualify.

Example: Carol is an accrual-based taxpayer who owns an eyeglass manufacturing company. One of her salesmen, Dawson, loses all his samples and asks Carol for a loan to replace them. Carol loans Dawson $3,000 to replace his eyeglass samples and sample bags. Dawson later quits his job without repaying the debt. Carol has a business-related bad debt that she may deduct as a business expense.

If a taxpayer receives property in partial settlement of a debt, the debt should be reduced by the property's FMV, which becomes the taxpayer's basis in the property. The remaining unpaid balance of the debt can be deducted as a bad debt when and if it becomes worthless.

An entity may later recover a debt that was previously written off as worthless. If a business recovers a bad debt that was deducted in a prior year, the recovered portion must be included as income in the current year tax return. There is no need to amend the prior year tax return on which the bad debt deduction was claimed.

Insurance Expenses

The following types of business-related insurance premiums are deductible:

- Property and casualty insurance (that covers fire, storm, theft, accident, or similar losses)
- Business interruption insurance (that reimburses a business if it is temporarily shut down due to a fire or similar disaster)

- Credit insurance that covers losses from business bad debts
- Liability insurance
- Malpractice insurance
- Contributions to a state unemployment insurance fund (deductible as taxes)
- Vehicle insurance that covers vehicles used in a business (not deductible if a business uses the standard mileage rate to figure vehicle expenses)
- Group-term life insurance for employees
- Group accident, health, long-term care, and workers' compensation insurance for employees

Note: If a partnership pays accident, health, or workers' compensation insurance premiums for its partners, it generally can deduct them as guaranteed payments to the partners. If an S corporation pays accident, health, or workers' compensation insurance premiums for its more-than-2% shareholder-employees, it generally can deduct them and must also include them in the shareholders' wages subject to federal income tax withholding.

As described in Unit 2, if a cash-basis business pays insurance premiums in advance, it may rely upon a 12-month rule and deduct amounts paid that do not extend beyond the earlier of the following: (1) 12 months after the benefit begins, or (2) the end of the tax year after the tax year in which payment is made.

Self-Employed Health Insurance Deduction

A self-employed individual may be able to deduct premiums paid for medical and dental insurance and qualified long-term care insurance for himself, his spouse, and his dependents.

To qualify, a taxpayer must have a net profit reported on his Schedule C (Form 1040), Schedule C-EZ, or Schedule F; be a partner with net earnings from self-employment reported on Schedule K-1; or be a more-than-2% shareholder in an S corporation who had premiums paid or reimbursed by the corporation and reported to him as wages on Form W-2. He cannot take the deduction for any month he was eligible to participate in any employer-subsidized health plan (including one that his spouse was eligible for), even if he or his spouse did not actually participate in the plan.

Interest Expense

A business can deduct interest paid or accrued during the tax year on debts related to a trade or business for which it is legally liable. It does not matter what type of property secures the loan.

A business deducts business-related interest as follows:

- **Cash Method:** A business may deduct interest paid during the tax year. It cannot deduct a promissory note given in payment of interest because it is a promise to pay and not an actual payment.
- **Accrual Method:** A business may deduct interest that has accrued during the tax year.

A taxpayer cannot accelerate a tax deduction by paying interest in advance of when it is due. If a business uses the accrual method, it cannot deduct interest owed to a related person who uses the cash method until payment is made and the interest is includable in the gross income of that person.

If the proceeds of a loan are used for more than one purpose, the related interest must be allocated based upon the use of the proceeds, among the following:

- Personal interest
- Investment interest
- Portfolio interest
- Interest related to a trade or business

Interest charged on income tax assessed on an individual's income tax returns is not a business deduction, even if the tax is related to income from a trade or business. This interest should be treated as a business deduction only in figuring a net operating loss deduction. Penalties on underpaid deficiencies and underpaid estimated tax are not interest and are not deductible.

Rent Expense

A business may deduct expenses for renting property, including real estate, machinery, and other items used to conduct business. However, the cost of acquiring a lease is not considered rent and must be amortized over the term of the lease.

Generally, rent paid in a trade or business is deductible in the year paid or accrued. However, if a taxpayer pays rent in advance, he can deduct only the amount that applies to his use of the rented property during the tax year. The rest of the payment can be deducted only over the period to which it applies.

If a taxpayer has both business and personal use of rented property, he may only deduct the amount actually used for business. To compute the business percentage, the taxpayer must compare the portion of the property used for business to the entire property. The resulting percentage is used to figure the business portion of the rent expense.

Example: Ainsley rents a business office to use both as a personal studio for painting and as a site to run her tutoring business. Her total rental payments for the year are $11,000. The office is 1,000 square feet; she uses 800 square feet for the tutoring business and the remaining 200 square feet for her art studio. Therefore, she uses the office 80% for her business and 20% for personal purposes. The deductible portion of the rent expense is $8,800 (80% × $11,000).

Home Office Deduction

A self-employed taxpayer may be able to deduct certain expenses related to part of his home if the space is used regularly and exclusively for business and it is:

- The taxpayer's principal place of business, and/or
- The place used to meet with patients, clients, or customers in the normal course of business; or
- A separate structure not attached to the home that is used in connection with the business.

A taxpayer can use any reasonable method to calculate the percentage of the home that is used for business. Typically, the square footage of the home used for business is divided by the home's total square footage. Because of the exclusive use rule, a taxpayer is not allowed to deduct business expenses for any part of the home that is used for both personal and business purposes.

A self-employed taxpayer must complete Form 8829, *Expenses for Business Use of Your Home,* and then transfer the total to his Schedule C (Form 1040).

Simplified Home Office Deduction: Under a new option introduced for 2013, a taxpayer may compute his home office deduction using a simplified calculation formula: a deduction of $5 per square foot is allowed for the space in the home that is used for business, up to a maximum allowable square footage of 300 square feet (for a maximum deduction of $1,500.)

Example: Rick is a self-employed insurance broker with a home office he uses exclusively for business. The office measures 15 × 15, or 225 square feet. Rick deducts $1,125 ($5 × 225) using the simplified option.

Note: More than 3.4 million taxpayers claim the home office deduction each year. The IRS estimates the simplified option will save taxpayers 1.6 million hours a year in paperwork and recordkeeping requirements.

Under this option, a taxpayer can claim the full amount of allowable mortgage interest, real estate taxes, and casualty losses on his home as itemized deductions on Schedule A. These deductions do not need to be allocated between personal and business use, as is required under the regular method. The simplified option does not include a deduction for depreciation.

Each year, a taxpayer may use either the simplified method or the regular method to calculate the home office deduction. If he chooses the regular method after having used the simplified method in an earlier year, depreciation is calculated using an optional depreciation table for the property.

Employee Use: The home office deduction is also available for an employee who uses part of his home for business. However, there are two additional tests that must be met:

- The business use must be for the convenience of the employer, and
- The employee must not rent any part of his home to his employer and use the rental portion to perform services as an employee for that employer.

Business Travel, Meals, and Entertainment

To be deductible for tax purposes, business expenses for travel, meals, and entertainment must be incurred while carrying on a genuine business activity. Generally, the taxpayer must be able to prove that entertainment expenses, including meals, are directly related to the conduct of business. Adequate records must be retained to support these expenses, including receipts, bills, or canceled checks. An exception is made for expenses other than lodging that cost less than $75.

Travel costs with a business purpose are generally 100% deductible. However, if the travel includes an element of personal travel, the personal portion of the expense may not be deductible. In some instances, the personal portion may be incremental costs related to a spouse's travel. In other cases, a business must determine the nondeductible portion of an expense by multiplying it by a fraction. The numerator of the fraction is the number of personal days during the travel period and the denominator is the total number of days spent traveling.

Example: Paul flies to New Orleans on business and takes his wife with him so she can vacation there. Paul pays $190 for each airline ticket and $200 for a double hotel room. The cost of a single hotel room is $150. Paul can deduct the cost of his plane ticket and $150 for the hotel room. His wife's expenses are not deductible as a business expense.

Only 50% of the cost is deductible for business meals or entertainment incurred while:

- Traveling away from home (whether eating alone or with others) on business
- Entertaining customers at a restaurant or other location
- Attending a business convention or reception, business meeting, or business luncheon
- Obtaining deductible educational expenses, such as meals during a continuing education seminar

Taxpayers are considered "traveling away from home" if their duties require them to be away from home substantially longer than an ordinary day's work and they need to sleep or rest to meet the demands of their work.

The following related expenses are also subject to the 50% limit:

- Taxes and tips on a business meal or entertainment activity
- Cost of a room in which the business holds a dinner or cocktail party

The cost of transportation to a business meal or a business-related entertainment activity is not subject to the 50% limit.

Example: Karen is a business owner who takes a client to lunch. The total restaurant bill is $88. She also pays cab fare of $10 to get to the restaurant. Karen's deductible expense is $54:

Deductible meal expense	$88 × 50% = $44
Deductible travel expense	$10
Total deductible expense	**$54**

Exceptions to the 50% Limit: The following meals are 100% deductible by the employer:

- Meals that are included in employees' wages as taxable compensation
- Meals that qualify as a de minimis fringe benefit, such as occasional coffee and doughnuts
- Meals that are made available to the general public as part of a promotional activity, such as a real estate broker who provides dinner to potential investors at a sales presentation
- Meals furnished to employees when the employer operates a restaurant or catering service
- Meals furnished to employees as part of a teambuilding activity
- Meals that are required by federal law to be furnished to crew members of certain commercial vessels
- Meals furnished on an oil or gas platform or drilling rig located offshore or in Alaska

Special Department of Transportation Rules: There is also an exception for certain individuals subject to the U.S. Department of Transportation (DOT) "hours of service" limits who are traveling away from their tax home. A business is allowed to deduct 80% of employees' meal costs when DOT hours of service limits apply to the following:

- Certain air transportation workers such as pilots, crew, and mechanics regulated by the Federal Aviation Administration
- Interstate truck operators and bus drivers regulated by the Department of Transportation
- Certain railroad employees such as engineers and conductors regulated by the Federal Railroad Administration
- Certain merchant mariners regulated by the Coast Guard

Per Diem Rates for Business Travel

To ease recordkeeping requirements, a business may use a federal per diem rate as an alternative to keeping track of employees' actual expenses during business travel away from home.

Per diem is a daily allowance paid by a business to its employees for lodging, meals, and incidental expenses incurred when traveling. The allowance is in lieu of paying actual travel expenses. There is a per diem rate for combined lodging and meal costs, and a per diem rate for meal costs alone. An employer may use either per diem method for reimbursing employee travel expenses. A self-employed person can only use a per diem rate for meal costs. Per diem payments not in excess of the federal rate are not included in an employee's taxable wages, if an employee submits an expense report to the employer.

The applicable per diem rates vary based on whether the travel is domestic and foreign, and also by location. For example, the per diem rate in large cities like Los Angeles and New York is higher than for smaller cities. The IRS publishes the per diem rates every year in Publication 1542, *Per Diem Rates.*

Deductible Entertainment Expenses

A business is allowed to deduct 50% of business-related entertainment expenses that are incurred for entertaining a client, customer, or employee, as long as either the directly-related test or the associated test described below is met. It is not necessary to prove that the entertainment actually resulted in business income or another business benefit.

The IRS looks at whether there is a "clear business setting" associated with the entertainment and whether there are "substantial distractions" at the location that prevent business from being conducted. If a taxpayer takes a client to a special event, he may not deduct more than 50% of the face value of the ticket, regardless of the amount paid.

Example: Following a day of business meetings, Erik wants to take his two best clients to a basketball game, but the tickets are sold out. So Erik pays a scalper $390 for three tickets. The face value of each ticket is $52. Erik may only use the face value of the tickets as a basis for his deduction, and he also must apply the 50% limit. Therefore, his deductible entertainment expense is $78, figured as follows:

Cost of three event tickets (face value of $52 × 3):	$156
Apply the 50% limit ($156 × 50%):	$78

Transportation Expenses: Ordinarily, expenses related to use of a vehicle for business can be deducted as transportation expenses. To claim a deduction for business use of a car or truck, business-related costs must have been incurred for one or more of the following:

- Traveling from one work location to another within the taxpayer's tax home area. (Generally, the tax home is the entire city or general area where the taxpayer's main place of business is located, regardless of where he actually lives.)[34]
- Visiting customers.
- Attending a business meeting away from the regular workplace.
- Traveling from home to a temporary workplace. A temporary workplace can be either within or outside the taxpayer's tax home area.

Self-employed individuals, including partners in a partnership, may choose to use either the standard mileage rate or actual car expenses in order to figure the deduction for vehicle expenses. C corporations generally cannot use the standard mileage rate. However, businesses, including C corporations, may reimburse an employee under an accountable plan for business-related use of his car using the standard mileage rate. Any amounts reimbursed in excess of the standard mileage rate are reportable on the employee's Form W-2 as wages.

Whether using the standard mileage rate or claiming actual expenses, a taxpayer must keep records that identify the vehicle and provide evidence of ownership or a lease. Further, he should maintain a daily log showing miles traveled, destination, and business purpose to support the total business miles claimed or the business use percentage to be applied to allocate actual expenses.

Actual vehicle expenses include the costs of the following items:

- Depreciation
- Lease payments
- Registration
- Garage rent
- Repairs and maintenance
- Gas, oil, and tires
- Insurance, parking fees, and tolls

If business use of the vehicle is less than 100%, expenses must be allocated between business and personal use, and only the business use portion is deductible.

Example: Brandon uses a delivery van in his landscaping business. He has no other car, so the van is used for his personal transportation on the weekends. Brandon chooses to deduct actual costs, rather than using the standard mileage rate. Based on his records, Brandon's total vehicle expenses in 2013 are $6,252, which includes the cost of diesel fuel, oil changes, tire replacement, and repairs. Brandon uses the vehicle 75% for business, so his allowable auto expense deduction using the actual expense method is $4,689 ($6,252 × 75%).

[34] Costs related to travel between an individual's home and regular place of work are commuting expenses and not deductible as business expenses.

For 2013, the standard mileage rate for business use of a vehicle is 56.5 cents per mile. A taxpayer who elects to use the standard rate may not deduct actual expenses of operating a vehicle, such as gas, oil, and insurance. However, business-related parking fees and tolls may be deducted in addition to the standard mileage rate.

A business is prohibited from using the standard mileage rate if it:

- Operates five or more cars at the same time
- Claimed a depreciation deduction using any method other than straight-line, including MACRS
- Claimed a section 179 deduction on the car
- Claimed the special depreciation allowance on the car
- Claimed actual car expenses for a car that was leased

Recordkeeping for Travel, Entertainment, & Gift Expenses				
Expense	**Amount**	**Date**	**Description**	**Business Purpose**
Travel	Record of each expense for travel, lodging, and meals.	Dates for each trip and number of days spent on business.	Destination (name of city, town, etc.)	Business purpose for the expense.
Entertainment	Cost of each separate expense.	Date of entertainment.	Location of place of entertainment.	Business purpose for the expense.
Gifts	Cost of the gift.	Date of the gift.	Description of the gift.	Business relationship.
Transportation	Cost of each separate expense.	Date of the expense.	The business destination.	Business purpose for the expense.

Business Gifts

A business may deduct business-related gifts to clients and customers. The deductible amount is limited to $25 for amounts given to any person during the year. If a taxpayer and a spouse both give gifts, they are treated as one taxpayer for this limit, even if they have separate businesses. A gift to the spouse of a business customer or client is generally considered an indirect gift to the customer or client.

The $25 limit for business gifts does not include incidental costs such as packaging, insurance, and mailing costs, or the cost of engraving jewelry, which may be deducted separately. Related costs are considered incidental only if they do not add substantial value to a gift.

Example: Hawaii Fruit Corporation gives a large fruit and nut basket to its best customer, Dominic's Produce Company. The fruit basket costs $57, and the shipping and mailing of the basket costs $17. Hawaii Fruit Corporation can deduct $25 for the basket and $17 for the cost of mailing, for a total deduction of $42.

Example: Miguel sells tools to Hammer's Hardware Store. He gives three candy boxes to each of the store's owners to thank them for their patronage. Miguel pays $80 for each package, or $240 total. He can deduct $75 ($25 limit × 3) for the packages.

Exceptions to the Gift Limit

The following items are considered promotional and not subject to the $25 gift limit:

- An item with the business name clearly imprinted on it that costs $4 or less (examples include imprinted pens, desk sets, and plastic bags)
- Signs, display racks, or other promotional materials to be used on the business premises of the recipient

A business may also deduct gifts to employees. Noncash gifts of nominal value that are distributed to employees to promote goodwill may be excluded from taxable compensation. Gifts of greater value and of cash or cash-equivalent items such as gift cards are considered compensation.

Example: Roggan Corporation gives each of its 75 employees a $25 turkey during the holidays. The company may deduct the cost of the turkeys ($1,875 = $25 × 75). The gift is not taxable to the employee, and the fair market value of the gift is not included in the employee's wages.

Charitable Contributions

Among business entities, only C corporations are permitted to deduct charitable contributions on their income tax returns. The deduction is limited to 10% of taxable income, and is explained further in Unit 13, *Corporate Transactions.*

Self-employed taxpayers may not deduct charitable contributions as business expenses, but may claim deductions on Schedule A if they itemize deductions. Contributions made by partnerships and S corporations are reported on their respective returns as separately stated items, and may be deductible by their partners and shareholders.

Miscellaneous Business Expenses

Additional expenses may be deductible by a business, including the following:

- Advertising
- Credit card convenience fees
- Certain franchise or trademark fees
- Education and training for employees
- Internet-related expenses, such as domain registration fees
- Interview expense allowances for job candidates

- Outplacement services provided to employees
- Legal and accounting fees directly related to operating the business
- Tax preparation fees for business returns
- License and regulatory fees paid annually to state or local governments
- Penalties paid for late performance or nonperformance of a contract
- Repairs to business property, including the cost of labor and supplies
- Subscriptions and memberships to trade magazines and professional organizations
- Supplies and materials used during year
- Utilities, including heat, lights, power, telephone service, and water and sewage

Deducted or Capitalized Costs

There are certain costs that businesses may choose to either deduct currently or capitalize as an addition to the basis of a related asset. There are specific rules about the circumstances in which each type of item may be deducted, or if capitalized, how its cost may be recovered through depreciation or amortization. The following are examples of costs that are generally capital in nature, but which a business may elect to deduct currently:

- Research and experimental costs
- Certain intangible drilling costs
- Certain domestic exploration and development costs for mines or other natural deposits (other than oil or gas wells)
- Circulation costs for publishers of newspapers and magazines
- Certain environmental cleanup costs
- Qualified cleanup or repair expenses in federally-declared disaster areas
- Reforestation costs up to $10,000
- Film and television production costs, for productions that begin by 2013

Nondeductible Expenses

The following expenses are not allowed as business deductions:

- Political contributions, including indirect contributions such as advertising in a convention program of a political party
- Lobbying expenses
- Dues for country clubs, golf and athletic clubs, and hotel and airline clubs, even if the club is used for business activity
- Penalties and fines paid to any governmental agency for breaking the law, such as parking tickets or fines for violating local zoning codes
- Legal and professional fees for work of a personal nature

Unit 4: Study Questions

1. Tom operates a computer service/repair business as a sole proprietorship. He drives a sedan when he visits clients, and each of his four technicians drives a van to make their repair visits. Which of the following methods may Tom use to claim deductions for the cost of these vehicles?

A. He can use the standard mileage rate for the sedan, but must use actual expenses for the vans.
B. He must use actual expenses for all of the vehicles.
C. He must use the standard mileage rate for the sedan, but can use actual expenses for the vans.
D. He can choose to use either method.

2. Alexa is a self-employed accountant who reports income and loss on Schedule C. She goes to a continuing education seminar out-of-state and incurs the following expenses:

- Seminar: $400
- Train ticket: $35
- Restaurant meal expense: $26
- Taxi fare to the restaurant: $10

A. $400.
B. $435.
C. $458.
D. $465.

3. In 2013, Helton Partnership, a cash-basis partnership, borrowed $50,000 to purchase machinery. Interest of $2,500 on the loan was due in December 2013. Rather than pay the interest, the partnership refinanced the loan and the interest due into a new loan of $53,800 on December 31, 2013: the original loan amount plus the interest due and an additional $1,300 in loan origination fees. The first payment on the new loan was due January 29, 2014. How much interest is deductible in 2013?

A. $0.
B. $2,500.
C. $2,800.
D. $3,800.

4. Norman is an interstate truck driver subject to the Department of Transportation rules for hours of service. During 2013, he incurs $3,064 in meal expenses while on the job. What is his deductible expense for business meals?

A. $1,532.
B. $2,298.
C. $2,451.
D. $3,064.

5. Kimberly is a sole proprietor and files a Schedule C. How should she report the $2,000 in charitable contributions she made on behalf of her business in 2013?

A. The contributions may be deducted on Schedule A as an itemized deduction.
B. The contributions may be deducted on Schedule C as a business deduction.
C. The contributions may not be deducted.
D. Up to 10% of the taxpayer's charitable contributions may be deducted on Schedule C. The remaining amount must be carried over to the next taxable year.

6. Which of the following is not required in order to meet the directly-related test for entertainment expenses to be deductible?

A. Business was engaged in during the entertainment event.
B. The main purpose of the entertainment was the conduct of business.
C. There was more than just the general expectation of business benefit.
D. The entertainment resulted in profit for the business.

7. Delia, a self-employed real estate agent, traveled to a business convention by train and incurred the following expenses:

- Train ticket: $100
- Meals: $80
- Hotel room: $90
- Computer game: $50

How much is deductible as a current business expense?

A. $190.
B. $230.
C. $280.
D. $320.

8. Marion operates a shoe repair shop in a building she owns. In 2013, she had the following income and expenses:

- Repairs to shop floor: $1,000
- Property tax on business assets: $2,000
- Assessment for sidewalks: $5,800
- Utilities for her store: $1,800

What is the tax treatment of the above expenditures?

A. Deduct repairs, property tax, and utilities as business expenses. The assessment must be added to the basis of the property and depreciated.
B. All of the above expenses are deductible.
C. The property tax must be deducted on Schedule A, and the rest of the expenses may be deducted as business expenses on Schedule C.
D. Only the utilities and repairs may be deducted.

9. Mountain Suppliers made a business loan to Sugarhill Corporation, a supplier, in the amount of $10,000. After paying $2,000, Sugarhill Corporation defaults, and the debt becomes worthless. How much may Mountain Suppliers deduct as a business bad debt?

A. $0.
B. $2,000.
C. $8,000.
D. $10,000.

10. Brady owns Super Sweets Company. He gives the following business gifts to one of his best customers:

- Glass display for Super Sweets: $500
- Coffee and tea gift basket: $50
- 20 pens imprinted with the Super Sweets name and logo: $35
- Postage for the gift basket: $20

How much can Brady deduct on his tax return?

A. $25.
B. $525.
C. $580.
D. $605.

11. Bob owns Jackpot Pawn Shop. He makes a business loan to a client in the amount of $5,000. Bob also loans his brother $1,000 so he can buy a car. His brother, Keith, used to work sporadically at the shop as an employee. Both of the loans are now uncollectible. How much can Bob deduct as a business bad debt expense?

A. $1,000.
B. $4,000.
C. $5,000.
D. $6,000.

12. Luxe Chocolate Corporation is a cash-basis, calendar-year business. On October 1, 2013, Luxe Chocolate pays $3,600 for a business insurance policy covering three years. The policy coverage begins October 1, 2013 and ends September 30, 2016. How does Luxe Chocolate treat the expense for its insurance policy?

A. The entire $3,600 may be deducted in 2013.
B. 2013 deduction $1,200; 2014 deduction $1,200; 2015 deduction $1,200.
C. 2014: deduction $1,500; 2015 deduction $1,200; 2016 deduction $900.
D. 2013: deduction $300; 2014 deduction $1,200; 2015 deduction $1,200; 2016 deduction $900.

13. Lily owns a dress shop. In 2010, she correctly deducted a $10,000 business bad debt after a fabric supplier defaulted on a loan. In 2013, the fabric supplier wishes to do business with Lily again and repays $9,000 of the loan. How must Lily report this payment?

A. She must amend her 2010 tax return to correct the previously reported bad debt deduction.
B. She must reflect this recovery of $9,000 as income in 2013.
C. She may deduct a loss of $1,000 on her 2013 tax return.
D. She is not obligated to report the $9,000 loan repayment.

14. Mike borrowed $100,000 to purchase a machine for his business. The machine cost $90,000. The rest of the money went into Mike's business account, and he purchased a jet ski with the money later in the year. However, the entire loan was secured by his business assets. Which of these statements is true?

A. Mike cannot purchase personal items with a business loan; therefore, none of the interest is deductible.
B. All of the interest is deductible, because it is secured by his business assets.
C. Only the amount of interest allocable to purchase of the business machine is deductible.
D. None of the answers is correct.

15. Maddie rents a small storage unit for her business on February 1, 2013. She is given a discount if she pays the full amount of the lease upfront, which is $1,620 for a three-year lease. What is the amount of Maddie's 2013 deductible expense for leasing the storage unit?

A. $495.
B. $540.
C. $560.
D. $1,620.

16. Garrett operates his printing business out of rented office space. He uses a truck to deliver completed jobs to customers. Which of the following statements is not correct?

A. Garrett can deduct the cost of round-trip transportation between customers and his print shop.
B. Garrett can deduct traveling costs between his home and the print shop.
C. Garrett can deduct the cost of mileage to deliver completed jobs to the post office for mailing.
D. Garrett can deduct the costs to travel to his customers who are disabled and cannot come to his shop.

17. The Castellano Partnership paid the following penalties in 2013. Which are deductible?

A. A penalty paid to the county for violating construction regulations.
B. A penalty imposed by the IRS for late filing of a Form 1065 partnership return.
C. A penalty paid to the city for violating its sign ordinance.
D. A penalty for late performance of a contract.

18. Which of the following costs qualify as business start-up costs?

A. State and local taxes.
B. Research and experimental costs.
C. A survey of potential markets.
D. Both B and C.

19. Only-a-Dollar is a retail store in Dallas. It pays a combined 8.25% sales tax to local and state taxing authorities when a customer purchases its merchandise. How should Only-a-Dollar treat this sales tax expense?

A. Include the amount in its gross receipts and its deductible expenses.
B. Add the amount to the depreciable basis of property of the items sold.
C. Capitalize the cost as a component of inventory of the items sold.
D. Exclude from its gross receipts and deductible expenses the sales taxes it collects and remits them to local and state taxing authorities.

20. Affordable Pool Supplies is an accrual-based taxpayer with a September 30 fiscal year-end, and gross receipts of $4 million in 2013. The company places a $5,000 order for chemical sanitizers on September 20, 2013 and receives the chemicals on September 29. Affordable Pool Supplies pays the bill for the chemicals on October 26, 2013. When should the company deduct the expense for the chemicals?

A. In its year ended September 30, 2013.
B. In its fiscal year ended September 30, 2014.
C. It may choose to deduct the expense in the year ended September 30, 2013 or September 30, 2014.
D. The cost of supplies is not a deductible business expense.

Unit 5: Employee Compensation & Fringe Benefits

More Reading:
Publication 535, *Business Expenses*
Publication 15-A, *Employer's Tax Guide*
Publication 15-B, *Employer's Tax Guide to Fringe Benefits*

Employee Compensation

An employer can deduct the compensation it provides its employees if all of the following tests are met:

- The payments must be ordinary and necessary expenses directly related to the trade or business.
- The amounts must be reasonable. Reasonable pay is the amount that like businesses would normally pay for the same or similar services. If the IRS determines pay is excessive, it can disallow deduction of the excess amount.
- There must be proof that services were actually performed (unless the compensation qualifies as supplemental wages, such as maternity leave, sick pay, or vacation pay).
- The expenses must have been paid or incurred during the tax year.

Supplemental wages refers to compensation paid in addition to an employee's regular salary or wages. In addition to the items mentioned above, supplemental wages may include the following:

- Bonuses
- Commissions
- Overtime pay
- Severance pay
- Taxable awards
- Prizes
- Back pay
- Retroactive pay increases
- Payments for nondeductible moving expenses

Supplemental wages are taxable to the employee just like regular wages and deductible as a wage expense by the employer.

Transfers of property to an employee can also be considered compensation. The fair market value of the property on the date of transfer is deductible by the business and taxable to the employee. The business would recognize a gain or loss on the transfer equal to the difference between the fair market value and its basis in the property.

In addition to deducting compensation payments to employees, a business may deduct amounts paid to independent contractors, such as those described in Unit 1.

Employment Taxes: A business's deduction for compensation paid to employees is not reduced by the Social Security, Medicare, and income taxes it is required to withhold from them.

Further, a business can deduct the amounts paid as the employer's share of Social Security and Medicare taxes, as well as state and federal unemployment and disability fund taxes.

Example: A partnership pays its secretary $18,000 a year. After withholding various taxes, the employee receives $14,500. The business pays an additional $1,500 of employment taxes. The full $18,000 can be deducted as wages. The business can also deduct the $1,500 paid as taxes.

A self-employed individual can deduct one-half of his self-employment tax as a business expense in figuring adjusted gross income. This deduction only affects income tax. It does not affect net earnings from self-employment or self-employment tax.

Fringe Benefits

A fringe benefit is a form of additional compensation that may be provided by a business to those who perform services, such as employees and independent contractors.

Study Tip: For Part 1 of the EA exam, you must understand fringe benefits from the employee's perspective. For Part 2 of the EA exam, you must know how these benefits are treated from the employer's perspective.

A business must include in a recipient's taxable compensation the amount by which the value of a fringe benefit is more than the sum of the following amounts:

- Any amount the law excludes from taxation
- Any amount the recipient paid for the benefit

If the recipient of a taxable fringe benefit is an employee, the benefit is subject to employment taxes and must be reported on Form W-2. If the recipient of a taxable fringe benefit is not an employee, the benefit is not subject to employment taxes, but it may have to be reported on Form 1099-MISC for independent contractors or Schedule K-1 for partners.

Generally, nontaxable benefits are not subject to income tax withholding, Social Security and Medicare taxes, or unemployment (FUTA) tax. However, there are exceptions for certain items. For example, an S corporation shareholder with ownership of more than 2% is not considered an employee for purposes of excluding certain fringe benefits, such as accident and health benefits, and this benefit is therefore subject to income tax withholding. Further, exclusion of an otherwise nontaxable benefit may be disallowed if there is discrimination in favor of highly compensated employees (as described below).

Cafeteria Plans

A cafeteria plan, including a flexible spending arrangement, is a written plan that provides employees an opportunity to choose between receiving at least one taxable benefit, such as cash, and one qualified (nontaxable) benefit. Employees may generally contribute a portion of their salaries on a pretax basis to pay for a portion of the qualified benefits. Having a salary reduction option is typically deemed sufficient to satisfy the requirement to provide a taxable option, even though the amounts are withheld on a pretax basis.

The plan may make benefits available to employees, their spouses, and their dependents. Qualified benefits may include:

- Accident and health benefits (but not Archer medical savings accounts or long-term care insurance)
- Adoption assistance
- Dependent care assistance
- Group-term life insurance
- Health savings accounts (HSAs)
- Flexible spending arrangements (FSAs)

A cafeteria plan cannot include certain other types of fringe benefits, which may nevertheless be deductible by the employer and nontaxable to the employee. Some of these additional items are addressed later in this unit under the heading "Other Types of Employee Fringe Benefits."

Highly Compensated/Key Employees: If a cafeteria plan favors either highly compensated employees (HCEs) or key employees as to eligibility to participate, contributions, or benefits, the employer must include in their taxable income the value of taxable benefits they could have selected. This is intended to discourage employers from offering tax-free benefits to their owners or highly compensated executives, while ignoring lower-paid employees.

An HCE is any of the following:

- An officer,
- A shareholder who owns more than 5% of the voting power or value of all classes of the employer's stock,
- An employee who is highly compensated based on the facts and circumstances, or
- A spouse or dependent of a person described above.

A key employee is defined as follows for 2013:

- An officer with annual pay of more than $165,000, or
- An employee who is either a 5% owner of the business or a 1% owner of the business whose annual pay was more than $150,000.

A plan is considered to have favored key employees if more than 25% of all the nontaxable benefits are given to key employees.

Accident and Health Benefits: Nontaxable accident or health benefits may include the following:

- Contributions to the cost of accident or health insurance, including long-term care insurance
- Contributions to a separate trust or fund that directly or through insurance provides accident or health benefits
- Contributions to Archer MSAs or health savings accounts

Adoption Assistance: An adoption assistance program provides payments or reimbursements for qualifying expenses related to adopting a child, with up to $12,970 excludable in 2013.

Dependent Care Assistance: An annual exclusion of up to $5,000 ($2,500 if MFS) may apply to benefits received by an employee under a dependent care assistance program that provides for a qualifying person's care and allows the employee to work. The exclusion cannot exceed the smaller of the earned income of either the employee or the employee's spouse.

> **Note:** Like the other cafeteria plan benefits described above, a dependent care assistance program cannot favor HCEs. However, for a dependent care assistance program, the definition of an HCE differs from the general guidelines above. In this case, and for most of the other types of fringe benefits described in this unit, an HCE is an employee who (1) was a 5% owner at any time during the year or the preceding year, or (2) received more than $115,000 in pay for the preceding year, unless he was not also in the top 20% of employees when ranked by pay in the preceding year.

Group-term Life Insurance Coverage: An employer can exclude the cost of up to $50,000 of group-term life insurance from the taxable wages of an insured employee. The value of insurance coverage that exceeds $50,000 is a taxable benefit and must be included in the employee's wages, after reduction for any amount the employee paid toward the insurance.

Health Savings Accounts: An HSA is an account owned by a company's employee or former employee. Any contributions an employer makes become the employee's property and cannot be withdrawn by the employer. Contributions to the account are used to pay current or future medical expenses of the account owner, his spouse, and any qualified dependent. The medical expenses must not be reimbursable by insurance or other sources.

A qualified individual must be covered by a high deductible health plan with a deductible in 2013 of at least $1,250 for self-only coverage or $2,500 for family coverage. Annual out-of-pocket expenses to the beneficiary are limited to $6,250 for self-only coverage and $12,500 for family coverage. There are no income restrictions on an individual's eligibility to contribute to an HSA; nor is there a requirement the account owner have earned income to contribute.

In 2013, an employer can contribute up to $3,250 for self-only coverage or $6,450 for family coverage to a qualified individual's HSA. The contribution limits are increased by $1,000 for qualified individuals who are age 55 or older at any time during the year. No contributions can be made to an individual's HSA after he becomes enrolled in Medicare Part A or Part B.

An employer's contribution amount to an employee's HSA must be comparable for all employees who have comparable coverage during the same period, or there will be an excise tax equal to 35% of the amount the employer contributed to all employees' HSAs. However, an employer is allowed to make larger HSA contributions for a non-highly compensated employee than for a highly compensated employee.

Flexible Spending Arrangements

An FSA is a form of cafeteria plan benefit that reimburses employees for expenses incurred for certain qualified benefits, such as child care or health benefits. The employee must substantiate his expenses, and the distributions from the FSA to the employee are tax-free. An FSA generally cannot provide a cumulative benefit to the employee beyond the plan year. However, beginning in 2013, an employer may choose to allow an employee either a short grace period after the plan year to use his balance or to carry over an unused balance up to $500 for each account.

For plan years beginning after December 31, 2012, a cafeteria plan may not allow an employee to request salary reduction contributions to a health FSA in excess of $2,500.

Working Condition Benefits

This exclusion from wages applies to property and services an employer provides so that the employee can perform his job. A common example is an employee's use of a company car for business purposes. An employer who provides a car for an employee can exclude the amount that would be allowed as a deductible business expense if the employee paid for its use.

Alternatively, an employer may include the entire annual lease value of a car in the employee's wages and the employee can then claim any deductible business expense for the car as an itemized deduction on his personal income tax return.

A qualified nonpersonal-use vehicle is one that an employee is unlikely to use more than minimally for personal purposes because of its design. Examples include fire trucks, police cars, hearses, school buses, cement mixers, and tractors.

Note: Any vehicle designed to carry cargo of over 14,000 pounds is a qualified nonpersonal-use vehicle. Pickup trucks and vans of 14,000 pounds or less are qualified nonpersonal vehicles if they have been specially modified for business purposes, such as marked with permanent decals, painted with advertising logos, or fitted with certain special equipment specific to the business.

An employer-provided cell phone is another common working condition benefit. There must be a substantial business reason to provide the employee a cell phone; it cannot simply be used to boost an employee's morale, to attract a prospective worker, or as a means of providing additional compensation to an employee.

Example: Evelyn is an advertising executive who frequently visits clients at their locations. She uses her employer-paid cell phone to keep in touch with clients and her own firm while she is out of her office. If Evelyn did not have a legitimate business reason for the phone, its value would be added to her wages and her firm could not deduct it as a business expense.

Accountable Plans

A business can reimburse employees for business-related expenses. There are two types of reimbursement plans:

- **Accountable Plans**: Amounts paid under an accountable plan are deductible by the employer but they are not taxable wages and are not subject to income tax withholding or payment of Social Security, Medicare, and FUTA taxes.
- **Nonaccountable Plans**: Amounts paid under a nonaccountable plan are taxable to employees as wages and are subject to all employment taxes and withholding. Generally, there are no substantiation requirements for a nonaccountable plan.

For expenses to qualify under an accountable plan, the employee must follow strict guidelines in order to have the expenses reimbursed. An accountable plan requires employees to:

- Have incurred the expenses while performing services as employees.

- Adequately account for the expenses, including travel, meals, and entertainment, within a reasonable period of time.
- Provide documentary evidence of travel, mileage, and other employee business expenses.
- Return any excess reimbursement or allowance to the employer within a reasonable period of time, if paid in advance. A cash advance must be reasonably calculated to equal the anticipated expense, and the employer must make the advance within a reasonable period of time.

Example: Dana is a cosmetics saleswoman for Sunshine Cosmetics. She takes two potential clients out to dinner and pays for the meal. She keeps track of her business mileage on a spreadsheet. The following week, she submits her receipts and the spreadsheet to Sunshine Cosmetics for reimbursement. Dana's employer reimburses her for the out-of-pocket expenses she incurred. This arrangement is considered an accountable plan. The reimbursement is not taxable to Dana and is deductible by the employer as a regular business expense (subject to the 50% limitation on deductibility of meal costs).

Example: Maggie is a loan agent who goes to various locations to sign mortgage paperwork. In April, Maggie's employer gives her a $1,000 advance to cover her flight, hotel, and transportation on a business trip to Alaska. Maggie spends $940 on her travel expenses during the trip. When she returns, she submits her receipts to substantiate the expenses. She also pays back the excess advance to her employer. She has met the requirements of an accountable plan, and the advanced funds are not included in her taxable wages.

Other Types of Employee Fringe Benefits

Employee Achievement Awards: Employers may generally exclude from an employee's wages the value of awards given for length of service or safety achievement. An employer's deduction and the tax-free amount for each employee are limited each year to the following:

- $400 for awards that are not qualified plan awards
- $1,600 for all awards, whether or not they are qualified plan awards

The exclusion for employee awards does not apply to awards of cash, gift cards, or other intangible property such as vacations or tickets to sporting events.

Athletic Facilities: The value of an employee's use of a health club or athletic facilities may be excluded from wages, but only if the facility is on premises that the employer owns or leases. If the employer pays for a gym membership or a fitness program provided to the employee at an off-site location, the value is included in the employee's compensation.

De Minimis (Minimal) Benefits: An employer may exclude the value of a de minimis benefit provided to an employee from the employee's wages. This is something an employer provides that has so little value that accounting for it would be impractical, such as coffee and doughnuts in the break room. Cash and cash equivalent items, such as gift cards or the use of a credit or debit card, are not excludable as de minimis benefits, except for occasional meal money or transportation fare.

Educational Assistance: An educational assistance program is a separate written plan that allows an employer to provide educational assistance to employees for the cost of tuition, fees, books, supplies, and equipment. The payments may be for either undergraduate or graduate-level courses, and do not have to be work-related.

Up to $5,250 of assistance may be excluded per year per employee. If an employer does not have an educational assistance plan or pays more than $5,250, the excess is taxed as wages to the employee unless the benefits are working condition benefits that the employee would be able to deduct as a business expense if he paid for them himself.

Tuition Reduction: An educational organization can exclude the value of a qualified undergraduate tuition reduction it provides to an employee, his or her spouse, or a dependent child. Graduate education only qualifies if it is for the education of a graduate student who performs teaching or research activities for the educational organization.

Employee Discounts: Employers can exclude from wages the price reductions they give to employees on services or property they offer to customers in the normal course of business, up to the following limits:

- For a discount on services, 20% of the price charged nonemployee customers for the service.
- For a discount on merchandise or property, the company's gross profit percentage multiplied by the price nonemployee customers pay.

Employee Stock Options: A corporation may grant stock options to its employees, as compensation for past service and an incentive for retention, that allow them to purchase the company's stock at a later date. If an employee receives stock options, he may have income when the options are granted, when he exercises them (to buy the company's stock), or when he sells or otherwise disposes of the options or the stock. The nature, timing, and amount of the employee's taxable income and the employer's deduction for compensation expense depend on whether the options are considered to be statutory or nonstatutory options. There are two types of statutory stock options:

- Incentive stock options (ISOs), which allow employees to purchase stock at a pre-established price (exercise price) that may be below the market price on the date of exercise.
- Options granted under employee stock purchase plans (ESPPs).

The tax advantage of a statutory stock option for the employee is that income is not reported when the option is granted or when it is exercised. However, the employer corporation cannot take a deduction for compensation expense. The employee does report income when he ultimately sells the stock. If he satisfies certain holding period requirements, the income is treated as capital gain. If not, it is treated as ordinary income, and the employer is entitled to a compensation deduction at that time.

Nonstatutory or nonqualified stock options (NSOs) also allow employees to purchase stock at a pre-established exercise price. The employee must recognize compensation income, either at the date of grant or on the exercise date, and the employer is entitled to a corresponding compensation expense deduction at the same time.

Meals and Lodging: An employer may exclude from taxable wages the value of meals and lodging it provides to employees if they are provided:

- On the employer's business premises, and
- For the employer's convenience.

For lodging, there is an additional rule: it must be required as a condition of employment. Lodging can be provided for the taxpayer, the spouse, and the taxpayer's dependents, and still not be taxable. The exclusion from taxation does not apply if the employee can choose to receive additional pay instead of lodging.

Situations in which meals may be provided to employees for the convenience of the employer on the employer's business premises include the following:

- Workers such as police officers, firefighters, and other emergency personnel need to be on call for emergencies during the meal period
- The nature of the business requires short meal periods
- Eating facilities are not available in areas near the workplace
- Meals are furnished to all employees on a regular basis, so long as meals are furnished to more than half of the employees for the convenience of the employer
- Meals are furnished immediately after working hours because the employee's duties prevented him from obtaining a meal during working hours

Example: An employer has pizza delivered to the office at a group meeting because the business requires the meeting be kept short, and there are no alternative restaurants in the immediate area.

Meals provided to restaurant employees during, or immediately before or after work hours are also considered furnished for the employer's convenience.

Meals provided to employees for the convenience of the employer are not subject to the normal 50% deductibility limit; they are 100% deductible by the employer.

Moving Expense Reimbursements: An employer can generally exclude qualifying moving expense payments or reimbursements from an employee's taxable wages if they are paid under an accountable plan for expenses that would otherwise have been deductible by the employee if he had paid or incurred them without reimbursement. Deductible moving expenses include only the reasonable expenses of:

- Moving household goods and personal effects from the employee's former home to the new home, and
- Traveling, including lodging, from the former home to the new home.

Expenses for meals are not included, and the move must meet both the distance test and the time test. The distance test is met if the new job location is at least 50 miles farther from the employee's old home than the old job location was. The time test is met if the employee works at least 39 weeks during the first 12 months after arriving in the general area of the new job location.

No-Additional-Cost Services: An employer can exclude from an employee's taxable income the value of a service provided to the employee if it does not create substantial additional cost for the business. Typically, no-additional-cost services are excess capacity services, such as airline, bus, or train tickets; hotel rooms; or telephone services provided free or at a reduced price to employees working in those lines of business.

Transportation: Employers may provide transportation benefits to their employees up to certain amounts without having to include the benefit in the employee's taxable income. Qualified transportation benefits include transit passes, qualified parking, rides in a commuter highway vehicle between the employee's home and workplace, and qualified bicycle commuting reimbursements.

In 2013, employees may exclude:

- $245 per month in combined commuter highway vehicle transportation and transit passes, and
- $245 per month in parking benefits.
- $20 per month for expenses incurred when commuting to work by bicycle

Employees may receive transit passes and benefits for parking during the same month; they are not mutually exclusive.

If an employer allows an employee to use a company vehicle for commuting or other personal use, the value of the vehicle's use is taxable to the employee.

Unit 5: Study Questions

1. For cafeteria plans, a "key" employee in 2013 is defined as all of the following except:

A. An officer with annual pay of more than $165,000.
B. A 1% owner of the business with annual pay of more than $150,000.
C. A 3% owner of the business.
D. Both A and B.

2. All of the following are fringe benefits that may be excluded from an employee's pay except ________________________:

A. Dependent care assistance of up to $5,000 a year.
B. A cell phone given to an employee for excellent job performance.
C. Moving expense reimbursements.
D. Adoption assistance.

3. The Pancake House provides the following benefits to its employees. Which of these is fully taxable to the employee?

A. Qualified group term life insurance of $50,000.
B. Qualified dependent care of up to $5,000.
C. A membership at the local athletic club with a value up to $1,200.
D. Free transit passes, up to $245 per month.

4. Heart-Wise Ambulance Services provides meals and lodging for ten paramedics at the workplace as a condition of employment because they are not allowed to leave the premises when they are on a shift. The employees eat and sleep for free. Which of the following is true?

A. All the costs of meals and lodging can be excluded from the employees' wages and deducted as an expense by the employer.
B. The meals and lodging are not taxable to the employee, but the employer can only deduct 50% of the meal expense.
C. The meals and lodging are taxable to the employees and deductible by the employer. The employee may then deduct the costs as employee business expenses.
D. None of the above.

5. All of the following are excludable from an employee's wages and deductible by the employer except:

A. An outstanding employee achievement award valued at $300.
B. Occasional snacks provided by the employer in the employee break room.
C. Employer-provided vehicles that employees may also use for personal purposes.
D. Meals furnished during work hours for the convenience of the employer.

6. Evermore Inc. reimburses employees for their business travel and transportation expenses. Which of the following is taxable to the employee?

A. Travel reimbursements made under an accountable plan.
B. Travel reimbursements made under a nonaccountable plan.
C. Parking passes at a cost of $245 per month.
D. A qualified bicycle commuting reimbursement.

7. Renee is a full-time employee of Right Angles Engineering, which offers its employees reimbursement through an education assistance program. In 2013, she takes graduate accounting courses and has $5,900 of tuition expenses and $300 of expenses for required books. Right Angles reimburses Renee for all the expenses. How should this reimbursement be treated?

A. All of the amounts are excluded from Renee's income, and the amounts are deductible by Right Angles as a qualified fringe benefit.
B. The first $5,250 of the educational expenses is excluded from Renee's wages as a qualified fringe benefit, and the remaining amount is taxable as wage income to her.
C. Only $5,900 (the tuition costs) of the educational expenses are excluded from the Renee's wages as a qualified fringe benefit, and the remaining amount is taxable as wage income to her The cost of the books is not a qualified educational expense.
D. All of the reimbursement is taxable as wages to Renee because graduate courses do not qualify for reimbursement under a fringe benefit plan.

8. Which of the following benefits must be included in an employee's income?

A. Child care reimbursed under a qualified flexible spending plan.
B. Employee discounts on products.
C. A holiday gift of a $50 gas card.
D. A holiday gift of a $25 canned ham.

Unit 6: Business Deductions & Credits

More Reading:
Instructions for Form 3800, *General Business Credit*
Publication 334, *Tax Guide for Small Business*
Publication 536, *Net Operating Losses for Individuals, Estates, and Trusts*
Instructions for Form 8903, *Domestic Productions Activities Deduction*
Instructions for Form 4626, *Alternative Minimum Tax-Corporations*

Net Operating Losses (NOLs)

A net operating loss (NOL) occurs when a business has tax deductions that exceed its income, resulting in negative taxable income for a tax year. C corporations NOLs are discussed in Unit 13. Partnerships and S corporations generally cannot use NOLs, but their partners and shareholders may be able to use their individual shares.

For an individual, estate, or trust to have an NOL, the loss must be caused by deductions from:

- A trade or business that result in an overall loss
- Work as an employee
- Casualty or theft losses (personal or business-related)
- Losses from rental property
- Moving expenses
- A farming business

Depending upon whether it had taxable income in prior years, a business may choose to carry back an NOL to offset prior year taxable income or to carry forward the NOL to offset taxable income in future years.

Example: Harrison is a sole proprietor who owns a flooring business. In 2013, his business has a net operating loss of $13,000. In 2012, Harrison's business had taxable income of $10,000 and in 2011 it had taxable income of $25,000. Harrison may carry back $10,000 to 2011 and $3,000 to 2012.

The default election is to carry back an NOL for up to two years. Any remaining NOL can be carried forward for up to 20 years.

Note: A net operating loss that is not used in the carryback and carryforward periods is lost and cannot be deducted in any other tax year.

A business may also elect not to carry back an NOL and only carry it forward. If a taxpayer fails to file a return on time and does not make the proper election, he is forced to carry back the NOL.

There are certain instances in which a business qualifies for a longer NOL carryback period. The following are exceptions to the two-year carryback rule:

- If the NOL is due to a farming loss, qualified farmers are eligible for a five-year carryback period.

- "Qualified small businesses"[35] may carry back a loss three years if the loss is due to a federally declared disaster.
- Net operating losses due to a casualty or theft may be carried back three years.
- Product liability losses have a ten-year carryback period. An example would be when a business sells an item that is later subject to a recall and lawsuits.

To claim a refund from an NOL, an individual taxpayer may choose to amend a prior year tax return or may use Form 1045, *Application for Tentative Refund*, to apply for a quick tax refund resulting from the carryback of an NOL.

If the taxpayer is self-employed, the net operating loss does not change the amount of self-employment tax to any of the years it is carried forward or back to. Also, if a business or individual owes interest and penalties in a prior year, the NOL carryback will not abate them.

Example: Gregory operates a farming business and files his return on Schedule F. In 2013, he has a net operating loss of $35,000. He had income of $25,000 in the prior year, so he elects to carry back his NOL in order to receive a refund of the income tax he paid. Gregory also owed self-employment taxes in 2012, and the NOL will not reduce this tax. The NOL only reduces the income tax liability. As a farmer, Gregory would be able to carry back the NOL up to five years.

The following items are not allowed when figuring an NOL:

- Any deduction for personal exemptions
- Capital losses in excess of capital gains
- The exclusion of gain from the sale of qualified small business stock
- Nonbusiness deductions in excess of nonbusiness income (hobby losses)
- A net operating loss from another year (a carryback or a carryforward)
- The domestic production activities deduction (DPAD)
- A self-employed taxpayer's contribution to a retirement plan

Income from other sources may eliminate or reduce a net operating loss for the year. For example, if a taxpayer has income from wages, as well as a net operating loss from a small business, the wage income and the NOL will offset taxable income.

Example: Jim runs an auto detailing business as a sole proprietor. In 2013, he had an $8,000 NOL from his Schedule C business. Jim files jointly with his wife, Elaine. She has $23,000 in taxable income from wages. On their jointly filed return, Jim's net operating loss is absorbed by Elaine's $23,000 in wages, making their joint AGI $15,000 ($23,000 - $8,000 NOL).

Business Credits

A variety of tax credits are available for businesses. Credits are generally more valuable than deductions because they are subtracted directly from a business's tax liability. However, most tax credits are available in limited situations, applying only to certain industries or to very specific activities.

---

[35] A "qualified small business" for purposes of this rule is a sole proprietorship or a partnership that has average annual gross receipts of $5 million or less during the three-year period ending with the tax year of the NOL.

General Business Credit

Many business credits fall under the umbrella of the general business credit (GBC). The GBC is not a single credit but is instead a combination of individual credits. Each business credit is claimed on a separate form; the credits are then reported in aggregate on Form 3800, *General Business Credit.*

The GBC is a nonrefundable credit that is subtracted directly from tax, reducing an entity's tax liability dollar for dollar. Generally, credits cannot be claimed to the extent that they would reduce a business's tax bill below its tentative minimum tax. Further, the GBC may not offset any of a business's employment tax liabilities.

If a business is unable to use its entire GBC in the year it was earned, it can generally be carried back to the prior year and forward for up to 20 years. A business's GBC consists of its carryforward of business credits from prior years plus the total of its current year business credits.

Study Note: In addition to eligibility for and deduction of the general business credit as a whole, Prometric's exam specifications reference only the Investment Credit and the Disabled Access Credit, suggesting they are the two most likely to be tested on the EA exam. However, the Work Opportunity Tax Credit has also been tested on previous exams.

The following are some of the more widely-used general business credits.

Investment Credit (Form 3468): The Investment Credit is the sum of the following five credits: Rehabilitation and Energy Credits, and the Advanced Coal, Advanced Energy, and Gasification projects.

- **Rehabilitation Credit:** This credit is available for businesses that rehabilitate pre-1936 buildings (10%) or certified historic structures (20%) of qualified expenditures.
- **Energy Credit:** This credit is available for businesses that use solar energy to generate electricity or that use geothermal deposits to power their equipment. The credit is between 10% and 30% for qualified fuel cell and other solar energy property.
- **Advanced Coal, Gasification, and Advanced Energy Project Credits:** These credits are designed to reduce greenhouse emissions by retrofitting existing technology to make it cleaner or spurring investment in alternative energy. In the case of the Advanced Energy Credit, qualifying projects must re-equip, expand, or establish a manufacturing facility for the production of solar, wind, or geothermal energy, or electric cars.

The Investment Credit allows businesses to take a deduction for a percentage of certain investment costs from their tax liability in addition to the normal allowances for depreciation. In general, a business cannot claim the Investment Credit for property that is:

- Used mainly outside the United States;
- Used by a governmental unit or foreign person or entity;
- Used by a tax-exempt organization;
- Used for lodging or in the furnishing of lodging; or
- Any property that has already been expensed under section 179 (accelerated depreciation).

Disabled Access Credit (Form 8826): This is a nonrefundable tax credit for an eligible small business that incurs expenses to provide access to persons who have disabilities. The expenses must be incurred for the business to comply with the Americans with Disabilities Act. The amount of the Disabled Access Credit is 50% of qualified expenses, with a maximum credit per year of $5,000. To be eligible, a business must have earned $1 million or less or had no more than 30 full-time employees during the year.

Work Opportunity Tax Credit (Form 5884): The WOTC provides a credit to for-profit employers of as much as $9,600 per veteran (or other qualified employee in eight targeted groups) who was hired and began work by the end of 2013. The credit for qualified tax-exempt organizations is a maximum of $6,240. The amount of this credit varies depending on factors such as the length of the employee's unemployment before being hired.

Credit for Small Employer Pension Plan Startup Costs (Form 8881): Employers may claim a tax credit equal to 50% of the cost to set up and administer the plan, up to a maximum of $500 per year, for each of the first three years of the plan.

Energy Efficient Appliance Credit (Form 8909): This credit is available for manufacturers of eligible dishwashers, clothes washers, refrigerators. The amount of the credit is based on how little energy a particular appliance uses.

Energy Efficient Home Credit (Form 8908): This credit ranges from $1,000 to $2,000, and is available for eligible contractors of certain energy-efficient homes sold as residences.

Alternative Motor Vehicle Credit (Form 8910): This is a credit for a new qualified fuel cell vehicle placed in service during the year. (Earlier credits allowed for qualified hybrid vehicles, alternative fuel motor vehicles, and advanced lean-burn technology vehicles have expired.)

This credit is unusual because it is allowed for both personal and business-use vehicles. If the credit is claimed for a personal vehicle, it is a nonrefundable personal credit and will reduce the taxpayer's regular tax as well as the alternative minimum tax.

If the credit is claimed for a business-use vehicle, the credit becomes part of the general business credit, so it is available for carryback and carryforward.

Alternative Fuel Vehicle Refueling Property Credit (Form 8911): This is a 30% credit for the cost of installing clean-fuel vehicle refueling property to be used in a business, up to $30,000 a year.

Qualified Plug-in Electric Drive Motor Vehicle Credit (Form 8936): This is a $2,500 to $7,500 credit for each new qualifying plug-in electric vehicle purchased or leased during the year.

Credit for Employer Social Security and Medicare Taxes Paid on Certain Employee Tips (Form 8846): This credit is generally equal to the employer's portion of Social Security and Medicare taxes paid on tips received by employees of restaurants and other food service establishments where tipping is customary. An employer must meet both of the following requirements to qualify for the credit:

- Have employees who received tips from customers for serving food or beverages, and
- Have paid employer Social Security and Medicare taxes on these tips.

The credit does not apply to other tipped employees, such as hairdressers or bell hops.

Credit for Employer Differential Wage Payments (Form 8932): This credit provides certain small businesses with an incentive to continue to pay wages to an employee performing services on active duty in the uniformed services of the United States for a period of more than 30 days.

Credit for Employer-Provided Childcare Facilities and Services (Form 8882): This credit applies to the qualified expenses a business incurs for employee childcare, childcare resources, and childcare referral services. The credit is up to 25% of the cost of the childcare facility plus 10% of resource and referral costs. A business is limited to a credit of $150,000 per tax year.

Credit for Small Employer Health Insurance Premiums (Form 8941): This credit applies to the cost of health insurance premiums that an eligible small business provides certain employees. For tax-exempt small businesses, the credit is generally limited to 25% of premiums paid. For all other small employers, the credit is generally 35% of premiums paid. For purposes of this credit, an eligible business must have had fewer than 25 full-time equivalent employees for the tax year, with average annual wages of less than $50,000.

Credit for Increasing Research Activities (Form 6765): A credit for expenses related to qualified research intended for use in developing new or improved technology that would be used in a taxpayer's business.

Other Credits: Other, more obscure, general business credits include ones for maintaining railroad tracks, training mine rescue teams, and for makers of orphan drugs and distilled spirits.

In addition to credits designed to spur specific economic investment, Congress frequently passes other specific incentives for businesses to engage in certain types of business activity. For example, through 2013, section 181 allows film and television producers to expense the first $15 million of production costs incurred in the United States ($20 million if in economically depressed areas), rather than capitalizing the costs under normal uniform capitalization rules.

Domestic Production Activities Deduction

The domestic production activities deduction (DPAD, authorized by IRC section 199) is designed to stimulate domestic manufacturing and farming. The DPAD is calculated on Form 8903, *Domestic Production Activities Deduction*. Individual taxpayers, including partners or shareholders in pass-through entities and beneficiaries of trusts and estates, claim the DPAD deduction as an adjustment to income on Form 1040. C corporations claim the deduction on Form 1120.

The DPAD is equal to 9% of the lesser of:

- Qualified production activities income (QPAI), or
- Adjusted gross income for an individual, estate, or trust (or taxable income for all other taxpayers) determined without regard to the DPAD.

However, the deduction is also limited to 50% of Form W-2 wages paid to employees for the year. Payments made to independent contractors and reported on Form 1099-MISC are not wages and do not qualify for purposes of the DPAD.

The following activities are qualified production activities eligible for claiming the DPAD:

- Manufacturing goods in the United States
- Selling, leasing, or licensing items that have been manufactured in the United States

- Selling, leasing, or licensing motion pictures that have been produced in the United States (except for pornography)
- Construction of real property in the United States
- Engineering and architectural services relating to a U.S.-based construction project
- Software development in the United States
- The production of water, natural gas, and electricity in the United States (simply transmitting or distributing these goods does not qualify)
- The growth and processing of agricultural products and timber

QPAI is the excess of domestic production gross receipts (DPGR) over the sum of:

- Cost of goods sold allocable to DPGR, and
- Other expenses, losses, and deductions (other than the DPAD) properly allocable to DPGR.

A business's gross receipts must be allocated between DPGR and non-DPGR, and its cost of goods sold must then be allocated to each. One of several methods must then be used to allocate other expenses, losses, and deductions. The use of certain of these methods is limited to small businesses that meet specified parameters.

Example: Brent Wise Corporation manufactures building components that it sells wholesale to building contractors. All of Brent Wise's manufacturing activity is in the U.S., and therefore qualifies for the DPAD. In 2013, Brent Wise had QPAI of $650,000 from its manufacturing activity and taxable income (without regard to the DPAD) of $800,000. It paid $225,000 in W-2 wages to its employees. Brent Wise's DPAD deduction would therefore be the lesser of:

- 9% of the $650,000 of QPAI, or
- 50% of the $225,000 of wages.

Thus, Brent Wise's DPAD would be $58,500 (.09 × $650,000).

Example: Raiser Ranch Inc. is a meat processor that has various slaughtering plant locations in the United States as well as two locations in Brazil. Although this type of production activity is qualified for the DPAD, only the U.S. production qualifies for the DPAD. Raiser Ranch must allocate its gross receipts between the factory production in the United States and Brazil to calculate DPGR and non-DPGR.

Gross receipts from the following are not considered DPGR and therefore not eligible for the DPAD:

- Construction services that are cosmetic in nature, such as drywall and painting.
- Leasing or licensing items to a related party.
- Selling food or beverages prepared at restaurants or dining establishments.
- The transmission or distribution of electricity, natural gas, or water (although the production of electricity, natural gas, or potable water in the U.S. is a qualified activity).
- Any advertising, product placement, customer service businesses, and other telecommunications services.
- Most service type businesses.

Unit 6: Study Questions

1. Which of the following does not qualify for the domestic production activities deduction?

A. Manufacturing goods in the United States.
B. Construction of buildings in the United States.
C. Selling food or beverages prepared at restaurants.
D. Software development in the United States.

2. Which of the following items is allowed when figuring a net operating loss?

A. Capital losses in excess of capital gains.
B. A net operating loss from another year (a carryback or a carryforward).
C. The domestic production activities deduction.
D. The loss from the theft of business property.

3. Stacy owns the Peach Pit Cannery. In 2013, she renovated her cannery to comply with the Americans with Disabilities Act. The Peach Pit Cannery had gross receipts of $750,000 and spent $15,000 on disabled access upgrades. What is Stacy's current year Disabled Access Credit?

A. $2,500.
B. $5,000.
C. $7,500.
D. $15,000.

4. Farthington Corporation could not use all of its general business credits in 2013. What is the carryover period for the GBC?

A. The GBC may be carried back two years and carried forward five years.
B. The GBC may be carried back five years and carried forward 10 years.
C. The unused GBC cannot be carried over to another tax year.
D. The GBC may be carried back one year and carried forward for 20 years.

5. The Work Opportunity Tax Credit provides a credit for businesses that ____________:

A. Provide job training for out-of-work veterans and other individuals in targeted groups.
B. Give severance to laid-off workers.
C. Invest in federal empowerment zones.
D. Hire unemployed veterans and other individuals in targeted groups.

6. Bettina owns her own photography business, and she has an NOL in the current year. She elects to carry back her losses. How long may she carry back and carry forward her NOL?

A. Back five years, forward 20 years.
B. Back two years, forward 20 years.
C. Back three years, forward 25 years.
D. Back two years, forward five years.

7. Which of the following is not part of the Investment Credit in 2013?

A. Gasification Project Credit.
B. Hydroelectric Power Credit.
C. Rehabilitation Credit.
D. Energy Credit.

8. Which event would create an NOL?

A. Selling a personal-use car for a loss.
B. Selling a primary residence for a loss.
C. Casualty loss from a fire at a business location.
D. Loss from the sale of corporate stock.

9. All of the following statements are correct regarding the DPAD except ___________:

A. The DPAD cannot be more than 25% of the wages a business pays its employees.
B. Businesses with both domestic and foreign business activity must use only their domestic income in calculating the DPAD.
C. The DPAD can be as much as 9% of a company's taxable income.
D. The DPAD is authorized by section 199 of the Internal Revenue Code.

10. The Disabled Access Credit conforms with applicable standards of the ____________?

A Architectural Standards Act.
B. U.S. Department of Labor.
C. Americans with Disabilities Act.
D National Organization on Disability.

11. Madhu is a sole proprietor who manufactures specialty swimming apparel for Muslim women. Her factory, which is located in the United States, pays employees W-2 wages of $440,000 in 2013. The company's QPAI was $2 million. Madhu's AGI was $165,000. What may she claim for the DPAD in 2013?

A. She is not eligible for the DPAD because she is a sole proprietor.
B. $220,000.
C. $180,000.
D. $14,850.

12. Alistair is a sole proprietor who files his return on Schedule C. He had the following profit and losses:

- 2010: Net profit $7,000
- 2011: Net profit $9,000
- 2012: Net profit $6,000
- 2013: Net operating loss $24,000

How should Alistair treat his net operating loss?

A. NOL carryback of $7,000 to 2010; NOL carryback of $9,000 to 2011; NOL carryback of $6,000 to 2012; NOL carryforward of $2,000.
B. NOL carryback of $9,000 to 2011; NOL carryback of $6,000 to 2012; NOL carryforward of $9,000.
C. NOL carryback of $24,000 to 2012.
D. NOL carryforward of $24,000.

Unit 7: Basis of Business Assets

More Reading:
Publication 551, *Basis of Assets*
Publication 547, *Casualties, Disasters, and Thefts*

A business asset is any type of property used in the conduct of a trade or business: land, buildings, machinery, furniture, trucks, patents, and franchise rights are examples. Some assets are tangible, and others are intangible. Taxpayers generally must capitalize the cost of business assets, rather than deduct them in the year the cost is incurred.

In order to compute gain or loss on the sale or other disposition of an asset, a business must be able to determine its basis.

Definition: Basis is the amount of a taxpayer's investment in an asset or property for tax purposes.

The basis of property is also used to determine tax deductions for depreciation, amortization, depletion, and casualty losses. If a business cannot determine the basis of an asset, the IRS will deem it to be zero.

The basis of property is usually its cost, the amount a business pays for the asset. An asset's cost basis also may include amounts paid for the following items:

- Sales tax on the purchase
- Freight to obtain the property
- Installation and testing costs
- Excise taxes
- Legal and accounting fees to obtain property
- Revenue stamps
- Recording fees
- Real estate taxes (if assumed by the buyer)
- Settlement costs for the purchase of real estate
- The assumption of any liabilities on the property

Example: Naomi pays $4,000 for a commercial dryer for her laundromat. Naomi also pays $500 for shipping and sales tax. The installation cost for the dryer is $250. These costs are added to the purchase price, resulting in a basis of $4,750.

If a business produces real or tangible personal property for use in a trade or business, it may be subject to the uniform capitalization rules described in Unit 2.

Generally, if a group of assets that makes up a trade or business is acquired and those assets involve goodwill or going concern value, the seller and purchaser must file Form 8594, *Asset Acquisition Statement.* This form is used to allocate the total consideration paid among the various categories, or classes, of assets acquired and to establish the purchaser's cost basis for each category.

Note: Certain events that occur during the period of ownership may increase or decrease basis, resulting in an ***adjusted basis***. For example, the basis of property is ***increased*** by the cost of improvements that add to the value of the property. The basis of property is ***decreased*** by depreciation deductions, insurance reimbursements for casualty and theft losses, and certain other items such as rebates.

Basis of Real Property

Real property, often called real estate, includes land and anything built on or attached to it. When a taxpayer buys real property, certain fees and other expenses become part of the cost basis in the property.

Settlement Costs: Certain settlement fees and closing costs related to buying a property are added to its basis. These include abstract fees; charges for installing utility services; legal fees, including title search and preparation of the sales contract and deed; recording fees; surveys; transfer taxes; owner's title insurance; and any amounts the seller owes that the taxpayer agrees to pay, such as charges for improvements or repairs and sales commissions.

However, the following settlement fees and closing costs cannot be included in the basis of a property:

- Casualty insurance premiums
- Rent or utility costs related to occupancy of the property before closing
- Any charges for acquiring a loan, such as mortgage insurance premiums, loan assumption fees, cost of a credit report, fees for appraisal reports, fees for refinancing a mortgage, and points. Points are prepaid interest on a loan and are generally deducted as interest over the life of the loan.

Real Estate Taxes: If a taxpayer pays real estate taxes on property he buys that the seller owed, those taxes are added to the basis and cannot be deducted currently.

Assumption of Mortgage: If a taxpayer buys property with an existing mortgage, the basis includes the amount paid in cash for the property plus the amount of the mortgage assumed.

Example: The Oceanside Partnership purchases a commercial building for $200,000 in cash and assumes a related mortgage of $800,000. The partnership also pays $5,500 in legal fees to a real estate attorney to handle the purchase. Oceanside's basis in the building is $1,005,500 ($200,000 + $800,000 + $5,500).

Constructing Assets: If a taxpayer builds property or has assets built, the costs of construction are included in the basis. In addition to the cost of land, these may include labor and materials; architect's fees; building permit charges; payments to contractors; rental equipment; inspections; employee wages paid for the construction work; and the cost of building supplies and materials used in the construction. The value of an owner's labor (if a sole proprietor rather than an employee-owner of a corporation) or any other labor for which payment is not made is not included in the basis.

Demolition Costs: Demolition costs increase an asset's basis because they are necessary to prepare the property for use. As such, costs incurred to demolish a building are added to the basis of the land on which the building was located. The costs of clearing land for construction also must be added to the basis of the land.

Example: Tony buys a lot with a badly damaged building on it for $25,000. He demolishes the building and prepares the land for a new structure. The demolition costs $13,000. Tony's adjusted basis in the land is $38,000 ($25,000 + $13,000).

Rehabilitation Costs: Rehabilitation costs increase basis. However, any rehabilitation credits allowed for the expenses must be subtracted.

Improvements to Business Property

The costs of making improvements to an asset are capitalized if the improvements:

- Add to the value of the asset,
- Appreciably lengthen the time a business can use it, or
- Adapt it to a different use.

Examples of improvements include installation of new electric wiring, a new roof, adding central air conditioning, or renovation of a kitchen.

In contrast, a repair keeps a property in operating condition but does not add to its value or substantially prolong its life. Examples include repainting a property or replacing broken windows. Unlike improvements, the costs of repairs can be deducted currently.

Example: Douglas repairs a leaky toilet in a rental duplex. The repair may be deducted as a current expense. The following year, Douglas replaces the entire plumbing system in the duplex with new pipes and bathroom fixtures. This is an improvement that increases the value of the property. Douglas must capitalize the cost of the new plumbing, increasing the property's basis, and depreciate the cost of this improvement over its useful life.

Repair vs. Improvements (Capitalization Rule Changes)

The IRS released final regulations during 2013 that require major changes in determining whether certain costs are repairs or improvements, and thus whether they must be expensed or capitalized. The regulations are effective in 2014. However, taxpayers have the option to apply them for tax years beginning January 1, 2012 or later. Under the changes, an improvement is redefined as a cost involving:

- The **betterment** of a unit of property (UOP),
- The **restoration** of a UOP, or
- The **adaptation** of a UOP to a new or different use.

The new regulations divide a building into nine different structural components called "building systems," such as those for plumbing, heating and air conditioning, and electrical, each of which may be a UOP, in addition to the building itself. Under the new, narrower definition of an improvement, costs must be evaluated for a specific building system, and not just for the building as a whole. This means it will become more difficult to classify costs as repairs and deduct them currently and more likely they will need to be capitalized.

For example, the cost to refurbish an elevator may "better" the elevator but would not be significant to the building as a whole, so under the prior rules the cost could have been deducted as a repair. Under the new rules, the cost may be significant to the elevator system and therefore must be capitalized.

Example: Curtis buys an apartment building in 2010 for $750,000. In 2013 he spends $8,000 to fix wiring in the electrical system. Under the old rules, the $8,000 cost likely would be considered a repair because it is relatively small compared to the overall cost of the building. Under the new rules, the electrical system is a separate structural component or building system. This means that the $8,000 must be compared with the cost of the electrical system alone, not the cost of the whole building. The cost is more significant in this context and thus is more likely to be deemed an improvement.

Materials and supplies costing $200 or less are now immediately deductible.

Safe Harbor Rules: The regulations provide several safe harbor rules. First, a de minimis safe harbor permits a business to deduct amounts expensed on its financial statements that do not exceed $5,000 per invoice or per item, as long as the business has a written capitalization policy or procedure that provides for expensing items with cost less than specified amounts or an economic useful life of 12 months or less.

If the business does not have qualifying financial statements, it may be permitted to deduct items that cost up to $500 per invoice or per item. A second safe harbor allows taxpayers with gross receipts of $10 million or less to expense as repairs, rather than capitalize as improvements, amounts up to the lesser of $10,000 or 2% of the unadjusted basis of a building property, as long as the unadjusted basis is $1 million or less. A third safe harbor allows for deduction of routine maintenance costs that are required more than once within a ten-year period for buildings, or more than once within the applicable class life period for non-building properties.

Other Changes to Basis of Business Property

Among the items that increase the basis of property are the following:

- The cost of extending service lines to the property
- Impact fees
- Legal fees, such as the costs of defending and perfecting title
- Zoning costs

Government assessments for items such as paving roads and sidewalks increase the value of a property, and therefore must be added to the property's basis. A business cannot deduct assessments as taxes, but may deduct charges for maintenance, repairs, or interest charges related to the improvements.

A business must decrease the basis of property by amounts that represent a recovery of the business's cost of the property. For example, rebates and casualty losses are among the items that decrease an asset's basis.

Example: Kristin buys a copier that costs $1,200 to use in her business. She sends in a rebate receipt and receives a $50 rebate from the manufacturer. The correct way to account for this rebate is to reduce the basis of the asset to $1,150 ($1,200 - $50).

Items that reduce the basis of property also include the following:

- Deductions for amortization, depreciation, section 179, and depletion (covered in Unit 8, *Depreciation of Business Assets)*
- Nontaxable corporate distributions
- Exclusion of subsidies for energy conservation measures
- Residential energy credits, vehicle credits, and the Investment Credit
- Certain canceled debt excluded from income
- Easements

Casualty and Theft Losses

Deductible casualty and theft losses and related insurance reimbursements reduce the basis of property. A casualty is defined as the damage, destruction, or loss of property resulting from an identifiable event that is sudden, unexpected, or unusual.

Deductible losses related to business and income-producing property (such as rental property) are reported on Form 4684, *Casualties and Thefts*, and are deductible without regard to whether they exceed the $100 and 10% of AGI thresholds that apply for personal-use property.

Example: A fire at Ramon's home destroys his couch and coffee table, which are personal-use property, for a loss of $5,000. This loss must be reduced by $100, and Ramon can deduct the portion that exceeds 10% of his AGI. The same fire also damages a business asset, a laptop computer that he had brought home that day in order to catch up on his work. The computer is destroyed, resulting in a business casualty loss of $3,000 that is fully deductible.

A casualty loss is not deductible if the damage or destruction is caused by progressive deterioration due to normal wear and tear from weather conditions or insect damage.

If an entity has business property that is stolen or destroyed, the deductible loss is figured as follows:

The taxpayer's adjusted basis in the property
MINUS
Any salvage value
MINUS
Any insurance or other reimbursement received

Theft may involve taking money or property by the following means: blackmail, burglary, embezzlement, extortion, kidnapping for ransom, larceny, and robbery. The taking of property must be illegal under the state law where it happened, and it must have been done with criminal intent.

Example: Jeff owns a sports shop that sells memorabilia. Two years ago, Jeff purchased a signed Mike Trout baseball jersey for display for $150. The jersey was stolen in 2013. The FMV of the jersey was $1,000 just before it was stolen, and insurance did not cover the loss. Jeff's deductible theft loss is $150, equal to his basis in the jersey.

Casualty losses are generally deductible only in the tax year during which the casualty occurred, even if a business does not repair or replace the damaged property until a later year. Theft losses can be deducted only in the year the business discovers the property was stolen.

Insurance Reimbursements: If a business has insurance coverage for property that is lost or damaged, it must file a claim for reimbursement or it will not be able to deduct the loss. The portion of the loss that is not reimbursable by insurance, such as a deductible, is not subject to this rule.

Example: Howard and Gayle are partners and have a gourmet food truck that is used for business purposes. Howard has an accident that causes $2,350 in damage to the truck. He and Gayle pay the repair bill out-of-pocket so their business insurance costs will not increase. The insurance policy has a $500 deductible. Because the insurance would not cover the first $500 of the loss, this amount is their deductible casualty loss. The amount of their loss in excess of $500 is not deductible because they did not file an insurance claim.

A business that has a casualty or theft loss must decrease its adjusted basis in the property by any insurance or other reimbursement it receives and by any deductible loss.

A business increases its basis in the property by the amounts spent, whether with proceeds of an insurance reimbursement or otherwise, on repairs that restore the property to, or beyond, its pre-casualty condition.

Basis of Securities

The basis of stocks, bonds, and other securities is the purchase price plus any costs of purchase, such as commissions and recording or transfer fees. A taxpayer must keep track of the basis per share of all stock purchases and sales.

Example: In 2013, Yuen Corporation purchases 2,000 shares of Catalyst Corporation stock. The cost of the stock is $24,000, and Yuen pays a broker's fee of $550 on the purchase and transfer. Therefore, the basis of the stock is $24,550 ($24,000 + $550).

Events that occur after the purchase of the stock can require adjustments to the basis per share of stock. The original basis per share can be changed by events such as stock dividends, stock splits, and DRIP (dividend reinvestment plan) activity.

- Stock dividends involve the issuance of additional shares to current shareholders. The shareholder's total basis is unchanged but is spread over more shares, which decreases the basis per share.

- A stock split is similar to a stock dividend. For example, a two-for-one stock split increases the number of outstanding shares two-fold and decreases the value and the basis per share by half.

As with a stock dividend, the total basis remains the same after a stock split. For example, if a taxpayer has 100 shares with a cost of $50 per share, his basis is $5,000. Assuming a two-for-one stock split, the taxpayer now has 200 shares with a basis per share of $25, which still equals a total basis of $5,000.

Example: In 2013, Zollinger Partnership purchases 100 shares of Better Electronics for $11,000. There is an additional $200 in broker's commissions, so the original basis per share is $112 ([$11,000 + $200] ÷ 100). Later in 2013, Zollinger receives 40 additional shares of Better Electronics' stock as a nontaxable stock dividend. The $11,200 basis must now be spread over 140 shares (100 original shares plus the 40-share stock dividend). The adjusted stock basis is $80 per share ([$11,200 ÷ 140).

Basis Other Than Cost

In certain cases, the adjusted basis of an asset is determined from something other than cost. For example:

Property Received for Services: If a taxpayer receives property for his services, he must include the property's FMV in income. The amount included in income is the taxpayer's basis in the property. If the services were performed for a price agreed on beforehand, this price may be used as the FMV of the property, as long as there is no evidence to the contrary.

When property is transferred in lieu of wages, the employer is entitled to deduct the property's fair market value at the time of the transfer and the same amount is taxable compensation for the employee. A gain or loss is realized if there is a difference between the fair market value and the adjusted basis of the property.

Bargain Purchases: A bargain purchase is a purchase of an item for less than its FMV. If, as compensation for services, a taxpayer buys goods or other property at less than the FMV, the difference between the purchase price and the property's FMV must be included in his income. His basis in the property is its FMV (the purchase price plus the amount included in income.)

Unit 7: Study Questions

1. Jade purchases a warehouse for her business, but it is in such bad condition that she decides to demolish it and build a new one. The demolition costs $15,600. How must Jade report this cost on her tax return?

A. The cost for the demolition is added to the basis of the land where the original demolished structure was located.
B. The demolition may be deducted on her tax return on Schedule E.
C. The demolition cost may be deducted on her tax return on Schedule C.
D. The demolition cost must be amortized over 180 months.

2. What item would not be included in an asset's basis?

A. Sales tax.
B. Installation charges.
C. Recording fees.
D. Interest paid on a loan to purchase the asset.

3. Ian buys a building. He makes a $15,000 down payment in cash. He also assumes a mortgage of $180,000 on it and pays $1,000 in title fees and $2,000 in points. What is Ian's basis in the building?

A. $15,000.
B. $195,000.
C. $196,000.
D. $198,000.

4. Alex is having financial difficulties, so he sells his office building to Cheryl, a real estate investor, who plans to use it as a business rental property. Alex was liable for $5,000 in delinquent real estate taxes on the property, which Cheryl agrees to pay. How should Cheryl treat this transaction?

A. Cheryl cannot deduct these taxes as a current expense; she must add the amount to the basis of the property.
B. Cheryl can deduct these taxes as a current expense on her Schedule A.
C. Cheryl can deduct these taxes as a current expense on her Schedule E.
D. Cheryl can deduct these taxes as a current expense on her Schedule C.

5. All of the following items decrease the basis of property except _______________:

A. Casualty or theft loss deductions and insurance reimbursements.
B. The cost of defending a title.
C. Depreciation.
D. Amortization.

6. Irina owns a yarn store. In 2013, she has a loss of $14,000 of business inventory due to water damage from a storm. The loss is completely covered by insurance. However, Irina will not be reimbursed by her insurance company until 2014. How should she treat this loss?

A. She should claim the entire loss as a casualty loss in 2013 and then claim the income from the insurance company reimbursement in 2014.
B. She must reduce the amount of her inventory loss in 2013. For 2014, she must include the insurance reimbursement as income.
C. She does not need to report this loss on her 2013 tax return, since she knows she will receive a reimbursement within a short period of time.
D. She must reduce her cost of goods sold in 2013 to reflect the loss and then claim the reimbursement as income in 2014.

7. Under new IRS rules, what are the categories for determining what constitutes an improvement to property?

A. Betterment, restoration, or adaptation.
B. Prolonging life and creating value.
C. Renovation, amelioration, or restoration.
D. Enhancement and repair.

8. How does a stock split affect basis?

A. There is no effect.
B. It increases the basis of stock.
C. It decreases the basis of stock.
D. It decreases the basis of a share of stock but does not affect the total basis of the stock.

9. Franco purchases 50 shares of Canine Country stock for $3,500. He pays a broker's fee of $100. He later receives 40 additional shares of Canine Country stock as a stock dividend. The following year, the company declares a two-for-one stock split. Calculate the total basis of Franco's Canine Country stock and his per share basis:

A. Stock basis: $3,500; per share basis: $38.88.
B. Stock basis: $3,500; per share basis: $19.44.
C. Stock basis: $3,600; per share basis: $20.
D. Stock basis: $3,600; per share basis: $40.

10. Priscilla's Pastries, a sole proprietorship, bought a building for $250,000 in cash in March 2013. Priscilla paid the title company $13,000 in settlement fees to purchase the property. She also assumed an existing mortgage of $35,000 on the property. Legal fees of $9,500 were incurred in a title dispute with the former owner in April 2013. The title was finally transferred to Priscilla in May 2013. Property taxes in the amount of $2,600 were incurred on the property after ownership was transferred. What is Priscilla's basis in the building in December 2013?

A. $250,000.
B. $285,000.
C. $307,500.
D. $310,100.

11. Arrowhead Model Builders is constructing a custom home. Calculate the basis of the property from the following information:

- $125,000 land purchase price
- $40,000 construction loan
- $3,000 points on construction loan
- $20,000 tear-down of existing home
- $10,000 clearing brush
- $50,000 construction workers' wages
- $300,000 construction materials

A. $227,000.
B. $505,000.
C. $548,000.
D. $545,000.

12. A hailstorm damages a van owned by Marjorie, a sole proprietor who offers mobile chiropractic services. The van's basis is $25,000, and her insurance company reimburses her $4,000 for the hail damage. Marjorie decides to replace the cracked windshield at a cost of $500 and pockets the rest of the insurance money. What is the adjusted basis of her van?

A. $21,500.
B. $28,500.
C. $29,000.
D. $19,500.

13. Chan Delivery Services is having cash-flow difficulties, so it transfers a pickup truck to Bonnie, an employee, in lieu of wages. The company owes Bonnie $7,000 in wages. At the time of the transfer, the truck had a fair market value of $7,000 and an adjusted basis to Chan Delivery of $5,500. How should the company report this transaction?

A. Wage expense of $7,000.
B. Wage expense of $5,500.
C. Wage expense of $2,500.
D. Wage expense of $7,000 and gain on sale of $1,500.

14. In 2013 Bramblewoods Partnership provides legal services to Andrews Cellular. Andrews Cellular then becomes insolvent. In lieu of payment, Bramblewoods Partnership accepts a set of gold coins with a fair market value of $5,000 and an electric scooter with a fair market value of $2,000 and an adjusted basis of $1,000. What amount of income must Bramblewoods Partnership report for this transaction?

A. $7,000.
B. $6,000.
C. $8,000.
D. $5,000.

15. Which is not a correct statement regarding repairs and improvements?

A. A repair generally may be deducted as a current business expense.
B. A repair keeps a property in operating condition but does not add to its value or substantially prolong its life.
C. An improvement adds value to an asset lengthens the time a business can use it.
D. A taxpayer may choose whether to expense or capitalize improvements.

Unit 8: Depreciation

More Reading:
Publication 946, *How to Depreciate Property*

As discussed in Unit 7, the costs of business assets and improvements must be capitalized. Capital expenditures are not currently deductible, unless they qualify for the section 179 deduction. Instead, these costs may be recognized as depreciation or amortization expense over lives assigned to individual assets.

Example: Better Produce, Inc. is a canning company that processes fruits and vegetables. In 2013, an older canning machine ceases to function properly. Better Produce has the option to purchase a new machine for $500,000, or completely rebuild its old machine, which will extend its useful life for another five years. Better Produce chooses to rebuild the machine at a cost of $125,000. The $125,000 cost must be capitalized and depreciated over its useful life, which in this case is five years.

Depreciation is an annual allowance for the wear and tear, deterioration, or obsolescence of an asset. Tax depreciation is based on the original, historical cost of the asset and is not indexed for inflation.

The cost of land and certain land improvements cannot be depreciated. Most other types of tangible property, such as buildings, machinery, vehicles, furniture, and equipment, are depreciable. Likewise, certain intangible property, such as patents, copyrights, and computer software, is amortizable.

In order to be depreciated or amortized, an asset must meet all the following requirements:

- The taxpayer generally must own the property. However, taxpayers may depreciate capital improvements for property they lease (for example, a fence that is built on property that the business leases from another party).
- The taxpayer must use the property in business or in an income-producing activity. If a taxpayer uses the property for both business and personal use, he can only deduct an amount of depreciation based on the business-use percentage.
- The property must have a determinable useful life of more than one year.

The property ceases to be depreciable when the business has fully recovered its cost or when it sells or retires the property from service, whichever happens first.

Depreciation Rules

In order to properly depreciate an asset, a taxpayer must determine the following:

- The depreciable basis of the property
- The depreciation method for the property
- The class life (which is representative of the asset's useful life)
- Whether the asset is listed property

- Whether the taxpayer elects to expense any portion of the asset
- Whether the taxpayer qualifies for any bonus first year depreciation

The following assets are not depreciable:

- Property with a useful life of one year or less
- Property placed in service and disposed of in the same year
- Equipment that is used to build capital improvements
- Section 197 intangibles such as copyrights and patents, which must be amortized, not depreciated.

> **Example:** Natalie is a self-employed accountant who must purchase new tax return preparation software every year. She cannot depreciate the software but may instead deduct its cost as a business expense since the item has a useful life of only one year.

Reporting Depreciation: Taxpayers must use Form 4562, *Depreciation and Amortization* to:

- Claim deductions for depreciation and amortization,
- Make an election under section 179 to currently expense certain depreciable property, and
- Provide information on the business/investment use of automobiles and other listed property.

Depreciation begins when a taxpayer places property in service in a trade or business or for the production of income.

> **Example:** Donald buys a machine for his business that is delivered on December 20, 2013. However, the machine is not installed and operational until January 12, 2014. It is not considered placed in service until 2014, and the first depreciation expense deduction can be claimed in 2014. If the machine had been ready and available for use when it was delivered, it would have been considered placed in service in 2013 even if it were not actually used until 2014.

> **Example:** On June 23, 2013, Sue bought a house to use as residential rental property. She made several repairs and had it ready for rent on September 5, 2013. At that time, she began to advertise the home for rent in the local newspaper. Sue can begin to depreciate the rental property in September because it is considered placed in service when it is ready and available for rent.

Salvage Value: An asset cannot be depreciated below its salvage (or scrap) value. Salvage value is the asset's estimated FMV at the end of its useful life. Salvage value is affected both by how a business uses the property and how long it uses it.

If it is the business's policy to dispose of property that is still in good operating condition, the salvage value may be relatively large. If the business's policy is to use property until it is no longer usable, its salvage value may be zero.

> **Example:** Cooper Trucking purchases a new delivery truck in 2013 for $125,000. The MACRS class life of the truck is five years. At the end of five years, Cooper Trucking estimates it will sell the used delivery truck at auction for $30,000, so it uses this amount as salvage value. The basis of the truck is $125,000, but the basis for depreciation is $95,000 ($125,000 - $30,000), since the business expects to recover $30,000 at the end of the asset's useful life.

Depreciation Methods

Once a business chooses a depreciation method for an asset, the business must generally use the same method for the life of the asset.

Straight-Line Depreciation: This is the simplest method. To use the straight-line method, a business must first determine the asset's basis, salvage value, and estimated useful life. If the asset has a salvage value, it is subtracted from the basis. The balance is the total depreciation expense deduction the business can take over the useful life of the property. If an asset originally cost $200, has an estimated salvage value of zero, and a five-year recovery period, the straight-line depreciation allowance would be $40 ($200 ÷ 5) each year for five years.

Straight-line Depreciation = (Cost - Salvage Value) ÷ Useful Life

A business may switch to the straight-line method at any time during the useful life of the property without IRS consent. However, after a business changes to straight-line, it cannot change back to any other method for a period of ten years without written permission from the IRS.

Example: On April 1, 2013, the Redstone Granite Corporation purchases a computer system for $40,000. The system has a five-year life. There is no salvage value. Depreciation is figured as follows:
Depreciation for 2013 = ($40,000 ÷ 5 years) × (9 months ÷ 12) = $6,000.
Depreciation for 2014 = ($40,000 ÷ 5 years) × (12 ÷ 12) = $8,000.

The Double-Declining Balance Method: This method uses a flat percentage depreciation rate over the life of the asset. For example, if five years is the asset's life, the double-declining balance method has a depreciation rate of [2 ÷ 5], or twice the straight-line depreciation rate. Instead of spreading the cost of the asset evenly over its life, this method expenses the asset by applying a constant rate to the declining balance of the asset, which results in declining depreciation expense each successive period.

The logic for the double-declining balance method is that there should be a greater deduction in the earlier years when the asset is more productive.

Example: For an asset that originally cost $200 and has a five-year life, double-declining balance depreciation is $80 = ([2 ÷ 5]× $200) in the first year; $48 = ([2 ÷ 5]×[$200 - $80]) in the second year; $28.80 = ([2 ÷ 5]×[$200 - $80 - $48]) in the third year; and so on.

Modified Accelerated Cost Recovery System (MACRS)

The modified accelerated cost recovery system (MACRS) is the depreciation method generally used for most tangible property.

Under MACRS, depreciable assets are divided into nine separate classes that dictate the number of years over which their cost will be recovered. Each MACRS class has a schedule that specifies the percentage of the asset's cost that is depreciated each year. For example, computers are depreciated over five years, and office furniture is depreciated over seven years.

Real property is depreciated using the straight-line method, with an equal amount of expense each year. Nonresidential real property, such as office buildings, shopping malls, and factories, is depreciated over a 39-year recovery period. Residential buildings, such as apartment complexes and residential rentals, are depreciated over a 27.5-year period.

The depreciation calculations allocate deductions of the asset's cost over a recovery period roughly consistent with the asset's estimated useful economic life.

MACRS Class Life Table

Property Class	Asset Type
3-year property	Certain tractor units; race horses over two years old; qualified rent-to-own property.
5-year property	Computers; office machinery; automobiles, taxis, buses, and trucks; breeding cattle and dairy cattle; appliances, carpets, and furniture used in residential retail activity; certain geothermal, solar, and wind property.
7-year property	Office furniture and fixtures; agricultural machinery and equipment; any other property that does not have a designated class life.
10-year property	Vessels and water transportation equipment; trees or vines bearing fruit or nuts; single purpose agricultural or horticultural structures.
15-year property	Improvements to land such as fences, roads, and bridges; municipal wastewater treatment plants; qualified restaurant and retail improvement property; qualified leasehold improvement property.
20-year property	Certain municipal sewers; farm buildings (other than single purpose agricultural or horticultural structures).
25-year property	Certain municipal sewers; water utility property.
27.5-year property	Residential rental property, if more than 80% of its gross rental income is from dwelling units.
39-year property	Section 1250 nonresidential real property, such as office buildings, stores, and warehouses.

Section 179 Deduction

The section 179 deduction is a special allowance that allows a business to elect to take a full deduction for the cost of new or used property in the first year it is placed in service, rather than depreciating it over its useful life. To qualify for the section 179 deduction, the property must meet all the following requirements:

- It must be eligible property.
- It must be acquired for business use (and used more than 50% for business in the year placed in service).
- It must have been acquired by purchase.

- It must not have been purchased from a related party, including a spouse, ancestors, or lineal descendants.

Eligible property generally includes the following:

- Tangible personal property, such as machinery and equipment
- Property contained in or attached to a building (other than structural components), such as refrigerators, grocery store counters, office equipment, printing presses, testing equipment, and signs
- Gasoline storage tanks and pumps at retail service stations
- Livestock, including horses, cattle, hogs, sheep, goats, and mink and other furbearing animals
- Off-the-shelf computer software
- Single purpose agricultural or horticultural property
- Storage facilities
- Qualified real property (as described below)

The section 179 deduction may not exceed taxable business income for the year, calculated without regard to the section 179 deduction itself and certain other items. However, an amount disallowed due to this limitation may be carried over for an unlimited number of years.

The deduction can be elected for individual qualifying assets, up to a maximum of $500,000 for 2013. The deduction amount may be increased by up to $35,000 for businesses in qualifying enterprise zones and up to $100,000 for businesses in federally declared disaster areas. However, to the extent the cost of qualifying section 179 property placed in service by the taxpayer exceeds $2 million, the maximum is reduced on a dollar-for-dollar basis, and eliminated if the total cost of qualifying property is at least $2.5 million.

Example: In 2013, Ashby Corporation purchases refurbished manufacturing equipment costing $2.1 million. The cost of the equipment is $100,000 more than the $2 million limit, so Ashby Corporation must reduce its section 179 deduction to $400,000 ($500,000 - $100,000). The remaining cost basis of $1.7 million ($2.1 million - $400,000 deducted under section 179) may be recovered using regular depreciation methods.

For partnerships, the section 179 limits described above apply to both the partnership and to each individual partner. The partnership determines its deduction subject to these limits, and then allocates the deduction among the partners. The partner considers the amounts allocated based upon his interest in the partnership and from any other sources in relation to the same limits.

Qualified Real Property: Businesses generally may not deduct the costs of real property under section 179. However, a special provision presently allows businesses to use up to $250,000 of the $500,000 limit described above for costs of qualified real property (QRP).

This provision applies only to the following:

- Qualified leasehold improvement property
- Qualified restaurant property (such as renovation of a restaurant building)
- Qualified retail improvement property (such as an interior upgrade of a retail clothing store)

Example: Armando owns an Italian restaurant. In 2013, he renovates the interior by upgrading the booths and remodeling the kitchen at a cost of $260,000. He also purchases a computer for use in his business at a cost of $5,000. Therefore, Armando has the following qualifying expenses for the section 179 deduction:

Computer:	$5,000
Qualified real property:	$260,000
Total asset purchases in 2013:	**$265,000**

Since the limit for expensing QRP under section 179 is $250,000, Armando may only expense $250,000 of the renovation costs. However, he may still take the section 179 deduction for the full cost of the computer, since the limit for other qualifying property is $500,000. Armando's allowable section 179 deduction is therefore limited to $255,000 ($5,000 computer + $250,000 of QRP). The excess amount of $10,000 may be depreciated over the useful life applicable for this type of real property.

Trade-in Property: If a business buys qualifying property with cash and a trade-in, its depreciable basis for purposes of the section 179 deduction includes only the cash portion of the purchase price.

Example: Fleet Feet, a retail athletic shoe store, traded two wood displays with a total adjusted basis of $680 for a new glass display that cost $1,320. Fleet Feet received an $800 trade-in allowance for the old displays and paid an additional $520 in cash for the new glass display. The shop also traded a used van with an adjusted basis of $4,500 for a new van costing $9,000. Fleet Feet received a $4,800 trade-in allowance on the used van and paid $4,200 in cash for the new van. Only the portion of the new property's basis paid with cash qualifies for the section 179 deduction. Therefore, Fleet Feet's qualifying costs for the section 179 deduction are $4,720 ($520 + $4,200).

Bonus Depreciation

If the cost of business property cannot immediately be deducted as a section 179 expense, a business may elect to take bonus depreciation for certain types of new property. This provision allows a business to write off 50% of certain property costs in the first year, with the remaining cost depreciated over the asset's useful life. Applicable section 179 deductions are generally used first, followed by bonus depreciation, unless the business has an insufficient level of taxable income.

The bonus depreciation allowance generally applies to tangible personal property with a recovery period of 20 years or less, as well as to certain buildings and leasehold improvements, office equipment, and purchased computer software.

Note: The property must be new and in original use condition (unlike the requirement for section 179 deductions, which are allowed for both new and used property.) Bonus depreciation is also not subject to the same $2 million phase-out as the section 179 deduction.

Listed Property

Special rules apply to *listed property,* which includes cars and other vehicles used for transportation; property used for entertainment, recreation, or amusement such as photographic or video-recording equipment; and certain computers and related peripheral equipment. Computer equipment used exclusively at a business location (including a qualified home office) is not considered listed property.

If an item is used for both business and personal purposes, deductions for depreciation and section 179 are limited to the percentage of business use. Further, if business use is not more than 50%, section 179 deductions and bonus depreciation allowances are not allowed, and depreciation must be calculated using the straight-line method.

Example: In 2013, Eleanor buys and places in service a new computer that costs $4,000. She uses the computer 80% for her business and 20% for personal purposes. She may deduct $3,200 under section 179 for the business portion of the cost (80% × $4,000).

The IRS no longer categorizes cellular telephones as listed property.

Heavy Sports Utility Vehicle Exception: A taxpayer cannot elect to expense under section 179 more than $25,000 of the cost of any heavy sport utility vehicle (SUV) and certain other vehicles placed in service during the tax year. This rule applies to vehicles weighing between 6,000 and 14,000 pounds.

Note: This use of the section 179 deduction used to be known as the "Hummer Tax Loophole" because it allowed businesses to buy large SUVs and write them off. The IRS has since modified the tax code with the limits described above. When you take the EA exam, you should be familiar with the limits on vehicle depreciation.

Ambulances, hearses, taxis, transport vans, clearly marked emergency vehicles, and other qualified nonpersonal use vehicles are not listed property and are excluded from the $25,000 limit.

Section 280F Depreciation Limits: For certain other passenger vehicles weighing less than 6,000 pounds and used more than 50% for business purposes, the total depreciation deduction is also limited, as outlined under section 280F.

The IRS releases guidance each year indicating the depreciation limits for each category of vehicles, adjusted for inflation. In 2013, bonus depreciation is capped at $11,160 for cars and $11,360 for trucks and vans for the year they are placed into service.

Amortization

Amortization is used to deduct the cost or basis of an intangible asset over its estimated life. With the exception of off-the-shelf computer software, intangible assets generally are not eligible for section 179 deductions. The basis of an intangible asset is usually the cost to buy or create it.

Definition: Intangible property is property that has value but it cannot be seen or touched.

Examples of intangible assets include goodwill, patents, copyrights, trademarks, trade names, franchises, and favorable relationships with customers or suppliers that are carried over from an acquired business.

A taxpayer may amortize certain start-up costs for purchasing an active trade or business. These include only the investigative costs that help the taxpayer decide whether to purchase the business. Costs incurred in an attempt to purchase a specific business are capital costs that cannot be amortized.

Certain intangible assets, including the preceding examples, are designated as Section 197 intangibles and must be amortized over a 15-year period (180 months). Another example is the cost of a covenant not to compete executed in connection with the acquisition of a trade or business. As a section 197 intangible asset, this cost would be amortized over 15 years, even though the covenant agreement may be in place for a shorter period.

Example: Heather is a podiatrist. Another podiatrist is retiring, so she is purchasing his business for $1 million. The practice has $750,000 of tangible assets, including medical equipment and office furnishings. The remainder of the purchase price ($250,000) is attributed to goodwill, which Heather must amortize over 15 years. Her goodwill deduction is $16,667 a year ($250,000 ÷ 15).

Depletion

Depletion is similar in concept to depreciation, and is the method of cost recovery for mining and agricultural activities. Depletion refers to the exhaustion of a natural resource as a result of production, such as by mining, quarrying, or cutting (of timber). Mineral property, timber, and natural gas are all examples of natural resources that are subject to the deduction for depletion. There are two ways of figuring depletion:

- Cost depletion
- Percentage depletion

Some businesses employ cost depletion at the outset of operations when a large number of units of the deposit are extracted and sold, and then convert to percentage depletion later when percentage depletion yields a more sizable deduction.

Cost Depletion: This method allocates the cost of a natural resource over the total anticipated volume to yield cost depletion per unit (expressed in tons, barrels, etc.) A depletion deduction is then allowed each year based on the units exploited.

After a business determines the property's basis, estimates the total recoverable units, and knows the number of units sold during the tax year, it can calculate the cost depletion deduction as follows:

Divide the property's basis for depletion by estimated total recoverable units =
Rate per unit
Multiply the rate per unit by actual units sold =
Cost depletion deduction

Example: In 2013, Brian buys a timber farm, and he estimates the timber can produce 300,000 units when cut. At the time of purchase, the adjusted basis of the timber is $24,000. Brian cuts and sells 27,000 units. Brian's depletion rate for each unit is $.08 ($24,000 ÷ 300,000). His deduction for depletion in 2013 is $2,160 (27,000 × $.08).

Percentage Depletion: Under this method, a flat percentage of gross income from the property is taken as the depletion deduction. Percentage depletion may not be used for timber and its use for oil and gas properties is subject to strict limits.

To figure percentage depletion, the business multiplies a certain percentage, specified for each mineral, by gross income from the property during the year. The percentage depletion deduction generally cannot be more than 50% (100% for oil and gas property) of taxable income from the property, calculated before the depletion deduction and the domestic production activities deduction (DPAD).

Unit 8: Study Questions

1. The maximum section 179 expense a business can elect to deduct for qualified real property placed in service in 2013 is:

A. $179,000.
B. $250,000.
C. $500,000.
D. $2 million.

2. The Friendship Spirit Partnership bought the Andrews Brothers Partnership. Goodwill and a covenant not to compete associated with the purchase were valued at $100,000. What is the number of years over which these intangible assets can be amortized?

A. 5 years.
B. 10 years.
C. 15 years.
D. 25 years.

3. Which of the following would not qualify for a depletion deduction?

A. Oil well.
B. Timber.
C. Diamond mine.
D. Gasoline refinery.

4. Levi owns a convenience store. He purchases two computers from his grandfather and places both in service in 2013 as part of a bona fide business transaction. The computers cost $750 each. Which of the following is true?

A. Levi can take a section 179 deduction for the computers.
B. Levi can take regular MACRS depreciation on the computers.
C. Levi is not allowed to depreciate the computers since they were purchased from a related party. But he may take a section 179 deduction for them.
D. Levi may take either section 179 or bonus depreciation on the computers.

5. Which of the following types of business property qualifies for the section 179 deduction?

A. A delivery truck.
B. A business building.
C. A residential rental property.
D. A patent.

6. Mary purchases a new computer for $1,100. She uses the property 75% for her business and 25% for personal purposes. What is Mary's section 179 deduction?

A. $0.
B. $275.
C. $825.
D. $1,100.

7. Lou is a sole proprietor who buys a cellular phone for $720 in 2013. Based on his phone records, Lou uses the cell phone 45% for business use and 55% for personal use. What is Lou's section 179 deduction for 2013?

A. $0.
B. $324.
C. $396.
D. $720.

8. Kerman Corporation is a calendar-year, cash-basis corporation that specializes in constructing office buildings. Kerman bought a truck on December 1, 2013 that had to be modified for use in the business. The truck is 100% business-use. Kerman accepted delivery of the modified truck on January 10, 2014. The truck was first used for its intended purpose on January 23, 2014. As of what date can Kerman start depreciating the truck?

A. December 1, 2013.
B. January 10, 2014.
C. January 23, 2014.
D. Never.

9. Which of the following property is a business not able to depreciate?

A. Property placed in service and disposed of in the same year.
B. Fruit trees.
C. Machinery.
D. Buildings.

10. Which of the following vehicles is considered listed property for tax purposes?

A. An ambulance.
B. A passenger automobile weighing 6,000 pounds or less.
C. A taxi.
D. A marked police car.

11. In 2013, Vanner Corporation placed in service section 179 property with a total cost of $2,025,000. The corporation's taxable income in 2013 was $600,000. What is Vanner's allowable section 179 deduction for 2013?

A. $0.
B. $475,000.
C. $500,000.
D. $600,000.

12. TJ buys and places in service professional video-recording equipment. He pays $15,000 cash and receives a $3,000 trade-in allowance for used video equipment. Both the old and the new video-recording equipment were used 90% for business and 10% for personal purposes. His allowable section 179 deduction is:

A. $16,200.
B. $13,500.
C. $12,600.
D. $15,000.

13. Lucy and Jessica are equal partners in a restaurant. In 2013, they purchase a new $30,000 pizza oven and want to take the section 179 deduction for the full cost of the oven. The partnership's ordinary income before the section 179 deduction is $25,000. There were no other qualifying section 179 purchases during the year. What is the amount of section 179 deduction that Lucy can deduct on her *individual* tax return?

A. $0.
B. $6,000.
C. $12,500.
D. $15,000.

14. Using MACRS, what is the recovery period for depreciating a commercial office building?

A. 20 years.
B. 25 years.
C. 27.5 years.
D. 39 years.

Unit 9: Disposition of Business Assets

More Reading:
Publication 544, *Sales and Other Dispositions of Assets*

A business may recognize a gain or loss for tax purposes if it:

- Sells property for cash
- Exchanges property for other property (and cash)
- Receives payment by a tenant for the cancellation of a lease (treated as if it were a sale of the property)
- Receives payment for granting the exclusive use of a copyright
- Receives property to satisfy a debt
- Abandons property
- Loses property or has it damaged as a result of casualty or theft (and if it receives a related insurance reimbursement for such a loss)

A taxpayer may fully depreciate an asset until its adjusted basis is zero, but continue to use the asset thereafter. If an asset is sold or otherwise disposed of, its adjusted basis is compared to any amounts received to determine whether there is a gain or loss.

The treatment of gains or losses reportable for tax purposes is dependent upon whether they are classified as capital gains and losses or as ordinary income (and whether the capital gains and losses are long-term or short-term). For individual taxpayers, capital gains may be subject to more favorable capital gains tax rates. To properly report the disposition of an asset, a taxpayer must determine whether it is a capital asset, a noncapital asset, or a section 1231 asset.

Gains and losses on dispositions of business assets are generally reported on Form 4797, *Sales of Business Property*.

Capital Assets: Capital assets include personal-use assets; collectibles; and investment property such as stocks, bonds, and other securities (unless held by a professional securities dealer).

Example: Jim owns 15 mechanical toy banks, which he collects as a hobby. He is not a professional dealer. Jim's mechanical banks are considered capital assets.

A gain from the disposition of personal-use property is a capital gain, but a loss is generally not deductible, except for certain casualty losses.

Noncapital Assets: Assets used in a trade or business or as rental property are noncapital assets, including the following:

- Inventory or any similar property held for sale to customers
- Depreciable property used in a business, even if it is fully depreciated
- Real property used in a trade or business, such as a commercial building or a residential rental
- Self-produced copyrights, transcripts, manuscripts, drawings, photographs, or artistic compositions
- Accounts receivable or notes receivable acquired by a business
- Stocks and bonds held by professional securities dealers

- Business supplies
- Commodities and derivative financial instruments

Example: In February 2013, Ines purchases a black-and-white copy machine for use in her business. In July, she decides she needs a color copier instead. Ines sells the used black-and-white copier for $3,000. The copier is a business asset held for less than a year, so it is treated as a noncapital asset.

Section 1231 Assets: Section 1231 assets include certain business (noncapital) assets that have been held for more than one year, as well as certain business and investment property disposed of in involuntary conversions.

The tax code gives special treatment to transactions involving disposition of section 1231 assets. If the taxpayer has a net loss from all section 1231 transactions, the loss is treated as ordinary loss. If the section 1231 transactions result in a net gain, the gain is generally treated as capital gain (except for depreciation recapture, which is taxed as ordinary income, as discussed below).

Example: Philip owns an antique vase that he purchased at auction two years ago. He also owns a residential rental property that he purchased three years ago and two vehicles. One is a pizza delivery van he bought five years ago and uses exclusively in his restaurant business. The second is his personal-use SUV that he uses for commuting and everyday errands. Phillip's assets are categorized as follows:

1. Antique vase: A capital asset, because it is a collectible
2. Residential rental property: Section 1231 (rental property held over one year)
3. Pizza delivery van: Section 1231 (business property held over one year)
4. SUV: A capital asset, because it is a personal-use vehicle

Gain or loss on the following transactions is subject to section 1231 treatment:

1. **Sale or exchange of cattle and horses:** They must be used for draft, breeding, dairy, or sporting purposes and held for 24 months or longer.
2. **Sale or exchange of other livestock:** Other livestock includes hogs, mules, sheep, goats, donkeys, and other fur-bearing animals. They must be used for draft, breeding, dairy, or sporting purposes and held for 12 months or longer.
3. **Sale or exchange of depreciable (or amortizable) property:** Business property that is held for more than one year. Examples include machinery and trucks, as well as amortizable section 197 intangibles such as patents or copyrights.
4. **Sale or exchange of business real estate:** The property must be used in a business activity and held for more than one year. Examples include barns and office buildings.
5. **Sale or exchange of unharvested crops:** The crops and land must be sold, exchanged, or involuntarily converted at the same time and to the same person, and the land must have been held longer than one year. Growing crops sold with a leasehold on the land, even if sold to the same person in a single transaction, are not included.

> **Example:** Six years ago, Superior Design Inc. purchased a computer for $10,000. The company sells it this year for $700. Superior Design had depreciated the computer down to its salvage value, which was estimated at $1,000. The company has a loss of $300 on the sale of the computer ($1,000 salvage value minus $700 sale price). The computer is a section 1231 asset and the loss is an ordinary loss.

The sale, exchange, or involuntary conversion of inventory is not a section 1231 transaction, even if the inventory has been held for more than one year.

> **Example:** Harwell Inc. manufactures shipping containers. Harwell has owned land and a building that houses its manufacturing operations for 15 years. The land and the building are therefore section 1231 assets, because they are used in a business and have been held for more than one year. Harwell also has unsold shipping containers in inventory. Inventory is not a section 1231 asset.

The sale of a copyright, literary, musical, or artistic composition is not a section 1231 transaction if a taxpayer's personal efforts created the property, or if it was received as a gift from a previous owner whose personal efforts created it. The sale of such property results in ordinary income.

> **Example:** Debbie is a self-employed writer who reports her income on Schedule C. She writes and publishes a popular crockpot cookbook. A few years later, Debbie sells the copyright of her manuscript to a publisher. This is not a section 1231 transaction, because the copyright was self-created, and it must be reported as ordinary income.

Depreciation Recapture

Depreciation recapture may be required when a business sells previously depreciated or amortized property at a gain. All or a portion of the gain attributable to depreciation (that would otherwise be treated as capital gain) may need to be recaptured as ordinary income. The balance of the gain in excess of the recaptured depreciation is treated as capital gain.

> **Example:** Mort runs Hammerton Dairy Farm, a calendar-year sole proprietorship. In February 2011, Mort buys a tractor (five-year property) that costs $10,000. MACRS depreciation deductions for the tractor are $1,500 in 2011 and $2,550 in 2012 (based upon MACRS table A-14 for 150% declining balance depreciation using a half-year convention). Mort sells the tractor in May 2013 for $7,000. The MACRS deduction in 2013 is $893 (½ of $1,785). The gain on the sale of the tractor that must be treated as ordinary income is figured as follows:

Amount received in the sale	$7,000
Original purchase price	$10,000
MACRS depreciation deductions ($1,500 + $2,550 + $893)	($4,943)
Adjusted basis	$5,057
Gain realized ($7,000 - $5,057)	**$1,943**

> The realized gain is less than the amount of depreciation subject to recapture, so the entire amount is treated as ordinary income.

In determining depreciable recapture for property sold at a gain, there is a critical distinction between two types of property: section 1245 and section 1250. For section 1245 property, any gain attributable to previous depreciation deductions is taxed as ordinary income. For section 1250 property, the depreciation recapture is limited to the portion of previously deducted depreciation in excess of deductions that would have been taken if computed using the straight-line method.

Section 1245

Section 1245 property is defined by either:

1. Personal (tangible or intangible) property, or
2. Other tangible property (not including buildings) that is depreciable and that is:
    a. Used as an integral part of certain specified activities (manufacturing, production, extraction, or furnishing transportation, communications, electrical energy, gas, water, or sewage disposal services), or
    b. A facility used for the bulk storage of fungible commodities.

Definition: A fungible good or asset is one that is essentially interchangeable with other goods or assets of the same type, such as a specific grade of a particular commodity. Examples of highly fungible commodities are crude oil and wheat.

A grain silo is considered section 1245 property rather than section 1250 property, even if it is attached permanently to the land. Storage structures for oil and gas and other minerals are considered section 1245 property.

Example: Several years ago, Crystal purchased a used binding machine for $1,000 for her business. She has claimed $400 in depreciation on the machine. In 2013, Crystal sells the machine for $1,100. Her gain is as follows:

Sale price of the machine:	$1,100
Minus adjusted basis ($1,000 - $400):	$600
Crystal's gain on the sale of the machine:	**$500**

A portion of the gain is ordinary income ($400 of depreciation recapture for section 1245 property), and the remainder of $100 is long-term capital gain.

Section 1250

Section 1250 property generally consists of buildings (including their structural components), most other permanent structures, and land improvements of general use and purpose. Examples of section 1250 property include residential rental property, factory buildings, and office buildings. Since buildings are generally depreciated using the straight-line method, taxpayers usually receive more favorable treatment of depreciation recapture for section 1250 property.

Example: Maeve has owned an apartment building for almost 20 years. She originally purchased the building for $2.5 million. After taking straight-line depreciation deductions, her adjusted basis in 2013 is $800,000 and she sells the property for $4.5 million. Her gain is as follows:

Sale price	$4,500,000
Minus adjusted basis	$800,000
Gain on sale	**$3,700,000**

Because the building is section 1250 property and Maeve has only taken straight-line depreciation, there is no depreciation recapture, and the entire amount of the gain is treated as long-term capital gain. Had the building been depreciated using an accelerated method, as was more common prior to the adoption of the current MACRS system, a portion of the prior year depreciation deductions might have been subject to recapture.

Installment Sales

An installment sale involves a disposition of property in which the seller receives at least a portion of the sales proceeds during a year subsequent to the year of the sale. The resulting gain is typically reported using the installment method. If a business elects out of using the installment method, it must report the entire gain in the year of the sale, even if it does not receive the remaining proceeds until later years. Each payment received on an installment sale transaction may include the following components:

- Return of the seller's adjusted basis in the property
- Gain on the sale
- Interest income (attributable to financing the sale over a period of time)

The taxpayer must calculate a gross profit percentage, representing the ratio of the gain on the sale (numerator) to the total proceeds to be paid less any interest income (denominator). The denominator will also equal the total of the gain and the return of the seller's adjusted basis in the property. Each year, including the year of sale, the total payments received less the portion attributable to interest is multiplied by the gross profit percentage to determine the portion of the gain that must be recognized.

Example: A business sells a machine for a price of $6,000, with a gross profit of $1,500, and it will receive payments totaling $6,000 plus interest over four years. The gross profit percentage is 25% ($1,500 ÷ $6,000). After subtracting the applicable interest portion from each payment, the business will apply the gross profit percentage to each installment, including any down payment, and report the resulting amount as installment sale income for each tax year in which it receives payments. The remainder of each payment is the tax-free return of the machine's adjusted basis.

The gain is reported on Form 6252, *Installment Sale Income.*

If the arrangement is modified at a later date or the full amount of the sale price is not paid, the resulting gross profit on the sale may also change.

Note: A taxpayer's gain, or gross profit, is the amount by which the selling price exceeds the adjusted basis in the property sold. The gross profit percentage is generally calculated by dividing the gross profit from the sale by the selling price. You may be required to understand how to calculate gross profit percentage for both Parts 1 and 2 of the EA exam.

Example: In 2013, the Greenbelt Partnership sells land under an installment sale. The land has a basis of $40,000, and the sale price is $100,000. Therefore, the gross profit is $60,000. Greenbelt receives a $20,000 down payment and the buyer's note for $80,000. The note provides for four annual payments of $20,000 each, plus 8% interest, beginning in 2014. Greenbelt's gross profit percentage is 60%. Greenbelt will report capital gain of $12,000 for each payment of $20,000 received. In 2015, Greenbelt and the buyer agree to reduce the purchase price to $85,000, and the remaining payments during 2015, 2016, and 2017 are each reduced to $15,000. The new gross profit percentage is 46.67% for the remaining payments. Greenbelt will report capital gain of $7,000 (46.67% of $15,000) for each of the $15,000 installments paid in 2015, 2016, and 2017.

In certain circumstances, a business may be treated as having received a payment, even though it has not received cash. For example, the receipt of property or the assumption of a mortgage by the buyer may be treated as a payment. If the buyer assumes or pays off a mortgage or other debt on the property sold, the calculation of gross profit percentage is affected.

The mortgage assumption is subtracted before calculating the gross profit percentage, except to the extent that it exceeds the adjusted basis of the property for installment sale purposes. In contrast, if the property is sold to a buyer who holds a mortgage on it and the mortgage is canceled rather than assumed, the cancellation is treated as a payment received in the year of the sale and is not subtracted in calculating the gross profit percentage.

If a business reports the sale of property under the installment method, any applicable depreciation recapture under section 1245 or 1250 is taxable as ordinary income in the year of sale, even if no payments are received in that year.

If the gain is more than the depreciation recapture amount, the remainder of the gain would be recognized using the installment method rules. An installment sale generally does not apply to:

- The sale of inventory, even if the business receives a payment after the year of sale
- Dealer sales of real or personal property in the normal course of business
- A sale that results in a loss
- The sale of stock or securities traded on an established market

Installment sales to related persons are generally allowed. However, if a taxpayer sells property to a related person who then sells or disposes of the property within two years of the original sale, the taxpayer will lose the benefit of installment sale reporting.

Example: Resort Properties Co. sells a motel to a 50% owner/shareholder of the corporation, Better Lodging Co. The sale price is $2 million, and Resort Properties realizes a profit on the sale of $250,000. Better Lodging agrees to pay in five installments of $400,000. Eighteen months later, Better Lodging sells the motel to another company. Resort Properties must report the entire profit of $250,000 on the sale, even though it has not received all of the installment payments. The installment sale method is disallowed on the related party sale, because the property was disposed of before the end of the two-year holding period.

Like-Kind Exchanges (Section 1031)

A section 1031 "like-kind" exchange occurs when a business or individual exchanges business or investment property for similar property. If an exchange qualifies under section 1031, the taxpayer does not pay tax currently on a resulting gain and may not deduct a loss until the acquired property is later sold or otherwise disposed of. To qualify for nonrecognition treatment, an exchange must meet all of the following conditions:

- The property must be held for investment or for productive use in a business.
- The property must not be "held primarily for sale" (such as inventory).
- There must be an actual exchange of two or more assets or properties. (The exchange of cash for property is treated as a sale, not as an exchange.)

The simplest form of 1031 exchange is a simultaneous swap of one property for another. Alternatively, it may be arranged as a deferred exchange, in which the disposition of one property and the later acquisition of a replacement property are mutually dependent parts of an integrated transaction. In contrast, simply selling a property and using the proceeds to purchase another similar property is a taxable transaction.

In a deferred exchange, the property to be received must be identified in writing (or actually received) within 45 days after the date of transfer of the property given up. Further, the replacement property in a deferred exchange must be received by the earlier of:

- The 180th day after the date on which the property given up was transferred, or
- The due date, including extensions, of the tax return for the year in which the transfer of that property occurs.

Example: A corporation purchases a medical office building for $300,000. After four years, the fair market value of the property is $350,000. If the corporation were to sell the property, it would recognize a gain of $50,000. If the corporation instead arranges a like-kind exchange and either receives a similar property in exchange or invests the proceeds from the sale of the building in a similar property, the taxable gain could be deferred.

A qualified intermediary must be used to facilitate a deferred exchange. This is an independent party who acquires the relinquished property and transfers it to a buyer. The intermediary holds the sales proceeds to prevent the taxpayer from having actual or constructive receipt of the funds. The intermediary then acquires the replacement property and transfers it to the taxpayer to complete the exchange within the allowable time limits.

Example: Otis owns a piece of land in Louisiana he wants to exchange, and he arranges a 1031 exchange transaction. When the land sale closes, his escrow company holds the proceeds. Within 45 days Otis identifies an apartment building he wants to buy in Arkansas and negotiates a contract to buy the building. Within the required 180 days, the escrow company releases the funds he needs to close the purchase, and the exchange transaction is complete. The escrow company is considered a qualified intermediary, and Otis has successfully postponed recognition of any gain related to disposition of the original property.

Qualifying Exchanges: To qualify under section 1031, an exchange must involve like-kind property, such as the trade of real property for real property or personal property for personal property.

An exchange of real property generally qualifies more easily as like-kind, regardless of how each property is used or whether each property is improved or unimproved. For instance, the exchange of a building for farmland would qualify, as would the exchange of an apartment building for an office building. In contrast, the exchange of factory machinery for a factory building is not a qualifying exchange.

An exchange of personal property must involve items that are at least similar enough to both be categorized within one of several asset classes established by the IRS. For example, the exchange of a panel truck for a pickup truck may qualify as a trade of like-kind property, but the exchange of a pickup truck for a semi-truck likely would not.

The exchange of equipment or business assets that are used within the United States for similar items used outside the United States would not be considered an exchange of qualifying like-kind property.

All of the following can be exchanged as like-kind property:

- Condos, land, apartment buildings, duplexes, commercial buildings, residential rentals, and retail buildings
- A single business property exchanged for two or more properties and vice versa
- Water rights, mineral rights, oil and gas interests, copyrights, trademarks, and other intangible assets (but not partnership interests or securities)
- Livestock (but not livestock of different sexes)

Exchanges involving the following types of property do not qualify for section 1031 exchange treatment:

- Inventory, or any property purchased for resale
- Stocks, bonds, notes, or other securities
- Real property within the United States and real property outside the United States
- Exchanges of shares of corporate stock in different companies
- Exchanges of partnership interests or LLC membership interests
- A personal residence, or personal-use property, such as a personal car
- Land under development for resale
- Corporation common stock

Definition: Boot is a term used to describe cash or other property that is included in an exchange to compensate for a difference in the values of the like-kind properties traded.

Boot: A taxpayer who receives boot in a section 1031 exchange may have to recognize a taxable gain to the extent of the cash and the FMV of unlike property received.

Example: Stephen and Tricia decide they will exchange rental properties. Stephen's rental property is more valuable, so Tricia agrees to exchange her rental property and an additional $10,000 in cash. Therefore, Stephen must recognize $10,000 of any gain he realizes on the transaction, even if Section 1031 tax deferral otherwise applies.

The taxable gain cannot exceed the amount of gain that would have been recognized if the property had been sold in a taxable transaction. The amount considered boot would be reduced by qualified costs paid in connection with the transaction.

Example: Andrew's relinquished rental property has an FMV of $60,000 and an adjusted basis of $30,000. His replacement property has an FMV of $50,000, and he also receives $10,000 in cash as part of the exchange. Andrew, therefore, has a realized gain of $30,000 on the exchange, but his taxable gain is only $10,000, equal to the cash (boot) received in the exchange. The rest of his gain is deferred until he disposes of the new property at a later date.

When an exchange involves property that is subject to a liability, assumption of the liability is treated as if it were a transfer of cash and thus considered boot by the party who is relieved of the liability. If each property in an exchange is transferred subject to a liability, a taxpayer is treated as having received boot only if he is relieved of a greater liability than the liability he assumes. This is called debt reduction boot, and it occurs most often when a taxpayer is acquiring a less expensive or valuable property.

Although a taxpayer may have to recognize gain on a partially taxable like-kind exchange, he would never recognize a loss. However, a loss on a like-kind exchange would affect the taxpayer's basis in the property received, and the tax treatment when it is ultimately sold or disposed.

If a taxpayer receives boot in connection with an exchange and recognizes gain, the basis of the property received is equal to the basis of the property given up plus the amount of gain recognized.

Basis of Property Received in a Like-Kind Exchange: The basis of the property received is generally the adjusted basis of the property transferred.

Example: Judy has a rental house with an adjusted basis of $70,000. In 2013, she trades the rental house for an empty lot with an FMV of $150,000. Judy's basis in the lot is $70,000, equal to the adjusted basis of the property she exchanged.

If a taxpayer trades property and also pays money as part of the exchange, the basis of the property received is the basis of the property given up, increased by any additional money paid.

Example: Peyton pays $43,000 cash for a new diesel truck for her business. She receives a trade-in allowance of $13,600 on her old truck, which she had paid $50,000 for two years ago. She has taken depreciation deductions of $39,500 on the old vehicle. She has a $3,100 gain on the exchange ($13,600 trade-in allowance minus her $10,500 adjusted basis for the old truck) but recognition of the gain is postponed under the rules for like-kind exchanges. Her basis in the new truck is $53,500, the total of the cash paid ($43,000) and her adjusted basis of $10,500 in the old truck.

Example: Jorge trades a plot of land (adjusted basis $30,000) for a different plot of land in another town (FMV $70,500). He pays an additional $4,000 in cash. Jorge's basis in the new land is $34,000: his $30,000 basis in the old land plus the $4,000 cash.

Related Party Transactions: Like-kind exchanges are allowed between related parties, including family members. However, if either party disposes of the property within two years after a 1031 exchange, the exchange is usually disqualified from nonrecognition treatment; any gain or loss that was deferred in the original transaction must be recognized in the year the disposition occurs. The two-year holding period rule may not apply:

- If one of the parties involved in the exchange dies
- If the property is subsequently converted in an involuntary exchange (such as a fire or a flood)
- If it can be established to the satisfaction of the IRS that the exchange and subsequent disposition were not done mainly for tax avoidance purposes

Example: Tim and Harry are brothers. Tim owns a residential rental property and Harry owns a tract of land. In 2013, they exchange the properties. Since they are related parties, each must hold the property he acquired for at least two years or the exchange may be disallowed and treated as a sale. In early 2013, Harry dies. In this case, the 1031 exchange is still valid, because the holding period rule does not apply if one of the parties in a related exchange dies before the two-year period expires.

For purposes of this rule, a related person includes:

- A close family member (siblings, spouses, ancestors, and lineal descendants).
- An entity (corporation or partnership) in which the taxpayer owns either directly or indirectly more than a 50% interest. This includes ownership by a spouse or a close family member.
- Two entities in which the same taxpayer owns directly or indirectly more than 50% of each.
- An estate in which the taxpayer is either the beneficiary of the estate.
- A trust for which the taxpayer is the fiduciary and the related party is a beneficiary either of that same trust or a related trust or a fiduciary of a related trust.

The IRS gives close scrutiny to exchanges between related parties because they can be used by taxpayers to evade taxes on gains.

Reporting: A taxpayer who transfers property in a like-kind exchange must file Form 8824, *Like-Kind Exchanges*, with his tax return for the year of the exchange. If the exchange involves a related party, the form must also be filed for each of the following two years.

Involuntary Conversions (Section 1033)

An involuntary conversion occurs when a taxpayer's property is lost, damaged, or destroyed, for which the taxpayer may receive an award, insurance reimbursement, or some other type of payment, as a result of:

- Theft
- Disaster,
- Condemnation, or threat of condemnation.

A taxpayer typically reports a gain or deducts a loss in the year the gain or loss is realized. However, under section 1033, a taxpayer can defer reporting gain on an involuntary conversion if he receives proceeds from insurance or another source and invests in property similar to the converted property. The gain on the involuntary conversion is then deferred until a taxable sale or exchange of the replacement property occurs at a later date.

Example: A hurricane destroys Denise's residential rental property that has an adjusted basis of $50,000. Denise receives insurance reimbursement for $100,000, the fair market value of the property. Denise buys a replacement rental property six months later for $100,000. Her gain on the involuntary conversion is $50,000 ($100,000 insurance settlement minus her $50,000 basis). However, Denise does not have to recognize any taxable gain because she reinvested all the insurance proceeds in another, similar property.

Replacement Period: The replacement period for an involuntary conversion generally ends two years after the end of the first tax year in which any part of the gain on the condemnation is realized.

Example: Seiji owns a trophy business. On May 30, 2013, a tornado destroys a garage with Seiji's trophies and other business supplies. His insurance company reimburses him for the entire loss. Seiji has until December 31, 2015 to replace the garage and supplies using the insurance proceeds. He is not required to report the insurance proceeds on his 2013 tax return. If he reinvests all the insurance proceeds in replacement property, he will not have taxable gain until he disposes of the replacement property.

A three-year replacement period is allowed for real property that is held for investment, such as office buildings or residential rentals. The replacement period is four years for livestock that is involuntarily converted because of weather-related conditions. If the property is subject to an involuntary conversion in certain federally declared disaster areas, the replacement period can be up to five years.

The replacement property must be purchased before the end of the tax year in which the replacement deadline applies. If the involuntary conversion property is not replaced within the allowed time period, an amended tax return would have to be filed for the year the involuntary conversion occurred, reporting a taxable transaction.

Usually, the taxpayer's basis in the new property will be its cost, reduced by any gain realized on the old property that was not recognized.

However, the basis may be increased by any gain the taxpayer recognizes on the involuntary conversion and decreased by the following:

- Any loss the taxpayer recognizes on the involuntary conversion
- Any reimbursement he receives and does not reinvest in similar property

Example: Cody is a general contractor whose business truck is destroyed in an accident. It had been partially depreciated, and its adjusted basis was $40,000. The insurance company sends a check for $55,000 to replace the truck. Two months later, Cody uses all the insurance money to purchase a replacement truck, paying an additional $2,000 out-of-pocket to purchase the new vehicle. The basis in the new truck is $42,000 ($40,000 basis of the old truck + $2,000 additional out-of-pocket cost). Another way of reaching the same answer is as follows: Cody paid a total of $57,000 for the new truck, including the insurance proceeds of $55,000 plus an additional $2,000. This cost is reduced by the amount of gain that he has not recognized on the involuntary conversion, $15,000 (replacement proceeds of $55,000 less adjusted basis of $40,000), to derive the basis of the new truck: $42,000. This does not have to be reported as a taxable transaction because it is a qualified involuntary conversion of business property.

Unit 9: Study Questions

1. The Drake Partnership owned a $20,000 business machine that had been depreciated by $12,000, so the partnership's adjusted basis in it was $8,000. In 2013, the partnership sold the machine for $25,000. What is the nature of the tax treatment resulting from the sale?

A. Capital gain of $17,000.
B. Ordinary income of $12,000 and capital gain of $5,000.
C. Ordinary income of $17,000.
D. Capital gain of $12,000 and ordinary income of $5,000.

2. Which of the following dispositions of depreciable property can trigger depreciation recapture?

A. Installment sale.
B. Gift.
C. Transfer at death.
D. Section 1031 exchange where no money or unlike property is received.

3. Which of the following is not section 1245 property?

A. Computer.
B. Office building.
C. Display shelving.
D. Grain silo.

4. Which of the following assets is not section 1231 property?

A. Office building.
B. Unharvested crops.
C. Business asset held for less than one year.
D. Patent.

5. Which of the following property types qualifies for section 1031 like-kind exchange?

A. A personal residence.
B. Inventory property.
C. Corporation common stock.
D. An empty lot held for investment.

6. Caraway Carwash paid $200,000 for business equipment in January 2013. Caraway sells the equipment for $180,000 in October 2013. Caraway had not taken any depreciation on the equipment. How will this transaction be reported?

A. Caraway has a section 1231 loss of $20,000 on the sale of the equipment. This is treated as an ordinary loss.
B. Caraway has a section 1231 loss of $20,000 on the sale of the equipment. This is treated as a capital loss.
C. This is an installment sale, with a loss of $20,000 that is treated as an ordinary loss.
D. Caraway has an ordinary loss.

7. On January 10, 2013, a rental office building owned by Clovis Investments Corporation burns down. The property had an adjusted basis of $260,000, and Clovis receives an insurance reimbursement of $310,000. Clovis buys another rental office property for $290,000 in March 2013. What is Clovis's taxable gain as a result of this transaction?

A. $0.
B. $20,000.
C. $30,000.
D. $50,000.

8. Barbara exchanges an apartment building with an adjusted basis of $125,000 for a business office building. The fair market value of Barbara's old property is $500,000. The fair market value of the business office building is $475,000. What is Barbara's basis in the new building?

A. $125,000.
B. $475,000.
C. $500,000.
D. $525,000.

9. Jennifer operates Right Hair Salon, a sole proprietorship. In 2013, she sells all of her salon chairs for $3,500 in order to buy new ones. She had purchased the chairs seven years ago for $15,000, and they were fully depreciated. Therefore, her basis in the chairs is zero. How should she report this transaction?

A. She reports a loss of $11,500 on Schedule C.
B. She reports a gain of $3,500 on Form 4797 and Schedule C. The entire $3,500 is treated as depreciation recapture, which is subject to ordinary income tax rates.
C. She reports a gain of $3,500 on Form 4797 and Schedule C. The entire $3,500 is taxed as a long-term capital gain.
D. She is not required to report this sale.

10. Arbordale Acres is a farming corporation. In 2013, Arbordale sells a used tractor for $25,000. The original cost of the tractor was $20,000, and it is fully depreciated. What is the tax treatment for Arbordale's sale of the tractor?

A. There is no gain or loss on the sale of the tractor.
B. Arbordale has a gain of $25,000. The first $20,000 is considered section 1245 recapture and is taxed as ordinary income. The remaining $5,000 is considered section 1231 capital gain.
C. Arbordale has a gain of $25,000. The first $15,000 is considered section 1245 recapture and is taxed as ordinary income. The remaining $10,000 is considered section 1231 capital gain.
D. The entire gain is considered section 1245 recapture and will be taxed as ordinary income.

11. Which of the following property exchanges does not qualify as a like-kind exchange?

A. Exchange of an apartment building for an office building.
B. Exchange of livestock of different sexes.
C. Exchange of improved property for unimproved property.
D. Exchange of farm machinery for factory machinery.

12. Scott has a plane that he used in his business for two years. Its adjusted basis is $35,000, and its trade-in value is $45,000. He trades his old plane for a new plane that costs $200,000 and pays the dealer an additional $155,000 in cash. What is Scott's basis of the new plane?

A. $35,000.
B. $155,000.
C. $190,000.
D. $200,000.

13. The Karabell Company trades a delivery truck with an adjusted basis of $11,000 and cash of $6,000 for a new truck with a fair market value of $25,000. How much gain must Karabell recognize in this exchange, and what is its basis in the new truck?

Gain	Basis of New Truck
A. $0	$17,000
B. $0	$25,000
C. $8,000	$17,000
D. $8,000	$25,000

14. Fran and Zachary are mother and son who complete a section 1031 exchange in March 2013. On January 29, 2014, Fran dies, and her property is inherited by her husband, who promptly sells it. Which of the following statements is true?

A. Since one of the properties in the exchange has been sold before the two-year time limit for related parties, the section 1031 exchange is disallowed, and both parties must pay tax on the transaction.
B. The section 1031 exchange is still valid.
C. Since this was a related party exchange, the section 1031 exchange is still valid for Zachary, but Fran's estate must pay tax on the exchange because her husband disposed of the property before the two-year waiting period.
D. The nonrecognition treatment is lost for both parties, but Fran's husband is liable for the tax on the exchange, since he was the owner of the property when it was sold.

15. Which of the following trades qualifies as a nontaxable like-kind exchange?

A. The exchange of a vacant lot in the city for farmland in the country.
B. The exchange of a Toyota Prius owned by one car dealer for a Ford C-Max Hybrid owned by another car dealer.
C. The exchange of shares of stock for units of bonds.
D. The exchange of an apartment building in New York City for an apartment building in Mexico City.

16. Angelina trades a laser printer used in her tax practice for a new color model. The cost of the original printer was $5,000 and she had taken $1,000 of depreciation. She exchanged her old printer as a trade-in and paid an additional $2,000 in cash to complete the exchange. What is Angelina's basis in the new printer?

A. $1,000.
B. $2,000.
C. $6,000.
D. $7,000.

17. Special rules apply to like-kind exchanges between related persons. For purposes of a section 1031 exchange, which of the following qualifies as a related person?

A. The taxpayer's spouse.
B. A corporation in which the taxpayer has a 51% ownership.
C. A partnership in which the taxpayer owns a 53% interest, and a partnership in which the taxpayer's spouse owns a 52% interest.
D. All of the above.

18. Cecil operates a sandwich shop as a sole proprietorship. During 2013, Cecil sold personal property that was used in the business for $100,000. The purchase price of the property was $120,000, and Cecil had claimed section 179 and depreciation deductions totaling $47,000. Based upon the information provided, what is the nature and amount of taxable income that will result from the sale of this property?

A. Capital gain of $27,000.
B. Ordinary income of $27,000.
C. No gain or loss.
D. Ordinary income of $47,000 and capital loss of $20,000.

19. Sergio is a self-employed carpenter who owns a compressor for use in his business. He trades the compressor (adjusted basis $3,000) for a large table saw (FMV $7,500) and pays an additional $4,000 cash to the seller in a qualified exchange. What is Sergio's basis in the saw?

A. $7,000.
B. $7,500.
C. $4,000.
D. $3,000.

20. Sadie owns a gym. She sells some used fitness equipment in 2013 for $65,000. She had purchased the equipment for $90,000. She has taken $50,000 of depreciation deductions, and a section 179 deduction of $10,000. Which of the following will Sadie report on the sale of the equipment?

A. Ordinary loss of $25,000.
B. Long-term capital gain of $35,000.
C. Ordinary income of $35,000.
D. Ordinary income of $10,000 and long-term capital gain of $25,000.

21. Ahmed sells a duplex with an adjusted basis of $150,000. The buyer agrees to pay Ahmed $300,000, with a cash down payment of $100,000 and $20,000 (plus 5% interest) in each of the next ten years. What is Ahmed's gross profit and gross profit percentage on the installment sale?

A. The gross profit is $5,000, and the gross profit percentage is 50%.
B. The gross profit is $10,000, and the gross profit percentage is 100%.
C. The gross profit is $150,000, and the gross profit percentage is 50%.
D. The gross profit is $5,000, and the gross profit percentage is 100%.

Unit 10: Partnerships in General

> **More Reading:**
> **Publication 541, *Partnerships***

Partnership Basics

As described in Unit 1, an unincorporated business with two or more owners is generally classified as a partnership for federal tax purposes. A partnership is a pass-through entity that is generally not directly taxed on its income. Instead, income and loss are determined at the partnership level and are taxable to the individual partners. In this respect, a partnership is similar to a sole proprietorship.

Unlike a corporation, a partnership does not require any formal legal documents. A partnership must have at least two partners and at least one of them must be a general partner. A joint undertaking merely to share expenses is not a partnership.

Certain entities with different legal structures may be classified as partnerships for tax purposes, either based upon their election by filing Form 8832, *Entity Classification Election,* or by default (as in the case of a domestic LLC with at least two members that is classified as a partnership unless it files Form 8832 and elects to be treated as a corporation). However, the following organizations are prohibited from being classified as partnerships:

- A corporation (although a corporation can be a partner in a partnership)
- A joint-stock company or joint-stock association
- An insurance company
- Certain banks
- A government entity
- An organization required to be taxed as a corporation by the IRS
- Certain foreign organizations
- Any tax-exempt (nonprofit) organization
- Any real estate investment trust (REIT)
- Any organization classified as a trust or estate
- Any other organization that elects to be classified as a corporation by filing Form 8832

The Partnership Agreement

The term *partnership agreement* refers to any written document or oral agreement that bears on the underlying economic arrangement of the partners, including allocations of income, gain, loss, deductions, and credits. Examples of such documents include:

- Loan and credit agreements
- Assumption agreements
- Indemnification agreements
- Subordination agreements
- Correspondence with a lender concerning terms of a loan
- Loan guarantees

A partnership agreement may be modified during the tax year and even after the tax year has closed. However, the partnership agreement cannot be modified after the due date for filing the partnership return for the year, not including extensions.

Example: Terry and Dawn run a cash-basis, calendar-year partnership. They split the partnership's proceeds 50-50. In 2013, they decide to alter their partnership agreement. They have until the due date of the partnership return to change the partnership agreement. Filing for an extension does not give them additional time.

Partnership Filing Requirements

A partnership must file a tax return unless it has no activity (and no income or losses for the year). A partnership reports its income and loss on Form 1065, which is due on the 15th day of the fourth month following the close of the tax year. Since most partnerships are calendar-year partnerships, their tax returns are generally due on April 15, like individual returns.

Note: A partnership may request a five-month extension to file (unlike individuals and corporations that may request a six-month extension). Therefore, a calendar-year partnership can request an extension until September 15 to file its tax return.

The extension is requested on Form 7004, *Automatic Extension of Time to File Certain Business Income Tax, Information, and Other Returns.*

The partnership return must show the name and address of each partner and the partner's distributive share of taxable income (or loss) on Schedule K-1. The partnership is also required to furnish a copy of each partner's Schedule K-1 to the partner by the due date (including extensions) of the partnership tax return. The individual partner then reports his share of partnership income on Schedule E of Form 1040.

Example: Lovett Partnership is a calendar-year, cash-basis partnership that is required to file Form 1065 every year. The partnership has five partners and each partner receives a Schedule K-1 for his share of partnership income and losses, which are then reportable on the partners' individual tax returns. Each partner must receive his Schedule K-1 by the due date of the partnership return (or by the extended due date, if the partnership requests an extension).

The IRS requires partnerships with more than 100 partners (Schedules K-1) to file their returns electronically. If a partnership fails to do so, it may be subject to penalty unless it was unable to file electronically (e.g., because the e-filing was rejected, the return required paper attachments, etc.) The partnership return must be signed by a general partner.

The penalty for late filing is $195 per month, per partner, for up to 12 months. For example, if a partnership has four partners and files its tax return two months late, it would be liable for a late filing penalty of $1,560 ($195 × 2 months × 4 partners). Additional penalties may apply if the partnership fails to furnish Schedules K-1 to its partners, fails to supply a tax identification number, or fails to furnish information on tax shelters. These penalties may not be imposed if the partnership can show reasonable cause for its failure.

Partners who work in the business are not employees and do not receive Forms W-2. Withholding from their distributions to pay the income and self-employment taxes that they report on their Forms 1040 is generally not required. General partners are considered to be self-employed and therefore must pay estimated payments just like other self-employed individuals. Limited partners are subject to self-employment tax only on guaranteed payments, such as salaries and professional fees for services rendered.

General Partnership vs. Limited Partnership

A partnership can either be a general partnership or a limited partnership. In a general partnership, the partners have unlimited liability for partnership debts. In a limited partnership, there must be at least one general partner and at least one limited partner. The limited partners have no obligation to contribute additional capital to the partnership and therefore do not have an economic risk of loss related to partnership liabilities. In this respect, a limited partner is like an investor in a corporation. Limited partners generally cannot participate in the management or the day-to-day administration of the partnership.

A limited partnership (LP or LLP) is formed under state limited liability law. Often, the owners of limited liability partnerships offer professional services (e.g., attorneys or doctors). This entity type protects individual partners from liability for the malpractice of other partners.

Family Partnerships

Members of a family can form a partnership together. However, family members will be recognized as partners only if one of the following requirements is met:

- If capital is a material income-producing factor, the family members must have acquired their capital interests in a bona fide transaction (even if by gift or purchase from another family member); actually own the partnership interests; and actually control the interests. This means that a family member who acquires a partnership interest from another family member needs to treat the activity as a bona fide business activity.
- If capital is not a material income-producing factor, the family members must have joined together in good faith to conduct a business. They must have agreed that contributions of each entitle them to a share in the profits and that some capital or service is provided by each partner.

Capital (investment) is a material income-producing factor if a substantial part of the gross income of the business comes from the use of capital. For example, this would apply if the operation of the business requires substantial inventories or investment in a plant, machinery, or equipment.

In general, capital is not a material income-producing factor if the income of the business consists principally of fees, commissions, or other compensation for personal services performed by members or employees of the partnership.

If a family member (or any other person) receives a gift of a capital interest in a partnership in which capital is a material income-producing factor, the donee's distributive share of partnership income is subject to both of the following restrictions:

- It must be figured by reducing the partnership income by reasonable compensation for services the donor provides the partnership.
- The donee's distributive share of partnership income attributable to donated capital must not be proportionately greater than the donor's distributive share attributable to the donor's capital.

Example: Ronald sold 50% of his business to his daughter, Cindy. The resulting partnership had a profit of $60,000. Capital is a material income-producing factor. Ronald performed services worth $24,000, which is reasonable compensation, and Cindy performed no services. The $24,000 must be allocated to Ronald as compensation. Of the remaining $36,000 of profit due to capital, at least 50%, or $18,000 must be allocated to Ronald since he owns a 50% capital interest. Cindy's share of partnership profit cannot be more than $18,000.

For purposes of determining a partner's distributive share, an interest purchased by one family member from another family member is considered a gift from the seller. The fair market value of the purchased interest is considered donated capital. For this purpose, members of a family include only spouses, ancestors, and lineal descendants (grandchild, daughter, son, stepchild, etc.)

Costs of Organizing and Starting a Partnership

The costs to organize a partnership and to start up a business are treated much like similar costs incurred by other types of businesses. As discussed in Unit 4, limited amounts of organizational and start-up costs can be deducted in the year the partnership's active trade or business begins. Amounts not deducted can be amortized ratably over a period of 180 months. The election to either amortize or capitalize these costs is irrevocable and applies to all organizational and start-up costs related to the trade or business. The partnership must complete and attach Form 4562, *Depreciation and Amortization*, to its tax return.

A partnership can amortize an organizational cost only if it meets all the following tests:

- It is for the creation of the partnership itself and not for starting or operating the partnership trade or business.
- It is chargeable to a capital account.
- It is incurred by the due date of the partnership return (excluding extensions) for the first tax year in which the partnership is in business.
- It is for a type of item normally expected to benefit the partnership throughout its entire life.

Qualifying partnership organizational costs include the following fees:

- Legal fees for services related to the organization of the partnership, such as negotiation and preparation of the partnership agreement
- Accounting fees for services related to the organization of the partnership.
- Filing fees

The following costs cannot be deducted or amortized:

- The cost of acquiring assets for the partnership or transferring assets to the partnership

- The cost of admitting or removing partners, other than at the time the partnership is first organized
- The cost of making a contract concerning the operation of the partnership trade or business including a contract between a partner and the partnership
- Syndication costs for issuing and marketing interests in the partnership, such as brokerage, registration, and printing costs

If a partnership is liquidated (ceases operations) before the end of the amortization period, the unamortized amount of qualifying organizational costs can be deducted in the partnership's final tax year, but only to the extent they qualify as a loss from a business.

Start-up costs include amounts paid or incurred in connection with an existing activity engaged in for profit and for the production of income in anticipation of the activity becoming an active trade or business. Start-up costs include amounts paid for the following:

- An analysis of potential markets, products, labor supply, transportation facilities, etc.
- Advertisements for the opening of the business
- Salaries and wages for employees who are being trained and their instructors
- Travel and other necessary costs for securing prospective distributors, suppliers, or customers
- Salaries and fees for executives and consultants, or for similar professional services

Special Partnership Allocations

Unlike S corporations, which must report all income and expenses in proportion to stock ownership, partnerships have more flexibility. Partnership agreements can be written to reflect special allocations of income, gain, loss, or deductions, as long as the allocations are consistent with the economic sharing arrangement among the partners. For example, the partnership agreement may allocate all of the depreciation deductions to one partner or specify that the partners share capital, profits, and losses in different ratios.

Example: Pandora, who has design and sewing skills, forms a partnership with Jayne, who has the money to invest in developing a clothing line. Jayne contributes $100,000 in cash to the partnership. Pandora and Jayne agree to split the business profits 20/80 until Jayne recovers her entire investment; thereafter, profits will be split 50/50. These special allocations are written into their partnership agreement.

Example: Nico and Rhoda form a partnership. Nico contributes $1,000 and Rhoda contributes $99,000. Due to Nico's expertise in management and his daily participation in the partnership's business, the partnership agreement provides that he will be allocated 20% of the partnership's taxable income and 2% of the partnership's losses. Thus, although Nico owns only 1% in partnership capital, his profit sharing ratio is 20%. This tax allocation between Nico and Rhoda is allowed because it reflects their underlying economic arrangement.

Example: Alicia and Becky form a partnership to run a cupcake bakery. The bakery is opened during the year, and the partnership has ordinary income of $10,000. The partnership agreement states they will share income and losses equally (50/50). Alicia and Becky agree that the $10,000 income will be distributed equally between them. However, for tax purposes, they want the income to be allocated as $7,500 to Alicia and $2,500 to Becky. The tax allocation (75/25) is not consistent with the underlying economic agreement on their partnership agreement (50/50). Unless the partnership agreement contains other provisions that justify this allocation, it has no economic effect and must be reallocated to the partners based on their economic sharing ratio.

Guaranteed Payments

A partnership may be required by the terms of its partnership agreement to make guaranteed payments to one or more partners without regard to whether the partnership has income or loss for the year.

Guaranteed payments are not the same as partnership distributions. They may compensate the partner for services or for the use of capital, as if they were made to a person who is not a partner. Guaranteed payments are generally deducted by the partnership on Form 1065 as a business expense and reported on Schedule K-1.

The partner who receives a guaranteed payment reports the full amount of the payment as ordinary income on Schedule E (Form 1040) of his individual tax return for the tax year in which the partnership's tax year ends, and also reports his distributive share of the partnership's ordinary income or loss. Guaranteed payments are not subject to income tax withholding.

Example: Erica is a partner in the Bookertown Partnership. Under the terms of her partnership agreement, she is entitled to a guaranteed payment of $10,000 per year, regardless of how profitable the partnership is. In 2013, Erica's distributive share of partnership income is 10%. Bookertown Partnership has $50,000 of ordinary income after deducting Erica's guaranteed payment. She must include ordinary income of $15,000 ($10,000 guaranteed payment + $5,000 [$50,000 × 10%] for her distributive share) on her individual income tax return.

Separately Stated Items

Many of the individual components of a partnership's income or loss are calculated similarly to those of an individual. However, some deductions are not allowed at the partnership level, and certain items of income and loss must be separately stated on the tax return. These separately stated items flow through to the partners with a specific character. For example, a partnership that makes charitable contributions must list them as a separately stated item. Each individual partner then reports his share of the charitable contributions on his Schedule A.

Each year, a partnership provides Schedules K-1 to each of its partners, indicating their respective shares of:

- **Ordinary income or loss,** and
- **Separately stated items.**

Study Note: For the EA exam, you should be able to distinguish the items that are separately stated on a partnership's tax return.

The following items must be separately stated:

- Net short-term capital gains and losses
- Net long-term capital gains and losses
- Charitable contributions
- Dividends eligible for a dividends-received deduction
- Taxes paid to a foreign country
- Taxes paid to a U.S. possession (Guam, Puerto Rico, etc.)
- Section 1231 gains and losses
- Section 179 deductions and bonus depreciation
- Any tax-exempt income and expenses related to the tax-exempt income
- Investment income and related investment expenses
- Rental income, portfolio income, and related expenses
- Any recovery items, such as bad debts

Example: The Stevenson Partnership operates as an accrual-based business. Its gross receipts for 2013 were $250,000. In addition, it had the following income and expenses:

•Liability insurance	($5,000)
•Charitable contributions	($2,000)
•Continuing education	($9,000)
•Rental income	$25,000
•Guaranteed payments to partners	($15,000)

Ordinary income for the Stevenson partnership is figured as follows:

Gross receipts	$250,000
Liability insurance	($5,000)
Continuing education	($9,000)
Guaranteed payments to partners	($15,000)
Total ordinary business income:	**$221,000**

The rental income and charitable contributions are not considered in determining ordinary income of the partnership. Instead, these are separately stated items that pass through to the partners and retain their character, just as they would for a sole proprietorship. Each individual partner receives a Schedule K-1 from the partnership, reporting his share of ordinary income or loss and each separately stated item. The partners report these amounts on their tax returns. Guaranteed payments are deductible by the partnership because they are treated like wages and are taxable to the partners who receive them.

Cash and Property Contributions to a Partnership

When a partnership is formed or new partners are added, the partners contribute property or cash in exchange for their partnership interests. Generally, neither the partner nor the partnership recognizes gain or loss in connection with contributions, whether made in connection with the partnership's formation or after it is operating. However, a partner's contribution can result in gain or loss recognition in the following situations:

- When property is contributed to a partnership that would be treated as an investment company if it were incorporated. A partnership is treated as an investment company if over 80% of the value of its assets is held for investment in cash or readily marketable items.
- When contributed property is distributed to a different partner within seven years of the original contribution date. The contributing partner would recognize gain on the difference between the fair market value and the adjusted basis of the property as of the contribution date. The character of the gain or loss will be the same as would have resulted if the partnership had sold the property to the distributee partner.
- When a partner contributes cash or property to a partnership and then receives a distribution of different property. In this case, the transaction may be considered a disguised sale. A disguised sale is not treated as a contribution and a subsequent distribution but as a sale of property, if:
    - The distribution would not have been made if the initial contribution had not occurred; and
    - The partner's right to the distribution does not depend on the success of partnership operations.

If a contribution and distribution occur within two years of each other, the transfers are presumed to be a sale unless the facts clearly indicate they are not. If the contribution and distribution occur more than two years apart, the transfers are presumed not to be a sale unless the facts clearly indicate they are.

Example: Alberta contributes land with a fair market value of $150,000 and a basis of $100,000 to her partnership. In the same year, the partnership distributes $100,000 of cash and marketable securities worth $50,000 to Alberta. This transaction would be considered a sale rather than a tax-free contribution and distribution of property.

When a partner contributes property to a partnership, the partnership's basis is generally the same as the adjusted basis of the partner, including any gain recognized by the partner in connection with the contribution. The partner's holding period for the property is also carried over. For example, if a partner contributes a building with an FMV of $100,000 and a basis of $50,000, the basis of the building in the hands of the partnership would generally be $50,000.

Contribution of Services to a Partnership

A partner can acquire an interest in a partnership as compensation for services performed or to be performed. The tax treatment depends upon whether the partner receives a capital interest or a profits interest.

If a partner receives a capital interest as compensation for services, the partner must recognize ordinary income equal to the fair market value of a partnership interest that is transferred in exchange for services. The amount is treated as a guaranteed payment and is included in the partner's gross income in the first tax year during which the partner can transfer the interest.

If a partner receives a profits interest as compensation for services, the receipt may not be taxable to the partner or the partnership, except in certain circumstances.

Example: Greer is an attorney who contributes her services to a partnership in exchange for a 10% partnership interest. It is deemed a capital interest, as the partnership agreement provides for distribution of assets to Greer in the event she withdraws from the partnership or the partnership liquidates. The fair market value of the partnership interest is $3,000. Greer is required to recognize $3,000 in ordinary income, and her basis in the partnership is $3,000. The payment is deducted by the partnership as a guaranteed payment and is taxable to Greer as ordinary income.

Basis of a Partner's Interest

A partner's basis in his partnership interest may be referred to as *outside basis*. This is in contrast to the partnership's basis in its assets, which is known as *inside basis*.

Study Note: Be familiar with these two terms, as the EA exam may use them in questions when you are asked to determine a partner's or a partnership's basis.

Inside basis and outside basis may be equal, but certain distributions of property from the partnership or transfers of partnership interests may disrupt this equality. By means of an IRC section 754 election, the partnership may be able to make upward or downward adjustments to the basis of its assets in order to restore the equality between inside basis and outside basis.

The initial basis of a partnership interest is generally equal to the cash plus the adjusted basis of any property the partner contributed. The adjusted basis of a partner's partnership interest is ordinarily determined at the end of the partnership's tax year. However, if there is a sale or exchange of all or part of a partner's interest or a liquidation of his entire interest in a partnership, the adjusted basis must also be determined on the date of the transaction.

Example: Sam and Harriet form a partnership. Sam contributes a machine to the partnership that has an adjusted basis of $400 and an FMV of $1,000. Harriet contributes $1,000 cash. The basis of Sam's interest is $400 and the basis of Harriet's interest is $1,000.

The following items increase a partner's basis in the partnership:

- The partner's additional cash contributions to the partnership
- The partner's increased liabilities
- The partner's increased share (or assumption of) partnership liabilities
- The partner's distributive share of taxable and nontaxable partnership income

- The partner's distributive share of the excess of the deductions for depletion over the basis of the depletable property

In addition, if a partner must recognize a gain as a result of his partnership contribution, the gain is added to the basis of his partnership interest. A partner may be required to recognize a gain when he contributes an asset to the partnership that is subject to liability (such as the contribution of a building that is subject to a mortgage), as the other partners are assuming part of his liability.

Any increase in a partner's liabilities because of his assumption of partnership liabilities is treated as if it were a contribution to the partnership by the partner. If a partner's share of partnership liabilities increases, this increase is treated as if the partner contributed cash or property to the partnership.

A partner's basis in the partnership is decreased by the following items:

- The money and adjusted basis of property distributed to the partner by the partnership.
- The partner's distributive share of the partnership losses.
- The partner's distributive share of nondeductible partnership expenses (but not capital expenditures). This includes the partner's share of any section 179 expenses, even if the partner cannot deduct the entire amount on his individual income tax return.
- The partner's deduction for depletion for any partnership oil and gas wells, up to the proportionate share of the adjusted basis of the wells allocated to the partner.

If a partner's share of partnership liabilities decreases or the partnership assumes any of the partner's individual liabilities, the amounts are treated as distributions to the partner by the partnership.

For example, if contributed property is subject to a debt and the debt is assumed by the partnership, the basis of the contributing partner's interest is reduced (but not below zero) by the portion of the liability assumed by the other partners. The partner must reduce his basis because the assumption of the liability is treated as a distribution to him. The other partners' assumption of the liability is treated as a contribution by them to the partnership.

Example: Ji-woo acquired a 20% interest in a partnership by contributing a moving van that had an adjusted basis to her of $8,000 and a related $4,000 loan balance. The partnership assumed the loan. The basis of Ji-woo's interest is:

Adjusted basis of contributed property	$8,000
Minus loan assumed by other partners (80% × $4,000)	($3,200)
Basis of Ji-woo's partnership interest	**$4,800**

A partner's basis can never go below zero. To avoid this, a partner must recognize gain equal to the amount by which cash distributions or a decrease in his share of partnership liabilities exceeds his basis.

Example: Raymond acquired a 20% interest in a partnership by contributing an asset that had an adjusted basis of $8,000 and a related $12,000 loan balance. Since his basis in the asset is less than the loan balance, the $1,600 difference between the loan assumed by the other partners, $9,600 (80% × $12,000), and his basis of $8,000 is treated as capital gain from the sale or exchange of a partnership interest. Raymond's partnership basis is zero.

Partnership Loss Limitations

The amount of a partnership's loss that a partner is allowed to deduct on his tax return is dependent on the partner's basis in the partnership. In general, a partner cannot deduct losses that exceed his partnership basis. Losses disallowed due to insufficient basis are carried forward until the partner can deduct them in a later year.

However, debts on behalf of the partnership can increase a partner's individual basis. For example, if a partner takes out a $50,000 loan to finance partnership operations and he personally guarantees the debt, the debt is considered part of his basis in the partnership for purposes of deducting partnership losses.

Example: Rebecca invests $1,000 in the Goldblatt Partnership in return for a 10% general partnership interest. The Goldblatt Partnership takes out a $500,000 loan and incurs $100,000 in losses during the first year. Rebecca's share of partnership liabilities would increase her basis to $51,000 [$1,000 cash investment + ($500,000 × 10%). Rebecca's share of the loss is $10,000 ($100,000 × 10%). Rebecca is allowed to deduct the entire amount, because her partnership basis was increased by debt basis.

This only applies if the partner is at risk for the loss. If the partner does not have any personal liability to satisfy the debt, deductible losses are limited by the at-risk rules. The at-risk rules limit the deductibility of losses to the partner's basis, not including his share of any nonrecourse debt.

This means that a partner is prohibited from taking losses based on partnership liabilities unless the partner would be forced to satisfy the debt with his personal assets. This is intended to prevent abusive deductions from real estate and other tax shelter activities.

A partner (or related person) is considered to assume a partnership liability when:

- He is personally liable for it,
- The creditor knows that the liability was assumed by the partner or related person,
- The creditor can demand payment from the partner or related person, and
- No other partner or person related to another partner will bear the economic risk of loss on that liability immediately after the assumption.

Example: Gary and Santiago form a general partnership, with cash contributions of $2,000 from each. Under the partnership agreement, they share all partnership profits and losses equally. The partnership borrows an additional $10,000 and purchases equipment. Both partners are liable for the debt. This debt is included in the partners' basis in the partnership. Each partner's basis would include his allocated share of the liability, or $5,000. Therefore, each partner's basis is now $7,000 (the initial $2,000 contribution + $5,000 share of the liability).

The effect of liabilities on the individual partner's basis depends mainly on two factors:

- Whether or not the liability is recourse or nonrecourse
- Whether or not the partner is a general or limited partner

A nonrecourse liability is usually secured by an asset or property, and its terms provide that the creditor has no claim against the owner of the property. At most, the creditor may have a claim against the property. An example of this would be a mortgage loan where the lender's only recourse in case of default is to repossess the property. A partnership liability is considered a nonrecourse liability if no partner has an economic risk of loss for that liability.

Example: Reuben purchases a used van for his business, but he is unable to make the payments. The loan is a nonrecourse loan because the only action the lender can take is to repossess the vehicle. The lender cannot seek payment from Reuben for the balance of the loan.

A partner's share of nonrecourse liabilities is proportionate to his share of partnership profits. A partner's basis in a partnership interest includes the partner's share of a partnership liability only if, and to the extent, the liability:

- Creates or increases the partnership's basis in any of its assets,
- Gives rise to a current deduction to the partnership, or
- Is a nondeductible, noncapital expense of the partnership.

A partnership liability is a recourse liability when the individual partners have an economic risk of loss. A partner has an economic risk of loss to the extent that partner or a related person would be obligated to make payments to a creditor in the event of a constructive liquidation. Generally, in a constructive liquidation, the following events are treated as occurring at the same time:

- All partnership liabilities become payable in full
- All of the partnership's assets have a value of zero, except for property contributed to secure a liability
- All property is disposed of by the partnership in a fully taxable transaction for no consideration
- All items of income, gain, loss, or deduction are allocated to the partners
- The partnership liquidates

Partners generally share recourse liabilities based on their ratios for sharing losses. A limited partner has no obligation to contribute additional capital to the partnership, and therefore does not have an economic risk of loss in the partnership's recourse liabilities. Therefore, unless a limited partner guarantees a partnership liability or makes a loan to the partnership, his basis will generally not be affected by the partnership's recourse liabilities.

The cancellation of debt exclusions described in Unit 3 are applied at the partner level rather than at the partnership level. Thus, for example, an individual partner would need to be insolvent to utilize the insolvency exclusion for his share of COD income passed through from an insolvent partnership. If a partner is able to use the exclusion, he would be required to reduce specified tax attributes, including loss and credit carryforwards and the basis of assets.

Unit 10: Study Questions

1. In 2013 Raj and Ellie formed Deep Clean, a calendar-year partnership, to provide janitorial services to residential customers. Before they began operations in November 2013, they incurred legal fees of $2,000 and consulting expenses of $1,000 to draft the partnership agreement and file the required forms. They also paid a commission of $600 to a broker to market partnership interests to other potential partners. How much of these expenses may be deducted or amortized?

A. $0.
B. $600.
C. $3,000.
D. $3,600.

2. Which of the following statements is true?

A. The IRS requires partnerships with more than 100 partners to file their returns electronically.
B. The IRS requires all partnerships to file electronically.
C. The IRS requires limited partnerships with more than 10 partners to file their returns electronically.
D. The IRS requires partnerships with 100 or more partners to file electronically.

3. Todd and Charlotte form a general partnership with cash contributions of $20,000 each. Under the partnership agreement, they share all partnership profits and losses equally. They borrow $60,000 and purchase depreciable business equipment. However, Todd has poor credit, so Charlotte is the only signer on the loan. Charlotte is required to pay the creditor if the partnership defaults, so she has an economic risk of loss related to the loan. The payments on the loan are made out of the partnership bank account. What is Charlotte's basis in the partnership, and what is Todd's basis?

A. Charlotte: $80,000, Todd: $20,000.
B. Charlotte: $60,000, Todd: $20,000.
C. Charlotte: $20,000, Todd: $20,000.
D. Charlotte: $60,000, Todd: $60,000.

4. Which of the following statements regarding limited partnerships is correct?

A. A limited partner has an economic liability for damages and an economic risk of loss.
B. A limited partner does not have an economic risk of loss in the partnership's recourse liabilities.
C. A limited partner does not have an economic risk of loss in the partnership's recourse liabilities; however, a limited partner may be required to contribute additional capital.
D. A limited partner is treated just like a general partner when it comes to the partnership's recourse liabilities.

5. Polly and Diane form P&D Partnership in 2013. Polly contributes $16,000 cash and Diane contributes equipment with a fair market value of $15,000 and an adjusted basis of $5,000. What amount should Diane report as a gain as a result of this transaction?

A. $0.
B. $3,000.
C. $5,000.
D. $8,000.

6. If a partnership requests additional time to file its return, how long will the filing deadline be extended?

A. Three months.
B. Five months.
C. Six months.
D. Nine months.

7. José and Carlos form a partnership. Each contributes $20,000 during the initial formation of the partnership. Their partnership agreement states that José will receive 35% of the distributive income and Carlos will receive 65%. In 2013, the partnership has income of $200,000. What is each partner's distributive share of the partnership profits?

A. José: $70,000, Carlos: $130,000.
B. José: $100,000, Carlos: $100,000.
C. José: $35,000, Carlos $65,000.
D. José: $77,000, Carlos $143,000.

8. The G&H Partnership has two partners, Gil and Hassid. They share profits and losses equally (50/50). The partnership has the following activity during the year.

Gross income from operations:	$200,000
Business expenses:	$30,000
Tax-exempt interest income:	$10,000
Rental income:	$120,000
Charitable contributions:	$4,000

What is Hassid's share of the partnership's ordinary income?

A. $85,000.
B. $91,000.
C. $100,000.
D. $105,000.

9. When payments are made by a partnership to partners without regard to partnership income, these payments are called:

A. Capital gains.
B. Ordinary distributions.
C. Passive income.
D. Guaranteed payments.

10. Racing Horses Partnership has seven partners. The partnership files its tax return three months late. What is the IRS penalty for late filing of the partnership return?

A. $0.
B. $585.
C. $780.
D. $4,095.

11. Carolyn and Jerome form a partnership in 2013. Each contributes $5,000 for an equal partnership interest. Their partnership agreement states that they will share income and losses equally. However, Carolyn will provide accounting services to the partnership and receive a guaranteed payment each year of $21,000, regardless of the partnership's income or loss. In 2013, the partnership earns $50,000 before deducting the guaranteed payment. What is Jerome's distributive share of partnership profits for 2013?

A. $0.
B. $14,500.
C. $22,500.
D. $25,000.

12. D&D Healthy Pet Stores operates as an accrual-based partnership and files Form 1065 for 2013. In addition to receipts from pet food sales of $250,000, the partnership has the following items of income and expenses for 2013:

• Salaries	$50,000
• Insurance	$5,000
• Charitable contributions	$5,000
• Licenses	$5,000
• Rental income	$25,000
• Guaranteed payments	$75,000

What is the ordinary income that D&D Healthy Pet Stores should report on its 2013 Form 1065?

A. $85,000.
B. $115,000.
C. $190,000.
D. $210,000.

13. Which of the following increases the basis of a partner's interest in a partnership?

A. A partner's share of tax-exempt interest from municipal bonds owned by the partnership.
B. A decrease in the partner's share of liabilities.
C. A distribution of $2,000 in cash to the partner.
D. A property distribution with an FMV of $5,000.

14. John, Robin, Shanette, and Theresa form a partnership. Each partner contributes $10,000 and receives an equal interest in the partnership (25%). Under the partnership agreement, they share partnership profits and losses equally. The partnership borrows $135,000 and purchases business equipment. All of the partners except for Theresa personally guarantee the liability. What is each partner's basis after this transaction?

A. Theresa's basis is zero, and the other partners each have a basis of $58,333.
B. Theresa's basis is $10,000, and the other partners each have a basis of $43,750.
C. Theresa's basis is $10,000, and the other partners each have a basis of $55,000.
D. Each partner has a basis of $43,750.

15. Daniel is a general partner in the Vrettos Partnership. During the year, Daniel personally assumes $100,000 of the partnership's liabilities. Which of the following statements regarding partnership liabilities is true?

A. The assumption of partnership debt by Daniel is treated as a distribution of cash to Daniel, and it decreases Daniel's partnership basis.
B. The assumption of partnership debt by Daniel increases his basis.
C. Daniel cannot assume partnership liabilities.
D. Only limited partners are allowed to assume partnership liabilities.

16. The Bissinger Cosmetics Partnership generated income and expenses as stated below. What is the amount of ordinary business income that Bissinger should report for 2013?

- Employee wages $15,000
- Rental real estate income: $20,000
- Charitable contributions: $500
- Cost of goods sold: $10,000
- Income from cosmetics sales: $75,000

A. $65,000.
B. $69,500.
C. $50,000.
D. $30,000.

17. Hatam Persian Restaurant operates as a calendar-year partnership. Hatam's two partne-s, Afsar and Ted, share profits and losses 60% and 40%, respectively. For tax year 2013, Hatam Restaurant had the following income and expense:

- Gross sales $270,000
- Cost of goods sold $80,000
- Bank interest income $2,500
- Wages paid $50,000
- Short-term capital loss $5,000

Compute the partnership's ordinary income and flow-through amounts to the partners:

A. Afsar: ordinary income $85,500 and short-term capital loss $3,000; Ted: ordinary income $57,000 and short-term capital loss $2,000.
B. Afsar: ordinary income $82,500; Ted: ordinary income $55,000.
C. Afsar: ordinary income $81,000, interest income $1,500, and short-term capital loss $3,000; Ted: ordinary income $54,000, interest income $1,000, and short-term capital loss $2,000.
D. Afsar: ordinary income $84,000, interest income $1,500, and short-term capital loss $3,000. Ted: ordinary income $56,000, interest income $1,000, and short-term capital loss $2,000.'

18. Monica contributes property to a partnership for a 40% interest. The property has a fair market value of $7,000, an adjusted basis of $4,000, and a related mortgage of $1,000 that the partnership assumes. What is Monica's basis in her partnership interest?

A. $4,000.
B. $3,000,
C. $6,000.
D. $3,400.

19. Bea acquired a 30% interest in a partnership by contributing property in which she had an adjusted basis of $25,000. The property's fair market value was $50,000, and it had a $40,000 mortgage that was assumed by the partnership. What is Bea's gain or loss on the contribution of her property to the partnership?

A. $0.
B. $3,000 gain.
C. $12,000 gain.
D. $10,000 loss.

20. A partner is not considered at risk for which of the following amounts?

A. The money and adjusted basis of any property the partner contributed to a partnership's activity.
B. The partner's share of income retained by the partnership.
C. A partnership's nonrecourse liability.
D. Certain amounts borrowed by the partnership for use in the activity if the partner is personally liable for repayment.

21. Derrick is a 10% partner in Hartville Roads Partnership. According to the partnership agreement, Derrick is entitled to a fixed annual guaranteed payment of $5,000. During the year, Hartville Roads has $55,000 of ordinary income before deducting the guaranteed payment. How much partnership income should Derrick report on his individual return for this year?

A. $11,500.
B. $16,000.
C. $10,000.
D. $5,000.

Unit 11: Partnership Distributions & Liquidations

More Reading:
Publication 541, *Partnerships*

Partnership Distributions

A partnership is not a taxable entity; its income and losses flow through and are reported on the partners' individual tax returns. Each partner is taxed on his distributive share of income, whether or not it is actually distributed. Therefore, when distributions are made to the partners, they are generally not taxable. Partnership distributions may include the following:

- Distributions of the partnership's earnings for the current or prior years
- A withdrawal by a partner in anticipation of the current year's earnings
- A complete or partial liquidation of a partner's interest
- A distribution to all partners in a complete liquidation of the partnership

A partnership distribution is not taken into account in determining the partner's distributive share of the partnership's income or loss. If a gain or loss from the distribution is recognized by the partner, it must be reported on his return for the tax year in which the distribution is received. Cash or property withdrawn by a partner in anticipation of the current year's earnings is treated as a distribution received on the last day of the partnership's tax year. A partner's adjusted basis in his partnership interest is decreased (but not below zero) by the cash and adjusted basis of property distributed to the partner.

A partnership generally does not recognize any gain or loss because of distributions it makes to partners. The partnership may be able to elect to adjust the basis of its undistributed property.

Example: The adjusted basis of Angela's partnership interest is $14,000. She receives a distribution of $8,000 cash and land that has an adjusted basis of $2,000 and a fair market value of $3,000. The distribution decreases the basis of her partnership interest to $4,000 [$14,000 – ($8,000 + $2,000)]. Because the distribution does not exceed the basis of her partnership interest, Angela does not recognize gain. Any gain related to the excess of the land's fair market value over its adjusted basis may be recognized if she later disposes of it.

Unless there is a complete liquidation of a partner's interest, the basis of property (other than cash) distributed to the partner is its adjusted basis to the partnership immediately before the distribution.

Example: The adjusted basis of Jin Yeon's partnership interest is $45,000. She receives a distribution of property that has an adjusted basis of $23,000 to the partnership and $6,000 in cash. Her basis in the property is $23,000.

However, a partner cannot have a negative partnership basis. Therefore, the basis of property distributed to a partner cannot be more than the adjusted basis of his interest in the partnership, reduced by any cash received in the same transaction.

Example: The basis of Mike's partnership interest is $10,000. He receives a distribution of $4,000 cash and a parcel of land that has an adjusted basis to the partnership of $8,000. His basis in the land is limited to $6,000 ($10,000 - $4,000, the cash he receives), since the total amount cannot exceed his partnership interest. After the distribution, his partnership basis would be zero.

When a partnership distributes the following items, the distribution may be treated as a sale or exchange of property rather than a distribution:

- Unrealized receivables or substantially appreciated inventory items distributed in exchange for any part of the partner's interest in other partnership property, including cash
- Other property, including cash, distributed in exchange for any part of a partner's interest in unrealized receivables or substantially appreciated inventory items

This treatment does not apply to the following distributions:

- A distribution of property to the partner who contributed the same property to the partnership
- Payments made to a retiring partner or successor in interest of a deceased partner that are the partner's distributive share of partnership income or guaranteed payments

A gain or loss on a sale or exchange of unrealized receivables or inventory items a partner received in a distribution is generally treated as ordinary income or loss.

Example: Marcia was a partner in Illuminated, a business that sold handmade candles. In 2013, the store closed and Marcia received, through dissolution of the partnership, inventory that had a basis of $19,000. She sold the entire inventory for $24,000. The $5,000 gain was taxed as ordinary income.

If a partner's losses for the year exceed his basis, the losses he can claim are limited to the basis of his partnership interest (with some exceptions to this rule in a partnership liquidation). Partnership losses and other deductions that exceed the partner's basis may be carried forward indefinitely until the partner's basis in the partnership increases sufficiently for them to be utilized.

If a partnership acquires a partner's debt and extinguishes the debt by distributing it to the partner, the partner will recognize capital gain or loss to the extent the fair market value of the debt differs from the basis of the debt. The partner is treated as having satisfied the debt for its fair market value. If the issue price of the debt exceeds its FMV when distributed, the partner may have to include the excess amount in income as canceled debt.

Sale of a Partnership Interest

A partnership interest is a capital asset. As a result, a gain or loss on the sale or exchange of a partnership interest is treated as a capital gain or loss. Gain or loss is calculated as the difference between the amount realized and the adjusted basis of the partner's interest in the partnership.

If the selling partner is relieved of partnership liabilities, he must include the liability relief as part of the amount realized for his interest.

An exchange of partnership interests generally does not qualify as a nontaxable exchange of like-kind property. This applies regardless of whether they are general or limited partnership interests or interests in the same or different partnerships.

Example: Selene became a partner in the Rincon Partnership by contributing cash to the formation of the partnership. The adjusted basis of her partnership interest at the end of 2013 is $20,000, which includes her $15,000 share of partnership liabilities. Selene sells her interest in the partnership for $10,000 in cash on December 31, 2013. At the time of the sale, she had been credited for her share of the partnership's income for the tax year. Selene realizes $25,000 from the sale of her partnership interest ($10,000 cash payment + $15,000 liability relief). She must report $5,000 ($25,000 realized – $20,000 basis) as a capital gain.

Liquidation of a Partnership

When a partnership dissolves or stops doing business, it is called a partnership liquidation. A partnership may dissolve when a partner dies, or when one partner drops out of the business.

The basis of property received in complete liquidation of a partner's interest is the adjusted basis of the partner's interest in the partnership reduced by any cash distributed to the partner in the same transaction.

A partner's holding period for property distributed to him includes the period held by the partnership. If the property was contributed to the partnership by a partner, the holding period includes the period held by that partner also.

Example: Merle's basis in his partnership interest is $20,000. In a distribution to liquidate his entire interest, he receives a delivery truck and a utility trailer. The truck has an adjusted basis to the partnership of $15,000 and an FMV of $15,000. The trailer has an adjusted basis to the partnership of $14,000 and an FMV of $4,000. To figure his basis in each property, Merle first assigns a basis of $15,000 to the truck and $14,000 to the trailer. This leaves a $9,000 basis decrease (the $29,000 total of the assigned basis minus the $20,000 allocable partnership basis). He allocates the entire $9,000 to the trailer to reflect its unrealized depreciation. Merle's basis in the truck is $15,000, and his basis in the trailer is $5,000 ($14,000 - $9,000).

If a partnership is liquidated or dissolved with unamortized organizational or start-up expenses, the unamortized amounts can be deducted in the partnership's final tax year.

Payments made by the partnership to a retiring partner or a deceased partner's estate or in liquidation of the interest of a retiring or deceased partner in exchange for his interest in partnership property are considered a distribution, not a distributive share or guaranteed payment that could give rise to a deduction for the partnership. A retiring or deceased partner is treated as a partner until his interest in the partnership has been completely liquidated.

In a partnership liquidation, the liquidating distributions are similar to regular distributions except that the partner may recognize a loss if the total basis of the cash and property received is less than his basis in the partnership. A partner cannot recognize a loss on a partnership distribution unless all of the following requirements are met:

- The adjusted basis of the partner's interest in the partnership exceeds the distribution.
- The partner's entire interest in the partnership is liquidated.
- The distribution is in cash, unrealized receivables, or inventory items.

Example: The Webb-Bruner Partnership is liquidating. Donnie's adjusted basis in the partnership is $80,000. He receives a liquidating distribution of $60,000 in cash. As Donnie's adjusted basis of his partnership interest exceeds the distribution, he has a capital loss of $20,000 ($80,000 - $60,000).

Partnership Termination

A partnership generally terminates when one of the following events takes place:

- All its operations are discontinued and no part of any business, financial operation, or venture is continued by any of its partners in a partnership.
- At least 50% of the total interest in partnership capital and profits is sold or exchanged within a 12-month period, including a sale or exchange to another partner.

The partnership's tax year ends on the date of termination. If a partnership is terminated before the end of its regular tax year, Form 1065 must be filed for the short tax year from the beginning of the tax year through the date of termination. The return is due on the fifteenth day of the fourth month following the date of termination.

If a partnership is converted into an LLC classified as a partnership, the conversion does not terminate the partnership, and there is no sale, exchange, or termination of partnership interests. The partnership's tax year does not close, and the LLC can continue to use the partnership's taxpayer identification number.

If a partnership terminates and one of the former partners is insolvent and cannot pay any of the partnership's debts, the other partners may be forced to pay more than their share of the liabilities. If another partner pays any part of an insolvent partner's share of the debts, he can take a bad debt deduction.

Related Party Transactions

A partnership cannot deduct a loss on the sale or trade of property if the transaction is directly or indirectly between related parties. Under the related party transaction rules, an individual is considered as also owning the partnership interest directly or indirectly owned by his family. Members of a family, for this purpose, include only brothers, sisters, half-brothers, half-sisters, spouses, ancestors, parents, and lineal descendants (children, grandchildren).

Losses will not be allowed from a sale or exchange of property (other than an interest in the partnership) directly or indirectly between a partnership and a person whose direct or indirect interest in the capital or profits of the partnership is more than 50%.

If the sale or exchange is between two partnerships in which the same persons directly or indirectly own more than 50% of the capital or profits interests in each partnership, no loss is allowed.

Example: George and Lynn are siblings. Lynn is a 60% partner in the BuildRite Machinery Partnership, and George is a 55% partner in the Schlutter Partnership. If the partnerships sell property to each other, no loss will be allowed in the transaction, because the partnerships are considered related parties. Losses will instead be suspended until the property is eventually disposed of in a non-related party transaction.

The basis of each partner's interest in the partnership is decreased (but not below zero) by the partner's share of the disallowed loss.

If the purchaser later sells the property, only the gain realized that is greater than the loss not allowed will be taxable. If any gain from the sale of the property is not recognized because of this rule, the basis of each partner's interest in the partnership is increased by the partner's share of that gain.

Unit 11: Study Questions

1. Davisville Partnership sold a capital asset to Winters Partnership at a loss of $50,000. Davisville had held the property for five months. Davisville is owned 30% by Marvin, 30% by LaTroy, and 40% by Geoff, Marvin's brother. Winters Partnership is owned 80% by Dixon Corporation. Marvin owns 25% of the stock of Dixon Corporation and Geoff's daughter owns 60% of Dixon Corporation. How much of the loss should Davisville Partnership recognize for tax purposes on their tax return for the year of the sale?

A. $0.
B. $3,000.
C. $35,000.
D. $50,000.

2. The adjusted basis of Allison's partnership interest is $24,000. She receives a distribution of $9,000 cash and machinery that has an adjusted basis of $1,000 and a fair market value of $7,000. How much gain should Allison recognize on this distribution?

A. $0.
B. $1,000.
C. $2,000.
D. $7,000.

3. The adjusted basis of Steve's partnership interest is $10,000. He receives a distribution of $4,000 cash and a van that has an adjusted basis to the partnership of $9,000 and a fair market value of $12,000. This was not a liquidating distribution. What is Steve's basis in the van?

A. $5,000.
B. $6,000.
C. $12,000.
D. $16,000.

4. Marty is retiring from Sunnyside Partnership this year. His adjusted basis in the partnership is $50,000. He receives a distribution of $65,000 in cash. How would Marty report this transaction?

A. $15,000 capital gain.
B. $50,000 capital gain.
C. $65,000 capital gain.
D. $65,000 ordinary income.

5. Bart and Ellen are equal partners in B&E Partnership. In 2013, the partnership breaks up. Bart is insolvent, and Ellen becomes responsible for paying a portion of his partnership debt. Which of the following statements is true?

A. Ellen cannot take a bad debt deduction for any debt that the partnership incurred.
B. Bart is not responsible for paying any of his liabilities after dissolution.
C. Ellen can take a bad debt deduction for any amount that she must pay that is not her share of the partnership debt.
D. None of the above.

6. In 2013, Laney sold her partnership interest for $45,000. Her adjusted basis at the time of the sale was $29,500, which includes her $12,500 share of partnership liabilities. When she initially invested in the partnership, she contributed $10,000 worth of equipment. There was no profit or loss at the partnership level that had not been credited at the time she sold her interest. What is the amount and nature of her income or loss from the sale of her partnership interest in 2013?

A. $7,500 ordinary loss.
B. $10,000 capital gain.
C. $12,500 ordinary income.
D. $28,000 capital gain.

7. Bill owns a 75% capital interest in the Shanahan Partnership. Bill's wife, Veronica, is a 65% owner in the Underdahl Partnership. Bill and Veronica file separate tax returns and keep all their books and records separate. Shanahan Partnership sells Underdahl Partnership a factory machine for $7,600. Shanahan's basis in the machinery is $10,000. What is Shanahan Partnership's deductible loss?

A. $0.
B. $2,400.
C. $7,600.
D. $10,000.

8. The adjusted basis of Adrian's partnership interest is $17,500. He received a distribution of $9,000 cash and a piece of land with an adjusted basis of $2,500 to the partnership and a fair market value of $4,000. What is the gain to be recognized at the time of these distributions?

A. $0.
B. $1,500.
C. $4,500.
D. $6,000.

9. Alice's outside basis in Dogan Tiles Partnership on January 1, 2013 was $11,000. She is a 50% partner and shares profits and losses in the same ratio. For 2013, the partnership's ordinary business income was $40,000 and its tax-exempt interest income was $700. If the partnership were to liquidate on December 31, 2013, what would be Alice's basis for determining gain or loss?

A. $24,900.
B. $30,750.
C. $31,350.
D. $30,300.

10. The basis of Hugo's partnership interest is $150,000. He receives a nonliquidating distribution of $80,000 cash and land that has an adjusted basis to the partnership of $100,000. What is the basis of the land in Hugo's hands?

A. $70,000.
B. $100,000.
C. $120,000.
D. $150,000.

11. Nina, a partner in the Maass Partnership, receives distributions of $1,000 in cash and property worth $2,000, in which Maass has a basis of $1,500. Nina's outside basis at the time of the distributions is $20,000. The partnership has assets of $40,000 and no outstanding liabilities. The distributions are made at the end of the year, after partnership income (loss) has been recorded. How much gain should Nina recognize on the distributions and what is her basis in the property received?

A. She recognizes a gain of $500 on the property received and her basis in the property is $2,000.
B. She recognizes gain of $1,500 on the property and cash received. Her basis in the property received is $3,500.
C. She recognizes no gain on the property received. Her basis in the property received is $1,500.
D. She recognizes a gain of $1,000. Her basis in the property received is $1,500.

Unit 12: C Corporations in General

More Reading:
Publication 542, *Corporations*
Publication 544, *Sales and Other Dispositions of Assets*
Instructions for Form 1120, *U.S. Corporation Income Tax Return*

Most major companies are C corporations, which are taxed under subchapter C of the Internal Revenue Code. A C corporation can own property in its own name and it can be sued directly. The shareholders who own stock in a corporation do not own its individual assets. Individual shareholders are protected from legal liability, except in very unusual circumstances.

The IRS requires certain businesses to be taxed as corporations. The following businesses formed after 1996 are automatically treated as corporations:

- A business formed under a federal or state law that refers to it as a corporation
- A business formed under a state law that refers to it as a joint-stock company or joint-stock association
- Insurance companies
- Certain banks
- A business owned by a state or local government
- A business specifically required to be taxed as a corporation by the IRC (for example, certain publicly-traded partnerships)
- Certain foreign businesses
- Any other business that elects to be taxed as a corporation and files Form 8832, *Entity Classification Election*

Basic concepts regarding C corporations include:

1. A C corporation enjoys perpetual life and limited liability.
2. Earnings of a C corporation may be taxed twice: first at the corporate level and again at the shareholder level if they are distributed as dividends. Shareholders of a C corporation cannot deduct corporate losses.
3. A corporation must maintain a list of all its shareholders, and generally must conduct at least one shareholder meeting per year.
4. A C corporation must file a charter, issue stock, and be overseen by a board of directors.
5. A C corporation may have a single owner-shareholder or an unlimited number of shareholders.
6. A corporation's existence starts when articles of incorporation are filed with the state office that handles incorporations (usually the Secretary of State), along with any required filing fees.
7. If a C corporation liquidates, it will recognize gain or loss on the sale or distribution of its assets. Corporate shareholders then recognize gain or loss on the surrender of their stock to the corporation.
8. A C corporation may sell common and/or preferred stock with different voting rights.
9. A C corporation's shareholder-employees can receive tax-free employee fringe benefits that are deductible by the corporation as a business expense.

Filing Requirements

A domestic corporation in existence for any part of a tax year (including corporations in bankruptcy) must file an income tax return, regardless of its taxable income. A C corporation typically files Form 1120, *U.S. Corporation Income Tax Return*, but it may file Form 1120-A if its gross receipts, total income, and total assets are each under $500,000. Tax-exempt organizations organized as corporations file Form 990 rather than Form 1120.

A corporation must continue to file tax returns even if there is no business activity or profits. However, it does not have to file after it has formally dissolved.

A corporation must file by the fifteenth day of the third month after the end of its tax year. Thus, a calendar-year corporation must file its tax return by March 15 of the following year.

Example: Finman Design Corporation's tax year ends December 31. It must file its Form 1120 by March 15.

Example: Greenbook Inc. is a domestic corporation with a fiscal year-end of March 31. Greenbook must file Form 1120 by June 15.

Electronic filing using the Electronic Federal Tax Payment System (EFTPS) is mandatory for C corporations with $10 million or more in assets and at least 250 or more returns of any type, including information returns such as Forms W-2 or Forms 1099.

A corporation must file Form 7004, *Automatic Extension of Time to File Certain Business Income Tax, Information, and Other Returns,* to request a six-month extension of time to file its income tax return. Form 7004 does not extend the time for paying the tax due on the return. Interest, and possibly penalties, will be charged on any part of the tax due and not paid. The interest is figured from the original due date of the return to the date of payment.

A penalty for late filing is assessed at 5% of any unpaid tax for each month the return is late, up to a maximum of 25% of the unpaid tax on the return. The late filing penalty is reduced by any late payment penalty for the same period. The minimum penalty for any return that is over 60 days late is the smaller of the tax due on the return, or $135. The penalty for late payment of corporate income tax is one half of 1% of the unpaid tax for each month that the tax is not paid, up to a maximum of 25% of the unpaid tax.

These penalties may not be imposed if the corporation shows reasonable cause for not paying or filing on time.

Estimated Tax Payments

Corporations are required to make estimated tax payments if they expect their tax due to be $500 or more during the taxable year. Penalties apply if estimated tax payments are not made on time. Most business entities, including corporations, are now required to use EFTPS to make their estimated tax payments.

Installments are due on a quarterly basis, on the fifteenth day of the fourth, sixth, ninth, and twelfth months of the corporation's taxable year. Thus, a calendar-year corporation is required to make estimated payments on April 15, June 15, September 15, and December 15.

Example: Longinotti Textiles Corporation's tax year ends January 31. Estimated tax payments are due on May 15, July 15, October 15, and January 15 (of the following year).

There is no penalty for underpayment of estimated tax if the tax is less than $500, or if each quarterly estimated tax payment is at least 25% of the corporation's current-year tax.

There is also no underpayment penalty if each estimated tax installment is at least 25% of the income tax on the prior year return. However, this provision will not apply in the following instances:

- If the prior tax year was a short year (less than 12 months)
- If the corporation did not file a return for the prior year
- If the prior year tax return showed zero tax liability
- If the corporation had at least $1 million of taxable income in any of the last three years

Corporate Refunds and Amended Returns

Corporations may use Form 1139, *Corporate Application for Tentative Refund,* or Form 1120X, *Amended U.S. Corporation Income Tax Return,* to apply for a refund. If a corporation does not file Form 1139, it must file Form 1120X to apply for a refund. Form 1120X must be filed within three years of the due date, including extensions, for filing the return for a year in which it sustains a loss.

A corporation cannot file Form 1139 before filing the return for a capital loss year, but it must file Form 1139 no later than one year after the year it sustains the capital loss.

If a corporation accidentally overpays its estimated tax, it may use Form 4466, *Corporation Application for Quick Refund of Overpayment of Estimated Tax,* to obtain a quick refund of its estimated tax payments. Form 4466 may be used if a corporation's overpayment is at least 10% of its anticipated tax liability and at least $500.

Corporate Taxation

Unlike a partnership or an S corporation, a C corporation is not a pass-through entity. This means that the earnings of a C corporation may be taxed twice. Corporate income is taxed when it is earned and then may be taxed again if it is distributed to shareholders as dividends. A corporation does not receive a tax deduction for the distribution of dividends to its shareholders.

A C corporation's income does not retain its character when it is distributed to shareholders. A corporation can have revenue from many different sources, including sales of products, services, and investment income. If, for example, a C corporation has rental income, it pays tax on this and any other sources of income at the corporate level.

When the corporation's after-tax income is distributed to shareholders, this portion does not retain its character as rental income. It is distributed merely as a dividend. This also applies if the corporation earns tax-exempt income. For example, a C corporation may earn tax-exempt income from investing in municipal bonds. If this income is used to make distributions to shareholders, its tax-exempt character is lost, and the distributions will be taxable dividends to the shareholders.

Example: Riden Paper Products, a C corporation, receives tax-exempt income from bonds. Riden subsequently distributes income to its shareholders as taxable dividends. Even though a portion of the income was tax-exempt to Riden, it does not retain its tax-exempt character when distributions are made to the shareholders. In contrast, in the case of an S corporation or a partnership, the income would have retained its character when it was passed through to the partners or S corporation shareholders.

Example: Super Sailing Inc. is a calendar-year C corporation with 20 shareholders. After deducting business expenses, Super Sailing has $150,000 in taxable net income in 2013. The corporation also earns $4,000 in interest from municipal bonds. The $4,000 of tax-exempt bond interest is excluded from the corporation's taxable income. In December 2013, Super Sailing distributes $120,000 to its shareholders. The company cannot take a tax deduction for the distribution. Each shareholder has an equal stake in the company, so each one receives $6,000 in dividend income ($120,000 ÷ 20 = $6,000). Each shareholder is required to recognize $6,000 of dividend income for 2013.

Accumulated Earnings Tax

A corporation is allowed to accumulate a reasonable portion of its earnings for possible expansion or other bona fide business reasons. However, a corporation may be subject to the accumulated earnings tax if it does not distribute enough of its profits to shareholders. This tax was instituted to prevent corporations from hoarding income in order to avoid income tax on distributions for its shareholders.

The tax is levied at a rate of 15% of accumulated taxable income. If the accumulated earnings tax applies, interest is also assessed from the date the corporate return was originally due, without extensions.

An accumulation of $250,000 or less is generally considered reasonable for most businesses. However, for personal service corporations, the limit is $150,000. Reasonable needs of the business include the following:

- Specific, definite, and feasible plans for use of the earnings accumulation in the business.
- The amount necessary to redeem the corporation's stock included in a deceased shareholder's gross estate, if the amount does not exceed the reasonably anticipated total estate and inheritance taxes and funeral and administration expenses incurred by the shareholder's estate.

The absence of a bona fide business reason for a corporation's accumulated earnings may be indicated by many different circumstances, such as a lack of regular distributions to its shareholders or withdrawals by the shareholders classified as personal loans. Actions to expand the business generally qualify as a bona fide reason for the accumulated income. Specific examples may include:

- The expansion of the company to a new area or a new facility
- Acquiring another business through the purchase of stock or assets
- Providing for reasonable estimates of product liability losses

The fact that a corporation has an unreasonable accumulation of earnings is sufficient to establish liability for the accumulated earnings tax unless the corporation can show the earnings were not accumulated to allow its shareholders to avoid income tax.

Corporate Alternative Minimum Tax

Tax laws give special treatment to some types of income and allow special deductions and credits for some types of expenses. As these laws allow some corporations with substantial economic income to significantly reduce their regular tax liabilities, the corporate alternative minimum tax (AMT) is intended to ensure that corporations pay at least a minimum amount of tax on their income. A corporation owes AMT if its tentative minimum tax is more than its regular tax.

Small corporations are exempt from corporate AMT. Most corporations will automatically qualify for the exemption in their first year of existence. After its first year, a corporation is considered a small corporation if its average annual gross receipts for the prior three years (or portion thereof) do not exceed $7.5 million ($5 million for its first three-year period).

If a corporation fails the $7.5 million test for any year, it will be ineligible for the AMT exemption for that year and all subsequent years. If a corporation fails to qualify under the initial $5 million limit, it will never qualify for the AMT exemption even if its gross receipts remain under the $7.5 million exemption limit.

The starting point for the determination of income for AMT purposes is the corporation's regular taxable income. Regular taxable income is modified by a series of additional computations called adjustments and preferences. Adjustments can either increase or decrease taxable income, whereas preferences are calculated on a property-by-property basis and only apply to the extent that they are positive. Adjustments include a portion of accelerated depreciation on buildings and equipment, amortization of pollution control facilities, mining exploration and development expenses, income reported under the completed contract method of accounting, and installment sales income.

Corporations use Form 4626, *Alternative Minimum Tax-Corporations*, to figure their minimum tax for AMT purposes. Corporations use Form 8827, *Credit for Prior Year Minimum Tax*, to figure the minimum tax credit, if any, for alternative minimum tax incurred in prior tax years and any minimum tax credit carry forward. A minimum AMT tax credit may be carried forward indefinitely.

Accounting Methods

Like other entities, C corporations may generally use any permissible accounting method for keeping track of income and expenses, as described in Unit 2.

The nonaccrual experience method is a method of accounting for bad debts. If a corporation uses the accrual method of accounting and qualifies to use the nonaccrual experience method for bad debts, it is not required to accrue service-related income that it expects to be uncollectible.

Accrual-method corporations are not required to maintain accruals for certain amounts from the performance of services that, on the basis of their experience, will not be collected, if:

- The services are in the fields of health, law, engineering, architecture, accounting, actuarial science, performing arts, or consulting (personal service corporations); or
- The corporation's average annual gross receipts for the three prior tax years do not exceed $5 million.

This provision does not apply if the corporation charges interest on late payments, or if it charges customers any penalty for failure to pay an amount timely. Further, a corporation cannot use this method for amounts owed from activities such as lending money, selling goods, or acquiring receivables.

Additional Form 1120 Schedules

Corporations may be required to complete certain additional schedules in connection with the preparation of Form 1120. Schedule L includes balance sheets as of the beginning and end of the year, based upon the corporation's books and records. Differences in accounting rules for financial reporting (book income) and tax reporting can lead to differences in the amounts of income reported to shareholders and tax authorities. Preparation of a C corporation's income tax return includes a reconciliation of book income to taxable income.

For small corporations with less than $10 million in assets, the differences in book and taxable income are reconciled in Schedule M-1 of Form 1120. Larger corporations with more than $10 million in assets use Schedule M-3, *Net Income (Loss) Reconciliation for Corporations with Total Assets of $10 million or More*.

Example: Armington Corporation had $8 million in assets in 2013. It uses Schedule M-1 to reconcile the difference between its book and taxable income. Marcus Corporation had $15 million in assets in 2013. It uses Schedule M-3 to reconcile the difference between its book and taxable income.

Schedule M-3 provides additional information and contains three main sections:

- Financial statement reconciliation
- Detail of income/loss items
- Detail of expenses/deductions

Examples of items that would be included in the reconciliation on Schedule M-1 or Schedule M-3, if applicable, are:

- Excess of capital losses over capital gains (nondeductible, as discussed in Unit 13.)
- Charitable contribution carryover (the amount of charitable contributions that are disallowed for tax purposes and must be carried over to the next taxable year.)
- Travel and entertainment in excess of the allowable 50% limit.
- Federal income taxes paid or accrued, which are deductible for accounting purposes but not for tax purposes.
- Other expenses recorded on books but not deductible on return.
- Advance rental income.
- Other income subject to tax that is not included in book income.
- Tax-exempt interest income.

- Other income included on books but not subject to tax.
- Deductions on return not charged against book income.

Generally, a foreign corporation that is required to file Form 1120-F must also complete Schedule M-2. However, the corporation is not required to complete Schedules M-1, M-2, or M-3 if its total assets at the end of the year per Schedule L are less than $25,000. Further, corporations with less than $250,000 of total receipts and total assets at the end of the year are not required to complete Schedules L, M-1, and M-2.

Contributions of Capital

A corporation is formed initially by a transfer of money, property, or services by prospective shareholders in exchange for stock in the corporation. A transfer of assets may take place when a business that previously operated as a partnership or sole proprietorship opts to become a corporation.

Contributions to the capital of a corporation are generally not taxable transactions to the corporation, whether or not they are made by the shareholders. A shareholder will not recognize gain when a cash contribution is made for stock. This is just like when a person purchases stock on the open market for cash. The shareholder's basis in the stock is the amount of cash contributed.

However, a transfer of property, rather than cash, to a corporation may have tax consequences to both the corporation and the shareholder. For example, if a shareholder contributes property to a corporation, he generally recognizes gain and the basis of the contributed property to the corporation is the same as the basis that the shareholder had in the property, after increase for any gain that the shareholder recognized in the exchange. There is an exception, however, for situations in which property is contributed and the shareholder controls the corporation immediately after the transfer. This is called a section 351 transfer, and is explained below.

The basis of property contributed to a corporation's capital by anyone other than a shareholder is zero.

Example: The city of Omaha, Nebraska gives Madera Corporation a plot of land as an enticement to locate its business operations there. Madera accounts for the property as a contribution to capital. The land has zero basis since the property was contributed by a non-shareholder.

If stock is exchanged for services, the recipient of the stock recognizes taxable income based upon fair market value of the services provided, and that amount is his basis in the stock.

Example: Justin is a web designer who provides web design services to a corporation. He agrees to accept stock as payment instead of cash. The stock is valued at $5,000. Justin must recognize ordinary income of $5,000 as payment for services he rendered to the corporation. His basis in the stock is $5,000.

Section 351: Nontaxable Corporate Transfers

If a taxpayer transfers property to a corporation in exchange for stock and immediately afterward the taxpayer controls the corporation, the exchange may not be taxable. This rule applies both to individuals and to entities that transfer property to a corporation. It also applies whether the corporation is being formed or is already in operation. The effect is to allow the investing shareholder to contribute assets to a corporation without immediate tax consequences, and to defer recognition of taxable gain until the stock received is later disposed.

This nonrecognition rule does not apply in the following situations:

- The corporation is an investment company.
- The taxpayer transfers the property in a bankruptcy proceeding in exchange for stock that is used to pay creditors.
- The stock is received in exchange for the corporation's debt (other than a security, such as a bond) or for interest on the corporation's debt (including a security) that accrued while the taxpayer held the debt.

In order to be considered in control of a corporation immediately after an exchange, the transferors must own at least 80% of the total combined voting power of all classes of stock entitled to vote and at least 80% of the outstanding shares of each class of nonvoting stock.

Example: Amanda owns an office building. Her basis in the building is $100,000. She organizes a corporation when the building has a fair market value of $300,000. Amanda transfers the building to the corporation for all its authorized capital stock. No gain is recognized by Amanda or the corporation on the transfer.

Example: Aaron and Pedro transfer property with a basis of $100,000 to a corporation in exchange for stock with a fair market value of $300,000. This represents only 75% of each class of stock of the corporation. The other 25% was already issued to someone else. Aaron and Pedro must recognize a taxable gain of $200,000 on the transaction.

This nonrecognition rule does not apply to services that are rendered in exchange for stock. The value of stock received for services is income to the recipient.

Example: Wayne is an architect. In 2013, he transfers property worth $35,000 and renders services valued at $3,000 to a corporation in exchange for stock valued at $38,000. Right after the exchange, Wayne owns 85% of the outstanding stock. No gain is recognized on the exchange of property. However, Wayne must recognize ordinary income of $3,000 as payment for services he rendered to the corporation.

If, in an otherwise nontaxable exchange of property for stock, the shareholder receives money or property in exchange for the contribution of property, he would recognize gain to the extent of the money and the fair market value of property received. If the corporation assumes the shareholder's liabilities, the assumption generally is not treated as if the shareholder received money or other property, unless:

- The liabilities the corporation assumes are more than the shareholder's adjusted basis in the property transferred, in which case gain is recognized up to the difference. However, if the liabilities assumed give rise to a deduction when paid, such as a trade account payable or interest, no gain is recognized.

- There is no good business reason for the corporation to assume the liabilities, or if the main purpose in the exchange is to avoid federal income tax.

The shareholder's basis in his stock must be reduced by the amount of the liabilities assumed by the corporation.

Example: Rasheda transfers machinery to a corporation in exchange for all of the corporation's outstanding stock. The machinery's FMV at the time of the transfer is $200,000. Rasheda's basis in the machinery is $80,000. The machinery is encumbered by an outstanding loan of $30,000, which the corporation assumes. In this example, the section 351 exchange is valid, and no gain or loss is recognized in the transaction. Rasheda's basis in the stock is $50,000 ($80,000 basis of property contributed minus the $30,000 loan that was assumed by the corporation.)

Both the corporation and certain stockholders involved in a nontaxable exchange of property for stock must attach to their income tax returns a complete statement of all facts pertinent to the exchange. This reporting requirement applies to stockholders who own 5% or more of a public company or 1% or more of a privately held company.

Exclusions from Nonrecognition Treatment

This nonrecognition rule does not apply when the property transferred is of a relatively small value when compared to the value of stock already owned, and the main purpose of the transfer is to qualify for the nonrecognition of gain or loss. Property transferred will not be considered to be of small value if its FMV is at least 10% of the FMV of the stock already owned or to be received by the transferor.

If a group of transferors exchanges property for corporate stock, each transferor may not receive stock in proportion to his interest in the property transferred. However, if a disproportionate transfer takes place, it may be treated as if the stock were first received in proportion to the interests in the property and then portions were used to make gifts, pay compensation for services, or to satisfy the transferor's obligations.

If a corporation transfers its stock in satisfaction of indebtedness and the fair market value of its stock is less than the indebtedness, the corporation has income to the extent of the difference from the cancellation of indebtedness. For example, if stock is given to an individual to pay for a debt, the transfer does not qualify for nonrecognition treatment.

Unit 12: Study Questions

1. Lightning Forecasting Corporation has net income for books of $3 million in 2013. What is its taxable income if it also has the following?

- Federal income tax expense of $1.5 million
- Travel and entertainment expenses of $200,000
- Tax-exempt interest income of $100,000
- Capital losses of $47,000 and capital gains of $18,000

A. $4,471,000
B. $1,529,000.
C. $4,729,000.
D. $4,529,000.

2. The accumulated earnings tax is imposed on C corporations that accumulate earnings beyond the reasonable needs of their businesses. Which of the following reasons would not be an example of a reasonable accumulation?

A. The expansion of the company to a new area or a new facility.
B. Acquiring another business through the purchase of stock or other assets.
C. Allowing the shareholders to take bona fide loans from the corporation.
D. Providing for reasonable estimates of product liability losses.

3. Which of these domestic business entities will be automatically taxed as a corporation?

1. A joint stock company.
2. An insurance company.
3. Any business formed under a state law that refers to it as a corporation.
4. A single member limited liability company (LLC).

A. All of the above.
B. 1, 2, and 3.
C. 3.
D. 2 and 3.

4. Nell transfers property with a basis of $200,000 and an FMV of $350,000 to a corporation in exchange for stock with a fair market value of $300,000. This represents 65% of the stock of the corporation. How much gain is recognized by Nell on this transaction?

A. $0.
B. $50,000.
C. $100,000
D. $150,000.

5. The accumulated earnings tax is levied at a rate of __________ on accumulated taxable income.

A. 5%.
B. 10%.
C. 15%.
D. 50%.

6. John transfers property worth $43,000 and renders services valued at $6,000 to a corporation in exchange for stock valued at $49,000. Right after the exchange, John owns 90% of the outstanding stock. How much income, if any, must he recognize in this transaction?

A. $0.
B. $3,000.
C. $6,000.
D. $49,000.

7. If a corporation's tentative minimum tax exceeds its regular tax, the excess amount is:

A. Payable instead of the regular tax.
B. Carried back to offset losses from prior years.
C. Carried forward to offset losses in future years.
D. Payable in addition to the regular tax.

8. What is the penalty for a corporation that fails to make estimated tax payments?

A. One-half of 1% per month, up to a maximum of 25%.
B. 5% per month, up to a maximum of 25%.
C. 5% per month, up to a maximum of 35%.
D. 5% per month, up to a maximum of 100%.

9. Lori and Marcus each transfer property with a basis of $10,000 to a corporation in exchange for stock with a fair market value of $30,000. The total stock received by them represents 75% of the corporation's stock. The other 25% of the corporation's stock was issued earlier to Anne, an unrelated person. The taxable consequences are:

A. None, because it is a transfer of property for stock.
B. Lori and Marcus each recognize a gain of $20,000.
C. Lori and Marcus each recognize a gain of $30,000.
D. 80% of the transaction is recognized as a taxable gain.

10. BRB Corporation's fiscal year ends June 30. Not counting extensions, what is the due date for its tax return?

A. September 15.
B. April 15.
C. October 15.
D. January 15.

11. Metro Street Cars Corporation had a profitable 2013 and was required to make estimated payments during the year totaling $19,000. However, because of serious economic difficulties, Metro expects to have a tax loss in 2014. Which statement is true about Metro's required estimated payments?

A. Metro must make a minimum estimated tax payment of $500.
B. Metro must make estimated payments of at least 90% of the prior year's tax liability.
C. Metro is required to pay 100% of the prior year tax liability.
D. Metro is not required to make estimated payments in 2014.

12. Kathleen transferred a factory building with an adjusted basis of $70,000 and a fair market value of $110,000 to the Carpenteria Corporation in exchange for 100% of Carpenteria Corporation stock and $20,000 cash. The building was subject to a mortgage of $25,000, which Carpenteria Corporation assumed. The fair market value of the stock was $75,000. What are the amounts of Kathleen's realized gain and her recognized gain?

A. $25,000 realized gain; $25,000 recognized gain.
B. $50,000 realized gain; $45,000 recognized gain.
C. $50,000 realized gain; $20,000 recognized gain.
D. $35,000 realized gain; $20,000 recognized gain.

13. Topcare Pet Products, a cash-basis corporation that operates on the calendar year, is required to make estimated tax payments. What are the due dates for the estimated payments?

A. April 15, June 15, September 15, and December 15.
B. January 15, March 15, June 15, September 15, and December 15.
C. March 1, June 1, September 1, and December 1.
D. None of the above.

14. Vihaan transferred a warehouse with an adjusted basis of $10,000 and a fair market value of $140,000 to the Data-Tech Corporation in exchange for 100% of Data-Tech stock. The building was subject to a mortgage of $25,000, which Data-Tech Corporation assumed. The fair market value of the stock was $150,000. What are the amounts of Vihaan's realized gain and his recognized gain?

A. $165,000 realized gain; $15,000 recognized gain.
B. $35,000 realized gain; $15,000 recognized gain.
C. $165,000 realized gain; $25,000 recognized gain.
D. $130,000 realized gain; $15,000 recognized gain.

Unit 13: Corporate Transactions

More Reading:
Publication 542, *Corporations*

The tax treatment of certain items is different for C corporations, as compared with individuals and other types of entities. C corporations are subject to their own tax rate schedules.

Capital Gains and Losses

Unlike the favorable capital gains' rates available to individuals, the capital gains of a C corporation are taxed at the same rate as its ordinary income. A corporation figures its capital gains and losses much like an individual. However, in the case of a C corporation, its capital losses are only deductible to the extent of its capital gains. A C corporation is not allowed to offset capital losses against its other income the way individuals can (up to a limit).

If a corporation has an excess capital loss, it may carry the loss back or forward to other tax years and deduct it from any net capital gains that occurred in those years. The default election is for a corporation to carry back its capital losses to the earliest of the three preceding years in which it had net capital gains; any remaining losses may be carried forward a maximum of five years.

A capital loss from another year cannot create or increase a net operating loss in the year to which it is carried. Further, capital losses can be carried only to years that would otherwise have had a net capital gain.

In rare instances, longer carryback and carryforward periods may be allowed. Capital losses that are a result of foreign expropriation[36] may not be carried back, but may be carried forward for ten years. In the case of a regulated investment company (RIC), net capital losses may be carried forward eight years.

When a corporation carries back or carries forward a capital loss, the loss does not retain its character as a long-term loss. All capital loss carryforwards and carrybacks are treated as short-term losses. A C corporation cannot carry back capital losses to any previous year when it was an S corporation.

Example: In 2013, Chambrun Canvas, a calendar-year C corporation, has a capital gain of $3,000 and a capital loss of $9,000. The capital gain offsets some of the capital loss, leaving a net capital loss of $6,000. Chambrun treats this $6,000 as a short-term loss when carried back or forward. The corporation carries the $6,000 short-term loss back to 2012. In 2012, Chambrun had a short-term capital gain of $8,000 and a long-term capital gain of $5,000 (a total of $13,000 in capital gains). It carries back the loss and subtracts the $6,000 short-term loss (carryback) first from the net short-term gain. This results in a net capital gain of $7,000 that consists of a net short-term capital gain of $2,000 ($8,000 - $6,000) and a net long-term capital gain of $5,000, which allows the corporation to receive a refund of income tax paid in 2012.

[36] This is when a foreign nation takes a corporation's assets for its own use.

Net Operating Losses (NOLs)

A C corporation figures and deducts a net operating loss (NOL) in the same manner as an individual, an estate, or a trust, and the same carryback (two years) and carryforward (up to 20 years) periods apply.

A corporation figures an NOL the same way it figures taxable income. It starts with gross income and subtracts its deductions. If its deductions are more than its gross income, the corporation has an NOL. However, the following rules apply for figuring NOLs:

- A corporation cannot increase its current year NOL by carrybacks or carryovers from other years in which it has a loss.
- A corporation cannot use the domestic production activities deduction to create or increase a current year NOL.
- A corporation can take the deduction for dividends received, without regard to the aggregate limits that normally apply.
- A corporation can figure the deduction for dividends on certain preferred stock of public utilities without limiting it to its taxable income for the year.

An NOL carryback can only be used to reduce income tax. If the corporation owes other taxes or penalties from a prior year, a carryback will not reduce the penalties.

Example: Artisan Cheese Corporation had taxable income of $30,000 in 2012. Business has slowed, and Artisan Cheese has an NOL of $20,000 in 2013. The company decides to carry back its NOL to recover a portion of the income taxes it paid in 2012. Artisan Cheese also incurred a $1,200 penalty in 2012 for failing to remit estimated taxes on time. The corporation cannot recover the amount paid for the estimated tax penalty.

A C corporation with a net operating loss can file for a refund by using Form 1139 or by amending a prior year tax return using Form 1120X. If a corporation elects to waive carryback and instead carry forward its NOL, it enters the carryover on Form 1120, Schedule K. If the corporation is filing a consolidated return, it must also attach a required statement or the election will not be valid.

If a corporation reasonably expects to have a net operating loss in its current year, it may automatically extend the time for paying income tax liability for the preceding year by filing Form 1138, *Extension of Time For Payment of Taxes by a Corporation Expecting a Net Operating Loss Carryback.*

Charitable Deductions

C corporations may deduct the amount of charitable contributions made to qualified organizations, up to 10% of taxable income. A corporation figures its taxable income for this limit without regard to the following:

- The deduction for charitable contributions
- The dividends-received deduction
- The domestic production activities deduction

- Any net operating loss carryback to the tax year
- Any capital loss carryback to the tax year

The rules regarding what qualifies as a charitable organization and required supporting documentation are the same for corporations as they are for individuals. Generally, no deduction is allowed for any charitable contribution of $250 or more unless the corporation obtains a receipt from the donee organization. The written receipt or acknowledgment should show the amount of cash contributed or a description of the property contributed. The receipt or acknowledgment should also give a description and a good faith estimate of the value of any goods or services provided in return for the contribution, or state that no goods or services were provided in return for the contribution.

If a corporation (other than a closely held or personal service corporation) claims a deduction of more than $500 for contributions of property other than cash, a schedule describing the property and the method used to determine its fair market value must be attached to the corporation's return. In addition the corporation should keep a record of:

- The approximate date and manner of acquisition of the donated property.
- The cost or other basis of the donated property held by the donor for less than 12 months prior to contribution.
- Any donation of a used vehicle, boat, or similar property if it takes a deduction larger than $500 for the donated vehicle.

If the deduction claimed for donated property exceeds $5,000, the corporation must complete Form 8283, *Noncash Charitable Contributions,* and attach it to its tax return. A corporation must obtain a qualified appraisal for all deductions of property claimed in excess of $5,000. A qualified appraisal is not required for the donation of cash, publicly traded securities, or inventory.

A corporation using the cash method deducts contributions in the tax year they are paid. A corporation using the accrual method can deduct unpaid contributions if the board of directors authorized the contributions during the year, and the corporation pays the contributions within 2.5 months after the close of the year. A declaration with a statement that includes the date that the board of directors adopted the resolution must accompany the return.

Example: Ladera Corporation is a calendar-year, accrual-basis corporation. Ladera's board of directors approves a charitable contribution of $5,000 to the United Way on December 15, 2013. Ladera Corporation deducts the contribution on its 2013 corporate tax return. Ladera does not have to pay the contribution until March 15, 2014, or 2.5 months after the close of its tax year.

A corporation can carry over charitable contributions made during the current year that exceed the 10% limit to each of the subsequent five years, subject to the same 10% limitation in each year. Any excess contributions not used within that five-year period are lost. No carryback is allowed for charitable contributions. A corporation cannot deduct a carryover of excess contributions to the extent it increases a net operating loss carryover.

Example: Hernandez Sporting Goods has net income of $600,000 in 2013 before taking into account its charitable contributions. The corporation donated $80,000 to a qualified charity in 2013. It also has a net operating loss carryover of $100,000 from a prior year. Therefore, the corporation's charitable deduction is limited to $50,000. The allowable contribution deduction is figured as follows:

($600,000 - $100,000 = $500,000) × 10% = $50,000

The charitable contribution that is not allowed in the current tax year can be carried forward for up to five years. If Hernandez Sporting Goods does not use the remainder at the end of five years, the deduction is lost.

Example: Gromwell Corporation, a calendar-year C corporation, makes a large charitable contribution in 2013. As a result, the corporation has a carryover of excess contributions paid in 2013 and it does not use all the excess on its return for 2014. Gromwell Corporation can carry the rest over to 2015, 2016, 2017, and 2018. After that time, it can no longer carry over the excess 2013 charitable contributions.

Dividends-Received Deduction

A corporation can deduct a percentage of certain dividends received from other corporations in which it has an ownership interest. The dividends-received deduction (DRD) is designed to reduce the consequences of double taxation. Without this deduction, corporate profits could be taxed to the corporation that earned them, then to its corporate shareholders, and then again to the individual shareholders of the parent corporation.

The DRD complements the consolidated return regulations, which allow affiliated corporations to file a single consolidated return for U.S. federal income tax purposes. It is available to C corporations but not to LLCs, S corporations, partnerships, or individuals.

Generally, if a corporation receives dividends from another corporation, it is entitled to a deduction of 70% of the dividends received. If the corporation receiving the dividend owns 20% or more of the other corporation, the deduction increases to 80% of the dividends received. If the corporation receiving the dividends owns more than 80% of the distributing corporation, it is allowed to deduct 100% of the dividends it receives. To summarize, the deduction for dividends received is based on the percentage of stock ownership in the distributing corporation:

Percentage of ownership	Dividends-Received Deduction
Less than 20%	70%
20 - 80%	80%
Greater than 80%	100%

The percentage of stock ownership is determined without regard to preferred stock.

Example: The Quincy Corporation owns 25% of LightStar Corporation. The Quincy Corporation has taxable income of $70,000 before taking into account its dividend income. In 2013, Quincy received $100,000 of dividends from LightStar. Quincy is allowed an 80% dividends-received deduction, figured as follows: $80,000 = ($100,000 × 80%). Therefore, only $20,000 of the dividends received from LightStar Corporation are taxable. In 2013, the Quincy Corporation's taxable net income is $90,000 ($70,000 + $20,000).

Example: JRD Corporation owns 85% of the outstanding stock in Humboldt Corporation. In 2013, JRD receives $250,000 of dividends from Humboldt. Because JRD has over 80% ownership of Humboldt, it may claim the 100% dividends-received deduction and the dividends are not taxable.

If a corporation is entitled to a 100% DRD, there is no taxable income limitation, and the corporation may deduct the full amount of the dividends received. However, if a corporation is entitled to a 70% DRD, it can deduct amounts only up to 70% of its taxable income. If a corporation is entitled to an 80% DRD, it can generally deduct amounts only up to 80% of its taxable income. In each case, the corporation would determine taxable income without the following items:

- The DRD
- The net operating loss deduction
- The domestic production activities deduction
- Any adjustment due to the nontaxable part of an extraordinary dividend
- Any capital loss carryback to the tax year

If a corporation has an NOL for a tax year, the DRD must be figured differently. The limit of 80% (or 70%) of taxable income does not apply if use of the unlimited DRD by the receiving corporation would result in a net operating loss.

Example: Verde Eco-Products Corporation loses $25,000 from its own business operations in 2013. Verde Eco-Products also receives $100,000 in dividend income from a 20%-owned corporation. Therefore, Verde Eco-Product's taxable income in 2013 is $75,000 ($100,000 - $25,000 loss) before the DRD. If Verde Eco-Products claims the full DRD of $80,000 ($100,000 × 80%) and combines it with a loss from operations of $25,000, it will create an NOL of ($5,000). Therefore, the 80% of taxable income limit does not apply. The corporation can deduct the full $80,000 DRD.

Example: Redwood Patio Corporation has a loss of $15,000 from business operations in 2013. However, it also has dividends of $100,000 from a corporation in which it holds an interest of 50%. Therefore, Redwood's taxable income is $85,000 before applying the DRD. After claiming the DRD of $80,000 ($100,000 × 80%), its taxable income is $5,000. Because Redwood would not have an NOL after applying a full 80% DRD, its allowable DRD is limited to 80% of its taxable income (before the DRD), or $68,000 ($85,000 × 80%).

Corporations cannot take a deduction for dividends received from the following entities:

- A real estate investment trust (REIT)
- A tax-exempt corporation
- A corporation whose stock was held less than 46 days
- A corporation whose preferred stock was held less than 91 days

- Any corporation, if another corporation is under an obligation to make related payments for positions in substantially similar property

Dividends on deposits in domestic building and loan associations, mutual savings banks, cooperative banks, and similar organizations are taxed as interest income—not dividends. They do not qualify for the DRD. Small business investment companies can deduct 100% of the dividends received from taxable domestic corporations.

Study Note: For the EA exam, you must understand how to calculate the dividends-received deduction and how it applies to a C corporation's taxable income and net operating losses.

Related Party Transactions

Strict rules apply to related party transactions. A corporation that uses the accrual method cannot deduct business expenses and interest owed to a related person who uses the cash method until the corporation makes the related payment and the amount is included in the related person's income. These rules also deny the deduction of a loss on the sale or trade of property (other than in the complete liquidation of a corporation) between related persons.

For purposes of these rules, the following persons are considered related to a corporation:

- A corporation that is a member of the same controlled group.
- An individual who owns, directly or indirectly, more than 50% of the value of the outstanding stock of the corporation.
- A partnership, if the same persons own more than 50% of the value of the outstanding stock of the corporation and more than 50% of the partnership.
- An S corporation, if the same persons own more than 50% of the value of the outstanding stock of each corporation.
- A trust fiduciary, when the trust or its grantor owns, directly or indirectly, more than 50% of the value of the outstanding stock of the corporation.
- An employee-owner of a personal service corporation, regardless of the amount of stock owned.

In determining whether a person directly or indirectly owns any of the outstanding stock of a corporation, the following rules apply:

- Stock directly or indirectly owned by or for a corporation, partnership, estate, or trust is considered owned proportionately by or for its shareholders, partners, or beneficiaries.
- An individual is considered to own the stock that is directly or indirectly owned by or for his family. Family includes only brothers and sisters (including half-brothers and half-sisters), a spouse, ancestors, and lineal descendants.
- An individual owning any stock in a corporation is considered to own the stock that is directly or indirectly owned by his partner.

Example: Robert is a 90% owner in Nampa Boots Corporation. His wife, Eileen, is a 55% owner of Terabyte Corporation. Robert is considered a related person for the purposes of ownership in Terabyte Corporation. Therefore, for the related-party transaction rules, Robert is also considered a 55% owner in Terabyte Corporation and Eileen is considered a 90% owner in Nampa Boots Corporation.

Closely Held Corporations

A closely held corporation generally has a small number of shareholders (often family members) and no public market for its stock. Corporate ownership and management often overlap. A corporation is considered to be closely held if both of the following apply:

- It is not a personal service corporation.
- At any time during the last half of the tax year, more than 50% of the value of its outstanding stock is, directly or indirectly, owned by or for five or fewer individuals. An individual in this case includes certain trusts and private foundations.

This designation matters because of at-risk rules for closely held corporations similar to those that apply to partners in a partnership. These rules dictate that a closely held corporation's losses are only deductible up to the amount at risk of financial loss in connection with an activity. The amount at risk generally equals:

- The money and the adjusted basis of property contributed by the taxpayer to the activity, and
- The money borrowed for the activity.

The at-risk amount also includes the FMV of property (adjusted for any liens or encumbered mortgages) that is pledged as security or collateral for the debts of the activity.

Example: Allworth Corporation is a closely held C corporation with only two shareholders: a father and son. Allworth Corp. invests $50,000 in a business venture, and also pledges the value of a factory building as collateral for a $100,000 loan that is used in the business venture. Allworth's factory building has a fair market value of $150,000 but is also secured by a lien of $125,000. Allworth Corp.'s amount at risk in the business venture is only $75,000 [$50,000 plus the $25,000 ($150,000 - $125,000) equity in the building].

The following items increase an entity's amount at risk:

1. A contribution of additional cash (or property) to the venture.
2. Any recourse loan for which the corporation is liable for repayment.

The amount at risk is decreased by the following items:

1. An investor's withdrawal of cash or property from the activity.
2. A nonrecourse loan where the corporation is not liable for repayment.

The amount at risk cannot be decreased below zero. If this occurs, suspended losses from prior years must be reduced.

Controlled Groups

A controlled group is a group of corporations that are related through common ownership, typically as either parent-subsidiary or brother-sister.

A **Parent-Subsidiary Controlled Group** involves a parent corporation that owns at least 80% or more of the voting power of at least one other corporation (with possible additional corporations that are at least 80% owned by either the common parent or one of the subsidiary entities).

A **Brother-Sister Controlled Group** involves situations in which five or fewer individuals, estates, or trusts own 80% or more of the combined voting power for multiple corporations, and have identical common ownership within the individual corporations of at least 50%.

Example of parent-subsidiary controlled group: Ciara Corporation owns:

- 90% of the stock of Shiffrin Corporation
- 80% of the stock of Kumagai Corporation
- 65% of the stock of Faruqi Corporation

Unrelated persons own the percentage of stock not owned by Ciara Corporation. As Ciara Corporation owns 80% or more of the stock of Shiffrin and Kumagai, it is the common parent of a parent-subsidiary group consisting of the three corporations. Faruqi Corporation is not a member of the group because Ciara Corporation's ownership is less than 80%.

Example of brother-sister controlled group: Kendrick Corporation and Leitzel Corporation are owned by four shareholders in the following percentages:

Shareholder	Kendrick Corp.	Leitzel Corp.
A	70%	30%
B	10%	50%
C	10%	10%
D	10%	10%
Total	**100%**	**100%**

The same five or fewer common owners must own more than 80% of stock or some interest in all members of the controlled group. In this example, the four shareholders together own 100% of the stock of each corporation, so the first test is met. They also meet the second test of owning more than 50% of the stock of each corporation, taking into account only the identical ownership in each corporation.

Shareholder	**Identical Ownership Percentage in Both Corporations**
A	30%
B	10%
C	10%
D	10%
Total	**60%**

A controlled group is allowed a single set of graduated income tax brackets, a single exemption amount for AMT purposes, and a single accumulated earnings credit of $250,000. In each case, these amounts must be allocated among the members of the group. Members of controlled groups are also subject to the rules regarding related party transactions that may require deferral of recognition for losses or expenses incurred by one party.

Unit 13: Study Questions

1. The Farber Corporation owns 10% of the Lewisville Corporation. In 2013, Farber receives $10,000 in dividends on Lewisville stock. What is the dividends-received deduction that Farber Corporation can take?

A. 10%.
B. 50%.
C. 70%.
D. 80%.

2. The Surf's Up Corporation had an NOL of $110,000. Which of the following statements is true?

A. The corporation can forgo the carryback period and choose to carry the entire loss forward to the next 20 years.
B. The corporation is required to carry back losses for two years and then forward for 15 years
C. The corporation can carry back losses five years and carry them forward for 25 years.
D. A corporation cannot carry back losses. It can only carry them forward.

3. Davidson Corporation owns 50% of Nguyen Corporation's outstanding common stock. Davidson has taxable income of $8,000, which includes dividends received of $10,000 from its investment in Nguyen Corporation. What is Davidson Corporation's taxable income after applying the dividends-received deduction?

A. $0.
B. $1,600.
C. $6,400.
D. $8,000.

4. BMD Corporation is a calendar-year corporation that uses the accrual method. What is the last day that the corporation can pay a charitable contribution and still deduct it on its 2013 tax return?

A. December 31, 2013.
B. January 15, 2014.
C. March 15, 2014.
D. April 15, 2014.

5. Xena Corporation is a cash-basis C corporation. In 2013, the corporation has a net short-term capital gain of $23,000 and a net long-term capital loss of $29,000. How should these capital gains and losses be treated?

A. The corporation may deduct a $6,000 long-term capital loss on its 2013 tax return.
B. The corporation may carry back the $29,000 long-term capital loss to a prior year, where it may only be deducted against long-term capital gains.
C. The corporation may carry back the $6,000 net capital loss to a prior year, where it may be deducted against short-term capital gains.
D. The corporation must carry forward the entire capital loss to the following tax year. Carryback of capital losses is not allowed.

6. In 2013, Mansour Corporation has a $15,000 loss from its business operations. In addition, Mansour has received $100,000 in taxable dividends from a 30%-owned corporation. Therefore, its taxable income is $85,000 before applying the dividends-received deduction. What is the corporation's dividends-received deduction?

A. $15,000.
B. $68,000.
C. $80,000.
D. $100,000.

7. McClimate Corporation owns 25% of Wilson Foods Corporation. In 2013, McClimate received $10,000 of dividends from Wilson Foods. Assuming no other limitations apply, McClimate's dividends-received deduction is ________:

A. $7,000.
B. $8,000.
C. $2,000.
D. $0.

8. In 2013 Real Time Corporation made contributions totaling $20,000 to qualified charitable organizations. Due to income limitations, Real Time Corporation could only deduct $15,000 of the contributions on its return. Which of the following statements regarding the excess contributions of $5,000 is correct?

A. Excess charitable contributions can be carried back for 2 years and carried forward for 20 years.
B. Excess charitable contributions can be carried forward for 20 years.
C. Excess charitable contributions can be carried back for 3 years and carried forward for 10 years.
D. Excess charitable contributions can be carried forward for 5 years. They cannot be carried back.

9. Which of the following statements about a controlled group of corporations is true?

A. Members of a controlled group are entitled to only one accumulated earnings tax credit.
B. A parent corporation and its 80% owned subsidiary would be considered members of a controlled group.
C. Members of controlled groups are subject to rules regarding related party transactions that may require deferral of recognition for losses or expenses incurred by one party.
D. All of the above.

10. Redd Beauty Products and Helena Mountain Coffee are domestic C corporations. Redd Beauty owns 25% of Helena Mountain Coffee. Redd Beauty's income from its business operations in 2013 is $500,000. In addition to its business income, Redd Beauty received dividends from Helena Mountain Coffee of $145,000. What is Redd Beauty's dividends-received deduction?

A. $36,250.
B. $101,500.
C. $116,000.
D. $145,000.

11. The Arbabi Plastics Corporation is a calendar-year C corporation. In 2013, it has $400,000 of taxable income before consideration of the following additional items:

- $50,000 of charitable contributions
- A dividends-received deduction of $70,000
- A domestic production activities deduction of $40,000

What portion of the charitable contributions is deductible in 2013?

A. $50,000.
B. $29,000.
C. $40,000.
D. $36,000.

12. During 2013, Bernardino Jewelry, a domestic C corporation, had the following income, expenses, and deductions:

Gross receipts:	$95,000
Net capital gains:	$10,000
Business expenses, (not including charitable contributions):	$65,000
Charitable contribution:	$20,000
NOL carryover from 2012:	$30,000

What is the amount of Bernardino Jewelry's allowable charitable contribution deduction for 2013?

A. $1,000.
B. $3,000.
C. $4,000.
D. $20,000.

13. Which of the following best describes a brother-sister controlled group?

A. A brother and sister each own 50% of a corporation, or a total of 100% of the corporation combined.
B. A parent corporation that owns at least 80% or more of the voting power of at least one other corporation, with at least two brothers and one sister or two sisters and one brother as owners.
C. Five or fewer individuals, estates, or trusts own 80% or more of the combined voting power for multiple corporations, and have identical common ownership within the individual corporations of at least 50%.
D. A corporation that controls at least two other corporations where a brother and sister are chief executive officers of the different corporations and each control over 50% of their respective corporations.

Unit 14: Corporate Distributions & Liquidations

More Reading:
Publication 542, *Corporations*

Corporate Distributions

Corporate distributions or dividends occur when cash, stock, or other property is distributed to shareholders based on the shareholders' ownership of the corporation's stock. When a corporation earns profits, it may retain the profits in the business (as retained earnings) or pay all or a portion of the profits as dividends to shareholders. The amounts a corporation pays as dividends are not deductible expenses. Dividends are most commonly paid in cash. However, a dividend can take the form of stock or other property.

The most common kinds of corporate distributions are:

- Ordinary dividends (either in cash or in property)
- Capital gain distributions
- Nondividend distributions
- Distributions of stock or stock rights

The FMV of distributed property becomes the shareholder's basis in the property. A distribution may be reduced by the following liabilities:

- Any liability of the corporation the shareholder assumes
- Any liability applicable to distributed property, such as mortgage debt the shareholder assumes in connection with distribution of ownership in a building

The amount of a distribution can never go below zero, no matter how much liability a shareholder assumes.

Reporting Requirements: A corporation must furnish Form 1099-DIV, *Dividends and Distributions,* to each of its shareholders who receives a dividend of $10 or more during a calendar year by January 31 of the following year. The corporation must also file copies of the Forms 1099-DIV with the IRS, along with Form 1096, *Annual Summary and Transmittal of U.S. Information Returns,* by February 28 (March 31 if filing electronically) of the year following the year of the distribution.

The corporation is allowed to furnish Forms 1099-DIV to shareholders any time after April 30 of the year of the distributions if the corporation has made its final distributions for the calendar year.

Distributions from Earnings and Profits

The amount of a C corporation's earnings and profits (E&P) determines the tax treatment of corporate distributions to shareholders.

The starting point for determining corporate E&P is the corporation's taxable income. The following transactions increase the amount of E&P:

- Long-term contracts reported on the completed contract method
- Intangible drilling costs deducted currently
- Mine exploration and development costs deducted currently
- Dividends-received deduction

The following transactions reduce the amount of E&P:

- Corporate federal income taxes
- Life insurance policy premiums on a corporate officer
- Excess charitable contributions (over 10% limit)
- Expenses relating to tax-exempt income
- Excess of capital losses over capital gains
- Corporate dividends and other distributions

Accumulated Earnings and Profits

Accumulated earnings and profits are E&P that the corporation accumulated before the current year and has not distributed to its shareholders. If a corporation's current year E&P are less than the total distributions made during the year, part or all of each distribution is treated as a distribution of accumulated E&P. Any part of a distribution from current-year earnings and profits or accumulated earnings and profits is reported as dividend income to the shareholder and is generally taxable as ordinary income to the shareholder rather than as capital gains.

If accumulated earnings and profits are reduced to zero, the remaining part of a distribution reduces the adjusted basis of the shareholder's stock. This is referred to as a nondividend distribution and it is not taxable to the shareholder until his basis in the stock is fully recovered. This nontaxable portion is considered to be a return of capital that he had previously invested in the corporation. If the corporation makes nondividend distributions to a shareholder that exceed the adjusted basis of his stock, the excess distribution is treated as a gain from the sale or exchange of property and is taxable to the shareholder as capital gain.

If nondividend distributions are made to shareholders, the corporation must report these distributions to the IRS on Form 5452, *Corporate Report of Nondividend Distributions*.

Example: Tobias is the only shareholder of Seaside Corporation, a calendar-year corporation. During the year, Seaside makes four $1,000 distributions to Tobias. At the end of the year (before subtracting distributions made during the year), the corporation has $10,000 of current year earnings and profits. Since the corporation's current year E&P ($10,000) were more than the amount of the distributions it made during the year ($4,000), all of the distributions are treated as distributions of current year E&P. The corporation must issue Form 1099-DIV to Tobias by January 31 to report the $4,000 distributed to him as dividends. Seaside Corporation must use Form 1096, *Annual Summary and Transmittal of U.S. Information Returns*, to report this transaction to the IRS by February 28 (March 31 if filing electronically). The corporation does not deduct these dividends on its income tax return.

Distributions of Property

A sale or exchange of property by a corporation to a shareholder who is not a corporation may be treated as a distribution to the shareholder, to the extent the FMV of the property on the date of the sale or exchange exceeds the price he paid.

A distribution of property is also treated as if the corporation had sold the property to the shareholder. A corporation (either a C corporation or an S corporation) recognizes gain on a distribution of property to a shareholder if the FMV of the property is more than its adjusted basis.

Example: Wright Stuff Construction Corporation distributes to a shareholder $65,000 in cash and an excavator with a $35,000 adjusted basis and a $50,000 FMV. Wright Stuff must recognize a $15,000 gain on the distribution of property because its FMV is more than its adjusted basis ($50,000 - $35,000 = $15,000).

For this purpose, the FMV is considered to be the greater of the property's actual FMV or the amount of liabilities the shareholder assumes in connection with the distribution. If the distributed property was depreciable or amortizable, the corporation may have to treat all or a portion of the gain as ordinary income from depreciation recapture.

These transactions may be taxable to the shareholder at FMV and are reported on Form 1099-DIV or Form 5452, *Corporate Report of Nondividend Distributions*. A corporation generally cannot recognize a loss on a distribution of property (i.e., where the property's FMV is less than the adjusted cost basis). However, a corporation is allowed to recognize losses when depreciated property is distributed to shareholders in complete liquidation (when the corporation ceases operations).

Stock Distributions

Stock distributions or stock dividends occur when a corporation issues additional shares of its own stock to shareholders, rather than paying a cash dividend or distributing property.

Stock rights, also known as stock options, may be distributed by a corporation to some or all of its shareholders to allow them to purchase additional shares at a set price.

Distributions by a corporation of its own stock or stock rights generally are tax-free to shareholders and not deductible by the corporation. However, they may be treated as taxable property distributions in certain situations, including when:

- The shareholder has the choice to receive cash or other property instead of stock or stock rights.
- The distribution gives cash or other property to some shareholders and an increase in the percentage interest in the corporation's assets or earnings and profits to other shareholders.
- The distribution is in convertible preferred stock.
- The distribution gives preferred stock to some shareholders and common stock to other shareholders.
- The distribution is paid based on ownership of preferred stock.

A corporation must capitalize, rather than deduct, the expenses of issuing a stock dividend, such as printing, postage, and any fees for listing on stock exchanges.

Constructive Distributions

A constructive distribution may occur when a corporation confers a benefit upon a shareholder. A transaction recorded by the corporation as an expense may be recategorized instead as a constructive distribution. This would make the transaction nondeductible to the corporation and in many instances taxable to the shareholder. Examples of constructive distributions include:

- **Payment of personal expenses:** If a corporation pays personal expenses on behalf of a shareholder, the amounts should be classified as a distribution rather than expenses of the corporation.
- **Unreasonable compensation:** If a corporation pays an employee-shareholder an unreasonably high salary considering the services actually performed, the excessive part of the salary may be treated as a distribution.
- **Unreasonable rents:** If a corporation rents property from a shareholder and the rent is unreasonably higher than the shareholder would charge an unrelated party for use of the property, the excessive part of the rent may be treated as a distribution.
- **Cancellation of a shareholder's debt:** If a corporation cancels a shareholder's debt without repayment by the shareholder, the amount canceled may be treated as a distribution.
- **Property transfers for less than FMV:** If a corporation transfers or sells property to a shareholder for less than its FMV, the excess may be treated as a distribution.
- **Below market or interest-free loans**: If a corporation gives a loan to a shareholder on an interest-free basis or at a rate below the applicable federal rate, the uncharged interest may be treated as a distribution.

Example: Arevalo Corporation rents office space from a 75% shareholder, Otto, who is the sole owner of the office building. The corporation pays Otto $15,000 a month for its space. He charges other tenants $5,000 a month for offices with the same square footage. The excessive rent of $120,000 ($15,000 - $5,000 = $10,000 × 12 months) in 2013 would likely be disallowed as an expense for Arevalo Corporation and recharacterized as a constructive distribution to Otto.

Stock Redemptions

A stock redemption occurs when a corporation buys back its own stock from a shareholder in exchange for cash or property. The stock acquired may be canceled, retired, or held as Treasury stock.

A shareholder is required to treat the amount realized on a stock redemption as either a dividend or a sale of stock. Stock redemptions are generally treated as dividends unless certain conditions are met, as follows:

- The redemption is not equivalent to a dividend, meaning that the shareholder's proportionate interest and voting power in the corporation has been substantially reduced.

- There was a substantially disproportionate redemption of stock, meaning that the amount received by the shareholder is not in proportion to his stock ownership.
- The redemption was due to a complete termination of a shareholder's interest in the corporation.
- The redemption is of stock held by a non-corporate shareholder and was part of a partial liquidation.
- The distribution is received by an estate and does not exceed the sum of death taxes plus funeral and administration expenses to be paid by the estate.

The corporation must realize a gain from the redemption, as if the property were sold at its fair market value to the shareholder. The corporation must recognize income on the distribution of depreciated property to the extent of depreciation or the amount realized, whichever is less. The corporation may not recognize a loss on a stock redemption unless:

- The redemption occurs in a complete liquidation of the corporation, or
- The redemption occurs on stock held by an estate.

Corporate Liquidations and Dissolutions

Liquidating distributions are distributions received by a shareholder during a complete or partial dissolution of a corporation. When a corporation dissolves, it redeems all of its stock in a series of distributions.

Complete liquidation occurs when the corporation ceases to be a going concern and its activities are merely for the purpose of winding up its affairs, paying its debts, and distributing any remaining balance to its shareholders. In certain cases in which the buyer is a corporation in control of the distributing corporation, the distribution may not be taxable. A corporate dissolution or liquidation must be reported on Form 966, *Corporate Dissolution or Liquidation*, within 30 days after the resolution or plan is adopted to dissolve the corporation or liquidate any of its stock. Exempt entities are not required to file Form 966, even if they are organized as corporations.

When property is distributed in a complete liquidation, the transaction is treated as if the corporation sold the assets to a buyer at fair market value. The corporation recognizes gain or loss on the liquidation in an amount equal to the difference between the FMV and the adjusted basis of the assets distributed. A corporation is allowed to recognize losses during the liquidation, except for losses resulting from transactions with related parties.

Amounts received by the shareholder in complete liquidation of a corporation are treated as full payment in exchange for the shareholder's stock. A liquidating distribution is considered a return of capital and is not taxable to the shareholder until the shareholder recovers all of his basis in the stock. After the basis of the stock has been reduced to zero, shareholders must report any additional amounts as a capital gain.

If a dissolving corporation distributes property that is subject to a liability, the gain or loss is adjusted to reflect assumption of the liability. If the liability is greater than the FMV of the property, the amount of the liability is treated as the FMV of the property. A corporation is required to provide each shareholder a Form 1099-DIV showing the amount of the liquidating distribution.

Example: The Maurer Farm Equipment Corporation is going through a complete liquidation. Saul, a shareholder, receives a liquidating distribution of property (a tractor). Maurer Corporation's basis in the tractor is $3,000. The fair market value of the tractor is $13,000. However, the tractor is encumbered by a liability of $15,000 (an unpaid loan), which Saul assumes. Because the remaining loan amount is more than the FMV of the tractor, the amount of the liability is treated as the FMV. The corporation must recognize a $12,000 gain on the distribution ($15,000 loan - $3,000 basis), and Saul is treated as having received a liquidating distribution of $15,000.

A corporation must file an income tax return for the year it goes out of business, even if it has no income or business activity in that year. If the dissolution is effective on any day other than the last day of the corporation's tax year, the final tax return is due on the fifteenth day of the third month following the close of its short tax year.

Unit 14: Study Questions

1. Which of the following statements about stock distributions is correct?

A. A stock distribution must be treated like a cash distribution that is taxable to the shareholder.
B. Stock distributions are usually taxable to the corporation when distributed to shareholders.
C. Stock distributions are deductible by a corporation as an expense.
D. Stock distributions are generally not taxable to shareholders and not deductible by the corporation.

2. Three years ago, Mark purchased 100 shares of Rock Star, Inc. for $10 per share. In 2013 Rock Star, Inc. completely liquidated and distributed $20,000 to Mark in exchange for all of his stock. Mark must report this distribution as a ____________________:

A. $20,000 long-term capital loss.
B. $19,000 short-term capital gain.
C. $19,000 long-term capital gain.
D. $19,000 ordinary gain.

3. Ryan is a shareholder in PRK Corporation with a basis of $20,000 in his stock. He also has an outstanding $10,000 loan that he owes to the corporation. In 2010, Ryan files for bankruptcy and defaults on the loan. PRK Corporation cancels Ryan's debt in 2013. How should this cancellation of debt be reported?

A. The debt cancellation is a $10,000 distribution to Ryan.
B. The debt cancellation is considered a return of capital to Ryan.
C. The debt cancellation is a charitable contribution to Ryan.
D. The debt cancellation is a $10,000 capital gain to Ryan.

4. All of the examples below are considered corporate distributions except ______________:

A. Ordinary dividends to a shareholder.
B. Capital gain distributions to a shareholder.
C. Constructive distributions to an employee-shareholder.
D. Wage compensation to an employee-shareholder.

5. Party Time Corporation distributes to a shareholder $75,000 in cash and a delivery truck with a $40,000 adjusted basis and a $60,000 FMV. What gain or loss, if any, must Party Time Corporation recognize?

A. No gain or loss is recognized in this transaction.
B. $20,000 gain.
C. $40,000 gain.
D. $20,000 loss.

6. Geraldine owns 1,000 shares of Kimball Software Corporation. Her shares were all acquired three years ago, and her basis in the stock is $20,000. Kimball Software completely liquidated in 2013 and distributed $56,000 in two payments to Geraldine. She received $16,000 in December 2013 and $40,000 in January 2014. How much gain or loss does Geraldine recognize in 2013 and 2014?

A. $4,000 loss in 2013 and $40,000 gain in 2014.
B. $4,000 loss in 2013 and $44,000 gain in 2014.
C. No gain or loss in 2013 and $40,000 gain in 2014.
D. No gain or loss in 2013 and $36,000 gain in 2014.

7. Distributions of stock rights are generally tax-free to shareholders. Which of the following statements is not correct?

A. Even if a shareholder has a choice to receive cash instead of stock rights, so long as the shareholder chooses to receive stock rights, the distribution will be tax-free.
B. Stock rights are distributions by a corporation of rights to acquire its own stock.
C. Stock rights are sometimes called stock options.
D. Stock rights can be taxable in some circumstances.

8. The Midwestern Grain Corporation distributes property with an adjusted basis of $1,000 and a fair market value of $4,000 subject to a liability of $6,000 to Joseph, a shareholder. What is the gain or loss, if any, Midwestern Grain must recognize as a result of the distribution?

A. $1,000 loss.
B. $3,000 gain.
C. $5,000 gain.
D. $0.

9. Buffalo Corporation displays a collection of fine artwork in its main office. When the 75% shareholder retires, he is presented with his choice from the art collection. He selects a painting with a FMV of $250,000. Buffalo Corporation's basis in the painting is $100,000. How should the transaction be reported on the Buffalo Corporation's tax return?

A. $150,000 loss.
B. $150,000 distribution.
C. $150,000 taxable gain.
D. $250,000 taxable gain.

10. April bought corporate stock five years ago for $1,000. In 2011, she received a return of capital distribution of $800. April did not include this amount in her income, but correctly reduced the basis of her stock to $200. She received another return of capital distribution of $300 in 2013. The first $200 of this amount reduced April's stock basis to zero. How should she report the remaining $100 distribution?

A. April must report $100 in long-term capital gain in 2013.
B. April does not have to report the additional return of capital.
C. April must report the $100 as ordinary income.
D. April must report any additional return of capital as a capital loss.

11. Six years ago, Sabine purchased 100 shares of Vitality Nature Co. stock for $50 per share. In 2013, the corporation liquidated. After paying its outstanding liabilities, Vitality Co. distributed $10,000 in cash and appreciated property worth $90,000 to its shareholders. Sabine's portion of the distributed assets and cash was $12,000. What must she report from this liquidating distribution in 2013?

A. $0 gain.
B. $3,000 capital gain.
C. $7,000 capital gain.
D. $10,000 capital gain.

12. Millerton Software is a C corporation that was formed in 2003. At the beginning of 2013, Millerton Software had accumulated earnings and profits of $100,000. The company makes a $5,000 distribution to its 100% shareholder in the first month of each quarter. In 2013, Millerton Software had $150,000 in gross income and $140,000 in expenses from ordinary business operations. Millerton also received $5,000 in fully tax-exempt interest from state bonds. What part of the second quarter distribution is treated as a distribution of accumulated earnings and profits?

A. $1,250.
B. $2,500.
C. $3,750.
D. $5,000.

Unit 15: S Corporations

More Reading:
Form 1120S and Instructions

The rules governing S corporations are found in subchapter S of the Internal Revenue Code. An S corporation has similarities to both a C corporation and a partnership. Like a partnership, an S corporation is a pass-through entity and is generally not taxed on its earnings. Instead, income and losses pass through to shareholders. Like a C corporation, an S corporation enjoys liability protection that a partnership does not.

S corporations do have some drawbacks. They are less flexible than partnerships. There are instances in which an S corporation is forced to pay tax on its earnings. There are restrictions on the number and types of shareholders an S corporation can have.

Electing S Corporation Status

To become an S corporation, a business must file an election on Form 2553, *Election by a Small Business Corporation.* The filing must be made within 2.5 months after the start of its tax year for the election to be effective at the beginning of the year. An election made after the first 2.5 months of the tax year becomes effective on the first day of the following tax year, unless the corporation receives IRS approval to make the election retroactive to the beginning of the tax year. The IRS will generally accept a late S election if the following requirements are met:

- The entity must qualify for S corporation status, except for not having filed Form 2553 in a timely manner.
- The entity had intended to be classified as an S corporation as of the effective date of the S corporation election.
- The entity applies for relief no later than six months following the due date of its tax return for the year.
- The corporation either had reasonable cause or inadvertently failed to file Form 2553 in a timely manner.
- The corporation has not yet filed a tax return for the first tax year for which it intends to file as an S corporation, or the corporation has filed its first tax return using Form 1120S and the shareholders properly reported their share of income in a manner consistent with the corporation's intention to be an S corporation.
- No shareholder has reported inconsistencies with the S election.

An S corporation generally may choose to use either the cash or the accrual method of accounting, subject to the requirements outlined in Unit 2.

S Corporation Requirements

The main requirements for S corporation status are:

- It must be a domestic corporation.
- It cannot have more than 100 shareholders.

- Shareholders generally must be U.S. citizens or residents, if individuals, or certain kinds of trusts, banks, estates, or certain tax-exempt corporations. Corporate shareholders and partnerships are generally excluded. However, certain tax-exempt corporations, including 501(c)(3) corporations, may be S corporation shareholders. In contrast, an S corporation is allowed to own a partnership interest or own stock in a C corporation. Nonresident aliens cannot be shareholders.
- A business must meet the definition of a small business corporation, per IRC section 1361.
- An S corporation can only have one class of stock, but that stock can be voting or nonvoting. The difference in voting rights allows one group of shareholders to retain voting control, while allowing other shareholders to benefit from corporate earnings. However, all the stock of an S corporation must possess identical rights to distribution and liquidation proceeds.
- Profits and losses must be allocated to shareholders in proportion to each one's interest in the business.
- All shareholders of an S corporation must give written consent for the S election.

If the S election is made during the corporation's tax year for which it first takes effect, each individual shareholder who holds stock at any time during the part of that year before the election is made must also consent to the election. This is true even if the person may have sold or transferred his stock before the election is made.

Example: Ron, Tara, and William are all equal shareholders in a C corporation. In January 2013, William decides to retire and sells all his shares in the C corporation to Sandra, an unrelated person. In February, Ron, Tara, and Sandra vote to elect S corporation status. All the current shareholders must agree to the election. William must also agree, even though he sold his stock before the election was made.

Example: A husband and wife own 90% of an S corporation and their son owns the remaining 10% of the stock. The son announces his marriage to a nonresident alien and he gives her one-half of his stock. The S corporation's status is revoked, because a nonresident alien cannot hold stock ownership in an S corporation.

For the 100-shareholder limit, related persons are considered one shareholder. Spouses are automatically treated as a single shareholder. A family, defined as a group of individuals descended from a common ancestor, plus spouses and former spouses of either the common ancestor or anyone lineally descended from that person, is considered a single shareholder so long as any family member elects such treatment.

When a shareholder dies, the deceased shareholder's spouse and the estate are still considered one shareholder for the shareholder limit. However, a husband and wife cannot be considered a single shareholder if they divorce, or if the marriage is dissolved for any other reason than death. Therefore, a shareholder's divorce can potentially increase the number of shareholders to a number in excess of the 100-shareholder limit. If an S corporation fails to meet this restriction, the S election is considered terminated, and the S corporation ceases to be an S corporation and is instead taxed as a C corporation.

The following entities cannot elect S corporation status:

- A bank or thrift institution that uses the reserve method of accounting for bad debts
- An insurance company
- A domestic international sales corporation (DISC)
- Any foreign entity

Filing Requirements

An S corporation files its tax return on Form 1120S, and allocated amounts of income, deductions, and credits pass through to individual shareholders and are reported on Schedule K-1. The return must be signed and dated by an authorized corporate officer or, in certain instances, by a fiduciary such as a receiver, trustee, or assignee, on behalf of the corporation.

An S corporation is always required to file a tax return, regardless of income or loss. The filing requirement ends only when the corporation is dissolved. The IRS mandates electronic filing for S corporations with $10 million or more in assets that file 250 or more returns of any type (W-2, 1099, K-1) per year. The tax return is due on the fifteenth day of the third month following the tax year end. For a calendar-year corporation, the tax return is due March 15. A corporation that has dissolved must generally file by the fifteenth day of the third month after the date it dissolved.

A six-month extension of time to file can be requested using Form 7004, *Automatic Extension of Time to File Certain Business Income Tax, Information, and Other Returns.*

Shareholders of an S corporation are required to pay estimated taxes in connection with their own returns. S corporations are only required to pay estimated taxes if $500 or more of certain corporate-level taxes apply.

Required Tax Year

As discussed in Unit 2, an S corporation must use one of the following as its tax year:

- A calendar year
- A natural business year
- An ownership tax year (the tax year that coincides with <50% ownership of the corporation)
- A fiscal year duly elected and approved by the IRS under section 444
- A 52-53 week year that ends with reference to a year listed above

An S corporation may always use a calendar year, or any other tax year for which it establishes a bona fide business purpose.

A new S corporation must use Form 2553, *Election by a Small Business Corporation*, to elect a tax year. An existing S corporation that wishes to change its existing tax year may use Form 1128, *Application to Adopt, Change, or Retain a Tax Year*. However, Form 8716, *Election to Have a Tax Year Other Than a Required Tax Year*, is used to apply for a tax year change under section 444.

Termination of an S Election

Once the S election is made, it stays in effect until terminated. In addition to the ways already discussed, the election will terminate automatically in any of the following cases:

- The corporation no longer qualifies as a small business corporation.[37]
- For each of three consecutive tax years, the corporation
    - Has accumulated earnings and profits,[38] and
    - Derives more than 25% of its gross receipts from passive investment income.
- The corporation creates a second class of stock.
- The shareholders willingly revoke the S election.

Absent an automatic termination due to failure to meet the requirements of S election status, an S election can be revoked only with the consent of the majority shareholders (those holding more than 50% of the corporation's stock, including nonvoting stock). The corporation must file a statement of revocation with the IRS that is signed by each shareholder who consents.

A shareholder revocation may specify an effective revocation date that is on or after the day the revocation is filed. If no date is specified and the revocation is made on or before the fifteenth day of the third month of that tax year, the revocation is effective at the start of a tax year. If no date is specified and the revocation is made after the fifteenth day of the third month of the tax year, the revocation is effective at the start of the next tax year. A revocation may be rescinded before it takes effect.

When an S election is terminated, two short tax years are created for the corporation. Income and loss must be allocated on a pro rata basis between the period the corporation operated as an S corporation and the period as a C corporation that was created when the S election was terminated. The entity must file Form 1120S for the S corporation's short year by the due date (including extensions) of the C corporation's short year return.

Example: On May 1, 2013, Zander Corporation, a calendar-year S corporation, exceeded 100 shareholders. This will create two short tax years—one for the S corporation and one for the C corporation. Zander must file a Form 1120S and a Form 1120; the due date for each return will be March 15, 2014.

If the IRS deems that a revocation was inadvertent (that the shareholders did not mean to revoke their S election or that the revocation was accidental), the corporation may be allowed to correct the error and retain its S election status.

Example: In 2013, Morrison Window Blinds, a calendar-year S corporation, inadvertently terminates its S status. The S corporation shareholders immediately correct the problem. Therefore, the S corporation status is considered to have been continuously in effect, and no termination is deemed to have occurred. Only a single S corporation tax return will need to be filed for tax year 2013.

---

[37] This termination of an election is effective as of the day the corporation no longer meets the definition of a small business corporation. A statement notifying the IRS of the termination and the date it occurred is attached to Form 1120S for the final year of the S corporation.

[38] This only applies to S corporations that were previously C corporations. An S corporation cannot accumulate earnings and profits as a C corporation can. However, it is possible for a C corporation to elect S corporation status and still have accumulated earnings and profits at the time of the election.

A terminating event will be considered inadvertent if the event was not within the control of the corporation, and the shareholders did not plan to terminate the election. Further, all of the following must occur:

- The S election must have involuntarily terminated either because:
  - The corporation no longer qualified as a small business corporation, or
  - It had accumulated earnings and profits from past C corporation activities.
- The IRS must agree that the termination was inadvertent.
- The corporation must take reasonable and immediate steps to correct the issue.
- The shareholders and the corporation must agree to any adjustments proposed by the IRS.
- The corporation must request a private letter ruling from the IRS for any inadvertent termination relief.

Note: If the status of an S corporation is terminated, either because the shareholders elect to become a C corporation or because a terminating event has occurred, the S corporation cannot elect to become an S corporation within the next five years. However, the IRS may choose to waive the five-year restriction.

S Corporation Income and Expenses

As with a partnership, all the income of an S corporation must be allocated to the shareholders, even if it is not distributed. Income, gains, losses, deductions, and credits are allocated to each shareholder on a pro-rata basis, according to the number of shares of stock held by the shareholder on each day of the corporation's tax year, and retain their character when they are passed through. The shareholder then reports the items on his tax return. Some of the items that pass through to shareholders on a pro rata basis and retain their character must be separately stated on an S corporation's tax return. These include:

These include:

- Net income or loss from rental real estate activity (rental income)
- Portfolio income or loss that include:
  - Interest income
  - Dividend income
  - Royalty income
- Capital gains or losses
- Section 1231 gain or loss
- Charitable contributions
- Section 179 expense deduction
- Foreign taxes paid or accrued
- Expenses related to portfolio income or loss
- Credits, including:
  - Low-income housing credit
  - Qualified rehabilitation expenses
- Investment interest expense
- Tax preference and adjustment items needed to figure a shareholder's AMT

- Nonbusiness bad debts

Unlike a C corporation, an S corporation is not eligible for a dividends-received deduction.

> **Example:** The Oliveira Company is an S corporation with a single shareholder. In 2013, it has \$100,000 in gross receipts; \$40,000 wage expense to its shareholder; \$15,000 in charitable contributions; \$10,000 in rental losses; and \$8,000 in capital gains. Its ordinary income is \$60,000 (\$100,000 gross receipts minus \$40,000 wages). The other items are all separately stated on Form 1120S but are not used to determine ordinary income or loss.

Limited Taxation of S Corporations

S corporations generally are not subject to taxation since they are primarily pass-through entities. However, in certain cases, S corporations are subject to taxes. A subchapter S corporation may have to pay income tax due to:

- Excess net passive investment income
- Built-in gains
- Investment credit recapture
- LIFO recapture

None of these taxes are deductible as business expenses by the S corporation. An S corporation may also be responsible for other taxes, such as payroll taxes if it has employees, and penalties, such as late filing penalties.

Excess Net Passive Income Tax: An S corporation that had been a C corporation previously and had accumulated E&P during that period may have to pay tax at the corporate level on excess net passive income (ENPI) if its passive investment income exceeds 25% of its gross receipts. The purpose of this requirement is to discourage a corporation with accumulated earnings and profits (E&P) from functioning as a holding company and gaining favorable tax treatment as an S corporation. For this purpose, passive investment income includes interest, dividends, rents, and royalties. If income is generated in the ordinary course of business, it is non-passive, or active, income. The tax rate on excess net passive income is 35% and is applied against the lesser of:

- Excess net passive income, or
- Taxable income figured as though the corporation were a C corporation

> **Example:** Trailblazer Inc. is an S corporation with accumulated E&P from earlier years when it was a C corporation. In 2013, Trailblazer has gross receipts of \$80,000, comprised as follows:
>
> - \$25,000 Rental income
> - \$10,000 Interest income
> - \$45,000 Additional gross receipts from business operations
>
> Trailblazer's passive investment income for the year is \$35,000, or 44% of its gross receipts. As this exceeds the 25% threshold, Trailblazer will be subject to the 35% excess net passive income tax on the lesser of its excess net passive income or its taxable income (calculated as if it were a C corporation).

If the corporation has always been an S corporation, it would not have accumulated E&P and the ENPI tax would not apply.

If the corporation has accumulated E&P at the end of the tax year and has ENPI in excess of 25% of its gross receipts for three consecutive taxable years, the S election is terminated as of the beginning of the fourth year.

Example: For 2011, 2012, and 2013, Herzing Corporation, a calendar-year S corporation, earned passive investment income in excess of 25% of its gross receipts. If Herzing Corporation has accumulated E&P from earlier years in which it was a C corporation, its S election would be terminated as of January 1, 2014, and the corporation would be taxed as a C corporation as of January 1, 2014.

Built-in Gains (BIG) Tax

The built-in gains (BIG) tax may apply to the following S corporations:

- An S corporation that was a C corporation before it elected to be an S corporation.
- An S corporation that acquired an asset with a basis determined by reference to its basis (or the basis of any other property) in the hands of a C corporation (a transferred-basis acquisition).

An S corporation must measure for each asset the amount of unrecognized appreciation that existed at the time an S election was made or an asset was acquired. The net amount of unrecognized built-in gains and built-in losses is subject to tax when those assets are sold, unless the assets are held for at least five years after conversion from a C corporation to an S corporation.

The S corporation pays tax on the recognized built-in gain at the highest corporate rate. The tax is reported on Form 1120S and is a deduction for the shareholders.

The built-in gains tax only applies to corporations that elected S status after 1986, and it only affects property dispositions during the five-year period beginning:

- On the first day of the first tax year for which the corporation is an S corporation, for an asset held when the S corporation was a C corporation, or
- On the date the asset was acquired by the S corporation, for an asset with a basis determined by reference to its basis in the hands of a C corporation.

Investment Credit Recapture: Business credit recapture is generally the responsibility of the entity that claims the credit. If a company is an S corporation when the credit originates, the credit passes through to the shareholders and they must report any subsequent recapture on Form 4255, *Recapture of Investment Credit*. However, if a C corporation claims the general business credit and then converts to S status, the S corporation itself may be responsible for the recapture.

LIFO Recapture Tax: A corporation that accounts for inventory using the last in, first out (LIFO) method is subject to a LIFO recapture tax in its final year as a C corporation after making an S corporation election. This tax is intended to address built-in gains in inventory that might not otherwise be recognized. The taxable LIFO recapture amount is the amount by which the amount of inventory assets calculated under the first in, first out (FIFO) method exceeds the amount under the LIFO method. If the LIFO value is higher than the FIFO value, no negative adjustment is allowed.

Inventory assets include stock in trade of the corporation, or other property of a kind that would properly be included in the inventory of the corporation if on hand at the close of the taxable year.

The LIFO recapture tax is paid in four equal installments, beginning on the due date of the final C corporation return. The three subsequent installments are payable on the due dates of the first three S corporation returns.

S Corporation Basis

To compute basis in the stock of an S corporation, a shareholder starts, just as for a C corporation, with his initial capital contribution or the initial cost of the stock purchased. However, his basis may vary based on how the stock was acquired (by purchase, gift, or inheritance).

In general, a shareholder's basis in S corporation stock is determined as follows:

Stock Acquired	How Stock Basis is Determined
Stock purchase	If the S corporation shares were purchased outright, initial basis is the cost of the shares.
S corporation capitalized	If the shares were received when the S corporation was formed under IRC §351, the basis in the stock is equal to cash invested and/or the basis of property transferred to the corporation, increased by any gain recognized on the transfer, and decreased by any boot received from the corporation (IRC §358).
Prior C corporation	Initial basis in S corporation stock is the basis in the C corporation stock at the time of conversion.
Gift	The recipient's basis in shares received by gift is generally the donor's basis (IRC §1015). Suspended passive activity losses can increase the basis of a gift (IRC §469).
Inheritance	The basis of inherited stock is its fair market value at the date of death or, if elected, the alternate valuation date (IRC §1014).
Services rendered to the S corporation	Basis in stock received in exchange for services is measured by the stock's fair market value, rather than by the value of the services (Treas. Reg. §1.61-2).

Both the taxability of a distribution and the deductibility of a loss are dependent on a shareholder's stock basis, and basis is adjusted annually, on the last day of the S corporation year, in the following order:

- Increased for income items and excess depletion
- Decreased for distributions
- Decreased for nondeductible, noncapital expenses and depletion
- Decreased for items of loss and deductions

S corporation shareholders must pay taxes on their share of the corporation's current year income, regardless of whether the amounts are distributed. The shareholder's Schedule K-1 reflects the income, loss, and deductions that are allocated to him but does not state the taxable amount of a distribution. The taxable amount of each distribution is contingent upon a shareholder's stock basis, and it is the shareholder's responsibility to track his individual basis.

Distributions from an S corporation must be paid to all shareholders on the same date, as a pro rata distributions based on the shareholders' individual ownership percentages.

S corporation distributions are generally not treated as dividends and not subject to income tax, except in cases where a corporation has accumulated E&P from years before it elected to become an S corporation. Distributions from an S corporation with no accumulated earnings and profits are considered a return of capital and reduce the shareholder's basis in the stock of the corporation.

Distributions that exceed the shareholder's adjusted stock basis are treated as capital gains and must be reported by the shareholder on Schedule D.

Example: Lucinda is the sole shareholder of an S corporation. Her basis as of January 1, 2013 is $25,000. She receives a distribution of $28,000 in December 2013, which reduces her basis to zero. She must report the excess $3,000 as a capital gain.

The amount of an S corporation distribution is equal to the sum of cash and the fair market value of the property received by a shareholder. If an S corporation distributes appreciated property, the distribution is treated as a sale to the shareholder. To the extent the FMV of the property exceeds the corporation's adjusted basis, the corporation would recognize gain. The gain passes through to the shareholders and increases the basis of their stock. No loss is recognized if the FMV of the distributed property is less than the corporation's basis.

S corporation shareholders are required to compute both stock basis and debt basis. A shareholder's basis in S corporation stock can never be reduced below zero.

The amount of loss that is deductible on a shareholder's tax return is limited to the shareholder's at-risk basis, and is applied in the following order:

- Cash and the adjusted basis of property that the shareholder contributed to the S corporation, subject to annual adjustments as described above (adjusted stock basis), and
- Any loans the shareholder makes to the corporation or any amounts that are borrowed for use by the S corporation for which the shareholder is directly liable (debt basis).

If a shareholder has S corporation losses and deductions in excess of his adjusted stock basis and those losses and deductions are claimed based on debt basis, the debt basis of the shareholder will be reduced by the claimed losses and deductions. If an S corporation repays reduced basis debt to the shareholder, part or all of the repayment is taxable to the shareholder.

Note: These concepts are complex and can be hard to visualize without specific details. The following example shows how S corporation stock and debt basis are calculated.

Example: Samuel, the sole shareholder of an S corporation, has $15,000 of stock basis on January 1, 2013. Samuel received a 2013 K-1 reflecting the following:

- ($20,000) of ordinary business income (loss)
- $4,000 of net section 1231 gain
- $5,000 of cash contributions (50%)
- $1,000 of nondeductible expenses
- $12,000 of distributions

Assume Samuel does not have any debt basis. Using the ordering rule, stock basis is first increased by items of income, so his initial stock basis of $15,000 is increased by the $4,000 net section 1231 gain. His stock basis before distributions is $19,000. Then he reduces stock basis by distributions of $12,000. Since Samuel has adequate stock basis before the distributions, the distributions reduce his stock basis to $7,000 and do not result in any taxable gain for him. Next, his stock basis is reduced by the $1,000 of non-deductible expenses. His stock basis before loss and deduction items is $6,000. Samuel has $25,000 of loss and deduction items:

- $20,000 of ordinary loss
- $5,000 of charitable contribution

The loss and deduction items exceed his stock basis. Since there is no debt basis, the loss and deduction items are pro-rated to determine the amounts currently allowable:

- 20,000/25,000 * 6,000 = $4,800 ordinary loss
- 5,000/25,000 * 6,000 = $1,200 charitable contribution

January 1, 2013 Stock basis:	**$15,000**
Plus: Net section 1231 gain	$4,000
Stock basis before distributions	$19,000
Less: Nondividend distributions	($12,000)
Stock basis before nondeductible expenses	$7,000
Less: Nondeductible expenses	($1,000)
Stock basis before loss and deductions	$6,000
Less: Ordinary business loss	($4,800)
Less: Cash contributions	($1,200)
December 31, 2013 Stock basis:	**$0**

The basis adjustment rules under IRC §1367 are similar to the partnership rules. However, while a partner has a unitary basis in his partnership interest, the adjustments to the basis of stock of an S corporation are applied on a separate share basis. The following additional rules apply:

- Losses and deductions not allowable in the current year due to basis limitations are suspended. However, if nondeductible expenses exceed basis, they do not get carried forward.

- Suspended losses and deductions retain their character in subsequent years. They are carried forward indefinitely until basis is increased in subsequent years or until the shareholder permanently disposes of the stock.
- If stock is sold, suspended losses are lost. The sales price does not have an impact on the stock basis. A stock basis computation should be reviewed in the year stock is sold or disposed of.
- If the current year has different types of losses and deductions that exceed the shareholder's basis, the allowable losses and deductions must be allocated pro rata based on the size of the particular loss and deduction items.
- In determining current year allowable losses, current year loss and deduction items are combined with the suspended losses and deductions carried over from the prior year, though the current year and suspended items should be separately stated.
- A shareholder only has debt basis to the extent he has personally lent money to the S corporation. A loan guarantee does not create debt basis.
- Part or all of the repayment of a reduced basis debt is taxable to the shareholder.

If an S corporation engages in rental activity or has a shareholder who does not materially participate in S corporation activities, the passive activity loss rules described in Unit 3 apply to the individual shareholders. If the passive activity loss rules apply, the shareholders' at-risk amounts must be reduced by the full amounts allowable as current deductions.

In contrast to the treatment applicable for a partnership, cancellation of debt income is applied at the entity level for corporations, including S corporations. The debtor is required to reduce specified tax attributes, including loss and credit carryforwards and the basis of assets.

Accumulated Adjustments Account (AAA)

If a C corporation elects to become an S corporation, it may have an accumulated adjustments account (AAA). The AAA is a corporate account that does not relate to individual shareholders. The S corporation maintains the account to track undistributed income that has been taxed during the period its S election is in effect.

S corporations with accumulated E&P must maintain the AAA to determine the tax effect of distributions during S years and, if applicable, during the period after termination of an S election. It is not mandatory to track AAA if the S corporation does not have prior year C corporation E&P (IRC section 1368). Nevertheless, if an S corporation without accumulated E&P engages in certain transactions where an AAA account is required, such as a merger into an S corporation with accumulated E&P, the S corporation must be able to calculate its AAA at the time of the merger. Therefore, it is recommended that the AAA be maintained by all S corporations. The AAA may have a negative balance at year end. The ordering rules for distributions from an S corporation with accumulated E&P are as follows:

- First, from the AAA, tax-free to the shareholders and a reduction of each shareholder's basis.
- Second, from E&P, and taxable as dividends.

- Third, if applicable, from the corporation's Other Adjustments Account (OAA), which includes accumulated tax-exempt interest income that has not been distributed previously, and reduce basis.
- Additional distributions are considered return of capital, up to the amount of each shareholder's basis in his stock.
- Distributions in excess of a shareholder's basis in his stock are considered capital gains from the sale of property.

Termination of a Shareholder's Interest

If a shareholder sells or disposes of his stock interest in an S corporation, it is treated in the same manner as the sale of stock in a C corporation. The shareholder reports the sale of the stock on Schedule D. The gain or loss that is recognized by the shareholder is the difference between the shareholder's basis and the sale price of the stock.

If a shareholder in an S corporation terminates his interest in a corporation during the tax year, the corporation, with the consent of all affected shareholders (including those whose interest is terminated), may elect to allocate income and expenses as if the corporation's tax year consisted of two separate short tax years, the first of which ends on the date of the shareholder's termination.

To make this election, the corporation must attach a statement to a timely filed original or amended Form 1120S for the tax year for which the election is made and state that it is electing to treat the tax year as if it consisted of two separate tax years.

The statement must also explain how the shareholder's entire interest was terminated (e.g., sale or gift), and state that the corporation and each affected shareholder consented to the election. A single statement may be filed for all terminating elections made for the tax year.

If this election is made, "section 1377(a)(2) Election Made" should be written at the top of each affected shareholder's Schedule K-1.

Reasonable Compensation

An S corporation may wish to pay little or no salary or wages to employees or officers who are also shareholders, as these amounts are subject to employment taxes while distributions to shareholders are not. However, if an S corporation is not paying a reasonable compensation to a shareholder-employee, distributions to him may be reclassified as wages subject to employment taxes. Therefore, an S corporation will be at risk if it attempts to avoid paying employment taxes by having its officers treat their compensation as cash distributions, payments of personal expenses, or loans rather than as wages.

There are no specific guidelines in the IRC or in IRS regulations for what is considered reasonable compensation. Factors considered by the courts in determining reasonable compensation for employees or officers of an S corporation include:

- Training and experience
- Duties and responsibilities
- Time and effort devoted to the business

- Dividend history
- Payments to non-shareholder employees
- Timing and manner of paying bonuses to key people
- Amounts that comparable businesses pay for similar services
- Compensation agreements
- The use of a formula to determine compensation

The regulations provide an exception for an officer of a corporation who does not perform any services or performs only minor services and receives no compensation. Such an officer would not be considered an employee for tax purposes.

Health Insurance Premiums for Shareholders

Fringe benefits paid to employees who are not shareholders or who have ownership of less than 2% are generally deductible by the S corporation and tax-free to the employees. However, for shareholder-employees who have at least 2% ownership, health and accident insurance premiums paid on their behalf are deductible by the S corporation as fringe benefits and are reportable as wages for income tax withholding purposes on the shareholder-employees' Forms W-2. The S corporation can exclude these health benefits from the wages subject to Social Security, Medicare, and FUTA taxes.

A 2% shareholder-employee is eligible for an AGI deduction for amounts paid during the year for health insurance premiums if the health insurance coverage is established by the S corporation. If the coverage plan is in the name of the shareholder rather than the name of the S corporation, the coverage can still be considered to be established by the S corporation if:

- The S corporation either paid or reimbursed the shareholder for the premiums, and
- It reported the premium payment as wages on the shareholder's Form W-2.

Neither Schedule K-1 (Form 1120S) nor Form 1099 can be used as an alternative to Form W-2 to report this additional compensation.

Example: Victory Energy Bars, an S corporation, provides health insurance coverage to its two owner-shareholders. Victory paid $5,000 in insurance premiums. The corporation treats the shareholders as having received the health insurance as additional compensation and reports the insurance premiums as W-2 wages.

An S corporation cannot take a deduction for amounts incurred during periods in which the shareholder-employee is eligible to participate in any subsidized health plan maintained by another employer (or the spouse's employer).

Example: Edward is the sole owner-shareholder in an S corporation. He pays the health insurance premiums for himself and his wife. His wife works full-time for an employer who has offered to provide family health coverage. Edward and his wife declined the coverage because they did not want to switch doctors. Because Edward had the option to participate in an employer plan (through his wife), the health insurance premiums paid on his behalf by his S corporation are not deductible.

Unit 15: Study Questions

1. Sydney owns 50% of the Verrengia Company, a calendar-year S corporation. As of January 1, 2013, Sydney's stock basis was $13,000. Verrengia has $2,000 of income in 2013 and distributes a large machine with an FMV of $7,000 and a basis of $3,000 to Sydney. How much income must Sydney report on her individual tax return in connection with distribution?

A. $0.
B. $3,000.
C. $2,000.
D. $7,000.

2. Greenhouse Gardens is an S corporation with four shareholders. The corporation has 10,000 shares outstanding. The shareholders have the following ownership:

Shareholder	Ownership
Jordan	4,500 shares
Mai	2,000 shares
Simon	2,000 shares
Nora	1,500 shares
Total	10,000 shares

Nora and Jordan wish to terminate the S election, but Mai and Simon do not. Which statement is true?

A. Jordan can elect to terminate the corporation's S status on his own.
B. All of the shareholders must agree to terminate the election.
C. Nora and Jordan have enough stock ownership to terminate the election.
D. At least 75% of the shareholders with active ownership must agree to the termination.

3. Close family members can be treated as a single shareholder for S corporation purposes. A family member in this instance includes:

A. A nonresident alien spouse.
B. A first cousin.
C. The estate of a shareholder's deceased spouse.
D. A divorced spouse.

4. What is the total amount of the separately stated income items of this S corporation?

Gross receipts	$700,000
• Rental real estate income	$300,000
• Interest income	$25,000
• Royalty income	$10,000
• Section 1231 gain	$20,000

A. $355,000.
B. $345,000
C. $700,000.
D. $720,000.

5. Francisco is the sole employee-shareholder of an S corporation that has no accumulated earnings and profits. At the beginning of the year, his stock basis was $50,000. The corporation had no income in 2013. The corporation distributed property to Francisco with an FMV of $75,000 and an adjusted basis of $62,000. What is the treatment of the distribution?

A. $63,000 as a return of capital and $25,000 taxable capital gain.
B. $50,000 as a return of capital and $12,000 taxable capital gain.
C. $60,000 as a return of capital and $15,000 taxable capital gain.
D. $62,000 as a return of capital and $0 taxable gain.

6. How much is the tax on excess net passive income?

A. 10%.
B. 15%.
C. 25%
D. 35%.

7. Which of the following events would cause the termination of an S corporation's status?

A. An S corporation that has an estate as a shareholder.
B. An S corporation that has a nonprofit corporation 501(c)(3) shareholder.
C. An S corporation that issues one share of stock to a C corporation.
D. An S corporation that owns one share of stock in a C corporation.

8. On January 1, 2013, Seth purchased 50% of the stock of Rancho Sendero, an S corporation, for $100,000, and also loaned the corporation $20,000. At the end of 2013, Rancho Sendero incurred an ordinary loss of $180,000. How much of the loss can Seth deduct on his personal income tax return for 2013?

A. $ 90,000.
B. $180,000.
C. $0.
D. $120,000.

9. On December 31, 2012, Adrienne had a $2,000 basis in Liaison Corporation, an S corporation. She owns 50% of Liaison's outstanding stock. At the beginning of 2013, Adrienne contributed a patent that she had acquired for $1,000 to Liaison. During 2013 Liaison received $5,000 in royalty income from that patent. Liaison also had $2,500 of ordinary income and $500 of section 179 deductions. At the end of 2013, Liaison returned ownership of the patent, which now had a fair market value of $5,000, to Adrienne. What is Adrienne's basis in Liaison Corporation at the end of 2013?

A. $1,000.
B. $3,500.
C. $2,500.
D. $5,000.

10. In which circumstance is a C corporation unable to elect to become an S corporation?

A. The C corporation has 50 shareholders.
B. The C corporation is incorporated in Canada.
C. The C corporation has common stock with voting and nonvoting rights.
D. The C corporation is on a fiscal year with a legitimate business purpose.

11. Bettendorf River Company is a calendar-year C corporation that wishes to elect S corporation status in 2013. What is the latest date that Bettendorf River Company can elect S status for tax year 2013?

A. March 15, 2013.
B. March 15, 2014.
C. January 1, 2013.
D. December 31, 2013.

12. A calendar-year S corporation operating on the accrual basis has the following income items and expenses. What is the ordinary income of this S corporation, not counting the separately stated items?

• Gross receipts	$300,000
• Interest income	$25,000
• Royalty income	$10,000
• Salary paid to shareholder	$20,000

A. $55,000.
B. $280,000.
C. $320,000.
D. $345,000.

13. Danielle is a 50% owner in Goodpaster Software Corporation, an S corporation. Danielle's basis in her stock at the end of 2012 is $5,000. At the end of 2013, Goodpaster Corporation reports $10,000 in ordinary income. In December 2013, Goodpaster makes a distribution to Danielle of appreciated property. It is a rare motorcycle originally purchased for $1,000 but now worth $8,000. How much income must Danielle report on her individual return in connection with the distribution?

A. $3,500.
B. $1,000.
C. $0.
D. $8,000.

14. An S corporation, regardless of when it became an S corporation, must use a permitted tax year. A permitted tax year is any of the following except ______________:

A. The calendar year.
B. A tax year elected under section 444.
C. A fiscal tax year with a legitimate business purpose.
D. A short tax year.

15. S corporations are generally not subject to taxation and are primarily pass-through entities. But in certain cases, S corporations are subject to taxes. Which of the following taxes do not apply to S corporations?

A. Excess net passive investment income.
B. Built-in gains tax.
C. Self-employment tax.
D. LIFO recapture.

16. In January 2013, Christopher and Eva are shareholders in Garabedian Company, a C corporation. Christopher owns 65% of the corporate stock and Eva owns the remainder. Christopher decides that he wants to convert to an S corporation. Which of the following statements is true regarding the conversion?

A. They must both consent to the conversion to the S corporation.
B. The election to become an S corporation is taken on Form 1120S.
C. Christopher may choose to convert the C corporation to an S corporation because he owns more than 50% of the stock.
D. They cannot elect S corporation status, because a C corporation cannot elect to become an S corporation.

17. Which of the following items is not a separately stated item on an S corporation return?

A. Charitable contributions.
B. Net short-term capital gains or losses.
C. Interest income.
D. Interest expense on a business loan.

18. On January 1, 2013, Gloria, Kristin, and Nancy are all equal shareholders in Fairview Heights Corporation, a calendar-year C corporation that has been in existence for four years. On March 1, 2013, Gloria sells her entire stock interest in the corporation to an unrelated party, Irving. Irving immediately wants to convert the corporation to an S corporation effective January 1, 2013. Whose consent is required for Fairview to convert to S status?

A. Irving may convert the corporation into an S corporation so long as Kristin and Nancy consent.
B. Gloria must also consent to the election, along with Kristin and Nancy.
C. Irving may convert the corporation to an S corporation on his own.
D. The corporation cannot convert to S status until it has been in existence for five years.

19. A C corporation may not elect to become an S corporation if:

A. It is a domestic corporation.
B. It has voting and nonvoting stock.
C. It has two classes of stock.
D. It has common stock.

20. Which of the following will not terminate an S corporation's status?

A. The S corporation no longer qualifies as a small business corporation.
B. The S corporation, for each of three consecutive tax years, has accumulated earnings and profits, and derives more than 25% of its gross receipts from passive investment income.
C. The S corporation creates a second class of stock.
D. The S corporation earns the majority of its revenue from passive activities.

21. On January 15, 2013, Elliott decides to voluntarily terminate his corporation's S status and convert to a C corporation. The termination was approved by the IRS. He later changes his mind and wishes to elect S corporation status again. How long does Elliott have to wait to elect S corporation status again?

A. 18 months.
B. Two years.
C. Four years.
D. Five years.

Unit 16: Farming Businesses

More Reading:
Publication 225, *Farmer's Tax Guide*

Farming businesses may be engaged in activities such as crop production, animal production, or forestry and logging. They may include stock, dairy, poultry, fish, fruit, and tree farms, as well as plantations, ranches, timber farms, and orchards.

A farming or fishing business operating as a sole proprietorship reports income and loss on Schedule F, *Profit or Loss from Farming*. A farmer is usually self-employed if he operates his own farm or rents farmland from others to engage in the business of farming. Self-employed farmers and fishermen must also complete Schedule SE.

Alternatively, a farming business may be organized as a partnership or a corporation.

Certain associated businesses are not considered farming businesses and instead must file on Schedule C (if a sole proprietorship). Examples include:

- Veterinary businesses
- Businesses that only supply farm labor
- Businesses that are only in the business of breeding, including those that raise or breed dogs, cats, or other household pets
- Businesses that provide agricultural services such as soil preparation and fertilization

Farm income does not include any of the following:

- Wages received as a farm employee
- Income received under a contract for grain harvesting with workers and machines furnished by the taxpayer
- Gains received from the sale of farm land and depreciable farm equipment
- Gains from the sale of securities, regardless of who owns the securities

Rental Income from Farmland

If a farmer rents his farmland for someone else to use, the related revenue is generally rent income, not farm income. This also applies to crop shares, when a tenant farmer pays a proportion of crop harvest proceeds to the land owner for use of his farmland. This passive activity income is reported on Form 4835, *Farm Rental Income and Expenses*. However, if a farmer materially participates in farming operations on the land he owns, the rent is considered farm income and is reported on Schedule F.

Estimated Taxes

Special rules apply to the payment of estimated tax by qualified farmers and fishermen.

If at least two-thirds of the business's gross income comes from farming or fishing activities, the following rules apply:

- The taxpayer does not have to pay estimated tax if he files his return and pays all the tax owed by the first day of the third month after the end of his tax year (usually March 1).

- If the taxpayer must pay estimated tax, he is required to make only one estimated tax payment (called the "required annual payment") by the fifteenth day after the end of his tax year (usually January 15).

Accounting Methods for Farming

Farmers may use the following accounting methods:

- **Cash Method** (subject to the limitations described in Unit 2)
- **Accrual Method**
- **Combination (Hybrid) Method** (using two or more of the methods listed)
- **Special Methods, including the Crop Method:** The IRS allows a number of different special methods of accounting that apply to items such as depreciation or farm business expenses or income. Among these is the crop method, which requires IRS approval and is allowed only for farming businesses. If crops are not harvested and disposed of in the same tax year they are planted, the farmer may deduct the entire cost of producing the crop, including the expense of seed or young plants, in the year income is realized.

Example: Will is a self-employed farmer who uses the accrual method. He keeps his books on a calendar-year basis. Will sells grain in December 2013, but he is not paid until January 2014. He must include the sale on his 2013 tax return. He may also deduct the costs incurred in producing the grain on his 2013 return.

Example: Miguel is also a self-employed farmer, but he uses the cash method. Miguel sells livestock in December 2013, but he is not paid until January 2014. Since Miguel uses the cash method and there was no constructive receipt of the sale proceeds in 2013, Miguel includes the sale proceeds in income in 2014, the year he receives payment.

The following farming businesses must use the accrual method:

- A corporation (other than a family farming corporation) that had gross receipts of more than $1 million for any tax year
- A family farming corporation that had gross receipts of more than $25 million for any tax year
- A partnership with a corporate partner
- A tax shelter (of any size or income)

To qualify as a family farming corporation, the business must meet at least one of the following requirements:

- Members of the same family own at least 50% of the corporation's stock
- Members of two families have owned since October 1976, either directly or indirectly, at least 65% of the corporation's stock
- Members of three families have owned since October 1976, either directly or indirectly, at least 50% of the corporation's stock

Example: Dave and Raymond are brothers. They are also the only shareholders of Da-Ray Farms Corporation, which is a qualified family farming corporation. Da-Ray Farms raises cattle, and in 2013 it has $20 million in gross receipts. Since Da-Ray is a qualified family farm, the entity is allowed to use the cash method of accounting.

The accrual method must generally be used in any case in which it is necessary to use an inventory. However, farmers are exempt from the usual code requirements to maintain an inventory. Most small farming businesses operate using the cash method of accounting. But since farming usually requires an inventory (of crops or livestock, for example), larger farming businesses are required to use the accrual method.

Farm Inventory

Farm inventory includes all items that are held for sale, purchased for resale, and for use as feed or seed, such as the following:

- Eggs in the process of hatching.
- Harvested farm products that are held for sale, such as grain, cotton, hay, or tobacco.
- Supplies that become a physical part of an item held for sale, such as containers, wrappers, or other packaging. A business may expense the cost of supplies consumed in operations during the year.
- Any livestock that is held primarily for sale or purchased for resale.
- Fur-bearing animals (such as mink, fox, or chinchilla) that are being held for breeding.
- Purchased farm products that are being held for seed or feed.

If livestock was purchased primarily for draft, breeding, sport, or dairy purposes, the farmer can choose to depreciate it, or include the livestock in inventory. Regardless of the method chosen, it must be consistent from year to year.

Note: Farm inventory does not include real property, such as land or buildings, or depreciable equipment, such as tractors.

Currently growing crops are generally not required to be included in inventory. However, if the crop has a pre-productive period of more than two years, the crop may have to be capitalized in connection with the uniform capitalization (UNICAP) rules described in Unit 2 and below.

Farmers may use the same inventory methods that are available to other businesses, such as cost and lower of cost or market, which were covered in Unit 2 under inventory methods. However, there are two other inventory methods that are unique to farming businesses:

Farm-Price Method: Under the farm-price method, each item, whether raised or purchased, is valued at its market price less the costs of disposition. The costs of disposition include broker's commissions, freight, hauling to market, and other marketing costs. If a farming business chooses to use the farm-price method, it must use it for the entire inventory, except that livestock can be inventoried under the unit-livestock-price method.

Unit-Livestock-Price Method: The unit-livestock-price method is an easier inventory method that allows farmers to group livestock together rather than track the costs of each animal. A farmer may classify livestock according to type and age and use a unit price for each animal within a class. The unit price must reasonably approximate the costs incurred in producing the animal.

If a farming business uses the unit-livestock-price method, it must include all raised livestock in inventory, regardless of whether they are held for sale or for draft, breeding, sport, or dairy purposes. This method accounts only for the costs incurred while raising an animal to maturity. It does not provide for any decrease in the animal's market value after it reaches maturity.

UNICAP: Except for corporations, partnerships, and tax shelters that are required to use the accrual method, farming businesses are not required to apply the UNICAP rules to the costs of:

- Raising plants for which the pre-productive period is two years or less
- Animals
- Replanting certain plants lost or damaged due to casualty

Most of these businesses may also elect not to apply the UNICAP rules in connection with the costs of plants for which the pre-productive period is more than two years.

A farmer can determine costs required to be allocated under UNICAP by using the farm-price or unit-livestock-price inventory method.

Example: Jane's accrual-basis farming business is subject to the UNICAP rules. She owns a peach orchard that produces an annual crop. The trees have a pre-productive period of more than two years. Absent an election not to, she must capitalize the direct costs of the orchard and an allocable part of indirect costs incurred due to the production of the trees. Jane is not required to capitalize the costs of producing the annual peach crop because its pre-productive period is two years or less.

For crops, pre-productive period costs include the costs of irrigation, pruning, spraying, and harvesting. For livestock, pre-productive costs include the costs of feed, maintaining pasture or pen areas, breeding, veterinary services, and bedding.

Sales of Farm Products and Farm Assets

When a self-employed farmer sells products raised on a farm, his entire proceeds are reported on Schedule F, in a manner similar to any other taxpayer who sells inventory and reports the sales proceeds on Schedule C. Gain on the sale of livestock raised on a farm is generally the gross sales price reduced by any expenses of the sale, such as commissions or freight charges. The basis of the animal sold is zero if the costs of raising it were deducted during the years the animal was being raised.

Example: In 2012, five goats were born on Lisa's farm. She deducted the cost of feed and other expenses of raising the goats on her 2012 tax return. In 2013, the goats were hauled to a nearby town for auction, where they sold for a total of $900, with $75 in sales expenses. Lisa will report a gain of $825 on her 2013 tax return ($900 - $75 = $825).

When a farmer sells farm products bought for resale, his profit or loss is the difference between his basis in the item (usually cost) and any payment received for it.

Example: In 2012, Oscar bought 20 feeder calves for $6,000 for resale. He sold them in 2013 for $11,000. Oscar reports the $11,000 sales price, subtracts his $6,000 basis, and reports the resulting $5,000 profit on his 2013 Schedule F.

However, income reported on Schedule F does not include gains or losses from sales or other dispositions of the following farm assets:

- Land
- Depreciable farm equipment
- Buildings and structures
- Livestock held for draft, breeding, sport, or dairy purposes (unless held as inventory or held primarily for sale)

The sale of these assets is reported on Form 4797, *Sales of Business Property*, and may result in ordinary or capital gains or losses.

Like other businesses, when a farming business disposes of depreciable property (section 1245 property or section 1250 property) at a gain, the taxpayer may have to recognize ordinary income under the depreciation recapture rules. Any gain remaining after applying the depreciation recapture rules may be section 1231 gain, which may be taxed as capital gain.

Section 1245: Part or all of the gain of the sale of section 1245 property is treated as ordinary income under the rules of depreciation recapture**.** Buildings and structural components are excluded under section 1245. However, "single purpose agricultural (livestock) or horticultural structures" are section 1245 property. So, for example, a barn that houses different animals and is used to store supplies would not be section 1245 property because it is not a single purpose facility.

Example: A greenhouse that is used only to grow plants would be single purpose and thus section 1245 property. If a cash register is installed in the greenhouse so that a farmer can sell plants in addition to growing them there, the greenhouse would no longer be section 1245 property because it is no longer single purpose.

Other examples of farming-related section 1245 property include a grain silo, fencing for the confinement of livestock, and wells for providing water to livestock.

Section 1231: Section 1231 assets include certain business (noncapital) assets that have been held for more than one year, as well as certain business and investment property disposed of in involuntary conversions.

Note: As discussed in Unit 9, section 1231 assets receive special tax treatment. If a taxpayer has a net loss from all section 1231 transactions, the loss is treated as ordinary loss. If the section 1231 transactions result in a net gain, the gain is generally treated as capital gain, with the exception of depreciation recapture, which is taxed as ordinary income.

Gain or loss on the following farm-related transactions is subject to section 1231 treatment:

1. Sale or exchange of cattle or horses held for draft, breeding, dairy, or sporting purposes and held for 24 months or longer.
2. Sale or exchange of other livestock held for draft, breeding, dairy, or sporting purposes and held for 12 months or longer. Other livestock includes hogs, mules, sheep, and goats, but does not include poultry.
3. Sale or exchange of depreciable property used in the farming business and held for longer than one year. Examples include farm machinery and trucks.

4. Sale or exchange of real estate used in the farming business and held for longer than one year. Examples are a farm or ranch, including barns and sheds.
5. Sale or exchange of unharvested crops.
6. Sale from cut timber.
7. The condemnation of business property held longer than one year. Condemnations of business property usually qualify for nonrecognition treatment if replacement property is purchased within a certain time period, under the involuntary conversion rules.

Postponing Gain Due to Weather Conditions

There are special rules for farmers regarding the postponement of gain due to weather conditions. If a farmer sells or exchanges more livestock (including poultry), than he normally would in a year because of a drought, flood, or other weather-related conditions, he may postpone reporting the income from the additional animals until the following year.

The taxpayer must meet all the following conditions to qualify:

- The principal trade or business must be farming.
- The farmer must use the cash method of accounting.
- The farmer must be able to show that he would not have sold or exchanged the additional animals in that year except for the weather-related condition.
- The area must be designated as eligible for federal disaster assistance.

The livestock does not have to be raised or sold in the affected area. However, the sale must occur solely because the weather-related condition affected the water, grazing, or other requirements of the livestock. The farmer must figure the amount to be postponed separately for each generic class of animals, such as hogs, sheep, and cattle.

Example: Yolanda is a calendar-year farmer, and she normally sells 100 head of beef cattle a year. As a result of drought, she sells 135 head during 2013 and realizes $70,200 from the sale. On November 9, 2013, because of drought, the affected area is declared a disaster area eligible for federal assistance. The income Yolanda can postpone until 2014 is $18,200 [($70,200 ÷ 135) × 35], which is the portion of the income attributed to the additional animals that she sold over her normal amount.

To postpone gain, the farmer must attach a statement to his tax return for the year of the sale providing specific information about the weather conditions and circumstances that led to the postponement of gain for each class of livestock. For a sale that qualifies as an involuntary conversion, the farmer can file this statement at any time during the replacement period. The replacement period for the sale of livestock due to weather-related conditions is four years, and up to five years if the property is subject to an involuntary conversion in a federally declared disaster area.

A weather-related sale or exchange of livestock held for draft, breeding, or dairy purposes (but in this case, not including poultry) may also qualify as an involuntary conversion.

Livestock that is sold or exchanged because of disease may not trigger taxable gain if the proceeds of the transaction are reinvested in replacement animals within two years of the close of the tax year in which the diseased animals were sold or exchanged.

Example: Paulo is a farmer who owns 3,000 head of cattle. In 2013, his herd is struck by virus and he is forced to send 1,500 to slaughter. His insurance company reimburses his losses, and he promptly reinvests all the insurance proceeds into new livestock. This is treated as an involuntary conversion.

Crop Insurance and Government Payments

Insurance proceeds, including government disaster payments, may be received as a result of destruction or damage to crops or the inability to plant crops because of drought, flood, or other natural disaster. These payments are generally taxable in the year they are received.

However, a farmer can elect to postpone reporting the income until the following year if he meets all of these conditions:

- The farming business must use the cash method of accounting.
- Crop insurance proceeds were received in the same tax year the crops were damaged.
- Under normal business practices, the farming business would have reported income from the damaged crops in any tax year following the year the damage occurred.

A statement must be attached to the tax return indicating the specific crops that were damaged and the total insurance payment received. To make this election to postpone income, the farmer must be able to prove that the crops would have been harvested or otherwise sold in the following year.

If a farmer forgoes the planting of crops altogether and receives agricultural program payments from the government, payments are reported on Schedule F, and the full amount of the payment is subject to self-employment tax.

Other Unique Tax Rules for Farmers

Other examples of tax rules that are unique to farming businesses include the following:

Car and Truck Expenses: Farmers can claim 75% of the use of a car or light truck as business use without any records if the vehicle is used in a farming business.

Soil Conservation: Farmers can choose to deduct as a business expense land-related expenses for soil or water conservation or for the prevention of erosion. Examples include leveling, eradication of brush, removal of trees, or planting of windbreaks. For most businesses, these would be considered capital expenses and would be added to the basis of the land.

Net Operating Losses: Farming losses qualify for longer carryback periods. The carryback period for farming losses is five years rather than the two-year carryback period that applies for other businesses.

Excise Tax Credits: Farmers may be eligible to claim a credit or a refund of federal excise taxes on fuel used on a farm.

Farm Income Averaging: Certain farmers that operate as sole proprietorships or partnerships may use Schedule J, *Income Averaging for Farmers and Fishermen,* to average all or some of their current year's farm income by allocating it to the three prior years. This may lower a farmer's current year tax liability if the current year is high and his taxable income from one or more of the three prior years was low.

Unit 16: Study Questions

1. Becky is a calendar-year, self-employed farmer who files on the cash basis. For purposes of the estimated tax for qualified farmers, all of the following statements are true except:

A. Becky does not have to make any estimated payments if she files by April 15 and pays all her taxes with her return.
B. Becky is a qualified farmer if at least two-thirds of her previous year's gross income is from farming.
C. The required annual estimated tax payment for farmers is due on the fifteenth day after the close of their tax year.
D. The required annual payment is two-thirds of the current year's tax or 100% of the previous year's tax.

2. Joel is a qualified farmer who usually sells 500 beef cattle every year. However, because of a severe drought, he was forced to sell 800 beef cattle. Which of the following statements is true?

A. Joel may choose to postpone all of the gain in this transaction.
B. Joel may choose to postpone a portion of his gain in this transaction.
C. Joel must use the accrual method in order to postpone gain.
D. Postponement of gain is not allowed.

3. All of the following should be included in farming inventory except ____________:

A. Farming equipment and machinery.
B. Livestock held primarily for sale.
C. Farm products held for feed or seed.
D. Supplies that become a physical part of items held for sale.

4. Which of the following statements about farmers is true?

A. Gross income from farming includes capital gains from the sale of equipment.
B. A farmer who is a sole proprietor may use income averaging to reduce his tax liability.
C. A farmer does not have to report income from crop insurance payments.
D. An individual who owns livestock as a hobby and grows a large garden can be considered a farmer for tax purposes.

5. All of the following are acceptable methods for valuation of farm inventory except ______:

A. Cost.
B. Harvest discount.
C. Farm-price method.
D. Unit-livestock-price method.

6. Jon owns a dairy business and has income from the following sources:

- Income from milk production: $50,000
- Sale of old dairy cows: $20,000
- Sale of feed: $15,000
- Sale of used machinery: $4,000

What amount of income should be reported on Jon's Schedule F, *Profit or Loss from Farming?*

A. $50,000.
B. $65,000.
C. $74,000.
D. $85,000.

7. Oliver is a farmer who receives agricultural program payments after refraining from growing any crops in 2013. How should these payments be reported?

A. As "other income" on the taxpayer's individual Form 1040.
B. On Schedule E, *Supplemental Income and Loss*.
C. As farm income on Schedule F, but not subject to self-employment tax.
D. As farm income on Schedule F, subject to self-employment tax.

8. Hope is a qualified farmer who grows soybeans. In 2013, her soybean crop was destroyed by flood. If the crop had not been destroyed, she would have harvested it in 2014. Hope receives federal disaster payments in 2013. Which of the following is true?

A. Hope can choose to postpone the income from this disaster payment until 2014.
B. Disaster payments are not taxable income.
C. Hope must report the income on her 2013 return.
D. Hope may delay recognition of the gain for two years.

9. Luke is a qualified farmer. A bull calf was born on his farm on 2012. Luke raised the calf for breeding purposes. Luke spent $750 in feed for the calf and it was sold for $5,000 for breeding use in 2013. How much is Luke's gain from the sale of the bull calf?

A. $0.
B. $4,250.
C. $4,750.
D. $5,000.

10. Andy owns 150 acres of farmland that he rents to other farmers. He does not actively participate in any of the farming activity. How should the income from this activity be reported?

A. As rental income on Form 4835.
B. As farming income on Schedule F.
C. As ordinary income on Schedule C.
D. As passive income on Schedule 4797.

11. To be eligible as a qualified farmer and not have to pay quarterly estimated taxes during the year, at least _____________ of a farmer's gross income must be from farming.

A. Half.
B. Two-thirds.
C. Three-quarters.
D. 80%.

12. All of the following would be considered section 1245 property except __________:

A. A greenhouse.
B. A grain silo.
C. A wire chicken coop.
D. A barn that houses cows and horses.

13. The carryback period for farming losses is ____________:

A. Two years.
B. Four years.
C. Five years.
D. Farmers are not allowed to carry back their losses.

14. Farm income averaging is computed on Schedule J, which may be filed:

A. For the current year when a taxpayer files Schedule F showing a farm loss.
B. For the current year when a taxpayer files Schedule F showing net income from farming.
C. For the current year, along with Schedule C.
D. As an amended return showing the past three years of farming income.

Unit 17: Exempt Organizations

More Reading:
Publication 4220, *Applying for 501(c)(3) Tax-Exempt Status*
Publication 557, *Tax-Exempt Status for Your Organization*
Publication 4221-PC, *Compliance Guide for 501(c)(3) Public Charities*
Publication 598, *Tax on Unrelated Business Income of Exempt Organizations*

Nonprofit organizations may qualify for exemption from the requirement to pay income taxes, but they are still subject to certain filing and recordkeeping requirements under federal tax law.

IRC Section 501(c)(3)

The majority of nonprofit organizations qualify for tax-exempt status under section 501(c)(3) of the IRC. They are exempt from paying income tax in connection with their charitable activities, and they are eligible to receive tax-deductible charitable contributions. To qualify for these benefits, an organization must file an application with the IRS and must meet the following requirements:

- **Organization:** It must be organized as a corporation, a trust, or an unincorporated association, and its purpose must be limited to those described in section 501(c)(3). A nonprofit entity may not be organized as a partnership or sole proprietorship.
- **Exempt Purpose:** It must have one or more exempt purposes as listed under section 501(c)(3): charitable, educational, religious, scientific, literary, fostering national or international sports competition, preventing cruelty to children or animals, and testing for public safety.
- **Operation:** A substantial portion of its activities must be related to its exempt purpose(s). Further, a 501(c)(3) organization must:
    - Refrain from participating in political campaigns of candidates
    - Restrict its lobbying activities to an "insubstantial" part of its total activities
    - Ensure that its earnings do not benefit any private shareholder or individual
    - Not operate for the benefit of private interests such as those of its founder, the founder's family, or its shareholders
    - Not operate for the primary purpose of conducting a trade or business that is not related to its exempt purpose

Applying for 501(c)(3) Status

Before applying for tax exempt status, an organization must be created by preparing an organizing document. This document must limit the organization's purposes to those set forth in section 501(c)(3) and must specify that the entity's assets will be permanently dedicated to the specified exempt purpose(s). The organizing document should also contain a provision for distributing funds if it dissolves.

To request exempt status under section 501(c)(3), entities use Form 1023, *Application for Recognition of Exemption*. An organization with annual gross receipts of no more than $5,000 is not required to file Form 1023. However, it must file Form 1023 to request formal exemption within 90 days of the end of the year in which it exceeds this threshold.

Example: An animal rescue organization that was created five years ago did not exceed the $5,000 gross receipts threshold until its fiscal year ended September 30, 2013. The organization must file Form 1023 to request formal tax exemption within 90 days (by December 30, 2013).

A private foundation is always required to request exemption, regardless of the amount of its gross receipts. Organizations that do not qualify for exemption under section 501(c)(3) may qualify for tax-exempt status by filing Form 1024, *Application for Recognition of Exemption Under 501(a).* An organization must generally request exemption from the IRS by the end of the fifteenth month after it is created, with a 12-month extension available.

An organization that files its application before the deadline may be recognized as tax-exempt from the date of its creation. An organization that files an application after the deadline also may be recognized as tax-exempt from the date of the application by requesting exemption retroactive to the date of creation. The IRS will review an organization's application and determine if it meets the requirements for exemption. If approved, the IRS will issue a letter recognizing the organization's exempt status and providing its public charity classification.

While an organization's Form 1023 is pending approval, the organization may operate as if it were tax-exempt. Donor contributions made while an application is pending would qualify, assuming the IRS later approves its 501(c)(3) status. If the application is not approved, these contributions would not qualify. The organization would also be liable for filing federal income tax returns unless its income is otherwise excluded from federal taxation.

Other Section 501(c) Organizations

In addition to 501(c)(3) organizations, there are other types of organizations that qualify for tax-exempt status. However, they may or may not qualify to receive contributions that are deductible by the donor. Examples include the following:

- 501(c)(4) Civic leagues and social welfare organizations
- 501(c)(5) Labor unions, agricultural, and horticultural organizations
- 501(c)(6) Business leagues
- 501(c)(7) Social and recreation clubs
- 501(c)(8) and 501(c)(10) Fraternal beneficiary societies
- 501(c)(4), 501(c)(9), and 501(c)(17) Employees' associations
- 501(c)(12) Local benevolent life insurance associations
- 501(c)(13) Nonprofit cemetery companies
- 501(c)(14) Credit unions and other mutual financial organizations
- 501(c)(19) Veterans' organizations

Note: 501(c)4 social welfare organizations were the subject of Congressional hearings in 2013 to investigate whether certain groups were unfairly targeted with heightened scrutiny during the application process. The IRS has proposed new regulations governing how much political activity tax-exempt 501(c)4 organizations may legitimately conduct. The regulations were not finalized in 2013 and should not be the subject of testing for the current EA exam. Test-takers should focus primarily on the tax requirements affecting 501(c)3 organizations.

Public Charity or Private Foundation

Every organization that qualifies for tax-exempt status under section 501(c)(3) is further classified as either a public charity or a private foundation. Tax-exempt entities are presumed to be private foundations, unless they fall into certain categories of organizations that are specifically excluded. Even if an organization falls into one of these excluded categories, it is presumed to be a private foundation unless it files a timely Form 1023 showing that it is not a private foundation.

The primary distinction between classification as a public charity or a private foundation is the organization's source of financial support. A public charity tends to have a broad base of support while a private foundation has more limited sources of support. Generally, an exempt organization will not be considered a private foundation if it receives more than one-third of its annual support from governmental units and/or the general public. This classification is important because different tax rules apply: deductibility of contributions to a private foundation is more limited than deductibility of contributions to a public charity. Further, there is an excise tax on the net investment income of domestic private foundations. This excise tax must be paid annually or, if the total tax for the year is $500 or more, in quarterly estimated tax payments.

All private foundations must file Form 990-PF, *Return of Private Foundation*, every year regardless of their income.

Filing Requirements

Every exempt organization must file an annual information return with the IRS, generally on Form 990, *Return of Organization Exempt from Income Tax*, unless it is specifically exempt from the filing requirement. The following organizations are not required to file:

- Churches and their affiliated organizations
- Government agencies

Tax-exempt organizations with gross receipts of $50,000 or less are required to file Form 990-N, *Electronic Notice for Tax Exempt Organizations Not Required to File Form 990.* This form is also called an "e-postcard" because it is filed electronically and is short. A small tax-exempt organization may voluntarily choose to file a long form (Form 990) instead.

An exempt entity may choose to file on a fiscal-year or a calendar-year basis. The applicable annual information return is due by the fifteenth day of the fifth month after the year ends. For a calendar-year entity, the due date is May 15. If the organization has been dissolved, the return is due by the fifteenth day of the fifth month after the dissolution.

An exempt entity may request a three-month extension of time to file by filing Form 8868, *Application for Extension of Time to File an Exempt Organization Return.* An additional three-month extension can be requested, if needed, using the same form. When filing a request for the first three-month extension, neither a signature nor an explanation is required. However, when requesting an additional three-month extension, both a signature and an explanation are required.

An organization must file Form 990 electronically if it files at least 250 returns during the calendar year and has total assets of $10 million or more at the end of the tax year. A private foundation is required to file Form 990-PF electronically if it files at least 250 returns during the calendar year. A section 501(c)(3) organization must make its application (Form 1023) and its three most recent annual returns (Form 990) available to the public. The IRS also makes these documents available for public inspection and copying.

Every tax-exempt entity must have an EIN, regardless of whether it has employees.

Penalties

An exempt organization that fails to file a required return must pay a penalty of $20 a day for each day the return is late. The same penalty may apply if the organization provides incorrect information on the return. Generally, the maximum penalty is the smaller of:

- $10,000, or
- 5% of the organization's gross receipts for the year.

However, for an organization that has gross receipts of more than $1 million for the year, the late filing penalty is $100 a day, up to a maximum of $50,000.

An organization's exempt status may be revoked for failure to file. Failure to file an annual information return for three years in a row will result in the automatic revocation of exempt status. In this case, the organization would be required to reapply for exemption. However, no penalty will be imposed if reasonable cause for failure to timely file can be shown.

If an organization's tax-exempt status was automatically revoked for failing to file a return or notice for three consecutive years, it must apply to have its tax-exempt status reinstated by filing either Form 1023 or Form 1024 and paying the appropriate fee.

Employment Tax Returns

Just like other businesses, exempt organizations are subject to the basic requirements for tax and wage reporting compliance, calculating withholding, making deposits, and keeping tax and reporting records.

Even though some organizations (such as a church or other religious organization) are not required to file Forms 990, any entity with employees must withhold and remit income and Social Security and Medicare taxes on its employees' wages, and some exempt organizations are also responsible for Federal Unemployment Tax (FUTA).

Example: Trinity Methodist Church is not required to file an application for exemption in order to be recognized as tax-exempt by the IRS. Trinity applies for an EIN as an exempt entity and begins regular worship. In 2013, Trinity Church hires three employees: a part-time pastor, a Sunday child care worker, and a music leader. Although Trinity does not have to file Form 990, the church is still required to file employment tax returns and remit and collect employment taxes from its employees. In this way, the exempt organization is treated like every other employer.

Unrelated Business Income Tax (UBIT)

Although an exempt organization must be operated primarily for tax-exempt purposes, it may engage in income-producing activities that are unrelated to those purposes, so long as these activities are not a substantial part of the organization's regular activities. Income from unrelated business activities is subject to a federal tax called the unrelated business income tax (UBIT). For most organizations, an activity is considered an unrelated business and subject to UBIT if:

- It is a trade or business,
- It is regularly carried on, and
- It is not substantially related to furthering the exempt purpose(s) of the organization.

An exempt organization that has $1,000 or more of gross income from an unrelated business must file Form 990–T by the fifteenth day of the fifth month after the tax year ends. An exempt organization must make quarterly payments of estimated tax on unrelated business income if it expects its tax for the year to be $500 or more.

Example: A university enters into a multi-year contract with a company to be its exclusive provider of sports drinks for the athletic department and concessions. As part of the contract, the university agrees to perform various services for the company, such as guaranteeing that coaches make promotional appearances on behalf of the company. The university itself is a qualified nonprofit organization, but the income received from the exclusive contract is subject to UBIT. The university is therefore required to file Form 990-T.

Example: A college negotiates discounted rates for the soft drinks it purchases for its cafeterias in return for an exclusive provider arrangement. Generally, discounts are considered an adjustment to the purchase price and do not constitute gross income to the purchaser. Thus, the amount of the negotiated discount is not includable in UBIT. The college is not required to file Form 990-T.

Summary of Exempt Entity Requirements

Exempt Entities: Financial Activity	Annual Information Return Required
Gross receipts normally ≤ $50,000	Form 990-N (e-postcard)
Gross receipts < $500,000 and Total assets < $1.25 million	Form 990-EZ or 990
Gross receipts $500,000 (or greater), or Total assets ≥ $1.25 million	Form 990
Unrelated business income of $1,000 or more	Form 990-T
Private foundation (must file every year, regardless of financial activity)	Form 990-PF
Churches and similar religious organizations	No annual return filing requirement, but may be required to file payroll returns if the entity has employees

Unit 17: Study Questions

1. Which of the following organizations does not qualify for tax-exempt status?

A. A charitable organization.
B. A religious organization.
C. A private foundation.
D. An educational partnership.

2. Child Rescue Inc. is a calendar-year nonprofit organization that helps prevent child abuse. It is required to file Form 990 in 2013. What is the due date of its tax return, not including extensions?

A. April 15.
B. March 15.
C. May 15.
D. October 15.

3. Which of the following statements is true?

A. If an exempt organization qualifies for tax-exempt status with the IRS, any contributions it receives are fully deductible by the donors.
B. A church is not required to file an annual information return (Form 990).
C. A religious entity does not have to file payroll tax returns if it has employees.
D. A church may be organized as a sole proprietorship.

4. Most organizations seeking recognition of exemption from federal income tax must use specific application forms prescribed by the IRS. Which form must be filed in order to request recognition as a 501(c)(3) nonprofit organization by the IRS?

A. Form 1023.
B. Form 1024.
C. Form 1040.
C. Form 990.

5. Which of the following exempt organizations is not required to file an annual information return?

A. A church with gross receipts exceeding $250,000.
B. An exempt literary organization with $6,000 in gross receipts.
C. A Chamber of Commerce with $26,000 in gross receipts.
D. A private foundation with income of less than $5,000.

6. All of the organizations listed below would qualify for tax-exempt status under the Internal Revenue Code except ________________:

A. A Christian church with only eight members.
B. A political action committee.
C. A trust for a college alumni association.
D. A local boys club.

7. The local Catholic church has two employees: Martha, who works as a secretary in the church rectory, and Jack, who is the church custodian. Which return(s) must the church file in order to fulfill its IRS reporting obligations?

A. Form 990.
B. Form 8300.
C. Employment tax returns.
D. Form 990-PF.

8. A charitable organization has $2,000 in unrelated business income in the current year. How is this income reported?

A. The organization must file a business tax return for the unrelated business income.
B. The organization is required to file Form 990-T.
C. The organization will have its exempt status revoked.
D. The organization must file Schedule C to correctly report the business income.

9. What action does the IRS take if a nonprofit with $500,000 in gross receipts fails to file its required information returns or notices?

A. Nothing. Information returns are voluntary.
B. A maximum penalty of up to $10,000 or 5% of the organization's gross receipts for the year.
C. Automatic revocation of tax-exempt status if the organization fails to file returns or notices for three consecutive years.
D. Both B and C are correct.

10. Which kind of organization is allowed to file an e-postcard?

A. A private foundation.
B. A nonprofit with gross receipts of $25,000 or less.
C. A nonprofit with gross receipts of $50,000 or less.
D. A nonprofit with gross receipts of $100,000 or less.

11. What does an organization that wishes to be recognized as a 501(c)(3) charity need to file with the IRS?

A. Form 990.
B. Form 990 and its organizing document.
C. Form 1023 and its organizing document.
D. Form 1023, its organizing document, a listing of its board of directors, and its bylaws.

Unit 18: Retirement Plans for Businesses

More Reading:
Publication 560, *Retirement Plans for Small Business*

Employers may establish retirement plans as fringe benefits for their employees. Self-employed taxpayers are also allowed to set up retirement plans for themselves.

There are numerous forms of retirement plans; they include Simplified Employee Pension (SEP) plans, Savings Incentive Match Plan for Employees (SIMPLE) plans, and qualified plans.

Note: The term **qualified** refers to certain IRS requirements that the plan and the employer must adhere to in order to obtain tax-favored status. SEP and SIMPLE plans must also meet certain requirements, but they are much less complex than those that apply to qualified plans. If retirement plans are structured and operated properly, businesses can deduct retirement contributions they make on behalf of their employees or, if self-employed, themselves. Both the contributions and the earnings are generally tax-free until distribution.

The rules vary depending on the type of business. Any business, including a sole proprietorship or a partnership, can deduct retirement plan contributions made on behalf of employees, even if the business has a net operating loss for the year.

Example: Gemma is self-employed and reports her income and losses from her catering business on Schedule C. She has a retirement account set up for herself and her five employees. In 2013, Gemma's catering business showed a loss from operations on her Schedule C, and Gemma has no other source of taxable income. She made regular contributions to her employees' retirement accounts in 2013, and she may deduct these contributions as a regular business expense. However, Gemma cannot make a retirement contribution for herself in 2013 because she has no self-employment income. Since her business showed a loss, she has no qualifying income for purposes of her own retirement plan contribution.

However, in the case of a sole proprietorship or partnership, if the owners of the business contribute to their own retirement accounts, they must take the deduction on Form 1040, and only if they have self-employment income. Self-employment income for the purpose of this deduction means net profits from Schedule C or Schedule F, or self-employment income from a partnership.

Since an S corporation is a pass-through entity, certain shareholder-employees in an S corporation are also required to report these deductions on their individual returns.[39]

However, as a C corporation is not a pass-through entity, the corporation deducts the expense on Form 1120, *US Corporation Income Tax Return,* whether the contributions are made for employee-shareholders, officers, or other employees.

Retirement plans generally must adhere to certain nondiscrimination requirements intended to ensure they do not favor owners or executives of the sponsoring employer over other employees. Depending upon the type of plan, these requirements may include:

[39] This rule applies to employee-shareholders who own more than 2% of the S corporation stock.

- Minimum coverage tests that limit elective deferral and employer contributions to highly compensated employees (HCEs) as percentages compared to the corresponding percentages for non-highly compensated employees.
- Prohibition of terms that favor HCEs' dollar amounts of contributions or benefits, or other rights.

Simplified Employee Pension (SEP) Plans

A SEP plan provides the simplest and least expensive method for employers to make contributions to a retirement plan for themselves and their employees. A SEP may be established as late as the due date (including extensions) of the company's income tax return for the year the employer wants to establish the plan. Employers must also make their contributions to the plan by the due date, including extensions. There is no requirement for a plan document such as those needed for qualified retirement plans. However, the employer must execute a formal written agreement to provide benefits to all eligible employees under the SEP. Except in certain circumstances, including when the employer also maintains a qualified plan, this can be done using Form 5305-SEP. Using this form will typically eliminate the need to file annual information returns with the IRS and the Department of Labor.

Contributions to a SEP can vary from year to year, so it is a very flexible option for small employers. A SEP can be set up for an individual person's business even if he participates in another employer's retirement plan.

Example: Mitch works for the post office, and also runs a profitable photo booth business with his wife on the weekends. They have self-employment income from the business. Mitch may set up a SEP for himself and his wife, even though he is already covered by the post office retirement plan.

Contributions to a SEP

Under a SEP, employers make contributions to an individual retirement arrangement (called a SEP-IRA), which must be set up for each eligible employee. The SEP-IRA is owned and controlled by the employee, and the employer makes contributions to the financial institution where the SEP-IRA is maintained. SEP-IRAs are funded exclusively by contributions from the employer. A SEP does not require employer contributions every year, but it cannot discriminate in favor of HCEs. An eligible employee is one who meets all the following requirements:

- Has reached age 21
- Has worked for the employer in at least three of the last five years
- Has received at least $550 in compensation in 2013

Note: If an employer sets up a SEP, all employees who are eligible employees must also be allowed to participate.

An employer can use less restrictive participation requirements than those listed, but not more restrictive ones. The following employees can be excluded from coverage under a SEP:

- Employees covered by a union agreement
- Nonresident alien employees who have received no U.S. source income from the employer

Example: Vazquez Company decides to establish a SEP for its employees. Vasquez has chosen a SEP because its industry is cyclical in nature. In good years, Vasquez can make larger contributions for its employees, and in down years it can reduce or eliminate contributions. Vasquez knows that under a SEP, the contribution rate (whether large or small) must be uniform for all employees. The financial institution that Vasquez identifies to be the trustee for its SEP has several investment funds for employees to choose from. Individual employees have the opportunity to divide their employer's contributions to their SEP-IRAs among these fund options.

Contributions to a SEP must be made in cash; an employer cannot contribute property to a SEP. However, plan participants may be able to transfer or roll over certain property from another retirement plan account to a SEP-IRA. Each year that an employer contributes to a SEP, it must contribute to the SEP-IRAs of all participants who had qualified compensation, including employees who die or terminate employment before the contributions are made. A SEP-IRA cannot be a Roth IRA. Employer contributions to a SEP-IRA do not affect the amount an individual can contribute to a Roth or traditional IRA. **SEP Contribution Limits:** The following SEP limits apply in 2013:

- For an employee: Contributions cannot exceed the lesser of 25% of the employee's compensation or $51,000.
- For a self-employed individual: Contributions cannot exceed the lesser of 20% of net self-employment income, after considering both the deduction for self-employment tax and the deduction for the SEP-IRA contribution, or $51,000.

Employers cannot make contributions conditional, or require that any part of the contribution be kept in the employee's account after the business has made its contributions.

SEP Distributions: Employees have control over their own SEP-IRAs, so employers cannot prohibit distributions from a SEP-IRA. As with traditional IRAs, money withdrawn from a SEP-IRA (and not rolled over to another qualified retirement plan or account) is subject to income tax for the year in which a distribution is received.

If an employee withdraws money from a SEP-IRA before age 59½, a 10% additional tax generally applies. Further, a participant in a SEP-IRA must begin receiving required minimum distributions (RMDs) by April 1 of the year following the year the participant reaches age 70½. However, unlike a traditional IRA, contributions can be made for participants over age 70½.

SEP RULES	Rules for Employers	Rules for Employees
Eligibility	Any business or self-employed individual may set up a SEP.	Employees aged 21 or older who have worked for the business for 3 of the last 5 years and earned at least $550 in the current year are eligible.
Contributions	Vesting is immediate.	Employees cannot contribute to a SEP.
Pros	Contributions can vary from year to year. Inexpensive to set up and administer.	Employers cannot prohibit distributions from a SEP, because vesting is immediate.
Drawbacks	A SEP must cover all qualifying employees. Employers cannot discriminate in favor of HCEs. Only employers can contribute.	Employees cannot contribute. Only employers and self-employed individuals can contribute to a SEP.

SIMPLE Plans

A SIMPLE (Savings Incentive Match Plan for Employees) plan provides another simplified way for a business and its employees to contribute toward retirement. Like SEPs, SIMPLE plans have lower start-up and annual costs than most other types of retirement plans.

If a business has 100 or fewer employees who received $5,000 or more in compensation during the preceding year, it can establish a SIMPLE plan.[40] The business cannot maintain another retirement plan unless the other plan is for a union workforce.

The business must continue to meet the 100-employee limit each year. However, if a business maintains a SIMPLE plan for at least one year and subsequently fails to meet the 100-employee limit, the business is allowed a two-year grace period to establish another retirement plan. Another exception may apply if the business fails to meet the 100-employee limit as a result of an acquisition, disposition, or similar transaction.

Employees can choose to make retirement plan contributions by allocating a portion of their salaries, and businesses can contribute matching or nonelective contributions. SIMPLE plans can only be maintained on a calendar-year basis. A SIMPLE plan can be structured in one of two ways: using SIMPLE IRAs or as a SIMPLE 401(k) plan, covered below.

SIMPLE IRAs

Unlike a SEP, SIMPLE IRAs allow employee contributions and require employer contributions. A SIMPLE IRA must be set up for each eligible employee. An eligible employee is generally one who received at least $5,000 in compensation during any two years preceding the current calendar year and is reasonably expected to receive at least $5,000 in the current calendar year, except for:

- Employees covered by a union agreement
- Nonresident alien employees who have received no U.S. source income from the employer

Prior to an election period (generally 60 days) preceding the start of the calendar year, employees must receive formal notice of their rights to participate and make salary reduction contributions, and information regarding the employer's planned contributions.

Contributions to a SIMPLE IRA

During the election period, an employee may execute or modify a salary reduction agreement to defer a portion of his salary (up to $12,000 for 2013.) Employees age 50 or over can also make a catch-up contribution of up to $2,500 (for a total of up to $14,500 for 2013). The salary reduction contributions under a SIMPLE IRA plan are elective deferrals that count toward an overall annual limit on elective deferrals an employee may make to this and other plans permitting elective deferrals.

Each year, the employer must choose to make either matching contributions or nonelective contributions. Employer matching of the employee's salary reduction contributions is generally required on a dollar-for-dollar basis up to 3% of the participant's compensation.

---

[40] For purposes of the 100-employee limitation, all employees employed at any time during the year are taken into account, regardless of whether all of them are eligible to participate in the SIMPLE plan.

The employer may elect to make matching contributions at less than 3%, but not lower than 1% for more than two years within a five-year period.

Instead of matching contributions, the employer may choose to make nonelective contributions of 2% of each eligible employee's compensation. An individual employee's compensation used for this contribution is limited to $255,000 in 2013. If the employer chooses to make nonelective contributions, it must make them for all eligible employees, regardless of whether they make salary reduction contributions. The employer must notify employees of its choice to make nonelective contributions within a specified period prior to the employees' annual period for making their own salary reduction contribution elections.

An eligible employee may choose not to make salary reduction contributions for a given year. In this case the employee would accrue no employer matching contributions but would receive an employer nonelective contribution if the employer elects to make this type of contribution for the year. Employee and employer contributions are 100% vested.

Definition: Vesting refers to a person's rights to receive some type of benefit, such as retirement benefits as discussed in this unit, or other employee benefits such as stock options. Vesting may occur on a gradual schedule, such as a certain percentage per year of employee service, or at a set time, such as five years after an employee has begun work for a company.

The money an employee has put aside plus employer contributions and net earnings from investments cannot be forfeited. The employee has the right to withdraw funds at any time, but those withdrawals may be subject to tax.

Salary reduction contributions must be deposited with the applicable financial institution within 30 days after the end of the month in which they would otherwise have been paid to the employee. Matching or nonelective contributions must be made by the due date (including extensions) for filing the company's income tax return for the year.

An employer can set up a SIMPLE IRA plan effective on any date from January 1 through October 1 of a year, provided the employer did not previously maintain another SIMPLE IRA plan. A new employer may set up a SIMPLE IRA plan as soon as administratively feasible after the business comes into existence.

A business cannot suspend its employer matching contributions mid-year or terminate its SIMPLE IRA plan mid-year. The business must maintain the plan for a full calendar year (except in the year the business first establishes the plan). The employer is required to make the contributions that were promised to the employees.

A SIMPLE IRA plan may not require a participant to be employed on a specific date to receive an employer contribution. If a participant terminates employment during the year after making a salary reduction contribution, he would still be entitled to an employer contribution.

SIMPLE IRA contributions are not included in the "Wages, tips, other compensation" box of Form W-2, *Wage and Tax Statement*. However, salary reduction contributions must be included in the boxes for Social Security and Medicare wages.

Distributions from a SIMPLE IRA

Distributions are subject to income tax in the year they are received. If a participant takes a withdrawal from a SIMPLE IRA before age 59½, an additional tax of 10% generally applies. If the withdrawal occurs within two years of beginning participation in the SIMPLE IRA plan, the additional tax is increased to 25%.

SIMPLE IRA contributions and earnings may be rolled over tax-free from one SIMPLE IRA to another. A rollover may also be made from a SIMPLE IRA to another type of IRA, or to another employer's qualified plan, but it will be tax-free only if it is made after two years of participation in the SIMPLE IRA plan. A participant in a SIMPLE IRA plan must begin receiving required minimum distributions by April 1 of the year following the year the participant reaches age 70½.

Example: Rockland Quarry Company is a small business with 50 employees. Rockland has decided to establish a SIMPLE IRA plan for all of its employees and will match its employees' contributions dollar-for-dollar up to 3% of each employee's salary. Under this option, if a Rockland employee does not contribute to his SIMPLE IRA, the employee does not receive any matching employer contributions. Elizabeth is an employee of Rockland Company. She has a yearly salary of $50,000 and decides to contribute 5% of her salary to her SIMPLE IRA. Elizabeth's yearly contribution is $2,500 (5% of $50,000). The Rockland matching contribution is $1,500 (3% of $50,000). Therefore, the total contribution to Elizabeth's SIMPLE IRA that year is $4,000 (her $2,500 contribution plus the $1,500 contribution from Rockland).

SIMPLE IRA Snapshot

	Rules for Employers	Rules for Employees
Eligibility	Any employer with 100 or fewer employees who received at least $5,000 in the preceding year. The employer cannot maintain another retirement plan in addition to the SIMPLE IRA.	Any employee who has earned at least $5,000 in any two prior years and who is expected to earn at least $5,000 in the current year.
Contribution Thresholds	Employers may choose to make either matching contributions at 1% to 3% of compensation for employees that make salary deferral contributions, or nonelective contributions at 2% of compensation for all eligible employees.	An employee can contribute up to $12,000 of his salary (or self-employment earnings, for a self-employed owner), plus an additional $2,500 if 50 or older for a total of $14,500.
Pros	Employees can make contributions. Vesting is immediate.	Employees can make contributions. Vesting is immediate.
Drawbacks	Employer matching is mandatory.	Employees with higher salaries may prefer a retirement plan option that allows them to contribute more.

SIMPLE 401(k) Plans

A SIMPLE 401 (k) plan can be adopted as part of a traditional 401(k) plan (see below) if the business meets the 100-employee limit discussed above for SIMPLE IRA plans and does not maintain another qualified retirement plan.

An employee can elect to make salary reduction contributions as a percentage of his compensation, but not more than $12,000 for 2013. An employee age 50 or over can also make a catch-up contribution of up to $2,500 (for a total of up to $14,500 for 2013).

Unlike a regular 401(k) plan, the employer must make either:

- A matching contribution up to 3% of compensation for each employee who makes a salary reduction contribution, or
- A nonelective contribution of 2% of compensation for each eligible employee who receives at least $5,000 of compensation from the employer that year.

Participants are fully vested in all contributions. SIMPLE 401(k) plans must file Form 5500, *Annual Return/Report of Employee Benefit Plan*, annually.

Pros and Cons of a SIMPLE 401(k)

- The plan is not subject to the discrimination rules that apply to traditional 401(k) plans.
- The plan may offer optional participant loans and hardship withdrawals to add flexibility for employees.
- No other retirement plans can be maintained.
- Withdrawal and loan flexibility adds an administrative burden for the employer.

Qualified Plans

There are two basic kinds of qualified retirement plans, defined contribution plans and defined benefit plans, and different rules apply to each. An employer is allowed to have more than one type of qualified plan, but maximum contributions cannot exceed annual limits.

All qualified plans are subject to federal regulation under the Employee Retirement Income Security Act (ERISA). The federal government does not require an employer to establish a retirement plan, but it provides minimum federal standards for qualified plans.

ERISA covers qualified retirement plans, as well as health and welfare benefit plans. Among other things, ERISA requires that individuals who manage plans (and other fiduciaries) meet certain standards of conduct. The law also contains detailed provisions for reporting to the government and for disclosure to participants. Further, there are provisions aimed at assuring plan funds are protected and participants receive their benefits. ERISA mandates minimum funding requirements to ensure that benefits will be available to employees when they retire. For defined benefit plans, it requires that plan funding be certified by an actuary.

ERISA also mandates that qualified plans meet specific requirements regarding eligibility, vesting, and communications with participants. The administrator of an employee benefit plan subject to ERISA must file an information return for the plan each year. Form 5500, *Annual Return/Report of Employee Benefit Plan*, must be filed by the last day of the seventh month after the plan year ends.

Defined Benefit Plans

A defined benefit plan (often called a traditional pension plan) promises a specified benefit amount or annuity after retirement. Most federal and state governments offer defined benefit plans to their employees. However, fewer companies now offer defined benefit plans because they are costly to administer and inflexible. The benefits in many defined benefit plans are protected by federal insurance. Contributions to a defined benefit plan are not optional. They are typically based on actuarial calculations. Contributions for self-employed taxpayers are limited to 100% of compensation. If the business does not have any income for the year, no contribution can be made.

Defined Contribution Plans

A defined contribution plan provides an individual account for each participant in the plan. It provides benefits to the participant based on the amounts contributed to the participant's account, along with subsequent income, expenses, gains, losses, and, in some instances, allocations of forfeitures among participant accounts.

The participant, the employer, or sometimes both may contribute to the individual participant accounts. The value of the account will fluctuate due to the changes in the value of investments that have been made with the amounts contributed. A participant's retirement benefits depend primarily on the amount of contributions made on his behalf, rather than upon his years of service with the employer or his earnings history.

Examples of defined contribution plans include 401(k) plans, 403(b) plans, and 457 plans.

Traditional 401(k) Plans

A 401(k) plan is a defined contribution plan that allows each eligible employee to defer receiving a portion of his salary, which is instead contributed on his behalf to the 401(k) plan. Deferrals generally are made on a pretax basis, although some plans allow employees the option to make them on an after-tax basis.

Pretax deferrals are not subject to income tax withholding, and they are not included in taxable wages on the employee's Form W-2. However, they are subject to Social Security, Medicare, and federal unemployment taxes.

Sometimes the employer will make matching contributions. Employee deferrals and any employer matching contributions are accounted separately for each employee. Earnings on the retirement account grow tax-free until distribution.

401(k) plans can vary significantly in their complexity. However, many financial institutions administer 401(k) plans, which can lessen the administrative burden on individual employers of establishing and maintaining these plans.

Distributions from Qualified Plans

Generally, distributions cannot be made from a qualified plan until one of the following occurs:

- The employee retires, dies, becomes disabled, or otherwise terminates employment
- The plan terminates

- The employee reaches age 59½ or suffers financial hardship

Unless a distribution is properly rolled over into another retirement plan or individual retirement account, it will be subject to income tax upon receipt.

If a distribution is made to an employee before he reaches age 59½, the employee may have to pay a 10% additional tax on the distribution. However, the additional 10% tax may not apply in the following situations:

- Distributions are for the taxpayer's medical care, up to the amount allowed as a medical deduction.
- Disability or death.
- Distributions in the form of an annuity.
- Distributions are made because of an IRS levy on the plan.
- Distributions are made to a qualified reservist (an individual called up to active duty).

Even if these distributions are not subject to the additional 10% tax, they would be subject to tax at the taxpayer's applicable rate.

Example: Lauren, age 43, takes a $5,000 distribution from her traditional IRA account. She does not meet any of the exceptions to the 10% additional tax, so the $5,000 is an early distribution. Lauren must include the $5,000 in her gross income for the year the distribution is received and pay income tax on it. She must also pay an additional tax of $500 (10% × $5,000).

Required Minimum Distributions: A participant in a qualified retirement plan must begin receiving distributions by April 1 of the first year following the later of:

- The calendar year in which he reaches age 70½
- The calendar year in which he retires from employment with the employer maintaining the plan

However, the plan may require distributions by April 1 of the year after the participant reaches age 70½ even if he has not retired. Further, if the participant is a 5% owner of the employer, he must begin receiving distributions by April 1 of the year after the year he reaches age 70½.

Penalties for not taking required minimum distributions (RMDs) can be severe. Penalties are assessed if an account owner fails to withdraw an RMD, fails to withdraw the full amount of the RMD, or fails to withdraw the RMD by the applicable deadline. The penalty is 50% of the amount that is not withdrawn from the account when required.

Limits on Benefits and Contributions

For 2013, the following overall limits apply:

The annual benefit for a participant in a defined benefit plan cannot exceed the lesser of $205,000 or 100% of the participant's average compensation for his highest three consecutive calendar years.

A combined limit of $17,500 applies to each employee's elective deferrals and salary reduction contributions, other than catch-up contributions, to all defined contribution retirement plans and any SIMPLE IRA plan under which he is covered. If the limit is exceeded, the amount that would otherwise have been nontaxable must be included in the employee's gross income. Catch-up contributions are limited to $2,500 for each participant in a SIMPLE plan and $5,500 for each participant in other defined contribution plans.

Annual contributions to the account of a participant in a defined contribution plan cannot exceed the lesser of $51,000 or 100% of the participant's compensation.

An employer's deduction for contributions to a defined contribution plan cannot be more than 25% of the compensation paid or accrued during the year for the eligible employees. The maximum compensation that can be considered for each employee is $255,000.

Penalties apply to excess contributions. An excise tax of 6% applies to excess amounts contributed by employees and self-employed individuals if these amounts and related earnings are not withdrawn by the due date of their returns (with or without extensions, depending upon the type of plan). An excise tax of 10% applies to excess employer contributions.

Prohibited Transactions

A prohibited transaction is a transaction between a retirement plan and a disqualified person that is prohibited by law. A disqualified person may include the following:

- A fiduciary of the plan
- A person providing services to the plan
- An employer, any of whose employees are covered by the plan
- An employee organization, any of whose members are covered by the plan
- An indirect or direct owner of 50% or more of the applicable employer or employee organization
- A member of the family of anyone described in the bullet points above
- A corporation, partnership, trust, or estate of which any direct or indirect owner described in the bullet points above holds a 50% or more interest
- An officer, director, 10% or more shareholder, or highly compensated employee of the entity administering the plan

An initial 15% tax is applied on the amount involved in a prohibited transaction for each year (or part of a year) in a taxable period. If the transaction is not corrected within the taxable period, an additional tax of 100% of the amount involved is imposed. These taxes are payable by any disqualified person who takes part in a prohibited transaction. If more than one person takes part, each can be jointly and severally liable for the entire amount of tax. Prohibited transactions include the following:

- A transfer of plan income or assets to, or use for the benefit of, a disqualified person
- Any act of a fiduciary by which plan income or assets are used for his own benefit
- The receipt of money or property by a fiduciary for his own account from any party dealing with the plan in a transaction that involves plan income or assets
- The sale, exchange, or lease of property between a plan and a disqualified person
- Lending money between a plan and a disqualified person
- Furnishing goods or services between a plan and a disqualified person

Example: A plan fiduciary had a prohibited transaction by investing in a life insurance company's group annuity contract, resulting in a 10% commission paid to his company on the investment. This is a prohibited transaction between a plan fiduciary and a retirement plan.

If a prohibited transaction is not corrected during the taxable period, the taxpayer usually has an additional 90 days after the day the IRS mails a notice of deficiency for the 100% tax to correct the transaction. This correction period (the taxable period plus the 90 days) can be extended if one of the following occurs:

- The IRS grants reasonable time needed to correct the transaction.
- The taxpayer petitions the U.S. Tax Court.

If the transaction is corrected within this period, the 100% tax may be abated.

Employer Credit for Pension Start-up Costs

Employers may be able to claim a tax credit equal to 50% of the cost to set up and administer a retirement plan, up to a maximum of $500 per year, for each of the first three years of the plan.

Employers can choose to start claiming the credit in the tax year before the tax year in which the plan becomes effective. In order to qualify for this credit, the employer must have had 100 or fewer employees who received at least $5,000 in compensation for the preceding year.

Further, the employees cannot be substantially the same group covered by another retirement plan sponsored by essentially the same employer during the preceding three-year period. This credit is part of the general business credit, which can be carried back or forward to other tax years if it cannot be used in the current year.

Comparison of Defined Benefit and Defined Contribution Plans

Rule	Defined Benefit Plan	Defined Contribution Plan
Employer Contributions	Employer contributions are required based upon actuarial calculation of amounts needed to fund plan benefits.	The employer may match a portion of employee contributions or contribute without employee contributions.
Employee Contributions	Employees often do not contribute.	For many plans, employees are the primary contributors.
Managing the Investments	The employer must ensure that contributions to the plan plus investment earnings will be enough to pay the promised benefits.	The employee often is responsible for managing the investments, choosing from investment options offered by the plan. For some plans, the plan administrator is responsible for investing the plan's assets.
Benefits Paid Upon Retirement	A promised benefit is based on a formula, often using a combination of the employee's age, years worked, and salary history.	The benefit depends on contributions made by the employee and/or the employer and investment earnings on the contributions.
Type of Retirement Benefit Payments	Traditionally, these plans pay the retiree monthly annuity payments that continue for life.	The retiree may transfer the account balance into an Individual Retirement Account (IRA) from which he may withdraw money. Some plans also offer monthly payments through an annuity.
Guarantee of Benefits	The government, through the Pension Benefit Guaranty Corporation (PBGC), may partially guarantee benefits.	No federal guarantee of benefits.

Unit 18: Study Questions

1. Jensen Biomedical Corporation maintains a SIMPLE IRA for its employees and has elected to make 3% matching contributions. A former employee, Grace, quit her job on January 27, 2013 after the business had already deducted $75 from her wages based upon her election to contribute to its SIMPLE IRA plan. Grace had earned $2,000 in wages before she quit. How must Jensen Biomedical treat this $75 deduction from Grace's wages?

A. Jensen must return Grace's $75 salary reduction contribution.
B. Jensen must deposit Grace's salary reduction contribution in her SIMPLE IRA account. The company must also match Grace's salary reduction contributions up to 3% of her $2,000 compensation ($60).
C. Jensen must deposit Grace's salary reduction contribution in her SIMPLE IRA account. However, the company is not required to make a matching contribution for an employee who has terminated employment.
D. Jensen is required to remit the $75 to the U.S. Treasury.

2. What types of employers cannot establish a SEP?

A. A self-employed taxpayer without any employees.
B. A corporation with 90 employees.
C. A nonprofit entity with five employees.
D. All of the above can establish a SEP.

3. "Prohibited transactions" are transactions between a retirement plan and a disqualified person. Which of the following is exempt from the prohibited transaction rules?

A. A fiduciary of the plan.
B. A person providing services to the plan.
C. An employer whose employees are covered by the plan.
D. A disqualified person who receives a benefit to which he is entitled as a plan participant.

4. Sarah runs her own business, and sets up a new defined benefit plan for her ten employees. In 2013, what is the maximum tax credit Sarah can receive for qualified retirement plan start-up costs?

A. $100.
B. $500.
C. $1,000.
D. $2,000.

5. Ram is a sole proprietor whose tax year is the calendar year. He made a contribution to his SIMPLE IRA on May 15, 2014. What is the earliest year for which he can deduct this contribution?

A. His 2013 tax return.
B. His 2014 tax return.
C. The contribution is not deductible on his tax return because it was made late.
D. None of the above.

6. Maura, age 26, began participating in a SIMPLE IRA retirement account on March 10, 2012. She took an early distribution from the account on December 26, 2013. She does not qualify for any of the exceptions to the early withdrawal penalty. The distribution amount was $10,000. What is the amount of additional tax that Maura must pay on the early distribution?

A. $1,000.
B. $1,500.
C. $2,500.
D. $3,000.

7. Can a SIMPLE IRA plan be maintained on a fiscal-year basis?

A. Yes, if the business is on a fiscal year.
B. Yes, even if the business uses a calendar year.
C. Yes, but only if the business requests a 444 election.
D. No, a calendar year must be used.

8. Huang Software, Inc. decides to establish a SEP for its employees. All of the following statements about Huang's retirement plan are correct except:

A. In good years, Huang can make larger contributions for its employees, and in down years it can reduce the amount.
B. Individual employees have the opportunity to divide the employer's contributions to their SEP-IRAs among the funds made available to Huang employees.
C. Under a SEP, the contribution rate can be different for each employee, based on length of service and sales performance.
D. Only employers and self-employed individuals can make contributions to SEPs.

9. Brenda owns the Fresh Berry Company, a sole proprietorship with 150 employees. All of the following plans are available for Brenda's company except ______________:

A. A qualified plan.
B. A defined benefit plan.
C. A SIMPLE IRA.
D. None of the above.

10. The Azalea City Partnership has 15 employees and contributes to their retirement accounts. How is this transaction reported?

A. The business can take the deduction for its contributions to its employees' retirement accounts on Form 1065, *Partnership Income Tax Return*.
B. The business cannot take a deduction for its contributions to its employees' retirement accounts. Instead, the amounts contributed are added to the partnership basis.
C. The individual partners are allowed to deduct contributions to the employee retirement accounts on their individual returns.
D. None of the above.

11. Leah is a sole proprietor who establishes a SEP. She has two employees. Leah has a net loss in 2013 on her Schedule C. Which of the following is true?

A. Because the business shows a loss, she is prohibited from contributing to her retirement account, as well as the retirement accounts of her employees.
B. Because the business shows a loss, she is prohibited from contributing to her retirement account, but she may contribute to the retirement accounts of her employees.
C. Leah may make a retirement contribution to her own retirement account as well as the accounts of her employees.
D. None of the above.

12. All of the following are requirements of ERISA (the Employee Retirement Income Security Act) except:

A. ERISA requires that employers file an annual report on Form 5500 for their sponsored retirement plans.
B. ERISA requires employers to set up retirement plans for their employees.
C. ERISA requires minimum funding standards for retirement plans.
D. ERISA requires certain communications with plan participants.

13. Under the rules for prohibited transactions, all of the following would be considered disqualified persons except:

A. A 5% shareholder of the entity administering the plan.
B. A fiduciary of the plan.
C. An employer whose employees are covered by the plan.
D. A person providing services to the plan.

14. A 401(k) is a type of ___________:

A. SEP-IRA.
B. Government pension plan.
C. Defined contribution plan.
D. Defined benefit plan.

15. Which of the following statements regarding a SEP-IRA is true?

A. Money can be withdrawn from a SEP-IRA by the employee at any time without tax or penalty.
B. Money can be withdrawn from a SEP-IRA by the employee at any time, but taxes may apply.
C. An employee must wait at least two years to withdraw money from a SEP-IRA.
D. An employee must wait at least three years to withdraw money from a SEP-IRA.

16. Josie works full-time and participates in her employer's retirement plan. She also has her own graphic design business. She does not have any employees. Can Josie set up a SEP for self-employment income, even though she is already participating in her employer's plan?

A. Yes, Josie can still set up a SEP for her business.
B. No, Josie cannot set up a SEP because she is covered by an employer plan.
C. No, Josie cannot set up a SEP because she is a prohibited individual.
D. Josie can set up a SEP only if she hires employees.

17. What are the penalties imposed on a disqualified person who takes part in a prohibited transaction?

A. 25% tax of the amount involved.
B. 50% tax of the amount involved.
C. An initial tax of 15% of the amount involved, and an additional tax of 100% if the transaction is not corrected within the taxable period.
D. An initial tax of 25% of the amount involved, and an additional tax of 100% if the transaction is not corrected within the taxable period.

18. Theresa is a small business owner who maintains a SEP plan for her employees. Which of the following employees can be excluded from the plan, if Theresa chooses?

A. Stan, a 32-year-old part-time employee who has worked for Theresa for five years.
B. Aldo, a 42-year-old seasonal employee and U.S. resident alien who has worked for Theresa for three years.
C. Noel, a 21-year-old part-time employee who is also a union member.
D. Millie, a 55-year-old full-time employee who has worked for Theresa for four years.

19. What happens if an eligible employee entitled to a contribution is unwilling to set up a SIMPLE IRA?

A. Eligible employees may decline to participate in an employer's SIMPLE IRA.
B. Eligible employees may not opt out of a SIMPLE IRA.
C. Eligible employees may choose to set up a ROTH IRA in lieu of a SIMPLE IRA.
D. None of the above.

20. The Esslinger Carpet Company has started a SEP plan for its employees. The company currently has four employees. Which of the following employees is the company not required to cover under the SEP plan?

A. Faye, age 45, a full-time employee for the last five years.
B. Larry, age 25, a part-time employee for the last three years.
C. Randolph, age 20, a full-time employee for the last three years.
D. Mack, age 42, a seasonal employee for the last six years.

21. Marcelo owns Perez Auto and sets up a SEP-IRA for all of his employees. In his benefits handbook, he makes the following statements regarding the shop's SEP-IRA plan. All are correct except:

A. Only employees age 21 and older are eligible.
B. An employee cannot withdraw from his SEP-IRA while he is employed by Perez Auto.
C. A SEP-IRA will be set up for all eligible employees.
D. An employee must have worked for Perez Auto for at least three of the last five years to be eligible.

Unit 19: Trusts and Estates

More Reading:
Publication 559, *Survivors, Executors, and Administrators*
Publication 950, *Introduction to Estate and Gift Taxes*
Publication 536, *Net Operating Losses (NOLs) for Individuals, Estates, and Trusts*

Estates and trusts are separate legal entities that are defined by the assets they hold. An estate is created when a taxpayer dies and the estate tax may be imposed on the assets held by the estate.

A trust is created while the taxpayer is alive or by a taxpayer's last will, and can determine how property will be distributed during his lifetime or at death. A trust can hold title to property for the benefit of one or more persons or entities. An estate or trust is generally required to obtain an employer identification number (EIN), like other legal entities.

Estates and trusts generally terminate when all of their assets and income have been distributed and all of their liabilities have been paid. If a trust or estate's existence is unnecessarily prolonged, the IRS can step in and terminate it after a reasonable period for completing the final administration. If an estate or trust has a loss in its final year, the loss can be passed through to the beneficiaries, allowing them deductions on their returns. Losses cannot be passed through to beneficiaries in a non-termination year.

Estates in General

For federal tax purposes, an estate is a separate legal entity that is created when a taxpayer dies. A person who inherits property from an estate is generally not taxed on the transfer. Instead, the estate itself is responsible for paying any applicable taxes before the property is distributed. However, if the estate's assets are distributed to beneficiaries before the taxes are paid, the beneficiaries can be held liable for the tax debt, up to the value of the assets distributed.

After a person dies, a personal representative, such as an executor named in his will or an administrator appointed by a court, will typically manage the estate and settle the decedent's financial affairs. If there is no executor or administrator, another person with possession of the decedent's property may act as the personal representative. The personal representative is responsible for filing the final income tax return and the estate tax return, if required. The personal representative is also responsible for determining any estate tax liability before the estate's assets are distributed to beneficiaries.

Either the personal representative or a paid preparer must sign the appropriate line of each of the following tax returns that may need to be filed:

- The final income tax return (Form 1040) for the decedent (for income received before death);
- Fiduciary income tax returns (Form 1041) for the estate for the period of its administration; and
- Estate Tax Return (Form 706).

Example: James was unmarried when he died on April 20, 2013. His only daughter, Lillian, was named as the executor of his estate. James earned wages in 2013 before his death. Therefore, a final tax return is required for 2013. Lillian asks her accountant to help prepare her father's final Form 1040, which will include all the taxable income that James received in 2013 before his death. The accountant also helps Lillian with the valuation of her father's estate. After determining the fair market value of all her father's assets, they conclude that James's gross estate is valued at approximately $7 million. As this exceeds the threshold of $5,250,000 for 2013, an estate tax return (Form 706) is also required to be filed. Depending upon the activity related to the estate's assets during the period from James's death until the assets are distributed, it may also be necessary to file Form 1041.

Decedent's Final Income Tax Return (Form 1040)

The personal representative must file the final individual income tax return of the decedent for the year of death and any preceding years for which returns have not been filed. Thus, if an individual died after the close of the tax year but before the return for that year was filed, the return for that year will not be the final return.

The taxpayer's final income tax return is filed on the same form that would have been used if the taxpayer were still alive, but "deceased" is written after the taxpayer's name. The filing deadline is April 15 of the year following the taxpayer's death, just like other individual income tax returns.

Example: Stephanie dies on March 2, 2014. At the time of her death, she had not yet filed her 2013 tax return. She earned $51,000 in wages in 2013. She also earned $18,000 in wages between January 1, 2014 and her death. Therefore, Stephanie's 2013 and 2014 tax returns must be filed by her representative.

On a decedent's final tax return, the rules for personal exemptions and deductions are the same as those that apply for any individual taxpayer. The full amount of the applicable personal exemption (subject to any phaseout limitations based on income) may be claimed on the final tax return, regardless of how long the taxpayer was alive during the year.

Income In Respect of a Decedent

Income in respect of a decedent (IRD) is any taxable income that was earned but not received by the decedent at the time of death. IRD is not taxed on the final return of the deceased taxpayer. It is reported on the tax return of the person (or entity) that receives the income. This could be the estate, the surviving spouse, or another beneficiary, such as a child. Regardless of the decedent's accounting method, IRD is subject to income tax when the income is received.

IRD retains the same tax character after death as if the taxpayer were still alive. For example, if the income would have been short-term capital gain to the deceased, it is taxed the same way to the beneficiary. IRD can come from various sources, including:

- Unpaid salary, wages or bonuses
- Distributions from traditional IRAs and employer-provided retirement plans

- Deferred compensation benefits
- Accrued but unpaid interest, dividends, and rent
- Accounts receivable of a sole proprietor

Example: Carlos was owed $15,000 in wages when he died. The check for these wages was not remitted by his employer until three weeks later and was received by his daughter and sole beneficiary, Rosalie. The wages are considered IRD, and Rosalie must recognize the $15,000 as ordinary income, the same tax treatment that would have applied for Carlos.

Example: Beverly died on April 30. At the time of her death, she was owed (but had not yet received) $1,500 in interest on bonds and $2,000 in rental income. Beverly's beneficiary will include $3,500 of IRD in gross income when the interest and rent are received. The income retains its character as interest income and passive rental income.

IRD is includible in the decedent's estate and may be subject to estate tax. It may also be subject to income tax if received by a beneficiary. Therefore, the beneficiary may take a deduction for estate tax paid on the IRD. This deduction is taken as a miscellaneous itemized deduction on Schedule A and is not subject to the 2% floor.

Fiduciary Income Tax Return (Form 1041)

Form 1041 is a fiduciary return used to report the following items for a domestic decedent's estate, a trust, or a bankruptcy estate:

- Current income and deductions, including gains and losses from disposition of the entity's property and excluding certain items such as tax-exempt interest (collectively, *distributable net income* or DNI);
- A deduction for income that is either held for future distribution or distributed currently to the beneficiaries (income distribution deduction) that is limited to DNI; and
- Any income tax liability.

An estate or trust may exist as a taxable legal entity until all of its assets have been distributed. Current income of an estate may include IRD, if it was received by the estate rather than specific beneficiaries. As investment assets will usually continue to earn income after a taxpayer has died, this income, such as rents, dividends and interest, must be reported. The expenses of administering an estate can be deducted either from the estate's income on Form 1041, in determining its income tax, or from the gross estate on Form 706, in determining the estate tax liability, but cannot be claimed for both purposes. Schedule K-1 is used to report any income that is distributed or distributable to each beneficiary and is filed with Form 1041, with a copy also given to the beneficiary.

The due date for Form 1041 is the fifteenth day of the fourth month following the end of the entity's tax year, but is subject to an automatic extension of five months if Form 7004 is filed. The tax year of an estate may be either a calendar or a fiscal year, subject to the election made at the time the first return is filed. An election will also be made on the first return as to method (cash, accrual, or other) to report an estate's income. Form 1041 must be filed for any domestic estate that has gross income for the tax year of $600 or more, or a beneficiary who is a nonresident alien (with any amount of income).

Distributable Net Income: Taxable income earned by an estate or trust is taxable to either the entity or the beneficiaries, but not to both. Distributable net income (DNI) is income that is currently available for distribution. If the beneficiary receives a distribution in excess of DNI, only the DNI is taxed. The income distribution deduction (IDD) is allowed to trusts and estates for amounts that are paid, credited, or required to be distributed to beneficiaries. The income distribution deduction is calculated on Schedule B (Form 1041) and is limited to the lesser of distributions less tax-exempt income or DNI less tax-exempt income.

Net Investment Income Tax: Estates and certain trusts are subject to the additional tax of 3.8% on net investment income that became effective in 2013 as a result of the Affordable Care Act. The provisions for this tax are generally similar to those for individuals, and it must be reported on Form 8960, *Net Investment Tax: Individuals, Estates, and Trusts.* For trusts and estates, the tax applies to the lesser of undistributed net investment income or the excess of adjusted gross income over the threshold amount ($11,950 for 2013) at which the highest tax bracket begins. The tax does not apply to tax-exempt trusts or to grantor trusts.

Net investment income that is subject to the tax includes:

- Interest
- Dividends
- Capital gains
- Rental and royalty income
- Non-qualified annuities
- Income from businesses involved in trading of financial instruments or commodities
- Income from businesses that are passive activities for the taxpayer

Form 706: The Estate Tax Return

An estate tax return is filed using Form 706, *United States Estate (and Generation-Skipping Transfer) Tax Return.* The estate tax applies to an individual's taxable estate, which is the gross estate less certain deductions. After the taxable estate is computed, it is added to the value of taxable gifts made during the decedent's lifetime. The applicable estate tax rate is applied to derive a tentative tax, from which any gift taxes paid or payable are subtracted to determine the gross estate tax. The maximum estate tax rate is 40% in 2013.

However, all or a portion of the gross estate tax may be eliminated after consideration of the estate's available:

- **Basic Exclusion Amount:** This amount is adjusted for inflation each year and may be used to reduce or eliminate gift and/or estate taxes. For 2013, the basic estate tax exclusion amount is $5.25 million.
- **Deceased Spousal Unused Exclusion (DSUE):** This is the unused portion of the decedent's predeceased spouse's basic exclusion (the amount that was not used to offset gift or estate tax liabilities). The predeceased spouse must have died on or after January 1, 2011 and a

portability election must have been made on Form 706 filed to claim the DSUE on behalf of the surviving spouse's estate.

Only estates valued in excess of the sum of these amounts need to file a return and pay estate tax. Essentially, this means that a surviving spouse's estate with value up to $10.5 million of estate value could be excluded from taxation if both spouses died during 2013, neither spouse had used any of his basic exclusion amount to offset gift tax liabilities, and the portability election for DSUE was properly made on Form 706 for the first spouse's estate.

Example: Marlene dies in 2013 and leaves an estate valued at $3 million. She had not previously used any of her basic exclusion amount to avoid paying gift taxes, so the entire exclusion amount of $5.25 million is available to her estate. As this amount exceeds the estate's value, no estate tax will be owed and an estate tax return does not need to be filed.

Example: Matt dies in early 2013 and leaves a gross estate valued at $9 million. His assets transfer to his wife, Leslie, and none are taxed because of the unlimited marital deduction. Thus, none of the $5.25 million basic exclusion amount available to Matt's estate is used (and none had been used to offset gift tax liabilities during his lifetime). Leslie dies later in the year. Assuming the appropriate portability election was made when Form 706 was filed for Matt's estate and Leslie had not used any of her basic exclusion amount, Matt's unused basic exclusion is added to Leslie's basic exclusion, for a total exclusion amount of $10.5 million. If Leslie's estate is valued at less than $10.5 million, the full amount can be excluded and no estate tax will be owed.

Applicable Credit: The gross estate tax described above is reduced by the applicable credit, also referred to as the unified credit, which is a tax credit amount that corresponds with the basic exclusion amount and, if applicable, the DSUE available to a surviving spouse. For example, an applicable credit amount of $2,045,800 in 2013 corresponds with the basic exclusion amount of $5.25 million.

Just as with the basic exclusion amount, any portion of the applicable credit amount used to avoid payment of gift taxes reduces the amount of credit available in later years that can be used to offset gift or estate taxes. For example, if someone had used the full $2,045,800 applicable credit to avoid payment of gift taxes during his lifetime, he would have exhausted his entire $5.25 million basic exclusion. If he then died in 2013, his estate would be liable for tax on the taxable estate without further offset.

Example: June, who is single, dies in 2013 and leaves an estate valued at $20 million. During her lifetime, she had used $1 million of her basic exclusion to offset payments of gift tax. That reduces the amount her estate may exclude to $4.25 million, which is then subtracted from her $20 million taxable estate. That leaves a total of $15.75 million to be taxed at a 40% rate, resulting in an estate tax liability of $6.3 million.

If required to be filed, the due date for Form 706 is nine months after the decedent's date of death. An automatic six-month extension may be requested by filing Form 4768. However, the tax is due by the due date and interest is accrued on any amounts owed that are not paid at that time. The assessment period for estate tax is three years after the due date for a timely filed estate tax return. The assessment period is four years for transfers from an estate.

The Gross Estate

The gross estate is based upon the fair market value of the decedent's property, which is not necessarily equal to his cost, and includes:

- The FMV of all tangible and intangible property owned by the decedent at the time of death.
- The full value of property held as joint tenants with the right of survivorship (unless the decedent and spouse were the only joint tenants)
- Life insurance proceeds payable to the estate, or payable to the heirs, for policies owned by the decedent.
- The value of certain annuities or survivor benefits payable to the heirs.
- The value of certain property that was transferred within three years before the decedent's death.

The gross estate does not include property owned solely by the decedent's spouse or other individuals. Lifetime gifts that are complete (so that no control over the gifts was retained) are not included in the gross estate.

Deductions from the Gross Estate: Once the gross estate has been calculated, certain deductions (and in special circumstances, reductions to value) are allowed to determine the taxable estate. Deductions from the gross estate may include:

- Funeral expenses paid out of the estate.
- Administration expenses for the estate (if not deducted on Form 1041).
- Debts owed at the time of death.
- The marital deduction (generally, the value of the property that passes from the estate to a surviving spouse).
- The charitable deduction (generally, the value of the property that passes from the estate to qualifying charities).
- The state death tax deduction (generally, any inheritance or estate taxes paid to any state).

The following items are not deductible from the gross estate:

- Federal estate taxes paid.
- Alimony paid after the taxpayer's death. These payments would be treated as distributions to a beneficiary.

Property taxes are deductible only if they accrue under state law prior to the decedent's death.

> **Study Tip:** For both Parts 1 and 2 of the EA exam, you should be familiar with what is included in the gross estate and the taxable estate.

The Marital Deduction: Transfers from one spouse to the other are typically tax-free. The marital deduction allows spouses to transfer an unlimited amount of property to one another during their lifetimes or at death without being subject to estate or gift taxes.

To receive an unlimited deduction, the spouse receiving the assets must be a U.S. citizen and a legal spouse, and have outright ownership of the assets. The unlimited marital deduction is generally not allowed if the transferee spouse is not a U.S. citizen (even if the spouse is a legal resident of the United States). If the receiving spouse is not a citizen, assets may be transferred tax-free only to the extent of an annual exclusion, which is $143,000 in 2013.

Decedent's Medical Expenses: Debts that were not paid before death, including medical expenses subsequently paid on behalf of the decedent, are liabilities of the estate and can be deducted from the gross estate on the estate tax return. However, if medical expenses for the decedent are paid out of the estate during the one-year period beginning with the day after death, the personal representative can alternatively elect to treat all or part of the expenses as paid by the decedent at the time they were incurred, and deduct them on the final tax return (1040) for the decedent.

Basis of Estate Property

The basis of property inherited from a decedent is generally one of the following:

- The FMV of the property on the date of death.
- The FMV on an alternate valuation date, if elected by the personal representative.
- The value under a special-use valuation method for real property used in farming or another closely-held business, if elected by the personal representative.
- The decedent's adjusted basis in land to the extent of the value excluded from the taxable estate as a qualified conservation easement.

Property that is jointly owned by a decedent and another person will be included in full in the decedent's gross estate unless it can be shown that the other person originally owned or otherwise contributed to the purchase price. The surviving owner's new basis in property that was jointly owned is calculated by adding his original basis in the property to the value of the part of the property included in the decedent's estate. Any deductions for depreciation of the property allowed to the surviving owner are subtracted from the sum.

If property is jointly held between husband and wife as tenants by the entirety or as joint tenants with the right of survivorship (if they were the only joint tenants), one-half of the property's value is included in the gross estate, and there is a step-up in basis for that one-half. If the decedent holds property in a community property state, half of the value of the community property will be included in the gross estate of the decedent, but the entire value of the community property will receive a step-up in basis.

Generation-Skipping Transfer Tax (Form 709)

The generation skipping transfer tax (GST) may apply to gifts during a taxpayer's lifetime or transfers occurring after his death, called bequests, made to "skip persons." A skip person is a person who belongs to a generation that is two or more generations below the generation of the donor. The most common scenario is when a taxpayer makes a bequest to a grandchild.

The GST is assessed when a property transfer is made, including instances in which property is transferred from a trust. The GST is based on the amounts transferred to skip persons, after subtracting the allocated portions of the GST exemption. In 2013, the GST exemption is $5.25

million and the GST tax rate is set at the maximum estate tax rate of 40%. The GST is imposed separately and in addition to the estate and gift tax.

Example: Patrick sets up a trust that names his adult daughter, Helene, as the sole beneficiary of the trust. In January 2013, Patrick dies, and the trust passes to Helene. However, later in the year, Helene also dies, and now the trust passes to her children (Patrick's grandchildren). Patrick's grandchildren are "skip-persons" for purposes of the GST, and the trust fund property may be subject to the GST.

Any payments that are made for tuition or medical expenses directly to an educational or medical institution on behalf of a skip person are exempt from gift tax and GST.

Example: Gordon wants to help support his grandchildren, but he wants to make sure that his gifts are not subject to gift tax, GST, or estate tax. In 2013, he offers to pay his grandchild's college tuition in full. Gordon writes a check directly to the college in the amount of $25,000. There is no tax consequence for this gift, and no reporting is required.

Trusts in General

A trust is an entity created under the laws of the state in which it is formed. A trust may be created during an individual's life (an inter-vivos trust) or at the time of death under a will (a testamentary trust). A trust can be created to hold property for the benefit of other persons. It may be created for the benefit of a disabled individual, or can be used to legally avoid certain taxes. The establishment of a trust creates a fiduciary relationship between three parties:

- **The Grantor:** The person who contributes property to the trust.
- **The Trustee (or Fiduciary):** The person or entity charged with the fiduciary duties associated with the trust.
- **The Beneficiary:** The person who is designated to receive the trust income or assets.

Example: AJ is having medical problems and decides to put her assets in a trust. She asks her attorney to create the trust and to manage the assets. The trust is structured so that it will pay AJ's living expenses, with the remainder of the assets going to her grandson after she dies. In this scenario, AJ is the **grantor**, the lawyer is the **trustee**, and AJ and her grandson are the **beneficiaries.**

Sometimes, a trust is used to transfer property in a controlled manner. For example, a parent may wish to transfer ownership of assets to his child, but does not want the child to waste the assets or spend them unwisely. The assets could be transferred to a trust, with the parent as both the grantor and the trustee. The child would be the beneficiary. The parent still has control over the assets, and the child is prevented from using them all up.

The accounting period for a trust is generally the calendar year. The filing due date for a calendar-year trust is April 15. A trust must file Form 1041, *U.S. Income Tax Return for Estates and Trusts* if it has:

- Any taxable income for the year (after subtracting the allowable exemption amount),
- Gross income of $600 or more (regardless of whether the income is taxable), or
- Any beneficiary who is a nonresident alien.

Example: The Russick Family Trust has $400 of tax-exempt interest from municipal bonds during the year. There is no other income. Normally, the trust would not be required to file a tax return because the income earned by the trust is tax-exempt. However, the Russick Family Trust has a beneficiary who is a nonresident alien. Therefore, the trust is required to file Form 1041.

A trust calculates its gross income in a manner similar to an individual taxpayer. Trusts are allowed an exemption, but the amount varies based on the type of trust. A trust that must distribute all of its income currently (a simple trust) is allowed an exemption of $300. Any other trust is allowed an exemption of $100 per year.

Most deductions and credits allowed to individuals are also allowed to trusts. However, there is one major distinction: a trust is a pass-through entity that is allowed a deduction for its distributions to beneficiaries. The beneficiaries (and not the trust) pay income tax on their distributive share of income. Schedule K-1 (Form 1041) is used to report income that a trust distributes to beneficiaries. The income must then be reported on the beneficiaries' income tax returns.

Simple and Complex Trusts

With regard to income distribution, there are two types of trusts: a simple trust and a complex trust. The IRC defines a simple trust as a trust that:

- Distributes all of its income currently;
- Makes no distributions from principal; and
- Makes no distributions to charity.

Any trust that is not a simple trust is automatically a complex trust. A complex trust:

- Is allowed to accumulate income;
- Can make discretionary distributions of income;
- Can make mandatory (or discretionary) distributions of principal; and
- Can make distributions to charity.

A trust may be a simple trust one year, and a complex trust in another year. For example, if a simple trust fails to distribute all its income in the current year, it becomes a complex trust. Unlike an estate or a simple trust, a complex trust reports its accounting income, which may differ from its taxable income and its DNI and may be more or less than distributions for the year, on Form 1041.

Grantor Trusts

A grantor trust is a valid legal entity under state law, but it is not recognized as a separate entity for income tax purposes.

The grantor (also known as trustor, settlor, or creator) creates the trust relationship and retains control over the trust. In the eyes of the IRS, the grantor is the owner of the trust for income tax purposes. The grantor establishes the terms and provisions of the trust relationship between the grantor, the trustee, and the beneficiary. These will usually include the following:

- The rights, duties, and powers of the trustee;
- Distribution provisions;

- Ability of the grantor to amend, modify, revoke, or terminate the trust agreement;
- The designation of a trustee or successor trustees; and
- The designation of the state under which the trust agreement is to be governed.

Example: The Kenneth Chiang Trust is a grantor trust. Kenneth is the grantor. During the year, the trust sold 100 shares of ABC stock for $1,010 in which it had a basis of $10 and 200 shares of XYZ stock for $10 in which it had a $1,020 basis. The trust does not report these transactions on Form 1041 or issue Kenneth a Schedule K-1. Instead, a schedule is attached to Form 1041 showing each stock transaction separately and in the same detail as Kenneth (grantor and owner) will need to report these transactions on his Schedule D (Form 1040). The trust does not net the capital gains and losses to show a $10 long-term capital loss.

Revocable Trusts: Revocable trusts, including revocable living trusts, are grantor trusts in which the grantor retains the right to make changes or end the trust during his lifetime. The trust assets are subject to estate tax upon the grantor's death. The trust is generally created to manage and distribute property. Many taxpayers use this type of trust instead of, or in addition to, a will.

Non-Grantor Trusts

A non-grantor trust is any trust that is not a grantor trust. A non-grantor trust is considered a separate legal entity from the individual or organization that created it. The trust's income and deductions are reported on Form 1041.

If a non-grantor trust makes distributions to a beneficiary, in general those distributions carry any taxable income to the beneficiary. Examples include:

1. **Irrevocable Trusts**: An irrevocable trust is a trust that cannot be revoked after it is created. The transfer of assets into this type of trust is generally considered a "completed gift" subject to gift tax.
2. **Disability Trusts:** A qualified disability trust is a non-grantor trust created solely for the benefit of a disabled individual under age 65. In 2013, a qualified disability trust can claim an exemption of up to $3,900; the exemption is subject to phaseout if modified AGI exceeds $250,000. This is a specific exception to the regular exemption of $600 that applies to most trusts.
3. **Charitable Trusts:** A charitable trust is a trust devoted to qualified charitable contribution purposes. Charitable trusts are irrevocable.

Example: Pamela creates a charitable trust. Its governing instrument provides that the Presbyterian Church (a qualified religious organization), and the SPCA (a 501(c)(3) charity) are each to receive 50% of the trust income for 10 years. At the end of the 10-year period, the corpus will be distributed to the American Red Cross, also a 501(c)(3) organization. Pamela is allowed an income tax deduction for the value of the assets placed in trust.

Abusive Trust Arrangements

Certain trust arrangements purport to reduce or eliminate federal taxes in ways that are not permitted under the law. These abusive or fraudulent trust arrangements may be used to hide the true ownership of assets and income or to disguise the substance of transactions. They frequently involve more than one trust, each holding different assets of the taxpayer (for example, the taxpayer's business, business equipment, home, automobile, etc.)

Some trusts may hold interests in other trusts, purport to involve charities, or be foreign trusts. Participants and promoters of abusive trust schemes may be subject to civil or criminal penalties.

Abusive or fraudulent trust arrangements may promise such benefits as:

- Deductions for personal expenses paid by the trust
- Depreciation deductions for an owner's personal residence
- A stepped-up basis for property transferred to the trust
- The reduction or elimination of self-employment taxes
- The reduction or elimination of gift and estate taxes

Although these schemes give the appearance of separating responsibility and control from the benefits of ownership, as would be the case with legitimate trusts, the taxpayer in fact controls them. When trusts are used for legitimate business, family, or estate planning purposes, either the trust, the beneficiary, or the grantor will pay the tax on the income generated by the trust.

Trusts cannot be used to transform a taxpayer's personal, living, or educational expenses into deductible items. A taxpayer cannot use a trust to avoid tax liability by ignoring either the true ownership of income and assets or the true substance of transactions.

Example: Hugo Edwards transfers his family residence and its furnishings to a trust, which rents the residence back to Hugo and his children. He deducts depreciation and the expenses of maintaining and operating the home, including landscaping, pool service, and utilities. Hugo's second trust transfers assets to the Edwards Charity Fund, which claims to be a charitable organization but is not an IRS-qualified exempt organization. The trust pays for personal, education, and recreational expenses on behalf of Hugo and his family. The trust then claims the deductions on its tax returns. Both the trusts Hugo created are fraudulent, and he would be subject to civil and criminal penalties.

Foreign Trusts: Foreign trusts are not always created to evade taxation. However, the IRS gives increased scrutiny to foreign trusts because of their growing popularity in foreign countries that provide financial secrecy and impose little or no tax on trusts. These are often in "tax haven" countries that are supposedly outside the jurisdiction of the U.S.

Typically, abusive foreign trust arrangements enable taxable funds to flow through several trusts or entities until the funds ultimately are distributed or made available to the original owner tax-free. Legally, however, the income from these arrangements is fully taxable.

Example: Shauna is a U.S. citizen with substantial business income. She forms an asset management company as a domestic trust, listing herself as the director and another individual as the trustee. She then forms a business trust, very similar to the domestic trust, with both intended to show she is not managing her own business. Next, Shauna forms a foreign trust in Bermuda, with the income from the business trust distributed to this foreign trust. Because the source of income is U.S.-based and there is a U.S. trustee, this foreign trust has filing requirements (discussed below). Her next step is to form a second foreign trust. The first foreign trust funnels all of its income to this second foreign trust, which has a foreigner as a trustee. Since the trustee and sources of income are now foreign, Shauna claims there are no U.S. filing requirements. In actuality, she retains control of the income in this second foreign trust and has set up an elaborate scheme to evade U.S. tax laws.

Since 1996, a trust is considered foreign unless a U.S. court supervises it and a U.S. fiduciary controls all substantial decisions. U.S. taxpayers are required to file Form 3520, *Creation of or Transfer to Certain Foreign Trusts*, Form 3520-A, *Annual Return of Foreign Trust with U.S. Beneficiaries*, and Form 926, *Return by a Transferor of Property to a Foreign Estate or Trust*, when contributing property to a foreign trust. These trusts are usually U.S. tax neutral and are treated as grantor trusts with income taxable to the grantor that should be included on Form 1040.

Foreign Accounts: Both individuals and entities including trusts may be required to report their foreign accounts to the IRS by filing an electronic Financial Crimes Enforcement Network (FinCEN) Form 114, *Report of Foreign Bank and Financial Accounts* (FBAR). The report must be e-filed by June 30, 2014 if:

- The taxpayer had a financial interest in or signature authority over at least one financial account located outside of the United States, and
- The aggregate value of all foreign financial accounts exceeded $10,000 at any time during the calendar year to be reported.

Certain exceptions apply to the filing requirement. For example, if the foreign financial accounts are owned by a governmental entity, international financial institution, participants or beneficiaries of a qualified retirement plan, or IRA owners and beneficiaries, they are exempt from the FBAR filing requirements.

Fun Fact (since you have successfully reached the end of your Book 2 study guide)

You may have heard the term "strawman" and not known what it meant. The IRS defines a strawman as a person whose trust receives another grantor's assets to be passed through the original trust to a second or possibly more trusts for the purpose of disguising the true identity or ownership of the trust.

Unit 19: Study Questions

1. Roger died in early 2013. His executor has elected to use a calendar year for Roger's estate and is preparing to file Form 1041. The estate has AGI of $211,950 that included the following:

- $15,000 of interest income
- $10,000 of dividends
- $65,000 of capital gains
- $25,000 of rental income
- $60,000 of income from an investment in a limited partnership
- $36,950 of salary that Roger earned before his death (paid to the estate as IRD)

What is the estate's liability for net investment income tax, if any, for 2013?

A. $0.
B. $7,600.
C. $6,650.
D. $3,800.

2. The Cormier Trust is required to distribute all its income currently. What is the yearly exemption amount for the Cormier Trust?

A. $0.
B. $100.
C. $300.
D. $600.

3. Carlton's will provides that each of his ten grandchildren would receive $1 million. Assuming that none of his GST exemption amount has previously been used in connection with gifts to the grandchildren or other skip persons, what portion of the total amount distributed to the grandchildren after his death in 2013 would be subject to GST?

A. $8,700,000.
B. $5,250,000.
C. $10,000,000.
D. $4,750,000.

4. The calculation of the gross estate includes all of the following except:

A. Life insurance proceeds payable to the decedent's heirs.
B. The value of certain annuities payable to the estate.
C. Property owned solely by the decedent's spouse.
D. The value of certain property transferred within three years before the taxpayer's death.

5. All of the following are required to file Form 1041 except:

A. An estate with gross income of $600.
B. An estate with $700 in exempt income.
C. An estate with $200 in gross income and a beneficiary who is a nonresident alien.
D. An estate with $500 in gross income and a beneficiary who is a resident alien.

6. All of the following are characteristics of a simple trust except:

A. The trust may distribute assets to charity.
B. The trust distributes all its income currently.
C. The trust makes no distributions from principal.
D. The trust makes no distributions to charity.

7. Virgil gave his granddaughter, Susannah, $30,000. Susannah is 14 years old and lives with her parents. Which of the following statements regarding the generation-skipping transfer tax is true?

A. Because the gift is subject to the generation-skipping transfer tax, it is not subject to the gift tax.
B. The gift is subject to both the gift tax and the generation-skipping transfer tax.
C. The gift is not subject to generation-skipping transfer tax because Susannah's parents are alive.
D. If Virgil had transferred the funds into a trust solely for his granddaughter's benefit, the gift would not be subject to the generation-skipping transfer tax.

8. Roberto died on May 3, 2013. The estate's tax year ends on December 31, 2013. The estate had the following items of income during the year:

- Interest of $250
- Dividends of $150
- Stock-sale proceeds, net of broker's commission, of $10,000
- Basis of the stock $9,900

The estate made no distributions during 2013. Based upon the information provided, which of the following statements is true?

A. The estate is not required to file an income tax return.
B. The estate is required to file an income tax return.
C. The estate is required to file a return on Form 706.
D. Both B and C.

9. Parker, a single taxpayer, died on March 3, 2013. Based on the following information, determine the value of his gross estate:

FMV on date of death	
Life insurance on Parker's life (payable to his estate)	$250,000
Parker's revocable grantor trust	$700,000
Liabilities owed by Parker when he died	$ 150,000

A. $250,000.
B. $800,000.
C. $950,000.
D. $1.1 million.

10. What is the amount of the applicable credit in 2013?

A. $600.
B. $2,045,800.
C. $1 million.
D. $1,772,800.

11. All of the following are examples of potentially abusive trusts except:

A. A taxpayer who claims charitable deductions from a charity trust he has created, without receiving an IRS exemption letter.
B. A taxpayer who forms a grantor trust and retains the power to control or direct the trust's income or assets.
C. A taxpayer who forms a foreign trust in a "tax haven" country so funds distributed will be outside the jurisdiction of the United States.
D. A taxpayer who transfers an ongoing business to a series of trusts to avoid taxation but continues to run the day-to-day activities of the business and control its income stream.

12. What is included in the gross estate?

A. The gross estate of the decedent includes everything the taxpayer owns at the date of death.
B. The gross estate of the decedent includes everything the taxpayer owns six months after the date of death.
C. The gross estate of the decedent includes everything the taxpayer owns at the date of death, including income that the taxpayer was owed but had not yet received.
D. The gross estate includes everything the decedent earned in the prior year, as well as income estimates for future years.

13. What is the due date for Form 706 for a decedent who died in 2013?

A. Six months after the date of death
B. Nine months after the date of death.
C. Twelve months after the date of death.
D. April 15, 2014.

14. Dominique, an American citizen, has a trust in Panama where she regularly deposits funds. Which of the following statements is true regarding the trust?

A. Income deposited in the Panama trust is shielded from all U.S. taxes.
B. Dominique is not subject to any filing requirements in connection with her foreign trust.
C. Dominique may have to pay gift taxes on funds distributed from the trust, but will not owe income tax.
D. All income in Dominique's foreign trust is fully taxable.

15. What is the maximum estate tax rate for 2013?

A. 10%.
B. 35%.
C. 40%.
D. There is no estate tax in 2013.

16. Luis died in March 2013. At the time of his death and when his estate was being settled, none of his basic exclusion amount had been used to reduce or eliminate payment of gift or estate taxes. Form 706 was filed in October 2013, and the full amount of deceased spousal unused exclusion (DSUE) was reported thereon. His wife Jenna died in December 2013. As was the case with Luis, none of her basic exclusion amount had been used previously to offset gift taxes that would otherwise have been payable. What amount must Jenna's taxable estate exceed in order to be subject to estate tax?

A. $5,120,000.
B. $2,045,800.
C. $5,250,000.
D. $10,500,000.

Answers to Practice Questions: Businesses

Unit 1: Businesses Quiz Answers

1. The answer is B. A domestic LLC with at least two members that does not file Form 8832 is classified as a partnership for federal income tax purposes.

2. The answer is A. They may choose to report their qualified joint venture as a sole proprietorship on two separate Schedules C, so long as they file jointly.

3. The answer is D. A partnership is not required to obtain a new EIN simply to add business locations. In all of the other circumstances, the entity would need to obtain a new EIN.

4. The answer is C. C corporations are subject to double taxation. The other statements are facts about C corporations but are not considered drawbacks.

5. The answer is A. If a taxpayer's net earnings from self-employment are less than $400, he should enter the net profit on line 12 of Form 1040 and attach Schedule C to the return. Schedule SE is not required unless he has net earnings from self-employment of $400 or more.

6. The answer is D. Mandy and Tammy are working as a partnership and should report their income and expenses on Form 1065, *U.S. Return of Partnership Income.* Each partner should receive a Schedule K-1 to report her individual share of the partnership's income on her Form 1040.

7. The answer is B. Julian must complete Schedule C to report his business income and expenses.

8. The answer is A. Only a C corporation may have an unlimited number of shareholders. An S corporation is limited to no more than 100 shareholders.

9. The answer is A. A sole proprietor who is required to file excise tax returns (or employment tax returns) must obtain an EIN. A sole proprietorship is not required to obtain a new EIN when it changes location or its business name. An individual may operate multiple businesses using the same EIN, so long as the businesses are sole proprietorships.

10. The answer is C. The principal activity of a personal service corporation is providing personal services to individuals or groups. PSCs are not eligible for graduated tax rates. They pay a 35% flat rate on their taxable income.

11. The answer is C. Federal law requires businesses to provide a Form 1099-MISC for each independent contractor paid at least $600 for services during a year. If a business makes payments to a corporation (rather than an individual), it is generally not required to issue a Form 1099-MISC.

12. The answer is B. Statutory employees are unique because they report their wages, income, and allowable expenses on Schedule C, like self-employed taxpayers. However, statutory employees are not required to pay self-employment tax because their employers treat them as employees for Social Security tax purposes.

13. The answer is C. Income level is not a factor in determining a worker's status. The main issue involves whether the employer or the worker has the right to direct or control how the work is done and to control the financial and business aspects of the job. This helps determine whether a worker should be classified as an employee or an independent contractor.

14. The answer is A. Family members who work for other family members are subject to different tax requirements. Only income tax is withheld from the paycheck of a child under age 18 who is working for a parent who is a sole proprietor.

15. The answer is C. A business must file Form 8300, *Report of Cash Payments Over $10,000 Received in a Trade or Business,* when it receives a cash payment of more than $10,000 from one transaction or from two or more related transactions.

16. The answer is D. A sole proprietorship without employees does not require an employer identification number. The other choices listed all require an EIN.

Unit 2: Businesses Quiz Answers

1. The answer is C. A fiscal tax year is any tax year that is 12 consecutive months and ends on the last day of any month except December. Answer A is incorrect because this is a calendar year, not a fiscal year. Answer B is incorrect because a fiscal year, other than a 52-53 week year or a short tax year, must end on the last day of the month. Answer D is incorrect because it is more than 12 consecutive months.

2. The answer is B. Shipping finished products to customers is not an expense that should be included in inventory. This cost is a current expense and would be deductible when incurred, rather than capitalized as a cost of the inventory.

3. The answer is D. The correction of a math error does not require prior approval from the IRS. Consent from the IRS is not required for the following changes:

- Correction of a math error for computing tax liability or other mathematical error
- A correction in depreciable life or correction of a depreciation error
- An adjustment to an asset's useful life

4. The answer is A. A family farming corporation may use the cash method of accounting if its average annual gross receipts are $25 million or less. A C corporation with gross receipts exceeding $5 million is required to use the accrual method. A tax shelter must always use the accrual method, regardless of its gross receipts. A corporation with long-term contracts must always use the accrual method.

5. The answer is B. April 15 is the IRS due date for individual tax returns but would not be the end of a tax year, except in a rare instance in which an entity's existence terminates or an individual dies on that date. Answer A is incorrect because January 31 is the last day of the month, which qualifies as a fiscal tax year-end. Answer C is incorrect because December 31 is a calendar year-end. Answer D is incorrect because a tax year that ends on the same day of the week every year is a 52/53-week tax year, which is a legitimate type of fiscal year.

6. The answer is A. Generally, an entity cannot use the cash method if it has average annual gross receipts exceeding $5 million. However, if a company has inventory, the threshold for gross receipts is $1 million. A qualified family farming corporation may use the cash method if its average gross receipts do not exceed $25 million.

7. The answer is D. To value inventory using the lower of cost or market method, compare the cost and the fair market value of each of the items in inventory, and choose the lower of the two tc obtain the inventory's value. The answer is calculated as follows:
(shirts $200 + shoes $200 + shorts $150) = $550 inventory valuation.

8. The answer is A. The income would be included in Banner's 2013 tax return, because Banner is using the accrual method of accounting for income and expenses. Under the accrual method, income is reported in the year earned and expenses are deducted in the year incurred. Since Banner sold the sofas in 2013, the income would be reported in 2013, regardless of when payment is received.

9. The answer is C. Since the corporation chose a calendar year, its first tax return is due March 15, 2014. This short period return will cover the period from April 1, 2013 through December 31, 2013. Corporate tax returns are due on the fifteenth day of the third month after the end of the corporation's tax year.

10. The answer is B. A taxpayer is subject to the uniform capitalization rules if he produces real or personal property for use in a trade or business. Producing items for personal use or as a hobby would not be subject to the UNICAP rules.

11. The answer is B. A taxpayer may use different methods of accounting for two distinct and separate businesses. Separate accounting books must be kept for each business.

12. The answer is C. According to the doctrine of constructive receipt, income is included in gross income when a person has an unqualified right to the funds. Constructive receipt must be more than just a billing, an offer, or a mere promise to pay. The amount promised to Ben as an IOU, therefore, does not have to be included in income for 2013.

13. The answer is A. Chris should include the consigned goods in his inventory, since he retains title to the goods on consignment until they are sold by the retailer. Merchandise sent COD is included in inventory until it reaches the buyer; at that time, title passes to the buyer when the item is delivered and paid for. Machinery and other fixed assets used by a business are not included in its inventory.

14. The answer is D. A corporation that produces audio recordings or films would be subject to UNICAP. Generally, the uniform capitalization rules apply to a taxpayer that produces property for use or resale in a business. A company that provides only services would not carry an inventory, so it is not subject to UNICAP. Independent (self-employed) authors, writers, and artists are exempt from the rules.

15. The answer is B. The shipping cost related to a purchase increases an asset's cost basis. If the property is merchandise bought for resale (such as inventory), the shipping cost is part of the cost of the merchandise and must be capitalized and later recovered as cost of goods sold when the watches are resold.

16. The answer is B. A business must adopt its first tax year by the due date (not including extensions) for filing a return for that year. A business adopts a tax year when it files its first income tax return.

17. The answer is A. Taxpayers must include direct and indirect costs in inventory. Taxpayers may claim a casualty or theft loss of inventory by increasing the cost of goods sold to properly report beginning and ending inventories. Taxpayers may choose to use different accounting methods for different businesses, so long as the businesses are kept separate and distinct accounting records are maintained for each.

18. The answer is A. Resellers of property with annual gross receipts of $10 million or less are exempt from UNICAP. A reseller with average annual gross receipts of $25 million would be subject to UNICAP.

19. The answer is B. The COGS is $26,600 ($15,600 beginning inventory + $20,000 purchases + $3,000 freight in, minus $12,000 ending inventory). Freight in and merchandise purchased for resale are part of the COGS.

Unit 3: Businesses Quiz Answers

1. The answer is D. Trade or business activities in which the taxpayer does not materially participate during the year are generally considered passive activities. Rental activities, even if the taxpayer does materially participate, are generally considered passive activities. However, there is an exception for real estate professionals. Portfolio income, such as interest, dividends, annuities, and royalties not derived in the ordinary course of a trade or business, or gain or loss from the disposition of property that produces these types of income or that is held for investment, is not passive activity income.

2. The answer is B. Canceled debt is not taxable income for a business to the extent that payment of the debt would have led to a business deduction.

3. The answer is B. The refundable security deposits are not taxable income, because those amounts are returned to the customer if the items rented are returned in good condition. The amounts included in gross income would be the rental income and the nonrefundable cleaning deposits ($50,000 + $1,500 = $51,500).

4. The answer is B. Certain items of income are excluded from gross income. Gross income does not include most types of compensation for physical injuries.

5. The answer is C. Under the rules of advance payment for services, Camille must recognize income from the eight lessons she gives in 2013 and the rest in 2014, regardless of whether she actually has given all of the lessons by the end of 2014.

6. The answer is A. Camille must include the entire payment in income in 2013 since some of the services may be performed after 2014.

7. The answer is D. In general, a rental activity cannot be grouped with a trade or business activity. However, they can be grouped together if the activities form an appropriate economic unit and:

- The rental activity is insubstantial to the trade or business activity,
- The trade or business activity is insubstantial in relation to the rental activity, or
- Each owner of the trade or business activity has the same ownership interest in the rental activity, in which case the part of the rental activity that involves the rental of items of property for use in the trade or business activity may be grouped with the trade or business activity.

8. The answer is B. Normally, rental income is not subject to employment taxes, and it is reported on Schedule E, *Supplemental Income and Loss*. However, as he is a real estate professional, Harley's income is subject to employment taxes and must be reported on Schedule SE as well as on Schedule C, *Profit or Loss for Business*.

9. The answer is D. Losses from passive activities that exceed the income from passive activities in a given year are generally disallowed. The losses may be carried forward to the next year. Generally, only when a taxpayer materially participates in a trade or business activity are his losses not limited.

10. The answer is A. Advance rental payments received under a lease must be recognized in the year received, regardless of which accounting method is used. This means that a taxpayer who owns rental properties and receives rent in advance cannot delay recognizing the income, even if the taxpayer is on the accrual basis.

11. The answer is C. Under the passive activity limitation rules, Sa'id would not be able to deduct the full amount of his losses in 2013. Since he had passive activity income of $31,000 in 2013, he can offset losses up to that amount. He can carry over the remaining losses of $6,500 to 2014.

12. The answer is D. As a cash-basis taxpayer, Allen's Exotic Pets would have been able to deduct the cost of the legal services as a business expense. It is therefore not required to recognize the canceled debt income.

13. The answer is C. Personal property has a similar name but should not be confused with "personal-use" property that a taxpayer uses for personal purposes rather than for business purposes. In a broad definition, personal property includes any asset other than real estate. Personal property is movable, unlike land and buildings that generally remain in one location.

14. The answer is D. A barter exchange of services between two sole proprietors would be business income. The fair market value of goods and services received in a barter exchange must be included in income by each party in the year received. If the two parties agree in advance to the fair market value of the goods or services being exchanged, the IRS will generally accept that amount as the FMV.

Unit 4: Businesses Quiz Answers

1. The answer is B. Many businesses, including self-employed individuals but not C corporations, may choose to use either the standard mileage rate or actual vehicle expenses in order to claim deductions for the cost of vehicles used in the business. However, a business is prohibited from using the standard mileage rate if it operates five or more vehicles at the same time.

2. The answer is C. The answer is $458 ($400 + $35 + $10 + [26 × 50%]). Her deductible meal expenses are subject to a 50% limit, but the taxi fare, the train ticket, and the seminar are fully deductible.

3. The answer is A. The partnership is on the cash basis; therefore, it can only deduct interest actually paid during the year. Since the partnership did not actually pay any interest, it does not have a deductible expense. The fact that the loan was refinanced has no bearing on the deductibility of the interest.

4. The answer is C. A taxpayer who is subject to the Department of Transportation's hours of service may deduct a larger percentage of his meal expenses when traveling away from his tax home. He would multiply his meal expenses incurred while away from home on business by the DOT hours of service limit of 80% ($3,064 × .80 = $2,451).

5. The answer is A. Self-employed taxpayers may deduct these contributions on Schedule A, subject to applicable AGI limits. The contributions cannot be deducted as a business expense on Schedule C. Only C corporations may deduct charitable contributions as a business expense, subject to a limit of 10% of taxable income.

6. The answer is D. The taxpayer is not required to prove that the entertainment event actually produced a profit. The taxpayer must meet either the directly-related test or the associated test in order to deduct an entertainment expense. The directly-related test requires that business was engaged in during the entertainment event; the main purpose was the conduct of business; and there was more than just the general expectation of business benefit.

7. The answer is B. Delia may deduct the cost of her hotel room, one-half of her meal expense, and her train ticket to attend the convention ($100 + $90 + (80 × 50%) = $230). The cost of the computer game is a personal expense and not deductible.

8. The answer is A. The repairs, property tax, and utilities are all deductible as business expenses. The property tax is deductible as a business expense on Schedule C (rather than on Schedule A) because it is assessed on business property. Assessments for streets, sidewalks, sewer lines, and other public services generally add value to the property and must be added to the basis of the property rather than deducted currently.

9. The answer is C. A loan to a client, customer, employee, or distributor for a business reason can be deducted as a business bad debt if it becomes worthless. The amount of the loan, minus what was repaid, is the deduction on Mountain Supplier's tax return: $10,000 - $2,000 = $8,000.

10. The answer is C. There is a $25 limit per person per tax year for business gifts; however, there are exceptions to this rule. Incidental costs, such as packaging, insuring, and mailing, are not included in determining the cost of a gift for purposes of the $25 limit, nor are certain promotional items. Therefore, the business may deduct $580($500 + $25 + $35 + $20) = $580:

- Glass display: $500
- Coffee and tea basket: $25 (only $25 is deductible as a gift expense)
- 20 imprinted pens: $35
- Postage for the gift basket: $20

11. The answer is C. Only the loan to the client would be deductible as a business bad debt expense. A loss related to a loan to a client, customer, employee, or distributor for a business reason can be deducted as a business bad debt. Since Keith is a related person and not a regular employee and the loan was for personal reasons, Bob may not deduct his loss on the loan to his brother as a business bad debt.

12. The answer is D. Since the advance payment covers more than 12 months (36 months), the $3,600 must be deducted ratably over the three-year period. To figure the monthly premium amount, the policy cost is divided by the coverage period: ($3,600 ÷ 36 = $100). The number of months of coverage in each tax year is then multiplied by the monthly premium:

- 2013: deduction $300 ($3,600 ÷ 36 × 3)
- 2014: deduction $1,200: ($3,600 ÷ 36 × 12)
- 2015: deduction $1,200 ($3,600 ÷ 36 × 12)
- 2016: deduction $900 ($3,600 ÷ 36 × 9)

13. The answer is B. Lily is not required to amend her prior year return to report the recovery of the bad debt. Since Lily recovered a bad debt that was deducted properly in a prior year, she must include the recovered portion as income in her current year tax return.

14. The answer is C. Generally, interest on a business loan is fully deductible. However, debt incurred for personal reasons is not deductible as a business expense. The amount of interest attributable to the portion of loan proceeds used to purchase the business machine is deductible, but not the amount for the jet ski, which is a personal expense.

15. The answer is A. If a taxpayer pays rent in advance, only the amount that applies to the current year is deductible. The balance must be deducted over the period to which it applies.

Supporting calculations:

Deductible lease expense for 2013:

\$1,620/36 (months) = \$45 per month

\$45 × 11 months (February-December 2013) = \$495

16. The answer is B. A taxpayer cannot deduct the costs of driving a car between his home and his main workplace. These costs are personal commuting expenses. The costs of driving to meet with clients or do other business-related errands are deductible.

17. The answer is D. Penalties paid for the late performance or non-performance of a contract are deductible. Penalties or fines paid to any government entity because of a violation of laws or regulations are not deductible.

18. The answer is C. A business may deduct up to \$5,000 in start-up costs. Start-up costs are costs incurred in creating an active trade or business or investigating the creation or acquisition of an active trade or business.

19. The answer is D. As a retailer, Only-a-Dollar acts as a collection agent for the taxing authorities. The amounts of taxes it collects and remits to them should be excluded from its taxable gross income and deductible expenses.

20. The answer is A. For an accrual-based taxpayer, business expenses are generally deducted or capitalized when both of the following apply:

- All events have occurred that fix the fact of liability, and the liability can be determined with reasonable accuracy.
- Economic performance has occurred: the property or services are provided or the property is used

In this instance, all events have occurred as of September 30, 2013 to fix the liability and the amount of the liability can be determined. There may, however, be a question as to whether economic performance has occurred by September 30, 2013, since it is unlikely that Affordable Pool Supplies would have used the entire shipment of supplies within two days of receipt. Nevertheless, an exception for recurring items allows certain expenses to be treated as incurred during the tax year even though economic performance has not occurred. The exception applies if all of the following requirements are met:

- The all-events test described above has been met.
- Economic performance occurs by the earlier of the following dates:
    - 8½ months after the close of the year.
    - The date the taxpayer files a timely return, including extensions, for the year.
- The item is recurring in nature and the taxpayer consistently treats similar items as incurred in the tax year in which the all-events test is met.
- And either:
    - The item is not material, or

- Accruing the item in the year in which the all-events test is met results in a better match against income than accruing the item in the year of economic performance.

It is likely that economic performance will have occurred within 8½ months after year-end, or by the time the tax return is filed for the 2013 year. Further, as a service business of modest size, Affordable Pool Supplies would not be required to maintain an inventory. Therefore, it may customarily record the full amount of supplies purchased as expenses when they are received and it could reasonably conclude that a shipment of $5,000 is not material to its operations. Accruing the expense as a deduction in its year ended September 30, 2013 would be consistent with the business's treatment of similar items in the past and thus result in better matching against 2013 income.

Unit 5: Businesses Quiz Answers

1. The answer is C. Under the rules for cafeteria plans, a key employee may include a 5% owner of the business, an officer with annual pay of more than $165,000, or a 1% owner of the business with annual pay of more than $150,000. Both A and B are correct in describing key employees.

2. The answer is B. The value of an employer-provided cell phone is only excludable from an employee's wages if it is given for a noncompensatory business purpose or is considered a de minimis benefit. A cell phone used to boost morale or in this case as a type of financial bonus would be taxable to the employee.

3. The answer is C. Employer-paid memberships at athletic facilities are generally taxable benefits. A workout area on the employer's premises is the exception.

4. The answer is A. Employers may exclude the value of meals and on-site lodging from an employee's wages if they are provided for the convenience of the employer. Meals provided to employees for the convenience of the employer are 100% deductible by the employer.

5. The answer is C. The value of a vehicle for personal use by an employee is a taxable benefit. If an employer provides a car for an employee's use, the amount that can be excluded as a working condition benefit is the amount that would be allowed as a deductible business expense if the employee paid for its use. There are exceptions for emergency personnel such as police officers who are required to use their emergency vehicles. Employee achievement awards may be exempt up to $1,600. Meals are exempt if either furnished for the employer's convenience or if considered de minimis, such as occasional snacks.

6. The answer is B. Travel reimbursements made under a nonaccountable plan are taxable to the employee as wages.

7. The answer is B. Although all of the expenses are qualified educational expenses, only the first $5,250 is excluded from Renee's wages as a qualified fringe benefit, and the remaining amount is taxable as wage income to her. If an employer pays more than $5,250 for educational benefits for an employee during the year, the excess is taxed as wages.

8. The answer is C. Gifts in cash or cash equivalents such as gift cards must be included in income. Fringe benefits that may be excluded from income include employee discounts, amounts reimbursed through a qualified flexible spending plan, and de minimis holiday gifts.

Unit 6: Businesses Quiz Answers

1. The answer is C. Selling food or beverages prepared at restaurants is specifically disallowed for purposes of the DPAD. Most U.S.-based manufacturing qualifies for the DPAD.

2. The answer is D. The losses due to the theft of business property would be allowed in figuring a net operating loss.

3. The answer is B. The amount of the Disabled Access Credit is 50% of the qualified expenses, but the maximum credit per year is $5,000.

4. The answer is D. Normally, businesses can carry back unused business credits one year and carry them forward for 20 years.

5. The answer is D. The WOTC offers credits to businesses who hire out-of-work veterans, as well as other individuals in eight different targeted groups.

6. The answer is B. In general, a net operating loss may be carried back to the two previous years, and the remaining loss may be carried forward to the subsequent 20 years.

7. The answer is B. The Investment Credit is the sum of five credits that are designed to spur investment in activity that reduces greenhouse emissions and rehabilitates historic property.
In 2013, the Investment Credit consists of the Rehabilitation and Energy Credits and the Advanced Coal, Advanced Energy, and Gasification Projects. There is no credit for hydroelectric power.

8. The answer is C. Only the casualty loss is potentially deductible for purposes of the net operating loss. Losses from the sale of stock are capital losses and cannot be used to create an NOL. Losses from the sale of personal-use property or a primary residence are not deductible.

9. The answer is A. The DPAD cannot be more than 50%, not 25%, of the wages a business pays its employees. All of the other statements are correct about this business deduction designed to stimulate manufacturing and other production activities in the United States.

10. The answer is C. The Disabled Access Credit is a nonrefundable tax credit for an eligible small business that pays expenses to provide access to disabled persons. The taxpayer must pay or incur the expenses to enable the business to comply with the Americans with Disabilities Act.

11. The answer is D. The DPAD is equal to 9% of the lesser of:

- Qualified production activities income (QPAI), or
- Adjusted gross income for an individual, estate, or trust (or taxable income for all other taxpayers) determined without regard to the DPAD.

Madhu's AGI of $165,000 was less than the company's QPAI of $2 million, so the answer is determined as follows: $165,000 × .9 = $14,850. The DPAD is also limited to 50% of Form W-2 wages paid to employees for the year, but this is not a factor since that amount is $220,000, much higher than Madhu's DPAD.

12. The answer is B. NOLs can generally be carried back two years. Any remaining amount of an NOL must be carried forward for up to 20 years.

Unit 7: Businesses Quiz Answers

1. The answer is A. Demolition costs or other losses related to the demolition of any building are added to the basis of the land.

2. The answer is D. Interest charges are not added to an asset's basis. Interest is a currently deductible expense.

3. The answer is C. Ian's basis is $196,000. The title fees, mortgage amount, and the down payment are added to figure the cost basis of the building. The points are not included in the basis.

4. The answer is A. Cheryl may not deduct the taxes as a current expense, since they are delinquent real estate taxes and the person who is legally liable for the debt is Alex. However, the taxes may be added to the property's basis and depreciated as part of her purchase price.

5. The answer is B. The cost of defending title to a property increases its basis.

6. The answer is C. Irina expects to be fully reimbursed for her loss, so reporting it on her 2013 return is not necessary. However, if Irina's insurance company reimbursement is ultimately either more or less than her loss, she may realize an additional gain or loss. Whether a gain would be taxable will depend on how she uses the insurance proceeds.

7. The answer is A. Under the new rules, an improvement is redefined as a cost involving a betterment of the unit of property, a restoration of the unit of property, or an adaptation of the unit of property to a new or different use.

8. The answer is D. A stock split increases the number of outstanding shares, which decreases the basis per share, but it does not change the basis of the stock as a whole.

9. The answer is C. The basis is the stock's purchase price plus the broker's fee ($3,500 + $100 = $3,600). After the stock split, Franco has 180 shares of stock [(50 shares + 40 shares) × 2 = 180]. The stock split reduces his per share basis by half to $20 ($3,600 ÷ 180 shares of stock = $20).

10. The answer is C. The basis is $307,500 ($250,000 + $13,000 + $35,000 + $9,500). The settlement fees, the mortgage assumed by the buyer, and the legal fees for defending the title are all included in the basis of the property. The property taxes are not included in the basis of the building because they were incurred when Priscilla was already the legal owner. Instead, the property taxes may be deducted as a current expense.

11. The answer is B. All items are added to the property's basis except for the points on the loan (an expense that is deducted over the life of the loan) and the construction loan ($125,000 + $20,000 + $10,000 + $50,000 + $300,000 = $505,000).

12. The answer is A. Marjorie must reduce the basis of her van by the portion of any insurance proceeds that are not used for repairs. Since she uses $500 of the proceeds to repair the windshield, the adjusted basis is $21,500 ($25,000 - $4,000 + $500 = $21,500.)

13. The answer is D. When property is transferred in lieu of wages, the employer is entitled to deduct its fair market value at the time of the transfer. A gain or loss is realized if there is a difference between the fair market value and the adjusted basis of the property. The transfer is treated as a sale, so Chan Delivery would have to report a gain. Chan Delivery should deduct $7,000 as wage expense and report the gain on the sale of the truck, figured as follows: ($7,000 - $5,500) = $1,500.

14. The answer is A. Bramble Partnership must include the FMV of the coins ($5,000) and the FMV of the scooter ($2,000) as income. Property exchanged for services must be included as income at its fair market value.

15. The answer is D. Improvements to a property cannot be deducted currently; they must be capitalized.

Unit 8: Businesses Quiz Answers

1. The answer is B. Taxpayers may deduct up to $250,000 of qualified real property (QRP) under section 179. This special allowance for QRP is included within the maximum $500,000 section 179 limit. For example, a taxpayer can claim $250,000 for QRP and $250,000 for other business property to use the $500,000 section 179 depreciation allowance.

2. The answer is C. Goodwill and a covenant not to compete are both section 197 intangible assets. A business must amortize over 15 years (180 months) the capitalized costs of section 197 intangibles.

3. The answer is D. A gasoline refinery would not qualify since its activity involves refining a product rather than the depletion of a natural resource. Depletion is the exhaustion of natural resources, such as mines, wells, and timber, as a result of production.

4. The answer is B. The computers do not qualify as section 179 property because Levi and his grandfather are related persons, meaning Levi cannot claim a section 179 deduction. However, Levi may still depreciate the computers using the MACRS depreciation schedule.

5. The answer is A. Tangible personal property generally qualifies for the section 179 deduction. With the exception of certain qualified real property (QRP), most real property generally does not qualify for section 179 treatment. Intangible assets do not qualify for section 179 treatment.

6. The answer is C. The business part of the cost of the property is $825 (75% × $1,100).

7. The answer is A. When a taxpayer uses property for both business and nonbusiness purposes, he can elect the section 179 deduction only if he uses the property more than 50% for business in the year the asset is placed into service. Lou may nevertheless claim depreciation deductions for the business portion of the phone.

8. The answer is B. Kerman may consider the truck to have been placed in service when it is ready for its intended purpose, which was on January 10, 2014. Kerman does not actually need to use it for that purpose in order to begin depreciation.

9. The answer is A. Property placed in service and disposed of in the same year is not depreciated.

10. The answer is B. Regular passenger automobiles weighing 6,000 pounds or less are listed property.

11. The answer is B. The corporation must reduce its section 179 dollar limit by $25,000, the amount of its qualifying purchases that exceeds the $2 million limit ($2,025,000 - $2,000,000). Its maximum section

179 deduction is $475,000 ($500,000 - $25,000). The corporation's taxable income from the active conduct of all its trades or businesses for the year was $600,000, so it can deduct the full $475,000.

12. The answer is B. The section 179 deduction applies only to the amount actually paid in cash and not to the value of his trade-in allowance, and further applies only to the portion used for business purposes. Thus, the deduction is limited to 90% of $15,000, or $13,500.

13. The answer is C. The partnership's section 179 deduction for the $30,000 oven is limited to the partnership's income of $25,000. The deduction is split between the two partners ($25,000 × 50%) = $12,500. Section 179 is a separately stated item on a partnership tax return. Assuming she has no section 179 deductions from other sources, Lucy's deduction would be $12,500.

14. The answer is D. Commercial real property is depreciated over a 39-year recovery period.

Unit 9: Businesses Quiz Answers

1. The answer is B. The total gain on the sale is $17,000 ($25,000 - $8,000). Because the machine is section 1245 property, the partnership must recognize ordinary income of $12,000 (to recapture depreciation deductions taken on the machine) and the remaining $5,000 ($17,000 - $12,000) is treated as a capital gain.

2. The answer is A. An installment sale can trigger recapture. If a business reports the sale of previously depreciated property using the installment method, any applicable depreciation recapture under section 1245 or 1250 is taxable as ordinary income in the year of sale.

3. The answer is B. Section 1245 property does not include real estate such as buildings and structural components. Storage structures such as oil and gas storage tanks, grain storage bins, and silos are not treated as buildings but as section 1245 property.

4. The answer is C. In order to qualify as section 1231 property, the property must have been held by the business for over one year.

5. The answer is D. Real property held for investment qualifies for like-kind exchange treatment. A personal residence, inventory, and common stock do not qualify under section 1031.

6. The answer is D. Because the business asset was held for less than one year, the business has an ordinary loss.

7. The answer is B. This transaction is treated as an involuntary conversion. Clovis recognizes a taxable gain of $20,000 ($310,000 - $290,000), equal to the portion of the insurance reimbursement that was not reinvested in replacement property. Clovis's unrecognized gain is $30,000, the difference between the $50,000 realized gain and the $20,000 recognized gain. The basis of the new property is as follows:

Cost of replacement property	$290,000
Minus gain not recognized	($30,000)
Basis of replacement property	**$260,000**

If Clovis had reinvested all the insurance proceeds in a new property, the entire gain would have been deferred.

8. The answer is A. Generally, an exchange of real property qualifies as a nontaxable exchange under section 1031. In a nontaxable exchange situation, the FMV of the properties exchanged may have no bearing on the basis of the property received. In this case, the basis of the new property is the same as the basis of the old property ($125,000).

9. The answer is B. Since the amount realized from the sale is less than Jennifer's original cost for the chairs, the entire gain of $3,500 is treated as depreciation recapture, which is subject to ordinary income tax rates. She reports the sale on Form 4797 and Schedule C.

10. The answer is B. The first $20,000 is considered section 1245 recapture and is taxed as ordinary income. The remaining $5,000 is considered section 1231 capital gain.

11. The answer is B. The exchange of livestock of different sexes does not qualify. The exchange of real estate for real estate and the exchange of business property for similar business property are exchanges of like-kind property.

12. The answer is C. Scott's basis is $190,000 ($155,000 of cash paid plus the $35,000 adjusted basis of the old plane).

13. The answer is A. This exchange qualifies as a nontaxable exchange for Karabell. Any gain on the exchange is deferred until the new asset is later disposed of. The $6,000 of cash is added to the basis of the old truck to determine the basis of the new truck.

14. The answer is B. In a related-party exchange, the nonrecognition treatment will generally be lost if either property in the exchange is disposed of within two years. However, the section 1031 exchange will still be valid if either party in the transaction dies, or if the property is subject to an involuntary conversion.

15. The answer is A. The exchange of a vacant lot for a tract of farmland qualifies for like-kind exchange treatment. Section 1031 specifically excludes exchanges of inventory; stocks, bonds, notes, or other securities; partnership interests; livestock of different sexes; and property used predominantly in the United States for property used predominantly outside the United States. Properties are like-kind if they are of the same nature or character, even if they differ in grade or quality.

16. The answer is C. The adjusted basis of the old printer was $4,000 ($5,000 - $1,000 depreciation). She paid an additional $2,000 to acquire the new printer. Therefore, the basis of the new model is:

Old model adjusted basis	$4,000
Cash paid	$2,000
Basis of new model	**$6,000**

17. The answer is D. A taxpayer and a member of his immediate family are related persons for purposes of like-kind exchanges. Any business in which the taxpayer has ownership of over 50% is also considered a related person.

18. The answer is B. The disposition of the property results in a gain of $27,000, equal to the proceeds of $100,000 less adjusted basis of $73,000 (purchase price of $120,000 less depreciation and section 179 deductions of $47,000). Because this was section 1245 property, the gain is characterized as ordinary income to the lesser of the actual gain or the amount of depreciation and section 179 expenses recaptured ($47,000).

Supporting calculations:

Purchase price	$120,000
Less depreciation and section 179 deductions	($47,000)
Adjusted basis at date of sale	**$73,000**

Proceeds	100,000
Gain on sale	**$27,000**
Potential depreciation recapture (as ordinary income)	**$47,000**

19. The answer is A. The basis of the saw is $7,000 (the $3,000 basis of the old asset plus the $4,000 paid).

20. The answer is C. Sadie has a gain of $35,000, equal to the difference between her sales proceeds of $65,000 and her adjusted basis of $30,000 (cost of $90,000 less accumulated depreciation of $60,000). Although she has had the property for more than one year, it is personal property classified as section 1245 property and therefore is subject to depreciation recapture to the extent of the entire amount of depreciation (and section 179 deductions) taken. Since this amount exceeds her gain, the entire amount of the gain is treated as ordinary income.

21. The answer is C. Ahmed's gross profit is $150,000 ($300,000 selling price - $150,000 adjusted basis), and the gross profit percentage is 50% ($150,000 ÷ $300,000). Ahmed must report half of each payment received as gain from the sale. He must also report all interest received as ordinary income.

Unit 10: Businesses Quiz Answers

1. The answer is C. The partnership may choose to either deduct or amortize the amounts for legal fees and consulting expenses ($2,000 + $1,000 = $3,000). However, the amount paid in commissions to a broker to market partnership interests must be capitalized and cannot be amortized or deducted. The costs for marketing and issuing interests in the partnership such as brokerage, registration, legal fees, and printing costs are syndication costs that are not deductible or amortizable.

2. The answer is A. The IRS requires partnerships with more than 100 partners (Schedules K-1) to file their returns electronically. Partnerships with 100 or fewer partners are not required to electronically file their returns.

3. The answer is A. This loan amount is included in Charlotte's basis in the partnership because she has an economic risk of loss related to this liability. An additional $60,000 of basis in the partnership's depreciable property was created as a result of incurring this debt. Her basis in the partnership would be $80,000 ($20,000 + $60,000), while Todd's basis would be only $20,000.

4. The answer is B. A limited partner generally has no obligation to contribute additional capital to the partnership. Therefore, absent some other factor such as the guarantee of a partnership liability by the limited partner or the limited partner making a loan to the partnership, a limited partner generally does not have an economic risk of loss in connection with the partnership's recourse liabilities.

5. The answer is A. Usually, neither the partner nor the partnership recognizes a gain or loss when property is contributed to the partnership in exchange for a partnership interest. This applies whether a partnership is being formed or is already operating. However, if an asset is encumbered by a liability, such as a mortgage, there is a possibility that the partner will recognize a gain in connection with the contribution.

6. The answer is B. Form 7004, *Automatic Extension of Time to File Certain Business Income Tax, Information, and Other Returns*, is used by partnerships to extend their filing deadline for five months.

7. The answer is A. The profits are allocated according to the partnership agreement. Jose's distributive share is calculated as follows: 35% × $200,000 = $70,000. Carlos's share is calculated as follows: 65% × $200,000 = $130,000.

8. The answer is A. The rental income, tax exempt income, and charitable contributions are all separately stated items that do not affect the calculation of ordinary income. Instead, each partner's share of the separately stated items is passed through to him. The partnership's ordinary income is split evenly, so Hassid's portion is as follows:

($200,000 - $30,000) = $170,000
$170,000 × 50% = $85,000

9. The answer is D. Guaranteed payments are made by a partnership to a partner and determined without regard to the partnership's income. A partnership treats guaranteed payments for services, or for the use of capital, as a business expense, just as if they were made to a person who is not a partner.

10. The answer is D. The penalty for late filing is $195 per month for each partner, for up to 12 months. The penalty is calculated as follows: $195 × 3 months × 7 partners = $4,095.

11. The answer is B. The guaranteed payment must be deducted before figuring each partner's distributive share. The answer is figured as follows:

$50,000 - $21,000 = $29,000
$29,000 × 50% = $14,500

Guaranteed payments are deducted from partnership income before determining the distributive share of income or loss for each partner.

12. The answer is B. All of the items listed are included in the calculation of ordinary income except the charitable contributions and the rental income, both of which must be separately stated on Form 1065. Thus, ordinary income will be $115,000 ($250,000 - $50,000 - $5,000 - $5,000 - $75,000). Like the other deductions listed, guaranteed payments to partners are treated as a deduction in determining ordinary income or loss.

13. The answer is A. Partnership income, including tax-exempt interest, increases a partner's basis in his partnership interest.

14. The answer is C. If a partner's share of partnership liabilities increases, this increase is treated as a contribution of money by the partner to the partnership. The debt is included in the bases of the three partners who signed the personal guarantees. Since Theresa does not have an economic risk of loss for this liability, the liability does not increase her basis. The basis for each of the other partners would include his or her share of the liability ([\$135,000 ÷ 3 partners] = \$45,000 + \$10,000 cash investment).

15. The answer is B. The assumption of partnership debt by Daniel increases his basis. If a partner's share of partnership liabilities increases, or a partner's individual liabilities increase because he assumes partnership liabilities, it is treated as if the partner made a contribution to the partnership.

16. The answer is C. Bissinger's ordinary income for 2013 is equal to its sales income less cost of goods sold and wages (\$75,000 - \$10,000 - \$15,000 = \$50,000). The income from rental real estate and the charitable contributions must be separately stated on the partnership's tax return.

17. The answer is D. Interest income and short-term capital losses are separately stated items that flow through to each partner and retain their character. The other items listed are components of ordinary income, determined as follows: gross sales of \$270,000, less cost of goods sold of \$80,000 and wages of \$50,000 = ordinary income of \$140,000. Absent any provisions in the partnership agreement to the contrary, both ordinary income and the separately stated items would be allocated according to the 60%/40% profit-sharing arrangement.

18. The answer is D. The basis of Monica's partnership interest is the adjusted basis of the property she contributes (\$4,000) less the portion of the related mortgage liability assumed by the other partners (60% × \$1,000 = \$600), or \$3,400.

19. The answer is B. The basis of Bea's partnership interest should be the adjusted basis of the property contributed (\$25,000) less the portion of the mortgage liability assumed by the other partners (70% × \$40,000 = \$28,000). However, this would result in a basis of negative \$3,000, and a partner's basis in a partnership can never go below zero. In order to avoid creating a negative basis, Bea must recognize a gain of \$3,000.

20. The answer is C. The at-risk rules limit the deductibility of losses to the partner's basis, not including his share of any of the partnership's nonrecourse debt.

21. The answer is C. Derrick must include \$10,000 of ordinary income from the partnership on his tax return. The answer is figured as follows:

1. \$55,000 - \$5,000 guaranteed payment = \$50,000 of ordinary income
2. \$50,000 × 10% = \$5,000 Derrick's share of the partnership's ordinary income
3. (\$5,000 guaranteed payment + \$5,000 (\$50,000 × 10%) distributive share) = \$10,000

Guaranteed payments are determined without regard to the partnership's income. They are deducted as a business expense when figuring the partnership's ordinary income. The individual partner who receives the guaranteed payments reports the payments on Schedule E (Form 1040) as ordinary income, along with his distributive share of the partnership's ordinary income.

Unit 11: Businesses Quiz Answers

1. The answer is A. A loss is not allowed from a sale or exchange of property directly or indirectly between a partnership and a person whose direct or indirect interest in the capital or profits of the partnership is more than 50%. In this case, Marvin and Geoff own a combined interest of 70% in the Davisville Partnership, and they indirectly own over 50% in Winters Partnership. (Since Marvin and Geoff's daughter own a combined interest of 85% in Dixon Corporation, their indirect interest in Winters Partnership is 85% × 80%, or 68%.)

2. The answer is A. Because the sum of cash and the adjusted basis of the property does not exceed the basis of her partnership interest, Allison does not recognize any gain on the distribution. Any gain on the machinery will be recognized when she sells it.

3. The answer is B. Steve's basis for the van is limited to $6,000 ($10,000 basis - $4,000, the cash he receives), equal to the remaining basis in his partnership interest after subtracting the cash received. After the distributions, his basis in the partnership interest is zero.

4. The answer is A. A retiring partner or the successor in interest of a deceased partner recognizes gain to the extent that any cash (and marketable securities treated as cash) distributed is more than the partner's adjusted basis in the partnership. Marty must recognize $15,000 of capital gain. This is the difference between his adjusted basis in the partnership and the amount of his distribution ($65,000 - $50,000).

5. The answer is C. If a business partnership dissolves and one of the former partners is insolvent and cannot pay his share of the partnership's debts, other partners may have to pay more than their respective shares. If a partner pays any part of the insolvent partner's share of the debts, she can take a bad debt deduction for the amount paid. Ellen is allowed to take a bad debt deduction for the liabilities she must pay that are in excess of her share of partnership liabilities.

6. The answer is D. When Laney sold her partnership interest, she was relieved of her $12,500 share of the partnership's liabilities, so her adjusted basis for purposes of calculating her gain on sale of the interest is $17,000 ($29,500 - $12,500). Thus, her gain is $28,000 (proceeds of $45,000 less adjusted basis of $17,000). Approached differently, the amount of liability relieved from Laney upon sale of her interest might be viewed as additional proceeds, but her gain would still be $28,000 ($45,000 + $12,500 - $29,500). As a partnership interest is a capital asset, any gain or loss recognized on the sale of the interest is typically treated as a capital gain or loss.

7. The answer is A. Shanahan Partnership's loss of $2,400 is not deductible. A loss on the sale or exchange of property between related persons is not deductible. This applies to both direct and indirect transactions. The fact that Bill and Veronica file separate tax returns does not prevent them from being related parties for purposes of this transaction.

8. The answer is A. Because the total of cash and the basis of property distributed ($9,000 + $2,500 = $11,500) does not exceed Adrian's adjusted basis of $17,500 in his partnership interest, he will recognize no gain as a result of the distribution. He assumes the partnership's adjusted basis of $2,500 in the property received, and will recognize gain or loss if he later sells this property.

9. The answer is C. Alice's basis on December 31, 2013 would be determined as follows:

Supporting calculation:
($11,000 + $20,000 + $350 = $31,350)

Basis at January 1, 2013	$11,000
50% share of ordinary business income	$20,000
50% share of tax-exempt interest income	$350
Basis at December 31, 2013	$31,350

10. The answer is A. Hugo's basis for the distributed property is limited to $70,000 ($150,000 - $80,000, the cash received). In a nonliquidating distribution, the basis of property (other than cash) distributed to the partner by a partnership is the adjusted basis to the partnership immediately before the distribution. However, the basis of the property distributed to the partner cannot be more than the adjusted basis of his interest in the partnership.

11. The answer is C. Nina recognizes no gain because the total of cash and the basis of property received does not exceed her basis in the partnership. She assumes the partnership's basis of $1,500 in the property received, and may recognize gain or loss if she later sells the property.

Unit 12: Businesses Quiz Answers

1. The answer is D. Based upon the information provided, Lightning Forecasting Corporation's taxable income would be calculated as follows:

Net income for books	$3,000,000
Plus federal income tax expense	1,500,000
Plus 50% of travel and entertainment expenses	100,000
Plus excess of capital losses over capital gains	29,000
Less tax-exempt interest income	(100,000)
Taxable income	**$4,529,000**

A corporation must generally report on either Schedule M-1 or Schedule M-3 the items that reconcile from net income (loss) on their books to taxable income reported on the return. Specific examples may include:

- Excess of capital losses over capital gains.
- Charitable contribution carryover (the amount of charitable contributions that are disallowed and must be carried over to the next taxable year.)
- Travel and entertainment in excess of the allowable 50% limit.
- Federal income taxes paid or accrued, which are deductible for accounting purposes but not for tax purposes.
- Advance rental income.
- Differences in book and tax depreciation.

2. The answer is C. Allowing shareholders to draw personal loans from a corporation is not a valid reason for a corporation to accumulate earnings. In fact, this is one of the items the IRS looks for that may lead to imposing the accumulated earnings tax upon a corporation. Making loans to shareholders would allow them to access the corporation's earnings without taking taxable distributions.

3. The answer is B. A single member LLC will be taxed as a sole proprietorship unless an election is made by filing Form 8832, *Entity Classification Election.* The rest of the choices are automatically required to be taxed as corporations.

4. The answer is C. Nell must recognize a taxable gain of \$100,000 (\$300,000 FMV of stock minus \$200,000 basis) on the transaction. IRC section 351 provides that no gain or loss will be recognized if property is transferred to a corporation solely in exchange for stock, if immediately after the exchange the shareholder is in control of the corporation. However, Nell did not control the corporation after the transfer. In order to be in control of a corporation, the transferor must own, immediately after the exchange, at least 80% of the total combined voting power of all classes of stock entitled to vote and at least 80% of the outstanding shares of each class of nonvoting stock. Since Nell owns only 65% of the shares, the exchange is taxable.

5. The answer is C. The accumulated earnings tax is levied at a rate of 15% of accumulated taxable income.

6. The answer is C. John recognizes ordinary income of \$6,000 as payment for services he rendered to the corporation. Normally, the exchange of money or property for a controlling interest in a corporation is treated as a nontaxable exchange. However, the exchange of services for stock does not qualify for this treatment. The value of stock received in exchange for services is taxed as income to the recipient.

7. The answer is D. If a corporation's tentative minimum tax exceeds the regular tax, the excess amount is payable in addition to the regular tax.

8. The answer is A. If a corporation fails to make estimated tax payments, there is a late payment penalty of one-half of one percent per month, up to a maximum of 25%.

9. The answer is B. If a shareholder contributes property to a corporation, he generally recognizes gain. The basis of the contributed property to the corporation is the same as the basis that the shareholder had in the property, after increase for any gain that the shareholder recognized in the exchange. There is an exception for situations in which property is contributed and the shareholder controls the corporation immediately after the transfer. In order to be considered in control of a corporation immediately after the exchange, the transferors must own at least 80% of the total combined voting power of all classes of stock entitled to vote and at least 80% of the outstanding shares of each class of nonvoting stock. In this case, Lori and Marcus do not own at least 80% of the corporation immediately afterward, so the exception does not apply.

10. The answer is A. The due date for BRB Corporation's income tax return is September 15. Generally, a corporation must file its income tax return by the fifteenth day of the third month after the end of its tax year.

11. The answer is D. The corporation does not have to make estimated payments if it expects to post a tax loss for the year. A corporation must make installment payments of estimated tax only if it expects its estimated tax for the year to be \$500 or more. However, it should be noted that payment of 100% of the prior year's liability, as in answer C, would provide a safe harbor in the event that the corporation does have taxable income and a related tax liability in 2013.

12. The answer is C. In situations where a shareholder contributes property for stock in a corporation and controls the corporation immediately after the transfer, she typically would not recognize gain. However, if the shareholder receives money or property in addition to the corporation's stock in exchange for her contribution of property, she would recognize gain to the extent of any money received plus the FMV of property received. In this case, Kathleen's realized gain is calculated as follows:

Fair value of stock received	$75,000
Cash received	$20,000
Mortgage assumed by corporation	$25,000
Total fair value received	$120,000
Adjusted basis of property	($70,000)
Realized gain	**$50,000**

Kathleen recognizes gain only to the extent of the cash received ($20,000).

13. The answer is A. Installments for corporations are due by the fifteenth day of the fourth, sixth, ninth, and twelfth months of the year. For example, a calendar-year corporation would have estimated tax due dates of April 15, June 15, September 15, and December 15.

14. The answer is A. In situations where a shareholder contributes property for stock in a corporation and controls the corporation immediately after the transfer, he typically would not recognize gain. However, if the shareholder receives money or property in addition to the corporation's stock in exchange for his contribution of property, he would recognize gain to the extent of any money received plus the fair market value of property received. If the corporation assumes the shareholder's liabilities, the assumption generally is not treated as if the shareholder received money for this property. However, if the liabilities the corporation assumes are more than the shareholder's adjusted basis in the property transferred, gain is recognized up to the difference. In this case, Vihaan's realized gain is calculated as follows:

Supporting calculations:

Fair value of stock received	$150,000
Mortgage assumed by corporation	$25,000
Total fair value received	$175,000
Adjusted basis of property	($10,000)
Realized gain	**$165,000**

Vihaan recognizes gain to the extent the mortgage assumed ($25,000) exceeds his basis in the property contributed ($10,000), or $15,000.

Unit 13: Businesses Quiz Answers

1. The answer is C. The dividends deduction for less-than-20% owned stock is generally 70%.

2. The answer is A. A corporation is not required to carry back losses. It may elect to forgo the carryback period. Net operating losses can be carried back to the two years before the loss year and forward for up to 20 years following the loss year.

3. The answer is B. Davidson Corporation cannot deduct the full $8,000 (80% × $10,000) dividends-received deduction that would normally apply based upon its 50% ownership because doing so would not result in a net operating loss. The deduction is instead limited to 80% of taxable income (before applying the DRD), which is $6,400 (80% × $8,000).

Taxable Income:	$8,000
Minus DRD:	($6,400)
Income after DRD:	**$1,600**

4. The answer is C. The corporation can have until March 15 of the following year to pay the contribution. A corporation using the accrual method can choose to deduct unpaid contributions for the tax year if the board of directors authorizes the contribution during the tax year, and the corporation pays the contribution within 2.5 months after the close of the year.

5. The answer is C. The corporation may carry back the $6,000 capital loss ($29,000 - $23,000) to the earliest of the three preceding years, where it may be deducted against short-term capital gains. Any remaining losses can be carried forward for up to five years. The corporation treats this $6,000 as a short-term loss when carried back or forward, because capital loss carrybacks and carryforwards do not retain their original character.

6. The answer is B. The corporation would not have an NOL after applying the full dividends-received deduction, so its allowable dividends-received deduction is limited to 80% of its taxable income (before applying the DRD), or $68,000 ($85,000 × 80%).

7. The answer is B. If a corporation receiving dividends owns 20% or more of the corporation issuing the dividends, it generally qualifies for a dividends-received deduction equal to 80% of the dividends received. It can deduct amounts up to 80% of its taxable income, calculated without regard to the DRD itself and certain other items.

8. The answer is D. The corporation can carry over excess charitable contributions made during the year that result from the 10% limit on deductibility to each of the subsequent five years. Any excess charitable contributions that are not used in this five-year period are lost. A corporation cannot carry back excess charitable contributions.

9. The answer is D. A parent-subsidiary controlled group involves a parent corporation that owns at least 80% or more of the voting power of at least one other corporation. A controlled group is allowed a single set of graduated income tax brackets, a single exemption amount for AMT purposes, and a single accumulated earnings credit of $250,000.
Members of controlled groups are also subject to rules regarding related party transactions that may require deferral of recognition for losses or expenses incurred by one party.

10. The answer is C. Generally, if a corporation receives dividends from another corporation in which it owns an interest of 20% to 80%, it is entitled to a deduction of 80% of the dividends received, subject to limitation based upon its taxable income without regard to the DRD and certain other items. Since Redd owns 25% of Helena, its DRD is $116,000 ($145,000 × 80%).

11. The answer is C. Arbabi Plastics' deductible charitable contributions are limited to 10% of its taxable income, before consideration of the following items:

- The deduction for charitable contributions
- The dividends-received deduction
- The domestic production activities deduction
- Any net operating loss carryback to the tax year
- Any capital loss carryback to the tax year

Qualifying contributions in excess of this limitation can be carried over for five years. In this case, $40,000 ($400,000 × 10%) would be deductible, and $10,000 would be carried over to the next year.

12. The answer is A. A C corporation may deduct charitable contributions made to qualified organizations, up to 10% of taxable income. Taxable income for this purpose is determined without regard to certain items, including the charitable contribution deduction itself and any net operating loss carryback (but not carryforward) to the tax year. Therefore, Bernardino Jewelry's charitable contribution deduction would be determined as follows:

Gross receipts	$95,000
Expenses	($65,000)
Net capital gains	$10,000
NOL from 2012	($30,000)
Taxable income before contribution deduction	$10,000
Deduction limit at 10%	$1,000

13. The answer is C. A brother-sister controlled group is when five or fewer individuals, estates, or trusts own 80% or more of the combined voting power for multiple corporations, and have identical common owner ship within the individual corporations of at least 50%. Despite the name, the owners do not have to be related as siblings.

Unit 14: Businesses Quiz Answers

1. The answer is D. Generally, distributions of stock and stock rights are not taxable to shareholders and not deductible by the corporation.

2. The answer is C. Mark has a $19,000 long-term capital gain. His basis in the stock was $1,000 [100 shares stock × $10], so his gain is figured as follows: ($20,000 - $1,000). Gain or loss recognized by shareholders on distributions in a corporate liquidation is generally determined by the difference between the total of the cash and property received by the shareholders and the basis of the stock they surrendered. The gain or loss will be long-term or short-term depending on the length of time the stock was held. Since Mark purchased the shares several years ago, his holding period exceeds one year and is therefore recognized as long-term capital gain on his return.

3. The answer is A. If a corporation cancels a shareholder's debt without repayment by the shareholder, the amount canceled is treated as a distribution to the shareholder.

4. The answer is D. Salaries or wages paid to an employee-shareholder are not considered a distribution. Instead, the wages would be treated as a business expense just like wages for the corporation's other employees. The wages are deductible by the corporation and taxable to the employee-shareholder.

5. The answer is B. A corporation will recognize a gain on the distribution of property to a shareholder if the FMV of the property is more than its adjusted basis ($60,000 FMV - $40,000 adjusted basis = $20,000 gain). This is the same treatment that would apply if the property were sold for its FMV.

6. The answer is D. The liquidating distribution is not taxable until the shareholder's stock basis ($20,000) has been recovered. Geraldine recovered $16,000 of her basis in 2013 and the remaining balance of $4,000 in 2014. Her recognized gain is $36,000 ($56,000 total distribution - $20,000 basis). She will recognize no gain or loss in 2013, but must recognize $36,000 of capital gain in 2014.

7. The answer is A. If the shareholder has an option to receive cash instead of stock rights, the distributions of stock and stock rights are taxable.

8. The answer is C. A distribution of property to a shareholder is treated as if the corporation had sold the property to the shareholder. The corporation recognizes gain on the distribution if the FMV of the property is more than its adjusted basis. The FMV is considered to be the greater of the property's actual FMV or the amount of liability the shareholder assumes in connection with the distribution. In this case, the FMV is considered to be the liability of $6,000 assumed by Joseph, so Midwestern Grain must recognize a gain of $5,000 ($6,000 – adjusted basis of $1,000).

9. The answer is C. The corporation must recognize a gain for any property distributed that has an FMV higher than its adjusted basis. This is the same treatment the corporation would receive if the property were sold for its FMV. The answer is figured as follows:

FMV of distribution	$250,000
Subtract adjusted basis	$100,000
Recognized gain	**$150,000**

It should be noted that the FMV of $250,000 is also reported as a distribution to the shareholder, and will be his basis in the painting.

10. The answer is A. When the basis of a shareholder's stock has been reduced to zero, the shareholder must report any additional return of capital received as a capital gain. Since April has held the stock for more than one year, the gain is reported as a long-term capital gain.

11. The answer is C. The capital gain is figured as follows: Her basis is $5,000 ($50 × 100 shares). The excess of her portion of the distribution over her basis ($12,000 distribution - $5,000 basis) results in a $7,000 capital gain.

12. The answer is A. Distributions from a C corporation are deducted first from current E&P, and then from any accumulated E&P. Any part of a distribution from current-year E&P or accumulated E&P is reported as dividend income to the shareholder. If a corporation's current E&P are less than the total distributions made during the year, part or all of each distribution is treated as a distribution of accumulated E&P. Since Millerton's distributions during the year ($20,000) were more than its current year E&P of $15,000 ($150,000 - $140,000 + $5,000), the amount of each distribution is treated as having been paid partially from current year E&P [in the ratio of current E&P for the year to total distributions for the year ($15,000/$20,000) × $5,000 = $3,750].The remainder of each distribution ($5,000 - $3,750 = $1,250) is treated as having been paid from accumulated E&P.

Unit 15: Businesses Quiz Answers

1. The answer is C. After recognizing her 50% share of Verrengia's income for the year, the basis of Sydney's stock is $14,000. In connection with the distribution, Verrengia recognizes a gain of $4,000, half of which is passed through to Sydney. Since her basis exceeds the FMV of the property distributed, the distribution itself is treated entirely as return of capital, and she recognizes no additional income. The calculations are as follows:

Adjusted basis – 1/1/2013	$13,000
S corp income × 50%	1,000
Adjusted basis before distribution	14,000
Gain from distribution	2,000
Subtotal	16,000
FMV of machine	(7,000)
Remaining basis	**$9,000**

2. The answer is C. An S election may be revoked if shareholders holding more than 50% of the stock consent. Since Nora and Jordan together own more than 50% of the outstanding stock, they can elect to revoke the S election.

3. The answer is C. Spouses are automatically treated as a single shareholder, and when a shareholder dies, the deceased shareholder's spouse and the estate are still considered one shareholder for the purpose of the shareholder limit. A husband and wife cannot be considered a single shareholder if they divorce, or if the marriage is dissolved for any reason other than death. An S corporation cannot have a nonresident alien member, so a nonresident alien spouse would not qualify.

4. The answer is A. All of the items, except for the gross receipts, must be separately stated on the S corporation's tax return. The total of the separately stated items is figured as follows:

• Rental activities:	$300,000
• Interest income	$25,000
• Royalty income	$10,000
• Section 1231 gain	$20,000
Total separately stated items	**$355,000**

5. The answer is A. Distributions from an S corporation with no accumulated E&P are generally treated as a nontaxable return of capital, up to the amount of the shareholder's adjusted stock basis. However, if an S corporation distributes appreciated property, the distribution is treated as a sale to the shareholder. To the extent the FMV of the property exceeds the corporation's basis, the corporation would recognize gain. The gain passes through to the shareholders and increases the basis of their stock. The answer is calculated as follows:

Adjusted basis 1/1/2013:	$50,000
S corporation net income	$0
Gain related to distribution	$13,000
Adjusted basis 12/31/13:	$63,000
Distribution	
FMV of property:	$75,000
Less shareholder's basis:	$63,000
Additional capital gain:	**$12,000**

Francisco must report $25,000 of capital gain income on his tax return. This includes the gain of $13,000 recognized by the corporation and passed through to him. In addition, since the distribution reduces the basis of his stock to zero, the amount exceeding his basis ($12,000) is also treated as capital gain.

6. The answer is D. Excess net passive income earned by S corporations is taxed at a rate of 35%.

7. The answer is C. An S corporation may own stock in a C corporation but it cannot have a C corporation as a shareholder. S corporation shareholders must generally be U.S. citizens or U.S. residents, and must be physical entities (persons), so corporate shareholders and partnerships are excluded. Certain estates, trusts, and tax-exempt corporations, including 501(c)(3) corporations, are also permitted to be shareholders.

8. The answer is A. An S corporation shareholder may deduct his share of the corporation's losses only to the extent of his stock and debt basis. Before consideration of Rancho Sendero's 2013 loss, Seth's stock basis and debt basis were $100,000 and $20,000, respectively. Therefore, he can deduct his entire 50% share of the company's ordinary loss.

9. The answer is B. Adrienne's basis is calculated as follows:

Basis at December 31, 2012	$2,000
Contribution of patent	$1,000
50% share of 2013 income:	
• Royalty income	$2,500
• Ordinary income	$1,250
Basis prior to consideration of distribution	$6,750
50% share of gain related to patent	$2,000
Distribution of patent, at FMV	(5,000)
Subtotal	**$3,750**
50% share of section 179 deduction	(250)
Basis at December 31, 2013	**$3,500**

10. The answer is B. A C corporation can elect to become an S corporation if it otherwise qualifies. Only domestic U.S. corporations are allowed to elect S status. An S corporation can only have one class of stock, but differences in voting rights are allowed. An S corporation can have a fiscal year if it has a legitimate business purpose for doing so.

11. The answer is A. An eligible corporation must make an S election within two months and 15 days from the start of its tax year (or within 2.5 months of its inception). Since Bettendorf is a calendar-year corporation, its tax year begins January 1. It must make the election on or before March 15, in order to be effective for that year.

12. The answer is B. Ordinary income would reflect the gross receipts of $300,000 less salary expense to the shareholder of $20,000, or $280,000. Interest income and royalty income would be separately stated items on Form 1120S, but would not be considered in determining ordinary income or loss. The amount is figured as follows: ($300,000 - $20,000 = $280,000).

13. The answer is A. If an S corporation distributes appreciated property, the distribution is treated as if the property had been sold to the shareholder. To the extent the FMV of the property exceeds the corporation's basis, the corporation would recognize gain. The gain passes through to the shareholders and increases the basis of their stock. In this case, the amount of the distribution ($8,000) is less than Danielle's adjusted stock basis after recognition of her share of the corporation's gain ($3,500). Therefore, she would reduce her basis by the distribution but would recognize no additional income from the transaction:

Danielle's basis as of 1/1/2013:	$5,000
S corp. ordinary income × 50%:	$5,000
Adjusted basis before distribution	$10,000
Distribution	
Gain on sale of $7,000 × 50%	$3,500
Less FMV of property distributed:	(8,000)
Adjusted basis as of 12/31/2013:	**$5,500**

14. The answer is D. A short tax year is only applicable when an S corporation is in its first year or its S status is terminated.

15. The answer is C. S corporations are not subject to self-employment tax. Self-employment tax only applies to individuals. The S corporation may have to pay tax due to:

- Excess net passive investment income
- Built-in gains
- Investment credit recapture
- LIFO recapture

16. The answer is A. All the shareholders must consent to an S election.

17. The answer is D. Charitable contributions, interest income, and short-term capital gains and losses are all separately stated items. The interest on a business loan is not a pass-through item; it is a business expense, as it would be for any other entity.

18. The answer is B. In order for the election to be made, Gloria must also consent to the election, even though she has sold all of her shares to Irving. All the shareholders must consent to the election. If the S election is made during the corporation's tax year for which it first takes effect, any individual shareholder who holds stock at any time during the part of that year before the election is made must also consent to the election, even though the person may have sold or transferred his stock before the election is made.

19. The answer is C. A corporation may not elect S corporation status if it has two classes of stock. A corporation may have both voting and nonvoting stock because they are not considered different classes of stock. A corporation must be a domestic corporation to qualify for S corporation status.

20. The answer is D. All of the following actions will terminate an S election:

- When the corporation no longer qualifies as a small business corporation.
- For each of three consecutive tax years, the corporation
  - Has accumulated earnings and profits, and
  - Derives more than 25% of its gross receipts from passive investment income.
- The S election may be willingly revoked by the shareholders.
- If the corporation creates a second class of stock (such as common and preferred stock).

21. The answer is D. A corporation must generally wait five years to make another S election.

Unit 16: Businesses Quiz Answers

1. The answer is A. If a farmer waits until April 15 to file her return, she must pay estimated taxes just like any other business. If the taxpayer is a qualified farmer, she can either:

- Pay all her estimated tax by the fifteenth day after the end of her tax year (this date is usually January 15)
- File her return and pay all the tax owed by the first day of the third month after the end of her tax year (usually March 1).

2. The answer is B. Joel may postpone a portion of his gain to the following year. If a farmer sells or exchanges more livestock, including poultry, than he normally would in a year because of a drought, flood, or other weather-related condition, he may postpone reporting the gain from the additional animals until the next year. The farmer must use the cash method of accounting in order to postpone gain in this manner.

3. The answer is A. Farming equipment is a depreciable asset and therefore not included in inventory.

4. The answer is B. Certain farmers may average all or some of their current year's farm income by allocating it to the three prior years. This may lower a farmer's current year tax if the current year is high and his taxable income from one or more of the three prior years was low. Income averaging is only available to farmers and fishermen who operate as sole proprietors or partnerships. It is reported on Schedule J, *Income Averaging for Farmers and Fishermen*.

5. The answer is B. The harvest discount method does not exist. All of the other inventory valuation methods listed are allowed for farming businesses.

6. The answer is B. The farming income reported is from milk production and sale of feed ($50,000 + $15,000 = $65,000). Gross income from farming activity is reported on Schedule F, and includes farm income, farm rental income, and gains from livestock that were raised specifically for sale on the farm, or purchased specifically for resale. The sale of old dairy cows and the sale of used machinery do not qualify. The sale of depreciable machinery and the sale of livestock used for dairy purposes are not reported on Schedule F. Instead, these amounts should be reported on Form 4797, *Sales of Business Property.*

7. The answer is D. An agricultural program payment is reported on Schedule F, and the full amount of the payment is subject to self-employment tax.

8. The answer is A. She can delay recognizing income on the payment until the following year. Payments for disaster relief may be included in income in the tax year following the year in which they were awarded. In order to make this election, the farmer must be able to prove that the crops would have been harvested or otherwise sold in the following year.

9. The answer is D. The basis of livestock is generally its cost. However, since the bull calf was born on the farm, its basis is zero. The cost of the feed is deductible and is listed on the return as a regular business expense and as a deduction from gross income. The cost of the feed is not added to the basis of the calf. The sale of livestock held for breeding is not included in regular farming income. Special rules apply to the sale of livestock held for draft, breeding, sport, or dairy purposes. In this case, the sale resulted in a capital gain of $5,000, which would be reported on Form 4797, *Sales of Business Property.*

10. The answer is A. The rent received for the use or rental of farmland is generally rental income, not farm income. If the farmer does not materially participate in operating the farm, the income is reported on Form 4835, *Farm Rental Income and Expenses*, and the income is not subject to self-employment tax.

11. The answer is B. An individual is a qualified farmer if at least two-thirds of his gross income from all sources was from farming.

12. The answer is D. Section 1245 typically excludes buildings and other structural components. However, there is an exception for single purpose agricultural or horticultural structures. A barn for cows and horses is not a single purpose structure so it would not be considered section 1245 property.

13. The answer is C. The carryback period for farming losses is five years. Other businesses are allowed to carry back their losses only two years.

14. The answer is B. If a farmer or fisherman elects income averaging, he must file Schedule J along with a Schedule F showing his net farming income.

Unit 17: Businesses Quiz Answers

1. The answer is D. A partnership does not qualify for exemption from income tax. A tax-exempt organization cannot be organized as a partnership or a sole proprietorship.

2. The answer is C. Since Child Rescue is on a calendar year, its tax return is due May 15. Each tax-exempt organization is required to file by the fifteenth day of the fifth month after its fiscal year ends.

3. The answer is B. A religious organization is not required to file an annual information return. However, a religious organization with employees is still responsible for filing employment tax returns.

4. The answer is A. The form required by the IRS to apply for 501(c)(3) status is Form 1023, *Application for Recognition of Exemption Under Section 501(c)(3) of the Internal Revenue Code.*

5. The answer is A. Only the church would not be required to file a tax return. Tax-exempt organizations must file a Form 990 or Form 990-N (e-postcard) unless specifically exempt. Private foundations must file a Form 990-PF, regardless of income.

6. The answer is B. A political action committee would not qualify. In general, if a substantial part of an organization's activities includes attempting to influence legislation, the organization's exemption from federal income tax will be denied.

7. The answer is C. Exempt churches, their integrated auxiliaries, and conventions or associations of churches are not required to file information returns. However, every employer is responsible for filing employment tax returns.

8. The answer is B. An exempt organization that has $1,000 or more of gross income from unrelated business activity must file Form 990–T.

9. The answer is D. Exempt organizations are subject to failure-to-file penalties and to automatic revocation if returns are not filed for three consecutive years. For exempt organizations with gross receipts of less than $1 million for the year, the maximum penalty is up to $10,000 or 5% of the organization's gross receipts for the year. For exempt organizations with gross receipts of more than $1 million a year, the maximum penalty is increased to $50,000.

10. The answer is C. A tax-exempt organization, other than a private foundation, with gross receipts of $50,000 or less may file the short "e-postcard" Form 990-N, *Electronic Notice for Tax Exempt Organizations Not Required to File Form 990*, instead of the longer information return, Form 990, if it so chooses.

11. The answer is C. Form 1023, *Application for Recognition of Exemption Under Section 501(c)(3 of the Internal Revenue Code*, must be filed with the IRS, along with the entity's organizing document. This document should contain the required information as to purposes and powers of the organization and disposition of its assets upon dissolution.

Unit 18: Businesses Quiz Answers

1. The answer is B. Jensen Biomedical Corporation must deposit Grace's salary reduction contribution in her SIMPLE IRA account. The company must also match Grace's salary reduction contributions at 3% of her $2,000 compensation ($60). An employer cannot return a salary reduction contribution after it has already deducted it from wages as a SIMPLE IRA plan contribution. A SIMPLE IRA plan may not require a participant to be employed on a specific date to receive an employer contribution. If a participant terminates service during the year after making a salary reduction contribution, she would still be entitled to an employer contribution, regardless of whether it is matching or nonelective.

2. The answer is D. Any employer or self-employed individual can establish a SEP.

3. The answer is D. It is not a prohibited transaction if a disqualified person receives a benefit to which he is entitled as a plan participant or beneficiary.

4. The answer is B. The maximum annual credit amount is $500. Employers may claim a tax credit of up to 50% of the first $1,000 of start-up costs if starting a new SEP, SIMPLE, or qualified plan.

5. The answer is A. Taxpayers can deduct contributions for a particular tax year if they are made by the due date (including extensions) of the federal income tax return for that year. Assuming the contributions made in May 2014 were within the applicable limits based upon his compensation for 2013, he could make deductible contributions until his extended due date of October 15, 2014 for his 2013 tax return.

6. The answer is C. Early withdrawals generally are subject to an additional tax of 10%. However, the additional tax is increased to 25% if funds are withdrawn within two years of beginning participation in a SIMPLE IRA. The answer is $10,000 × 25% = $2,500.

7. The answer is D. A SIMPLE IRA plan may only be maintained on a calendar-year basis.

8. The answer is C. Under a SEP, the contribution rate must be uniform for all employees. Employers may contribute less when they have less income, but the plan cannot discriminate among employees.

9. The answer is C. Brenda cannot set up a SIMPLE IRA for her employees, because her company exceeds the 100-employee threshold, unless at least 50 of the employees earned less than $5,000 in the prior year.

10. The answer is A. A partnership may deduct contributions to an employee's retirement plan, just as it would deduct any other ordinary business expense. However, the rules are different for contributions to the retirement accounts of the partners. Contributions made on behalf of the partners are passed through to each of them on Schedule K-1.

11. The answer is B. Leah is self-employed, so she must have compensation in order to contribute to her own retirement plan. However, she is not prohibited from contributing to her employees' retirement plan, even if the business has a loss.

12. The answer is B. ERISA does not require that employers set up retirement plans for their employees.

13. The answer is A. A 10% or more shareholder of the entity administering the plan would be a disqualified person under the rules for prohibited transactions (not 5% as stated in Answer A).

14. The answer is C. A 401(k) is a very common type of defined contribution plan in which employees contribute to their own accounts, generally on a pretax basis. Earnings grow tax-free until distribution. Employers often supplement or match employee contributions.

15. The answer is B. Although income tax may apply, including an additional 10% tax for withdrawals prior to age 59½, participants are allowed to withdraw money from a SEP-IRA at any time. Withdrawals can be rolled over tax-free to another SEP-IRA, to another traditional IRA, or to another employer's qualified retirement plan.

16. The answer is A. Josie can set up a SEP. A SEP can be established for a person's independent business activity even if she participates in an employer's retirement plan.

17. The answer is C. An initial 15% tax is applied on the amount involved in a prohibited transaction for each year in a taxable period. If the transaction is not corrected within the taxable period, an additional tax of 100% of the amount involved is imposed. These taxes are payable by any disqualified person who takes part in a prohibited transaction.

18. The answer is C. Employers may choose to exclude employees covered by a union agreement. Since Aldo is a resident alien, he still qualifies to participate. Only nonresident aliens who do not have any U.S.-source income may be excluded.

19. The answer is B. An eligible employee may not opt out of participation. However, any eligible employee may choose not to make salary reduction contributions for a year. In that case the employee would accrue no employer matching contributions for the year, but would still receive an employer nonelective contribution (if the plan provides for such contributions for the year.)

20. The answer is C. Randolph is not an automatically eligible employee because he is not at least 21 years old. For purposes of a SEP, an eligible employee is an individual who meets all the following requirements:

- Has reached age 21
- Has worked for the employer in at least three of the last five years
- Has received at least $550 in compensation

An employer can use less restrictive participation requirements than those listed, but not more restrictive ones.

21. The answer is B. Employers cannot prohibit distributions from a SEP-IRA. Employers also cannot make their contributions contingent on the condition that any part of them must be kept in the account. All of the other statements are correct regarding SEP-IRA plans.

Unit 19: Businesses Quiz Answers

1. The answer is C. Roger's estate is subject to NIIT on the lesser of $175,000 (its NII) or $200,000 (the amount by which its AGI of $211,950 exceeds the threshold of $11,950 for 2013). The estate owes NIIT of $6,650 ($175,000 × 3.8% = $6,650).

2. The answer is C. A trust that distributes all its income currently is allowed an exemption of $300. All other trusts are allowed an exemption of $100 per year.

3. The answer is D. The aggregate portion of his estate distributed to his grandchildren ($10 million) would be reduced by his exclusion amount for GST ($5,250,000) and the remainder of $4,750,000 would be subject to GST.

4. The answer is C. The gross estate does not include property owned solely by the decedent's spouse or other individuals.

5. The answer is D. An estate with $500 in income and a beneficiary who is a resident alien is not required to file a tax return. An estate with a nonresident alien beneficiary would be required to file Form 1041, regardless of the amount of income earned.

6. The answer is A. The IRC defines a simple trust as one that distributes all its income currently, makes no distributions from principal, and makes no distributions to charity. Any trust that is not a simple trust is automatically a complex trust.

7. The answer is B. The GST tax is imposed separately and in addition to the estate and gift taxes.

8. The answer is A. An income tax return (Form 1041) must be filed for any domestic estate that has gross income for the tax year of $600 or more, or a beneficiary who is a nonresident alien, regardless of the estate's gross income. Roberto's estate has gross income of $500 ($250 + $150 + $100 gain from stock sale). Since the gross income is below the $600 exemption amount, an income tax return is not required to be filed for 2013.

9. The answer is C. Life insurance payable to a trust and assets held in a grantor trust are included in a decedent's gross estate. Liabilities of the decedent are not included in the gross estate. However, they are an allowable deduction from the gross estate in determining the taxable estate.

10. The answer is B. The applicable credit amount in 2013 is $2,045,800. A taxpayer must subtract the applicable credit amount from any gift or estate tax he owes. Any applicable credit used against gift tax in prior years reduces the amount of credit he can use against gift or estate taxes in later years.

11. The answer is B. A grantor trust is a legitimate form of trust. All of the other trusts described are potentially abusive. Trusts cannot be used to transform a taxpayer's personal, living, or educational expenses into deductible items. A taxpayer cannot use a trust to avoid tax liability by ignoring either the true ownership of income and assets or the true substance of transactions.

12. The answer is A. The gross estate of the decedent includes everything the taxpayer owns at the date of death.

13. The answer is B. The estate tax return is generally due nine months after the date of death.

14. The answer is D. Although foreign trusts are often established in certain countries in an effort to evade taxation, the income from such arrangements is fully taxable under U.S. law. Dominique would also be subject to an annual filing requirement, Form 3520-A, *Annual Return of Foreign Trust with U.S. Beneficiaries.*

15. The answer is C. The maximum estate and gift tax rate for 2013 is 40%.

16. The answer is D. When Luis died in 2013, his estate qualified for the full basic exclusion amount of $5,250,000. As a result of having reported the DSUE when Form 706 was filed for his estate, the amount of the DSUE is available in addition to Jenna's basic exclusion amount of $5,250,000. Therefore, the amount of her taxable estate would have to exceed $10,500,000 in order to be subject to estate tax.

Part 3: Representation

Unit 1: Legal Authority of the IRS

More Reading:
Circular 230, *Regulations Governing Practice Before the Internal Revenue Service*
Publication 947, *Practice Before the IRS and Power of Attorney*

Overview of SEE Part 3

Part 3 of the EA exam concerns the ethics, laws, and regulations that govern the tax profession: rules that tax preparers must follow; standards that the tax profession is held to; who may represent taxpayers before the IRS; IRS procedures for conducting audits and assessing and collecting taxes; and penalties that tax preparers face if they violate the law.

Specifically, Part 3 of the exam is broken down into the following sections and corresponding percentage of questions: *Practice and Procedures*, 35%; *Representation before the IRS*, 30%; *Specific Types of Representation*, 30%; and *Completion of the Filing Process*, 5%.[41]

Issues of ethics, practice, and representation are dealt with in detail in Treasury Department Circular No. 230,[42] which underwent a sweeping revision in 2011. The update of Circular 230 is part of a series of steps designed to increase oversight of federal tax return preparation. All practitioners who represent taxpayers before the IRS and paid tax return preparers are subject to the rules and regulations set forth in Circular 230.

Federal Tax Law

The Internal Revenue Code (IRC) is the main body of tax law of the United States. The IRC is enacted by Congress and published as Title 26 of the United States Code. Other tax law is promulgated by individual states, cities, and municipalities. The IRS enrolled agent exam deals only with federal tax laws and not with the laws of any individual state or municipality.

Tax law is determined by all three branches of our federal government, although the legislative branch (Congress) has the primary function of originating tax laws. The executive branch (the president) is responsible for income tax regulations, revenue rulings, and revenue procedures. The judicial branch is responsible for court decisions.

The IRS is the federal agency that enforces tax law. It is the collection arm for the U.S. Treasury, which is responsible for paying various government expenses. The IRS takes the specifics of the laws enacted by Congress and translates them into the detailed regulations, rules, and procedures of the IRC. The IRS produces several kinds of documents that provide guidance to taxpayers, including the following:

1. Treasury regulations
2. Revenue rulings
3. Revenue procedures

---

[41]Specifications for tests administered during the May 1, 2013 to February 28, 2014 exam cycle.

[42]Regulations governing practice are set forth in Title 31, Code of Federal Regulations, Subtitle A, Part 10, and were published in pamphlet form as Treasury Department Circular No. 230 on June 3, 2011.

4. Private letter rulings
5. Technical advice memoranda
6. IRS notices

Each of these carries varying degrees of authority in providing the basis of tax law and establishing precedents for the future. Under IRC §6662, sources of "substantial authority" include the following: provisions of the Internal Revenue Code, temporary and final regulations, court cases, administrative pronouncements, tax treaties, and Congressional intent as reflected in committee reports.

The list was later expanded to include proposed regulations, private letter rulings, technical advice memoranda, IRS information or press releases, notices, and any other similar documents published by the IRS in the Internal Revenue Bulletin.[43]

Treatises and articles in legal periodicals are not considered substantial authority under this statute.

Treasury Regulations

Treasury regulations are the U.S. Treasury Department's official interpretations of the Internal Revenue Code. The IRC authorizes the Secretary of the Treasury to "prescribe all needful rules and regulations for enforcement" of the code. All regulations are written by the IRS's Office of the Chief Counsel and approved by the Treasury secretary. The courts give weight to Treasury regulations and will generally uphold the regulations so long as the IRS's interpretation is reasonable.

Note: The IRS is bound by its regulations, but the courts are not. U.S. Treasury regulations are authorized by law, but U.S. courts are not bound to follow administrative interpretations.

The three types of Treasury regulations are legislative, interpretative, and procedural.

Legislative regulations are created when Congress expressly delegates the authority to the Treasury secretary or the commissioner of the IRS to provide the requirements for a specific provision of the IRC. A legislative regulation has a higher degree of authority than an interpretative regulation. A legislative regulation may be overturned if any of the following conflicts apply:

- It is outside the power delegated to the U.S. Treasury.
- It conflicts with a specific statute.
- It is deemed unreasonable by the courts.

Interpretive regulations are issued under the IRS's general authority to interpret the IRC. An interpretative regulation only explains the meaning of a portion of the code. Unlike a legislative regulation, there is no grant of authority for the promulgation of an interpretative regulation, so these regulations may be challenged on the grounds that they do not reflect Congress's intent.

Procedural regulations concern the administrative provisions of the code and are issued by the commissioner of the IRS and not the secretary of the Treasury. They often concern minor issues, such as when notices should be sent to employees.

[43] The Committee Report for the Revenue Reconciliation Act of 1989.

Regulations are further classified as proposed, temporary, or final:

- **Proposed regulations** are open to commentary from the public. Various versions of proposed regulations may be issued and withdrawn before a final regulation is issued.
- **Temporary regulations** may remain in effect for three years, and may never be finalized.
- **Final regulations** are issued when the regulation becomes an official Treasury decision.

Revenue Rulings and Revenue Procedures

The IRS issues revenue rulings and revenue procedures to inform and guide taxpayers. Neither has the force of Treasury Department regulations, but they may be used as precedents. A *revenue ruling* typically states the IRS position, while a *revenue procedure* provides instructions concerning that position.

Revenue rulings are intended to promote uniform application of the IRC. The national office of the IRS issues revenue rulings, which are published in issues of the Internal Revenue Bulletin and the Federal Register. A revenue ruling is not binding in Tax Court or any other U.S. court. However, revenue rulings can be used by taxpayers as guidance to avoid certain IRS penalties.

The numbering system for revenue rulings corresponds to the year the ruling was issued. Thus, for example, revenue ruling 80-20 was the twentieth revenue ruling issued in 1980.

Revenue procedures are official IRS statements of procedure that affect the rights or duties of taxpayers under the IRC. A revenue procedure may be cited as precedent, but it does not have the force of law.

Example: A *revenue ruling* will announce that taxpayers may deduct certain automobile expenses. A *revenue procedure* will then explain how taxpayers must deduct, allocate, or compute these automobile expenses.

IRS Written Determinations

Private Letter Ruling (PLR): A taxpayer who has a specific question regarding tax law may request a private letter ruling (PLR) from the IRS. A PLR is a written statement issued to a taxpayer that interprets and applies tax laws to the taxpayer's specific case. It is issued to communicate the tax consequences of a particular transaction before the transaction is consummated or before the taxpayer's return is filed.

A PLR is legally binding on the IRS, but only if the taxpayer fully and accurately described the proposed transaction in the request and carried out the transaction as described. A PLR may not be relied on as precedent by other taxpayers or IRS personnel.

PLRs are made public after the taxpayer's private, identifiable information has been redacted (removed or blacked out).

Technical Advice Memorandum (TAM): A TAM is written guidance furnished by the IRS Office of Chief Counsel upon the request of an IRS director. A TAM is issued in response to a technical or procedural question that develops during:

- The examination of a taxpayer's return
- Consideration of a taxpayer's claim for refund or credit

- A request for a determination letter
- Processing and considering non-docketed cases in an Appeals office

Technical advice memoranda are issued only on closed transactions and provide the interpretation of proper application of tax laws, tax treaties, regulations, revenue rulings, or other precedents.

The advice rendered represents the position of the IRS, but it only relates to the specific case in question. Technical advice memoranda are made public after private information has been removed that could identify a specific taxpayer.

IRS Notices

An official IRS notice is a public pronouncement that may contain guidance involving substantive interpretations of the IRC or other provisions of the law. Information commonly published in IRS notices includes:

- Weighted average interest rate updates
- Inflation adjustment factors
- Changes to IRS regulations
- Presidentially declared disaster areas
- IRS requests for public comments on changes to regulations, rulings, or procedures

Internal Revenue Bulletin

The Internal Revenue Bulletin (IRB) is the authoritative source of official IRS tax guidance. It is a weekly collection of items of substantial interest to the professional tax community. The IRB announces official IRS rulings and publishes Treasury decisions, executive orders, tax conventions, significant legislation, and court decisions.

Anyone may search the IRS website, www.irs.gov, for past issues of the IRB. Issues after June 2003 are available in both HTML and PDF file formats; earlier issues are in PDF only.

The IRS often releases individual items in advance of their publication in the IRB. Tax professionals may subscribe to the IRS GuideWire service to receive automated email notifications about these items.

Internal Revenue Manual

The Internal Revenue Manual (IRM) is the single official compilation of policies, delegated authorities, procedures, instructions, and guidelines relating to the organization, functions, administration, and operations of the IRS. It is primarily used by IRS employees to guide them in all facets of operations.

As of early 2014, the manual has 35 separate parts, which include sections on the processing of tax submissions, examinations, collection, and appeals. Criminal investigations, legal advice, and litigation in the courts are also included in the manual.

Twenty-two parts of the IRM are available for the public to access.

IRS Publications, Forms, and Instructions

The IRS disseminates information to both taxpayers and preparers through its publications. For example, Publication 17 covers the general rules for filing a federal income tax return for individuals. Publication 17 supplements information contained in the tax form instruction booklet and explains the law so taxpayers pay only the tax they owe and no more. Its guidance, along with information in other official IRS publications, is an important document for practitioners who prepare income tax returns. Although the information in publications is drawn from the IRC, Treasury regulations, and other primary sources of authority, publications themselves are not considered to have "substantial authority."

IRS tax forms and schedules are used by taxpayers to report financial information to the IRS and calculate taxes to be paid or disclose other information as required by the Internal Revenue Code. There are more than 800 forms and schedules in use. Many of them also have accompanying instructions for taxpayers. Forms, schedules, and instructions are updated whenever necessary due to changes in the tax code.

All publications, forms, and instructions are listed and available for download on the IRS website at *www.irs.gov*, usually in both HTML and PDF file formats. Updated versions of publications are listed with the date revisions were made, so taxpayers may know they are using the most current information. Many libraries and post offices offer free tax forms to taxpayers during the filing season, as do the more than 400 Taxpayer Assistance Centers across the country where the IRS offers face-to-face help to taxpayers. Taxpayers may also call the IRS to order current year tax forms, instructions, and publications by mail. Due to the growth in electronic filing and the availability of free access to tax forms, the IRS no longer automatically mails paper tax packages to taxpayers.

Case Law

Often, taxpayers and tax preparers will disagree with the IRS's interpretation of the IRC. In these cases, it is up to the courts to determine Congress's intent or the constitutionality of the tax law or IRS position that is being challenged. There are many instances where tax laws are either disputed or overturned. Court decisions then serve as guidance for future tax decisions.

In most instances, the IRS chooses whether or not to acquiesce to a court decision. This means that the IRS may choose to ignore the decision of the court and continue with its regular policies regarding the litigated issue. The IRS is not bound to change its regulations due to a loss in court. The only exception to this rule is the U.S. Supreme Court, whose decisions the IRS is obligated to follow.

The IRS does not announce acquiescence or non-acquiescence in every case. Sometimes its position is withheld. When it does announce its position, the IRS publishes its acquiescence and non-acquiescence first in the Internal Revenue Bulletin.

Study Note: The enrolled agent exam is based largely on IRS publications, and exam candidates will not be tested on court cases unless the law has already made its way into an IRS publication. Similarly, exam candidates will not be tested on any pending tax law or legislation; the exam is based on tax law from the prior year. However, EA candidates must understand the basics of tax law, the court system, and how it relates to the taxpayer.

Freedom of Information Act Requests (FOIA)

The Freedom of Information Act (FOIA) is a law designed to ensure public access to U.S. government records. Upon written request, federal agencies, including the IRS, are required to disclose requested records, unless they can be withheld under certain exceptions allowed in the FOIA. Under the terms of the act, agencies may charge reasonable fees for searching, reviewing, and copying records that have been requested.

The IRS may withhold a record that falls under one of the FOIA's nine exemptions and three exclusions. The exemptions protect against the disclosure of information that would harm national security, the privacy of individuals, the proprietary interests of business, the functioning of the government, and other important recognized interests. Exclusions involve especially sensitive law enforcement records related to criminal, FBI, counterintelligence, and international terrorism investigations.

When a record contains some information that qualifies as exempt, the entire record is not necessarily exempt. Instead, the FOIA specifically provides that any portions of a record that can be set apart must be provided to a requester after deletion of the exempt portions.

The IRS generally has 20 business days to say whether it will comply with a FOIA request. When a request is denied, the IRS must give the reason for denial and explain the right to appeal to the head of the agency.

A taxpayer may contest the type or amount of fees charged in the processing of the records request. A taxpayer also may appeal any other type of adverse determination under the FOIA, such as the failure of the IRS to conduct an adequate search for requested documents.

A person whose request was granted in part and denied in part may appeal the part that was denied. If the IRS has agreed to disclose some but not all of the requested documents, the filing of an appeal does not affect the release of the documents that can be disclosed.

Unit 1: Study Questions

1. Which branch of government is the main source of tax law in the United States?

A. Legislative.
B. Executive.
C. Judicial.
D. All three branches contribute equally to the creation and adoption of tax law.

2. Which of the following would have the highest authority in establishing precedence for tax law?

A. Private letter ruling.
B. Treasury regulation.
C. IRS publication.
D. Technical advice memorandum.

3. In matters of tax law, the IRS must acquiesce in all decisions rendered by the _______:

A. U.S. Tax Court.
B. U.S. Supreme Court.
C. U.S. Court of Appeals.
D. Both A and B.

4. Which of the following statements regarding revenue rulings is correct?

A. Revenue rulings cannot be used to avoid certain IRS penalties.
B. Revenue rulings can be used to avoid certain IRS penalties.
C. Revenue rulings are not official IRS guidance.
D. None of the above.

5. What is a private letter ruling?

A. A private letter that a taxpayer writes to the IRS.
B. A private letter issued by the U.S. Tax Court.
C. A written statement issued to a taxpayer that interprets and applies tax laws to the taxpayer's specific case in response to the taxpayer's request.
D. A request by the IRS to Congress about tax issues.

6. Which has the highest level of authority?

A. Revenue ruling.
B. Procedural regulation.
C. Interpretative regulation.
D. Legislative regulation.

7. A private letter ruling is legally binding on the IRS if _________________.

A. The taxpayer fully and accurately described the proposed transaction in his request and carried out the transaction as described.
B. The IRS is notified of any discrepancies on a taxpayer's return.
C. The taxpayer goes to the Tax Court and requests a formal decision.
D. None of the above.

8. Which of the following statements is true regarding IRS acquiescence?

A. The IRS may choose whether or not to acquiesce to any court decision.
B. The IRS must change its regulations due to a loss in court.
C. The IRS will announce acquiescence or non-acquiescence in every case.
D. The IRS is bound to follow U.S. Supreme Court decisions.

9. Which of the following does not meet the substantial authority test?
A. Proposed regulations.
B. Legal opinion.
C. Congressional intent as reflected in committee reports.
D. Information from an IRS press release.

Unit 2: Practice Before the IRS

More Reading:
Circular 230, *Regulations Governing Practice Before the Internal Revenue Service*
Publication 947, *Practice Before the IRS and Power of Attorney*
Publication 470, *Limited Practice Without Enrollment*

Practice before the IRS includes all matters connected with a presentation before the IRS, or relating to a taxpayer's rights, privileges, or liabilities under laws or regulations administered by the IRS. Practice before the IRS includes:

- Corresponding and communicating with the IRS
- Representing a taxpayer at conferences, hearings, or meetings with the IRS
- Preparing and filing documents, including tax returns, with the IRS
- Providing written advice that has a potential for tax avoidance or evasion

Example: Trina is a CPA. Her client, Samuel, has a large tax debt. Samuel does not wish to communicate directly with the IRS, but he wants to set up an installment agreement. Trina has Samuel sign Form 2848 giving her power of attorney and calls the IRS on his behalf to set up the installment agreement for him. This action is considered *practice before the IRS*.

U.S. citizenship is not required to practice before the IRS.

Practitioners

The IRS defines *practitioners* as attorneys, CPAs, enrolled agents, enrolled retirement plan agents, or enrolled actuaries authorized to practice before the IRS. Other individuals may qualify to practice temporarily or engage in limited practice before the IRS. However, they are not referred to as practitioners.

The following individuals may represent taxpayers and practice before the IRS by virtue of their licensing, unless they are currently under suspension or disbarment:

Attorneys: An attorney who is a member in good standing of the bar of any state, possession, territory, commonwealth, or of the District of Columbia.

Certified Public Accountants (CPAs): A CPA who is duly qualified to practice as a CPA in any state, possession, territory, commonwealth, or the District of Columbia.

Enrolled Agents (EAs): An enrolled agent in active status may represent clients before any office of the IRS. Like attorneys and CPAs, EAs are unrestricted as to which taxpayers they can represent and what types of tax matters they can handle.

Enrolled Actuaries: The practice of an individual enrolled as an actuary by the Joint Board for the Enrollment of Actuaries is limited to certain Internal Revenue Code sections that relate to his area of expertise, principally those sections governing employee retirement plans.

Enrolled Retirement Plan Agents (ERPAs): The practice of an enrolled retirement plan agent is limited to certain Internal Revenue Code sections that relate to his area of expertise, principally those sections governing employee retirement plans.

Unenrolled Tax Return Preparers

Individuals who prepare tax returns for other taxpayers but who are not practitioners (EAs, CPAs, attorneys, ERPAs, or enrolled actuaries) have limited practice rights before the IRS. These unenrolled tax return preparers may represent taxpayers only during an IRS examination of the taxable year or period covered by the tax return or claim of refund they prepared and signed. This representation may occur only before revenue agents, customer service representatives, or similar officers and employees of the IRS, including the Taxpayer Advocate Service.

Unenrolled tax return preparers cannot do the following:

- Represent taxpayers before appeals officers, revenue officers, counsel, or similar officers or employees of the IRS or Department of Treasury
- Execute closing agreements
- Extend the statutory period for tax assessments or collection of tax
- Execute waivers
- Execute claims for refund
- Sign any document on behalf of a taxpayer

Example: Louie is an unenrolled tax preparer. The IRS is conducting an audit of a client's income tax returns for the years 2010, 2011, and 2012. Louie prepared only his client's 2013 return. Since he is not a practitioner, he may not represent his client before the IRS because he did not prepare the tax returns for the period under examination.

Students: Students who work in a Low Income Taxpayer Clinic (LITC) or Student Tax Clinic Program (STCP) may request permission to represent a taxpayer before the IRS. Students must be supervised by a practitioner, and the request must be authorized by the Office of Professional Responsibility.

Registered Tax Return Preparers (*DESIGNATION STRUCK DOWN*): Under the terms of Circular 230, any individual other than an attorney, CPA, enrolled agent, enrolled actuary, or ERPA who prepares a tax return and signs it as a paid preparer must be a registered tax return preparer (RTRP). The IRS had wanted anyone who prepares tax returns for compensation to pass an IRS competency test and be subject to annual continuing education requirements.

However, a district court ruling in January 2013 blocked the IRS from enforcing the regulatory requirements for registered tax return preparers.[44] The court found that the IRS "lacks statutory authority to promulgate or enforce the new regulatory scheme for 'registered tax return preparers' brought under Circular 230." On February 11, 2014, the D.C. Circuit Court of Appeals upheld the district court ruling that invalidated the RTRP program.[45]

The IRS is not expected to pursue the litigation by appealing to the U.S. Supreme Court. The district court's ruling allows the RTRP exam to be offered on a voluntary rather than a compulsory basis, which the IRS has said it is exploring. However, the RTRP exam is not expected to be offered in 2014, and the designation of "RTRP" does not have any current legal standing.

---

[44] *Loving*, No. 12-385, U.S. District Court for the District of Columbia, January 18, 2013.

[45] *Loving*, No. 13-5061, D.C. Circuit Court of Appeals, February 11, 2014.

Limited Practice Due to 'Special Relationship'

Other individuals who are not practitioners may represent taxpayers before the IRS because of a special relationship with the taxpayer, without having prepared the tax return in question.

An individual (self-representation): An individual may always represent himself before the IRS, provided he has appropriate identification, such as a driver's license. He does not have to file a written declaration of qualification and authority. Even a disbarred individual may represent himself before the IRS.

> **Example:** Gary was a tax attorney who was disbarred because of a felony conviction in 2012. An individual who is disbarred is not eligible to represent other taxpayers before the IRS. Gary was audited by the IRS in 2013. Despite being disbarred, Gary may still represent himself before the IRS during the examination of his own return.

A family member: An individual may represent members of his immediate family. Family members include a spouse, child, parent, brother, or sister of the individual.

> **Example:** Jim's mother is being audited by the IRS. Even though Jim is not enrolled to practice before the IRS, he is allowed to represent his mother because of the family relationship.

An officer: A bona fide officer of a corporation (including a parent, subsidiary, or affiliated corporation), association, organized group, or governmental agency may represent its corporation, association, organized group, or governmental agency before the IRS.

A partner: A general partner may represent the partnership before the IRS but limited partners may not.

An employee: A regular full-time employee can represent his employer. An employer can be an individual, partnership, corporation, association, trust, receivership, guardianship, estate, or organized group; or a governmental unit, agency, or authority.

> **Example:** Angelique is a full-time bookkeeper for her employer. In 2013, the IRS sent her employer a notice regarding some unfiled payroll tax returns. Angelique may file Form 2848, *Power of Attorney and Declaration of Representative*, and speak with the IRS on her employer's behalf because of the employee-employer relationship.

A fiduciary: A fiduciary (trustee, executor, personal representative, administrator, receiver, or guardian) is considered to be the taxpayer and not a representative of the taxpayer.

> **Example:** Tony was named the executor of his mother's estate after she passed away. He is allowed to represent his mother's estate before the IRS because he is the fiduciary for the estate.

Authorization for Special Appearances: In rare circumstances, the Commissioner of the IRS or a delegate will authorize a person who is not otherwise eligible to practice before the IRS to represent another person for a particular matter. The request is made to the Office of Professional Responsibility (OPR). If granted, the written consent will detail the specific circumstances related to the appearance.

Ineligible to Practice Before the IRS: Individuals not previously described are generally not eligible to practice before the IRS. Corporations, associations, partnerships, and others that are not individuals also are not eligible to practice before the IRS.

Even if named in a power of attorney as a representative, an individual will not be recognized if he has lost his eligibility to practice before the IRS. Reasons for losing eligibility include suspension or disbarment by the OPR, being placed in inactive retirement status, and not meeting the requirements for renewal of enrollment, such as continuing professional education.

Actions That Are Not Practice Before the IRS

Practice before the IRS does not include:

- Representation of taxpayers before the U.S. Tax Court. The Tax Court has its own rules of practice and its own rules regarding admission to practice.
- Merely appearing as a witness for the taxpayer. In general, individuals who are not practitioners may appear before the IRS as witnesses—but they may not advocate for the taxpayer.

Additional issues related to representation of taxpayers are examined in greater detail in Unit 3.

Tax Return Preparers

The IRS defines *tax return preparers* as individuals who participate in the preparation of tax returns for taxpayers for compensation. This includes return preparers who are in business, casual or part-time preparers who receive fees for preparing tax returns, and certain e-file providers.

Under Circular 230, the IRS requires the following:

- All paid tax return preparers must register with the IRS and obtain a preparer tax identification number (PTIN). Specifically, Circular 230 states that "any individual who for compensation prepares or assists with the preparation of all or substantially all of a tax return or claim for refund" must have a PTIN.[46]
- Tax preparers who register must undergo a limited tax compliance check to ensure they have filed their own personal and business tax returns.

PTIN Requirements

The PTIN (preparer tax identification number) is a nine-digit number that preparers must use when they prepare and sign a tax return or claim for refund. In 2011, use of the PTIN became mandatory on all federal tax returns and claims for refund prepared by a paid tax preparer. This requirement includes all enrolled agents and many attorneys and CPAs. Attorneys and CPAs do not need to obtain PTINs if they do not prepare federal tax returns.

Example: Helen is a CPA who specializes in audit work. She works for a CPA firm with a tax practice, but she does not prepare tax returns herself. Helen is not required to obtain a PTIN.

[46] The IRS's loss in the court case regarding the RTRP designation does not apply to the IRS's requirement for all paid tax preparers to obtain PTINs. The judge ruled in Loving v. IRS that the PTIN program was valid and could be enforced by the IRS.

Multiple individuals cannot share one PTIN. A PTIN is assigned to a single preparer to identify that he is the preparer of a particular return. When applicable, the PTIN is included in the "Paid Preparer" section of a tax return.

An applicant must be at least 18 years old to obtain a PTIN. Felony convictions and failure to meet federal tax obligations may affect an individual's ability to obtain a PTIN.

All tax preparers are required to pay a fee and renew their PTINs online each year between October 16 and December 31.[47] Preparers who fail to list a valid PTIN on tax returns they sign are subject to penalties of $50 per return, up to a maximum of $25,000 a year. Preparers may also be subject to disciplinary action by the Office of Professional Responsibility.

Note: In late January, the IRS sent expiration notices to tax preparers who had not renewed their PTINS for 2014. The IRS says it will continue to process renewals throughout the year.

Supervised Preparers

Supervised preparers are also required to have PTINs. These are individuals who do not sign tax returns as paid return preparers but are:

- Employed by a law firm, EA office, or CPA practice, and
- Are directly supervised by an attorney, CPA, EA, ERPA, or enrolled actuary who signs the returns prepared by the supervised preparer as the paid tax return preparer.

Supervised preparers may not:

- Sign any tax return they prepare or assist in preparing
- Represent taxpayers before the IRS in any capacity
- Identify themselves as Circular 230 practitioners

When applying for or renewing a PTIN, supervised preparers must provide the PTIN of their supervisor.

Non-1040 Preparers

Non-Form 1040 series preparers are required to obtain PTINs. These are individuals who do not prepare or assist in the preparation of any Form 1040 series tax returns or claims for refund, except Forms 1040-PR or Forms 1040-SS, for compensation. Both forms are for residents of Puerto Rico only.

Exceptions to PTIN Requirements

An individual who prepares a tax return with no agreement for compensation is not considered a tax return preparer for IRS purposes. This is true even if the individual receives a gift or a favor in return. The agreement for compensation is the deciding factor as to whether or not the IRS considers an individual a tax preparer.

[47] The IRS delayed the start of the 2014 PTIN renewal period to October 30, 2013 due to the federal government shutdown.

> **Example:** Terri is a retired CPA who only prepares tax returns for her close family members. She does not charge her family to prepare their tax returns. Sometimes, a family member will give Terri a gift in return. This year, she received home-baked cookies from her sister and a sweater from her niece. However, Terri does not ask for any gifts or expect them. She is not a tax return preparer for IRS purposes, and she is not required to obtain a PTIN.

An individual is not considered an income tax return preparer and would not be required to obtain a PTIN in the following instances:

- A person who gives an opinion about events that have not happened (such as tax advice for a business that has not been created).
- A person who furnishes typing, copying, or mechanical assistance.
- A person who prepares a return of his employer (or of an officer or employee of the employer) by whom the person is regularly and continuously employed.
- A fiduciary who prepares a tax return for a trust or estate.
- An unpaid volunteer who provides tax assistance under Volunteer Income Tax Assistance (VITA) or Tax Counseling for the Elderly (TCE) programs.
- An employee of the IRS who performs official duties by preparing a tax return for a taxpayer who requests it.

> **Example:** Thomas is a CPA. His neighbor, Ross, consults with Thomas about a business he is thinking about starting. Thomas gives Ross an opinion regarding the potential business and taxes. In this case, the IRS does not consider Thomas a tax preparer. This is because Thomas is merely giving an opinion about events that have not yet happened.

> **Example:** Ginny is a bookkeeper for Creative Candies Corporation. She is a full-time employee, and she prepares the payroll checks and payroll tax returns for all of the employees of Creative Candies. As a full-time employee, Ginny is not considered a tax preparer since her employer is ultimately responsible for the accuracy of the payroll tax returns.

> **Example:** Francisco is an EA who has a PTIN. He employs an administrative assistant, Claudia, who performs data entry during tax filing season. At times, clients call and provide Claudia with information, which she records in the system. Using the data Claudia has entered, Francisco meets with his clients and provides tax advice as needed. He then prepares and signs their returns. Claudia is not a tax preparer and is not required to have a PTIN.

> **Example:** Bob is a retired tax professional. He does not have a PTIN. Bob volunteers during the tax filing season at a VITA site, where he prepares individual tax returns for lower-income individuals for free. Bob is not a tax return preparer and is not required to have a PTIN.

Preparation of tax returns outside the U.S. is included in these rules. Tax preparers who work on U.S. tax returns overseas are still subject to Circular 230 regulations.

The Substantial Portion Rule

Only the person who prepares all or a "substantial portion" of a tax return is considered the preparer of the return. A person who merely gives advice on a portion or a single entry on a tax return is considered to have prepared only that portion. If more than one individual is involved in the preparation of a tax return, the preparer is the person with the primary responsibility for the overall accuracy of the return and the one who must sign the return.

In order to identify who is responsible for a substantial portion of the return, the following guidelines may be used. A portion of a tax return is not typically considered to be substantial if it involves only minor dollar amounts of:

- Less than $2,000, or
- Less than 20% of the adjusted gross income on the return.

Usually, a single IRS schedule would not be considered a substantial portion of a tax return unless it represents a major portion of the income.

Example: Greg and Eli are partners in a tax practice. In March, Eli finishes a few returns that Greg had started before he left on vacation. Later, one tax return comes up for audit, and it is determined that the return has a gross misstatement. Greg prepared Schedule C on the return, and Eli prepared the rest of the return. Schedule C represents 95% of the income and expenses shown on the return. Therefore, for purposes of any potential penalty, Greg is considered the preparer of this return, since he prepared the schedule that represents the majority of the income and expenses on the return.

Enrolled Agent Licensing

As outlined in Circular 230, there are two tracks to becoming an enrolled agent. An individual may receive the designation by passing a three-part exam, or by virtue of past employment with the IRS.

Exam Track: For the first track, an EA candidate must apply for a PTIN and register to take the Special Enrollment Examination (SEE), also known as the EA exam, by filling out Form 2587, *Application for Special Enrollment Examination*. An applicant must be at least 18 years old. A candidate then must:

- Achieve passing scores on all three parts of the SEE.
- File Form 23, *Application for Enrollment to Practice before the Internal Revenue Service*, to apply for enrollment within one year from the date of passing the exam.
- Pass a background check conducted by the IRS. The tax compliance check makes sure the applicant has filed all necessary tax returns and has no outstanding tax liabilities. The suitability check determines whether an applicant has engaged in any conduct that would justify suspension or disbarment.

Previous Experience Track: For the second track, an EA candidate must possess a minimum of five years of past service with the IRS and technical experience as outlined in Circular 230. Application must be made within three years from the date the employee left the IRS. Factors considered with this second track are the length and scope of employment and the recommendation of the superior officer. The applicant then must:

- Apply for enrollment on Form 23.

- Pass a background check, which includes a tax compliance and suitability check.

Former IRS employees who become enrolled agents without taking the EA exam may be granted limited or unlimited representation rights.

The IRS's Return Preparer Office (RPO) makes the determination on applications for enrollment to practice. The RPO was created to provide oversight of all matters related to the authority to practice before the IRS, including competency testing, enrollment and renewal, and continuing education.

Form 23 takes about 60 days to process. Once an individual's application is approved, the RPO will issue an enrollment card, and enrollment becomes effective on that date.

Denial of Enrollment

Any individual who is involved in disreputable conduct is subject to disciplinary action or denial of enrollment. Disreputable acts alone may be grounds for denial of enrollment, even after the candidate has passed the EA exam. Failure to timely file tax returns or to pay one's taxes may also be grounds for the Return Preparer Office to deny an application for enrollment.

The RPO must inform the applicant of the reason he is denied enrollment. The applicant may then file a written appeal to the Office of Professional Responsibility within 30 days from the date of the notice. The appeal must be filed along with the candidate's reasoning why the enrollment application should be accepted.

Example: Todd passed all three parts of the EA exam in 2012. He properly filed Form 23 requesting enrollment. Because he had failed to file numerous tax returns in the past, his application was denied. Todd filed an appeal with the Office of Professional Responsibility, explaining that he had been seriously injured years ago and therefore had failed to file his tax returns on time. He attached supporting evidence, including copies of medical bills and a letter from his doctor. Todd also provided evidence that all his tax returns had been properly filed after his recovery. The OPR accepted Todd's appeal and granted him enrollment.

Renewal of Enrollment

Enrolled agents must renew their enrollment status every three years. To renew, an EA must file Form 8554, *Application for Renewal of Enrollment to Practice before the Internal Revenue Service*, and submit the required nonrefundable fee. If an EA does not renew his enrollment, he may not continue to practice before the IRS.

The three successive enrollment years preceding the effective date of renewal is referred to as the IRS enrollment cycle. Applications for renewal of enrollment must be submitted between November 1 and January 31 prior to April 1 of the year that the next enrollment cycle begins. The last digit of a practitioner's Social Security number determines when he must renew enrollment. If the candidate's SSN ends in:

- 0, 1, 2, or 3 –The next enrollment cycle begins April 1, 2016.
- 4, 5, or 6 – The next enrollment cycle begins April 1, 2014.
- 7, 8, or 9 – The next enrollment cycle begins April 1, 2015.

EAs who do not have an SSN must use the "7, 8, or 9" renewal schedule.

As part of the renewal process, the IRS will check the EA's filing history to verify that he has filed and paid all federal taxes on time. If the practitioner owns or has an interest in a business, the IRS will also check the tax compliance history of the business. In addition, the IRS will check that the EA has completed all necessary professional continuing education requirements.

The IRS sends a reminder notice when an EA is due for renewal. However, an enrolled agent is not excused from the obligation to renew if he does not receive the notice. An EA must inform the Return Preparer Office of an address change within 60 days of a move.

Continuing Education for Enrolled Agents

During each three-year enrollment cycle, an EA must complete 72 hours of continuing education credit. A minimum of 16 hours, including two hours of ethics or professional conduct, must be completed during each enrollment year.

For a new EA, the month of initial enrollment begins the CE requirement. They must complete two hours of CE for each month enrolled, which must include two hours of ethics. Enrollment for any part of a month is considered enrollment for the entire month. When an EA's new three-year enrollment cycle begins, he will be required to satisfy the full 72-hour continuing education credit requirement.

Example: Cammie became a new EA on September 30, 2013, which was the third year of the enrollment cycle based on her SSN. She is required to take two hours of CE per month prior to January 1, 2014, which equals eight hours for the period of September through December. Two of those hours must be on the topic of ethics. Since her initial enrollment came during the final year of the enrollment cycle, Cammie must renew her enrollment status in 2014 and will be subject to the full 72-hour CE requirement during her renewal period.

Ethics courses must be taken every year. If a candidate takes more than two hours of ethics courses during a single year, the additional hours may count toward the overall requirements of 16 hours per year and 72 hours per cycle. However, an enrolled agent may not take additional ethics courses in the current year and neglect to take them in future years.

Exception: If an enrolled agent retakes and passes the SEE again since his last renewal, he is only required to take 16 hours of CE, including two hours of ethics, during the last year of his current enrollment cycle.

CE Providers: Individuals and companies who wish to offer continuing education to EAs must pay a registration fee and apply as providers. Providers are issued a provider number and may display a logo that says "IRS Approved Continuing Education Provider."[48] Course providers must renew their status every year.

Approved Programs: Qualifying programs include traditional seminars and conferences, as well as correspondence or individual self-study programs on the Internet, so long as they are

[48] The IRS contracts with a private company to maintain an updated list of qualified providers at http://ssl.kinsail.com/partners/irs/publicListing.asp.

approved courses of study by approved providers. In order to qualify as CE, a course must be designed to enhance professional knowledge in federal taxation or federal tax-related matters. Courses related to state taxation do not meet the IRS requirement, unless at least 80% of the program material consists of a comparison between federal and state tax laws.

Contact Hours: Continuing education programs are measured in terms of contact hours. The shortest recognized program is one hour. In order for a course to qualify for CE credit, it must feature at least 50 minutes of continuous participation. Individual segments at conferences and conventions are considered one total program. For example, two 90-minute segments (180 minutes) at a continuous conference count as three contact hours.

Instructor Credit: A tax professional may receive continuing education credit for serving as an instructor, discussion leader, or speaker on federal tax matters for approved educational programs. One hour of CE credit is awarded for each contact hour completed. Two hours of CE credit is awarded for actual subject preparation time for each contact hour completed as an instructor, discussion leader, or speaker at such programs. The maximum credit for instruction and preparation may not exceed six hours annually.

Verifying CE Hours: After completing CE coursework, an EA will receive a certificate from the course provider. The course provider will also report completed continuing education to the IRS, using the PTINs of the individual participants. Tax professionals may check their online PTIN accounts to see a display of the CE programs they have completed, as reported by providers. CE hours completed prior to 2013 are not included. EAs are required to keep their own records related to continuing education hours for four years following the date of renewal.

CE Waiver

An EA may request a full or partial waiver of CE requirements from the RPO. Qualifying circumstances may include:

- Health issues
- Extended active military duty
- Absence from the United States for employment or other reasons
- Other reasons on a case-by-case basis

The request for a waiver must be accompanied by appropriate documentation, such as medical records or military paperwork. If the request is denied, the enrolled agent will be placed on the inactive roster. If the request is accepted, the EA will receive an updated enrollment card reflecting his renewal.

Example: Santiago is an EA who is also an Army reservist. He was called to active duty in a combat zone for two years. During this time, he was unable to complete his CE requirements for his enrolled agent license. Santiago requested a waiver based on his deployment, which was granted by the RPO.

Inactive and Terminated EAs

The RPO notifies any EAs who fail to comply with the requirements for eligibility for renewal of enrollment. The notice via first class mail explains the reason for noncompliance and provides the individual an opportunity to furnish the requested information, such as missing CE credits, in writing. An EA has 60 days from the date of the notice to respond to this initial notice. If no response is received, the EA will move to inactive status as of April 1.

To be eligible for renewal after missing one full enrollment cycle, an EA must pay fees for both the prior and current renewal cycles and verify that the required CE hours have been taken.

In July 2013, the RPO sent letters to all EAs whose enrollment status was being inactivated or terminated because of failure to renew. Those with Social Security numbers of 0, 1, 2, or 3 who did not renew for the 2013 cycle had their enrollment placed in inactive status. Those with Social Security numbers of 0, 1, 2, or 3 who had not renewed since the 2007 cycle had their enrollment terminated.

To have his termination status reconsidered, an EA must file a written protest within 30 days and provide a valid reason for not renewing timely. Reasons may include serious illness or extended travel out of the country.

Losing the Eligibility to Practice

Preparers may lose their eligibility to practice before the IRS for the following reasons, among others:

- Failure to meet the yearly educational requirements for enrollment.
- Failure to renew a PTIN or pay required fees.
- Requesting to be placed on inactive/retirement status.
- Being disbarred by state regulatory agents (in the case of attorneys and CPAs.) An attorney or CPA who is disbarred from practice at the state level is also disbarred from practice at the federal level, and cannot practice before the IRS as long as his disbarment or suspension is active.

Unit 2: Study Questions

1. Denise and Gabriela are best friends. They are not family members. Gabriela must appear before the IRS for an examination. Denise wants to appear before the IRS on her best friend's behalf, though she is not a practitioner. Which of the following statements is true?

A. Denise may represent Gabriela before the IRS without Gabriela being present.
B. Denise may advocate for Gabriela to the best of her ability.
C. Denise may appear before the IRS as a witness and communicate information.
D. Denise may not appear before the IRS in any capacity.

2. Enrolled agents must complete continuing education credits for renewed enrollment. Which of the following describes the credit requirements?

A. A minimum of 72 hours must be completed in each year of an enrollment cycle.
B. A minimum of 24 hours must be completed in each year of an enrollment cycle.
C. A minimum of 80 hours must be completed for the entire enrollment cycle.
D. A minimum of 16 hours must be completed in each year of the enrollment cycle, including two hours of ethics credits.

3. Which of the following individuals is required to obtain a PTIN?

A. A CPA who does not prepare any tax returns.
B. An EA who works for a CPA firm, but does not sign any tax returns.
C. A tax attorney who only does representation before the Supreme Court.
D. A retired accountant who prepares tax returns for free for his family.

4. Matthew is a full-time employee for Parkway Partnership. He is not an EA, attorney, or CPA. Parkway requests that Matthew represent the partnership in connection with an IRS audit. Which of the following statements is true?

A. Matthew is allowed to represent the partnership before the IRS.
B. Matthew is not allowed to represent the partnership before the IRS.
C. Matthew is only allowed to represent individual partners before the IRS.
D. None of the above.

5. What is the enrollment cycle for enrolled agents?

A. The enrollment cycle is the year after the effective date of renewal.
B. The enrollment cycle means the three successive enrollment years preceding the effective date of renewal.
C. The enrollment cycle is the method by which the RPO approves exam candidates.
D. The enrollment cycle is the method Prometric uses to choose EA exam questions.

6. All of the following are potential grounds for denial of enrollment except:

A. Failure to timely file tax returns.
B. Failure to pay taxes.
C. Felony convictions.
D. A candidate who is only 18 years old.

7. Barry helps his friend, José, who does not speak English fluently. Barry appears before the IRS and translates for José at an IRS examination. Which of the following is true?

A. Barry is practicing before the IRS.
B. José must sign a power of attorney form authorizing Barry to represent him.
C. Barry is not considered to be practicing before the IRS.
D. The IRS prohibits unrelated persons from being present at an IRS examination.

8. EAs who do not comply with the requirements for renewal of enrollment will be contacted by the Return Preparer Office. How much time does the EA have to respond to the RPO?

A. 30 days from the date of the notice.
B. 60 days from the date of the notice.
C. 60 days from the date of receipt.
D. 90 days from the date of the notice.

9. Which of the following is considered a tax return preparer under Circular 230 regulations?

A. A full-time bookkeeper working for an employer who prepares payroll tax returns.
B. A retired attorney who prepares tax returns under the VITA program.
C. A person who furnishes typing, reproducing, or mechanical assistance.
D. A full-time secretary who also prepares tax returns for pay part-time from home during tax season.

10. Practice before the IRS does not include:

A. Communicating with the IRS on behalf of a taxpayer regarding his rights or liabilities.
B. Representing a taxpayer at conferences, hearings, or meetings with the IRS.
C. Preparing and filing documents for the IRS.
D. Representation of clients in the U.S. Tax Court.

11. Andrea has been enrolled to practice before the IRS for many years. Her records show that she had the following hours of qualified CE in 2013:

- January 2013, 7 hours: General tax CE
- May 2013, 1 hour: Ethics
- December 2013, 9 hours: General tax CE

Has Andrea met her minimum yearly CE requirements?

A. Yes, Andrea has met her minimum yearly CE requirements.
B. No, Andrea has met her ethics requirement, but not the overall minimum requirement for the year.
C. No, Andrea has not met her ethics requirement.
D. None of the above.

12. Everett is an EA with a PTIN. His firm employs a bookkeeper named Fernanda. She gathers client receipts and invoices and organizes and records all information for Everett. Everett then uses the information that his bookkeeper has compiled and prepares all the tax returns. Which of the following statements is true?

A. Fernanda needs to have a PTIN, and she is required to become an EA because she assists in the preparation of returns.
B. Fernanda needs to have a PTIN, but she is not required to become an EA.
C. Fernanda is not a tax return preparer and is not required to have a PTIN.
D. None of the above.

13. What action should an EA take if he chooses to appeal termination from enrollment?

A. Call the Office of Professional Responsibility to complain.
B. File a written protest within 30 days of the date of the notice of termination.
C. File a written protest within 60 days of the date of the notice of termination.
D. File a written protest within 90 days of the date of the notice of termination.

14. Adele is a CPA with a bookkeeper, Kazuo, who assists in the preparation of returns. Kazuo has a PTIN and qualifies as a supervised preparer. He is not an EA or other practitioner. Kazuo may not:

A. Sign any tax return he prepares or assists in preparing.
B. Represent taxpayers before the IRS in any capacity.
C. Identify himself as a Circular 230 practitioner.
D. All of the above.

15. Enrolled agents who apply for renewal to practice before the IRS must retain information about CE hours completed. How long must CE documentation be retained?

A. For one year following the enrollment renewal date.
B. For four years following the enrollment renewal date.
C. For five years if it is an initial enrollment.
D. The individual is not required to retain the information if the CE provider has agreed to retain it.

16. To determine which preparer is responsible for a "substantial portion" of a tax return, each of the following guidelines is used except:
A. Whoever has the primary responsibility for the accuracy of the return.
B. Whoever actually owns or manages the tax practice.
C. Whoever prepares the portion of the return that declares the greatest amount of adjusted gross income.
D. All of the above.

17. Which of the following individuals does not qualify as a practitioner under Circular 230?

A. Certified public accountant.
B. Enrolled actuary.
C. Registered tax return preparer.
D. All of the above are considered practitioners.

18. When does a new EA's enrollment take effect?

A. On the date he applies for enrollment with the IRS.
B. On the date listed on his enrollment card.
C. On the date he receives his enrollment card.
D. On the first day of January after he receives his enrollment card.

19. Eleanor failed to complete her continuing education requirements. She plans to request a waiver so that she can renew her EA license. All of the following are reasons the RPO may accept as it considers whether to grant her waiver except:

A. Financial hardship.
B. Absence from the United States for an extended period of time.
C. Back surgery that required lengthy rehabilitation.
D. Deployment to Afghanistan as a member of the Army Reserve.

20. Khan is a CPA who employs Amy, an accounting student, to assist in the preparation of tax returns. Khan signs all of the tax returns. Which of the following statements is true?

A. Amy and Khan can share one PTIN.
B. Amy is required by law to sign the returns that she has prepared.
C. Amy is required to obtain a PTIN.
D. Amy cannot assist with the preparation of tax returns until she becomes a CPA.

21. Stan is an EA with a PTIN. What must he do to retain his existing PTIN?

A. Nothing. Stan is allowed to retain his PTIN so long as he is current in his enrollment status.
B. Stan must renew his PTIN every three years when he renews his enrollment status.
C. Stan cannot retain his existing PTIN. He must apply for a new PTIN every year.
D. Stan must renew his existing PTIN each year and pay a required fee.

22. Cameron is an EA whose Social Security number ends with the number seven. When does the next cycle begin for him to renew his enrollment?

A. On the anniversary date of his initial enrollment.
B. Beginning April 1, 2014.
C. Beginning April 1, 2015.
D. Beginning April 1, 2016.

23. All of the following are permitted to represent the taxpayer before the IRS except:

A. The taxpayer's best friend who is an attorney licensed to practice law in the state where the taxpayer lives.
B. The taxpayer's brother who is not an attorney, CPA, or enrolled agent.
C. An unregistered tax return preparer who did not prepare the taxpayer's return.
D. All of the above are permitted to represent the taxpayer before the IRS.

Unit 3: Authorizations and Disclosures

More Reading:
Publication 947, *Practice Before the IRS and Power of Attorney*
Instructions for Form 2848
Publication 216, *Conference and Practice Requirements*
Publication 4019, *Third Party Authorization, Levels of Authority*

Powers of Attorney

A power of attorney (POA) is a taxpayer's written authorization for an individual to act on the taxpayer's behalf in tax matters. The power of attorney gives an eligible individual, which includes all practitioners, the ability to represent a taxpayer before the IRS. Often, this occurs when a taxpayer wants to be represented at a conference with the IRS or to have a written response prepared and filed with the IRS.

When a taxpayer wishes to use a representative, he should fill out and sign Form 2848, *Power of Attorney and Declaration of Representative.* In doing so, the taxpayer authorizes a specific individual or individuals to receive confidential tax information and to perform the actions detailed on the form. On Form 2848, the taxpayer describes the tax matters the representative is authorized to handle, the time periods allowed, and the specific acts that are authorized or not authorized. A separate Form 2848 must be completed for each taxpayer who wishes representation; even joint filers must submit separate Forms 2848.

The types of tax and dates of a Form 2848 must be specific. The IRS will reject Forms 2848 with general references such as "all years" or "all taxes." In preparing the form, any tax years or periods that have already ended may be listed under "tax matters." For future tax periods, the period specified is limited to no later than three years after the date the POA is received by the IRS.

A representative must be eligible to practice before the IRS in order to sign Form 2848, and the duty may not be delegated to an employee. An enrolled agent must provide his PTIN and use his own name as the representative, rather than the name of his business.

Example: Caitlyn is an EA who operates Caitlyn Rivera's Tax Prep Co. When she prepares Form 2848, she must represent her client as an individual. Caitlyn is granted permission to represent her client, but her corporation and other members of her firm are not.

If a tax professional is disbarred or suspended, his power of attorney will not be recognized by the IRS. Unenrolled individuals may also be authorized to represent a taxpayer under Form 2848, if specifically permitted in limited circumstances (such as a family member representing a taxpayer, an executor representing an estate, or an unenrolled tax preparer who prepared the specific tax return at issue.)

Non-IRS Powers of Attorney (Durable Power of Attorney)

The IRS will accept a non-IRS power of attorney, such as a durable power of attorney, but it must contain all of the information included on a standard Form 2848.

Note: A durable power of attorney is not subject to a time limit and will continue in force after the incapacitation or incompetency of the individual. It is terminated upon the death of the individual.

Specifically, a non-IRS power of attorney must contain the following information:

- The taxpayer's name, mailing address, and taxpayer identification number
- The name and mailing address of the representative
- The types of tax involved and the federal tax form number in question
- The specific periods or tax years involved
- For estate tax matters, the decedent's date of death
- A clear expression of the taxpayer's intention concerning the scope of authority granted to the representative
- The taxpayer's signature and date

A signed and dated statement made by the representative should also be attached to the non-IRS power of attorney.

Example: Ronald signs a durable power of attorney that names his neighbor, Erik, as his representative. The durable power of attorney grants Erik the authority to perform all acts on Ronald's behalf. However, it does not list specific tax-related information such as types of tax or tax form numbers. Shortly after Ronald signs the power of attorney, he is declared incompetent. Later, a tax matter arises concerning a prior year return filed by Ronald. Erik attempts to represent Ronald before the IRS, but is rejected because the durable power of attorney does not contain required information. If Erik attaches a statement (signed under penalties of perjury) that the durable power of attorney is valid under the laws of the governing jurisdiction, he can sign a completed Form 2848 and submit it on Ronald's behalf. If Erik is eligible to practice before the IRS, he can name himself as the representative on Form 2848.

Unless a particular act is specifically not authorized by the taxpayer, a representative, with the exception of unenrolled tax preparers, can generally perform the following acts:

- Represent a taxpayer before any office of the IRS
- Record an interview or meeting with the IRS
- Sign an offer or a waiver of restriction on assessment or collection of a tax deficiency, or a waiver of notice of disallowance of claim for credit or refund
- Sign consents to extend the statutory time period for assessment or collection of a tax
- Sign a closing agreement
- Receive (but never endorse or cash) a tax refund check

The rights of unenrolled tax preparers are limited to representing taxpayers in examinations of the tax returns they prepared and signed.

A qualified representative can represent a taxpayer before the IRS without the taxpayer present, so long as the proper power of attorney is signed and submitted to the IRS.

Example: Delia is an enrolled agent with a signed Form 2848 for Mark, who is being audited by the IRS. Delia did not prepare Mark's tax return, but she is still eligible to represent him by virtue of her status as an EA. Mark does not have to appear at the examination hearing. If Delia were an unenrolled tax preparer, her representation rights would be restricted to the particular tax returns she had prepared for Mark that were under examination. She would be able to represent Mark only before IRS revenue agents and not revenue officers or appeals officers.

Revocation or Withdrawal of a POA: A power of attorney is valid until revoked by the taxpayer or until the representative withdraws from representation. If the taxpayer is revoking the power of attorney, he must write **"REVOKE"** across the top of the first page with his signature and the date below it. If the representative is withdrawing from representation, he must write **"WITHDRAW"** across the top of the first page with his signature and the date below it. The revocation or withdrawal must be mailed or faxed to the IRS. It must clearly indicate the applicable tax matters and periods.

Example: Nicola is an EA who had a power of attorney for her former client, Edwin. Nicola fired Edwin for nonpayment, but she continued to receive IRS notices on his behalf. Nicola writes "WITHDRAW" on the POA and submits it to the IRS, notifying the IRS that she no longer represents Edwin.

If a taxpayer or representative does not have a copy of the power of attorney, a statement of revocation or withdrawal must be sent to the IRS.

A newly filed power of attorney concerning the same matter will revoke a previously filed power of attorney. For example, if a taxpayer changes preparers and the second preparer files a power of attorney on behalf of the taxpayer, the old power of attorney on file will be rescinded. Unless the taxpayer specifically requests that the old power of attorney remain active, a power of attorney is automatically rescinded when a newer power of attorney is filed.

A power of attorney is generally terminated if the taxpayer becomes incapacitated or incompetent.

Updating a Power of Attorney: Any update or modification to a power of attorney must be submitted in writing to the IRS. A recognized representative may substitute or delegate authority if the taxpayer has specifically given him the power to do so. The representative must file the following items with the IRS offices where the power of attorney was filed:

- A written notice of substitution or delegation signed by the recognized representative.
- A written declaration of representation made by the new representative.
- A copy of the power of attorney that specifically authorizes the substitution or delegation.

After a substitution is made, only the newly recognized representative will be considered the taxpayer's representative.

Representative Signing in Lieu of the Taxpayer

A representative named under a power of attorney is generally not permitted to sign a personal income tax return unless both of the following are true:

- The signature is permitted under the Internal Revenue Code and the related regulations.
- The taxpayer specifically grants signature authority on the power of attorney.

For example, IRS regulations permit a representative to sign a taxpayer's return if the taxpayer is unable to sign for any of the following reasons:

- Disease or injury (for example, a taxpayer who is completely paralyzed or who has a debilitating injury)
- Continuous absence from the United States (including Puerto Rico) for a period of at least 60 days prior to the date required by law for filing the return
- Other good cause if specific permission is requested of and granted by the IRS

Example: Geoffrey is an EA with a client named Sally who travels extensively for business. She had signed Form 2848 specifically granting Geoffrey the right to sign her tax returns in her absence. Sally is currently traveling outside the U.S. for business and will not return until four months after the due date of her returns. Geoffrey is allowed to sign Sally's return.

When a tax return is signed by a representative, it must be accompanied by a copy of the power of attorney authorizing the representative to sign the return.

Tax Information Authorization, Form 8821

IRS Form 8821, *Tax Information Authorization* (TIA), authorizes any individual, corporation, firm, organization, or partnership to inspect or receive confidential information for the type of tax and periods listed. Any third party may be designated to receive tax information.

Form 8821 is used by tax preparers, employers, banks, and other institutions to receive financial information on behalf of an individual or a business. It is only a disclosure form, so it does not give an individual authority to represent a taxpayer before the IRS. Similar to a POA form, Form 8821 requires the taxpayer to list the type of tax, the tax form number, the year or periods the authorization covers, and the specific tax matters that apply. Any prior tax years may be specified, but only future tax periods ending no later than three years after the date the TIA is received by the IRS are recognized.[49] Form 8821 must be received by the IRS within 120 days of the date the taxpayer signs the form.

Centralized Authorization File (CAF)

The centralized authorization file (CAF) is the IRS's computer database that contains information regarding the authorizations that taxpayers have given representatives for their accounts. When a power of attorney or disclosure authorization document is submitted to the IRS, it

[49] In September 2013, the IRS removed the disclosure authorization application from its online e-services because of low usage and budget cuts. That means users have to either mail or fax Forms 2848 and 8821 to the appropriate IRS location rather than file them electronically.

is processed for inclusion in the CAF. A CAF number is assigned to a tax practitioner or other authorized individual when either a Form 2848 or Form 8821 is filed.

Example: Josie is not a tax return preparer. In 2013, Josie's son, David, is audited by the IRS. David is 21 years old and does not wish to speak directly with the IRS. Josie files a Form 2848 and becomes the authorized representative for her son. She is issued a CAF number.

Joint filers must complete and submit separate Forms 2848 to have the power of attorney recorded in the CAF. Alternative power of attorney forms, such as a durable power of attorney, will not be recorded in the CAF unless a Form 2848 is also attached.

The issuance of a CAF number does not indicate that a person is either recognized or authorized to practice before the IRS. It merely confirms that a centralized file has been established for the representative under that number.

Example: Darren is an EA who recently submitted Form 2848 to the IRS on behalf of his client, Jennifer. He later called the IRS to check the status of Jennifer's tax refund. The IRS employee requested Darren's CAF number, which he provided. The IRS employee found Jennifer's power of attorney information in the CAF system and gave Darren the information about his client's refund.

Having a CAF number also enables the IRS to automatically send copies of notices and other IRS communications to a representative.

Third Party Authorizations

A third party authorization is when a taxpayer authorizes an individual (usually his tax preparer) to communicate with the IRS on his behalf. This authorization allows the IRS to discuss the processing of a taxpayer's current tax return, including the status of refunds, with whomever the taxpayer specifies. The authorization automatically expires on the due date of the next tax return.

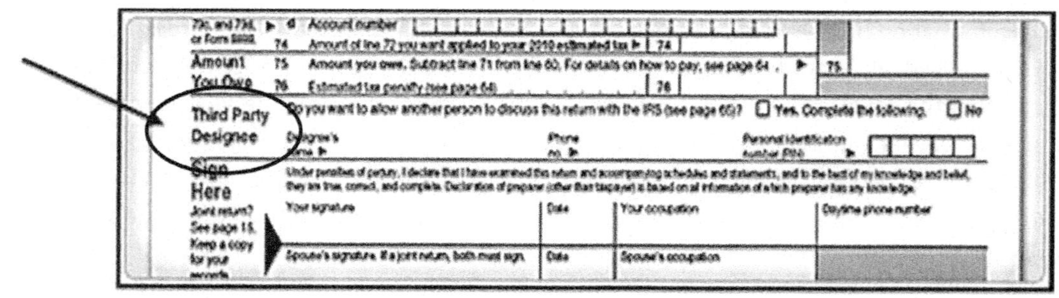
Amount You Owe
75 Amount you owe. Subtract line 71 from line 60. For details on how to pay, see page 64
76 Estimated tax penalty (see page 64)
Third Party Designee
Do you want to allow another person to discuss this return with the IRS (see page 65)? Yes. Complete the following. No
Designee's name | Phone no. | Personal identification number (PIN)
Sign Here
Joint return? See page 15. Keep a copy for your records.
Your signature | Date | Your occupation | Daytime phone number
Spouse's signature. If a joint return, both must sign. | Date | Spouse's occupation

A taxpayer can choose a third party designee by checking the "yes" box on his tax return, which is why it is known as "Check Box" authority. The taxpayer then enters the designee's name and phone number and a self-selected five-digit PIN, which the designee must confirm when requesting information from the IRS. The designee can exchange verbal information with the IRS on return processing issues and on refunds and payments related to the return. The designee may also receive written account information including transcripts, upon request. A designee cannot receive a tax refund check on a client's behalf.

Example: Rashid named his EA, Patty, as his third party designee on his tax return. A few months after filing his return, Rashid still had not received his refund. He asked Patty if she could check the status of his refund. Patty called the IRS and was given the information over the phone, because she was listed as a third party designee on Rashid's return. No further authorization was necessary for Patty to receive this confidential taxpayer information.

The third party designee authorization is more limited than the authority given by Form 8821, *Tax Information Authorization* (TIA). Form 8821 can be used to allow discussions with third parties and disclosures of information to third parties on matters other than a taxpayer's current return.

Tax Return Copies and Transcripts

If a taxpayer needs an actual copy of his own tax return that has been filed and processed, he may use Form 4506, *Request for Copy of Tax Return.* Copies are generally available for the current year and the past six years. The IRS charges a fee for mailing the copy.[50]

Form 4506-T, *Request for Transcript of Tax Return,* is used when a taxpayer wants to authorize an individual or organization to receive or inspect confidential tax return information.

This form is often used by financial institutions to verify tax compliance or income, such as when a taxpayer is applying for a mortgage. Form 4506-T does not authorize an individual to represent a taxpayer before the IRS.

The taxpayer must specify on the form what type of information is needed. If a "return transcript" is requested, the IRS will provide most of the line items of a filed tax return. It does not reflect any changes made after the original return was filed. If an "account transcript" is requested, the IRS will provide information on the financial status of the account, such as payments made and penalty assessments. Requesting a "record of account" produces the most detailed information as it combines the return transcript and account transcript information. The record of account is available for the current year and the three prior tax years. The IRS does not charge a fee for providing tax return transcripts. [51]

Privacy of Taxpayer Information (§7216)

The IRS has enacted strict privacy regulations designed to give taxpayers more control over their personal information and tax records. The regulations limit tax professionals' use and disclosure of client information, and explain precise and limited exceptions in which disclosure is permitted.

Internal Revenue Code §7216 is a criminal provision enacted by Congress that prohibits tax return preparers from knowingly or recklessly disclosing or using tax return information.

---

[50] In 2013, the fee was $57 for each tax year requested.

[51] In early 2014, the IRS added a new online request option called "Get Transcript" that allows individual taxpayers to instantly view and print a copy of tax transcripts. Five types of transcripts are available: tax account, tax return, record of account, wage and income, and verification of non-filing.

A preparer may be fined up to $1,000, imprisoned up to one year, or both, for each violation of §7216. There is also a civil penalty of $250 for improper disclosure or use of taxpayer information, outlined in IRC §6713. However, unlike §7216, this code section does not require that the disclosure be "knowing or reckless."

Tax preparers must generally obtain written consent from taxpayers before they can disclose information to a third party or use the information for any purpose other than the preparation of tax returns. The consent form must meet the following guidelines:

- Identify the purpose of the disclosure.
- Identify the recipient and describe the authorized information.
- Include the name of the preparer and the name of the taxpayer.
- Include mandatory language that informs the taxpayer that he is not required to sign the consent, and if he does sign the consent, he can set a time period for the duration of the consent.
- Include mandatory language that refers the taxpayer to the Treasury Inspector General for Tax Administration if he believes that his tax return information has been disclosed or used improperly.
- If applicable, inform the taxpayer that his tax return information may be disclosed to a tax return preparer located outside the U.S.
- Be signed and dated by the taxpayer. Electronic (online) consents must be in the same type as the website's standard text and contain the taxpayer's affirmative consent (as opposed to an opt-out clause).

Unless a specific time period is specified, the consent is valid for one year.

These privacy regulations apply to paid preparers, electronic return originators, tax software developers, and other persons or entities engaged in tax preparation.

The regulations also apply to most volunteer tax preparers, such as Volunteer Income Tax Assistance and Tax Counseling for the Elderly volunteers, and to employees and contractors employed by tax preparation companies in a support role.

Allowable Disclosures

In certain circumstances, a preparer may disclose information to a second taxpayer who appears on a tax return. The preparer may disclose return information obtained from the first taxpayer if:

- The second taxpayer is related to the first taxpayer.
- The first taxpayer's interest is not adverse to the second taxpayer's interest.
- The first taxpayer has not prohibited the disclosure.

Example: Zach is an EA with two married clients, Serena and Tyler, who file jointly. Serena works long hours, so she is unavailable when Tyler meets with Zach to prepare their joint tax return. Later, Serena comes in alone to sign the return. She also has a question regarding the mortgage interest on the joint tax return. Zach is allowed to disclose return information to Serena because it is a joint return, Tyler has not prohibited any disclosures, and both Serena and Tyler's names are on the return.

A taxpayer is considered related to another taxpayer in any of the following relationships:

- Husband and wife, or child and parent
- Grandchild and grandparent
- General partner in a partnership
- Trust or estate and the beneficiary
- A corporation and shareholder
- Members of a controlled group of corporations

A tax preparer may also disclose tax return information that was obtained from a first taxpayer in preparing a tax return of the second taxpayer, if the preparer has obtained written consent from the first taxpayer. For example, if an unmarried couple lives together and splits the mortgage interest, the preparer may use or disclose information from the first taxpayer to the second so long as the preparer has written consent.

Note: The IRS's definition of **tax return information** is broad and encompasses the following: "All the information tax return preparers obtain from taxpayers or other sources in any form or matter that is used to prepare tax returns or is obtained in connection with the preparation of returns. It also includes all computations, worksheets, and printouts preparers create; correspondence from the IRS during the preparation, filing and correction of returns; statistical compilations of tax return information; and tax return preparation software registration information."

Disclosure Consent Not Required: A tax preparer is not required to obtain disclosure consent from a client if the disclosure is made for any of the following reasons:

- A court order or subpoena issued by any court of record whether at the federal, state, or local level. The required information must be clearly identified in the document (subpoena or court order) in order for a preparer to disclose information.
- An administrative order, demand, summons, or subpoena that is issued by any federal agency, state agency, or commission charged under the laws of the state with licensing, registration, or regulation of tax return preparers.
- To report a crime to proper authorities. Even if the preparer is mistaken and no crime has occurred, he will not be subject to sanctions if he makes the disclosure in good faith.
- For purposes of peer reviews.

A tax preparer may disclose private client information to his attorney or to an employee of the IRS, in connection with an IRS investigation of the preparer.

Example: The IRS is investigating a CPA named Harry for possible misconduct. Harry has an attorney who is assisting in his defense. As it turns out, Harry was the victim of embezzlement because his bookkeeper was stealing client checks. He only discovered the embezzlement when the IRS contacted him about client complaints. Harry may disclose confidential client information to his attorney in order to assist with his own defense. Harry may also disclose confidential client information to the IRS during the course of its investigation.

A tax preparer may disclose tax return information to a tax return processor. For example, if a tax preparer uses an electronic or tax return processing service, he may disclose tax return information to that service in order to prepare tax returns or compute tax liability.

Confidentiality Privilege for Practitioners

Practitioners and their clients are granted limited rights of confidentiality protection. This confidentiality privilege applies to attorneys, CPAs, enrolled agents, enrolled actuaries, and certain other individuals allowed to practice before the IRS.[52]

The confidentiality protection applies to communications that would be considered privileged if they were between the taxpayer and an attorney and that relate to:

- Noncriminal tax matters before the IRS, or
- Noncriminal tax proceedings brought in federal court by or against the United States.

This confidentiality privilege cannot be used with any agency other than the IRS.

The confidentiality privilege does not apply:

- In criminal tax matters
- To any written communications regarding the promotion of a tax shelter
- In state tax proceedings
- To the general preparation of tax returns

There is a long history of court decisions that deny confidentiality of information disclosed to an attorney for purposes of preparing tax returns. In a key 1983 ruling, the court stated that "information transmitted for the purpose of preparation of a tax return, though transmitted to an attorney, is not privileged information. When information will be transmitted to a third party (in this case on a tax return,) such information is not confidential."[53] This restriction on the confidentiality privilege related to tax preparation applies to other practitioners, including enrolled agents and CPAs, as well as to attorneys.

Identity Theft

Identity theft occurs when someone uses another individual's personally identifiable information, such as his name, Social Security number, or credit card number, without his permission to commit fraud or other crimes. Fraudulent refunds have become a major issue, and identity theft is considered one of the biggest challenges facing the IRS.

---

[52] IRC §7525.

[53] *United States v. Lawless*, 709 F.2d 487 (7th Cir. 1983.)

Stolen Identity Refund Fraud (SIRF): This growing type of crime occurs when thieves file fraudulent refund claims using a legitimate taxpayer's identifying information, which they have stolen. In 2012, the IRS issued $4 billion in fraudulent tax refunds to people using stolen identities.[54] Tax refund fraud involving the use of stolen identities is now referred to as SIRF, for Stolen Identity Refund Fraud.

Enforcement: The IRS has doubled the number of employees working on identity theft cases since 2011. In fiscal year 2013, the IRS started 1,492 criminal investigations into the use of tax returns to commit identify theft, a 66% increase. Among those prosecuted was a Florida woman who was ordered to forfeit $2.2 million.

Theft Prevention: To help stop identity thieves, the IRS says it now has dozens of identity theft screening filters in place to protect tax refunds. To educate taxpayers, the IRS has added a guide to identity theft on its website. Taxpayers are advised to be on the alert for possible identity theft if they receive an IRS notice or letter stating that any of the following has occurred:

- There was more than one tax return filed by the taxpayer.
- The taxpayer has a balance due, refund offset, or has had collection actions taken against him for a year in which he did not file a tax return.
- IRS records indicate the taxpayer received wages from an unknown employer.

The IRS will never seek financial or personal information by initiating contact with taxpayers by email, text messages, social media, or any other form of electronic communications. Many phishing scams attempt to collect taxpayer Social Security numbers by contacting taxpayers using these methods.

As part of its crackdown, the IRS is issuing an identity protection personal identification number (IP PIN) to any taxpayer who has:

- Reported to the IRS he has been the victims of identity theft
- Given the IRS information that verifies his identity
- Had an identity theft indicator applied to his account

For 2013 tax returns, the IRS assigned 1.2 million IP PINs to identity theft victims, nearly double the number from the previous year.

The IP PIN helps prevent the misuse of a taxpayer's Social Security number or taxpayer identification number. It is used on both paper and electronic returns. If the taxpayer attempts to file an electronic return without his IP PIN, the return will be rejected. If it is missing on a paper return, there will likely be a delay in processing, as the IRS will have to validate the taxpayer's identity.

The IP PIN is only valid for a single year. A taxpayer will receive a new IP PIN every year for three years after reporting the identity theft incident to the IRS. If a spouse also has an IP PIN, only the person whose SSN appears first on the tax return needs to input his PIN.

---

[54] Treasury Inspector General for Tax Administration report, November 7, 2013. The IRS sent a total of 655 tax refunds to a single address in Lithuania, and 343 refunds to a single address in Shanghai, China. Florida had the highest number of fraudulent returns in the U.S., partly because of the number of older residents living there. Thieves often steal Social Security numbers from people who do not have to file tax returns, including the young, old, and people who have died.

Preparer Security Precautions

Since practitioners are required to obtain and store client information, they have an important role to play in keeping this information secure. To help prevent identity theft, the IRS suggests preparers confirm identities and taxpayer identification numbers of taxpayers, their spouses, dependents, and Earned Income Credit qualifying children on the returns to be prepared. TINs include Social Security numbers (SSNs), adopted taxpayer identification numbers (ATINs), and individual taxpayer identification numbers (ITINs). To confirm identities, the preparer can request a picture ID showing the taxpayer's name and address, and Social Security cards or other documents providing the TINs for all other individuals to be listed on the return.

Additional steps practitioners can take to guard against identity theft include the following:

- File clients' returns early when possible.
- E-file returns, in order to be notified of duplicate return notices more quickly.
- Let clients know that refunds may take longer in future years as additional system security steps are taken.
- Be very careful about confirming the identity of new online clients.

Since tax return preparers are at risk of having their identities, and those of their clients, stolen, they should take special precautions to safeguard their clients' sensitive information. Industry recommendations include the following:[55]

- Locking desk drawers and file cabinets
- Using encrypted flash drives and using other encrypted procedures in electronically transferring a client's information to a third party
- Redacting or truncating SSNs and other personal information
- Using couriers and certified mail to ensure that the correct person receives the correspondence
- Installing and requiring antivirus and other security software on all of the firm's computers

[55] American Institute of CPAs' written statement to the IRS Oversight Board, May 1, 2013.

Unit 3: Study Questions

1. All of the following statements regarding the signature requirements for tax returns are correct except:

A. A tax preparer may sign a taxpayer's return in lieu of the taxpayer, if the taxpayer cannot sign his own tax return due to a physical disability.
B. A tax preparer may sign a taxpayer's return in lieu of the taxpayer, if the taxpayer cannot sign his own tax return due to an extended absence from the United States.
C. A tax preparer is allowed to copy a taxpayer's signature if he has a signed power of attorney.
D. A tax preparer must have a signed power of attorney in order to sign on the taxpayer's behalf.

2. The Centralized Authorization File (CAF) is ________________.

A. An IRS computer data base with information regarding the authority of individuals appointed under powers of attorney or designated under tax information authorizations.
B. A file containing a practitioner's personal tax return files, in order to assist with compliance regulation and monitoring of enrolled individuals.
C. An automated list of disbarred tax preparers.
D. An automated file of taxpayer delinquencies.

3. Darrell is an EA who has a third party designee authorization from his client, Annalise. All of the following actions are allowed with this type of authorization except:

A. Darrell can receive written account information on Annalise's behalf.
B. Darrell can receive Annalise's tax transcripts upon request.
C. Darrell can check the status of tax refund processing.
D. Darrell can receive Annalise's refund check.

4. Which designation or form gives the appointed person the greatest rights to represent a taxpayer?

A. Third party designee, also known as "Check Box" authority.
B. Form 8821, *Tax Information Authorization*.
C. Form 2848, *Power of Attorney and Declaration of Representative*.
D. Form 4506-T, *Request for Transcript of Tax Return*.

5. The IRS has created a system of IP PINs as a step toward combating __________:

A. Practitioner fraud.
B. Unenrolled preparer fraud.
C. Identity fraud.
D. Taxpayer abuse of the Earned Income Credit.

6. In what situation is a preparer allowed to disclose information without first obtaining written permission from a client?

A. When he is issued a subpoena by a state agency that regulates tax return preparers.
B. When he is contacted by a reporter investigating a possible crime committed by his client.
C. When the information is requested by his client's uncle who helps support the client financially.
D. When the information is needed by a preparer who volunteers with VITA.

7. For taxpayers who want someone to represent them at an examination with the IRS, all of the following statements are correct except:

A. The taxpayer must furnish that representative with written authorization on Form 2848, *Power of Attorney and Declaration of Representative*, or any other properly written authorization.
B. The representative can be an attorney, CPA, or EA.
C. The representative can be an unenrolled preparer who prepared the taxpayer's current year tax return but not the year of the return under examination.
D. Even if the taxpayer appointed a representative, the taxpayer may choose to attend the examination or appeals conference and may act on his own behalf.

8. Which statement is true regarding the privacy regulations in IRC §7216?

A. The regulations do not apply to e-file providers.
B. The improper disclosure must be "knowing or reckless" for criminal provisions to apply.
C. A practitioner may be fined up to $500 and imprisoned for up to one year for each violation of this code.
D. Tax practitioners must obtain oral consent from taxpayers before they can use information for anything other than the actual preparation of tax returns.

9. How long is a power of attorney authorization valid?

A. One year.
B. Three years.
C. Until it is revoked or superseded.
D. Until the due date of the next tax return.

10. Form 8821, *Tax Information Authorization*, may be used to authorize the following:

A. Any individual, corporation, firm, organization, or partnership to receive confidential information for the type of tax and periods listed on Form 8821.
B. Any designated third party to receive tax information.
C. Both A and B.
D. For unenrolled preparers to indicate a representative relationship with a taxpayer and to authorize practice before the IRS.

11. Willa is an EA with a signed Form 2848 from her client, who is currently under audit. Which of the following actions is not correct?

A. Willa may record the audit meeting with the IRS examiner.
B. Willa may sign a consent to extend the statutory time period for assessment of tax.
C. Willa may receive and endorse a tax refund check on her client's behalf.
D. Willa may represent her client before the IRS Appeals office, without the taxpayer present.

12. A durable power of attorney remains in effect until an individual ____________________.

A. Gets divorced.
B. Becomes mentally incompetent or incapacitated.
C. Dies.
D. Both B and C.

13. When does the authorization for a third party designee expire?

A. Three months after the return is filed.
B. One year after the return is filed.
C. Three years after the return is filed.
D. On the due date of the next tax return.

14. For future tax periods, Form 2848 is valid for a period of no later than ______________ after the date the POA is received by the IRS.

A. One year.
B. Two years.
C. Three years.
D. Five years.

15. Taxpayers are granted a confidentiality privilege with any federally authorized practitioner. This is the same confidentiality protection that a taxpayer would have with an attorney, with some exceptions. Confidential communications include all of the following except:

A. Written tax advice.
B. Matters that would be confidential between an attorney and a client.
C. Participation in a tax shelter.
D. Noncriminal tax matters before the IRS.

16. If a preparer no longer wishes to represent a taxpayer, he should take the following action:

A. Nothing. A taxpayer is the only one who can revoke power of attorney authorization.
B. Write the word "REVOKE" on the POA form and mail or fax it to the IRS.
C. Write the word "WITHDRAW" on the POA form and mail or email it to the IRS.
D. Write the word "WITHDRAW" on the POA form and mail or fax it to the IRS.

17. Which is not necessary in connection with Form 2848?

A. For all signatures to be notarized.
B. For the form to be filed with the IRS.
C. For the preparer to include his PTIN.
D. All of the requirements above are necessary in connection with Form 2848.

Unit 4: Tax Preparer Responsibilities

More Reading:
Circular No. 230, *Regulations Governing Practice Before the IRS*
Publication 947, *Practice Before the IRS and Power of Attorney*
Publication 216, *Conference and Practice Requirements*

Circular 230 Regulations

The Treasury Department's Circular 230 sets forth regulations that govern all paid tax preparers, including enrolled agents, CPAs, attorneys, and others who practice before the IRS. Circular 230 imposes professional standards and codes of conduct for tax preparers and tax advisors. It prohibits certain actions, requires other actions, and details penalties for ethical violations and other misconduct by tax preparers.

In the next two units, we will look at the various sections of Circular 230 that describe tax preparer responsibilities and standards.

Diligence as to Accuracy (§10.22)

Central to the Circular 230 regulations is the mandate for practitioners to exercise due diligence when performing the following duties:

- Preparing or assisting in preparing, approving, and filing of returns, documents, affidavits, and other papers relating to IRS matters
- Determining the correctness of oral or written representations made to the Department of the Treasury
- Determining the correctness of oral or written representations made to clients related to any matter administered by the IRS

The Circular 230 statement does not specify exactly what due diligence entails.

In letters sent to selected tax preparers in 2013,[56] the IRS further described a preparer's due diligence responsibility to his clients, saying it involves multiple steps to prepare accurate tax returns for clients. These steps include "reviewing the applicable tax law to establish the relevance and reasonableness of income, credits, expenses, and deductions on a return."

Reliance on Others: A practitioner will be presumed to have exercised due diligence if he relies on the work product of another person, assuming that the practitioner used reasonable care in engaging, supervising, training, and evaluating that person.

Best Practices (§10.33)

Circular 230 explains the broad concept of *best practices*. Tax preparers must provide clients with the highest quality representation concerning federal tax matters by adhering to best practices in providing advice and in preparing documents or information for the IRS.

---

[56] IRS Return Preparer Visitation Project: Letters 5102 and 5105 sent in January 2013 to preparers who had Schedule C returns that indicated a high rate of errors.

Tax preparers who oversee a firm's practice should take reasonable steps to ensure that the firm's procedures for all employees are consistent with best practices.

Best practices include the following:

- Communicating clearly with the client regarding the terms of the engagement.
- Establishing the facts, determining which facts are relevant, evaluating the reasonableness of any assumptions, relating the applicable law to the relevant facts, and arriving at a conclusion supported by the law and the facts.
- Advising the client of the conclusions reached and the impact of the advice rendered; for example, advising whether a taxpayer may avoid accuracy-related penalties if he relies on the advice provided.
- Acting fairly and with integrity in practice before the IRS.

Knowledge of Client's Omission (§10.21)

A practitioner who knows that his client has not complied with the revenue laws or who has made an error or omission on his tax return has the responsibility to advise the client promptly of the noncompliance, error, or omission, as well as its consequences.

The practitioner is not responsible for correcting the noncompliance once he has notified the client of the issue, or for notifying the IRS of a client's noncompliance.

Example: Jeremy is an EA with a new client, Monique, who has prepared her own returns in the past. Jeremy notices that Monique has been claiming head of household status on her tax returns, but she does not qualify for this status, because she does not have a qualifying person. Jeremy is required to promptly notify Monique of the error and tell her the consequences of not correcting the error. However, Jeremy is not required to amend Monique's prior year tax returns to correct the error. Nor is he required to notify the IRS of Monique's claim of incorrect status.

The §10.21 obligations are not limited to practitioners preparing returns, so the discovery of an error in the course of a tax consulting or advisory engagement will also trigger its requirements.

Example: Gina is an EA who takes over another tax preparer's practice. She discovers that the previous preparer has been taking section 179 deductions on assets that do not qualify for this treatment. Gina must notify her clients of the errors and the consequences of not correcting the errors. She is not required to correct the errors.

Conflicts of Interest (§10.29)

A conflict of interest exists if:

- The representation of one client will be directly adverse to another client; or
- There is a significant risk that the representation of one or more clients will be materially limited by the practitioner's responsibilities to another client, a former client, a third person, or by a personal interest of the practitioner.

A tax professional may represent a client when a conflict of interest exists if:

- The practitioner reasonably believes that he will be able to provide competent and diligent representation to each affected client;
- The representation is not prohibited by law; and
- Each affected client waives the conflict of interest and gives informed consent, confirmed in writing.

If there is a potential conflict of interest, the practitioner must disclose the conflict and be given the opportunity to disclose all material facts. The written consent must be retained for at least 36 months from the date representation ends. At minimum, the consent should adequately describe the nature of the conflict and the parties the practitioner represents.

Example: Christa is an EA who prepares tax returns for Jana and Brett, a married couple. In 2013, they go through a contentious divorce, and Christa believes there is potential for conflict of interest relating to the services she would provide for each of them. She prepares a written statement explaining the potential conflict of interest. Jana and Brett still want Christa to prepare their returns, so she has each sign a written consent. Christa must retain the record of their consent for at least 36 months after she last represents either party.

IRS Information Requests (§10.20)

Under Circular 230 §10.20, when the IRS requests information, a practitioner must comply and submit records promptly.

If the requested information or records are not in the practitioner's possession, he must promptly advise the requesting IRS officer and provide any information he has regarding the identity of the person who may have possession or control of the requested information or records. The practitioner must also make a "reasonable inquiry" of his client regarding the location of the requested records.

However, the practitioner is not required to make inquiry of any other person or to independently verify any information furnished by his client. Further, the practitioner is not required to contact any third party who might be in possession of the records.

Example: An IRS revenue agent submitted a lawful records request to Randall, an EA, for accounting records relating to a former client who was under IRS investigation. However, earlier in the year, Randall had fired his client for nonpayment and returned his records. Randall promptly notified the IRS officer that he no longer had the records. He also attempted to contact his former client, but the phone number was disconnected. Randall is not required to contact any third parties to discover the location of the requested records. Therefore, Randall has fulfilled his obligations under §10.20.

A practitioner may not interfere with any lawful effort by the IRS to obtain any record or information unless he believes in good faith and on reasonable grounds that the record or information is privileged under IRC §7525. A practitioner can also be exempted from these rules if he believes in good faith that the request is of doubtful legality.

If the IRS's Office of Professional Responsibility requests information concerning possible violations of the regulations by other parties, such as other preparers or taxpayers, the practitioner must furnish the information and be prepared to testify in disbarment or suspension proceedings.

Return of Client Records (§10.28)

A practitioner is required to return a client's original records upon request, whether or not his fees have been paid. Client records include:

- All documents a client provided to a practitioner that pre-existed their business engagement.
- Any materials that were prepared by the client or a third party that were provided to the practitioner relating to the subject matter of the representation.
- Any document prepared by the practitioner that was presented to the client relating to a prior representation if such document is necessary for the taxpayer to comply with his current federal tax obligations.

Client records generally do not include the tax practitioner's work product. However, they may include any work product that the client has already paid for, such as a completed copy of a tax return. Client records do not include any return, claim for refund, schedule, affidavit, appraisal, or any other document prepared by the practitioner if he is withholding these documents pending the client's payment of fees.

The practitioner must, at the request of a client, promptly return any and all records that are necessary for the client to comply with his federal tax obligations. The practitioner must also allow the client reasonable access to review and copy any additional records retained by the practitioner that are necessary for the client to comply with his federal tax obligations.

Example: Leroy is an EA with a client, Samantha, who becomes upset after he tells her she owes substantial penalties to the IRS. Samantha wants to get a second opinion, and she does not want to pay Leroy for his time. Leroy is required to hand over Samantha's tax records, including copies of her W-2 forms and any other information she brought to his office. Leroy returns her original records, but he does not give her a copy of the tax return he prepared, since she did not pay his fee for the return.

Example: Clara is an EA who does substantial tax work for a partnership, Greenway Landscaping. Greenway has been slow to pay in the past, so Clara asks that the owners of Greenway pay for the tax returns when they pick them up. Greenway refuses and demands the tax returns anyway. Clara decides to discontinue all contact with Greenway. Clara must return Greenway's original records, but she is not required to give Greenway work product that the owners have not paid for.

The practitioner may retain copies of the records returned to a client.

Signature Requirements

Signature requirements for the preparation of tax returns are as follows:

1. **Preparer Signature and PTIN:** A preparer is required by law to sign the tax return, include his PTIN, and fill out the preparer areas of the form. The preparer's declaration on signing the return states that the information contained in the return is true, correct, and complete based on all information he has. This statement is signed under penalties of perjury. The preparer must sign the return after it is completed but before it is presented

to the taxpayer for signature. The preparer can sign original returns, amended returns, or request for filing extensions by rubber stamp, mechanical device (such as a signature pen), or computer software program.

2. **Taxpayer Signature:** Regardless of whether a paid preparer or someone else has prepared a return, a taxpayer must sign his own return, affirming it is correct under penalties of perjury. A taxpayer is legally responsible for the accuracy of every item on the return.
3. **More Than One Preparer:** If the original preparer is unavailable for signature, another preparer must review the entire preparation of the return or claim and then must manually sign it. For purposes of the signature requirement, the preparer with primary responsibility for the overall accuracy of the return or claim is considered the preparer, if more than one preparer is involved. The other preparers do not have to be disclosed on the return.

A preparer may sign on behalf of the taxpayer in the client's signature area only if certain standards are met (covered previously in Unit 3.)

Copies of Tax Returns (§6107)

Tax preparers are required to give a completed copy of a tax return or claim for refund no later than the time the return or claim is presented for the taxpayer's signature.

Preparers are required to keep copies of all returns they have prepared or retain a list of clients and tax returns prepared. At a minimum, the list must contain the taxpayer's name, taxpayer identification number, tax year, and the type of return prepared. The copies of tax returns or the lists must be retained for at least three years after the close of the return period. The close of the return period is defined as June 30, meaning the three-year period to retain records begins July 1.

Note: In practice, most preparers keep scanned, digital, or hard copies of client tax returns rather than simply a list of the returns prepared.

Tax Preparer Employer Records (§6060, Employer of Tax Preparers): The employer of tax return preparers must keep a record of all those employed and make it available for IRS inspection upon request. The records must include the name, taxpayer identification number, and place of work of each tax return preparer employed. Records must be retained for at least three years following the close of the return period.

Other Duties and Prohibited Acts

No Delay Tactics Allowed (§10.23): A practitioner must not unreasonably delay the prompt disposition of any matter before the IRS.

Example: Emory is an enrolled agent who is representing a client in an IRS examination. Emory has repeatedly rescheduled appointments with an IRS revenue agent in an attempt to delay proceedings. He has also delayed furnishing certain documents that the IRS has requested, and when he does provide them, the records are incomplete. Emory's actions are in violation of Circular 230.

No Employment of Disbarred or Suspended Persons (§10.24): A tax practitioner may not knowingly employ a person or accept assistance from a person who has been disbarred or suspended from practice. This restriction applies even if the duties of the disbarred or suspended person would not include actual preparation of tax returns. In addition, a practitioner may not accept assistance from a former government employee in matters in which the former employee personally and substantially participated in the particular matter while employed by the government.

Practice by Former Government Employees (§10.25): A former government employee (and his partners and associates) cannot represent or knowingly assist a taxpayer if the representation would violate any law of the United States. A government employee who personally and substantially participated in a particular matter cannot represent or assist a taxpayer in the same particular matter after leaving his government position. §10.25 also places other restrictions on former government employees, including former IRS workers, in order to avoid conflicts of interest during representation.

Performance as a Notary (§10.26): A tax practitioner who is a notary public and is employed as counsel, attorney, or agent in a matter before the IRS or who has a material interest in the matter cannot engage in any notary activities related to that matter.

Negotiations of Taxpayer Refund Checks (§10.31): Tax return preparers must not endorse or negotiate (cash) a refund check issued to the taxpayer. For example, a preparer may not use Form 8888, *Allocation of Refund (Including Savings Bond Purchases)*, to obtain his tax preparation fee by entering his own account. Form 8888 instructions state that entering an account in someone else's name, such as a preparer's, causes the direct deposit request to be rejected and the taxpayer to be sent a paper check instead. A preparer could also be subject to a penalty under §6695(f).

Example: Jeffrey is an enrolled agent with a new client who will receive a $500 refund on her 2013 tax return. The client has not yet paid Jeffrey's tax preparation fee, so he enters his own preparer account number, rather than his client's, on Form 8888, *Allocation of Refund (Including Savings Bond Purchases)*. Jeffrey plans to take his $200 fee from the refund and give his client the remaining $300. However, this action is expressly forbidden, and Jeffrey could be subject to a preparer penalty for improper negotiation of a client's check.

Practice of Law (§10.32): Nothing in the regulations or in Circular 230 may be construed as authorizing persons who are not attorneys to practice law.

Practitioner Fees (§10.27)

The IRS prohibits practitioners from charging "unconscionable fees." Although that term has not been defined, it is generally believed to refer to fees that the courts would consider grossly disproportionate in relation to the services provided.

A practitioner may not charge a contingent fee (for example, a percentage of the taxpayer's refund) for preparing an original tax return, amended tax return, or claim for refund or credit. A contingent fee also includes a fee that is based on a percentage of the taxes saved or one that depends on a specific result.

Additionally, a contingent fee includes any fee arrangement in which the practitioner agrees to reimburse the client for all or a portion of the client's fee in the event that a position taken on a tax return or other filing is not successful. The OPR has announced it will aggressively seek out and sanction tax preparers who are collecting unauthorized contingent fees.

However, the IRS does allow a practitioner to charge a contingent fee in limited circumstances, including:

- Representation during the examination of an original tax return; during the examination of an amended return or claim for refund where the amended return or claim for refund was filed within 120 days of the taxpayer receiving a written notice of examination or a written challenge to the original tax return.
- Services rendered in connection with a refund claim for credit or refund filed in conjunction with a penalty or interest charge assessed by the IRS.
- Services rendered in connection with any judicial proceeding arising under the Internal Revenue Code.

Advertising Restrictions (§10.30)

A practitioner may not use any form of advertising that contains false, deceptive, or coercive information, or that is in violation of IRS regulations.

Practitioners may not use official IRS insignia in their advertising.

Practitioners are **prohibited** from using the following logos:

Practitioners who are authorized e-Service providers may use the IRS e-file logo.

Acceptable Terms: In describing their professional designation, enrolled agents may not use the term "certified" or imply any type of employment relationship with the IRS. Examples of acceptable descriptions for EAs are "enrolled to represent taxpayers before the Internal Revenue Service," "enrolled to practice before the Internal Revenue Service," and "admitted to practice before the Internal Revenue Service."

Solicitation Restrictions: A practitioner may, in certain circumstances, solicit his professional services. The solicitation may not violate federal or state law, or other applicable rules (such as attorneys who are bound to conduct guidelines in their particular states.) For example, a practitioner may seek new business from a current or former client, or a client's family. However, a practitioner may not continue to contact a prospective client who has communicated that he does not wish to be solicited.

Mail Advertising: Mail advertising is allowed, but a solicitation must be clearly labeled as such and, if applicable, the source of information used in choosing the recipient must be identified. In the case of direct mail and e-commerce communications, the practitioner must retain a copy of the communication, along with a list of persons to whom the communication was mailed or distributed, for at least 36 months.

Practitioners may also send solicitations to other practitioners indicating their availability to provide professional services (such as bookkeeping or payroll services). The advertising and communications must not be misleading, deceptive, or in violation of IRS regulations.

Fee Information: A practitioner may publish and advertise a fee schedule. A practitioner must adhere to the published fee schedule for at least 30 calendar days after it is last published.

Example: Gracie is an EA who publishes an advertisement in her local newspaper. The ad includes a published fee schedule for preparing certain tax return forms at deeply discounted rates. Gracie is inundated with calls and decides that the ad was a mistake. Regardless, she must adhere to the published fee schedule for at least 30 days after it was published.

Fee information may be published in newspapers, telephone directories, mailings, websites, e-mail, or by any other method. A practitioner may include fees based on the following:

- Fixed fees for specific routine services
- Hourly rates
- A range of fees for particular services
- A fee charged for an initial consultation

Radio and Television Advertising: When advertising fees on radio or television, the broadcast must be recorded, and the practitioner must retain a copy of the recording for at least 36 months from the date of the last transmission or use.

Example: Travis is an EA who pays for a radio commercial about his services. It plays for four months during tax season. Travis is required to keep a copy of the radio commercial for at least 36 months from the last date that the commercial aired.

Unit 4: Study Questions

1. Which does not constitute a "best practice" for tax return preparers under the guidelines of Circular 230?

A. Consulting other professionals when questions arise about a particular tax issue.
B. Acting fairly and with integrity in practice before the IRS.
C. Communicating clearly with the client regarding the terms of the engagement.
D. Advising the client regarding the consequences of advice rendered.

2. Melanie is an EA who submits her clients' returns via IRS e-file. In order to save paper, she does not give a copy of the prepared tax return to her clients if they do not request it. Melanie allows her clients to have a copy of the return, so long as they pay a small fee. Which of the following is true?

A. Melanie is not in violation of Circular 230.
B. Melanie is in violation of Circular 230.
C. Melanie is not in violation of Circular 230 if she gives clients the option of receiving a copy of their return for a small fee.
D. Melanie may offer a copy of the return to the client only if the client asks for it.

3. If an EA knows that a client has filed an erroneous tax return, he is legally required to ________________________.

A. Correct the error.
B. Advise the client about the error and the consequences of not correcting the error.
C. Do nothing if the EA was not the one who prepared the erroneous return.
D. Disengage from any further business with the client if the client does not agree to correct the error.

4. The rules and regulations of Circular 230 apply to:

A. Anyone who prepares tax returns.
B. Only practitioners, including CPAs and EAs.
C. All paid tax preparers.
D. All of the above.

5. Dennis, an enrolled agent, wants to hire his friend, Brandon, who is also an enrolled agent. Brandon has been disbarred from practice by the IRS for misconduct. Brandon has appealed the disbarment, and it is currently under review. Which of the following statements is true?

A. Dennis can still hire Brandon as a tax preparer, provided Brandon does not represent any taxpayers.
B. Dennis can still hire Brandon, provided Brandon does not prepare or sign any tax returns.
C. Dennis cannot hire Brandon.
D. Dennis can hire Brandon while his appeal is pending.

6. Which of the following statements is correct regarding a client's request for his original records in order to comply with federal tax obligations?

A. The practitioner may choose not to return records to the client even if he requests their prompt return.
B. A fee dispute relieves the practitioner of his responsibility to return a client's records.
C. The practitioner must, at the request of the client, promptly return a client's records, regardless of fee disputes.
D. The practitioner must, at the request of the client, return client records within three months of the request.

7. Enrolled agents may advertise their services in the following manner:

A. With the phrase "Certified by the IRS."
B. With the phrase "Enrolled to practice before the IRS."
C. With the phrase "An IRS-approved practitioner."
D. With the phrase "A Certified Tax Accountant."

8. Which of the following statements is correct?

A. Conflicts of interest apply only to attorneys and not to other tax professionals.
B. Practitioners may represent clients who have a conflict of interest if waivers are signed by both parties.
C. Practitioners may represent clients who have a conflict of interest if the taxpayer informs both parties by phone.
D. Practitioners may not represent clients who have a conflict of interest.

9. Sarah, an enrolled agent, buys a practice owned by Mark, an EA who is retiring. As she reviews the records from Mark's practice, she learns he has been incorrectly claiming dependents for certain taxpayer clients. What should Sarah do?

A. Notify the clients of the error and the consequences of not correcting the error.
B. Inform the clients that she will refuse to prepare their taxes if they do not file amended returns.
C. Contact the IRS to alert agents about the error and to request audits of those clients' prior year returns.
D. Inform the clients that Mark had made mistakes on their returns.

10. Which of the following statements is true regarding practitioners?

A. Practitioners cannot notarize documents of the clients they represent before the IRS.
B. Practitioners cannot be notaries.
C. Practitioners are required to be notaries.
D. A notary who is also a practitioner will not be eligible for the e-file program.

11. Whit is an EA who decides to advertise his fee schedule in the local newspaper. Which of the following fee arrangements is prohibited?

A. Hourly fee rates.
B. Fixed fees for tax preparation.
C. Contingent fees for original returns.
D. Flat fees for initial consultations.

12. Ryan is an EA with a client named Hannah who has had significant income from a partnership for the past five years. However, Ryan did not see a Schedule K-1 from the partnership among the information Hannah provided to him this year. What does due diligence require Ryan to do?

A. Attempt to estimate the amount that would be reported as income on the Schedule K-1 based on last year's Schedule K-1 and include that amount on Hannah's return.
B. Call Hannah's financial advisor and ask him about Hannah's investments.
C. Nothing, because Ryan is required to rely only on the information provided by his client, even if he has reason to believe the information may not be accurate.
D. Ask Hannah why she did not provide him with the partnership's Schedule K-1, as she had in previous years.

13. All of the following statements regarding a tax preparer's responsibility to provide information requested by the IRS are correct except:

A. He must promptly turn over all records relating to the IRS request, no matter what the circumstances.
B. If the records are not in his possession, he must make a "reasonable inquiry" of his client about their whereabouts.
C. He is not legally obligated to contact any third party who might possess the requested records.
D. If he believes in good faith and on reasonable grounds that the requested material is legally privileged information, a preparer may choose to decline a records request.

14. In which instance is a tax preparer allowed to charge a contingent fee?

A. When his regular fee is "unconscionable."
B. When the fee is based on a claim for refund only.
C. When the fee is based on preparing an original tax return.
D. When he renders services in connection with an IRS court proceeding.

15. How long must a practitioner retain records relating to clients who have provided their consent for representation in conflict-of-interest cases?

A. One year from the date representation ends.
B. Two years from the date representation ends.
C. Three years from the date representation ends.
D. Five years from the date representation ends.

16. What should a practitioner do if he knows that the taxpayer has failed to comply with the revenue law on an earlier tax return?

A. Report the taxpayer to the IRS.
B. Refuse to prepare a tax return until the taxpayer amends the earlier, noncompliant return.
C. Advise the taxpayer promptly of the error and its consequences.
D. All of the above.

17. Under Circular 230 §6107, what is a tax preparer required to keep for at least three years after the close of the return period?

A. A list of clients and tax returns prepared.
B. Copies of all tax returns prepared.
C. Both a list of clients and copies of all tax returns prepared.
D. Either A or B.

18. If more than one preparer is involved in preparing a tax return, who is required to sign?

A. Any preparer involved in the preparation of the return.
B. Only the preparer with primary responsibility for the accuracy of the return; however, the other preparers must be disclosed on the return.
C. Only the preparer with primary responsibility for the accuracy of the return; the other preparers do not need to be disclosed on the return.
D. Only the taxpayer.

19. An employee of a tax accounting firm has spent hours constructing a spreadsheet used in determining a client's estimated tax payments. The client has yet to pay the firm for fees charged in connection with his tax return. Which of the following best describes the firm's responsibility regarding the client's request of a copy of the spreadsheet?

A. The firm is under no obligation to hand over the spreadsheet. It is also not required to give the client access to view or copy it.
B. The firm is required to hand over the spreadsheet.
C. The firm is not required to hand over the spreadsheet, but is required to allow the client access to view or copy it.
D. None of the above.

20. With the taxpayer's properly signed power of attorney, an EA may:

A. Receive a taxpayer's refund check, but not endorse or cash the check.
B. Receive and endorse a taxpayer's refund check and invest the proceeds in the taxpayer's own mutual fund.
C. Receive a taxpayer's refund check and endorse it in order to pay tax preparation fees only.
D. None of the above.

Unit 5: Tax Preparer Standards & Advice

More Reading:

Circular 230, *Regulations Governing Practice Before the IRS*

Circular 230 outlines broad standards for practitioners when it comes to tax positions taken on income tax returns, as well as other forms of written advice they provide clients. Practitioners who fail to meet these standards are subject to penalties and other sanctions.

Standards for Tax Returns and Documents (§10.34)

Information from Clients: When preparing income tax returns, a practitioner is not required to verify all the information furnished by his clients. In general, a practitioner may:

- May rely in good faith without verification of information that a client provides.
- Should not ignore the implications of the information.
- Make reasonable inquiries if the information appears to be incorrect, inconsistent, or incomplete.

Example: Jay is an EA who conducts an interview with his client, Barbara. She states she made a $50,000 charitable contribution of real estate during 2013; however, this is not true, and Jay fails to make reasonable inquiries to Barbara about the contribution. He does not ask about the existence of a qualified appraisal and he does not complete an IRS-required substantiation form. Jay includes the deduction for the charitable contribution on Barbara's tax return, which results in an understatement of tax liability. Barbara's return is later audited, and the charitable deduction is disallowed. Jay is in violation of §10.34 and would be subject to a preparer penalty for his negligence.

Tax Positions

A practitioner may not willfully sign a tax return or claim for refund that the practitioner knows (or reasonably should know) contains a position that:

- Lacks a reasonable basis.
- Is an unreasonable position as described in IRC §6694(a)(2).[57]
- Is a willful attempt by the practitioner to understate the liability for tax or a reckless or intentional disregard of rules or regulations.

In determining potential penalties, the IRS will take into account a pattern of conduct to assess whether a practitioner acted willfully, recklessly, or through gross incompetence.

Standards for Submittal of Documents to the IRS: A practitioner may not advise a client to submit a document, affidavit, or other paper to the IRS:

- The purpose of which is to delay or impede the administration of the federal tax laws;
- That is frivolous; or

[57]Section 6694(a) imposes penalties on paid preparers who prepare returns reflecting an understatement of liability due to an unreasonable position if the preparer knew (or reasonably should have known) of the position. No penalty is imposed, however, if it is shown that there is reasonable cause for the understatement and the preparer acted in good faith.

- That contains or omits information in a manner that demonstrates an intentional disregard of a rule or regulation unless the practitioner also advises the client to submit a document that evidences a good faith challenge to the rule or regulation (such as a disclosure statement).

A practitioner must not knowingly sign a frivolous return. A frivolous position is defined as one that the practitioner knows is in bad faith and is improper. A practitioner may sign a return with a tax position that meets at least one of two standards:

- The position is "more likely than not" to be sustained on its merits, or
- The position has a "reasonable basis."

Tax Position Definitions

More Likely Than Not: There is a greater than 50% likelihood that the tax treatment will be upheld if the IRS challenges it. If a preparer is unsure that a position meets this standard, he may generally avoid penalties by disclosing the position on the return. However, a disclosure statement will not protect the preparer if the position is patently frivolous.[58] The "more likely than not" standard must be used for tax shelters and reportable transactions.

Reasonable Basis: This is the minimum standard for all tax advice and preparation of tax returns. The IRS defines it this way: "Reasonable basis is a relatively high standard of tax reporting that is significantly higher than not frivolous or not patently improper. The reasonable basis standard is not satisfied by a return position that is merely arguable." The precise likelihood that a reasonable basis position will be upheld on its merits is not defined in Circular 230. For purposes of avoiding §6694 penalties, the reasonable-basis standard applies only if the relevant tax position is disclosed on the return or document so that the IRS is aware of a potential issue.

Advising Clients on Potential Penalties

A practitioner is required to inform a client of any penalties that are reasonably likely to apply to a position taken on a tax return if:

- The practitioner advised the client with respect to the position; or
- The practitioner prepared or signed the tax return.

The practitioner also must inform the client of any opportunity to avoid penalties by disclosure of the position and of the requirements for adequate disclosure. This rule applies even if the practitioner is not subject to a penalty under the Internal Revenue Code related to the position or to the document or tax return submitted.

Disclosure Statements: A tax return that requires a disclosure to the IRS must include either Form 8275, *Disclosure Statement*, or Form 8275-R, *Regulation Disclosure Statement*.

Form 8275 is used by taxpayers and preparers to disclose items or positions on a tax return that are not otherwise adequately disclosed. It is primarily used to avoid accuracy-related penalties so long as the return position has a reasonable basis and the taxpayer (and preparer) acted in good faith in taking the position.

[58] See Regulation 1.6694-1(e) for more information.

Example: Amanda is an EA with a client who has a very complex tax situation. She notices that the IRS publications reflect one position, but there is a recent court case that may allow a more favorable position for her client. There are also two other similar cases being litigated, but the outcome of those cases is currently unknown. Amanda believes that the position has a 30% chance of prevailing on its merits. Amanda thinks that the client's position has a reasonable basis and decides to disclose the position on the tax return. Even though the position is contrary to the IRS's current guidance, Amanda may take the position on the return, so long as it is disclosed. She must file Form 8275 along with the tax return stating the position, referencing the court case or any other basis she has for the position.

Form 8275 cannot be used to avoid the portion of the accuracy-related penalty attributable to certain types of misconduct, including the following:

- Negligence
- Disregard of regulations
- Any substantial understatement of income tax on a tax shelter item

A disclosure statement cannot be used for a preparer to avoid penalties if the position has no reasonable basis.

Covered Opinions (§10.35)

The Circular 230 requirements apply to all written forms of federal tax advice. There are especially strict rules for the written advice on *covered opinions*, which are sometimes referred to as "tax shelter advice." The rules are extremely complex and are in the process of being revised.[59]

Not all tax shelters are prohibited. A pretax retirement plan, for example, is considered a legal tax shelter. However, some tax shelters are unlawful.

IRS regulations dictate mandatory requirements for practitioners who provide covered opinions, which relate to the following:

- Any transaction the IRS has determined is a tax-avoidance transaction, or any plan or arrangement that has tax avoidance as a "significant purpose."
- Any written advice that is:
    - A reliance opinion
    - A marketed opinion
    - Subject to conditions of confidentiality
    - Subject to contractual protection

Reliance Opinion: Written advice that is more likely than not (greater than 50%) to result in the federal tax issue being sustained in the taxpayer's favor. Under Circular 230, written advice will not be treated as a reliance opinion if the practitioner "prominently discloses in the written advice that it was not intended or written by the practitioner to be used, and that it cannot be used by the taxpayer, for the purpose of avoiding penalties that may be imposed on the taxpayer."

---

[59] In September 2012, the IRS submitted proposed revisions to Section 10.35 of Circular 230. The revisions would revoke the complicated rules regarding covered opinions and substitute a single, basic new standard governing all written tax advice. As of publication, these new rules had not yet become final; thus, exam-takers should study the current rules of Circular 230 covered in this unit.

Marketed Opinion: Written advice that is used by a person other than the practitioner in promoting, marketing, or recommending an investment plan to one or more taxpayers.

Under the rules, unless the advice contains a disclaimer such as the one cited above, the practitioner providing advice in a covered opinion must comply with all of the following requirements:

1. **Know all the relevant facts:** A practitioner must describe a legitimate business purpose for the transaction, and he must use reasonable efforts to get the factual information correct.
2. **Relate law to the facts:** The opinion must relate the applicable law, including applicable court decisions, to the relevant facts.
3. **Evaluation of significant federal tax issues:** The opinion must provide that the taxpayer will prevail (more likely than not) on the merit of the issues contained in the opinion.
4. **Overall conclusion:** The practitioner must provide an overall conclusion that the tax treatment is proper and give reasons for that conclusion.
5. **Practitioner competence:** The practitioner must be competent and knowledgeable about the issues addressed in the opinion.

Note: Many practitioners now routinely add a disclaimer to any written communication, including e-mails, regardless of whether the communication contains tax advice. According to the IRS, this practice may actually discourage compliance with ethical requirements because some practitioners believe a disclaimer allows them to disregard the current §10.35 standards governing written tax advice. This issue is one of the factors behind the IRS's proposal to overhaul the covered opinion regulations.

Reporting Requirements for Tax Shelter Activities

There are certain types of tax shelter activities that must be reported to the IRS. A *reportable transaction*, also called a *listed transaction*, is one that the IRS has determined has the potential for tax avoidance or evasion.

The rules for reportable transactions apply to all individuals and entities (including trusts, estates, partnerships, S corporations, etc.) Form 8886, *Reportable Transaction Disclosure Statement*, must be attached to a taxpayer's return for any year that he participates in this type of tax shelter. A separate statement must be filed for each reportable transaction.

The fact that a tax shelter transaction must be reported on this form does not necessarily mean the IRS will disallow its tax benefits.

If a reportable transaction is not disclosed and results in an understatement of tax, an additional penalty of 30% of the understatement may be assessed. A taxpayer may request a ruling from the IRS to determine whether a transaction must be disclosed.

The following are not considered reportable transactions:

- Losses from casualties, thefts, and condemnations
- Losses from Ponzi schemes
- Losses from the sale or exchange of an asset with a qualifying basis
- Losses arising from any mark-to-market treatment of an item

A person who sells (or otherwise transfers) an interest in a tax shelter must provide the taxpayer the tax shelter registration number or be subject to a $100 penalty.

If the taxpayer claims any deduction, credit, or other tax benefit because of a tax shelter, he must attach Form 8271, *Investor Reporting of Tax Shelter Registration Number*, to the tax return to report this number. A taxpayer may have to pay a penalty of $250 for each failure to report a tax shelter registration number on a return.

Excluded Advice

Some forms of written tax advice are not subject to the rules for covered opinions under Circular 230. Certain types of excluded advice that do not qualify as covered opinions include:

- Advice from in-house employees to their employers.
- Written advice solely for one taxpayer after the taxpayer has already filed a tax return.
- Written advice that does not resolve a federal tax issue in the taxpayer's favor. This is also called "negative advice," in which an advisor tells a client a transaction will not provide the purported tax benefit.
- Written advice regarding qualified plans, state and local bonds, or SEC-filed documents.
- Any written advice if the practitioner is reasonably expected to provide subsequent written advice that satisfies the covered opinion requirements.

Example: An accountant is working full-time as an employee for Baker's Dozen Corporation. The accountant gives incorrect advice to his employer regarding a tax shelter, and the employer is subject to penalties. The employee is not subject to Circular 230 penalties for covered opinions because he was acting as an in-house professional for his own employer.

Firm Compliance Procedures (§10.36)

A practitioner (or practitioners, if the duty is shared) who oversees a firm's practice must ensure adequate procedures are in place for every member, associate, or employee to comply with the covered opinion requirements, as well as the other requirements specified in Circular 230 governing the preparation of tax returns and other documents submitted to the IRS.

A practitioner(s) who does not take reasonable steps to ensure the firm has adequate procedures in place to comply with Circular 230 requirements may face disciplinary action. He may also be subject to sanctions if he knows of other members of the firm who are engaging in a pattern of noncompliance, and he fails to take prompt action to correct the noncompliance.

Requirements for Other Written Advice (§10.37)

Circular 230 also outlines expectations for other types of written advice a practitioner gives a client. The practitioner:

- Must not make unreasonable factual or legal assumptions.
- Must not have an unreasonable reliance on taxpayer information or third party information.
- Must consider all relevant facts and law.
- Must not use the possibility of an IRS audit as a factor in providing the written advice.

Unit 5: Study Questions

1. Glen is a CPA who prepares income tax returns for his clients. One of his clients submits a list of expenses to be claimed on Schedule C of the return. Glen is required to comply with which one of the following?

A. Glen is required to independently verify the client's information.
B. Glen can ignore the implications of information known by him.
C. Inquiry is not required if the information appears to be incorrect or incomplete.
D. Appropriate inquiries are required to determine whether the client has substantiation for his Schedule C expenses.

2. Bethany is an EA with a client, Dylan, who wishes to claim a deduction for a large business expense. However, there is a question about whether the expense is "ordinary and necessary" for his business. If the deduction were disallowed, there would be a substantial understatement of tax (over 25%). Bethany researches the issue and tells Dylan that the position should be disclosed. Dylan does not want to disclose the position on the return, because he is afraid that the IRS will disallow it. What are the repercussions for Bethany?

A. None. All the penalties apply to the client.
B. Bethany may be liable for preparer penalties.
C. Bethany will not be liable for preparer penalties so long as she explains the potential penalties to the client.
D. None of the above.

3. A tax professional cannot sign ________________.

A. A tax return for a family member.
B. A tax return that is not prepared for compensation.
C. A tax return with a properly disclosed tax shelter position.
D. A frivolous return with a disclosure.

4. Which of the following types of written advice would fall under the Circular 230 rules for covered opinions?

A. Advice from in-house employees to their employers.
B. Written advice solely for one taxpayer after the taxpayer has already filed a tax return.
C. Written advice that does not resolve a federal tax issue in the taxpayer's favor.
D. A plan or arrangement whose principal purpose is the avoidance of tax.

5. A practitioner is required to inform a client of penalties that are reasonably likely to apply to a position taken on a tax return if:

A. The taxpayer decides to self-prepare a return.
B. The practitioner gave the client professional advice on the position.
C. The IRS has the taxpayer under examination.
D. The taxpayer is deceased.

6. When it comes to professional tax advice, the IRS defines "more likely than not" as:

A. A tax position that has a reasonable basis of being upheld in court.
B. A tax position that has at least a 50% likelihood that the position will be upheld if the IRS challenges it.
C. A tax position that has a greater than 50% likelihood that the position will be upheld if the IRS challenges it.
D. A tax position that is disclosed.

7. Which of the following positions requires disclosure on a tax return?

A. When there is reasonable basis for the position.
B. When there is substantial authority for the position.
C. When the position is unreasonable.
D. All of the above.

8. Which type of transaction must always be reported to the IRS?

A. Listed transaction.
B. Reliance opinion.
C. A loss from a Ponzi scheme.
D. Marketed opinion.

9. A marketed opinion is defined as:

A. Written advice concerning tax shelters.
B. An opinion that has a more likely than not chance of being sustained in the taxpayer's favor.
C. A form of due diligence related to marketing a preparer's tax practice.
D. An opinion that is used by a person other than the practitioner in promoting, marketing, or recommending an investment plan to one or more taxpayers.

10. Creighton is a tax preparer with a client who insists he wants to claim an unreasonable position on his tax return. If Creighton goes along with his client's wishes, how can he avoid a preparer penalty for understatement of tax due to an unreasonable position?

A. Hope the IRS will not audit the return.
B. Disclose the position, and have the taxpayer sign a statement saying he is willing to take the risk but that Creighton does not believe the position is correct.
C. If there is substantial authority for the position.
D. There is no relief from the preparer penalty for an understatement due to an unreasonable position.

11. What is a covered opinion?

A. A disclaimer a preparer must file to avoid accuracy-related penalties.
B. Written advice on a federal tax issue that the IRS has determined is a tax-avoidance transaction.
C. Any position with a reasonable basis.
D. Any position that is considered more likely than not to be upheld on its merits.

12. Under Circular 230, the type of opinion concluding that one or more tax issues could be resolved in the taxpayer's favor is a _______________ opinion.

A. Marketed.
B. Covered.
C. Reliance.
D. All of the above.

Unit 6: Earned Income Credit for Preparers

More Reading:
www.eitc.irs.gov
Publication 596, *Earned Income Credit*
Publication 4687, *EITC Due Diligence Requirements*
Publication 4808, *Disability and EITC*

The Earned Income Credit (EIC)[60] is a refundable federal income tax credit for low to moderate income working individuals and families. When the EIC exceeds the amount of taxes owed, it results in a tax refund to those who claim and qualify for the credit. Any taxpayer who is claiming the EIC must have a valid Social Security number. The same is true for any qualifying child who is listed on an EIC return. An ITIN or ATIN is not sufficient.

The EIC due diligence rules for tax preparers have expanded in recent years, and are more stringent than they are for other tax returns. This is because the number of individuals claiming the EIC is high, and the number of erroneous claims is also high. In fiscal year 2012, the IRS estimated an error rate of 21 to 25%, or about $13 billion, that was paid out in error on returns claiming the Earned Income Credit.

Paid preparers must meet four additional due diligence requirements on returns with EIC claims or face possible penalties. IRS regulations specify these EIC due diligence requirements and set a performance standard for the *knowledge requirement:* what a reasonable and well-informed tax return preparer, knowledgeable in the law, would do.

Knowledge Requirement for EIC Returns

Under the knowledge requirement, a preparer must:

- Apply a common sense standard to the information provided by the client.
- Evaluate whether the information is complete and gather any missing facts.
- Determine if the information is consistent; recognize contradictory statements and statements the preparer knows are not true.
- Conduct a thorough, in-depth interview with every client, every year.
- Ask enough questions to reasonably know the return is correct and complete.
- Document in the file any questions he asked and his client's responses.

Preparer Compliance Requirements

The four due diligence requirements for preparers related to the EIC are as follows:

1) **Complete and Submit the EIC Checklist:** A preparer must complete Form 8867, *Paid Preparer's Earned Income Credit Checklist*, to make sure he considers all EIC eligibility criteria for each return prepared. A preparer is required to submit Form 8867 to the IRS with every EIC claim.
    a) The preparer must ask and explain each of the questions in Part 1 of the checklist to every EIC client, and all of the questions in Parts II or III that apply. Part 1 deals with basic

[60] The IRS uses both the terms "Earned Income Tax Credit" (EITC) and "Earned Income Credit." They are the same credit. For consistency's sake, we will refer to it as the Earned Income Credit, or EIC.

questions including filing status, Social Security numbers, and amount of investment income. Part II applies only to taxpayers with a child or children. Part III applies to taxpayers without children.

b) The preparer must personally answer the due diligence questions in Part IV and Part V (see more detail on the next page.)

c) The form may be submitted to the IRS either electronically or on paper, along with any return or claim for refund.

2) **Compute the Credit:** A preparer must complete the EIC worksheet in the Form 1040 series instructions or the one in Publication 596, *Earned Income Credit*. The worksheet shows what is included in the computation (i.e. self-employment income, total earned income, investment income, and adjusted gross income.) Most tax preparation software has the computation worksheet, but the IRS emphasizes that using software is not a substitute for knowledge of EIC tax law.

3) **Retaining Records:** A preparer must retain the following five records for each EIC claim:
   a) Form 8867
   b) EIC worksheet(s) or his own worksheet
   c) Copies of any taxpayer documents he relied on to determine eligibility for or amount of EIC
   d) A record of how, when, and from whom the information used to prepare the form and worksheet(s) was obtained
   e) A record of any additional questions the preparer asked and his client's answers

All records should be kept for at least three years in either paper or electronic format, and they must be produced if the IRS asks for them.

4) **Knowledge:** A preparer must not know (or have reason to know) that the information used to determine eligibility or to compute the amount of the credit is incorrect. A preparer must ask his client additional questions if the information furnished seems incorrect or incomplete.

Example: Esther is an EA. A new 28-year-old client, Charlie, wants to claim two sons, ages 14 and 15, as qualifying children for the EIC. Esther is concerned about the age of the children, since Charlie's age seems inconsistent with the ages of the children. Esther asks additional questions and discovers the boys are both adopted, which explains the age inconsistency. She completes the EIC Worksheet and Form 8867, and submits Form 8867 to the IRS. She retains copies of these records, as well as the adoption records that Charlie provides her and notes of her client interview, for a period of three years. Esther has complied with her due diligence requirements.

Form 8867

The IRS has updated and expanded Form 8867. It includes six questions in Part IV that preparers must ask taxpayers in order to comply with due diligence requirements. It also includes a new Part V that a preparer must use to identify the documents the taxpayer provided and the preparer used to determine EIC eligibility.

Questions in Part IV concern the eligibility of a qualifying child of a nonparent taxpayer, tiebreaker rules, and possible consequences of another person claiming the child. The preparer is warned that he has not complied with his due diligence requirements and faces a penalty if he answered "no" to any of the six questions in Part IV.

Example: Alonso is an EA. His client, Maria, states that she is separated from her spouse. Her daughter lives with her and she wants to claim the EIC as head of household. In reviewing Maria's records, Alonso notes that she earns a minimal income, which appears insufficient to support a household. As the preparer, Alonso must ask appropriate questions to determine Maria's correct filing status, determine how long the child lived with each parent during the year, and probe for any additional sources of income. He must interview her thoroughly and document her answers. He must also fill out Form 8867, *Paid Preparer's Earned Income Credit Checklist*, and complete the EIC worksheet. After asking various questions, Maria discloses that she receives child support, which is not taxable or reportable on the return. She also receives food stamps and other public benefits, which also help support her daughter. Food stamps are also not taxable. Alonso notes this information in his workpapers and is more confident that he can prepare Maria's return accurately.

In determining the residency of qualifying children, a preparer must specify in Part V whether he relied upon documents such as school, medical, or social service records. In determining the disability of a qualifying child, a preparer must answer whether he relied upon documents such as a statement from a doctor, other health care provider, or social services agency.

Example: Judd is an EA. His new client, Thelma, 62, wants to take a dependency exemption for her son, Randy, who is 32. She also wants to claim the Earned Income Credit and the Dependent Care Credit for her son. Since Randy is beyond the age limit for these credits, Judd makes reasonable inquiries and Thelma produces a doctor's statement that says Randy is severely disabled and incapable of self-care. Therefore, Thelma may claim her son as a dependent, and the credits will be allowed regardless of Randy's age. Judd has fulfilled his due diligence requirement by conducting a thorough interview with his client, asking enough questions to understand an individual tax situation, documenting the answers, and seeking appropriate supporting evidence. He completes his due diligence requirements by submitting Form 8867 to the IRS.

If a Schedule C is included with the tax return, the preparer must answer whether he determined EIC eligibility by relying upon any documents the taxpayer provided in connection with the business. These documents may include a business license, Forms 1099, records of gross receipts and expenses, or bank statements.

Example: Tonya is an EA. Mai is a new client who wants to claim the EIC. She has two qualifying children. She tells Tonya she had a Schedule C business and earned $10,000 in income but had no expenses. This information appears incomplete because it would be unusual that someone who is self-employed has no business expenses. Tonya is required to ask reasonable questions to determine if the business exists and if the information about Mai's income and expenses is correct. Tonya must submit Form 8867 to the IRS and keep copies of any documents Mai provides for at least three years.

Common EIC Errors

The three issues that account for more than 60% of all EIC errors are:

- Claiming a child who does not meet the age, relationship, or residency requirement
- Filing as single or head of household when married
- Over or underreporting income or business expenses to maximize the credit

A common method of EIC fraud is the "borrowing" of dependents. Unscrupulous tax preparers will "share" one taxpayer's qualifying child or children with another taxpayer in order to allow both to claim the EIC.

Example: Reggie has four children, but he only needs the first three children to receive the maximum EIC credit. The preparer lists the first three children on Reggie's return and lists the other child on another return. The preparer and Reggie are "selling" the dependents and will then split a fee or split the refund. This is an example of tax fraud that involves both the preparer and the taxpayer.

Since tax professionals prepare more than 70% of EIC claims, the quality of their work has a significant impact on reducing erroneous claims. Preparers who file high percentages of questionable EIC claims or returns with a high risk of EIC error may be subject to on-site audits. IRS agents will review preparer records to verify due diligence compliance, including whether they are meeting the knowledge requirement. Penalties may be assessed when noncompliance is identified.

In November and December 2013, the IRS sent letters to preparers suspected of filing inaccurate EIC claims. The letters detailed the critical issues identified on the returns and explained the consequences of filing inaccurate EIC claims. The IRS warned these preparers that their future EIC claims would be monitored closely.[61]

Note: For tax year 2012, the IRS sent notice of penalty letters to nearly 800 preparers who had received a warning letter and continued to submit EIC claims without Form 8867. For tax year 2013, the IRS says it will penalize all preparers who do not submit or attach Form 8867 with both electronic and paper EIC returns or claims for refund.

Penalties for Incorrect EIC Returns

The penalties for failing to exercise due diligence with EIC claims can be severe. Preparers face a penalty of $500 for each failure to comply with the requirements. There is no maximum dollar penalty amount.

Taxpayers also face consequences. If the IRS examines a taxpayer's return and disallows all or part of the EIC, the taxpayer:

- Must pay back the amount in error with interest;
- May need to file Form 8862, *Information to Claim Earned Income Credit after Disallowance*;

[61] In December 2013, the Treasury Inspector General for Tax Administration reported that there was an increasing level of noncompliance by tax preparers with the EIC due diligence requirements. As of March 2, 2013, TIGTA had identified more than 122,000 tax preparers who had prepared more than $2 billion in EIC claims but who had failed to attach Form 8867.

- Cannot claim the EIC for the next two years if the IRS determines the error is because of reckless or intentional disregard of the rules; or
- Cannot claim the EIC for the next ten years if the IRS determines the error is because of fraud.

Further, if the IRS examines an EIC claim and it is determined that the preparer did not meet all four due diligence requirements, he can be subject to penalties even beyond the $500 penalty for each failure to comply.

The preparer may also be subject to:

- A minimum penalty of $1,000 if the IRS finds any part of the amount of taxes owed is due to an unreasonable position.
- A minimum penalty of $5,000 if the IRS finds any part of the amount of taxes owed is due to reckless or intentional disregard of rules or regulations.

If a preparer receives a return-related penalty, he may also face:

- Disciplinary action by the OPR
- Suspension or expulsion from IRS e-file
- Injunctions barring him from preparing tax returns

The IRS has streamlined procedures for faster referrals to the U.S. Department of Justice to prohibit preparers from making fraudulent EIC claims. These preparers could be permanently or temporarily barred from any type of federal tax preparation.

Example: Stephanie is a preparer working for a large chain. She has knowingly prepared false EIC claims for several years. Eventually, the office is subject to an IRS audit, and the fraud is discovered. Stephanie is disbarred and fined. Her employer is also subject to penalties and can be assessed a fine for each fraudulent claim.

Unit 6: Study Questions

1. Which statement is correct about the EIC?

A. Information obtained by the preparer may be discarded after the client interview.
B. Interfering with IRS efforts to investigate EIC fraud is allowed.
C. Incorrectly reporting income is acceptable so long as the client signs a release.
D. Preparers are required to ask additional questions if the information provided by a client appears incorrect, inconsistent, or incomplete.

2. The IRS can impose the following ban related to the EIC:

A. The IRS cannot ban a taxpayer from claiming the EIC.
B. Ten year ban for fraud.
C. Two year ban for fraud.
D. Permanent ban for fraud.

3. What is the penalty for preparers who fail to comply with due diligence requirements for the EIC?

A. $500 for each failure.
B. $1,000 for each failure.
C. There is no preparer penalty, but there is a taxpayer penalty for fraud.
D. A formal reprimand by the OPR, but there is no monetary penalty.

4. A client tells a preparer:

- She has no Form 1099.
- She was self-employed cleaning houses.
- She earned $12,000.
- She had no expenses related to the cleaning business.

What is the best course of action for the preparer in this case?

A. Refuse to prepare the return based on the client's information.
B. Ask probing questions to determine the correct facts and ask for proof of income or any expenses.
C. Accept the taxpayer's word so long as she fills out a legal liability release form.
D. Make the client swear to the truthfulness of her statements before an IRS officer.

5. When must a tax preparer complete a client checklist for the EIC?

A. Every year.
B. With every new client.
C. Every other year.
D. The client checklist is recommended, but is not required.

6. All of the following are EIC due diligence requirements except:

A. To evaluate the information received from the client.
B. To apply a consistency and reasonableness standard to the information.
C. To verify the taxpayer's information with the appropriate third parties.
D. To make additional reasonable inquiries when the information appears to be incorrect, inconsistent, or incomplete.

7. All of the following are common errors taxpayers make in claiming the EIC except:

A. Incorrectly reporting income or expenses.
B. Incorrectly claiming a child who does not meet the specific EIC requirements.
C. Filing as head of household when married.
D. Listing earned income for the year.

8. All of the following are possible penalties for preparers who file fraudulent EIC claims except:

A. Suspension or expulsion from IRS e-file.
B. Criminal action undertaken by the OPR.
C. A ban from preparing tax returns.
D. A preparer penalty of $5,000 if the IRS finds any part of the amount of taxes owed is due to reckless or intentional disregard of rules or regulations.

9. Mack and Judy have valid ITINs. They have two children, both of whom have valid SSNs. Assuming they meet the income requirements, can Mack and Judy claim the EIC?

A. They may claim the EIC for themselves and their children.
B. They may claim the EIC for their children, but not for themselves.
C. They cannot claim the EIC, regardless of whether their children have valid SSNs.
D. Their dependents can claim the EIC, but only if they file separate returns.

10. Which is not one of the due diligence requirements preparers are expected to follow for EIC claims?

A. Maintaining records for two years.
B. Completing the eligibility checklist.
C. Computation of the credit.
D. The knowledge standard.

11. To fulfill the due diligence requirements for the earned income credit, a preparer must complete and submit to the IRS _______________ along with the taxpayer's EIC claim.

A. Notes from the client's interview.
B. The EIC worksheet.
C. The knowledge requirement worksheet.
D. Form 8867.

Unit 7: Obligations, Fraud, & Penalties

More Reading:
Publication 583, *Starting a Business and Keeping Records*
Publication 552, *Recordkeeping for Individuals*
Publication 947, *Practice Before the IRS and Power of Attorney*

Recordkeeping Requirements

There are basic recordkeeping requirements expected of U.S. taxpayers that tax preparers need to be familiar with and make sure their clients understand. Various types of recordkeeping requirements are tested on all three parts of the EA exam. Part 3 focuses on the substantiation of items and on records retention.

Except in a few cases, tax law does not require specific kinds of records to be kept. However, records that clearly demonstrate income, expenses, and basis should be retained.

Taxpayers may scan records and retain them electronically, as the IRS generally does not require a taxpayer to keep original paper records. However, a taxpayer must be able to store, preserve, retrieve, and reproduce electronic records when needed.

Statute of Limitations for Records Retention: A taxpayer should keep all relevant records as long as they may be needed for the administration of any provision of the Internal Revenue Code. As a practical matter, this means he must retain relevant records until the statute of limitations for each tax return expires. For assessment of tax owed, this period is generally three years from the date the return was filed or the return was due, whichever is later. For filing a claim for credit or refund, the period to make the claim generally is three years from the date the original return was filed or two years from the date the tax was paid, whichever is later.

Property Records: Records relating to the basis of property should be retained as long as they may be material to any tax return involving the property. The basis of property is material until the statute of limitations expires for the tax year an asset is sold or disposed of. A taxpayer must keep these records to figure the asset's basis, as well as any depreciation, amortization, or depletion deductions.

Example: Cory sells a vacation home he has owned for eight years. He uses records relating to the purchase of the property and improvements made on it to compute the basis and his gain. He reports the sale on his 2013 tax return. He must retain the records relating to the sale until the statute of limitations for the tax return expires, usually three years from the date of filing or the due date of the return, whichever is later.

Employment Tax Records: A business is required to retain payroll and employment tax records for at least four years after the tax becomes due or is paid, whichever is later. This rule also applies to businesses that employ other tax preparers.

Example: Joelle is an EA who employs five other preparers in her office. She is required to keep the employment tax records relating to her employees for at least four years.

Applicable employer tax records must be made available for IRS review. These include employer identification numbers; amounts and dates of wages, annuity, and pension payments;

amounts of tips reported; names, addresses, Social Security numbers, and occupations of employees; dates of active employment and sick leave; records of fringe benefits provided; Forms W-4; dates and amounts of tax deposits; and copies of all employment returns filed.

Other Retention Periods: Longer record retention periods may apply in some cases. For example, if a taxpayer files a claim from a loss of worthless securities, the period to retain records related to the transaction is seven years. If a taxpayer fails to report income that exceeds 25% of the gross income shown on his return, the statute of limitations is six years from when the return is filed. There is no statute of limitations to assess tax when a return is fraudulent or when no return is filed.

Statute of Limitations	
Type of Record/Return	**Applicable Statute or Retention Period**
Normal tax return	The latter of 3 years from due date or filing date
Omitted income that exceeds 25% of the gross income shown on the return	6 years from filing date
Fraudulent return	No limit
No return filed	No limit
A claim for credit or amended return	The latter of 3 years from filing original return or 2 years after tax was paid
A claim for a loss from worthless securities	7 years
Employment and payroll tax records	The latter of 4 years after tax becomes due or is paid
Fixed assets, real estate	Until the statute of limitations expires for the tax year in which the asset is disposed of

Test-takers should memorize these retention periods as they are often tested on the EA exam.

Supporting Documentation

As an essential part of due diligence, it is a practitioner's responsibility to request appropriate supporting documentation from clients in order to prepare an accurate tax return. A preparer must review prior year tax returns to identify relevant issues, such as items that need to be carried forward to the current year and tax years going forward.

In addition, depending on the type of tax return being prepared, a practitioner may need to see the following types of supporting documentation:

- **Financial documents:** Canceled checks, bank statements, credit card statements, receipts, brokerage records.
- **Legal documents:** Birth certificates, divorce decrees, lawsuit settlements.
- **Business entity supporting documents:** Partnership agreement, corporate bylaws, corporate minutes.

- **Expense records:** Mileage logs, receipts for business expenses such as travel, meals, entertainment, and lodging; and receipts and written acknowledgements from charitable organizations, particularly for non-cash contributions and expenses of $250 or more.

Example: A teacher tells her tax return preparer she had $23,000 in unreimbursed employee business expenses during the tax year. She provides no documentation, and her preparer does not ask to see any receipts. The IRS audits her return and disallows the expenses, which include a deduction for an $8,000 Mediterranean cruise. The preparer's failure to request receipts from his client shows a lack of due diligence.

Example: A taxpayer claims numerous deductions for her volunteer work in caring for feral cats. The U.S. Tax Court disallows expenses that were $250 or more because she failed to meet the substantiation requirement that required contemporaneous acknowledgement from the charitable organization.[62]

Tax Avoidance vs. Tax Evasion

The U.S. system of federal taxation operates on the concept of voluntary compliance; it is the taxpayer's responsibility to report all income. When a taxpayer fails to pay what officials say he owes, the IRS can collect back taxes and assess penalties. The Internal Revenue Code imposes many different kinds of penalties, ranging from civil fines to imprisonment for criminal tax evasion.

The term *tax avoidance* is not defined by the IRS, but it is commonly used to describe the legal reduction of taxable income, such as through deductions, credits, and adjustments to income. Most taxpayers use at least a few methods of tax avoidance in order to reduce their taxable income and therefore lower their tax liability.

Example: Nate contributes to his employer-sponsored retirement plans with pretax funds. He also uses an employer-based flexible spending account for his medical expenses, which reduces his taxable income by making all of his medical expenses pretax. He owns a home and claims a deduction for interest he pays on his mortgage. Nate is using legal tax avoidance to reduce his taxable income.

Tax evasion, on the other hand, is an illegal practice in which individuals or businesses intentionally avoid paying their true tax liability. Although most Americans comply with their tax obligations, the U.S. government estimates that 3% of taxpayers do not file tax returns at all. Those caught evading taxes are subject to criminal charges and substantial penalties.

For each year a taxpayer does not file a tax return, the penalty can include a fine of up to $25,000 and a prison sentence of up to one year. If it can be demonstrated that the taxpayer deliberately did not file in an attempt to evade taxation, the IRS can pursue a felony conviction, which can include a fine of up to $100,000 and a maximum prison sentence of five years.

Penalties Imposed Upon Taxpayers

The IRS can assess penalties on individual taxpayers who fail to file, fail to pay, or both. The failure-to-file penalty is generally greater than the failure-to-pay penalty. If someone is unable to

[62] Both examples are drawn from 2011 Tax Court cases.

pay all the taxes he owes, he is better off filing on time and paying as much as he can, as the IRS will consider payment options with individual taxpayers.

A taxpayer will not have to pay either penalty if he shows he failed to file or pay on time because of reasonable cause and not willful neglect.

Penalties are payable upon notice and demand. They are generally assessed, collected, and paid in the same manner as taxes. The taxpayer will receive a notice that contains:

- The name of the penalty,
- The applicable code section, and
- How the penalty was computed.

Failure-to-File Penalty: The penalty for filing late is usually 5% of the unpaid taxes for each month or part of a month that a return is late. This penalty will not exceed 25% of a taxpayer's unpaid taxes. The penalty is based on the tax that is not paid by the due date, without regard to extensions.

If both the failure-to-file penalty and the failure-to-pay penalty apply in any month, the 5% failure-to-file penalty is reduced by the failure-to-pay penalty. However, if a taxpayer files his return more than 60 days after the due date or extended due date, the minimum penalty is the smaller of $135 or 100% of the unpaid tax.

If a taxpayer is owed a refund, he will not be assessed a failure-to-file penalty.

Failure-to-Pay Penalty: If a taxpayer does not pay his taxes by the due date, he will be subject to a failure-to-pay penalty of ½ of 1% (0.5%) of unpaid taxes for each month or part of a month after the due date that the taxes are not paid. This penalty can be as much as 25% of a taxpayer's unpaid taxes.

The failure-to-pay penalty rate increases to a full 1% per month for any tax that remains unpaid the day after a demand for immediate payment is issued, or ten days after notice of intent to levy certain assets is issued. For taxpayers who filed on time but are unable to pay their tax liabilities, the failure-to-pay penalty rate is reduced to ¼ of 1% (0.25%) per month during any month in which the taxpayer has a valid installment agreement with the IRS.

Accuracy-Related Penalties

IRC §6662 describes penalties for accuracy-related violations of underpaying income tax, including penalties for substantial understatement, substantial overvaluation, and negligence or disregard of rules or regulations. These penalties are calculated as a flat 20% of the net understatement of tax. In addition to other penalties, if the taxpayer provides fraudulent information on his tax return, he can be subject to a civil fraud penalty.

Penalty for Substantial Understatement: For individual taxpayers, an understatement is considered substantial if it is more than the larger of:

- 10% of the correct tax, or
- $5,000.

Penalty for Substantial Overvaluation Misstatement: This penalty applies when a taxpayer incorrectly reports an asset's value or its adjusted basis on a tax return, resulting in an underpayment of tax.

A substantial valuation misstatement exists if the value of any property claimed on a tax return is 150% or more of the amount determined to be the correct amount. The penalty jumps to 40% of the net understatement of tax if the taxpayer claims a value in property on a tax return that is 200% or more of the correct amount. This is known as a *gross valuation misstatement*.

Example: A business makes a widget with an actual cost of $1 but falsely claims the cost is $10. The business reports it sold the widget for $1. Overstating the cost of the widget allows the business to claim a loss of $9, which it then uses to reduce tax on other income. This is one way a taxpayer might benefit by overvaluing its assets. In this case, the business would face a 40% penalty for underpayment of tax because it was a gross valuation misstatement.

A taxpayer may avoid both the substantial understatement and the substantial overvaluation penalties if he has substantial authority for his position or the position has a reasonable basis and is adequately disclosed.

Negligence and Disregard of the Rules and Regulations Penalty: IRC §6662 defines negligence as "any failure to make a reasonable attempt to comply with" the internal revenue laws. The penalty may be imposed on taxpayers who carelessly, recklessly, or intentionally disregard IRS rules and regulations by taking positions on their returns with little or no effort to determine whether the positions are correct or who knowingly take positions that are incorrect.

Civil Fraud Penalty: If there is any underpayment of tax due to fraud, a penalty of 75% of the underpayment will be assessed against the taxpayer. In the case of a joint return, the penalty will apply to both spouses only if some part of the underpayment is due to the fraud of each spouse.

Definitions: Negligence or simple ignorance of the law does not constitute fraud. The IRS characterizes fraud as a deliberate action for the purpose of "deceit, subterfuge, camouflage, concealment, some attempt to color or obscure events, or make things seem other than what they are."

Examples include omissions of specific items where similar items are included, concealment of bank accounts or other assets, failure to deposit receipts to business accounts, and covering up sources of receipts.

Criminal Fraud Penalty: In addition to being a civil offense, fraud may also be a criminal offense. A criminal offense must generally include an element of willfulness, meaning a voluntary and intentional violation of a known legal duty. If IRS examiners find evidence of criminal fraud in the course of an audit, they will refer the case to the IRS Criminal Investigation Division.

Frivolous Tax Return Penalty: A frivolous tax return is one that does not include enough information to figure the correct tax or that contains information clearly showing that the tax reported is substantially incorrect.

A taxpayer faces a penalty of $5,000 ($10,000 if MFJ) if he files a frivolous return or other frivolous submissions. This penalty is in addition to any other penalties provided by law. Frivolous submissions include tax protester arguments, such as contentions that filing of a tax return or payment of income tax is voluntary; that only foreign-source income is taxable; or that a taxpayer is not a "citizen" of the United States and thus not subject to federal income tax.

Frivolous submissions also include taxpayers who alter or strike out the preprinted language above the space provided for a signature. This declaration is called the jurat.

Third Party Designee	Do you want to allow another person to discuss this return with the IRS (see instructions)? ☐ **Yes.** Complete below. ☐ **No**				
	Designee's name ▶	Phone no. ▶		Personal identification number (PIN) ▶	
Sign Here	Under penalties of perjury, I declare that I have examined this return and accompanying schedules and statements, and to the best of my knowledge and belief, they are true, correct, and complete. Declaration of preparer (other than taxpayer) is based on all information of which preparer has any knowledge.				
Joint return? See instructions. Keep a copy for your records.	Your signature	Date	Your occupation	Daytime phone number	
	Spouse's signature. If a joint return, **both** must sign.	Date	Spouse's occupation	If the IRS sent you an Identity Protection PIN, enter it here (see inst.)	
Paid Preparer Use Only	Print/Type preparer's name	Preparer's signature	Date	Check ☐ if self-employed	PTIN
	Firm's name ▶			Firm's EIN ▶	
	Firm's address ▶			Phone no.	

Civil penalties for altering a jurat may include:

- A $500 penalty imposed under §6702;
- Additional penalties for failure to file a return, failure to pay tax owed, and fraudulent failure to file a return; and
- A penalty of up to $25,000 under §6673 if the taxpayer makes frivolous arguments in the United States Tax Court.

Example: A taxpayer files Form 1040 for the 2013 tax year. The taxpayer signs the form but crosses out the jurat on the return and writes the word "void" across it. This return is now considered frivolous and is subject to penalties.

Failure to Provide SSN

If a taxpayer does not include a Social Security number or the SSN of another person where required on a return, statement, or other document, he is subject to a penalty of $50 for each failure. The taxpayer also faces the $50 penalty if he refuses to give the SSN to another person (such as a tax preparer) when it is required on a tax return.

Trust Fund Recovery Penalty (TFRP)

As authorized by IRC §6672, the trust fund recovery penalty involves the income and Social Security taxes an employer withholds from the wages of employees. These taxes are called trust fund taxes because they are held in trust on behalf of employees until they are remitted to the government. Sometimes, business owners neglect to remit these taxes to the IRS.

A trust fund recovery penalty equal to 100% of the amount of unpaid trust fund taxes can be assessed against anyone who is considered a "responsible person" in the business. This may include corporate officers, directors, stockholders, and rank-and-file employees. The IRS has assessed the penalty against accountants, bookkeepers, and even clerical staff, if they have authority to sign checks.

A person must be both "responsible" and "willful" to be liable for an employer's failure to collect or pay trust fund taxes. This means that he knew (or should have known) that the payroll taxes were not being remitted to the IRS, and that he also had the power to correct the problem.

Example: Shelly works for Wilsonville Construction as a full-time bookkeeper and processes all the payroll tax forms. She also has check-signing authority, so she can pay the bills when her boss is working off-site. In 2013, her boss has a heart attack, and his wife, Doreen, takes over the business in his absence. Doreen cannot manage the business properly and Wilsonville Construction is unable to meet all of its financial commitments. Doreen tells Shelly to pay vendors first. The business continues to withhold payroll taxes from employee paychecks, but does not remit the amounts to the IRS. Eventually, the business declares bankruptcy. Doreen disappears, and Shelly is contacted by the IRS. Even though Shelly was "just an employee," the IRS can assess the trust fund recovery penalty against her because (1) she had check-signing authority, and (2) she knew that the business was not remitting payroll taxes to the IRS as required.

Client Fraud

The IRS encourages tax preparers to look for client fraud. Sometimes, the taxpayer is merely negligent or careless, or may have an honest difference of opinion regarding the deductibility of an expense. However, there are some common "badges of fraud" that the IRS looks for. Examples include:

- The understatement of income or improper deductions
- Personal items deducted as business expenses
- The overstatement of deductions or taking improper credits
- Accounting irregularities, such as making false entries in documents or destroying records
- Not cooperating with the IRS or avoiding IRS contact
- Concealing or transferring assets
- Inadequate recordkeeping
- Failing to file tax returns
- All-cash businesses

Certain of these items on their own do not necessarily indicate taxpayer fraud. However, since direct proof of fraudulent intent is rarely available, the IRS looks for a pattern of consistent abuses or multiple red flags.

Tax Preparer Fraud

Preparer fraud typically involves the preparation and filing of false income tax returns for their clients. The returns may have inflated personal or business expenses, false deductions, unallowable credits, or excessive exemptions. Preparers may also manipulate income figures to obtain fraudulent tax credits, such as the Earned Income Credit.

A preparer's clients may or may not know about the fraudulent items on their tax returns. Fraud may benefit preparers financially by:

- Diverting a portion of taxpayers' refunds for their own benefit;
- Increasing their clientele by developing a reputation for obtaining large refunds; and/or
- Charging inflated fees for return preparation.

Penalties for Preparing Fraudulent Returns (§6694)

If a tax return preparer willfully understates a client's tax liability, he is subject to penalties. Under IRS regulations, "understatement of liability" means:

- Understating net tax payable
- Overstating the net amount creditable or refundable

Under §6694, there are two specific penalties when an income tax preparer understates a taxpayer's liability.

Understatement Due to an Unreasonable Position: If there is an understatement on a tax return due to an unreasonable position, the penalty is the greater of:

- $1,000 per tax return, or
- 50% of the income the preparer received in fees for preparing the tax return with the understatement.

As described in Unit 5, this applies when a preparer knows, or reasonably should have known, that the position was unreasonable and would not have been sustained on its merits. If the position is adequately disclosed on a tax return, this penalty generally will not apply. However, in the case of a patently frivolous position (such as a tax protester position), the penalty will apply whether or not it is disclosed.

A preparer may be excused from the penalty if he acted in good faith and there was reasonable cause for the understatement.

Understatement Due to Negligent or Willful Disregard: If a tax preparer shows negligent or willful disregard of IRS rules and regulations, and makes a willful or reckless attempt to understate tax liability, the penalty is the greater of:

- $5,000 per tax return, or
- 50% of the income the preparer received in fees for preparing the tax return with the understatement.

If a tax preparer is subject to a penalty for understatement of liability and this includes a change to the Earned Income Credit, the preparer may be subject to additional penalties for failure to exercise due diligence while claiming the EIC.

IRC §6694 states that the understatement penalty will be abated if, under final judicial decision, it is found that there is no actual understatement of liability. Sometimes this occurs when a Tax Court case is decided in favor of the taxpayer.

Tax Return Preparation Penalties (§6695)

IRC §6695 lists the penalties that may be assessed in connection with the preparation of tax returns for other persons. The penalty is $50 for each violation of the following:

- Failure to furnish a copy of a return or claim to a taxpayer
- Failure to sign a return or claim for refund
- Failure to furnish an identifying number (PTIN) on a return
- Failure to retain a copy or list of a return or claim
- Failure to file correct information returns

A preparer faces a $500 fine for each time he improperly cashes a taxpayer's check. He also faces a $500 fine for each failure to comply with the EIC due diligence requirements.

Under §6695, the maximum penalty imposed by the IRS on any tax return preparer cannot exceed $25,000 in a calendar year or return period.

Additional Preparer Penalties

Abusive Tax Shelter (§6700): A tax preparer who organizes, sells, or promotes an abusive tax shelter is subject to penalties of $1,000 for each activity, or 100% of the gross income derived from the activity, whichever is less.

Aiding and Abetting Understatement of Tax Liability (§6701): The penalty is $1,000 for a tax preparer who aids and abets in an understatement of a tax liability. The penalty increases to $10,000 if the conduct relates to a corporation's tax return.

Disclosure or Use of Information by Preparers of Returns (§6713): The penalty is $250 for each unauthorized disclosure or use of information furnished for, or in connection with, the preparation of a return. The maximum penalty is $10,000 in a calendar year.

Disclosure or Use of Information by Preparers of Returns (§7216): Unlike §6713 this is a misdemeanor criminal charge, not a civil penalty. It is levied against a tax preparer who "knowingly or recklessly" discloses information furnished in connection with a tax return or uses the information for any purpose other than preparing or assisting in the preparation of such return. If convicted, a preparer faces a fine of up to $1,000, imprisonment for up to one year, or both.

Fraudulent Returns, Statements, or Other Documents (§7207): This is a misdemeanor criminal charge. Upon conviction, a preparer faces a fine of up to $10,000, imprisonment of up to one year, or both. The fine increases to $50,000 in the case of a corporation.

Fraud and False Statements (§7206): This is a felony charge. A tax preparer who is found guilty could face a fine of up $100,000, imprisonment for up to three years, or both. The fine increases to $500,000 in the case of a corporation.

Exam Tip: Specific penalties that may be imposed on both preparers and taxpayers are frequently tested on Part 3 of the EA exam. Although it is not generally necessary to memorize the IRC section numbers, test-takers should be familiar with each of the penalties listed in this PassKey study guide.

If a penalty is assessed against a tax preparer and he does not agree with the assessment, he may request a conference with the IRS officer or agent and explain why the penalty is not warranted. The preparer may also wait for the penalty to be assessed, pay the penalty within 30 days, and then file a claim for refund.

Preparer Penalties		
IRC Section	**Violation**	**Penalty**
§6695	Furnish a copy of return/claim for refund to taxpayer	$50 per failure
	Sign a return/claim for refund	$50 per failure
	Furnish a PTIN on a return	$50 per failure
	Retain a copy or list for a return/claim for refund	$50 per failure
	File correct information returns	$50 per failure
	Endorse, cash, or deposit taxpayer's refund check	$500 per failure
	Comply with EIC due diligence requirements	$500 per failure
	Maximum fines under this code section	$25,000 maximum fine per year

§6694	Understatement due to an unreasonable position	$1,000 per return, or 50% of fees derived by preparer for return
	Understatement due to negligent/willful disregard	$5,000 per return, or 50% of fees derived by preparer for return

§6700	Sells, organizes, or promotes abusive tax shelter	Lesser of $1,000 per activity, or 100% of gross income derived from activity
§6701	Aiding/abetting understatement of tax liability	$1,000 per individual return, $10,000 per corporate return
§6713	Unauthorized disclosure of client information (civil)	$250 per disclosure (not per return), $10,000 maximum/year
§7216	Unauthorized disclosure of client information (criminal)	$1,000 fine and/or up to one year in prison
§7207	Fraudulent returns/statements/documents (criminal)	$10,000 and/or up to one year in prison ($50,000 for corporate returns)
§7206	Fraud and false statements (felony criminal)	$100,000 and/or up to three years in prison ($500,000 for corporate returns)

Unit 7: Study Questions

1. IRC §6695 lists the penalties that may be assessed relating to the preparation of tax returns for other persons. For these violations, what is the maximum penalty per year a preparer may face?

A. $10,000.
B. $25,000.
C. $50,000.
D. $100,000.

2. Colleen owns a business and has never filed a tax return. How long should she keep her records?

A. Three years if she owes additional tax.
B. Seven years if she files a claim for a loss from worthless securities.
C. For an unlimited period of time if she does not file a return.
D. None of the above.

3. What penalty does a tax preparer face for failing to include his PTIN on a client's return?

A. A warning letter from the IRS.
B. A fine of $50.
C. A fine of $100.
D. A fine of $500.

4. What is the penalty a preparer faces for understating income on a tax return due to an unreasonable position?

A. $1,000 per tax return or 50% of the income the preparer received in fees for preparing the tax return with the understatement.
B. $5,000 per tax return.
C. 50% of the understatement.
D. No penalty, if the preparer failed to adequately disclose the position on the return.

5. Siobhan hires a friend, Gus, to prepare her income tax returns. Gus has prepared returns for several years but is not a CPA, an attorney, or an enrolled agent. Although he knows that Siobhan is single and childless, he prepares her tax return based on head of household filing status with two qualifying children so that Siobhan may qualify for the Earned Income Credit, and thus a larger refund. Siobhan reviews a copy of the tax return and signs it. Gus also signs the return and submits it to the IRS for processing. If the IRS detects the fraudulent credit, which of the two, if either, will face potential penalties?

A. Gus only.
B. Siobhan only.
C. Both Gus and Siobhan.
D. Neither. Since Gus is not a CPA, attorney, or enrolled agent, he is not governed by IRS rules of conduct. Siobhan is not responsible for any penalties because she relied upon Gus's professional advice in preparing her return.

6. All of the following statements regarding the fraud penalty are correct except:

A. If there is any underpayment of tax due to fraud, a penalty of 75% of the underpayment will be assessed against the taxpayer.
B. The fraud penalty on a joint return will automatically apply to each spouse.
C. IRS examiners who find strong evidence of fraud may refer the case to the IRS Criminal Investigation Division for possible criminal prosecution.
D. Negligence or simple ignorance of the law does not constitute fraud.

7. Under IRS rules, which penalty is greater: failure-to-file or failure-to-pay?

A. The failure-to-file penalty.
B. The failure-to-pay penalty.
C. Both have the same penalties.
D. None of the above.

8. Which of the following statements is true?

A. Tax avoidance and tax evasion are always illegal.
B. Taxpayers who commit fraud are subject to civil penalties only.
C. The IRS will assess a failure-to-file penalty or a failure-to-pay penalty but never both.
D. A felony conviction against a taxpayer who deliberately failed to file taxes could mean a fine of up to $100,000 and a prison sentence of up to five years.

9. What is the minimum penalty for failing to file a tax return more than 60 days late (assuming the taxpayer is not owed a refund)?

A. 100% of the unpaid tax.
B. $135.
C. The smaller of $135 or 100% of the unpaid tax.
D. A minimum of 25% of a taxpayer's unpaid tax.

10. What percentage of tax must a taxpayer pay if he is guilty of a substantial understatement penalty?

A. 5% of the net understatement of tax.
B. 10% of the net understatement of tax.
C. 20% of the net understatement of tax.
D. 25% of the net understatement of tax.

11. All of the following statements about the trust fund recovery penalty are correct except:

A. This penalty is equal to 100% of the amount that has not been properly paid.
B. The IRS primarily targets employees for this penalty.
C. This penalty involves payroll taxes withheld from the wages of employees.
D. The penalty can be assessed against anyone who is considered a responsible person and has failed to remit trust fund taxes to the U.S. government.

12. Records for a claim of loss from a worthless security should be kept for:

A. Three years.
B. Four years.
C. Six years.
D. Seven years.

13. What is the penalty for a taxpayer who has filed a return that is considered frivolous?

A. $500, plus any other penalty provided by law.
B. $1,000, plus any other penalty provided by law.
C. $5,000, plus any other penalty provided by law.
D. $10,000, plus any other penalty provided by law.

14. All of the following statements are correct except:

A. If no other provisions apply, the statute of limitations for an IRS examination of a return is three years after the return was filed or the return was due, whichever is later.
B. If more than 25% of gross income has been omitted from the tax return, the statute of limitations is six years after the return was filed.
C. If a fraudulent return is filed, the statute of limitations is seven years.
D. If a tax return is not filed at all, there is no statute of limitations.

15. What is not considered a "badge of fraud" by the IRS?

A. Sloppy recordkeeping.
B. Taking improper credits.
C. All-cash businesses.
D. Deductions for foreign travel.

16. If there is substantial unreported income (over 25%), the IRS may audit tax returns for up to __________ after the filing date.

A. Three years.
B. Four years.
C. Six years.
D. Indefinitely.

17. All of the following statements regarding preparer penalties are correct except:

A. A preparer who has been assessed a penalty may request a conference with an IRS officer to dispute the fine.
B. A preparer who makes a "willful or reckless" attempt to understate tax liability faces a fine of $10,000 per return.
C. There may be additional penalties for understatement of income if the preparer has not exercised due diligence related to the EIC.
D. A tax preparer may avoid penalties if he relied on the advice of another preparer in good faith.

18. Carlos owns a business with three employees. How long is Carlos required to keep payroll tax records?

A. Three years.
B. Four years.
C. Six years.
D. Seven years.

19. What penalty does a tax return preparer face if he cashes a client's tax refund check?

A. Nothing. This is acceptable so long as the client has given permission to do so.
B. A fine of $50 for each violation.
C. A fine of $100 for each violation.
D. A fine of $500 for each violation.

20. Accuracy-related penalties in IRC §6662 are imposed for substantial understatement of income tax and for ____________________:

A. Substantially or grossly undervaluing assets.
B. Substantially or grossly overvaluing assets.
C. Substantial overstatement of income tax.
D. Both A and B.

Unit 8: Preparer Misconduct & Sanctions

More Reading:
Publication 947, *Practice Before the IRS and Power of Attorney*

Office of Professional Responsibility

As reorganized by the revisions to Circular 230, the OPR has the authority over all matters related to practitioner conduct, discipline, and practice before the IRS.

This authority includes:

- Receiving and processing referrals regarding allegations of misconduct under Circular 230; and initiating disciplinary proceedings against individuals or entities relating to allegations or findings of practitioner misconduct consistent with the applicable disciplinary rules under Circular 230.
- Making final determinations on appeal regarding return preparer eligibility or suitability decisions; and recommending and imposing sanctions for violations under Circular 230.
- Making determinations on whether to appeal administrative law judge decisions and reviewing and determining petitions from preparers seeking reinstatement to practice.

Preparer Misconduct

There are four broad categories of preparer misconduct, all of which may be reasons for the OPR to initiate disciplinary action:

- Misconduct while representing a taxpayer
- Misconduct related to the practitioner's own return
- Giving a false opinion knowingly, recklessly, or through gross incompetence
- Misconduct not directly involving IRS representation (such as a felony conviction)

Circular 230 §10.51 outlines many instances in which the OPR might sanction a practitioner for incompetence or disreputable conduct. These instances include, but are not limited to:

- Conviction of any criminal offense under federal tax laws.
- Conviction of any criminal offense involving dishonesty or breach of trust.
- Conviction of any felony under federal or state law in which the conduct renders the practitioner unfit to practice before the IRS.
- Giving false or misleading information, or participating in any way in the giving of false or misleading information to the Department of the Treasury.
- Soliciting employment as prohibited under Circular 230 or making false or misleading representations with intent to deceive a client.
- Willfully failing to file a federal tax return, or willfully evading any assessment or payment of any federal tax.
- Willfully assisting a client in violating any federal tax law, or knowingly counseling a client to evade federal taxes.
- Misappropriating funds received from a client for purposes of payment of taxes.

- Attempting to influence any IRS officer by the use of threats, false accusations, duress, coercion, or bribery.
- Disbarment or suspension from practice as an attorney, CPA,[63] or actuary.
- Knowingly aiding and abetting another person to practice before the IRS during a period of suspension, disbarment, or ineligibility of such other person.
- Contemptuous conduct in connection with practice before the IRS, including the use of abusive language, making accusations or statements knowing them to be false, or circulating or publishing malicious or libelous matter.
- Willfully disclosing or using private tax return information.
- Willfully failing to sign a tax return.
- Willfully failing to e-file a return.
- Willfully signing a tax return without a valid PTIN.
- Willfully representing a taxpayer before the IRS without appropriate authorization.

The IRS may sanction a practitioner for any of these violations, or for engaging in reckless conduct.

This is defined as an "extreme departure from the standards" a practitioner should normally observe. The IRS will consider a practitioner's pattern of conduct to assess whether it reflects gross incompetence, meaning "gross indifference, preparation which is grossly inadequate under the circumstances, and a consistent failure to perform obligations to the client."

Disciplinary Sanctions

The OPR may impose a wide range of sanctions upon practitioners and tax preparers:

Reprimand— A reprimand is the least severe sanction. It is a private letter from the director of the OPR, stating the practitioner has committed some kind of misconduct under Circular 230. Although the issuance of a reprimand is kept private, it stays on a practitioner's record.

Censure— Censure is a public reprimand, with the practitioner's name published in the Internal Revenue Bulletin. The facts of the case that triggered the censure are not published. Unlike disbarment or suspension, censure generally does not prevent a practitioner from representing taxpayers before the IRS. However, in certain situations, a censure may place conditions on a practitioner's future representations in order to promote high standards of conduct.

Monetary Penalty— A monetary penalty may be imposed on an individual who engages in conduct subject to sanction or on an employer, firm, or entity if the individual was acting on its behalf and if it knew, or reasonably should have known, of the individual's conduct. This fine may be in addition to or in lieu of any other sanction imposed.

Suspension from Practice before the IRS— An individual who is suspended is not eligible to represent taxpayers before the IRS during the term of the suspension. Suspensions may be imposed for a period of one to 59 months.

[63] For example, a CPA who is disbarred at the state level would also be disbarred at the federal level.

Disbarment from Practice before the IRS— An individual who is disbarred is not eligible to represent taxpayers before the IRS. Disbarment lasts a minimum of five years, and Circular 230 requires the practitioner to demonstrate that he has regained fitness to practice before the IRS before he may be reinstated.

As a result of suspension or disbarment, the practitioner will have his PTIN revoked and the matter published in the Internal Revenue Bulletin.

Example: Tim is a CPA whose personal tax returns were audited by the IRS. The audit found he was improperly claiming personal expenses as business deductions and he had not timely filed his own tax returns. Even though no misconduct was discovered that related to his clients, Tim was suspended from practice by the OPR for a period of three years. The Internal Revenue Bulletin listed his name, length of time of the suspension, and personal tax compliance issues as the reason for the disciplinary action.

Complaints Against Tax Return Preparers

Any taxpayer may file a complaint against a tax return preparer by using Form 14157 and submitting it to the Return Preparer Office, which will undertake an initial investigation before referring a case to the OPR. The form divides complaints into the following categories: theft of refund, e-file issues, preparer misconduct, PTIN issues, false items/documents, employment taxes, and other issues.

Anonymous complaints are allowed. However, if a taxpayer chooses to submit his name and other personal information when he files a complaint, the information will not be shared with the individual or business being reported. A preparer who is reporting another preparer for misconduct should obtain his clients' consent before sharing any protected tax information, even with the IRS.

OPR Complaint Process

The OPR's response to a complaint or other referral about possible misconduct will vary depending on the seriousness of the allegation. In some cases, the OPR may simply contact a practitioner to discuss the matter informally. In other cases, the OPR will investigate the matter further and initiate a more formal contact with a practitioner or other parties concerning the allegations. A formal proceeding does not have to be instituted in order for the OPR to confer with other parties regarding alleged misconduct.

A practitioner may consent to be sanctioned in lieu of a formal proceeding. The director of the OPR may, in his discretion, accept or reject the practitioner's consent to a sanction. The director may accept a revised offer submitted in response to his rejection or may counteroffer and act upon any accepted counteroffer.

If the OPR issues a formal complaint against a practitioner, the complaint must:

- Name the respondent.
- Provide a clear and concise description of the facts.
- Be signed by the director of the OPR.

- Describe the type of sanction.

The complaint may be served to the practitioner in the following ways: certified mail; first class mail if returned undelivered by certified mail; private delivery service; in person; or by leaving the complaint at the office of the practitioner. Electronic delivery, such as e-mail, is not a valid means of serving a complaint. The complaint must specify a date by which the practitioner is required to respond, which must be at least 30 days after it is served. Within ten days of serving the complaint, copies of the evidence against the practitioner must also be served. If the practitioner fails to respond to an OPR complaint, it constitutes an admission of guilt and sanctions may be imposed without a hearing.

If a practitioner responds to a complaint, a hearing will be scheduled for an administrative law judge to hear the evidence and decide whether the OPR has proven its case. During a hearing, the practitioner may appear in person or be represented by an attorney or another practitioner. The director of the OPR may be represented by an attorney or by another employee of the IRS. If either party fails to appear, the administrative law judge may make his decision by default. Within 180 days of the conclusion of a hearing, the administrative law judge must enter a decision.

Example: Carolyn is an EA. The OPR sends her a complaint by certified mail that alleges she charged unconscionable fees, gave irresponsible advice to clients, and falsified documents. Thirty days later, Carolyn offers a response in writing. The case goes before an administrative judge who listens to evidence presented by the OPR and by Carolyn's attorney. The judge later hands down his ruling agreeing with the OPR's recommendation for Carolyn to be disbarred. She chooses not to appeal and is banned from practice before the IRS. She also faces separate monetary fines for her misconduct.

If there is no appeal, the decision becomes final. However, either party—the OPR or the practitioner—may appeal the judge's decision with the Secretary of the Treasury within 30 days. The Secretary of the Treasury, or his delegate, will then make a final determination on the case.

Prohibited Actions during Suspension or Disbarment

During disbarment or suspension, a practitioner will not be allowed to practice in any capacity before the IRS (except to represent himself). A disbarred or suspended practitioner may not:

- Prepare or file documents, including tax returns, or other correspondence with the IRS. The restriction applies regardless of whether the individual signs the documents and regardless of whether the individual personally files, or directs another person to file, documents with the IRS.
- Render written advice with respect to any entity, transaction, plan, or arrangement having the potential for tax avoidance or evasion.
- Represent a client at conferences, hearings, and meetings.
- Execute waivers, consents, or closing agreements; receive a taxpayer's refund check; or sign a tax return on behalf of a taxpayer.
- File powers of attorney with the IRS.

- Accept assistance from another person (or request assistance) or assist another person (or offer assistance) if the assistance relates to a matter constituting practice before the IRS, or enlist another person for purposes of practicing before the IRS.
- State or imply that he is eligible to practice before the IRS.

However, a disbarred individual or suspended is still allowed to:

- Represent himself in any matter.
- Appear before the IRS as a trustee, receiver, guardian, administrator, executor, or other fiduciary if duly qualified/authorized under the law of the relevant jurisdiction.
- Appear as a witness for a taxpayer.
- Furnish information at the request of the IRS or any of its officers or employees.
- Receive IRS information pursuant to a valid tax information authorization. However, simply receiving this information does not entitle him to practice before the IRS on behalf of that taxpayer.

Note: A practitioner who has been disbarred may petition the OPR for reinstatement after five years. The OPR may reinstate the practitioner if it determines that his conduct is not likely to be in violation of regulations and if granting the reinstatement is not contrary to the public interest.

Unit 8: Study Questions

1. Which of the following types of disciplinary actions allow a practitioner to continue practicing before the IRS?

A. Disbarment.
B. Suspension from practice.
C. Public censure.
D. All the disciplinary actions listed above will prevent a practitioner from practicing before the IRS.

2. An administrative judge ruled that Melissa, an EA, should be disbarred for gross misconduct in violation of Circular 230. Which of the following is true?

A. Melissa has a right to appeal the decision to the Secretary of the Treasury.
B. Melissa has a right to appeal the decision to the Office of Professional Responsibility.
C. Melissa has a right to appeal the decision to the Return Preparer Office.
D. Melissa has a right to appeal the decision to the Commissioner of the IRS.

3. What type of sanction will not be imposed by the OPR?

A. Disbarment.
B. Suspension.
C. Incarceration.
D. Censure.

4. A suspended or disbarred individual may:

A. Appear before the IRS as a trustee, receiver, guardian, administrator, executor, or other fiduciary, if duly authorized under the law of the relevant jurisdiction.
B. File documents on a taxpayer's behalf.
C. Represent a client at conferences, hearings, and meetings.
D. Execute a closing agreement for a client, so long as the practitioner has a valid power of attorney.

5. Following disbarment, a tax practitioner may petition the OPR for reinstatement after a period of ______________________.

A. One year.
B. Five years.
C. Ten years.
D. Never. Disbarment is always permanent.

6. What type of behavior would not subject a tax practitioner to being sanctioned by the OPR?

A. Misconduct while representing a taxpayer.
B. Misconduct related to the practitioner's own return.
C. When the practitioner is unable to pay his personal taxes due.
D. Misconduct not directly involving IRS representation.

7. Which of the following statements is true?

A. The IRS may not disbar a preparer without first seeking criminal prosecution.
B. Even without bringing a criminal prosecution, the IRS may disbar a tax return preparer.
C. A preparer is not liable for any preparer penalties if he diverts a portion of the refund to himself with the client's permission.
D. None of the above.

8. Which of the following is not listed in Circular 230 as conduct that could cause a practitioner to be censured, suspended, or disbarred?

A. Abusive language in connection with practice before the IRS.
B. Willfully failing to sign a federal tax return.
C. Conviction of a felony charge.
D. Indictment on a criminal offense charge.

9. If a practitioner has been disbarred, which of the following actions is he not allowed to do?

A. Serve as a witness at a friend's examination before the IRS.
B. Furnish information to the IRS at the request of a revenue officer.
C. Sign a tax return on behalf of a taxpayer.
D. Prepare his own federal tax return.

Unit 9: Payments & the IRS Collection Process

More Reading:
Publication 594, *The Collection Process*
Publication 1035, *Extending the Tax Assessment Period*
Publication 971, *Innocent Spouse Relief*
Publication 556, *Examination of Returns, Appeal Rights, and Claims for Refund*
Publication 1660, *Collection Appeal Rights*

Taxpayers generally have several options to make payments of any amounts owed on their tax returns or for estimated taxes.

The following methods of payments are accepted by the IRS:

1. Direct debit
2. Credit card
3. Personal check
4. Installment agreement requests
5. Electronic Federal Tax Payment System (EFTPS)
6. Electronic funds withdrawal
7. Federal Tax Application (same day wire transfer)
8. Direct Pay (new in 2014)

Balance-due payments may be made by check. Payments do not have to be mailed at the same time an electronic return is transmitted. For example, the return may be transmitted in January and the taxpayer may mail the payment at a later date. As long as the payment is mailed by the due date of the return, it will be considered timely.

On all checks or money orders, the practitioner should write the taxpayer's EIN, TIN, or SSN; the type of tax return; and the tax year to which the payment applies. The check or money order should be made payable to "United States Treasury."

Electronic Federal Tax Payment System (EFTPS)

For any type of payment due the IRS at any time of the year, taxpayers can use the Electronic Federal Tax Payment System (EFTPS). Taxpayers and businesses enroll in EFTPS by using an online application.

Businesses and individuals can pay all their federal taxes using EFTPS. Individuals can pay their quarterly estimated taxes, and they can make payments weekly, monthly, or quarterly. Businesses can schedule payments up to 120 days in advance of their tax due date. Individuals can schedule payments up to 365 days in advance of their tax due date. Domestic corporations must deposit all income tax payments by the due date of the return.

Note: In January, the IRS launched its first free electronic payment option, Direct Pay. It allows individual taxpayers with a valid Social Security number to make IRS payments directly from their checking or savings accounts. Taxpayers may pay their tax bill or make an estimated tax payment using the service, and will receive instant confirmation that their payment was submitted.

Tax Refunds

Taxpayers have a number of options related to their tax refunds. They may:

- Apply a refund to next year's estimated tax.
- Receive the refund as a direct deposit.
- Receive the refund as a paper check.
- Split the refund, with a portion applied to next year's estimated tax and the remainder received as direct deposit or a paper check.
- Use the refund (or part of it) to purchase U.S. Series I Savings Bonds. Taxpayers can purchase up to $5,000 in bonds for themselves or others.

The direct deposit option is the fastest way to receive refunds. Refunds may be designated for direct deposit to qualified accounts in the taxpayer's name. Qualified accounts include savings, checking, share draft, or retirement accounts (for example, IRA or money market accounts). Direct deposits cannot be made to credit card accounts. Qualified accounts must be in financial institutions within the United States.

Preparers are required to accept any direct deposit election to a qualified account at an eligible financial institution designated by the taxpayer. A preparer may not charge a separate fee for direct deposit.

Taxpayers may split their deposits between as many as three different accounts. Most e-file and tax preparation software allows taxpayers to split refunds.

The preparer must advise the taxpayer that a direct deposit election cannot be rescinded once a return is filed. In addition, changes cannot be made to routing numbers of financial institutions or to the taxpayer's account numbers after the IRS has accepted the return. Preparers should verify account and routing numbers with the taxpayer each year.

Refund Anticipation Loans

A refund anticipation loan (RAL) is a financial product offered by some tax offices. An RAL is not a tax refund. It is a loan: the taxpayer borrows money based on his anticipated tax refund.

The IRS is not involved in RALs or financial products. Further, there are no guarantees that the IRS will deposit a taxpayer's refund within a specified time. For example, a refund may be delayed due to processing problems or it may be withheld to pay for back taxes, child support, or other amounts that the taxpayer owes. The IRS is not liable for any loss suffered by taxpayers, practitioners, or financial institutions resulting from reduced refunds or dishonored direct deposits.

Tax preparers who assist taxpayers in applying for RALs have additional responsibilities and may be sanctioned by the IRS if they fail to adhere to the following requirements. If a preparer offers RALs, he must:

- Ensure the taxpayer understands that by agreeing to an RAL or other financial product he will not receive his refund from the IRS. Instead, it will be sent to the financial institution.
- Advise the taxpayer that an RAL is an interest-bearing loan and not a quicker way of receiving his actual refund from the IRS.

- Advise the taxpayer that if a direct deposit is not received by the financial institution within the expected time frame, for whatever reason, the taxpayer may be liable to the lender for additional interest and other fees.
- Advise the taxpayer of all fees and other known deductions to be paid from his refund and the remaining amount he will actually receive.
- Obtain the taxpayer's written consent to disclose information to the lending institution.
- Ensure that the preparer does not have a related party conflict with the financial institution that makes an RAL agreement.
- Adhere to advertising standards.

Fee Restrictions for RALs: A practitioner may not base his tax preparation fees on a percentage of the refund amount or compute his fees using any amount from the tax return. He must charge an identical flat fee to all customers applying for RALs, meaning the fee cannot correspond to the amount of a refund for an individual client.

Tax Payment Options

For taxpayers who are unable to pay the tax they owe, a number of options are available, including extensions of time to pay, installment agreements, and offers in compromise.

Extension of Time for Payment (Form 1127): A taxpayer should file Form 1127, *Application for Extension of Time for Payment of Tax Due to Hardship*, by the due date of his return, or by the due date for the amount determined as a deficiency. The types of taxes covered by Form 1127 include income taxes, self-employment taxes, and gift taxes.

The term "undue hardship" does not mean a taxpayer will simply be inconvenienced by paying the tax. Rather, for the IRS to grant a Form 1127 request, a taxpayer must show he will sustain a substantial financial loss if he pays tax on the date it is due.

In the request for extension, a taxpayer must:

- Enter the date he proposes to pay the tax
- Provide a detailed explanation of the undue hardship that would result if he paid the tax on or before the due date
- Provide supporting documentation, including a statement of assets and liabilities and an itemized list of income and expenses for each of the three months prior to the due date of the tax

Example: Luis had serious health issues in 2013 and has been hit hard by hospital bills. He does not have the money to pay the $8,500 of income tax he owes. To settle the debt he would have to sell his car at a sacrifice price. Doing so would create an undue hardship because he would not have reliable transportation, which could cause him to lose his job. Prior to the April 15 tax deadline, Luis files Form 1127 to request an extension of time to pay tax due to an undue hardship. He provides a full explanation of his financial difficulties as well as the other required documentation.

The IRS generally will not grant an extension of more than six months to pay the tax shown on a return. An extension to pay an amount determined as a deficiency is generally limited to 18 months from the date payment is due.

Installment Agreements: Installment agreements are arrangements in which the IRS allows taxpayers to pay liabilities over time. A taxpayer who files electronically may apply for an installment agreement once the return is processed and the tax is assessed. Taxpayers must either submit Form 9465, *Installment Agreement Request*, or apply online if they qualify. The IRS charges a one-time user fee to set up an installment agreement.

An agreement will only be granted if it provides for full payment of the account. This means the taxpayer must agree to pay the full balance due; he cannot use an installment agreement to negotiate a lower tax liability. During the term of the installment agreement, penalties and interest continue to accrue. Future refunds are applied to the tax debt until it is paid in full.

Equal monthly payments are specified in the agreement, but the taxpayer may choose to pay more than the required monthly amount. The minimum monthly payment is $25. Taxpayers may pay a variety of ways, including by check, credit card, payroll deduction, or direct debit.[64] Qualified taxpayers who owe $25,000 or less may have their Notice of Federal Tax Lien withdrawn after entering into a direct debit installment agreement.

A taxpayer who owes $10,000 or less in tax cannot be turned down for an installment agreement, assuming that the following apply:

- He (and spouse, if married) has timely filed all income tax returns and paid all tax due during the past five years.
- The IRS has determined the taxpayer cannot pay the tax owed in full when it is due.
- The taxpayer agrees to pay the full amount he owes within three years.

A taxpayer with $50,000 or less in combined tax, penalties, and interest can set up his installment agreement online. If a taxpayer owes more than $50,000, he may still qualify for an installment agreement, but Form 433-F, *Collection Information Statement*, must be submitted. The IRS will typically notify a taxpayer within 30 days if his request for an agreement is approved or denied. The IRS generally will not take collection actions:

- When an installment agreement is being considered
- While an installment agreement is in effect
- For 30 days after an agreement request is rejected
- During the period the IRS evaluates an appeal of a rejected or terminated agreement

If a taxpayer fails to make a payment on an installment agreement, an automatic 30-day notice is generated. The IRS generally charges a fee for reinstating an installment agreement that has gone into default.

IRS Offer in Compromise Program: An offer in compromise (OIC) is an agreement between a taxpayer and the IRS that settles the taxpayer's tax liabilities for less than the full amount owed. Generally, the IRS will accept an offer if it represents the most the agency can expect to collect within a reasonable period of time. Absent special circumstances, an offer will not be accepted if the IRS believes that the liability can be paid in full as a lump sum or through a payment agreement.

---

[64] Under the IRS's Fresh Start program, taxpayers who owe up to $50,000 can pay monthly over a period of 72 months (six years) so long as they use direct debit.

The IRS will consider each taxpayer's unique set of facts and circumstances in determining whether to grant an OIC, including his ability to pay, income, expenses, and asset equity.

An offer in compromise can be applied to all taxes, including interest and penalties. A taxpayer may submit an OIC on three grounds:

Doubt as to Collectability

Doubt exists that the taxpayer could ever pay the full amount of tax liability owed within the remainder of the statutory period for collection.

Example: Elise owes $80,000 for unpaid tax liabilities and agrees that the tax she owes is correct. Elise is terminally ill and cannot work. She does not own any property and does not have the ability to fully pay the liability now or through monthly installment payments.

Doubt as to Liability

A legitimate doubt exists that the assessed tax liability is correct.

Example: Sofia was vice president of a corporation from 2005 to 2012. In 2013, the corporation accrued unpaid payroll taxes and she was assessed a trust fund recovery penalty. However, by 2013, Sofia had resigned from the corporation, prior to the payroll taxes accruing. Since there is legitimate doubt that the assessed tax liability is correct, she may apply for an OIC under doubt as to liability.

Exceptional Circumstances (Effective Tax Administration)

There is no doubt that the tax is correct and there is potential to collect the full amount of the tax owed, but an exceptional circumstance exists. A taxpayer must demonstrate that the collection of the tax would create serious economic hardship or would be unfair.

Example: Brad and Stacy Snyder have assets sufficient to satisfy their tax liability. However, they provide full-time care to their dependent child, who has a serious long-term illness. The unpaid taxes were a result of the Snyders providing needed medical care for their sick child. They will need to continue to use their assets to provide for basic living expenses and ongoing care for the child. There is no doubt that the tax is correct, but to pay the tax would endanger the life of their child and would create a serious hardship.

To apply for an OIC on grounds of doubt as to collectability or exceptional circumstances, a taxpayer must submit an application fee and initial nonrefundable payment along with Form 656, *Offer in Compromise*. Fees may be waived for low income taxpayers. There is no fee or initial payment required to apply for an OIC on grounds of doubt as to liability and Form 656-L is used instead.

The taxpayer may appeal a rejected offer in compromise within 30 days.

As part of its Fresh Start initiative, the IRS has expanded and streamlined the OIC program. The agency has more flexibility when analyzing a taxpayer's ability to pay, which makes the program available to a larger group of taxpayers. Taxpayers may use the OIC pre-qualifier tool at www.irs.gov to see if they may be eligible for an OIC.

IRS Collection Process

The IRS has wide powers when it comes to collecting unpaid taxes. If a taxpayer does not pay in full when filing his tax return, he will receive a bill from an IRS service center. The first notice explains the balance due and demands payment in full. It will include the amount of the unpaid tax balance plus any penalties and interest calculated from the date the tax was due. This first notice starts the collection process, which continues until the taxpayer's account is satisfied or until the IRS may no longer legally collect the tax, such as when the collection period has expired.

Note: The IRS generally has ten years from the date of assessment to collect a tax debt from a taxpayer.

However, the ten-year collection period can be suspended in the following cases:

- While the IRS and the Office of Appeals consider a request for an installment agreement or an offer in compromise
- From the date a taxpayer requests a collection due process (CDP) hearing
- While the taxpayer is residing outside the United States
- For tax periods included in a bankruptcy

The amount of time the suspension is in effect will be added to the time remaining in the ten-year period. For example, if the ten-year period is suspended for six months, the time left in the period the IRS has to collect will increase by six months. The IRS is required to notify the taxpayer that he may refuse to extend the statute of limitations.

Bankruptcy: A filing in bankruptcy court immediately stops all assessment and collection of tax. This is called an *automatic stay*, and it remains in effect until the bankruptcy court lifts the stay or discharges liabilities, meaning they are eliminated or no longer legally enforceable.

Income tax debt that may be forgiven in bankruptcy must meet the following conditions:

- The tax debt must be related to a return that was due at least three years before the taxpayer filed for bankruptcy.
- The tax return must have been filed at least two years ago.
- The tax assessment must be at least 240 days old.

The taxpayer cannot be guilty of tax evasion, and the tax return cannot be fraudulent or frivolous.

Taxpayer's Ability to Pay

When there is a delinquent tax liability or when the taxpayer makes a request for an installment agreement or an offer in compromise, the IRS may use a variety of methods to assess the taxpayer's ability to pay. The IRS may consider the taxpayer's general financial health, including factors such as cash flow and assets, lawsuits against the taxpayer, garnishments, and whether the taxpayer has filed bankruptcy. They may also use third party research such as property assessments, asset values, and state and local tax information.

Collection Financial Standards: The IRS *Collection Financial Standards* are used to evaluate a taxpayer's ability to pay a delinquent tax liability. These standards are used to determine allowable living expenses that are necessary to provide for a taxpayer's (and his family's) health and welfare and/or production of income while his tax debt is being repaid.

Allowances for housing, utilities, and transportation vary by location, while standard amounts are allowed nationwide for food, clothing, out-of-pocket health care expenses, and other items. In most cases, the taxpayer is allowed the amount actually spent, or the local standard, whichever is less. For the items based on national standards, taxpayers are allowed the total amounts applicable for their family size, without regard to the amounts actually spent. Generally, the number of persons for whom necessary living expenses are allowed is the same as the number of exemptions on the taxpayer's most recent income tax return.

The IRS uses these standards for taxpayers who do not qualify for streamlined installment agreements, which require little financial analysis or substantiation of expenses. If a taxpayer believes he needs a higher amount for basic living expenses than the *Collection Financial Standards* allow, he must provide documentation to explain why.

Collection Information Statements: The information described above regarding allowable living expenses may be used to prepare a *Collection Information Statement*, using Form 433-A, Form 433-B, or Form 433-F. This statement also contains detailed financial information about the taxpayer's income, his bank and retirement accounts, real estate and other assets, and his outstanding debts. Further, it may include information concerning the taxpayer's obligations for court-ordered payments, such as child support and alimony, since the taxpayer will generally have little flexibility regarding these obligations.

Currently Not Collectible: The IRS can declare a taxpayer to be *currently not collectible* if the agency has received evidence that a taxpayer has no ability to pay his tax debts. Generally, this action is taken only when other options, such as an offer in compromise, are not feasible because the taxpayer's financial situation is so bad he cannot even afford to make monthly payments.

Before this status will be declared, the IRS will require a taxpayer to submit Form 433-F in order to demonstrate that after paying necessary living expenses he has no money left to make monthly payments to the IRS. Further, he must prove he has no assets that could be liquidated or sold to make a lump sum payment to the IRS.

Once a taxpayer is placed into currently not collectible status (also known as *Status 53),* the IRS must stop all collection activities, such as levies. A taxpayer is guaranteed this status for at least one year, or until his income increases. While in currently not collectible status, penalties and interest continue to be added to the tax debt.

IRS Actions to Collect Unpaid Taxes

Congress has given the IRS broad powers to compel taxpayers to produce information it requires to determine tax liability or to collect tax. The IRS is permitted to do the following:

- Examine any books, papers, records, or other data;
- Summon a taxpayer or any other person, requiring the person to appear, to produce books and records, and to give testimony under oath, and
- Take testimony under oath.

These powers are most commonly used in connection with collection proceedings, such as when a taxpayer refuses to provide information voluntarily, and in IRS audits, referred to as *examinations.*[65]

IRS enforcement actions to collect unpaid taxes may include the following:

[65] Even though the IRS uses the term "examination" rather than "audit," the terms mean essentially the same thing.

- Issuing a notice of levy on salary and other income, bank accounts, or property (legally seizing property to satisfy the tax debt).
- Issuing a summons to secure information to prepare unfiled tax returns or determine the taxpayer's ability to pay. IRS employees will prepare "substitute returns"[66] when taxpayers do not file voluntarily.
- Filing a Notice of Federal Tax Lien.
- Offsetting a taxpayer's refund.
- Applying future federal tax refunds to any prior amount due.

A state income tax refund may also be applied to a taxpayer's federal tax liability.

Federal Tax Lien

A federal tax lien is a legal claim against a taxpayer's property, including property that the taxpayer acquires after the lien is filed. By filing a Notice of Federal Tax Lien, the IRS establishes its interest in the taxpayer's property as a creditor and as security for his tax debt, and publicly notifies the taxpayer's other creditors of its claim.

A Notice of Federal Tax Lien may be filed only after:

- The IRS assesses the taxpayer's liability;
- The IRS sends a notice and demand for payment; and
- The taxpayer neglects to pay the debt.

Once these requirements are met, a lien is created for the amount of the taxpayer's debt. The lien attaches to all the taxpayer's property (such as a house or car) and to all the taxpayer's rights to property (such as accounts receivable, in the case of a business).

Under the IRS's Fresh Start program, the filing threshold for the amount taxpayers can owe before a Notice of Federal Tax Lien is issued has been increased from $5,000 to $10,000 in most cases. Once a lien is filed, the IRS generally cannot release it until the taxes are paid in full or until the government may no longer legally collect the tax.

Notice of Levy

An IRS seizure is the legal act of confiscating a taxpayer's property to satisfy a tax debt, as authorized by an earlier filed tax lien. If a tax lien is the IRS's authorization to act by seizing property, then the IRS levy is the actual act of seizure. A levy allows the IRS to confiscate and sell property, which may include cars, boats, or real estate. The IRS may also levy wages, bank accounts, Social Security benefits, and retirement income.

There are special rules regarding IRS seizures. The IRS generally must wait at least 30 days from the date of the notice of intent to levy before it can make a seizure. However, if the IRS has determined that collection of tax is in jeopardy, it may immediately seize property without the normal waiting period.

[66] These substitute returns generally do not give credit for deductions and exemptions a taxpayer may be entitled to receive. Even if the IRS has already filed a substitute return, a taxpayer may still file his own return. The IRS will generally adjust the taxpayer's account to reflect the correct figures.

Typically, the IRS may not seize property in the following circumstances:

- When there is a pending installment agreement
- While a taxpayer's appeal is pending
- During the consideration of an offer in compromise
- During a bankruptcy (unless the seizure is authorized by the bankruptcy court)
- If the taxpayer's liability is $5,000 or less in a seizure of real property
- While innocent spouse claims are pending

The IRS may not seize a main home without prior approval from the IRS district director or assistant district director; judicial approval is also generally required for seizure of a main home.

Further, the following items are exempt from IRS levy:

- Wearing apparel and school books.
- Fuel, provisions (food), furniture, personal effects in the taxpayer's household, arms for personal use, or livestock, up to $8,790 in value for tax year 2013.
- Books and tools necessary for the trade, business, or profession of the taxpayer, up to $4,400 in value for tax year 2013.
- Undelivered mail.
- Unemployment benefits and amounts payable under the Job Training Partnership Act.
- Workers' compensation, including amounts payable to dependents.
- Certain annuity or pension payments, but only if payable by the Army, Navy, Air Force, Coast Guard, or under the Railroad Retirement Act or Railroad Unemployment Insurance Act. Traditional or Roth IRAs are not exempt from levy.
- Judgments for the support of minor children (child support).
- Certain public assistance and welfare payments, and amounts payable for Supplemental Security Income for the aged, blind, and disabled under the Social Security Act. Regular Social Security payments are not exempt from levy.

If an IRS levy creates an immediate economic hardship, it may be released. A levy release does not mean the taxpayer is exempt from paying the balance.

Collection Appeal Rights

A taxpayer may appeal an IRS collection action to the IRS Office of Appeals. The Office of Appeals is separate from and independent of the IRS Collection offices that initiate the collection actions. The IRS ensures the independence of the Appeals office through a strict policy prohibiting *ex parte* communication[67] with the IRS Collection office about the accuracy of the facts or the merits of each case without providing the taxpayer an opportunity to participate at that meeting.

The two main ways that taxpayers use to appeal an IRS collection action are "collection due process" and the "collection appeals program."

---

[67]An ex parte communication occurs when one party to a case receives communications about issues in the case without the other party's knowledge. Revenue Procedure 2000-43 has more information about Appeals' mandatory independence and ex parte communication, and is available at *www.IRS.gov*.

Collection Due Process Hearings (CDP)

A taxpayer who wants to protest an IRS collection notice may complete Form 12153, *Request for a Collection Due Process or Equivalent Hearing,* and submit it to the address listed on the IRS notice. Collection due process is available for the following notices:

- Notice of Federal Tax Lien Filing
- Final Notice: Notice of Intent to Levy
- Notice of Jeopardy Levy and Right of Appeal
- Notice of Levy on a State Tax Refund
- Post Levy Collection Due Process (CDP) Notice

A collection notice will be mailed, given to the taxpayer, or left at his home or office. A taxpayer has 30 days from the date of a notice to request a CDP hearing. Before the hearing, the taxpayer may attempt to work out a solution with the Collection office that sent the notice. If the issue cannot be resolved, the case will be forwarded to Appeals for the taxpayer (or his representative) to schedule a conference with an Appeals officer. The conference may be by telephone, correspondence, or face-to-face for taxpayers who qualify.

Many taxpayers ignore IRS notices until they receive a final notice or a notice of intent to levy. Often, by the time this happens, it is too late to help the taxpayer solve these issues, and the IRS has already begun the collection process in earnest. Issues that may be discussed during a collection due process hearing include:

- Whether or not the taxpayer paid all the tax owed
- Whether the IRS assessed tax and sent the levy notice when the taxpayer was in bankruptcy
- Whether the IRS made a procedural error in the assessment
- Whether the time to collect the tax (the statute of limitations) has expired
- Whether the taxpayer wishes to discuss collection options
- Whether the taxpayer wishes to make a spousal defense (innocent spouse relief)

In a CDP hearing, a taxpayer may request specific action regarding a lien against his property. For example, he may request a *lien withdrawal* on the grounds the IRS filed the Notice of Federal Tax Lien prematurely or did not follow established procedures. Or he may request a *lien discharge* that removes a federal tax lien from a specific property.

Example: The IRS placed a federal tax lien on Pete's vacation condo in the Florida Keys. Pete's attorney attends a CDP hearing and asks that the lien be discharged so Pete may sell the condo and use the sales proceeds to pay the tax he owes.

After a CDP hearing, the Appeals officer will issue a written determination letter. If the taxpayer disagrees with the determination, he can request judicial review by petitioning the U.S. Tax Court. The petition must be made within the time period specified in the Appeals' determination letter. The taxpayer cannot raise any issues with the Tax Court that he did not already raise during the appeals hearing.

If a taxpayer timely files a CDP hearing request, no collection action can be taken until a final determination is made following the hearing or a subsequent appeal to the Tax Court.

Collection Appeals Program (CAP)

The collection appeals program (CAP) is generally quicker than a CDP hearing and available for a broader range of collection actions. However, the taxpayer cannot go to court to appeal if he disagrees with a CAP decision. Also, under CAP, the taxpayer may not contest the underlying tax liability.

CAP is available in the following instances:

- Before or after the IRS files a Notice of Federal Tax Lien
- Before or after the IRS levies or seizes a taxpayer's property
- After the termination of an installment agreement
- After the rejection of an installment agreement

To appeal an installment agreement that has been rejected or that the IRS is proposing be modified or terminated, the taxpayer should appeal by completing Form 9423, *Collection Appeal Request*. The form should be submitted within 30 days to the IRS office or revenue officer who took the action regarding the installment agreement.

Form 9423 is also used in the cases of liens, levies, and seizures. Generally, the taxpayer would first try to resolve the disagreement by telephone with an IRS employee, manager, or revenue officer. If the issue cannot be resolved, the taxpayer would submit a written request for Appeals consideration by completing Form 9423. The taxpayer must explain why he disagrees with the collection action and how he proposes to resolve his tax problem.

In the appeals hearing, a taxpayer may represent himself, or he may appoint a qualified representative (attorney, CPA, EA, spouse, or family member). In the case of a business, the entity may be represented by a regular full-time employee, a general partner, or a bona fide officer.

Once the IRS makes a determination under CAP, it is binding on both the taxpayer and the IRS. It cannot be appealed to the Tax Court.

Seeking Relief from Joint Liability

Married taxpayers often file jointly because of benefits this filing status affords. In the case of a joint return, both taxpayers are liable for the tax and any interest or penalties, even if they later separate or divorce. *Joint and several liability* means that each taxpayer is legally responsible for the entire liability. This is true even if only one spouse earned all the income, or if a divorce decree states that a former spouse is responsible for any amounts due on previously filed joint returns.

In some cases, however, a spouse who filed joint returns can receive relief from joint and several liability:

Innocent Spouse Relief: Provides relief from additional tax if a spouse or former spouse failed to report income or claimed improper deductions.

Separation of Liability Relief: Provides for the allocation of additional tax owed between the taxpayer and his spouse or former spouse because an item was not reported properly on a joint return. The tax allocated to the taxpayer is the amount for which he is responsible.

Equitable Relief: May apply when a taxpayer does not qualify for innocent spouse relief or separation of liability relief for items not reported properly on a joint return and generally attributable to the taxpayer's spouse. A taxpayer may also qualify for equitable relief if the correct amount of tax was reported on his joint return but the tax remains unpaid.

Requesting Innocent Spouse Relief

The taxpayer must meet all of the following conditions in order to qualify for innocent spouse relief:

- The taxpayer filed a joint return that has an understatement of tax directly related to his spouse's erroneous items.
- The taxpayer establishes that, at the time he signed the joint return, he did not know and had no reason to know that there was an understatement of tax.
- Taking into account all the facts and circumstances, it would be unfair for the IRS to hold the taxpayer liable for the understatement.

In order to apply for innocent spouse relief, a taxpayer must submit Form 8857, *Request for Innocent Spouse Relief*, and sign it under penalty of perjury.

A request for innocent spouse relief will be denied if the IRS proves that property was transferred between the taxpayer and the spouse or former spouse as part of a fraudulent scheme to defraud the IRS or another third party.

If a taxpayer requests innocent spouse relief, the IRS cannot enforce collection action while the request is pending, but interest and penalties continue to accrue.

Example: Nancy and Allen are married and file jointly. At the time Nancy signed their joint return, she was unaware her husband had a gambling problem. The IRS examined their return and determined that Allen's unreported gambling winnings were $25,000. Nancy was able to prove that she did not know about, and had no reason to know about, the additional $25,000, because Allen had concealed his gambling winnings. The understatement of tax due to the $25,000 qualifies for innocent spouse relief.

Requesting Separation of Liability Relief

To qualify for separation of liability relief, the taxpayer must have filed a joint return and be no longer married (including a taxpayer who is widowed), legally separated, or living apart for the 12 months prior to the filing of a claim. Living apart does not include a spouse who is only temporarily absent from the household, in which case the taxpayer would not qualify for separation of liability relief.

The spouse or former spouse who is applying for separation of liability relief must not have known about the understatement of tax at the time of signing the return. An exception is made for spousal abuse or domestic violence, if the taxpayer had been afraid that failing to sign the return could result in harm or retaliation.

Example: Lenora and Martin have lived apart since 2012 and divorced in 2013. In 2011, they filed a joint return showing Lenora's wages of $35,000 and Martin's self-employment income of $15,000. In an audit, the IRS found that Martin failed to report $25,000 of self-employment income, which resulted in a $7,500 understatement of tax. Since she is now divorced from Martin, Lenora filed Form 8857 to request relief by separation of liability. However, the IRS was able to prove that Lenora knew about the $25,000 of additional income at the time she signed the joint return, so she is not granted separation of liability relief.

Requesting Equitable Relief

A taxpayer who does not qualify for innocent spouse relief or separation of liability relief may qualify for equitable relief. The taxpayer must establish, based upon all the facts and circumstances, that it would be unfair to hold him liable for the understatement or underpayment of tax. The IRS considers a taxpayer's current marital status, whether there is a legal obligation under a divorce degree to pay the tax, and whether he would suffer significant economic hardship if relief were not granted.

Example: Paula and Joshua were married in 2012 and filed a joint return that showed they owed $10,000. Paula had $5,000 of her own money and she took out a loan to pay the other $5,000. Paula gave Joshua the money to pay the $10,000 liability. Without telling Paula, Joshua spent $5,000 rather than paying the full tax liability. The couple was divorced in 2013. Paula had no knowledge at the time she signed the return that the tax would not be paid. These facts indicate to the IRS that it may be unfair to hold Paula liable for the $5,000 underpayment.

The following factors weigh in favor of equitable relief:

- Abuse by the spouse or former spouse
- Poor mental or physical health on the date the taxpayer signed the return or requested relief

New streamlined procedures should make equitable relief available to more taxpayers, which the IRS used to grant only in rare circumstances. Under new guidelines,[68] the IRS defines abuse in a much broader fashion than before, which generally required evidence of physical abuse. A spouse whose access to financial information was restricted by the other spouse may also qualify. In cases of either abuse or financial control, the requesting spouse may have known about the tax understatement or underpayment, but may not have been able to challenge the treatment of items on the tax return for fear of retaliation.

Further, the IRS has expanded the amount of time to request equitable relief. Under prior rules, taxpayers were allowed only two years to file for relief. Now taxpayers have up to ten years to file, the same time period the IRS has to collect the tax. If the taxpayer is making a claim for refund, he must file his request within the statute of limitations for refunds. More time may be allowed for taxpayers who are physically or mentally unable to manage their financial affairs or who live in federally declared disaster areas.

---

[68] Revenue Procedure 2013-34, published in the Internal Revenue Bulletin on October 7, 2013.

Injured Spouse Claims

Innocent spouse relief should not be confused with an injured spouse claim. A taxpayer may qualify as an injured spouse if he filed a joint return and his share of the refund was applied against past due amounts owed by his spouse.

An injured spouse may be entitled to recoup only his share of a tax refund. When a joint return is filed and the refund is used to pay one spouse's past-due federal tax, state income tax, child support, spousal support, or federal nontax debt (such as a delinquent student loan), the other spouse may be considered an injured spouse. The injured spouse can request his share of the refund using Form 8379, *Injured Spouse Allocation*.

Example: Trudy and Brent marry in 2012 and file jointly in 2013. Unknown to Trudy, Brent has unpaid child support and delinquent student loan debt. Their entire refund is retained to pay Brent's outstanding debts. Trudy may qualify for injured spouse treatment and recoup her share of the tax refund. The IRS will retain Brent's share of the refund to pay the delinquent debts.

Abatement of Penalties and Interest

In certain cases, the IRS will waive or abate penalties and interest assessed a taxpayer.

Penalties: A taxpayer may qualify for penalty relief in the following circumstances:

- When the penalty is incurred due to a major disaster or emergency affecting a large number of taxpayers in a given geographical area. Relief is often provided in the form of extensions of time to file or pay.
- When the penalty is due to an IRS computation or assessment error.
- When the penalty is incurred as a result of the taxpayer relying on advice of a tax advisor. This is generally limited to issues considered highly technical or complicated, and only relates to accuracy-related penalties.
- When the penalty is incurred as the result of erroneous written advice provided by an IRS employee.

Penalty relief may also be provided due to *reasonable cause*. This is when a taxpayer has established that, despite the "exercise of ordinary business care and prudence," he was assessed a penalty due to circumstances beyond his control.

Under a special program, the IRS will use the reasonable cause standard to consider abatement of a taxpayer's first-time penalty charge on a one-time basis. This penalty relief is only available for failure to file, failure to pay, and failure to deposit penalties. The IRS will consider this relief option only if the taxpayer has filed all returns and paid, or arranged to pay, all tax currently due.

Interest: Reasonable cause is not allowed as the basis for abatement of interest.

Interest may be abated or waived in the following instances:

- When it is excessive, barred by statute, or erroneously or illegally assessed.
- When it is assessed on an erroneous refund.
- When it was incurred on an account while the taxpayer was in a combat zone or in a declared disaster area.

Further, the IRS will waive interest that is the result of certain errors or delays caused by an IRS employee. The IRS will abate the interest only if there was an unreasonable error or delay in performing a managerial or ministerial act (defined below). The taxpayer cannot have caused any significant aspect of the error or delay. In addition, the interest can be abated only if it relates to taxes for which a notice of deficiency is required, which includes income taxes and estate and gift taxes.

Definition: A **managerial act** is an administrative act that occurs during the processing of the taxpayer's case involving the temporary or permanent loss of records or the exercise of judgment or discretion relating to management of personnel.

Example: A revenue agent is examining Margaret's tax return. During the course of the examination, the agent is sent to an extended training course. The agent's supervisor decides not to reassign the audit case, so the examination is unreasonably delayed until the agent returns. Interest caused by the delay can be abated since the decision to send the agent to the training class and the decision not to reassign the case are both managerial acts.

Definition: A **ministerial act** is a procedural or mechanical act that does not involve the exercise of judgment or discretion and that occurs during the processing of the taxpayer's case.

Example: Calvin moves to another state before the IRS selects his tax return for examination. Notice of the examination was sent to his old address and then forwarded to his new address. When Calvin gets the letter, he requests that the examination be transferred to the area office closest to his new address. The examination group manager approves his request. However, the original examination manager fails to transfer the file for six months. The transfer is a ministerial act. The IRS can reduce the interest Calvin owes because of the unreasonable delay in transferring the case.

A taxpayer may request an abatement of interest on Form 843, *Claim for Refund and Request for Abatement.* The taxpayer should file the claim with the IRS service center where the examination was affected by the error or delay. If a request for abatement of interest is denied, an appeal can be made to the IRS Appeals office or the U.S. Tax Court. When a portion of interest is abated, the IRS must recalculate the amount of remaining interest the taxpayer owes.

Taxpayer Advocate Service

The Taxpayer Advocate Service (TAS) is an independent organization within the IRS whose goal is to help taxpayers resolve problems with the IRS. A taxpayer may be eligible for TAS assistance when he is facing the following situations:

- Economic harm or significant cost (including fees for professional representation)
- A significant delay to resolve a tax issue
- No response or resolution to a problem by the date promised by the IRS
- Irreparable injury or long-term adverse impact if relief is not granted

The Taxpayer Advocate Service is free and confidential, and is available for businesses as well as individuals. A taxpayer may call a toll free telephone line or submit Form 911, *Request for Taxpayer Advocate Service Assistance.*

Unit 9: Study Questions

1. A taxpayer may qualify as an injured spouse if ________________.

A. He files a joint return and his share of the refund is applied against past due amounts owed by a spouse.
B. He files a joint return and fails to report income.
C. He files a separate return and has the refund offset by past due student loan obligations.
D. He files for bankruptcy protection.

2. The statute of limitations on collection activity can be suspended in certain instances. The ten-year collection period may be suspended in each of the following cases except:

A. While the IRS and the Office of Appeals consider a request for an installment agreement or an offer in compromise.
B. From the date a taxpayer requests a collection due process (CDP) hearing.
C. While the taxpayer is in prison.
D. While the taxpayer lives outside the United States.

3. If the IRS rejects an offer in compromise, a taxpayer may appeal within ____________:

A. 30 days.
B. 60 days.
C. 90 days.
D. There is no time limit to appeal an offer in compromise.

4. Belinda and Neil file jointly. They report $15,000 of income, but Belinda knows that Neil is not reporting $3,000 of dividends. The income is not hers, and she has no access to it since it is in Neil's bank account. She signs the joint return. The return is later chosen for examination, and penalties are assessed. Does Belinda qualify for innocent spouse relief?

A. No, because she knew about the understated income.
B. Yes, because she had no control over the income.
C. No, but she is eligible for injured spouse relief.
D. None of the above.

5. Which of the following is true regarding refund anticipation loans?

A. A preparer may compute his RAL fee using any amount on the tax return.
B. A preparer may charge an identical flat fee to all customers applying for RALs.
C. A preparer may accept a fee that is contingent upon the amount of the refund or an RAL.
D. The IRS is responsible for paying any RAL fees associated with the preparation of a return.

6. A levy allows the IRS to __________.

A. Confiscate and sell property to satisfy a tax debt.
B. Publicly notify a taxpayer's creditors of a claim against his property.
C. Collect tax beyond the statute of limitations.
D. Sell property on behalf of the taxpayer.

7. Lena owes $20,000 for unpaid federal tax liabilities. She agrees she owes the tax, but she has a serious medical problem and her monthly income does not meet her necessary living expenses. She does not own any real estate and does not have the ability to fully pay the liability now or through monthly installment payments. What type of relief may she qualify for?

A. Doubt as to collectability.
B. Doubt as to liability.
C. Effective tax administration.
D. Collection advocate procedure.

8. Separation of liability relief does not apply to taxpayers who are _______________.

A. Divorced.
B. Legally separated.
C. Widowed.
D. Single (never married).

9. If a taxpayer believes the IRS is not handling his case in a timely and appropriate manner, he should contact the _______________ for assistance.

A. IRS Help Line.
B. U.S. Tax Court.
C. Taxpayer Advocate Service.
D. IRS Appeals office.

10. Which statement is correct regarding the process of a taxpayer appealing an IRS collection action?

A. The decision in a collection due process hearing is final, and a taxpayer may not appeal even if he is unhappy with the determination.
B. A disposition in the collection appeals program is typically slower than in a CDP, but the taxpayer has the right to appeal if he is unhappy with a CAP determination.
C. Innocent spouse relief may not be discussed during a CDP hearing.
D. If a taxpayer disagrees with the Appeals officer's determination after a CDP hearing, he can appeal to another court.

11. Which of the following amounts is the IRS least likely to challenge when evaluating a taxpayer's offer in compromise?

A. Rent.
B. Prescription drugs.
C. Child support.
D. Food.

12. All of the following property is exempt from an IRS levy except:

A. Undelivered mail.
B. Child support payments.
C. Social Security payments.
D. Unemployment benefits.

13. How does the IRS begin the process of collections?

A. With an email to the taxpayer shortly after he files his tax return.
B. With a certified letter to the taxpayer immediately after a tax return is flagged for audit.
C. With a written examination notice when the taxpayer is notified of the possibility of an audit.
D. A first notice will be sent, which is a letter that explains the balance due and demands payment in full.

14. The IRS may not pursue collection enforcement action against a taxpayer who has been placed in "currently not collectible status" for a minimum of ________________.

A. Six months.
B. One year.
C. Two years.
D. No specified time limit.

15. Sheila and Dale were married in 2013. They are owed a refund on their joint return, but the refund is offset against Dale's past-due child support. Does Sheila have any recourse to recover her portion of the refund?

A. No. Since they filed jointly, Sheila's portion of the refund cannot be recovered.
B. Sheila can request injured spouse relief.
C. Sheila can request innocent spouse relief.
D. Both B and C.

16. If the IRS has filed a notice of seizure, how long must it wait before actually seizing a taxpayer's nonexempt property?

A. Immediately, with the exception of a taxpayer's home, which requires judicial approval.
B. Seven days.
C. Thirty days.
D. Sixty days.

17. All of the following statements regarding IRS installment agreements are correct except:

A. During the course of the installment agreement, penalties and interest continue to accrue.
B. A taxpayer who owes $10,000 or less in taxes will be automatically approved for an installment agreement.
C. An installment agreement allows a taxpayer to pay a set amount toward a tax liability on a monthly basis.
D. IRS levies may be served during an installment agreement.

18. Noah discovers he owes $1,000 on his 2013 income tax return, but is unable to make the payment in full by the April 15 deadline. All of the following are payment options except:

A. Requesting an offer in compromise.
B. Requesting an installment agreement.
C. Requesting his state tax refund be applied toward the tax deficiency.
D. Requesting an extension of time to pay due to hardship.

19. All of the following statements about the IRS statute of limitations are true except:

A. The IRS generally has ten years following an assessment to begin proceedings to collect the tax by levy or in a court proceeding.
B. The IRS is required to notify the taxpayer that he may refuse to extend the statute of limitations.
C. The IRS does not allow the taxpayer the right to extend the statute of limitations.
D. The statute of limitations on collection activity may be suspended in certain cases.

20. Rosalyn is receiving a tax refund this year. Which of the following methods is not available for Rosalyn to receive her IRS refund?

A. She may apply the refund to next year's estimated tax.
B. She may receive the refund as a direct deposit to her retirement account.
C. She may use her federal tax refund to purchase U.S. Series I Savings Bonds.
D. She may direct deposit her refund to her credit card account.

21. An installment agreement allows a taxpayer to do all of the following except:

A. Pay his tax debt in equal monthly payments over a period of time.
B. Negotiate with the IRS for a lower tax liability.
C. Pay his tax debt in variety of ways, including by check, credit card, payroll deduction, or debit.
D. Avoid IRS collection actions, including levies.

22. Penalties and interest continue to accrue on a taxpayer's unpaid tax liability in which of the following instances?

A. When an installment agreement is in place.
B. When a taxpayer has been declared "currently not collectible."
C. When a taxpayer requests innocent spouse relief.
D. All of the above.

23. How much extra time will the IRS generally grant for a taxpayer to pay his tax liability under the "undue hardship" extension?

A. Three months.
B. Six months.
C. One year.
D. 18 months.

24. Art owes $40,000 to the IRS. He would like to set up an installment agreement. Which of the following statements regarding his payment options is true?

A. Art may qualify for an installment agreement, but a *Collection Information Statement*, Form 433-F, must be completed.
B. Art does not qualify for an installment agreement because he owes more than $25,000.
C. Art may qualify for an installment agreement, but an offer in compromise must first be completed.
D. Art must enroll in EFTPS and have automatic withdrawals in order to have his installment agreement approved.

25. The IRS may legally seize property in which of the following circumstances?

A. During the consideration of an offer in compromise.
B. If the collection of tax is in jeopardy.
C. If the taxpayer's liability is $5,000 or less in a seizure of real property (real estate).
D. While innocent spouse claims are pending.

Unit 10: The IRS Examination Process

More Reading:
Publication 556, *Examination of Returns, Appeal Rights, and Claims for Refund*
Publication 1, *Your Rights as a Taxpayer*
Publication 3498, *The Examination Process*

Overview of IRS Audits

The IRS accepts most tax returns as they are filed, but selects a small percentage for examination.

Statistics: In fiscal year 2013, the IRS audited .96% of the total number of individual tax returns filed, the lowest rate since 2005. Higher income earners were audited much more heavily than those who earned less. The IRS reports the audit rate for individual returns with total income of $1 million or more was 10.85%. Of the individual returns audited in 2011, nearly a third were returns with EIC claims.[69]

An IRS examination is a review of the accounts and financial information of an organization or individual. An examination evaluates whether information on a tax return is being reported correctly and according to the tax laws, and verifies that the amount of tax reported is accurate. Due to disclosure requirements, the IRS will notify a taxpayer about an examination by telephone or mail, but never by e-mail.

Selecting a return for examination does not necessarily suggest that the taxpayer has made an error or has been dishonest. Filing an amended return does not affect the selection process for original returns. Amended returns go through a separate screening process and may be selected for audit.

The responsibility to provide support for entries, deductions, and statements made on a tax return is known as the *burden of proof.* The taxpayer must be able to substantiate expenses in order to deduct them. Taxpayers can usually meet this burden of proof by having the receipts for the expenses.

After the examination, if any changes to the taxpayer's return are proposed, he can disagree with the changes and appeal the IRS's determination. This is done through the appeals process, which we cover in Unit 11.

The IRS conducts most examinations entirely by mail. In these *correspondence audits,*[70] a taxpayer will receive a letter asking for additional information about certain items shown on the return, such as proof of income, expenses, and itemized deductions.

Correspondence audits typically occur when there is a minor issue that the IRS needs to clarify. For example, the IRS may have detected a math error or there may be a discrepancy between the tax return and the 1099 statements sent by brokers, banks, or mutual funds. Other times, the IRS simply requests evidence that a particular transaction has transpired.

---

[69] IR-2012-36, The IRS Data Book.

[70] IRS Data Book: In fiscal year 2011, 75% of all examinations were correspondence audits.

Example: The IRS selects Sarah's return for examination. Sarah had claimed her older half-brother as a qualifying child based on his permanent disability, and she had also claimed head of household status. The IRS asks for proof of disability and residency, and Sarah provides copies of doctors' records and additional evidence that her brother lived with her full-time. The IRS accepts Sarah's documents and closes the case as a no-change audit. Sarah never has to meet with the IRS auditor, as the entire audit is conducted by mail.

How Returns are Selected for Examination

When tax returns are filed, they are compared against the norms for similar returns. The IRS selects returns for examination using a variety of methods, including:

- **Potentially Abusive/Tax Avoidance Transactions:** Some returns are selected based on information obtained by the IRS through efforts to identify promoters of and participants in abusive tax avoidance transactions.
- **Computer Scoring/DIF Score:** Tax returns may be chosen for examination on the basis of computer scoring. A computer program called the Discriminant Inventory Function System (DIF) assigns a numeric score to each individual and certain corporate tax returns after they have been processed. [71]
- **Information Matching:** Some returns are examined because third party reports, such as Forms W-2 from employers or Forms 1099, do not match the applicable amounts reported on the tax return.
- **Related Examinations:** Returns may be selected for audit when they involve issues or transactions with other taxpayers, such as business partners or investors, whose returns were selected for examination.
- **Third Party Information:** Returns may be selected as a result of information received from other third-party sources or individuals. Sources may include state and local law enforcement agencies, public records, and individuals. The information is evaluated for reliability and accuracy before it is used as the basis of an examination or investigation.

Example: Perry is an EA with a client, Lila, who received an audit notice this year. Lila's tax return was selected because she had a large number of credits and very little taxable income. However, her tax return was prepared correctly. Lila had adopted four special-needs children in 2013 and was able to take a large adoption credit. Perry provided proof of the adoptions to the examining officer, which resulted in a positive outcome for Lila and a no-change audit.

[71] IRS computers automatically check tax returns and assign a DIF score based on the probability that the return contains errors, excessive tax deductions, or other issues. This does not necessarily mean that the return was prepared incorrectly. However, the screening is intended to identify aberrations and questionable items. If a taxpayer's return is assigned a high score under the DIF system, the return has a high probability of being chosen for audit. The IRS does not release information about how it calculates a taxpayer's DIF score.

Example: Van embezzled money from his employer and was arrested for felony embezzlement. The case was made public, and the police shared its information with the IRS. The IRS then contacted Van and proposed adjustments to his tax returns, assessing additional tax, interest, and penalties for fraud for failing to report the embezzled funds as income. This is an example of third party information that can trigger an IRS investigation.

In general, a taxpayer's odds of being audited become greater if his income is over $200,000, he is self-employed, or his itemized deductions were much higher than other taxpayers with similar incomes. Other issues that may draw IRS attention are taking large charitable deductions; claiming the home office deduction; claiming rental losses; deducting business meals, travel, and entertainment; claiming 100% business use of a vehicle; writing off a loss for a hobby activity; running a cash business; failing to report a foreign bank account; and engaging in currency transactions.

Audit Location

The IRS chooses to conduct some audits face-to-face, which are known as field audits. Examinations that are not handled by mail may take place at:

- The taxpayer's home or place of business
- An IRS office
- The office of the taxpayer's authorized representative

Most often, a taxpayer's return is examined in the area where he lives. But if the return can be examined more conveniently in another area, such as where the taxpayer's records are located, he may request the audit be transferred to that area.

Example: Joyce runs a marketing business, and she travels frequently in order to promote her business. She lives in Los Angeles; however, her CPA is in Chicago. In 2013 Joyce's tax return is selected for examination and she chooses to have her CPA represent her. Her CPA requests that the examination be transferred to Chicago where Joyce's records are located. The transfer is granted.

The IRS may make exceptions for extenuating circumstances. For example, if the taxpayer is currently on active duty in a combat zone, the examination will be temporarily suspended. However, the IRS will make the final determination of when, where, and how the examination will take place.

Taxpayer Examination Rights

The taxpayer has a number of rights during the IRS examination process. These rights include:

- A right to professional and courteous treatment by IRS employees
- A right to privacy and confidentiality about tax matters
- A right to know why the IRS is asking for information, how the IRS will use it, and what will happen if the requested information is not provided
- A right to representation, either by oneself or an authorized representative

- A right to appeal disagreements, both within the IRS and before the courts

Notice of IRS Contact of Third Parties

During the examination process, the IRS may contact third parties regarding a tax matter without the taxpayer's permission. Third parties may include neighbors, banks, employers, or employees. However, the IRS must give the taxpayer reasonable notice before contacting other persons about his individual tax matters.

The IRS must provide the taxpayer with a record of persons contacted on both a periodic basis and upon the taxpayer's request. This requirement does not apply:

- To any pending criminal investigation
- When providing notice would jeopardize collection of any tax liability
- When providing notice may result in reprisal against any person
- When the taxpayer has already authorized the contact

Example: The IRS selects Max's tax return for audit because it suspects unreported income due to criminal drug activity. Max is also being investigated by the FBI. Because this is a pending criminal investigation, the IRS is not required to give Max reasonable notice before contacting third parties about his tax matters.

The Taxpayer's Representative

The taxpayer may always represent himself during an examination. Alternatively, a taxpayer may use a qualified representative before the IRS. The taxpayer does not have to attend the audit if the representative has the proper power of attorney authorization and is a practitioner per Circular 230; a family member; or an unenrolled preparer who is the representative during an examination of the taxable year or period covered by the return he prepared.

Example: Emily is an EA. A taxpayer named Seth hires her to represent him before the IRS during the examination of his tax return. Seth does not want to attend the audit. He signs Form 2848 indicating that Emily is now his authorized representative for all his tax affairs. Emily attends the examination on Seth's behalf.

Example: DeShawn is an accounting student who is not a practitioner. The IRS is auditing his sister, who has designated DeShawn as her authorized representative via Form 2848. DeShawn may practice before the IRS in this limited circumstance. His sister is not required to be present during the examination.

When a jointly filed tax return is selected for examination, only one spouse is required to meet with the IRS.

Examination Procedures

In examinations not handled by mail, the taxpayer or the taxpayer's representative must make an appointment to meet with the IRS. The examining officer will notify the taxpayer of any records that are required. The IRS officer must explain any proposed changes to the taxpayer's return. The examination interview may be recorded by the taxpayer or his representative, or by the IRS, but whoever initiates the recording must notify the other party ten days in advance in writing. The taxpayer may request a copy of the IRS's recording.

If a taxpayer becomes uncomfortable during the audit and wishes to consult with a tax advisor, the IRS must suspend the interview and reschedule it.

Revenue Agent Reports (RAR): When the field work portion of an examination is completed, the revenue agent must prepare a detailed written report on his findings, known as a revenue agent report (RAR). A RAR is supposed to clearly state the amount of adjustments to a taxpayer's return and demonstrate how the tax liability was computed. Taxpayers have the right to disagree with a RAR and may choose to contest the agent's findings.

If the taxpayer agrees with the IRS's proposed changes in a RAR, he may immediately sign an agreement. The taxpayer is responsible for paying interest and penalties on any additional tax. If the taxpayer pays any additional tax owed when he signs the agreement, the interest and penalties are calculated from the due date of the tax return to the date of the payment.

If the taxpayer does not pay the additional amounts when he signs the agreement, he will receive a bill that includes interest. If the taxpayer pays the amounts due within ten business days of the billing date, he will not have to pay any more interest or penalties. This period is extended to 21 calendar days if the amount due is less than $100,000.

Audit Determinations

An audit can be closed in one of three ways:

- **No change:** An audit in which the taxpayer has substantiated all of the items being reviewed and which results in no changes.
- **Agreed:** An audit in which the IRS proposes changes and the taxpayer understands and agrees with the changes.
- **Disagreed:** An audit in which the IRS proposes changes and the taxpayer understands, but disagrees with the changes. A conference with an IRS manager may be requested for further review of the issues. In addition, the taxpayer may request fast track mediation or an appeal. The taxpayer may also choose to go to court and contest the IRS determination.

The IRS will not typically reopen a closed examination case to make an unfavorable adjustment unless:

- There was fraud or misrepresentation,
- There was a substantial error based on an established IRS position existing at the time of the examination, or
- Failure to reopen the case would be a serious administrative omission.

Repeat Examinations

The IRS tries to avoid repeat examinations of the same items, but sometimes this happens. If a taxpayer's return was audited for the same items in the previous two years and no change was proposed to tax liability, the taxpayer may request the IRS discontinue the examination.

Example: Kelly donates a large percentage of her salary to her church. For the last two years, the IRS has selected Kelly's return for examination based on her large donations. In both instances, Kelly was able to substantiate her donations and no change was made to her tax liability. Kelly's tax return is selected again for the same reason in 2013. Kelly contacts the IRS to request that the examination be discontinued, and the examining officer agrees to do so.

Example: Terrell's tax return has been selected for examination three years in a row. In 2011 and 2012, his tax return was selected to verify compliance for the EIC. There was no change to his tax liability in either year. In 2013, Terrell's tax return is selected for audit again. This time, the IRS is questioning his education deductions. Terrell cannot request that the examination be discontinued because it is for a different item than in the previous two examinations.

Partnership (TEFRA) Examinations

IRS audits of partnerships can be complicated since partnerships are regarded as pass-through entities, and they do not pay tax on the income they report. Income, gain, loss, deductions, and credits are all reported on the partners' individual tax returns, and generally do not result in tax for the partnership itself.

When a question arises about the accuracy of a partnership return, it may be impractical for the IRS to audit each individual partner's return. Under the Tax Equity and Fiscal Responsibility Act of 1982 (TEFRA), the IRS will first audit the partnership as a single entity, with a tax matters partner (TMP) serving as the main contact.

IRS examiners will attempt to determine whether partnership losses were properly treated and recorded. If the IRS determines that losses were not properly treated, it will assess tax at the partnership level. The TMP would then decide whether to appeal the decision.

There is an exception under TEFRA for small partnerships consisting of ten or fewer partners. These partnerships may still elect, however, to be covered by the TEFRA provisions.

IRS examiners have strict procedures to follow during a TEFRA audit, including mandatory completion of check sheets to detail correct procedures.

Audit Reconsideration

In certain cases, the IRS will reevaluate the results of a prior audit where additional tax was assessed and remains unpaid or a tax credit was reversed. A taxpayer may request reconsideration if he disagrees with an earlier audit assessment, but he must provide additional information, with documentation, that was not considered during the original examination. The IRS is generally under no obligation to approve a request to reopen an audit. However, the taxpayer retains the right to appeal an IRS assessment, which is covered in the next unit.

Unit 10: Study Questions

1. Frank's tax return was chosen by the IRS for examination. He moved a few months ago to another state, but the IRS notice says that his examination will be scheduled in the city where he used to live. Which of the following statements is true?

A. Frank can request that his tax return examination be moved to another IRS service center since he has moved to another area.
B. Frank must schedule the examination in his former city of residence, but he can have a professional represent him.
C. Frank is required to meet with the auditor at least once in person in order to move the examination to another location.
D. None of the above.

2. For a jointly filed tax return that has been selected for examination, which of the following statements is true?

A. Both spouses must be present during an examination because both spouses signed the return.
B. Only one spouse must be present.
C. Each spouse must have his or her own representative.
D. Neither spouse may use a representative.

3. What is a DIF score?

A. A computer scoring process that the IRS uses to select some returns for audit.
B. A report that is transmitted with each filed return.
C. A score that an auditor gives to the tax practitioner.
D. An IRS scoring process for Tax Court procedures.

4. The IRS generally will not reopen a closed examination case. However, all of the following are reasons why the IRS would reopen a closed audit case except:

A. There was fraud or misrepresentation.
B. There was a substantial error based on an established IRS position existing at the time of the examination.
C. Failure to reopen the case would be a serious administrative omission.
D. The taxpayer filed a request for fast track mediation.

5. The IRS has begun an examination of Elaine's income tax return. The IRS would like to ask her neighbors questions related to the examination. There is no pending criminal investigation into the matter, and there is no evidence that such contact will result in reprisals against the neighbors or jeopardize collection of the tax liability. Before contacting the neighbors, the IRS must:

A. Provide Elaine with reasonable notice of the contacts.
B. Make an assessment of Elaine's tax liability.
C. Ask the court for a third-party record keeper subpoena.
D. Mail Elaine a Statutory Notice of Deficiency.

6. According to the IRS, tax returns are selected for audit based on a number of different reasons. All of the following are reasons a return may be chosen for audit except:

A. Potential abusive transactions.
B. Computer scoring.
C. Because the taxpayer is a foreign investor.
D. Information received from other third-party sources or individuals.

7. When a taxpayer is chosen for an IRS audit, which of the following statements is true?

A. The taxpayer must appear before the IRS in person.
B. A taxpayer may choose to be represented before the IRS and is not required to appear if he so wishes.
C. An audit case may not be transferred to a different IRS office under any circumstances.
D. If a taxpayer feels that he is not being treated fairly during an IRS audit, he cannot appeal to the auditor's manager.

8. When the IRS needs to examine the records of a partnership, it must do so under the rules of TEFRA. All of the following statements are correct except:

A. Partnerships with more than ten partners are exempt from the TEFRA rules.
B. Because TEFRA audits are so complicated, the IRS must follow special procedures when it initiates and conducts examinations.
C. A tax matters partner will be the main contact with examiners during a TEFRA audit.
D. Under TEFRA, the IRS will examine tax issues at the partnership level, rather than examine each individual partner's return.

9. If a taxpayer or his representative wishes for an audit to be recorded, which of the following must he do?

A. Make a request the same day as the examination.
B. Notify the examiner ten days in advance, in writing.
C. Notify the examiner one week in advance, in writing.
D. Nothing. All examinations are automatically recorded by the IRS to ensure compliance of regulations by all parties.

10. When do the IRS rules regarding notice of third parties not apply?

A. To any pending criminal investigation.
B. When providing notice would jeopardize collection of any tax liability.
C. When providing notice may result in reprisal against any person.
D. All of the above.

11. What is a revenue agent report?

A. An agreement a taxpayer makes with the IRS after an examination.
B. A report detailing the in-person interview of a taxpayer or his representative.
C. A concluding report by a revenue agent that states the amount of adjustments to a taxpayer's return.
D. A preliminary report by a revenue agent that is made when a taxpayer's return is first flagged for audit.

Unit 11: The Appeals Process

More Reading:
Publication 5, *Your Appeal Rights & How to Prepare a Protest If You Don't Agree*
Publication 556, *Examination of Returns, Appeal Rights, and Claims for Refund*
Publication 4227, *Overview of the Appeals Process*
Publication 4167, *Appeals: Introduction to Alternative Dispute Resolution*

Because taxpayers often disagree with the IRS on tax matters, the IRS has an appeals process. The Appeals office is independent of any other IRS office and serves as an informal administrative forum for any taxpayer who wishes to dispute an IRS determination.

IRS Appeals is a venue where disagreements concerning the application of tax law can be resolved on an impartial basis without having to go to court. Appeals officers are directed to give serious consideration to settlement offers by taxpayers or their representatives.[72]

Reasons for an appeal must be supported by tax law. An appeal cannot be based solely on moral, religious, political, constitutional, conscientious, or similar grounds.

Appeal System Overview

A taxpayer has three choices when he wishes to protest an IRS determination on his taxes:

1. He may appeal either formally or informally within the IRS appeals system.
2. He may take his case directly to the U.S. Tax Court.
3. He may bypass both IRS Appeals and the Tax Court and take his case to the U.S. Court of Federal Claims or to a U.S. district court.

The contested tax does not have to be paid first if a taxpayer opts for either IRS Appeals or the Tax Court. But if the taxpayer goes directly to the Court of Federal Claims or a U.S. district court, he must pay the tax first and then sue the IRS for a refund.

An IRS appeal does not abate penalties and interest on the tax due. These continue to accumulate until the balance of the debt is paid, or unless the taxpayer wins his appeal and he is granted a no-change audit.

Appealing after Examination

The 30-Day Letter: Within a few weeks after a taxpayer's closing conference with an IRS examiner, he will receive what is commonly called a 30-day letter. This letter includes:

- A notice explaining the taxpayer's right to appeal the proposed changes within 30 days
- A copy of the revenue agent report explaining the examiner's proposed changes
- An agreement or waiver form

[72] Internal Revenue Manual 1.2.17.16: "Appeals will ordinarily give serious consideration to an offer to settle a tax controversy on a basis which fairly reflects the relative merits of the opposing views in the light of the hazards which would exist if the case were litigated. However, no settlement will be made based upon nuisance value of the case to either party."

- A copy of Publication 5, *Your Appeal Rights and How to Prepare a Protest If You Don't Agree*

The taxpayer has 30 days from the date of notice to accept or appeal the proposed changes.

If the taxpayer chooses to appeal an examiner's decision through the IRS system, he can contact a local Appeals office, which is separate and independent of the IRS office that conducted the examination.

Conferences with Appeals office personnel may be conducted in person, through correspondence, or by telephone with the taxpayer or his authorized representative. Only practitioners are allowed to represent taxpayers before an IRS appeals hearing. The taxpayer does not need to attend if his representative has power of attorney authorization via a signed Form 2848 or any other properly written POA authorization. An unenrolled tax preparer may be a witness for a taxpayer at an appeals conference but may not serve as a representative for the taxpayer.

Small Case Request: Within the IRS appeals system, a taxpayer may file a small case request if the total amount of tax, penalties, and interest for each tax period involved is $25,000 or less. To make a small case request, the taxpayer must send a brief written statement requesting an appeals conference. He must specify why he does not agree with the proposed tax assessment.

Filing a Formal Protest: A taxpayer generally needs to file a formal protest to Appeals if the total amount of tax, penalties, and interest for each tax period exceeds $25,000. The protest statement must go into greater detail than the small case request. It must include the facts supporting the taxpayer's position and the law or authority that the taxpayer is relying upon in making his case. The protest must be signed under penalties of perjury.

If an enrolled agent or other practitioner prepares and signs the protest for a taxpayer, he must substitute a declaration that states whether he knows personally that the facts in the protest and accompanying documents are true and correct.

Example: Carl is an enrolled agent who represents a sole proprietor named Sasha. The IRS audited her tax return and found discrepancies on her Schedule C. Sasha receives a 30-day letter stating that she owes an additional $32,000 in tax. Sasha disagrees with the amount, so Carl files a formal protest within 30 days with the Appeals office. In the protest, Carl details why the proposed assessment is incorrect and the legal basis for his argument. He also submits the required practitioner declaration. Carl then schedules a conference with an Appeals officer. When they meet, they discuss the matter and reach a settlement agreeable to each party. Since the IRS has a signed Form 2848 authorizing Carl to be Sasha's representative, she was not required to attend the appeals hearing.

The 90-Day Letter: If a taxpayer does not respond to a 30-day letter or if he cannot reach an agreement with an Appeals officer, the IRS will send him a *Notice of Deficiency*, which is also known as the 90-day letter. A Notice of Deficiency is required by law and is used to advise the taxpayer of his appeal rights to the U.S. Tax Court.

A Notice of Deficiency must be issued before a taxpayer can go to the Tax Court. The taxpayer has 90 days (150 days if addressed to a taxpayer outside the United States) from the date of this notice to file a petition with the Tax Court.

If the taxpayer does not file the petition in time, the tax is due within ten days, and the taxpayer may not take his case to Tax Court. If the taxpayer does file a petition in time and the case is docketed before the Tax Court, his file will again go to an IRS Appeals office to see if it can be resolved before going to court. More than 90% of all tax cases are resolved before going to Tax Court.

U.S. Tax Court

The U.S. Tax Court is a federal court where taxpayers may choose to contest their tax deficiencies without having to pay the disputed amount first. The court issues both regular and memorandum decisions. A regular decision is when the Tax Court rules on an issue for the first time. Memorandum decisions are cases where the U.S. Tax Court has previously ruled on identical or similar issues. The Tax Court has jurisdiction over the following tax disputes:

- Notices of deficiency
- Review of the failure to abate interest
- Notices of transferee liability
- Adjustment of partnership items
- Administrative costs
- Worker classification (employee versus independent contractor)
- Review of certain collection actions

The Tax Court has jurisdiction over the following types of tax:

- Income tax
- Estate tax and gift tax
- Certain excise taxes
- Re-determine transferee liability
- Worker classification
- Relief from joint and several liability on a joint return
- Whistleblower awards

An individual taxpayer may represent himself before the U.S. Tax Court. However, EAs and CPAs must be admitted to practice before the Tax Court by first passing a separate exam specific to this purpose. Licensed attorneys are not required to pass the Tax Court exam before practicing before the court.

Tax Court Small Tax Case Procedure

Small tax case procedures (also known as S-case procedures) in the Tax Court are one avenue to resolve disputes between taxpayers and the IRS. Small tax cases are handled under simpler, less formal procedures than regular cases. Often, decisions are handed down quicker than in other courts. The taxpayer and the Tax Court must both agree to proceed with the small case procedure. Generally, the Tax Court will agree with the taxpayer's request if the taxpayer otherwise qualifies.

However, the Tax Court's decision in a small tax case cannot be appealed by the taxpayer. The decision is final, as the IRS is not allowed to appeal either if it loses the case. In contrast, either the taxpayer or the IRS can appeal a decision in a regular, non-S case to a U.S. Court of Appeals.

Dollar limits for the Tax Court Small Case Division vary:

- For a Notice of Deficiency: $50,000 is the maximum amount, including penalties and interest, for any year before the court.
- For a Notice of Determination: $50,000 is the maximum amount for all the years combined.
- For a Notice of Deficiency related to a request for relief from joint and several liability: $50,000 is the maximum amount of spousal relief for all the years combined.
- For an IRS Notice of Determination of Worker Classification: The amount in the dispute cannot exceed $50,000 for any calendar quarter.

A decision entered in a small tax case is not treated as precedent for any other case and is not typically published.

Since the taxpayer cannot appeal a decision by the Small Tax Case Division, he must consider whether using the S-case procedure is worth the risk. A taxpayer who pursues his case via the regular U.S. Tax Court retains the right to appeal to a higher court.

Delay Tactics

If a taxpayer unreasonably fails to pursue the internal IRS appeals system, if the case is filed primarily to cause a delay, or if the taxpayer's position is frivolous, the Tax Court may impose a penalty of up to $25,000.[73]

Frivolous positions include those that contend that:

- The income tax is not valid,
- Payment of tax is voluntary,
- A person or a type of income is not subject to tax, or
- Espouse other arguments that the courts have previously rejected as baseless.

The Tax Court may also impose sanctions of up to $25,000 on those who misuse their right to a to a court review of IRS collection procedures merely to stall their tax payments. This rule is targeted at taxpayers who do not have a legitimate complaint and are instead using the Tax Court simply to delay collection action in their case.

[73] The IRS makes public the names and cases of taxpayers who have been assessed these §6673 penalties by the Tax Court. The cases are published on the IRS website as well as in the Tax Court Historical Opinion area.

Other Court Appeals

The vast majority of taxpayers choose to appeal their disputes in the Tax Court. However, a minority of taxpayers choose to challenge the IRS in a U.S. district court or Court of Federal Claims. In this case, a taxpayer must pay the contested tax deficiency first.

Example: The IRS issues Peg a deficiency notice of $45,000. Peg disagrees with the examiner's findings and does not wish to contest the tax through the IRS Appeals office or the Tax Court. Instead, she wants to go straight to a U.S. district court. She must first pay the contested liability and then sue the IRS for a refund.

If either party loses at the trial court level, the court's decision may be appealed to a higher court.

Note: Although enrolled agents have unlimited rights of representation before all levels and officers of the IRS, they cannot represent taxpayers in disputes with the IRS before U.S. district courts, bankruptcy courts, courts of appeal, or the U.S. Supreme Court. That authority is only available to tax attorneys.

Taxpayer Rights to Bring Civil Action: The government cannot ask a taxpayer to waive his right to sue the United States or a government employee for any action taken in connection with the tax laws. However, a taxpayer's right to sue can be waived if:

- He knowingly and voluntarily waives that right.
- The request to waive the right is made in writing to his attorney or other federally authorized practitioner.
- The request is made in person and his attorney or other representative is present.

Burden of Proof: In most cases, the burden of proof lies with the IRS during court proceedings, assuming the taxpayer has complied with all of the following issues:

- Adhered to IRS substantiation requirements
- Maintained adequate records
- Cooperated with reasonable requests for information from the IRS
- Introduced credible evidence relating to the issue
- In the case of a trust, corporation, or partnership, the taxpayer had net worth of $7 million or less and not more than 500 employees at the time of contested tax liability

Recovering Court Costs

If the court agrees with the taxpayer on most issues in the case and finds that the IRS's position is unjustified, the taxpayer may be able to recover the expenses he incurred to defend his position. The taxpayer may be able to recover reasonable litigation or administrative costs if all of the following conditions apply:

- The taxpayer is the prevailing party.
- The taxpayer has exhausted all administrative remedies within the IRS.

- The taxpayer's net worth is below certain limits.
- The taxpayer does not unreasonably delay any IRS proceeding.

The taxpayer will not be treated as the prevailing party if the IRS establishes that its position was substantially justified. The position of the IRS is not considered substantially justified if either of the following applies:

- The IRS did not follow its applicable published guidance (such as regulations, revenue rulings, notices, announcements, private letter rulings, technical advice memoranda, and determination letters issued to the taxpayer) in the proceeding.
- The IRS has lost in courts of appeal for other circuits on substantially similar issues.

In order to request the recovery of litigation costs from the IRS, the taxpayer must meet certain net worth requirements:

- For individuals, net worth cannot exceed $2 million as of the filing date of the petition for review. For this purpose, individuals filing a joint return are treated as separate individuals.
- For estates, net worth cannot exceed $2 million as of the date of the decedent's death.
- For charities and certain cooperatives, the entity cannot have more than 500 employees as of the filing date of the petition for review.
- For all other taxpayers, net worth cannot exceed $7 million and the entity must not have more than 500 employees as of the filing date of the petition for review.

The taxpayer may apply for recovery of litigation and administrative costs within 90 days of the date of the mailing of the decision of the IRS Office of Appeals regarding the tax, interest, or penalty.

Unit 11: Study Questions

1. Which of the following statements is correct about an IRS appeal?

A. An appeal does not abate the interest, which continues to accrue.
B. A taxpayer must pay the disputed tax before filing an appeal with the IRS.
C. The IRS is prohibited from filing a federal tax lien if the taxpayer is outside the U.S.
D. Taxpayers who do not agree to the IRS changes may not appeal to the U.S. Tax Court.

2. The Statutory Notice of Deficiency is also known as:

A. A 30-day letter because the taxpayer generally has 30 days from the date of the letter to file a petition with the Tax Court.
B. A 90-day letter because the taxpayer generally has 90 days from the date of the letter to file a petition with the Tax Court.
C. An Information Document Request because the taxpayer is asked for information to support his position regarding liability for tax.
D. A federal tax lien.

3. Aaron wants to appeal the findings of an examination, but his tax return was prepared by an unenrolled tax preparer. Aaron does not wish to be present during the appeals process. What are his options?

A. Aaron may only represent himself at IRS Appeals.
B. Aaron may represent himself or hire a practitioner (CPA, attorney, or EA) to represent him at the appeals level.
C. Aaron may be represented by the unenrolled tax preparer, so long as the unenrolled preparer is the one who prepared the tax return that is at issue.
D. Aaron may ask an IRS employee to represent him at IRS Appeals.

4. Abigail received a Statutory Notice of Deficiency from the IRS. Abigail's permanent address is in Scotland. How many days does she have to respond and file a petition with the Tax Court?

A. 30 days.
B. 90 days.
C. 150 days.
D. 365 days.

5. At the beginning of each examination, the IRS auditor must explain _______________.

A. A taxpayer's appeal rights.
B. A taxpayer's right to a fair trial.
C. A taxpayer's right to remain silent.
D. A taxpayer's right to confidentiality.

6. Karl had his 2011 and 2012 income tax returns examined, resulting in adjustments. He has earlier appealed the adjustments through the IRS appeals process. Some of the adjustments were sustained, resulting in income tax deficiencies in the amounts of $25,000 for 2011 and $27,000 for 2012. Karl now wants to appeal his case to the U.S. Tax Court. He will handle the case himself since he cannot afford a lawyer or other representative. Which of the following is true?

A. Karl has forfeited his rights to the small tax case procedure by going to appeals first.
B. Karl is entitled to elect the small tax case procedure.
C. Karl is not entitled to the small tax case procedure because his disputed amount exceeds $50,000.
D. Karl must appeal to a U.S. district court first.

7. Alyssa disagrees with the IRS examiner regarding her income tax case. Her appeal rights are explained to her, and she decides to go to Tax Court. Which of the following is true?

A. Alyssa must receive a Notice of Deficiency before she can go to Tax Court.
B. Alyssa must wait for the IRS examiner to permanently close her audit case.
C. Alyssa must request a collection due process hearing before going to Tax Court.
D. Alyssa cannot go to Tax Court unless she agrees with the auditor's findings.

8. An enrolled agent may represent a taxpayer in a dispute before ____________

A. An IRS revenue agent.
B. An IRS revenue officer.
C. A U.S. district court judge.
D. Both A and B.

9. Kevin and Javier are partners in a body shop business. Both had their individual returns examined and both disagreed with the IRS. Kevin decided to take his case to the IRS Appeals office. After the conference, he and the IRS still disagreed. Javier decided to bypass the Appeals office altogether and go directly to court. Which of the following is true?

A. Both Kevin and Javier can take their cases to the following courts: U.S. Tax Court, U.S. Court of Federal Claims, or the U.S. District Court.
B. Only Kevin may petition the U.S. Tax Court, because he went through the IRS appeals process first.
C. Neither may petition the U.S. Tax Court.
D. Both can take their cases to the U.S. Tax Court, but not to other U.S. courts.

10. Which of the following statements is correct regarding a taxpayer's right to appeal a tax assessment?

A. A taxpayer must first pay the contested tax before he can appeal in the U.S. Tax Court, or U.S. district or federal courts.
B. A taxpayer has the right to appeal a tax assessment on the basis of religious, political, or constitutional grounds.
C. The IRS Appeals office is an arm of the IRS Collection division.
D. A taxpayer must first pay the contested tax before he can appeal in a U.S. district or federal court.

11. Danielle owes a substantial sum to the IRS. She files a petition with the U.S. Tax Court. Her case is later determined to be frivolous, wholly without merit, and merely to cause delay. What is the potential repercussion of Danielle's actions?

A. The Tax Court may impose a penalty of up to $10,000.
B. The Tax Court may impose a penalty of up to $25,000.
C. The Tax Court may impose a penalty of up to $50,000.
D. The Tax Court may impose a penalty of up to $25,000 and one year in prison.

12. If a taxpayer wishes to challenge the IRS in a district court, the taxpayer must ____________________:

A. First attempt to resolve the contested tax with the IRS Appeals office.
B. Pay the contested liability first and then sue the IRS for a refund.
C. Pay a retainer to the IRS for a refund.
D. Go first to the U.S. Tax Court before appealing to a U.S. district court.

Unit 12: IRS E-File

More Reading:
Publication 3112, *IRS e-file Application and Participation*
Publication 1345, *Handbook for Authorized IRS e-file Providers of Individual Income Tax Returns*

The IRS e-file program allows taxpayers to transmit their returns electronically. In 2013 more than 82% of American taxpayers filed electronically. According to the IRS, the processing of e-file returns is not only quicker but also more accurate than the processing of paper returns. However, as with a paper return, the taxpayer is responsible for ensuring an e-filed return contains accurate information and is filed on time.

Tax preparers who prepare more than ten individual returns a year are required to e-file income tax returns. The mandate covers returns for individuals, trusts, and estates.[74] Tax firms must estimate the aggregate number of returns they reasonably expect to file. If that number is 11 or more for the calendar year, all members of the firm must e-file the returns they prepare and file. This is true even if, on an individual basis, a member prepares and files fewer than the threshold.

Example: Elena is an EA who works for a CPA firm. She also has a side business doing tax returns from her home. For the coming tax year, Elena expects to prepare and file five Forms 1041 (for estates and trusts) while working for the CPA firm. She also expects to prepare and file seven Form 1040 tax returns as a self-employed preparer. Since she expects to file 11 or more forms, Elena is required to e-file.

Applying to the E-File Program

To begin e-filing tax returns, a preparer must first apply and be accepted as an authorized IRS e-file provider. There is no fee to apply, and the process takes up to 45 days. The first step is to create an IRS e-Services account by providing required personal information including a Social Security number and an address where confirmation of the account will be mailed.

After being approved for an e-Services account, applicants begin the comprehensive process to become an *IRS e-file provider*, which is an umbrella term for anyone authorized to participate in e-file, from software developers to transmitters. Preparers who want to e-file for clients must be approved as *electronic return originators* (ERO). The application must also identify a firm's principals and at least one responsible official.

Each person on an e-file provider application must:

- Be a United States citizen or a legal U.S. alien lawfully admitted for permanent residence;
- Be at least 21 years of age as of the date of application; and

[74] Financial institutions and fiduciaries that file Forms 1041 as a trustee or fiduciary are not required to e-file and are not subject to the mandate. The e-file mandate also does not apply to payroll tax returns.

- Meet applicable state and local licensing and/or bonding requirements for the preparation of tax returns.

All applicants must be fingerprinted. The IRS then conducts a suitability check on the firm and on each person listed on the application as either a principal or responsible official. Suitability checks may include the following:

- A criminal background check
- A credit history check
- A tax compliance check to ensure that the applicant's personal returns are filed and paid
- A check for prior noncompliance with IRS e-file requirements

When a business is accepted to participate in IRS e-file, it is assigned an electronic filing identification number (EFIN). All preparers in a firm based in the same physical location are covered by the same number. For example, a tax preparation business with ten employee-preparers in one location would all file using the same EFIN. Each preparer would then use his own PTIN on the returns that he individually prepares.[75]

Electronic Return Originators: An ERO is the authorized IRS e-file provider who originates the electronic submission of tax returns to the IRS. Although an ERO may engage in tax return preparation, and many do, tax preparation is a distinct and separate activity from the electronic submission of tax returns to the IRS. An ERO submits a tax return only after the taxpayer has authorized the e-file transmission. The return must be either:

- Prepared by the ERO; or
- Collected from a taxpayer who has self-prepared his own return and is asking the ERO to e-file it for him.

An ERO is required to:

- Timely submit returns.
- Submit any required supporting paper documents to the IRS.
- Provide copies to taxpayers.
- Retain records and make records available to the IRS.
- Work with the taxpayer and/or the transmitter to correct a rejected return.
- Enter the preparer's identifying information (name, address, and PTIN).
- Be diligent in recognizing fraud and abuse, and reporting it to the IRS
- Cooperate with IRS investigations by making documents available to the IRS upon request.

An ERO who originates returns that he has not prepared but only collected becomes an income tax return preparer when he makes substantive changes to the tax return. A non-substantive change is a correction limited to a transposition error, misplaced entry, spelling error, or arithmetic correction. The IRS considers all other changes substantive. As such, the ERO may be required to sign the return as the preparer.

[75] The IRS requires firms with multiple physical locations to obtain separate EFINs for each location.

Example: Diana is an ERO. A taxpayer brings a self-prepared tax return for Diana to e-file. She notices gross errors on the tax return and talks with the client about the mistakes. The taxpayer agrees to correct the return, and Diana makes the necessary adjustments in return for a small fee. Diana is now required to sign the return as a preparer.

Transmitters: After an ERO submits a tax return, it is sent to an authorized transmitter, which submits it to the IRS.

Example: Patrick is a preparer and an ERO who uses Ultra TaxPro software to prepare returns. Once he has completed a tax return, he gives a copy to the client, who gives signature authorization to e-file the return. Patrick transmits the return to Ultra TaxPro, which is an authorized transmitter. Ultra TaxPro then transmits the return to the IRS. Most tax practitioners use this method; all the major tax preparation software companies have e-file transmission options.

Once received at the IRS, the return is automatically checked for errors. If it cannot be processed, it is sent back to the originating transmitter to clarify any necessary information.

After correction, the transmitter retransmits the return to the IRS. Within 48 hours of electronically sending the return, the IRS sends an acknowledgment to the transmitter stating the return is accepted for processing. This is called an electronic postmark, and it is the taxpayer's proof of filing and assurance that the IRS has the return.

Authorized e-file providers must retain a record of each electronic postmark until the end of the calendar year and provide the record to the IRS upon request. Most tax software packages automatically retain a record of the return transmission report and electronic postmark.

Electronic Signature Requirements

Electronically filed returns have signature requirements, just as paper tax returns do. For e-filed tax returns, both taxpayers and preparers must complete Form 8879, *IRS e-file Signature Authorization*. The form includes a taxpayer's consent to electronic filing; a declaration that the e-filed return is true, correct, and complete; and which method of signature authorization is used on the e-filed return. The form must be retained for three years from the return due date or the IRS received date, whichever is later. Unless the IRS requests to see the form, it is not submitted.

If an e-filed return does not have an appropriate electronic signature via a personal identification number (PIN), it will be rejected. This requirement also applies to volunteers at VITA and TCE sites who provide free tax assistance and e-filing.

- The **Self-Select PIN** allows a taxpayer to electronically sign his e-filed return by selecting and entering a five-digit PIN as his signature. The IRS uses the taxpayer's prior year adjusted gross income or prior year PIN to validate the signature. The taxpayer may also authorize an ERO to enter or generate his PIN.
- The **Practitioner PIN** is an 11-digit number that includes the ERO's six-digit EFIN and the preparer's five-digit self-selected PIN. The ERO uses the same practitioner PIN for the entire tax year.

Form 8453, *U.S. Individual Income Tax Transmittal for an IRS e-file Return,* is used to send any required paper forms or supporting documentation that may be needed with an e-filed return. Form 8453 must be mailed to the IRS within three business days after receiving acknowledgment that the IRS has accepted the electronically-filed return. If the ERO is signing the tax return as a representative, Form 2848, *Power of Attorney and Declaration of Representative,* must be attached to Form 8453.

Example: Mitchell is an enrolled agent and ERO. He has power of attorney for a client, Al, who is working overseas for several months. Mitchell uses his practitioner PIN and signs Al's tax return on his behalf. He e-files the return and then mails Form 8453 to the IRS the next day. Mitchell attaches Form 2848 showing that he is Al's authorized representative to sign his tax return.

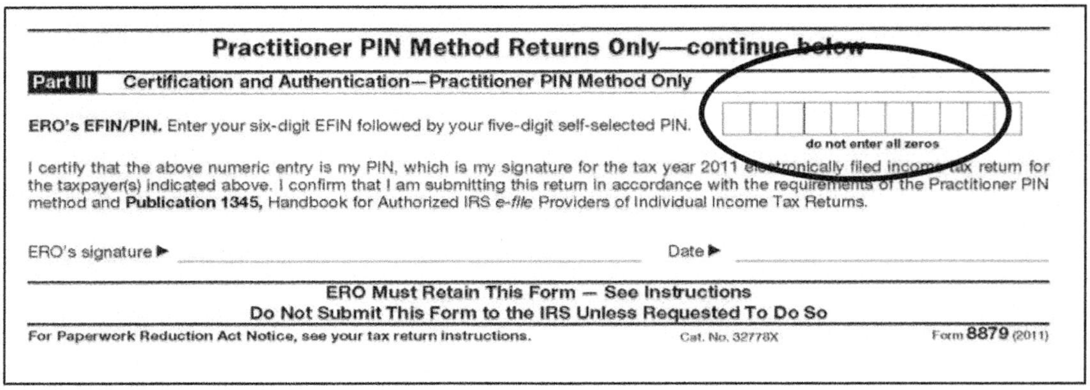

Practitioner PIN Method Returns Only—continue below

Part III **Certification and Authentication—Practitioner PIN Method Only**

ERO's EFIN/PIN. Enter your six-digit EFIN followed by your five-digit self-selected PIN.

do not enter all zeros

I certify that the above numeric entry is my PIN, which is my signature for the tax year 2011 electronically filed income tax return for the taxpayer(s) indicated above. I confirm that I am submitting this return in accordance with the requirements of the Practitioner PIN method and **Publication 1345,** Handbook for Authorized IRS *e-file* Providers of Individual Income Tax Returns.

ERO's signature ▶ Date ▶

ERO Must Retain This Form — See Instructions
Do Not Submit This Form to the IRS Unless Requested To Do So

For Paperwork Reduction Act Notice, see your tax return instructions. Cat. No. 32778X Form **8879** (2011)

E-File Rejections

The due dates for filing paper income tax returns also apply to electronic returns. If the IRS rejects an e-filed return and the preparer cannot rectify the reason for the rejection, the preparer must inform the taxpayer of the rejection within 24 hours. The preparer must provide the taxpayer with the IRS reject codes accompanied by an explanation.

If the taxpayer chooses not to have the electronic return corrected and retransmitted to the IRS, or if the IRS cannot accept the return for processing, the taxpayer must file a paper return. In order to timely file, the taxpayer must file the paper return by the later of:

- The due date of the return; or
- Ten calendar days after the date the IRS gives notification that it rejected the e-filed return. This is called the *ten-day transmission perfection period*; it is additional time the IRS gives a preparer and taxpayer to correct errors in the electronic filing and resubmit a tax return without a late filing penalty.

If a taxpayer files on paper after an e-file rejection, the following information must be included:

- An explanation of why the paper return is being filed after the due date
- A copy of the rejection notification
- A brief history of actions taken to correct the electronic return

The taxpayer should write in red at the top of the first page of the paper return:

"REJECTED ELECTRONIC RETURN-(DATE)."

The date should be the date of the first e-file rejection. The paper return must be signed by the taxpayer. The PIN that was used on the rejected e-filing may not be used as the signature on the paper return.

If an e-file submission is rejected, a return can be corrected within the ten-day transmission period and not be subject to a late filing penalty but this is not the case for a late payment penalty. If a return is rejected on the due date, an electronic payment should not be transmitted with the return, because a tax payment must still be submitted or postmarked by the due date.

Example: Russ is an EA who e-files a tax return for his client, Charita, on April 15, 2014. The next day, Russ receives an IRS notice that the return was rejected. Russ notifies Charita of the rejection within 24 hours. The issue cannot be corrected, so she must file a paper return. Russ mails the return on April 17, 2014 and gives Charita a copy. The tax return will be considered filed timely, because the paper return was filed within ten days of the rejection and the original e-filing of the return was attempted in a timely manner. If Charita had owed tax, she would have needed to send payment by the April 15 due date.

Rejected individual e-filed returns can be corrected and retransmitted without new signatures or authorizations if the changes do not differ from the amount on the original electronic return by more than $50 to "total income" or "AGI," or more than $14 to "total tax," "federal income tax withheld," "refund," or "amount you owe."

Entity E-File Requirements

Certain corporations, partnerships, and tax-exempt organizations are required to e-file. Corporate taxpayers, including tax-exempt organizations, with $10 million or more in assets and that file at least 250 returns (information returns and others, such as Forms 1099 and W-2) are required to e-file regardless of whether they use a paid preparer.

Partnerships with more than 100 partners are required to e-file. Partnerships with 100 or fewer partners (Schedules K-1) may voluntarily file their returns electronically, but are not required to do so.

A preparer's e-file application must be current and must list all the form types (1120, 1065, 990, etc.) that he will transmit to the IRS. If the preparer does not list a certain form on his application and later attempts to transmit that form, he will receive a rejection for return type.

Example: Karen is an EA. When she first applied to be an e-file provider, she only prepared individual returns. In tax year 2013, she prepares a partnership return. However, Karen forgets to update her e-file application. When she submits the partnership return online, it is rejected. Karen will have to update her e-file application in order to submit partnership returns electronically.

Paper Returns

A taxpayer may choose to file a paper return that has been prepared by a paid preparer. The taxpayer must mail the return himself and include a hand-signed and dated statement documenting his choice to file on paper. A preparer is required to attach Form 8948, *Preparer Explanation for Not Filing Electronically*, to a client's paper return.

A preparer may also request a hardship waiver from the IRS to be exempt from e-filing. The IRS says it will grant waivers only in rare cases and usually not for more than one calendar year. It will deny waivers if the request is made because the preparer does not have appropriate software or simply prefers not to e-file.

Some returns are impossible to e-file for various reasons and are therefore exempt from the e-file requirement. The IRS also may grant administrative exemptions when technology issues prevent specified preparers from filing returns electronically.

E-File Advertising Standards

"IRS e-file" is a brand name, but acceptance to the IRS e-file program does not imply an endorsement by the IRS. A practitioner must not use improper or misleading advertising in relation to IRS e-file, including promising a time frame for refunds and refund anticipation loans (RALs).

Practitioners may not use the regular IRS logo (the eagle symbol) or IRS insignia in their advertising, or imply any type of relationship with the IRS. They may use the IRS e-file logo, but cannot combine the e-file logo with the IRS eagle symbol, the word "federal," or with other words or symbols that might suggest a special relationship with the IRS.

Advertising materials must not carry the FMS, IRS, or any other Treasury seals.

The IRS e-file logo, which practitioners may use

If an e-file provider uses radio, television, Internet, signage, or other methods of advertising, the practitioner must keep a copy and provide it to the IRS upon request. Copies of any advertising must be retained until the end of the calendar year following the last transmission or use.

Practitioners may not advertise that individual income tax returns may be e-filed without using Forms W-2. For example, a firm may not advertise that it can file a tax return using only pay stubs or earnings statements.

E-file Revocations and Sanctions

The IRS may revoke e-file privileges if a firm is either:

- Prohibited or disbarred from filing returns by a court order, or
- Prohibited from filing returns by any federal or state legal action that forbids participation in e-file.

Example: Steve was a CPA who was convicted of felony embezzlement. He was also stripped of his license by his state accountancy board. The IRS revoked his e-file privileges without prior notice.

The IRS may also sanction any e-file provider who fails to comply with e-file regulations. Before sanctioning, the IRS may issue a warning letter that describes specific corrective action the provider must take. The IRS categorizes the seriousness of infractions as Level One (the least serious), Level Two, and Level Three (the most serious). A Level One sanction may result in an e-file provider receiving a written reprimand from the IRS. A Level Two sanction may result in a provider being suspended from participation in e-file for one year. A Level Three suspension may result in a provider being suspended from participating in e-file for two years or permanently expelled from the program. If a principal or responsible official is suspended or expelled from participation in IRS e-file, every entity listed on the firm's e-file application may also be expelled.

Providers who are denied participation in IRS e-file usually have the right to an administrative review. In order to appeal, a provider must mail a written response within 30 days addressing the IRS's reason for denial or revocation and include supporting documentation. During this administrative review process, the denial of participation remains in effect.

In certain circumstances, the IRS can immediately suspend or expel an authorized IRS e-file provider without prior notice.

Unit 12: Study Questions

1. Which of the following tax preparers would be subject to the mandate that requires preparers to e-file their clients' returns?

A. Dean, a bookkeeper who prepares a tax return for himself.
B. RJ, an EA who only prepares payroll tax returns for her employer.
C. Scott, who files six individual tax returns and seven estate returns for compensation.
D. Chon, a CPA who files 100 returns for the Volunteer Income Tax Assistance (VITA) program.

2. Which individual or business is not required to e-file tax returns?

A. A partnership with 100 partners.
B. A corporation with $8 million in assets that files more than 500 information returns.
C. An EA who prepares ten Forms 1040EZ through VITA, five Forms 1040 for a small fee for neighbors, and six Forms 1041 through the tax firm she works for.
D. Both A and B.

3. The IRS may sanction providers who fail to comply with e-file regulations. It uses a specific system of categorizing how serious infractions are. Which is the most serious?

A. Level One.
B. Level Two.
C. Level Three.
D. Level Four.

4. Katie is an EA subject to the e-file mandate. She has power of attorney authority for her client, Timothy. What must she do to e-file Timothy's return?

A. Use Form 8453 and submit Form 2848, *Power of Attorney and Declaration of Representative,* as an attachment.
B. Use Form 8879 and submit Form 2848, *Power of Attorney and Declaration of Representative,* as an attachment.
C. Use the Practitioner PIN method as her signature requirement.
D. Katie is not allowed to e-file Timothy's return in this instance. She must file it on paper.

5. If the IRS rejects an e-filed tax return for processing and the reason for the rejection cannot be rectified with the information already provided to the ERO, what is the ERO's responsibility at that point?

A. The ERO is not legally required to notify the taxpayer.
B. The ERO must attempt to notify the taxpayer within 24 hours and provide the taxpayer with the rejection code accompanied by an explanation.
C. The ERO is required to notify the taxpayer in writing within 72 hours.
D. The ERO is required to file the tax return on paper within 24 hours.

6. Electronic filing identification numbers (EFINs) are issued ______________.

A. On a firm basis.
B. On a preparer basis.
C. On a client basis.
D. Only to foreign firms.

7. The IRS may excuse a preparer from the mandate to e-file in all of the following instances except:

A. Administrative exemptions due to technology issues.
B. An individual case of hardship documented by the preparer.
C. Lack of access to tax preparation software.
D. All of the above.

8. Tammy is an EA who e-files a return for her client, Rick. However, Rick's e-filed return is rejected by the IRS. They cannot resolve the rejection issue, and the return must be filed on paper. In order to timely file Rick's tax return, what is the deadline for filing a paper return?

A. The due date of the return.
B. Ten calendar days after the date the IRS rejects the e-filed return.
C. Forty-eight hours after the date the IRS rejects the e-filed return.
D. The later of either A or B.

9. Which of the following statements is true?

A. Separate fees may be charged for direct deposits.
B. An e-file provider may not charge contingent fees based on a percentage of the refund.
C. An e-file provider may not charge a fee for paper returns under any circumstances.
D. An e-file provider is not allowed to charge a fee for e-filing.

10. What is the first step of the process for an individual to become an authorized e-file provider?

A. Apply for a PTIN.
B. Be fingerprinted and undergo a background check by the IRS.
C. Become a federally authorized practitioner.
D. Create an authorized e-Services account online.

11. Which logo may a practitioner use in his advertising?

A. The official IRS logo.
B. The IRS e-file logo.
C. The official seal of the U.S. Treasury.
D. The IRS eagle symbol.

Answers to Practice Questions: Representation

Unit 1: Representation Quiz Answers

1. The answer is A. Although both the judicial and executive branches play important roles in interpreting, implementing, and enforcing tax laws, the legislative branch (Congress) is the main source of tax law in the United States. Congress is responsible for passing tax laws, which are published as the Internal Revenue Code, issued separately as Title 26 of the United States Code.

2. The answer is B. A treasury regulation is the Treasury Department's official interpretation of the Internal Revenue Code. It has substantial authority in establishing precedence for tax law.

3. The answer is B. The Internal Revenue Service is required to obey all decisions rendered by the highest court of the land, the U.S. Supreme Court. It is not obligated to change its regulations in matters of tax law that are decided by other U.S. courts.

4. The answer is B. Revenue rulings can be used to avoid certain IRS penalties. Taxpayers may rely on revenue rulings as official IRS guidance on an issue to make a decision regarding taxable income, deductions, and how to avoid certain IRS penalties.

5. The answer is C. A private letter ruling is a written statement issued to a taxpayer that interprets and applies tax laws to the taxpayer's specific case. It is initiated at the taxpayer's request. It cannot be used as a precedent by other taxpayers or the IRS.

6. The answer is D. A legislative regulation is authorized by Congress to provide the material requirements of a specific IRC provision. If written correctly, a legislative regulation carries the same authority as the IRC itself. It can only be overturned if it is outside the power delegated to the U.S. Treasury; it conflicts with a specific statute; or it is deemed unreasonable by the courts.

7. The answer is A. A PLR is binding on the IRS if the taxpayer fully and accurately described the proposed transaction in his request and carried out the transaction as described. A PLR may not be relied on as precedent by other taxpayers or IRS personnel.

8. The answer is D. The IRS may generally choose whether or not to acquiesce to a court decision. The only exception to this rule is a case decided by the U.S. Supreme Court, whose decisions the IRS is obligated to follow. With other courts, the IRS is not bound to change its regulations due to a loss in court. The IRS does not announce acquiescence or non-acquiescence in every case. Sometimes the IRS's position is withheld.

9. The answer is B. A legal opinion does not have substantial authority. Sources of substantial authority are as follows: the Internal Revenue Code, temporary and final regulations, court cases, administrative pronouncements, tax treaties, Congressional intent as reflected in committee reports, proposed regulations, private letter rulings, technical advice memoranda, IRS information or press releases, IRS notices, and any other similar documents published by the IRS in the Internal Revenue Bulletin.

Unit 2: Representation Quiz Answers

1. The answer is C. Simply appearing as a witness before the IRS is allowed and not considered practice before the IRS. Individuals who are not practitioners may appear before the IRS as witnesses or communicate to the IRS on a taxpayer's behalf—but they may not advocate for the taxpayer.

2. The answer is D. A minimum of 16 hours of continuing education credit, including two hours of ethics credits, must be completed in each year of the enrollment cycle. An EA must complete a minimum of 72 hours of continuing education during each three-year period.

3. The answer is B. All EAs are required to obtain PTINs as a condition of their licensing (the PTIN must be included on Form 23, which is the application form to become an enrolled agent). Attorneys and CPAs do not need to obtain a PTIN unless they prepare tax returns for compensation. Someone who prepares returns for free is not considered a tax return preparer by the IRS and does not need a PTIN.

4. The answer is A. Matthew is a full-time employee for Parkway Partnership, so in that capacity he may represent his employer before the IRS. A regular full-time employee of an individual employer may represent the employer.

5. The answer is B. The enrollment cycle means the three successive enrollment years preceding the effective date of renewal. After the initial enrollment period, regular renewal enrollments are required every three years. This is known as an enrollment cycle.

6. The answer is D. The minimum age for enrollment is 18, so anyone over 17 would not be denied enrollment based on his age. Failure to timely file tax returns or pay taxes, and felony convictions are all potential grounds for denying an application for enrollment. The Return Preparer Office will review all of the facts and circumstances to determine whether a denial of enrollment is warranted.

7. The answer is C. Simply appearing as a witness or communicating information to the IRS does not constitute practice before the IRS. Barry is merely assisting with the exchange of information and is not advocating on José's behalf. An example of an individual assisting with information exchange but not practicing would be a taxpayer's friend serving as a translator when the taxpayer does not speak English.

8. The answer is B. Enrolled agents who fail to comply with the requirements for eligibility for renewal of enrollment will be notified by the Return Preparer Office by first class mail. The notice will explain the reason for noncompliance. The enrolled agent has 60 days from the date of the notice to respond.

9. The answer is D. A person who prepares tax returns for compensation is a tax return preparer, even if the activity is only part-time. A person who prepares and signs a tax return without compensation (such as for a family member or as a volunteer) is not considered a tax return preparer for purposes of the preparer penalties. An employee who prepares a tax return for his employer or for another employee is not a preparer under Circular 230. The employer (or the individual with supervisory responsibility) has the responsibility for accuracy of the return.

10. The answer is D. Practice before the IRS does not include the representation of clients in the U.S. Tax Court. The Tax Court is independent of the IRS and has its own rules of practice and its own rules regarding admission to practice.

11. The answer is C. The IRS requires a 16-hour minimum of CE per year, and requires two hours of ethics or professional conduct per year. Andrea has only completed one hour of ethics CE. She has met her yearly general CE requirement, but she has not met the ethics requirement for the year, so her minimum requirements have not been met.

12. The answer is C. Fernanda is not a tax return preparer and is not required to have a PTIN. An individual who provides only typing, reproduction, or other mechanical assistance, but does not actually prepare returns is not considered a tax preparer by the IRS.

13. The answer is B. An EA who has been terminated from enrollment should file a written protest within 30 days of the date of the notice. The protest must be filed with the Office of Professional Responsibility.

14. The answer is D. Supervised preparers may not:

- Sign any tax return they prepare or assist in preparing
- Represent taxpayers before the IRS in any capacity
- Identify themselves as Circular 230 practitioners

Individuals who apply for a PTIN under this provision are required to certify on their application that they are supervised by an attorney, CPA, or EA who signs the tax return.

15. The answer is B. Each individual applying for renewal must retain information about CE hours completed for four years following the enrollment renewal date.

16. The answer is B. Ownership or management of a tax practice is immaterial in determining the substantial portion rule. The most important determination is whoever has the primary responsibility for the accuracy of the return. If several people are involving in preparing a return, the person who prepares the part of the return that declares the greatest amount of income would be considered the preparer who must sign the return.

17. The answer is C. The registered tax return preparer designation is under suspension due to litigation. An RTRP is considered an unenrolled preparer and not a practitioner; unenrolled preparers have limited rights of practice before the IRS. An unenrolled preparer may only represent a taxpayer for the tax return or claim of refund he personally prepared and signed. This representation may occur only before revenue agents and similar employees of the IRS, and not before appeals or revenue officers. An unenrolled preparer also may not sign any document on behalf of a taxpayer.

18. The answer is B. An EA's enrollment becomes official on the date listed on his enrollment card, whether he has actually received the card or not.

19. The answer is A. Although the Return Preparer Office will consider each waiver request on a case-by-case basis, it will typically grant waivers based on the following reasons: active military duty; absence from the U.S. for an extended period of time provided the individual does not practice before the IRS during that period; and health issues. Financial hardship is generally not considered a legitimate reason to fail to complete CE requirements.

20. The answer is C. Amy must obtain a PTIN. Every individual who prepares or assists in the preparation of a tax return or claim for refund for compensation must have her own PTIN.

21. The answer is D. The IRS requires all paid preparers to have a preparer tax identification number (PTIN). Stan must pay a fee and renew his existing PTIN each year before the December 31 deadline. He may renew online at the IRS website or by mailing in Form W-12 along with his payment.

22. The answer is C. For EAs whose Social Security numbers end in 7, the next enrollment cycle begins April 1, 2015. If the candidate's SSN ends in:

- 0, 1, 2, or 3, the next enrollment cycle begins April 1, 2016.
- 4, 5, or 6, the next enrollment cycle begins April 1, 2014.
- 7, 8, or 9, the next enrollment cycle begins April 1, 2015.

EAs who do not have an SSN must use the "7, 8, or 9" renewal schedule.

23. The answer is C. Unenrolled tax preparers have only limited rights of representation before the IRS. They are not permitted to represent a taxpayer except in the examination of a tax return they prepared.

Unit 3: Representation Quiz Answers

1. The answer is C. A preparer is never allowed to copy a taxpayer's signature. A preparer may sign in lieu of the taxpayer in certain situations. For example, rules permit a representative to sign a taxpayer's return if he is unable to do so himself for any of the following reasons:

- Disease or injury
- Continuous absence from the United States for a period of at least 60 days prior to the date required by law for filing the return
- Other good cause if specific permission is requested of and granted by the IRS

When a return is signed by a representative, it must be accompanied by a power of attorney authorizing the representative to sign the return.

2. The answer is A. The CAF contains information on third parties authorized to represent taxpayers before the IRS and/or receive and inspect confidential tax information on active tax accounts or those accounts currently under consideration by the IRS.

3. The answer is D. In order to receive a tax refund check on a client's behalf, a Form 2848 (power of attorney) must be filed. A third party designee authorization is not sufficient. With a third party designee authorization, Darrell can exchange verbal information with the IRS on return processing issues and on refunds and payments related to the return. Darrell can also receive written account information, including transcripts, upon request.

4. The answer is C. Only Form 2848, *Power of Attorney and Declaration of Representative,* allows a third party to represent a taxpayer before the IRS. The other consents are much more limited and only allow the third party to receive or inspect tax account information.

5. The answer is C. Identity fraud is a growing problem for the IRS, which is issuing identity protection personal identity numbers (IP PINs) to taxpayers who have reported they have been victims of identity theft; have given the IRS information that verifies their identity; and had an identity theft indicator applied to their accounts. An IP PIN is good for only one year. It is designed to protect a taxpayer's taxpayer identification number. If a taxpayer with an IP PIN attempts to file a tax return without using it, the return will be rejected.

6. The answer is A. A preparer who is issued a subpoena or court order, whether at the federal, state, or local level, is not required to obtain disclosure permission from a client. In all the other cases, disclosure is not allowed unless there has been prior written consent.

7. The answer is C. Only persons eligible to practice before the IRS, including attorneys, CPAs, and EAs, have unlimited rights to represent taxpayers before the IRS. The representation rights of unenrolled preparers are much more limited. An unenrolled preparer who did not prepare and sign the specific tax return under examination would not be allowed to represent the taxpayer.

8. The answer is B. IRC §7216 is a criminal code that limits tax professionals' use and disclosure of client information. "B" is correct because criminal penalties will apply only if the improper disclosure is "knowing or reckless," rather than simply negligent. The other answers are incorrect because the regulations do apply to e-file providers; a practitioner may be fined up to $1,000, not $500, and imprisoned for up to a year for each violation; and written consent, not oral, is generally required before taxpayer information can be disclosed.

9. The answer is C. A power of attorney is valid until revoked or superseded. It may be revoked by the taxpayer or withdrawn by the representative, or it may be superseded by the filing of a new power of attorney for the same tax and tax period.

10. The answer is C. Form 8821, *Tax Information Authorization*, authorizes any individual, corporation, firm, organization, or partnership to receive confidential information for the type of tax and periods listed on the form. Any third party may be designated by the taxpayer to receive confidential tax information. Form 8821 is only a disclosure form, so it will not give an individual any power to represent a taxpayer before the IRS. It may be used only to obtain information, such as copies of tax returns.

11. The answer is C. Form 2848 may authorize a tax practitioner to receive (but never endorse or cash) a refund check drawn on the U.S. Treasury. All of the other actions listed are permitted, so long as the tax practitioner is qualified to practice before the IRS. In this case, Willa is an enrolled agent, so her practice rights are unlimited before all offices of the IRS.

12. The answer is C. A durable power of attorney is not subject to a time limit. It remains in effect until the death of the individual.

13. The answer is D. The designee may address any issue arising out of a tax return for a period not to exceed one year from the due date of the tax return. The designee may also receive written account information including transcripts upon request. The third party designee authorization expires on the due date of the next tax return.

14. The answer is C. The types of tax and dates listed on Form 2848 must be specific. Tax years or periods that have already ended may be listed under "tax matters." For future tax periods, the period specified is limited to no later than three years after the date the POA is received by the IRS.

15. The answer is C. The confidentiality privilege does not apply in the case of communications regarding the promotion of or participation in a tax shelter. A tax shelter is any entity, plan, or arrangement whose significant purpose is to avoid or evade income tax. The confidentiality privilege is also not extended to matters related to the general preparation of tax returns.

16. The answer is D. A preparer must write the word "WITHDRAW" on the first page of the POA form; include his signature and the date; and mail or fax the form to the IRS. Email is not an acceptable means of contact. The form must clearly indicate the applicable tax matters and periods. In contrast, if a taxpayer chooses to end a previously authorized power of attorney, he must write the word "REVOKE" on the form; include his signature and the date; and mail or fax the form to the IRS.

17. The answer is A. The signatures on Form 2848 are not required to be notarized.

Unit 4: Representation Quiz Answers

1. The answer is A. Although it may be a good idea to consult with other tax professionals when particular tax questions arise, this is not listed as one of the "best practices" in Circular 230.

2. The answer is B. Melanie is in violation of Circular 230. Paid preparers must furnish copies of completed returns and claims for refund to all their clients. This must be done no later than when clients sign the original documents.

3. The answer is B. If an EA knows that a client has filed an erroneous tax return, he must advise the client to correct the error. The EA is not required to amend the return, but he must advise the client about the error and the consequences of not correcting the error. He is not required to notify the IRS about his client's error.

4. The answer is C. The Treasury Department's Circular 230 sets forth regulations that apply to all paid tax preparers.

5. The answer is C. Dennis cannot knowingly hire a disbarred practitioner, regardless of whether that person would prepare tax returns. A practitioner may not knowingly employ a person or accept employment from a person who has been disbarred or suspended by the Office of Professional Responsibility, even if that person's case is under appeal.

6. The answer is C. Client records must generally be returned promptly upon client demand, regardless of fee disputes. Client records are defined as any original records belonging to the client, including any work product that he has already paid for, such as a completed copy of a tax return. However, the practitioner is allowed to withhold the return of his own work papers or preparer work product until the client has resolved any outstanding payment issues.

7. The answer is B. An EA may state that he is "enrolled to practice" before the Internal Revenue Service. The other phrases are not allowed.

8. The answer is B. A practitioner can represent clients who have a conflict of interest if the clients are notified and waivers are signed by each party. The notification must be in writing. A phone call is insufficient.

9. The answer is A. Under the rules of Circular 230, a tax preparer has a duty to advise a client about issues of noncompliance, errors, or omissions, in addition to the consequences of the errors. However, the preparer is not obligated to correct the error, inform the IRS of the error, or insist the client file an amended return. The duty to advise also applies when a preparer discovers an error or omission in the course of tax consulting or an advisory engagement.

10. The answer is A. Practitioners cannot notarize documents of the clients they represent before the IRS. However, they are not prohibited from performing notary services for clients in connection with other matters.

11. The answer is C. A practitioner may never charge a contingent fee based on the refund amount for an original return. A practitioner may publish and advertise a fee schedule. All the other fee structures are acceptable.

12. The answer is D. Ryan must ask Hannah about the missing Schedule K-1. A practitioner who has reason to believe his client has not complied with the revenue laws or has made an error in or omission from any return, document, affidavit, or other required paper has the responsibility to advise the client promptly of the noncompliance, error, or omission

13. The answer is A. Although Circular 230 dictates that a preparer comply promptly with information and record requests, there are limited circumstances when records do not have to be turned over. A preparer may decline to do so if he believes in good faith that the request is not legal or that the information is privileged. A preparer also does not have to contact any third party to inquire about the records; he must simply make a reasonable inquiry of his client.

14. The answer is D. There are strict rules for when preparers are permitted to charge contingent fees (for example, as a percentage of the taxpayer's refund). Only in limited instances are these fees allowed, such as when a preparer offers services in connection with any IRC-related litigation or judicial proceeding.

15. The answer is C. In conflict of interest cases, a preparer must obtain consent in writing and retain the records for at least 36 months (three years) from the date representation ends.

16. The answer is C. Under Circular 230 §10.21, if a tax preparer knows a taxpayer has failed to comply with the revenue law, the preparer is obligated to inform the taxpayer of the noncompliance, as well as its consequences. The preparer is not obligated to report the situation to the IRS; it is the taxpayer's choice whether or not to amend the return. As long as the error or omission on the prior return does not prevent completion of an accurate return for the current year, the preparer may go ahead and prepare the current year return.

17. The answer is D. Under Circular 230 §6107, a tax preparer must keep copies of all returns he has prepared or a list of clients and tax returns prepared. The list must include the taxpayer's name, taxpayer identification number, tax year, and the type of tax return prepared. The copies or list must be kept for at least three years after the close of the return period.

18. The answer is C. Only the preparer with primary responsibility for the accuracy of the return is considered the preparer and is thus required to sign the return under penalties of perjury. The other preparers do not need to be disclosed on the return. The taxpayer is also required to sign the return, whether prepared by a preparer or not. The taxpayer is legally responsible for the accuracy of every item on his tax return.

19. The answer is A. The firm is under no obligation to hand over its own work product to a client who has not paid his fees. A preparer is required only to return a client's original records. The client must also be given reasonable access to review and copy any additional records retained by the preparer that are necessary for the client to comply with his federal tax obligations. The spreadsheet is not necessary for the client to comply with his federal tax obligations.

20. The answer is A. With proper authorization, an EA may receive a refund check issued to the taxpayer. Practitioners are not allowed to negotiate taxpayer refunds under any circumstances, regardless of whether the client has given permission or not.

Unit 5: Representation Quiz Answers

1. The answer is D. A practitioner is not required to independently examine evidence of deductions. He may rely in good faith without verification upon information furnished by the taxpayer if it does not appear to be incorrect or incomplete. However, the practitioner must make reasonable inquiries about the validity of the information.

2. The answer is B. If the return does not adequately disclose the position and it is later examined by the IRS, she may be subject to a preparer penalty. The disclosure form is filed to avoid the potential for penalties due to disregard of rules regarding the substantial understatement of income tax.

3. The answer is D. A tax professional cannot sign a frivolous return, even if the return has a disclosure. A frivolous position is defined as one that the preparer knows is in bad faith or is improper.

4. The answer is D. The rules regarding covered opinions apply to written advice regarding a plan or arrangement whose principal purpose is the avoidance or evasion of any tax.

5. The answer is B. A practitioner is required to inform a client of any penalties that are reasonably likely to apply to a position taken on a tax return if:

- The practitioner advised the client with respect to the position; or
- The practitioner prepared or signed the tax return.

6. The answer is C. The IRS defines "more likely than not" as a position that has a greater than 50% likelihood that the tax position will be upheld if the IRS challenges it.

7. The answer is A. A position that has reasonable basis, but not substantial authority, should be disclosed on a tax return

8. The answer is A. A listed transaction, also called a reportable transaction, is a type of tax shelter activity that must be reported to the IRS. Form 8886, *Reportable Transaction Disclosure Statement*, must be attached to a taxpayer's return for any year that he participates in this type of tax shelter.

9. The answer is D. A marketed opinion is subject to the guidelines of §10.35. It is an opinion that is used by a person other than the practitioner in promoting, marketing, or recommending an investment plan to one or more taxpayers.

10. The answer is D. If Creighton files a tax return with an unreasonable position, he would face a preparer penalty. Answer "C" is incorrect because an unreasonable position has no substantial authority. Answer "B" is also incorrect, although some preparers mistakenly believe this is a solution. This type of signed statement will not prevent the preparer penalty for understatement due to an unreasonable position.

11. The answer is B. A covered opinion relates to written advice on tax shelters. More formally, Circular 230 refers to covered opinions as "written advice (including electronic communications) by a practitioner concerning one or more federal tax issues arising from a transaction that is the same as or substantially similar to a transaction that, at the time the advice is rendered, the Internal Revenue Service has determined to be a tax-avoidance transaction."

12. The answer is C. A reliance opinion is written advice that is more likely than not (greater than 50%) to result in the federal tax issue being sustained in the taxpayer's favor. Practitioners often will use disclosure statements in order for their written advice not to be categorized as reliance opinions.

Unit 6: Representation Quiz Answers

1. The answer is D. During the EIC interview with a client, preparers are required to ask additional questions if the information appears incorrect, inconsistent, or incomplete.

2. The answer is B. The IRS can impose the following types of bans related to the EIC:

- Two year ban for reckless or intentional disregard of EIC rules, or
- Ten year ban for fraud.

3. The answer is A. A tax return preparer who fails to comply with due diligence requirements for the EIC can be liable for a penalty of $500 for each failure.

4. The answer is B. The best course of action would be to ask probing questions and ask for proof of income. The preparer must document the client's answers as part of his due diligence requirements.

5. The answer is A. For any client claiming the EIC credit, a preparer must either complete Form 8867 or an equivalent checklist every year. The preparer is required to keep a copy of the checklist in his records for at least three years.

6. The answer is C. A tax preparer is not required to verify a taxpayer's answers with third parties. The EIC due diligence requires a preparer to:

- Evaluate the information received from the client,
- Apply a consistency and reasonableness standard to the information,
- Make additional reasonable inquiries when the information appears to be incorrect, inconsistent, or incomplete, and
- Document additional inquiries and the client's response.

7. The answer is D. To qualify for the EIC, a taxpayer must have earned income during the tax period. Assuming it is reported correctly, listing earned income is not an error made in claiming the EIC. The IRS cites the other three errors as common issues it sees with EIC claims.

8. The answer is B. The OPR may initiate disciplinary actions against preparers who violate rules related to the EIC. However, the OPR never initiates or prosecutes criminal cases.

9. The answer is C. If a primary taxpayer, the spouse, or both have ITINs, they are ineligible to receive the Earned Income Credit, even if their dependents have valid SSNs. A taxpayer (and his spouse, if married) must have valid Social Security numbers in order to receive the EIC. Qualifying children also must have valid SSNs.

10. The answer is A. Under the record retention portion of the EIC due diligence requirements, records must be maintained for at least three years, not two.

11. The answer is C. Form 8867, *Paid Preparer's Earned Income Checklist*, must be completed and submitted with each EIC claim. The records in answer "D" must be retained for at least three years but, other than Form 8867, they do not have to be submitted to the IRS.

Unit 7: Representation Quiz Answers

1. The answer is B. Under the terms of IRC §6695, the maximum penalty imposed on any tax return preparer cannot exceed $25,000 in a calendar year for these specific violations.

2. The answer is C. A taxpayer must keep records as long as they are needed for the administration of any provision of the IRC. Taxpayers must keep records that support an item of income or deduction on a tax return until the statute of limitations for that return runs out. If a tax return is not filed, there is no time limit.

3. The answer is B. Under IRC §6695, the IRS lists the penalties that may be assessed when it comes to the preparation of tax returns for other persons. The penalty is $50 for each violation of the following:

- Failure to furnish a copy of a return or claim to a taxpayer
- Failure to sign a return or claim for refund
- Failure to furnish an identifying number (PTIN) on a return
- Failure to retain a copy or list of a return or claim
- Failure to file correct information returns

4. The answer is A. A preparer faces an understatement penalty of $1,000 per tax return or 50% of the income the preparer received in fees for preparing the tax return with the understatement. If the position is adequately disclosed on the return, the penalty generally will not apply.

5. The answer is C. The taxpayer is ultimately responsible for the accuracy of her own return. However, a tax return preparer, whether officially licensed or not, also signs a tax return attesting to its accuracy under penalties of perjury. Both Gus and Siobhan could face penalties and other legal action in relation to the fraudulently claimed Earned Income Credit.

6. The answer is B. The fraud penalty on a joint return does not automatically apply to a spouse unless some part of the underpayment is due to the fraud committed by that spouse.

7. The answer is A. The penalty for filing late is usually 5% of the unpaid taxes for each month that a return is late. The penalty for not paying taxes by the due date is less—½ of 1% (0.5%). The IRS advises that if someone is unable to pay all the taxes he owes, he is better off filing on time and paying as much as he can.

8. The answer is D. This is the maximum penalty and prison sentence in a tax evasion case. The other statements are false. Tax avoidance is not illegal. Taxpayers who commit fraud are subject to criminal penalties as well as civil. The IRS may assess both failure-to-file and failure-to-pay penalties.

9. The answer is C. The minimum penalty is the smaller of $135 or 100% of the unpaid tax.

10. The answer is C. The substantial understatement penalty is calculated as a flat 20% of the net understatement of tax. A taxpayer may also face additional fraud-related penalties if he has provided false information on his tax return.

11. The answer is B. This penalty is generally levied against employers, or other responsible persons, who have failed to pay the appropriate payroll taxes to the U.S. government.

12. The answer is D. A taxpayer may file an amended return to take a loss on a worthless security up to seven years after the original filing date, so records should be kept for that length of time.

13. The answer is C. Any taxpayer who files a return found to be frivolous may be fined $5,000, in addition to any other penalties provided by law. This penalty may be doubled on a joint return.

14. The answer is C. If a fraudulent tax return is filed, there is no statute of limitations. Under federal law, a tax return is fraudulent if the taxpayer files it knowing that the return either omits taxable income or claims one or more deductions that are not allowable.

15. The answer is D. IRS auditors are trained to spot common types of deception and attempts to defraud on tax returns. These acts are known as badges of fraud and include deducting personal items as business expenses, the overstatement of deductions, and the understatement of income. Simply having deductions for foreign travel is not an indication of illegal behavior on the part of a taxpayer.

16. The answer is C. In most cases, tax returns can be audited for up to three years after filing. However, the IRS may audit for up to six years if there is substantial unreported income (over 25%).

17. The answer is B. A preparer who makes a "willful or reckless" attempt to understate tax liability faces a penalty of $5,000 per tax return or 50% of the additional income upon which the penalty was imposed, whichever is greater.

18. The answer is B. A taxpayer or business is required to keep records relating to employment taxes for at least four years after filing the fourth quarter for the year. Employment and payroll records must be available for IRS review. Examples include copies of employees' income tax withholding allowance certificates (Forms W-4) and dates and amounts of payroll tax deposits made.

19. The answer is D. It is illegal for return preparers to negotiate (cash) taxpayers' refund checks. A preparer faces a fine of $500 for each violation.

20. The answer is B. IRC §6662 imposes penalties on taxpayers who overvalue assets in order to reap tax benefits. The penalty is 20% of the net understatement of tax for assets incorrectly valued at 150% or more than the correct amount of valuation or adjusted basis. The penalty increases to 40% of the net understatement of tax for assets incorrectly valued at 200% or more than the correct amount of valuation or adjusted basis.

Unit 8: Representation Quiz Answers

1. The answer is C. A practitioner who is censured by the OPR is still eligible to practice before the IRS. Censure is a public reprimand. Unlike disbarment or suspension, censure does not affect an individual's eligibility to represent taxpayers before the IRS, but the OPR may subject the individual's future representation of taxpayers to conditions designed to promote high standards of conduct.

2. The answer is A. An enrolled agent has a right to appeal an administrative law judge's decision for disbarment to the Secretary of the Treasury.

3. The answer is C. OPR sanctions include disbarment, suspension, and censure. Although a tax preparer may be subject to criminal prosecution in some cases, the OPR would not be responsible for applying this penalty.

4. The answer is A. A disbarred practitioner may appear before the IRS as a trustee, receiver, guardian, administrator, executor, or other fiduciary, if duly qualified or authorized under the laws of the relevant jurisdiction.

5. The answer is B. A practitioner may petition the OPR for reinstatement after a period of five years.

6. The answer is C. Not being able to pay one's taxes on time would be unlikely to subject a tax practitioner to OPR sanctions. In general, the OPR defines four broad categories of misconduct which may be subject to disciplinary action: (1) misconduct while representing a taxpayer; (2) misconduct related to the practitioner's own return; (3) giving a false opinion, knowingly, recklessly, or through gross incompetence; (4) misconduct not directly involving IRS representation.

7. The answer is B. Even without bringing a criminal prosecution, the IRS may disbar or suspend a tax return preparer who engages in misconduct.

8. The answer is D. Circular 230 §10.51 details a large number of violations related to disreputable conduct for which a preparer may face sanctions from the OPR. The statute specifically cites "conviction" of criminal offense or felony charges, rather than indictment on criminal offense or felony charges. Circular 230 also does not specify that conviction of misdemeanor charges is a sanctionable offense. However, the statute also warns that preparers may be sanctioned for other offenses that are not listed.

9. The answer is C. A practitioner who has been disbarred (or suspended) may not sign a tax return on behalf of a taxpayer, file powers of attorney with the IRS, prepare tax returns for compensation, or any number of other actions that are considered practice before the IRS. The other actions listed are allowed, even for a practitioner who has been disbarred or suspended.

Unit 9: Representation Quiz Answers

1. The answer is A. A taxpayer may qualify as an injured spouse if he filed a joint return and his share of the refund was applied against past due amounts owed by a spouse. The injured spouse may be entitled to recoup only his share of a tax refund.

2. The answer is C. The ten-year collection period is not suspended when a taxpayer is in prison. The ten-year collection period is suspended in the following cases:

- While the IRS considers a request for an installment agreement or an offer in compromise
- From the date a taxpayer requests a collection due process (CDP) hearing
- For tax periods included in a bankruptcy
- While the taxpayer is residing outside the United States

3. The answer is A. The IRS requires a taxpayer whose offer in compromise has been rejected to file an appeal within 30 days.

4. The answer is A. Belinda is not eligible for innocent spouse relief because she knew about the understated income. She signed the return knowing that the income was not included, so the IRS will not grant her relief.

5. The answer is B. A preparer may charge an identical flat fee to all customers applying for RALs, meaning the fee cannot be based upon the amount of a refund for an individual client.

6. The answer is A. A levy allows the IRS to confiscate and sell property to satisfy a tax debt. An IRS levy refers to the actual seizing of property authorized by an earlier filed tax lien. Answer "B" refers to a lien, which gives the IRS a legal claim to a taxpayer's property as security for his tax debt.

7. The answer is A. Lena may apply for an offer in compromise under doubt as to collectability. Doubt exists that she could ever pay the full amount of tax liability owed within the remainder of the statutory period for collection.

8. The answer is D. To qualify for separation of liability relief, the taxpayer must have filed a joint return, meaning the taxpayer must have been married at one time. Separation of liability applies to taxpayers who are no longer married (including a taxpayer who is widowed); legally separated; or living apart for the 12 months prior to the filing of a claim.

9. The answer is C. Congress created the Taxpayer Advocate Service, an independent function within the IRS, to help taxpayers resolve issues with the IRS and recommend changes that will prevent future problems. Every year, the TAS helps thousands of taxpayers find solutions to their tax issues. There is no charge to taxpayers who use the service.

10. The answer is D. In a collection due process hearing, the taxpayer retains the right to appeal, unlike in the collection appeals program where the determination is final.

11. The answer is C. The IRS *Collection Financial Standards* are used to evaluate a taxpayer's ability to pay a delinquent tax liability. These standards help determine allowable living expenses that are necessary to provide for a taxpayer's (and his family's) health and welfare and/or production of income while his tax debt is being repaid. Allowances for housing, utilities, and transportation vary by location, while standard amounts are allowed nationwide for food, clothing, out-of-pocket health care expenses, and other items. Consideration is also given to the taxpayer's income, his bank and retirement accounts, real estate and other assets, and his outstanding debts. Further, the taxpayer may have obligations for court-ordered payments, such as child support and alimony. Since the taxpayer will generally have little flexibility regarding these obligations, the IRS would be unlikely to challenge amounts that are supported by evidence the taxpayer provides.

12. The answer is C. Regular Social Security payments are not exempt from IRS levy.

13. The answer is D. If a taxpayer does not pay in full when filing his tax return, he will receive a bill from an IRS service center. The first notice will explain the balance due and demand payment in full. It will include the amount of the tax plus any penalties and interest added to the taxpayer's unpaid balance from the date the tax was due.

14. The answer is B. If the IRS has determined a taxpayer's status is currently not collectible, it is prohibited from pursuing all collection activities for at least one year, or until the taxpayer's income has increased.

15. The answer is B. Sheila can file Form 8379, *Injured Spouse Allocation*, and request injured spouse relief. If married taxpayers filed a joint return and the refund was offset, an injured spouse can file Form 8379 to request the portion of the refund attributed to him or her.

16. The answer is C. After the IRS has filed a notice of intent to seize, it must wait 30 days before actually seizing a taxpayer's nonexempt property. It legally cannot seize items such as clothing, food, fuel, furniture, and personal effects up to a specified, inflation-adjusted amount. Undelivered mail and books and tools of the trade needed for the taxpayer's business are also exempt, up to a certain amount. Unemployment benefits, worker's compensation, child support payments, and certain disability and public assistance payments are also exempt from seizure. However, most Social Security benefits and retirement fund proceeds may be seized to fulfill a taxpayer's debt obligation. Before a taxpayer's home is seized, there generally must be judicial approval.

17. The answer is D. No levies may be served during installment agreements. During the course of the installment agreement, penalties and interest continue to accrue. A taxpayer who owes less than $10,000 in taxes will automatically be approved for an installment agreement.

18. The answer is C. The IRS provides several ways for a taxpayer to pay his tax liability when he does not have sufficient funds to cover the deficiency. Offers in compromise, installment agreements, and extensions of time to pay due to hardship are all legitimate options. Requesting that a state tax refund be applied toward a tax deficiency is not an option.

19. The answer is C. The taxpayer may choose to extend the statute of limitations or he may refuse to extend the statute. If a taxpayer does not file a tax return, the statute of limitations does not expire. The statute of limitations on collection activity may also be suspended in certain instances. The amount of time the suspension is in effect will be added to the time remaining in the ten-year period.

20. The answer is D. A taxpayer may not designate a credit card account for direct deposit of her federal tax refund.

21. The answer is B. An installment agreement allows a taxpayer to pay his tax liability over a period of time, if he cannot pay the amount when it is due. An installment agreement cannot be used to negotiate with the IRS for a lower tax bill. During the time an installment agreement is in place, penalties and interest continue to accrue.

22. The answer is D. The IRS will continue to assess penalties and interest on a taxpayer's unpaid tax liability in most circumstances, including during the period when an installment agreement is in place, when a taxpayer has been declared "currently not collectible," and when a taxpayer requests innocent spouse relief.

23. The answer is B. The IRS generally will not grant an extension of more than six months to pay the tax due on a return. A taxpayer may file Form 1127, *Application for Extension of Time for Payment of Tax Due to Hardship*, to explain why he cannot pay the tax. He must provide a detailed explanation of the undue hardship that would result if he paid the tax when it is due and provide adequate documentation of his financial situation.

24. The answer is A. If a taxpayer owes more than $25,000, he may still qualify for an installment agreement, but the taxpayer will also need to complete Form 433-F, *Collection Information Statement*.

25. The answer is B. The IRS may seize or levy property if the collection of tax is in jeopardy, and may do so without the normal waiting period if a jeopardy assessment has been made. Typically, the IRS may not seize property in the following circumstances:

- When there is a pending installment agreement
- While a taxpayer's appeal is pending
- During the consideration of an offer in compromise
- During a bankruptcy (unless the seizure is authorized by the bankruptcy court)
- If the taxpayer's liability is $5,000 or less, in a seizure of real property
- While innocent spouse claims are pending

Unit 10: Representation Quiz Answers

1. The answer is A. If a taxpayer has moved or if his books and records are located in another area, he can request that the location of his audit be changed to another IRS service center.

2. The answer is B. For taxpayers who file jointly, only one spouse is required to meet with the IRS. Alternatively, the taxpayers can use a qualified representative to represent them before the IRS.

3. The answer is A. The Discriminant Inventory Function System (DIF) score rates returns for audit probability, based on past IRS experience with similar returns. IRS personnel screen the highest-scoring returns, selecting some for audit and identifying the items on these returns that are most likely to need review.

4. The answer is D. Requesting fast track mediation during the examination is not a reason for the IRS to reopen a closed audit case. In general, the IRS will not reopen a closed examination case to make an unfavorable adjustment unless:

- There was fraud or misrepresentation,
- There was a substantial error based on an established IRS position existing at the time of the examination, or
- Failure to reopen the case would be a serious administrative omission.

5. The answer is A. Pursuant to IRC §7602(c), a third-party contact is made when an IRS employee initiates contact with a person other than the taxpayer. A third party may be contacted to obtain information about a specific taxpayer's federal tax liability, including the issuance of a levy or summons to someone other than the taxpayer. The IRS does not need permission to contact third parties, but it must generally notify the taxpayer that the contact with third parties will be made.

6. The answer is C. A taxpayer would not be chosen for audit simply because he is a foreign investor. The IRS selects returns using a variety of methods, including participants in potentially abusive tax transactions; computer scoring; information matching; and randomly.

7. The answer is B. The taxpayer is not required to be present during an IRS examination if he has provided written authorization to a qualified representative per Circular 230.

8. The answer is A. "A" is incorrect because partnerships with ten partners or fewer are typically exempt from the TEFRA rules under a special small partnership exception.

9. The answer is B. If a taxpayer, his representative, or the IRS examiner wishes for an audit to be recorded, he must notify the other parties in writing ten days in advance. If the IRS records the interview, the taxpayer may request a copy.

10. The answer is D. During the examination process, the IRS must give the taxpayer reasonable notice before contacting other persons about his individual tax matters. This provision does not apply:

- To any pending criminal investigation.
- When providing notice would jeopardize collection of any tax liability.
- When providing notice may result in reprisal against any person.

11. The answer is C. An IRS examiner files a revenue agent report (RAR) after he has completed the field work part of an examination. The report should clearly state the amount of adjustments to be made to a taxpayer's return and demonstrate how the tax liability was computed. A taxpayer may agree with the RAR and pay any additional tax owed, or he may contest the agent's findings. He may appeal to the IRS or fight the tax in court.

Unit 11: Representation Quiz Answers

1. The answer is A. An IRS appeal does not abate the interest, which continues to accrue until the balance of the debt is paid, or until the taxpayer wins his appeal and he is granted a no-change audit. A no-change audit means the IRS has accepted the tax return as it was filed.

2. The answer is B. The Statutory Notice of Deficiency, or 90-day letter, gives the taxpayer 90 days to file a petition in the U.S. Tax Court challenging the proposed deficiency.

3. The answer is B. Aaron can appear before IRS Appeals by himself, or hire a qualified representative to appear on his behalf. If he wants to be represented by someone else, he must choose a person who is eligible to practice before the IRS. Only practitioners (usually, attorneys, CPAs, and EAs) are allowed to represent taxpayers before an appeals hearing.

4. The answer is C. The taxpayer normally has 90 days to respond to a Notice of Deficiency. However, a taxpayer is granted 150 days if the notice is addressed to a taxpayer outside the United States.

5. The answer is A. At the beginning of each examination, the IRS auditor must explain a taxpayer's appeal rights.

6. The answer is B. A taxpayer may elect the small tax case procedure (also known as S case procedure) for cases involving up to $50,000 in deficiency per year, including penalties and other additions to tax, but excluding interest. Trials in small tax cases generally are less formal and result in a speedier disposition. However, small tax court cases may not be appealed. Decisions are final for both the taxpayer and the IRS.

7. The answer is A. A Notice of Deficiency (90-day letter) must be issued before a taxpayer can go to Tax Court. Once the taxpayer receives the Notice of Deficiency, she then has 90 days to respond and file a petition with the court.

8. The answer is D. An enrolled agent may represent taxpayers at all levels of the IRS, but does not have the same practice rights in the U.S. court system.

9. The answer is A. Both Kevin and Javier can take their cases to court. A taxpayer is not required to use the IRS appeals process. If a taxpayer and the IRS still disagree after an appeals conference or a taxpayer decides to bypass the IRS appeals system, the case may be taken to the U.S. Tax Court, the U.S. Court of Federal Claims, or a U.S. district court.

10. The answer is D. A taxpayer has the right to appeal a tax assessment through the IRS Appeals office, the U.S. Tax Court, or a U.S. district or federal court. However, if the taxpayer opts to have his appeal heard in a district or federal court, he must first pay the contested tax and sue the IRS for a refund.

11. The answer is B. If a taxpayer unreasonably fails to pursue the internal IRS appeals system, if the case is filed primarily to cause a delay, or if the taxpayer's position is frivolous, the Tax Court may impose a penalty of up to $25,000.

12. The answer is B. In order to appeal in a district court, the taxpayer must first pay the contested liability and then sue the IRS for a refund. If either party loses at the trial court level, the court's decision may be appealed to a higher court.

Unit 12: Representation Quiz Answers

1. The answer is C. Any paid preparer who files 11 or more individual or trust returns in aggregate in a calendar year is required to e-file. There are limited exceptions, such as for returns that cannot be e-filed (returns that require paper attachments, nonresident returns, etc.) The e-file mandate does not apply to payroll tax returns, volunteer preparers, or returns prepared under the Volunteer Income Tax Assistance (VITA) program.

2. The answer is D. A partnership with more than 100 partners must e-file. A partnership with 100 or fewer partners is not required to e-file, though it may choose to do so. A corporation with $10 million or more in assets must e-file if it files at least 250 returns. The EA in Answer C is required to e-file because she prepares 11 tax returns for compensation, which is the minimum number that triggers the e-file mandate. VITA volunteers are not covered under the e-file mandate.

3. The answer is C. Under the IRS system of rating e-file infractions, Level One is the least serious, Level Two is moderately serious, and Level Three is the most serious. There is no Level Four infraction.

4. The answer is A. Katie must use Form 8453, *U.S. Individual Income Tax Transmittal for an IRS e-file Return,* and also submit Form 2848, *Power of Attorney and Declaration of Representative,* as an attachment. Form 8879, *IRS e-file Signature Authorization,* is used by EROs but only submitted to the IRS upon request.

5. The answer is B. If the IRS rejects an e-filed tax return for processing and the reason for the rejection cannot be rectified, the ERO must take reasonable steps to inform the taxpayer of the rejection within 24 hours. The ERO must provide the taxpayer with the rejection code(s) accompanied by an explanation. After receiving a rejection, the ERO is not required to file a tax return on paper. The ERO and the client should attempt to correct the e-file. However, if the return continues to be rejected, the taxpayer may be forced to file on paper.

6. The answer is A. Electronic filing identification numbers (EFINs) are issued on a firm basis. All tax return preparers in the firm are covered by a single EFIN. Providers need an EFIN to electronically file tax returns.

7. The answer is C. An individual preparer's dislike of using a computer or not having appropriate software are not considered legitimate reasons to grant a hardship waiver. The IRS will grant e-file waivers in cases when technology makes it impossible to filing electronically. E-file waivers due to hardship will also be granted, but only on a rare, case-by-case basis and typically only for a single year.

8. The answer is D. In order to timely file a tax return, the taxpayer must file a paper return by the later of:

- The due date of the return; or
- Ten calendar days after the date the IRS gives notification that it rejected the e-filed return.

This is called the "Ten-Day Transmission Perfection Period." This is not an extension of time to file; rather, this is additional time that the IRS gives a preparer and taxpayer to correct and resubmit a tax return without a late filing penalty.

9. The answer is B. An e-file provider may not charge a contingent fee based on a percentage of the refund of an original tax return. Separate fees may not be charged for direct deposits. However, a practitioner is allowed to charge a fee for e-filing.

10. The answer is D. To become an authorized e-file provider, an individual must first register with the IRS by creating an IRS e-Services account online. The individual will need to provide personal information including a Social Security number and an address where confirmation of the account will be mailed.

11. The answer is B. A practitioner may use the IRS e-file logo, but may not use the IRS logo or insignia in his advertising, or imply a relationship with the IRS. A preparer may not combine the e-file logo with the IRS eagle symbol, the word "federal," or with other words or symbols that suggest a special relationship between the IRS and the logo. Advertising materials must not carry the IRS or other Treasury seals.

Index

About the Authors

Richard Gramkow, EA

Richard Gramkow is an Enrolled Agent with more than 17 years of experience in various areas of taxation. He holds a master's degree in taxation from Rutgers University and is currently a tax manager for a publicly held Fortune 500 company in the New York metropolitan area.

Collette Szymborski, CPA

Collette Szymborski is a Certified Public Accountant and the managing partner of Elk Grove CPA Accountancy Corporation. She specializes in the taxation of corporations, individuals, and exempt entities. Elk Grove CPA also does estate planning.

David V. Sherwood, CPA, EA

David V. Sherwood is a Certified Public Accountant and an Enrolled Agent with over 35 years of professional experience. He received his BBA in Accounting from The College of William and Mary, and later was a partner with a predecessor firm of PriceWaterhouseCoopers. He has provided accounting, auditing, and consulting services to a diverse group of private and publicly traded clients.

Christy Pinheiro, EA ABA®

Christy Pinheiro is an Enrolled Agent, Accredited Business Accountant, and writer. Christy was an accountant for two private CPA firms and for the State of California before going into private practice. She is a member of the California Society of Enrolled Agents and CalCPA

CPSIA information can be obtained at www.ICGtesting.com
Printed in the USA
BVOW08s2242110914

366521BV00003B/9/P

9 781935 664291